PAKISTAN: A MODERN HISTORY

IAN TALBOT

Pakistan
A Modern History

HURST & COMPANY, LONDON

First published in the United Kingdom by
C. Hurst & Co. (Publishers) Ltd,
41 Great Russell Street, London WC1B 3PL
Enlarged and updated editions, 2005, 2009
First published 1988
© Ian Talbot, 1998, 2005, 2009
All rights reserved.
Printed in India

A Catalogue record for this book is available
from the British Library.

ISBNs
978-1-85065-989-1 *paperback*

PREFACE AND ACKNOWLEDGEMENTS

The task of writing Pakistan's history since independence is an onerous one. The tumultuous and contested nature of the country's political development compounds the problems relating to source material for contemporary history. Documents relating to such controversial events as the break-up of the country in 1971, the Rawalpindi and Argatala Conspiracy cases and the circumstances of General Zia-ul Haq's death may never be made available to the historian. Indeed few countries' histories can be so marked by conspiracy theories, allegations and unresolved mysteries concerning a gamut of subjects from election riggings and attempted coups, to riots, massacres and assassinations.

This book seeks to make sense of Pakistan's history by examining the interplay between colonial inheritances and contemporary strategic and socio-economic environments. Equally important is the interplay between the regional and national levels of politics. The state's response to pressures for increased political participation and devolution of power has been of crucial importance, as has the perception by minorities of the 'Punjabisation' of Pakistan. Finally the work draws attention to the long-term problems of weak political institutionalisation and viceregalism which are rooted in the colonial past.

This study has emerged out of a longstanding interest in the history of the creation of Pakistan. Many friends and colleagues have helped in my journey of intellectual understanding. I would like to thank the following for their assistance and encouragement in the writing of this particular study: Professor Leslie Wolf-Philips for his comments on an earlier draft of Chapter 8, Dr Iftikhar Malik, Dr Yunas Samad, Dr Muhammad Waseem and Dr Gurharpal Singh for their encouragement and advice, and Professor James Manor for enabling me to be a Research Fellow at the Institute of Commonwealth Studies during the completion of the text. The work could not have been undertaken so expeditiously without a British Academy Senior Research Fellowship. I am also grateful to The Scouloudi Foundation Historical Awards for financially supporting my period of research at the India Office Library and to The Nuffield Foundation for supporting what proved to be a highly productive research visit to Washington, DC.

I am also grateful to the library staff at Coventry University for courteously dealing with what must have seemed an unending list of requests for inter-library loan materials. Thanks are due to all those who generously gave of their time during the interviews for this work. I am once again indebted to Lois for her forbearance and to Martin for his patience in the restrictions on his computer time at the end of the production of this manuscript. Finally, I am grateful to Michael Dwyer of C. Hurst & Co. for his encouragement during all stages of the production of this work. Any errors of fact or omission are my responsibility alone.

Coventry and London,   IAN TALBOT
March 1998

PREFACE TO THE THIRD EDITION

2007 was earmarked for Pakistan's third transition to democratic rule. When President Pervez Musharraf finally stepped down as President the following August, Pakistan had experienced one of the most tumultuous periods in its sixty year history and faced an uncertain future. Musharraf's fortunes had declined to the backdrop of his miscalculated Emergency and the prolonged crisis arising from the dismissal of the independent-minded Chief Justice Iftikhar Mohammad Chaudhry. The return of Benazir Bhutto and Nawaz Sharif to Pakistan in the Autumn of 2007 had held out the promise of a brighter democratic future and symbolised the narrowing options for an increasingly embattled President. The assassination of Benazir Bhutto just ninety days after her return from political exile, however, brought Pakistan into unchartered territory. Her death in Rawalpindi raised fears for the future of the federation and called into question the holding of the long-awaited national elections. When they went ahead on 18 February, the outcome generated great euphoria following the triumph of the mainstream opposition parties at the expense of the 'King's Party', the PML-Q and of the religious parties in the Frontier and Balochistan. The weeks of horse-trading which were to follow dampened down expectations of a decisive shift in Pakistan's political development. More realistically, in keeping with the country's history as revealed in this volume, it became clear that change would be incremental, dependent both on the strengthening of civil society and increased political institutionalisation. The outcome of a single election would not wrest power from the army and its political allies.

Hopes for democratic consolidation appeared increasingly shaky as the coalition between the PPP and PML-N unravelled, but not before it had achieved the goal of disposing of Musharraf under the threat of impeachment. The worsening economic situation increased the gloom, as did the stalling in the composite dialogue with India. Even more disconcerting was the tension in relations between Pakistan and its Western partners in the 'War on Terror.' The ANP preference for dialogue with militant groups enabled the already entrenched Taliban and Al-Qaeda groups to strengthen their sanctuaries in FATA . Growing casualties amongst western troops in south Afghanistan as a result of cross-border 'terrorist activity' increased US inclination for a policy of 'hot pursuit.' At the same time fears within Pakistan grew of a 'creeping' Talibanisation' in the settled districts of NWFP with some seeing threats emerging even to Peshawar and Islamabad. All the while the newly elected democratic forces appeared more concerned with their quarrels over the future of the judges and the President than with tackling growing economic and security threats. Musharraf's resignation rather than consolidating the power of the February victors, introduced a further element of uncertainty as it became clear that the PPP under the leadership of Asif Ali Zardari had abandoned the consensual approach to politics trumpeted at the time of the polls and instead sought to control the main levers of power. Nawaz Sharif in the 1990s had adopted a similar attitude in associating democratic consolidation with ever increasing power. His actions had provided the military with a 'legitimate' reason for intervention. Zardari does not possess any of Sharif's earlier stock of goodwill among the generals. While he possesses initial western support because of his pronouncements to pursue the 'War on Terror', even at the beginning of his tenure questions have emerged concerning his ability to maintain domestic political stability.

The goal of democratic consolidation and of a total normalisation of civil-military relations appears as distant as ever.

This edition not only brings the historical narrative up to date, but sets the rush of contemporary developments within the framework of Pakistan's past. Lessons can be drawn from this along with an appreciation of the continuities and imperatives which shape domestic political developments. The challenges and opportunities arising from the current process of democratic transition can be more profoundly understood in the light of earlier episodes at the end of the Ayub Khan and Zia-ul Haq eras. Similarly expectations of the outcome of the current dialogue with India can be more realistically entertained in the light of previous temperature changes in the relationship between the two 'distant neighbours.'

Important works which have been published since May 2005 have informed the argument in the Epilogue. They are also cited in the updated Bibliography. The appendices introduce fresh biographical and institutional material for reference purposes. Pakistan's future development remains uncertain at the time of writing. What is clear is that the country will remain the centre of international focus in the coming months and years ahead.

Southampton, September 2008

CONTENTS

Preface and Acknowledgements   page v
Preface to the Third Edition   vii
Tables   xv
Abbreviations   xvii

Introduction   1

Part I: THE HISTORICAL INHERITANCE

1. Pakistan: Land, Society and Economy   21

   East Bengal and the problem of national integration   24
   Language and political identity in Pakistan   25
   Islam   27
   Biraderi politics and feudalism   30
   Pakistan since 1971   31
   Post-1971 social and economic change   38
   Population growth   39
   Migration   41
   The growth of the middle classes   46

2. Colonial Rule, Authoritarianism and Regional History in North-West India   53

   Colonial administration in the Muslim-majority areas   53
   The British security state in North-West India   54

3. The Pakistan Movement: its Dynamics and Legacies   66

   Punjab   67
   The Unionist legacy   71
   The legacy of the campaign for Pakistan   73
   Sindh   74
   The North-West Frontier Province   81
   The Frontier Muslim League   83
   Bengal   87

*The All-India Muslim League and Pakistan's future
    political development*   91

4. Picking up the Pieces: Pakistan, 1947-49   95

    The economic and geographical inheritance   95
    Strategic and institutional inheritances   99
    Massacres and migrations   101
    The political inheritance from the refugee situation   106
    The crisis in Indo-Pakistan relations   112
    The Kashmir conflict   113
    The survival of Pakistan   120

Part II: THE DESTRUCTION OF PAKISTAN'S
DEMOCRACY AND UNITY

5. The Destruction of Democracy in Pakistan   125

    Pakistani politics: processes and perceptions   126
    The formative phase, 1947-51   134
    The collapse of democracy, 1951-58   139

6. Solon among the Subalterns   148

    The making of a leader   149
    Political developments, 1958-65   153
    Economic and social reform   164
    Economic development   169
    Foreign affairs   172
    The descent from power   179

7. Things Fall Apart   185

    Yahya's inheritance from Ayub   188
    Administrative and constitutional developments   190
    The 1970 elections   194
    The drift to civil war and the creation of Bangladesh   201

Part III: FROM BHUTTO TO ZIA

8. People's Power: Hopes and Impediments   215

    The PPP in power   218
    Preferential politics   220

Bhutto, the Army and the bureaucracy   222
Constitutional developments   228
Economic and social reforms   230
The Bhutto regime and nationalisation   233
Foreign policy   234
The March 1977 elections   239
The PNA agitation   241

9. Islam Changes Everything?   245

    The world of a dictator   254
    Political and constitutional change, 1977-85   256
    Political developments, 1985-88   262
    Pakistan and the war in Afghanistan   267
    Islamisation   270
    Women, the minorities and Islamisation   279
    A stormy summer   283

Part IV: EVER-DECREASING CIRCLES:
PAKISTAN POLITICS SINCE 1988

10. Democracy Restored? Pakistan Politics, 1988-93 287

    Democratisation, democracy and Pakistan: some
        theoretical contexts   290
    Benazir and the PPP are back   293
    The politics of confrontation and regional identity 298
    The PPP and the crisis in Sindh   303
    Azad Kashmir   308
    The PPP and the military-bureaucratic establishment 308
    The 1990 elections and Nawaz Sharif's rise to power 310
    Nawaz Sharif in power, 1990-93   315
    The Gulf War   315
    Islamisation and the IJI government   317
    Successes and setbacks   318
    Confrontation with the PPP   320
    Sindh   323
    The IJI and the military-bureaucratic establishment 325

11. Democracy in Crisis: Pakistan Politics, 1993-98 327

    Constitutional Crisis   327

Rule by the IMF?   329
The 1993 elections   331
Benazir Bhutto's second administration, 1993–96   333
Foreign policy   335
Political problems and confrontations   337
Islamic militancy and sectarianism   339
Civil war in Karachi   342
Punjab   344
The fall from grace   345
The caretakers   349
The election campaign   352
Fair and free polls?   355
The results   356
Future prospects   358

12. Conclusion   368

EPILOGUE
Musharraf's Pakistan: coup, crisis and conflict   375

The Coup of 12 October 1999   375
Musharraf's leadership and relationship with the army hierarchy   378
Musharraf's reforms and achievements   380
'Decentralisation of power'   381
Civil society   385
The Aftermath of 9/11   391
The October 2002 elections   401
The polls   403
Rapprochement with India   410
Pakistan since October 2002   412
A Troubled Transition   417

The Black Coat Revolt   417
President Musharraf's re-election   419
The Emergency   420
The Lal Masjid Affair   422
The troubled tribal areas   424
The Return of Benazir Bhutto and Nawaz Sharif   426
The Assassination of Benazir Bhutto   428
The February 2008 polls and their aftermath   429
Musharraf's resignation and its aftermath   436
The presidential election   438

Appendices
Pakistan Heads of State and Government   441
Biographical Notes   443
Pakistan Political Parties and Organisations   481

Select Bibliography   497
Index   517

TABLES

1.1.	Language distribution in Pakistan	27
1.2.	Pakistan population by area, 1981	32
1.3.	Pakistan religion by area, 1982	34
1.4.	Increase in consumer goods	46
6.1.	The military elite in Pakistan, 1955	162
6.2.	Central Secretariat elite posts, 1955	162
6.3.	Industrial development in West Pakistan, 1969-70	170
7.1.	National Assembly election results, 1970-1	200
7.2.	Provincial Assembly election results, 1970-1	201
8.1.	The quota system in public sector employment	221
8.2.	National Assembly election results, March 1977	241
10.1.	Provincial Assembly election results, 1988	296
10.2.	National Assembly election results, 1990	314
11.1.	National Assembly election results, 1993	332
11.2.	Party positions in the National and Provincial Assembly seats, February 1997 polls	357
Ep.1.	National Assembly results, 2002: seats	405
Ep.2.	Privincial Assembly results, 2002: seats	405

ABBREVIATIONS

AIML	All-India Muslim League
AK	Azad Kashmir
AKMC	Azad Kashmir Muslim Conference
AKPP	Azad Kashmir People's Party
ANP	Awami National Party
APMSO	All-Pakistan Mohajir Students' Organisation
APWA	All-Pakistan Women's Association
ARD	Alliance for the Restoration of Democracy
BJP	Bharatiya Janata Party
CCI	Council of Common Interests
CDNS	Council of Defence and National Security
CENTO	Central Treaty Organisation
CIA	Central Intelligence Agency (USA)
CII	Council of Islamic Ideology
COAS	Chief of Army Staff
COG	Commonwealth Observer Group
COP	Combined Opposition Parties
CPP	Communist Party of Pakistan
CSP	Civil Service of Pakistan
EBDO	Elective Bodies (Disqualification) Order
ECO	Economic Cooperation Agency
ESAF	Enhanced Structural Adjustment Facility
FATA	Federally Administered Tribal Areas
FSF	Federal Security Force
HUA	Harkat-ul-Ansari
IAEA	International Atomic Energy Agency
IDBP	Industrial Development Bank of Pakistan
IJI	Islami Jamhoori Ittehad
IJM	Islami Jamhoori Mohaz
IJT	Islami Jamiat-i-Tuleba
ISI	Inter Services Intelligence Agency
JCSC	Joint Chiefs of Staff Committee
JI	Jamiat-i-Islami
JKLF	Jammu and Kashmir Liberation Front
JUI	Jamiat-ul-Ulema-i-Islam
JUI(F)	— (Fazlur Rahman faction)
JUP	Jamiat-ul-Ulema-i-Pakistan
KPP	Krishak Praja Party
KSP	Krishak Sramik Party
KT	Khaksar Tehrik

LFO	Legal Framework Order
MFLO	Muslim Family Laws Ordinance
MMA	Muttahida Majlis-i-Amal
MQM	Mohajir Qaumi Mahaz
MQM(A)	— (Altaf Husain faction)
MQM(H)	— (Afaq Ahmed faction)
MRD	Movement for the Restoration of Democracy
NAP	National Awami Party
NDP	National Democratic Party
NEFA	North-East Frontier Agency
NICFC	National Industrial Credit and Finance Corporation
NPP	National People's Party
NWFP	North-West Frontier Province
OIC	Organisation of the Islamic Conference
PATA	Provincially Administered Tribal Areas
PDA	Pakistan Democratic Alliance
PDP	Pakistan Democratic Party
PIA	Pakistan International Airlines
PICIC	Pakistan Industrial and Credit Investment Corporation
PIF	Pakistan Islamic Front
PKMAP	Pushtunkhwa Milli Awami Party
PML	Pakistan Muslim League
PML(J)	— (Junejo faction)
PML(N)	— (Nawaz Sharif faction)
PML(P)	— (Pagaro faction)
PML(QA)	— (Quaid-e-Azam)
PODO	Public Offices (Disqualification) Order
PPP	Pakistan People's Party
PPP(SB)	— (Shaheed Bhutto faction)
PPPP	Pakistan People's Party Parliamentarians
PRODA	Public and Representative Offices (Disqualification) Act
PSF	People's Student Federation
PTV	Pakistan Television
RAW	Research and Analysis Wing (Indian Intelligence Agency)
SAARC	South Asian Association for Regional Cooperation
SEATO	South-East Asia Treaty Organisation
SKMH	Shaukat Khanum Memorial Hospital
SMP	Sipah-e-Muhammad Pakistan
SSP	Sipah-i-Sahaba-i-Pakistan
TI	Tehrik-i-Istiqlal
TNFJ	Tehrik-e-Nifaz-e-Shariat-e-Jafria
TNSM	Tehrik-e-Nifaz-e-Shariat-e-Muhammadi
UAE	United Arab Emirates
UDF	United Democratic Front
UP	Uttar Pradesh/United Provinces
USIS	United States Information Service
WAF	Women's Action Forum
WAPDA	Water and Power Development Authority

Bibliographic abbreviations occurring in the Notes

FMA	Freedom Movement Archives
IOL	India Office Library
IOR	India Office Records
Fr	Fortnightly Report
NAI	National Archives of India
NAP	National Archives of Pakistan

INTRODUCTION

Pakistan for much of its history has been a state searching for a national identity. The overlap of regional, Pakistani and religious identities was articulated most clearly by the Pushtun nationalist Wali Khan nearly a decade ago when he declared that he had been a Pushtun for 4,000 years, a Muslim for 1,400 years and a Pakistani for forty years.[1] Five decades after its creation the question remains whether Pakistan is a land for Muslims or a nation of Muslims moving towards its destiny as an Islamic state? Language and religion, rather than providing a panacea for unity in a plural society, have opened a Pandora's box of conflicting identities. Centrist state structures have reinforced a sense that Pakistani nationalism is being imposed from above in the service of the 'Punjabisation' of the state.

Successive bouts of authoritarian rule have reinforced centrifugal ethnic, linguistic and regional forces. This was seen most dramatically in the Bengali nationalists' struggle with the state which culminated in civil war and the separation of East Pakistan in 1971. Following the trauma of the Bangladesh War, Zulfiqar Ali Bhutto and Zia ul-Haq turned successively to populism and Islam in an attempt to strengthen a sense of national identity. Populism raised expectations which could not be met by an increasingly authoritarian regime; Islam proved a broken reed because it raised the question of whose Islam? and what Islam? should be implemented by the state.

The complex reasons why the Pakistan state has been manifestly unsuccessful in accommodating cultural diversity emerge during the narrative. This leads to the conclusion that the following three factors have been especially important: the tendency to regard all dissent as a law and order rather than a political issue; the manipulation and repression of popular forces by successive authoritarian regimes; and the uneven relationship between the Punjab and other regions in the conduct of national affairs.

The narrative also reveals that a state-centric approach is inadequate. Attention must also be paid to the socio-economic environment and

---

[1] Cited by A.S. Ahmed in his lecture 'Identity and Ethnicity', New Hall College, Cambridge, 7 November 1990. In his submission to the Supreme Court in 1976, Wali Khan claimed he was a 6,000-year-old Pathan.

1

its attendant political culture and to the circumstances which surrounded Pakistan's creation. It is there for example that we will find clues both to the Muslim League's failure to act as a nation-building institution, unlike its Indian Congress counterpart, and to the dysfunction between the state's subsequent development and the confederal text of the 'foundational' 1940 Lahore Resolution.[2]

Pakistani politics are ephemeral, displaying a bewildering array of shifting allegiances and alliances. Personalities count rather than ideologies or party institutionalisation. This is evidenced first by the impact of patron-client ties on voting behaviour; second by parties putting up candidates with names similar to their opponents to confuse the voters; third by the prevalence of 'one man band' parties; fourth by parties' passing over activists when allocating election tickets which instead are given to men of 'local influence'; and finally by the leading figures' multi-seat contests. Imran Khan, the former international cricketer turned politician, for example, stood unsuccessfully for no less than 8 seats in the 1997 elections. This political approach ensures that by-elections for the seats vacated follow immediately on general elections. In 1993 there were twelve National Assembly and ten Provincial Assembly contests within weeks of the October polls.

Electoral politics are dominated by elite families, many of whom regard the high costs of campaigning[3] as an 'investment' for access to the 'spoils system'. The Khans and the Sharifs are recent entrants to the Punjab's political families of Noons, Daultanas and Tiwanas. Indeed Nawaz Sharif's younger brother Shahbaz became Chief Minister of Punjab following the former's crushing 1997 national election victory. Pakistan's most famous political dynasty however remains the Bhuttos. Yet, despite the presence of high profile female politicians such as the Bhutto ladies, politics remain an overwhelmingly male preserve. There were only five female candidates from the Punjab in the February 1997 elections, and just one from Balochistan. Further evidence of the patriarchal nature of Pakistani society was provided by the threat of elders and religious leaders to punish tribesmen who registered their

---

[2] There has been great controversy surrounding the intentions of the Resolution which envisaged demarcation of geographically contiguous units into regions 'which should be so constituted with such territorial adjustments as may be necessary, that the areas in which the Muslims are numerically in a majority, as in the North-western and Eastern Zones of India, should be grouped to constitute *Independent States in which the constituent units shall be autonomous and sovereign*' (emphasis added). S.S. Pirzada (ed.), *Foundations of Pakistan: All-India Muslim League Documents 1906-1947*, vol. 2 (Karachi, 1969-70), p. 341.

[3] In a bid to curb the worst excesses, the 1997 electoral laws put a ceiling of Rs. 600,000 for Provincial Assembly candidates and of Rs. 1 million for those contesting for the National Assembly.

womenfolk as voters in the Federally Administered Tribal Areas (FATA) which, for the first time since Pakistan's creation, were able to vote on the basis of adult franchise in the 1997 polls. Under-registration of female voters has persisted in tribal areas of the Frontier, Balochistan and Punjab.[4]

The proliferation of parties and the presence of strong leaders has bequeathed instability and immaturity, rather than vitality and development. It was not until December 1970 that the first direct national elections were held. The proliferation of elections since 1988 is an equally unhealthy sign, as they have resulted from the dismissal of elected governments, none of which has seen through a full term in office. The persisting confrontational character of Pakistani politics was clearly demonstrated at the time of the 1993 polls, when the Election Commission felt it necessary to issue a code of conduct which banned the branding of opponents as *kafir* (infidel) or *ghaddar* (traitor).[5]

Powerholders harass their opponents who cry foul in a discourse dominated by concerns with corruption. Charges of national betrayal have been readily bandied about in a political system peculiarly prone to conspiracy theories. The belief for example that Bengali political demands in the early 1950s were not genuine, but instigated by a fifth-columnist Hindu population and by India is a striking instance of the dangerous consequences of such theories. The military and their bureaucratic allies have frequently inserted themselves into this unedifying and chaotic scene. Indeed for almost two decades of its existence, Pakistan has been administered by martial law regimes. At other times the army has more discreetly pulled the strings of puppet democratic dispensations. The formation of the Council of Defence and National Security (CDNS) shortly before the February 1997 polls sought to formalise the army's role in the power structure, thereby instituting a guided democracy. The military's repeated political intervention has led Pakistan to be variously termed a 'praetorian state'[6] or to possess 'a political economy of defence' in contradistinction to India's 'political economy of development'.[7]

Spending on the Punjabi-dominated armed forces[8] has drained Pakistan's resources with around 30 per cent of governmental expenditure

---

[4] Another problem has been bogus voting at polling stations, as women's identity cards do not carry photographs.

[5] M. Waseem, *The 1993 Elections in Pakistan* (Lahore, 1994), p. 228.

[6] Praetorianism is not just military intervention in politics, but unmediated politics in which the cooperative strategies for the resolution of conflict break down.

[7] See A. Jalal, *Democracy and Authoritarianism in South Asia: A Comparative and Historical Perspective* (Cambridge, 1995), in particular pp. 29–65.

[8] Armed forces personnel stood at 590,000 in 1994, a 22 per cent increase since 1987.

and 8 per cent of the GNP being devoted to defence. In the 1996-7 budget,[9] for example, 131 billion rupees was earmarked for defence, a 14 per cent increase on the previous year – this compared with a meagre Rs. 1,625 million for education and Rs. 3,219 million for health expenditure. The annual development programme expenditure was set at about 30 per cent less than this gargantuan military spending. Yet despite Pakistan spending nearly twice as great a percentage of its GNP on defence than India, the gap has widened between the absolute expenditures of the two countries, as the latter's greater population and industrial development has enabled it to outstrip its rival. The overdevelopment of the unelected institutions of the Pakistan state has perpetuated the problem of weak legitimisation as well as exacerbating ethnic politics by reinforcing the regional elites' claims of a Punjabisation of Pakistan.

Pakistan's post-independence political history has thus been a fruitless search for stability with frequent changes of government and regime. During the country's two opening decades, it experimented with two constituent assemblies, one constitutional commission and three constitutions. There have been numerous false starts, turning points which failed to turn and cul-de-sacs. The Bhutto regime of the early 1970s raised expectations with its cry of '*roti, kapra aur makan*' ('Food, Clothes and Shelter'). Similarly, the restoration of democracy which followed Zia's death in 1988 was hailed both within the country and internationally as part of the 'third wave' of democratisation sweeping the globe, marking a new beginning. The high hopes have since given way to profound gloom as successive elected governments have presided over economic decline, mounting corruption and ethnic conflict. What have been termed 'constitutional coups' successively removed the governments of Benazir Bhutto (1990), Nawaz Sharif (1993) and Bhutto again in 1996. The failure to realise earlier high expectations has contributed to a sense of cynicism and pessimism among the intellectual elites and many writers on Pakistan.

Like all new states, Pakistan possesses its foundational myths. The circumstances of its birth and the vagaries of post-independence politics have given these 'conjuring tricks' added influence.[10] The official reading of history still maintains that the Muslims of the subcontinent were a separate nation from their Hindu neighbours. On this 'two nation theory' the Pakistan demand was based. Viewed through this prism, post-independence regional identities are seen as a barrier to nation-building and as traitorous to the state's foundational unity of purpose.

[9] For further details see *Newsline* 7, 12 June 1996, pp. 24-40.

[10] A. Jalal, 'Conjuring Pakistan: History as Official Imagining', *International Journal of Middle East Studies* 27 (1995), p. 74.

The Zia regime further reworked the foundational myth to posit Jinnah and the Muslim League leadership as demanding Pakistan in order to establish not just a homeland for the nation of Indian Muslims, but an Islamic state. Thus only by returning to the pristine Islamic intentions of its creators could Pakistan establish its true identity and achieve national unity.

The reality of the Pakistan movement was that it was not monolithic. Indian Muslims adopted an identifiable Muslim political platform because of the encouragement they received from the colonial state and the contingencies arising from their relative economic and political backwardness *vis-à-vis* the Hindu majority. Jinnah's genius was to recognise the realities of the divisions in Muslim society and to forge what in fact approximated to a marriage of convenience between the Muslim professional classes of the Hindu dominated areas and the landlords of the future Pakistan regions. Local allegiances were what counted in political mobilisation rather than an understanding of a Muslim/Pakistani nationalism. Moreover, Jinnah's aim and that of the professional elite who controlled the League was to wrest a state in which Muslim economic, political and cultural interests could be safeguarded, but not to create an Islamic state. The secular outlook of the Muslim League lay beneath the temporary millenarian enthusiasm of the closing stages of the Pakistan movement. Many religious leaders were well aware of this fact and hence opposed the Muslim League, despite its demand for a state in the name of religion.

The idea that the Pakistan movement represented a golden age of idealism and that only a state–sponsored Islamisation process can recapture it is erroneous. The patronage politics of contemporary Pakistan are by no means unique. If Pakistan is to return to the past to safeguard the future,[11] it is not to the mythical theocratic intentions of its founders. It is rather to the original ideals of the famous 1940 Lahore Resolution that emphasised the decentralisation of power to the federating units of a Muslim state. Secondly it is to the consociational, accommodationist politics of the Muslim League's Unionist Party rivals in the Punjab during the 1940s. The selective memory of official history has in fact removed precisely those elements which could form the components of a viable political system. By throwing out Unionist power-sharing along with their opposition to the Pakistan struggle, the official discourse has reinforced the political culture of intolerance and confrontation which grew out of the feudal values of the Pakistan areas.

---

[11] Such dissident politicians as G.M. Syed by the early 1990s were questioning the entire Pakistan enterprise. As one of his options for the emancipation of the Sindhi nation he suggested that with 'minor adjustments in the British Cabinet Mission Plan of 1946, the confederacy of the Indian subcontinent be established.' *Dawn*, 18 January 1991.

Pakistan's historical realities are complex and messy and suit neither the rantings of Islamic ideologues, nor the precision of political science theorising about an ideal type category of the post-colonial state. Pakistan of course shares in common with many developing countries such features as class, gender and regional inequalities and conflicts between nation-building and ethnicity, modernity and tradition. But its complexities and paradoxes can only be understood in terms of an historical analysis, despite the charms of systems analysis and model building. The Pakistan state's capacity to resolve many of the conflicts arising from ethnicity for example are constrained by the past, both in terms of the authoritarianism of the modern state bequeathed by colonialism and the ambiguous relationship between Muslim nationalism and ethnic identities during the freedom struggle. This dual historical inheritance which has equated pluralism with a threat to modern Pakistani statehood has ironically resulted in undermining its legitimacy establishing a gulf between state and society. Many social science understandings lack this historical awareness and are shallow as a result.

The intention here however is not to lapse into mere description ignorant of theory. Useful insights as opposed to overarching explanations of Pakistan's instability can be gleaned from theoretic understandings. Weak political institutionalisation helps partly explain the persisting legitimacy problems of successive regimes in Pakistan, while the concepts of ethnic stereotyping,[12] ethnic discrimination and depoliticisation shed some light on the origins of the Bangladesh crisis. Rational choice theory's[13] concept of ethnic activists and political entrepreneurs may be applied with some utility to the rise of the MQM (Mohajir Qaumi Mahaz) in mid-1980s Karachi. Linked with the concept is the understanding that ethnic and linguistic self-determination movements in India have been dissipated by the state's co-opting of them in such regions as Assam and Tamil Nadu.

The historical persistence of identity politics in the Pakistan regions and their shifting bases around the symbols of religion, language and ethnicity can be understood in terms of the theoretical insight regarding the plasticity and contingency of identity and in Gramscian 'hegemonic' terms. Yunas Samad, for example, has argued that the Muslim nationalism of the freedom struggle and post-independence linguistic/ethnic nationalism are alike vehicles for minorities' counter-hegemonic aspirations. In the first instance, the Muslim League in the 1940s was mobilising against the exclusivist ideology of Indian nationalism. Bengali, Sindhi, Pushtun and other ethnic movements since independence have arisen

---

[12] For a discussion of this concept see D. Horowitz, *Ethnic Groups in Conflict* (Berkeley, CA, 1985).

[13] See R. Hardin, *One for All: The Logic of Group Conflict* (Princeton, 1995).

to challenge the hegemonic discourse of the Pakistan state which has failed to 'accommodate notions of cultural difference'.[14] The arms race in the subcontinent which has distorted Pakistan's political and economic development may be understood in part by the political scientist John Hertz's concept of the 'security dilemma'.[15]

Social scientists have variously labelled Pakistan as an 'over-developed state',[16] a 'bureaucratic polity'[17] and a 'garrison state'.[18] Lying behind these theoretical approaches is an emphasis on the geopolitical context and the role of the state in the development of Pakistan's politics.[19] Hence, Kamal Azfar has declared that 'Pakistan is a garrison state surrounded by three of the world's top four military powers, haunted by a history of wars with India.'[20] Meanwhile authoritarianism has been linked by a number of writers to the autonomous character of the Pakistani state. Hamza Alavi has understood the distance between state and society in terms of the Marxian concept of Bonapartism.[21] He sees this as resulting from the powerlessness of the national bourgeoisie in comparison with the highly developed state apparatus in the conditions of peripheral capitalism. The civilian and military controllers of the state apparatus moved from arbitration between the competing social classes, none of which is able to develop a hegemonic or dominant position, to overt control.

The lack of legitimacy and elite fear of subversion of state-building by ethnic and subaltern forces has according to some theorists been a fundamental and insoluble problem. It has given rise to the 'fearful state' in which pluralism is seen as a source of weakness rather than strength. Ruling elites have adopted policies of coercion rather than

---

[14] Y. Samad, 'Reflections on Partition: Pakistan Perspective', *International Journal of Punjab Studies* 4, no. 1 (January-June 1997), special issue on the partition of Punjab, pp. 43-63.

[15] The acquisition of 'defensive' military capabilities can be seen as threatening by neighbouring states who arm themselves, thereby resulting in the 'security dilemma' in which efforts to enhance security may actually undermine it. See J. Hertz, 'Idealist Internationalism and the Security Dilemma', *World Politics* 20, no. 2 (January 1950).

[16] See, for example, Jamal Naqvi, 'Policies and economics of a dependent state' in Naqvi, Ali and Ali, *Inside Pakistan* (New Delhi, 1986), pp. 71-2.

[17] S.H. Hashmi, Foreword in C.H. Kennedy, *Bureaucracy in Pakistan*, (Karachi, 1987).

[18] K.L. Kamal, *Pakistan The Garrison State* (New Delhi, 1982).

[19] See A. Whaites, 'The State and Civil Society in Pakistan', *Contemporary South Asia* 4, no. 3 (1995), pp. 229ff.

[20] Kamal Azfar, *Pakistan Political and Constitutional Dilemmas* (Karachi, 1987), p. 138.

[21] See Alavi's article in H. Gardezi and J. Rashid, *Pakistan: the Roots of Dictatorship. The Political Economy of a Praetorian State* (London, 1981).

co-option when responding to 'sub-nationalist' movements. An escalation of conflict, writers such as S. Mahmud Ali have maintained, inevitably followed.[22] Ishtiaq Ahmed[23] has similarly emphasised the way in which state repression has made ethnic conflict intractable. He has also linked the inability of South Asian states to resolve these conflicts to the condition of economic dependency in such peripheral capitalist countries.[24]

Much of the foregoing analysis rests on a general understanding of the post-colonial state. Christopher Clapham along with other theorists of the third-world state has maintained that its hallmark is the combination of both power and fragility.[25] The reason for the latter characteristic is not merely a lack of capacity, but the absence of a 'merging of state and society as common expressions of a set of shared values'.[26] Mehran Kamrava has reiterated this argument, maintaining that 'third world political cultures are marked by a sharp dichotomy between the political cultures of elites and that of the masses,' the uniformly weak political nexus between state and society creating a political orientation in the population that is either apathetic or extremist.[27] The state-society divide is of course intensified in many post-colonial situations because of the disjunction between cultural and territorial boundaries.

Institutionalist explanations for Pakistani authoritarianism are similarly set within the wider comparative politics context of Samuel Huntington's understanding of order and stability in post-colonial states. According to this model, poverty, regional, linguistic and religious group conflicts do not of themselves create instability. It only occurs when institutions are too weak to cope with the conflict over scarce resources which results from increased social and political mobilisation. In this situation, newly emergent groups are not socialised into the system, nor are their demands absorbed. Instead they enter it on their own terms and 'civic politics' are replaced by disorder which in turn results in praetorianism.[28] This prevents the political system from further 'over-heating' and enables it to strengthen its institutional capacity.

---

[22] S.M. Ali, *The Fearful State: Power, People and Internal War in South Asia* (London, 1993).

[23] Ishtiaq Ahmed, *State, Nation and Ethnicity in Contemporary South Asia* (London, 1996).

[24] See Gurharpal Singh's review article, 'What is Happening to the Political Science of Ethnic Conflict?', *International Journal of Punjab Studies* 3, no. 2 (July-December 1996), pp. 229-41.

[25] C. Clapham, *Third World Politics: An Introduction* (London, 1985), p. 39.

[26] *Ibid.*, p. 42.

[27] M. Kamrava, *Politics and Society in the Third World* (London, 1993), p. 168.

[28] For the classic exposition of this model see S.P. Huntington, *Political Order in Changing Societies* (New Haven, CT, 1968).

This model of analysis has been deployed by a number of scholars to explain military intervention in Pakistan.[29] Lawrence Ziring for example has linked the introduction of Pakistan's first martial law regime in 1958 with the institutional weakness resulting in part from the collapse of the Muslim League.[30] K. B. Sayeed in more colourful language adopts a similar analysis:

> Pakistan (during 1951-8) was very much like Hobbes' state of nature where every political or provincial group fought against every other group. [...] It was a ceaseless and ruthless struggle for power. [...] Pakistan needed a desperate remedy for this malady. And martial law was the Leviathan which emerged to maintain law and order and public good at the point of the sword.[31]

Veena Kukreja has similarly understood this period as one of general decay in political institutionalisation resulting in a crisis of legitimacy. She declares that 'in sum, Pakistan seems to aptly fit Huntington's model of praetorian society where military interventions are only specific manifestations of the broader phenomenon of underdevelopment and general politicisation of social forces and institutions.'[32] Maleeha Lodhi analyses the army's 1977 intervention in the same terms of the institutional weakness of Zulfikar Ali Bhutto's Pakistan People's Party (PPP) which lost its effectiveness as an instrument of political participation and recruitment when it substituted the co-option of local influentials for organisational development. Unaware of the simmering discontent, Bhutto miscalculated in calling the ill-fated 1977 elections.[33] Whether or not one agrees with this understanding of Bhutto's demise, it is undeniable that Pakistan's politics are personalistic and in one writer's words, 'as the charisma wears off, the popular base of each party has begun to decline.'[34] In such circumstances, patronage alone

[29] Both Kalam Siddiqui and Tariq Ali however put forward a different analysis of Ayub's coup, regarding it as an 'anticipatory' coup because the military feared the establishment of an East Pakistani dominated democratic order following promised national elections. See K. Siddiqui, *Conflict, Crisis and War in Pakistan* (London, 1972), pp. 130-1; Tariq Ali, *Can Pakistan Survive? The Death of a State* (Harmondsworth, 1983).

[30] L. Ziring, *Pakistan: The Enigma of Political Development* (Boulder, CO, 1980), p. 82.

[31] K.B. Sayeed, 'The Collapse of Parliamentary Democracy in Pakistan', *Middle East Journal*, 13, no. 4 (autumn 1959), pp. 389-90.

[32] V. Kukreja, *Civil-Military Relations in South Asia: Pakistan, Bangladesh and India* (New Delhi, 1991), p. 45.

[33] M. Lodhi, 'Pakistan in Crisis', *The Journal of Commonwealth and Comparative Politics* 16, no. 1 (March 1978), p. 65.

[34] A. Ahmad, 'The rebellion of 1983: A Balance Sheet', *South Asia Bulletin* 4, no. 1

can secure party cohesion and stability. This reached its logical absurdity in August 1996 when out of forty-three members of the Balochistan Provincial Assembly, no less than thirty-one held official positions in the government of Nawab Zulfiqar Ali Magsi.

Common to much political science writing on Pakistan however is a lack of historical and behavioural empirical data. David Gilmartin's and Theodore Wright's pioneering work notwithstanding,[35] the role of the *biraderi* (kinship group) in political mobilisation for example has received   nothing like the attention of caste in the Indian context.[36] Standard accounts have thus missed some of the real štuff of political activity and have presented parties as too 'modern' in their organisation and electioneering methods. *Biraderi* rivalries were particularly important in the 'partyless' February 1985 and April 1962 elections. At the time of the latter the influential Urdu daily paper *Nawa-i-Waqt* (Voice of the Times) lamented that it was 'regrettable so many election campaigns are being waged on the basis of sectarian and regional loyalties', and *Zamindar* asked the electorate, 'not to vote for persons who appeal only in the name of castes and factions'.[37] It is in fact impossible to understand the volatile politics of the Punjab's Gujrat district of the past three decades without reference to such *biraderi* feuds and loyalties.[38] When Arif Nakai's new PPP-PML(J) (Pakistan Muslim League – Junejo faction) cabinet was sworn into office in Punjab in September 1995, the local papers' main interest lay in comparing the number of seats held by Rajputs, Gujars and Jats.[39] At the time of the 1993 general elections, Adnan Adil produced a map of the *biraderi* belts in Punjab.[40]

Earlier 'high politics' accounts of the British transfer of power similarly disembodied political developments from their social realities. The growing use of literary sources to uncover the human dimension of

---

(Spring 1984), p. 36.

[35] D. Gilmartin, '*Biraderi* and Bureaucracy: The Politics of Muslim Kinship Solidarity in Twentieth Century Punjab', *International Journal of Punjab Studies* 1, no. 1 (January-June 1994), pp. 1-29; Theodore P. Wright Jr, 'Biraderis in Punjabi Elections', *The Journal of Political Science*, 14, nos 1 and 2 (1991).

[36] For a classic analysis of caste, politics and social change in India see: R. Kothari (ed.), *Caste in Indian Politics* (New Delhi, 1970), and M.N. Srinivas, *Caste in Modern India and Other Essays* (Bombay, 1962).

[37] American Consul Lahore to Department of State, 18 April 1962, 790D/00/4-1862, National Archives at College Park.

[38] See Mazhar Zaidi, '*Biraderi*-in-Arms', *Newsline* 8, no. 2 (August 1996), pp. 44-51.

[39] I.A. Rehman, 'A Question of Culture?', *Newsline* 7, no. 3 (September 1995), p. 38.

[40] Adnan Adil, 'Rajputs, Jats, Arains and Syeds Dominate Punjab Elections', *Friday Times*, 16-22 September 1993.

partition[41] could be deployed with equal effect for the post-colonial era. A starting point could be Shaukat Siddiqi's justly acclaimed novel *Khuda Ki Basti*.[42] Its themes of corruption, political manipulation and the degradation of the urban poor are the focus of much political science literature on Pakistan, but these take on a fresh starkness when given a human face through such characters as Niyaz, Khan Bahadur Farzand Ali, Nausha, Raja and Shami.

Similarly, theories of the geopolitical context, institutional decay and the distance between state and society lack sufficient historical contextualisation to convincingly explain Pakistani authoritarianism. A historical understanding of the marginalisation of the Pakistan areas in the freedom movement is necessary to understand the concept of the state's autonomy from society, while the concept of a garrison state needs to be set in the context of colonial army recruitment policies and the circumstances of the 1947 partition. Ayesha Jalal[43] has begun to examine the precise situations in which state building was emphasised over political participation, but a wider acknowledgement is required of the fact that Pakistan inherited from the Raj what has been termed a 'viceregal' tradition which strongly emphasised the supremacy of the executive over representative institutions. Its strength in the future Pakistan regions resulted from the fact that British rule came late to Muslim north-west India and was prompted by strategic rather than commercial considerations. Successive Pakistani regimes have suppressed popular participation by working within this tradition. Ayub Khan's government for example issued a decree at the time of the promulgation of the 1962 Constitution which enabled the colonially derived authoritarian Frontier Crimes Regulation to be applied throughout West Pakistan.[44] Pakistan's political development thus cannot be treated as if it

---

[41] See for example, Ian Talbot, 'Literature and the Human Drama of the 1947 Partition', *South Asia*, 18, special issue (1995), pp. 37-56; *Freedom Cry: The Popular Dimension in the Pakistan Movement and Partition Experience in North-West India*, (1996).

[42] The title comes from the following Urdu verses:

> '*khuda ki basti men khuda ke bandon pe kya guzri*
> *khuda par yaqin hai lekin khuda ki basti par nahin.*'
> 'God gave us our country; we toil and we plod.
> We can't trust our land, but we trust in our God.'

The work has been published under the title of *God's Own Land: A Novel of Pakistan*, (transl) D.J. Matthews (Sandgate, 1991).

[43] A. Jalal, *The State of Martial Rule: The Origins of Pakistan's Political Economy of Defence* (Cambridge, 1990).

[44] American Consul Lahore to Department of State, 6 March 1962, 790D.00/3-162, National Archives at College Park.

were inscribed on a *tabula rasa*, although this has been the approach of some social scientists.

There is a similar lack of historical understanding in 'process' explanations of the post-1988 democratisation. For it is extremely likely that the strategic choices of political actors during democratic transitions will be influenced by the legacies of the *ancien régime* from which they are departing. Moreover, the very nature of transitions requires historical analysis with its emphasis on change over time. Similarly, instrumentalist understandings of ethnic conflicts at best provide an inadequate understanding. They lack not only a sense of the historic role which ideas have played in political mobilisation, but a convincing understanding of the precise circumstances which trigger the transition from ethnic awareness to a politicisation of ethnic identity.

The division of labour between historians of the Pakistan region and political scientists has thus not served scholarship well. The abrupt termination of historical narratives in 1947 has helped obfuscate the continuities between the colonial and contemporary eras. Although Pakistan emerged as a state with a new identity, its political culture and characteristics were profoundly influenced by historical inheritances from the colonial era. The importance of five such influences are stressed in this study. The first was the clash between regional identity and Muslim nationalism, which was barely hidden in both Sindh and Bengal during the Pakistan struggle. The second was the problematic relationship between Islam and Muslim nationalism. Paradoxically, while Pakistan was created in the name of religion, many of the '*ulama* opposed nationalism as un-Islamic. The third was the culture of political intolerance[45] forged in the Muslim League's desperate struggle against Congress and such powerful regional opponents as the Punjab Unionists. The stakes were so high as the League clawed its way to power that all opposition was regarded as illegitimate. Such opponents as the Unionist Party Prime Minister Khizr Hayat Tiwana were denounced as 'infidels' and 'traitors' to Islam. The Muslim League identified its own interests with those of the whole Indian Muslim community. These attitudes were carried over into the independence era, when Liaquat and other Muslim League leaders denounced political opposition as anti-state and even Indian-inspired.

At the celebrations of the late Quaid-e-Azam's eighty-fifth birth

---

[45] Yunas Samad goes further than calling this a political culture of intolerance, maintaining that an exclusive hegemonic discourse in the Gramscian sense links the pre-independence and post-colonial eras. The Muslim League responded to the Congress's hegemonic discourse by adopting an identity politics 'mobilised around the cultural markers and idioms of religion.' Similarly, linguistic and 'new identity' politics have emerged since independence in response to the state sponsored official nationalist hegemonic discourse. Y. Samad, 'Reflections on Partition: Pakistan Perspective'.

anniversary in December 1961 a Majlis-i-Istaqlal-i-Pakistan (Committee for Independence of Pakistan) meeting in Lahore unanimously resolved that a committee should list those who had opposed Jinnah and the Pakistan movement during the period 1940-6 and that 'anti-Pakistan elements' should be deprived of their rights of political expression, they should be debarred from seeking election to any future parliament or government and a ceiling should be imposed on their property.[46] The seeds were thus sown for a political culture of intolerance which has become the hallmark of successive elected as well as non-elected regimes. It has brought in its wake not only curbs on civil liberties and selective political accountability, but violence in the absence of a consensual and accommodationist political culture. This in turn has encouraged military intervention under the pretext of restoring law and order.

The fourth inheritance is the colonial state's practice of ruling indirectly through intermediaries such as landlords, tribal chiefs and princes. The British tied them into their rule by elaborate networks of patronage and ensured that the tribal chiefs, landowners and Sufi *pirs'* predominance was unchallenged by agricultural commercialisation and the increasing introduction of representative institutions. Indeed many constituencies coincided with local patterns of power based on tribes, *biraderis* and landed estates. West Pakistan was thus to inherit a landlord's country in which little progress had been made in removing glaring social inequalities in the countryside.

Finally, Pakistan inherited historical traditions unique to each of the regions which were to comprise it. These have frequently been neglected in national level political studies, but have proved of immense importance in shaping post-colonial developments. In Sindh for example it is possible to discern in the 1930s the beginnings of a 'national' consciousness reacting to the presence of 'outsider others'. These were Punjabi agriculturalists who were encouraged to migrate following the opening of the Sukkur barrage. Sindhi sentiment against outsiders was submerged during the religious mobilisation of the freedom struggle, but re-emerged after independence in the wake of waves of *mohajir*, Pushtun, Punjabi and Baloch migrants. The nationalist leader G.M. Syed stated this resentment most baldly at the time of his eighty-eighth birthday celebrations, when he declared that all those who had entered Sindh after 1954 should be deprived of their civic and political rights and the influx of aliens be stopped.[47]

In Balochistan, British rule froze the ethnic division of Baloch and Pushtun territory and prevented the gradual incorporation of the more

---

[46] American Consul Lahore to Department of State, 29 December 1961, 790D/00/2-56, National Archives at College Park.

[47] *Dawn*, 18 January 1991.

egalitarian Pushtun lineages into Baloch and Brahui society. It also encouraged greater economic development in the northern Pushtun areas which were directly administered in British Balochistan than in the Baloch and Brahui areas of the Kalat States Union. The economic causes of the Baloch-Pushtun ethnic violence of the 1980s were thus not just the result of the tensions generated by the Afghan War, but possessed deeper historical roots. The rise of the ethnic Pushtunkhwa Milli Awami Party (PKMAP) at the time of the 1993 elections must also be understood against this background. Similarly, both the Pushtunistan issue in the post-independence Frontier and the increasing alienation of Bengalis from the centre cannot be understood without recourse to their regional pre-independence histories. At the time of the abortive 1946 Cabinet Mission for example, the Pushtun leader Abdul Ghaffar Khan opposed compulsory grouping and maintained that 'we are happy in framing our own destiny by ourselves'. Allah Nawaz Khan, Speaker of the Frontier Provincial Assembly articulated even more clearly the basis for a Pushtun identity when he declared in words reminiscent of the Lahore Resolution,

> 'Pathans[48] and Punjabis are two major nations by any definition or test of a nation and the idea and very thought of grouping the NWFP with the Punjabis is revolting to the Pathan mind. We are a nation of three million, and what is more, we, the Frontier Pathans, are a body of people with our own distinctive culture, civilisation, language, literature, art and architecture, names and nomenclature and sense of values and proportion, legal and moral codes, customs and calendar, history and traditions, and aptitudes and ambitions. In short, we have our own distinctive outlook on life and by all canons of international law a Pathan is quite separate from a Punjabi.'[49]

Anti-Punjabi sentiments are held quite widely by contemporary political leaders in the minority provinces. Some scholars have spoken in terms of the Punjabisation of Pakistan.[50] The region, which accounts for 56 per cent of the total population, has become the arbiter of national authority not just under periods of martial law, but also as Benazir Bhutto's first ministry (1988-90) found to its cost during periods of

[48] 'Pathan' is a popular Hindustani rendering of Pushtun or Pakhtun.

[49] S.A. Rittenberg, *Ethnicity, Nationalism and Pakhtuns: The Independence Movement in India's North-West Frontier Province, 1901-1947* (Durham, NC, 1988), p. 337.

[50] See for example, Yunas Samad, 'Pakistan or Punjabistan: Crisis of National Identity' in G. Singh and I. Talbot (eds), *Punjabi Identity: Continuity and Change* (New Delhi, 1995), pp. 61-87.

a democratic dispensation.[51] The region's political importance was recognised almost from the outset of the new state. The Pakistan Prime Minister, Liaquat Ali Khan moved his own office from Karachi to Lahore during the campaign for the March 1951 Punjab Provincial Assembly elections.[52] Punjabi dominance in the state's power elite and economic life has carried a high cost, creating Bengali and later Sindhi and Balochi alienation from the centre.

Punjab's political predominance was greatly increased with the breakaway of East Pakistan in 1971. But it can only be fully understood in terms of the colonial inheritance. This laid the basis for its agricultural prosperity, industrial development and association with army recruitment. Following partition, the same Rajput tribes of the Pothwar plateau were recruited to the Pakistan Army.[53] The continuation of colonial policies of making land available to servicemen has created a nexus of interest between the landowners and military. Many servicemen acquired redistributed land at knockdown prices after the 1959 land reforms.[54] Their entry into the rural and industrial elite continued apace during the Zia martial law period. Punjabi domination of the Army has had immense political repercussions, for the Army has been the most important institution in the state and the self-appointed upholder of Pakistani stability and national identity.[55]

Criticism of Punjab's role in Pakistani politics[56] should not however be allowed to obscure the reality of cultural and economic differentiation within the province. Four distinct economic and cultural regions can be identified. The northern region which corresponds to the administrative boundaries of the Rawalpindi division contains approximately 10 per cent of the province's population. From the colonial era onwards the inhabitants of this hilly region have supplemented low agricultural earnings with army recruitment and latterly with remittances from the Gulf. The Punjabi-dominated army of journalistic and polemical rhetoric is in reality an army recruited largely from the Attock, Rawalpindi and

---

51 Nawaz Sharif's provincial government in Lahore had continuously harried the Federal Government. The clash between the two power centres had a considerable influence on the undermining of the Bhutto administration.

52 A. Jalal, *The State of Martial Rule*, p. 145.

53 Three-quarters of all ex-servicemen come from just three districts of the Punjab (Rawalpindi, Jhelum and Campbellpur) and two adjacent disticts of the Frontier (Kohat, Mardan). S.P. Cohen, *The Pakistan Army* (Berkeley, CA, 1984), p, 44.

54 See Chapter 6 for a detailed examination of these reforms and their impact.

55 The most authoritative account of the Pakistan Army is still contained in S.P. Cohen, *The Pakistan Army*.

56 See for example, I.A. Rehman, 'Big Brother vs the Rest', *Newsline*, October 1995, pp. 67-8.

Jhelum districts, although it is true that the economic multiplier effects of military recruitment ripple out to other areas of the province.

Central Punjab contains virtually half of the province's population and includes not only the industrialised region around Faisalabad (Lyallpur) but also the fertile agricultural districts of Lahore and Gujranwala. The concentration of population makes this the most politically important region of the province with 55 out of 112 National Assembly seats. South-west Punjab, which contains around a fifth of the province's population comprises the Multan and Bahawalpur divisions. The Cholistan Desert forms the boundary with India, and the canal irrigation of the colonial era has transformed other previously barren tracts into major cotton growing areas. The poorest region of the Punjab remains the western districts including Jhang district and the Sargodha and Dera Ghazi Khan divisions. In contrast with central Punjab, its agrarian society and economy is organised on a feudal basis.

Cultural differences overlay these socio-economic and climatic variations. To the north of the Salt Range, Hindko and Pothwari are spoken alongside Punjabi as regional languages, whereas in the south-western Punjab Siraiki, which is closely related to Sindhi, is spoken as a mother-tongue by a considerable section of the population.[57] By the mid-1980s its leading organisation, the Siraiki Suba Mahaz, was calling for a Siraiki Suba (province). The regional variations in Punjab were reflected in the 1993 National Assembly election results: the PPP lost badly to the Muslim League in the northern Punjab, but captured 22 out of 36 seats in the Siraiki-speaking divisions of Multan, D.G. Kham, Rahimyar Khan and Bahawalpur.

The dangers of an unrepresentative army increased during periods of martial law and on the numerous occasions it was called on to restore order. Bengali separatist sentiment during the 1960s was undoubtedly fuelled both by the lack of Bengali representation in the military elite and by the discrimination towards the new East Bengal Regiment.[58] In 1962 Yahya Khan, who was to later preside over the débâcle of the Bangladesh secession, rather unconvincingly explained the slow increase in Bengali army recruitment in terms of the poor communications with the villages in East Pakistan. The army he declared were 'seeking peasant boys rather than city boys'.[59] Two decades after the Bangladesh

[57] See C. Shackle, 'Saraiki: A Language Movement in Pakistan', *Modern Asian Studies* 11, no. 3 (1979), pp. 379-403.

[58] In 1955 just 14/894 Army Officers came from East Bengal. Bengali Muslims from the World War Two Pioneer Corps, together with those who had served in the Bihar Regiment of the Indian Army formed the two battalion strong East Bengal Regiment.

[59] American Consul Dacca to Department of State, 14 December 1962, 790D.00/2-762, National Archives at College Park.

breakaway, Sindhi alienation from the centre was reinforced by the presence of a Punjabi 'colonising' force.

Karachi is the only other local political arena which is significant nationally. Successive waves of migration from India and within Pakistan have resulted in over 5 per cent of the total population congregating in its urban sprawl, drawn by the hope of finding employment in its Pakistan's only major port and retains its dominant commercial and industrial position, accounting for approximately a quarter of Pakistan's manufacturing base and two thirds of the country's banking transactions. This pivotal economic importance propelled the largely Karachi-based MQM to national political importance in the late 1980s. The state's inability to maintain law and order in the city was an important factor in the dismissal of both the first Benazir Bhutto administration (1990) and that of her successor Nawaz Sharif (1993). The charge sheet drawn up by President Farooq Leghari in November 1996 against Benazir Bhutto placed high on its list the prevalence of extra-judicial killings by the police and the rangers during 1995-6 in the campaign to snuff out MQM militancy.

While Karachi could break national governments, it nevertheless lacked the Punjab's political preponderance. Finally it is important to note the economic interconnection between Punjab and Karachi. All of the Punjab's foreign trade is transported through the latter region, the petroleum on which it depends also comes from the port and refineries of Karachi. Despite Punjab's dominance within the Pakistani economy as a whole, Karachi plays a vital role in its functioning.

It is clear even from this brief overview that historical and regional inheritances along with the legacy of the freedom struggle itself provide an important insight into Pakistan's post-independence politics. The state's contested national identity, uneven development, bureaucratic authoritarianism and imbalance between a weak civil society and dominant military can all be traced to the colonial era.

In stating this argument however, it is important not to ignore earlier historical influences. The British system of governance with its centralised administrative structure and the political co-option of local elites was based on Mughal practice. The work of Shaikh Ahmad Sirhindi (1564-1624) and Shah Wali-Allah (1703-62) to reform popular Islam and bring about a Sunni Islamic revival pre-date the establishment of British power. Resistance to obscurantist religious authority is associated not just with nineteenth-century Islamic modernism, but with the earlier writings of Varis Shah (1720?-84?). Another Sufi, Shah Inayat of Jhok who distributed land to the downtrodden peasants of Sindh and was martyred in January 1718 reveals a long established tradition of social activism and resistance to state oppression. The 1983 rebellion in Sindh against Zia's regime was not only heir to this, but drew inspiration from the verses of the great mystical poet Shah Abdul Latif of Bhit (1689-1752).

The Punjabi PPP leader and Interior Minister in Benazir Bhutto's first administration, Aitzaz Ahsan[60] has recently seized on such traditions to argue that the creation of Pakistan was not an historical aberration or the outcome of colonial divide and rule policies as Indian nationalist historiography has claimed; it was rather the culmination of a long-established cultural and historical Indus tradition which has moulded the Pakistani personality as distinct from the Indian. The attempt on the eve of the fiftieth anniversary of the British departure to establish a Pakistani identity rooted in the soil and history rather than in an 'obscurantist mould' was in itself interesting. The leading American analyst, Selig Harrison refutes such 'ingenuity' and understands Pakistan's post-independence political instability partly in terms of the 'artificiality' of the Pakistan state. Religion alone has proved an insufficient means of building a nation out of disparate ethnic groups who had never previously coexisted except under colonialism. He points out that during the Mughal era, Punjab was an outlying province and the Pushtuns and Baloch were pitted against the authorities in Delhi. Moreover, the Punjabis' contemporary ethnic assertiveness could be linked with their historical memory of rule by Afghan, Sikh and British outsiders.[61]

An emphasis on the significance of the colonial inheritance therefore not only runs the risk of overlooking earlier historical influences, but of producing a stereotype of Pakistan which in the words of Alan Whaites portrays it as 'a static state stuck in a continuing cycle of military and feudal government'.[62] There has been considerable social transformation since 1947, although this has not been reflected in post-1988 electoral politics, partly because constituencies remain tied to the outmoded 1981 Census. A striking change in the half century since independence seldom remarked upon is the establishment of a large Pakistani overseas community with a range of transnational linkages with the 'homeland'. Overseas mobilisation as a result of a new sense of ethnic consciousness has impacted upon the development of both the MQM within Pakistan and the Jammu and Kashmir Liberation Front (JKLF) in Azad Kashmir (AK),[63] although little has been written on this subject.[64]

---

60 A. Ahsan, *The Indus Saga and the Making of Pakistan* (Karachi, 1996).

61 Interview with Selig Harrison, Washington, 12 November 1996.

62 Whaites, 'The State and Civil Society in Pakistan', p. 230.

63 Since 1985 there has been an institutional recognition of the importance of the Kashmiri diaspora within the politics of AK with the addition of an overseas representative to the Legislative Assembly. The seat's holder is appointed by the Azad Kashmir Prime Minister. P. Ellis and Z. Khan, 'Partition and Kashmir: Implications Fifty Years On for the Region and the Diaspora', p. 9. Paper presented to 14th European conference on 'Modern South

Better documented discontinuities include the accelerated post-colonial ethnicisation of Sindh's politics as a result both of the preferential policies in the federal public employment sector from 1972 onwards and the acceleration of Punjabi and Pushtun immigration in the Zia era. The task of nation building in Pakistan has been hampered not only by unresolved conflicts between regional, religious and nationalist identity inherited from the freedom movement, but by the attempts of successive martial law regimes to forcibly impose a national identity rather than achieve it by consensus. Furthermore, ethno-nationalist movements have not been rooted in historically derived immutable traits and identities (despite the claims of primordialists), but rather on the shifting sands of political strategies and circumstances. Increasing Baloch and Pushtun access to federal levers of power during the past two decades has defused earlier regionalist movements. The Pakistan state has thus been unstable not just because of its inheritances from the colonial era; it is in fact precisely the interplay between these and the response of the power elites to rapid socio-economic change within the country and to political developments worldwide, especially the growing strategic asymmetry in the subcontinent, which hold the key to understanding Pakistan's dilemmas at the close of the twentieth century.

Our opening chapter provides the reader with both an introduction to Pakistan's geopolitical, economic and social setting and an overview of the changes and challenges since the separation of Bangladesh in 1971. Chapter 2 focuses on the administrative, economic and political legacies of British rule in the regions which were to form Pakistan, while Chapter 3 examines the character and legacies of the Pakistan movement. This is followed by a brief study of the seemingly insurmountable problems which faced Pakistan on its creation. Two key questions are raised. How was Pakistan able to overcome the difficulties which threatened to strangle it at birth? And in what ways did the crisis management of 1947-8 influence the state's future political trajectory? Chapter 5 surveys the chaotic political period which culminated in the military coup of 1958. It draws out both the causes and significance of the Muslim League's collapse and also looks at the establishment of the close strategic ties with the United States. There then follows an assessment of the successes and ultimate failures of the Ayub era. The Bangladesh breakaway is analysed in Chapter 7 in terms of both the depoliticisation and economic imbalances of the Ayub era and East Bengal's longer term history.

Asian Studies', Copenhagen, 21-24 August 1996.

64 An exception is the pioneering paper by P. Ellis and Z. Khan cited in note 63 above.

Chapter 8 sets the ultimate failure of the populist interlude of Zulfiqar Ali Bhutto in its regional and international historical context. Particular attention is drawn to the regime's economic and political reforms and to centre-province relations. The next chapter examines Zia's Pakistan and its legacy for the contemporary period, focusing on both the Islamisation process and the changing international context. The final two chapters seek to explain why democratisation in Pakistan since 1988 has gone hand in hand with a growing crisis of governability. The historic roots of Pakistan's zero-sum politics are examined along with the constraints placed upon the state by the late-twentieth-century new world order and economic globalisation.

Part I: THE HISTORICAL INHERITANCE

1

PAKISTAN: LAND, SOCIETY AND ECONOMY

Contemporary Pakistan, with an area of 803,943 square miles (twice the size of California), is strategically located to the east of the Persian Gulf and in close proximity to China and Russia. Its geopolitical position particularly during the Cold War era gave it greater international interest than its size and economy would otherwise warrant. Much of the country's foreign relations and domestic priorities have been diverted to counter-balancing what is seen as the threat posed to its existence by the neigh-bouring Indian state. Pakistan's resulting ties with America and, to a much smaller extent, with China have profoundly influenced its internal politics.

Pakistan's geopolitical situation in the new world order of the early 1990s seemed more favourable than at any period since the 1971 secession of East Pakistan. The military threat of the former Soviet Union had been removed and India could no longer rely on it for diplomatic and economic assistance or for supplies of cheap weapons. The emergence of the six Central Asian republics further opened up the possibility of economic, cultural and commercial links. They were admitted to an expanded and reactivated Economic Cooperation Agency (ECO) early in 1992.[1] Finally, the coming to power of a post-partition generation in both India and Pakistan held out the hope of improved relations and a much needed peace dividend. It seemed as though this was about to be realised early in 1991 following a series of agreements on troop movements and the opening of air corridors.

In Europe the euphoria engendered by the fall of the Berlin Wall

---

1 The ECO had originally included Pakistan, Iran and Turkey.

turned to disillusionment in the bloody Balkan conflict. Pakistan's hopes dissolved in the chaos of post-communist Afghanistan and in the intensification of the cold war with India. The turbulence in Afghanistan threatened not only an overspilling of violence into the Pushtun areas of the Frontier, but closed off the trade route from Central Asia to the Arabian Sea at Karachi. Iran increasingly emerged as an alternative trade outlet. The unofficial Pakistani support for the Taliban movement in Afghanistan must be viewed in the light of trade as much as Islamic policy.

Indo-Pakistan hostility fuelled the subcontinental arms race and destroyed any short-term prospect of South Asian regional economic cooperation in a world increasingly dominated by trading blocs.[2] Indo-Pakistan relations had worsened in the wake of the Kashmiri separatist uprising and the 1992 demolition of the Babri Masjid at Ayodhya in India. In March 1992 the Pakistan Government had to deploy paramilitary forces in Azad Kashmir to prevent protest marches by the JKLF across the ceasefire line. New Delhi continuously claimed that Pakistan was waging a covert war in Kashmir and that its Inter Services Intelligence Agency (ISI) had planted the bombs which killed 300 people in Bombay in March 1993. Islamabad for its part accused RAW (the Indian Intelligence Services) agents of being behind the random shootings in Karachi. The continued deterioration of relations in 1994[3] culminated in the closure of the two country's consulates in Bombay and Karachi respectively.[4] India's improved relations with Pakistan's traditional Chinese ally carried an even greater threat, as it freed upwards of five Indian divisions and thus upset the strategic balance still further. This exacerbated the effect of the loss of the US military prop. The economic strain in attempting to keep up with India was brought home in 1995 when rising defence expenditure forced Pakistan to break its accord with the IMF.[5] Such economic compulsions, both sides of the Wagah border, provide the most likely reason for a long overdue rethinking in Indo-Pakistan relations, although people-to-people diplomacy as

---

[2] The South Asian Association for Regional Cooperation (SAARC) had been founded in 1985. But it has made only limited headway in comparison with regional organisations elsewhere in the world, not just because of Indo-Pakistan suspicions, but also tensions between India and Sri Lanka and even India and Nepal.

[3] Benazir Bhutto warned of the dangers of a missile race following the test firing in June of the Prithvi surface-to-surface missile.

[4] Tahir Amin, 'Pakistan in 1994: The Politics of Confrontation', *Asian Survey* 35, no. 2 (February 1995), p. 146.

[5] S. Gordon, 'South Asia After the Cold War: Winners and Losers', *Asian Survey* 35, no. 10 (October 1995), p. 894.

epitomised by the India-Pakistan Forum for Peace and Democracy may make some headway in bridging the great divide of 1947.

In socio-economic terms Pakistan can be best typified as a populous, rapidly growing middle income country in which agriculture is losing its predominance. Arable land still remains the principal natural resource with 25 per cent of the country's total area under cultivation thanks to one of the most extensive irrigation systems in the world. However, social welfare has lagged behind economic growth, bringing with it marked rural-urban and gender disparities. Again, as in many developing countries, external and internal budget deficits are high.

The country's population was estimated at 128 million in 1994 with an annual increase of 3 per cent, one of the highest in the world. Rapid rates of economic growth (6.2 per cent during the 1980s and early 90s) have lifted Pakistan to the status of a middle income country with a GDP of $52 billion by 1993-4. Agriculture's share of the GDP has declined from 53 per cent in 1947 to around 26 per cent. Social welfare has lagged behind Pakistan's considerable economic progress since independence. This is demonstrated most starkly by such figures as 26 per cent literacy and an infant mortality rate of 97 out of 1000 births in 1993. Life expectancy stands at fifty-nine for both men and women. Gender inequalities are particularly marked in education where only 11 per cent of Pakistani women are literate and only a tenth of school-age girls in the countryside receive education.

Despite rapid growth, the economy is highly vulnerable to both internal and external shocks and indebtedness is a major problem. The exceptional flooding and political instability of 1993 for example, caused the balance of payments deficit to rise to $3.7 billion and the reserves were almost completely depleted. Pakistan's large external debt of about $19.2 billion in 1993 was considered to be manageable, although amortisation accounted for 23 per cent of export earnings in that year. Wheat is the main crop for domestic consumption and the major exports are rice, fish, fruits and vegetables. Despite attempts at diversification, cotton textiles and clothing account for about 50 per cent of all exports. These amounted to $6.6 billion for the year 1993-4 and went to Japan, the United States, Britain and Saudi Arabia. Imports of wheat, crude oil, cooking oil, fertilisers and machinery for the same financial year cost $8.8 billion. Pakistan received around $2.6 billion in grants/loans from such institutions as the International Monatary Fund, the World Bank and the Asian Development Bank as well as bilateral donors. By 1996 they appeared increasingly unwilling to bail Pakistan out of its debt crisis and there appeared a real possibility of defaulting on earlier loans. The crisis which coincided with the dismissal of Benazir Bhutto's second government was narrowly averted by recourse to short term high interest loans and by what opponents called a further surrender of economic decision making to international lenders.

Pakistani society is overwhelmingly Islamic in its values and ideas. However its Islam is not monolithic or for that matter monochrome, with significant sectarian differences and a lively Sufi tradition. Outside the tribal areas, the main social networks are formed by *biraderis* and Sufi brotherhoods. The countryside, especially in Sindh and south-western Punjab, is marked by uneven feudal power relationships. Society is strictly patriarchal. Competing with these social forces and identities in political mobilisation have been ethnic loyalties. These are grounded in both linguistic and cultural inheritances and a sense that Punjabis have controlled the Pakistan state apparatus to the disadvantage of others. Together all these influences, many of which were reinforced during the period of colonial rule, have established a political culture which is inimical to the growth of a participant democracy.

In keeping with the major concerns of this work, special attention will be paid in this chapter both to the inheritances from the colonial state and the changes brought about by the separation of East Pakistan in 1971. The chapter will conclude by examining Pakistan's post-independence socio-economic development.

East Bengal and the problem of national integration

East Bengal, which until 1971 comprised one-sixth of Pakistan's total area, was a monsoon-saturated delta land which extended some 300 miles north of the Bay of Bengal. Most of the province was barely above sea-level, broken only by a narrow band of hills along the Burmese border. It contrasted with West Pakistan not only in topography and climate, but in population density and religious composition. East Pakistan contained over half of the state's total population (some 45 million) in 1947, the 1,000-plus people per square mile making it one of the most densely settled regions of the world. Even in the most thickly populated rural areas of West Pakistan, the density was no more than 350 people per square mile. While just under 3 per cent of West Pakistan's population was non-Muslim according to the 1951 Census, the figure for the eastern wing was 23 per cent.[6] Caste Hindus accounted for the majority of the non-Muslim population. In the western wing the minorities comprised Punjabi and Goan Christians and Scheduled Caste Hindus from Sindh. The relative sizes of the two wings' minority populations inevitably influenced responses to the issue of Islamisation.

East Bengal's most striking feature was its 1,000-mile separation

6 E.H. Slade, *Census of Pakistan 1951* (Karachi, 1951), vol I, Table 6, pp. 6-2.

from West Pakistan by Indian territory. This distance from the seat of national power compounded the problem of forging a sense of national identity which could reach across regional, linguistic and religious differences. The economic imbalances between West and East Pakistan also hindered national integration. India retained the main industrial enclaves at the time of Partition, with the result that Pakistan inherited an overwhelmingly agrarian economy. The industrial base consisted of only a few cement plants, flour and rice mills and cotton-ginning factories, and nearly all of these were situated in the western wing. East Pakistan provided a market for West Pakistan's goods and, through the export of raw jute,[7] the foreign exchange for its infrastructural development. Economies of scale and the siting of the federal capital in West Pakistan perpetuated the inter-wing imbalance, and as the result there were destabilising political repercussions.

East and West Pakistan's agrarian structures also contrasted sharply. Peasant proprietors predominated in East Bengal where just under a half of the cultivable area was owned by families having 5 acres or less. Sindh and parts of the Punjab possessed large landed estates. Differing political priorities and styles emanated from the societies of the eastern and western wings. The Bengalis' more radical and democratic urges were denied in the realm of national politics because their demographic majority was converted to an equality with the less progressive West Pakistan under the principle of parity enshrined in the 1956 and 1962 Constitutions.

The Bengali elites' sense of marginalisation is clearly displayed in the following quotation from a speech by Ataur Rahman Khan during a debate in the Constituent Assembly early in 1956. 'I feel a peculiar sensation when I come from Dacca to Karachi', the then Chief Minister declared; 'I feel physically, apart from mental feeling, that I am living here in a foreign country. I did not feel as much when I went to Zurich, to Geneva...or London as much as I feel here in my own country that I am in a foreign land.'[8]

Language and political identity in Pakistan

Language has acted as an important marker of identity and source of political mobilisation in South Asia as is evidenced, for example, by the Telegu movement in the Indian state of Andhra Pradesh and the Dravidian movement and rise of the Dravida Munnetra Kazhagam in Tamil Nadu. Language politics rest first on cultural

[7] East Pakistan supplied three-quarters of the world's raw jute.

[8] Cited in I.H. Malik, *State and Civil Society in Pakistan: Politics of Authority, Ideology and Ethnicity* (Basingstoke, 1997), p. 63.

reactions both in India and Pakistan to the centralising attempts to impose a national language on a Babel of tongues; second on elite fears of disadvantage in the competition for public employment if the mother tongue is relegated in status. Muslim separatism in colonial India was rooted of course in the Urdu-Hindi controversy in the United Provinces (UP) at the beginning of this century. From the time of Muhsin al-Mulk's foundation of an Urdu Defence Association in 1900 onwards, the Urdu language became a major symbol of Muslim political identity.

For this reason the Prime Minister Liaquat Ali Khan rejected a motion in the Constituent Assembly in February 1948 that Bengali be used along with Urdu. He opined that 'Pakistan has been created because of the demand of a hundred million Muslims in this subcontinent and the language of a hundred million Muslims is Urdu. [...] It is necessary for a nation to have one language and that language can only be Urdu and no other language.'[9] Such statements were contradicted by a reality in which only around 7 per cent of the population spoke Urdu[10] as their mother-tongue. Attempts at strengthening Urdu as part of the na-tion-building enterprise proved counterproductive as was demonstrated most clearly in East Bengal. Even after 1971, as Table 1.1 reveals, Urdu has remained a minority language, despite its status as the national language.

The eminent Pakistani scholar Akbar Ahmed has seen rapid social mobility as aiding the process of 'Pakistanisation'[11] by its strengthening of Urdu as a common *lingua franca*.[12] However Urdu has proved much less effective in promoting a national Pakistani identity than Bengali, Sindhi, Pashto, Siraiki or Balochi have been in articulating ethnic identity. In fact Balochi existed only as an oral language until after independence and was widely regarded as a dialect of Persian.[13] From the 1950s onwards it was established as a literary

[9] Cited in H. Zaheer, *The Separation of East Pakistan: The Rise and Realization of Bengali Muslim Nationalism* (Karachi, 1994), p. 21.

[10] Despite this Urdu became the national language in 1947. This decision, which alienated Bengalis, was taken because of the symbolic role it had acquired in the growth of Muslim separatism in India. Its relationship with the regional languages can be further examined in Y.A. Mitha, 'Linguistic Nationalism in Pakistan: With Special Reference to the Role and History of Urdu in the Punjab', unpubl. M.Phil. Thesis, University of Sussex, 1985.

[11] Akbar S. Ahmed, 'Identity and Ideology in Pakistan: an interview' *Third World Quarterly* 10, no. 4 (October 1989), pp. 69-70.

[12] Although it should be noted that less than 20 per cent of the population of ten-year-olds was enumerated as literate in Urdu in 1981.

[13] See C. Jahani, 'Poetry and Politics: Nationalism and Language Standardization in the Balochi Literary Movement' in P. Titus (ed.), *Marginality and Modernity: Ethnicity and Change in Post-Colonial Balochistan* (Karachi, 1996), pp. 105-38.

language and nationalist figures such as Gul Khan Nasir (1914-83) were prominent poets and writers. In the early 1980s Urdu finally emerged as a major political rallying point, but for a *mohajir* ethnic identity rather than Pakistani nationalism.

Table 1.1. LANGUAGE DISTRIBUTION IN PAKISTAN
(1981 Census)

	Percentage	No. of speakers (millions)
Punjabi	48.17	60.9
Pashto	13.14	16.8
Sindhi	11.77	15.0
Siraiki	9.83	12.6
Urdu	7.60	9.7
Balochi	3.02	3.8
Hindko	2.43	3.1
Brahvi	1.21	1.5
Others	2.81	3.6

Source: T. Rahman, 'Language and Politics in a Pakistan Province: The Sindhi language Movement', *Asian Survey* 35, no. 11 (November 1995), p. 1006.

Language has formed an important element in Sindhi identity, along with territory and cultural traditions relating to dress – especially the wearing of the *ajrak* (shawl of Sindhi design), poetry and Sufism. Indeed it was Sufi poems (*kafi*) which helped to establish linguistic traditions, despite their ancient origins. During the era of British rule Sindhi was standardised in the Arabic script, formerly having also been written in Nagri and Gurumukhi. Sindhi is today the most developed regional language in Pakistan.

Islam

As befits a Muslim state created in the name of religion, Islam has exerted a major influence on Pakistani politics. What has been more striking is its divisive impact. Sectarian violence has become endemic in parts of Punjab. In order to make sense of the complex interaction between Islam and Pakistani politics, it is necessary to understand the conflicting Islamic ideological responses to the eighteenth-century decline of Muslim power in north India.[14] It is also important to understand

14 The development of Islamic modernism owed much to the Aligarh movement of Sir Syed Ahmad Khan (1817-98). Islamic revivalism owes its roots to the writings of Shah Waliullah (1703-62) although modern Islamist understanding was formulated by Syed Abul Ala Maududi (1903-79).

the importance of Sufism for rural Pakistani Muslims. Both of these themes will be outlined here, in preparation for a fuller treatment in later chapters.

We can broadly identify four major responses to the crisis brought on by the loss of Muslim political power and the rise of an alien Christian rule. These are modernism, reformism, traditionalism and Islamism, often called fundamentalism. They were represented respectively by the Aligarh, Deoband, Barelvi[15] and Jamaat-i-Islami movements. The institutions and ideas which they forged during the colonial era continue to profoundly influence Pakistani society and politics, as does their history of confrontation. During the Zia era this was intensified as well as externalised towards the Shia and non-Muslim minorities.

The modernist reformism of the Aligarh movement possessed a twofold aim; first to encourage Muslims to engage with Western scientific thought and second to reconcile the Islamic concept of the sovereignty of God with the nation state. The Pakistan demand was thus very much an Aligarh enterprise. It was opposed by both Deobandi reformists and Jamaat-i-Islami supporters. The former were not prepared to compromise Islamic law by modernist reasoning and understanding, although they were in many cases unconcerned with the politics of the colonial state. Islamists were opposed to the creation of Pakistan, seeing the establishment of a secular Muslim nation-state as blasphemous. Their disquiet had been increased by Jinnah's incorporation of the notion of discretion in choosing between Islamic law and customary law during the passage of the Muslim Personal Law Bill in the Central Legislature in 1937.

In post-independence Pakistan, the modernist approach reached its high-water mark during the Ayub era with the introduction in 1961 of the Pakistan Muslim Family Laws Ordinance (MFLO).[16] Islamist understandings have been articulated most forcefully through the Jamaat-i-Islami (JI) which achieved its greatest influence in the early Zia period. Even at this juncture however the perpetual disunity in the ranks of the *'ulama* undermined their attempts to transform Pakistan into an 'ideological state'. In addition to the Sunni-Shia divide,[17] there has always

---

[15] The Deoband movement was founded by Muhammad Qasim Nanautvi and Rashid Ahmad Gangohi. From the outset, it emphasised education and scriptualism. See B.D. Metcalf, *Islamic revival in British India: Deoband, 1860-1900* (Princeton, 1982). The Barelvi movement was founded by Ahmad Riza Khan (1856-1921) of Bareilly.

[16] See Fazlur Rahman, 'The controversy over the Muslim Family Laws' in D.E. Smith (ed.), *South Asian Politics and Religion* (Princeton, 1966), pp. 414-27.

[17] The Shias form around 20 per cent of the population. There has traditionally always been tension with Sunnis during the Muharram period when Shias mourn the tragic martyrdom of Hazrat Hussain and his family at the battle of Karbala. Shia revivalism in Iran, together with Zia's state-sponsored Sunni Islamisation in Pakistan have added to Shia-Sunni tensions.

been a bitter rivalry between the Barelvis and the Deobandis. The former uphold the 'traditional' Islam of *pir* and shrine, the latter represent the orthodox revivalist movement which aimed at purifying Indian Islam from such 'un-Islamic' practices. The Barelvis, unlike the Deobandis had unequivocally supported the Pakistan movement.[18] Barelvi interests have been articulated in Pakistani politics through the Jamiat-ul-Ulema-i-Pakistan (JUP). Unlike the JI it distanced itself from the Zia regime from the outset. Deobandis have worked for an Islamic state through the Jamiat-ul-Ulema-i-Islam (JUI) whose main support has been based in the Frontier and Balochistan.[19] It has been less influential however, than the more disciplined JI which has avoided the JUI's factional splits and has developed a more comprehensive ideology of reconstructing Pakistani society on a 'truly Islamic basis.'

Both modernists and those steeped in Sufi tradition have expressed hostility to attempts to create a '*mullahocracy*' in Pakistan. The uneducated and hypocritical *mullah* has emerged as a stereotype in Pakistani literature and in the folklore of the region. The *pirs*' popular religious influence, however, provides them with immense moral and temporal authority, and many have also acquired large landholdings. Their influence is rooted in the belief that they have inherited *baraka* (religious charisma believed to be transmitted by a saint to his descendants and his shrine) from their ancestors – the Sufi saints who since the eleventh century had played a major role in the region's conversion to Islam.

Relations between the '*ulama*, the custodians of Islamic orthodoxy, and the *pirs* have been uneasy. The reformist '*ulama* of the Deobandi and Ahl-i-Hadith movements from the second half of the nineteenth century onwards unequivocally condemned the 'un-Islamic' practices of saint worship at the shrines. While one should not exaggerate the differences between *pirs* and '*ulama* – an individual could be both an Islamic scholar and a mystic – the two groups have clashed both religiously and in their attitude to the role of Islam in the state.

The works of Sarah Ansari,[20] David Gilmartin and the present

---

[18] '*Ulama* from Deoband were active in the Jamiat-ul-Ulema-i-Hind which opposed the Pakistan demand because it would have 'a wordly' rather than a 'religious' government. The Deobandi *alim* Shabbir Ahmad Uthmani (1887-1949) was a notable exception. His followers supported the Pakistan demand through the Jamiat-ul-Ulema-i-Islam which was founded in Calcutta in November 1945.

[19] For an examination of the activities of both the JUP and JUI, see S. Akhtar, 'Pakistan Since Independence: The Political role of the Ulema', unpubl. D.Phil. thesis, University of York, 1989.

[20] S. Ansari, *Sufi Saints and State Power: The Pirs of Sind, 1843-1947* (Cambridge, 1992); D. Gilmartin, *Empire and Islam; Punjab and the Making of Pakistan* (Berkeley, CA, 1988); and 'Religious Leadership and the Pakistan Movement', *Modern Asian Studies* 13, no. 3 (1979), pp. 485-517; I. Talbot, *Punjab and the Raj, 1849-1947* (New Delhi, 1988).

author have highlighted the important role which the colonial state accorded the *pirs* and their significant influence in popularising the Pakistan message. The mass mobilisation of Muslims in 1946-7 would not have been possible without the support of the *pirs*. The '*ulama* lacked their influence amongst the rural voters and were in any case ambivalent about the Pakistan movement with its emphasis on Muslim nationalism and its Western-educated leadership.

Pirs have retained influence in Pakistan's post-independence history. Ayub Khan, despite his modernist outlook, sought their support because they provided religious fire-breaks from the incandescent attacks of Islamist groups and parties such as the JI. The *pirs* grouped in the Jamiat-i-Mashaikh threw their weight behind him in the 1965 presidential elections.[21]

Biraderi politics and feudalism

The *biraderi* (brotherhood, kinship group) forms an important locus of political authority especially in the central areas of the Punjab. Patrilineal descent lies at the heart of the *biraderi* as a social institution, although its boundaries vary with marriage connections, bonds of reciprocal obligation and political structures. *Biraderi* solidarity has appeared strongest among independent peasant proprietors, although 'tribal' and landed elites deploy its idiom for political mobilisation. Indeed since the colonial era, *biraderi* identity has played a crucial role in local electoral politics. Although the Muslim League stressed an Islamic identity which transcended the primordial allegiance to the *biraderi*, it could not ignore its political salience in the 1946 Punjab elections which held the key to the creation of Pakistan.[22] *Biraderi* influence has continued since independence because of weak party institutionalisation in the localities. Its high point was in fact reached in the 1985 'partyless' elections.

However, the unequal rural power relationships inherent in the feudal system have, in the eyes of some scholars, been even more influential in shaping Pakistani politics than Islam or *biraderi* loyalties. A vast economic and social gulf exists between the landholding elite and the rural masses. Indeed the continued power of the feudal elite

---

[21] The Pir of Dewal Sharif was Ayub Khan's most influential supporter. Only Pir Taunsa supported Fatima Jinnah who opposed him in the election. See S.R. Sherani, 'Ulema and Pir in Pakistani Politics' in H. Donnan and P. Werbner (eds), *Economy and Culture in Pakistan* (Basingstoke, 1991), pp. 233ff.

[22] See I. Talbot, 'The 1946 Punjab Elections', *Modern Asian Studies* 14, no. 1 (February 1980), p. 87.

is seen as Pakistan's bane by the professional classes.[23] The state's existence is owed neverthless to the Muslim League's strategic alliances with the large landholders. During Pakistan's opening turbulent decades, the landlords exerted a dominant influence which prevented effective land reform and hindered economic and political development within the countryside. The full sway of the landlords' power was displayed in provincial politics, but their predominance was also reflected in national politics. In the 1962 and 1965 National Assemblies landlords accounted for 58 out of 96 and 34 out of 82 members respectively.[24] As in the colonial era, power was primarily sought to bolster local prestige and access development funds. It could also be used to veto administrative and socio-economic reform in the localities. Votes were sought in an atmosphere of both 'coercive localism' and extravagant display.

Critics of Pakistani 'feudalism' have produced a threefold charge sheet arising from the landholders' predominance: first, the bulk of the agricultural population has remained effectively depoliticised; second, the perpetuation of feudal power relations has contributed to Pakistan's distinctive political culture of violence and intolerance; and third, the parochial and personalist character of Pakistan's political parties with their rapidly changing loyalties is rooted in this predominance of the landlords.[25]

Pakistan since 1971

The breakaway of East Bengal in 1971 remains the most important discontinuity in Pakistan's history. Indeed its consequences are still being worked out. As the causes of the secession are examined later, it is suffitient merely to draw attention here to its main demographic, religious and political legacies before turning to the rapid socio-economic change of the past two decades.

The secession of East Pakistan reinforced Punjabi domination of the state. Table 1.2 illustrates Punjab's demographic dominance. The region's economic predominance was rooted in its existing infrastructural

---

23 For a typical assessment see I.H. Malik, *State and Civil Society in Pakistan*, Chapter 4.

24 Maleeha Lodhi, 'The Pakistan People's Party', unpubl. Ph.D. thesis, London School of Economics, 1979, p. 51.

25 Keith Callard in his classic work on Pakistan politics observed: 'The system of political parties ... bears little resemblance to that of most other democratic countries. [...] In Pakistan politics is made up of a large number of leading persons who, with their political dependants, form loose agreements to achieve power and to maintain it. Consequently rigid adherence to a policy or a measure is likely to make politicians less available for office.' K. Callard, *Pakistan: A Political Study* (London, 1957) p. 67.

TABLE 1.2. PAKISTAN POPULATION BY AREA, 1981
(× *1,000*)

		% change (1973-81)	% of total (1981)	% urban (1981)
Punjab	47,116	26.3	56.2	27.5
Islamabad	335	42.6	.4	60.2
NWFP	10,885	29.8	13.0	15.2
FATA	2,175	−12.7	2.6	–
Sindh (exc. Karachi)	13,863	30.3	16.5	22.5
Karachi	5,103	45.2	6.1	100.0
Balochistan	4,305	77.2	5.1	15.6
Pakistan	83,782	28.3	100.0	28.3

Adapted from Main Findings of the 1981 Census (1983), cited in C. Baxter *et al.*, *Government and Politics in South Asia*, 3rd. edn. (Boulder, 1993) p. 169.

and educational advantages and in the considerable agricultural and industrial development of the Zia era. It also received the lion's share of remittances from the Middle East during the oil bonanza years.[26] Aijaz Ahmad has pointed to the depoliticisation arising from the 'Gulf factor'[27] and Omar Noman has similarly linked the political tranquility of the Punjab during the Zia era (1977-88) to the prosperity arising from migrants' remittances. Its absence in the interior of Sindh, which sent no migrants to the Gulf, undoubtedly contributed to the sense of relative deprivation which fuelled the anti-Zia protests.[28]

Punjab's big brother status in the post-1971 Pakistan state has been a cause of increasing resentment among Sindhi, Baloch, Pushtun and *mohajir* nationalists. Indeed their communities' identity formation was in part constructed around anti-Punjabi sentiments. Despite the importance of the Hindi heartland, there is no Indian equivalent of Punjab's pre-eminence in Pakistan. Comparative political frameworks are still drawn with India because of the historical commonalities of Mughal and British rule.[29] In the light of the country's intra-regional and ethnic imbalances it might be equally appropriate to consider Pakistan's development with that of Nigeria, Indonesia or Sudan.

[26] Pakistan was receiving $2.2 billion a year in remittances in the early 1980s, 85 per cent of which came from migrant labourers in Arab countries. J. Piscatori, 'Asian Islam: International Linkages and their Impact on International Relations' in J.L. Esposito (ed.), *Islam in Asia: Religion, Politics and Society* (New York, 1987), p. 248.

[27] A. Ahmad, 'The Rebellion of 1983: A Balance Sheet', p. 33.

[28] O. Noman, 'The Impact of Migration on Pakistan's Economy and Society' in Donnan and Werbner (eds), *Economy and Culture in Pakistan*, p. 90.

[29] See, for example, Ayesha Jalal, *Democracy and Authoritarianism in South Asia*.

Post-1971 ethnic clashes have been particularly bitter in Balochistan and Sindh. Indeed it might be argued that the genocide unleashed in East Pakistan in 1971 made later episodes of state repression in these provinces more politically acceptable. What is most chilling in such accounts as those of Anthony Mascarenhas[30] is not the level of the violence unleashed on 25 March 1971, but the meticulous planning which accompanied it. Parallels with the Nazi Holocaust immediately spring to mind. While its perpetrators were brought to trial, the 'butcher' of Dhaka, Lieutenant-General Tikka Khan, was to be rapidly rehabilitated and promoted in post-1971 Pakistan. State terrorism in the name of national security thereafter secured a political legitimacy with profound future consequences.

The state's violent response to ethno-regional grievances and identities is rooted in what has been termed a 'fragility syndrome' in the thinking of the ruling elites. It is based on a sense of increased insecurity *vis-à-vis* India and on the fear that ethno-nationalist movements in such provinces as Sindh, Balochistan and the Frontier may follow the Bengali precedent. A 'fearful state' has emerged which is repressive of internal dissent and defensive in its relations with India. These anxieties have encouraged widespread support in the political establishment for the acquisition of nuclear weapons, as demonstrated in May 1998.

Regarding Islamisation, the separation of East Pakistan contributed to the trend in three ways: first, as Table 1.3 reveals, it cut at a stroke the numerical strength of the non-Muslim minority; second it strengthened anti-Hindu and anti-Indian sentiment because of the credence given to conspiracy thesis interpretations of East Bengal's secession; third it demolished the 'two nation theory', the secular Pakistani nationalist ideology, thereby reinforcing Islam as an ideological cement for the state. These trends were encouraged by the oil boom in the Gulf and by the Iranian revolution and Afghan *jihad*. The latter's backwash effects included increased militancy and the growth of a 'kalashnikov culture'.

Since 1971, Pakistan has increasingly resembled a Middle Eastern rather than South Asian society. Mosques have mushroomed and numerous attempts have been made to bring legal and economic practices in conformity with Islam. Trade and investment have been increasingly directed towards the Islamic world. By 1981 over 30 per cent of both Pakistan's exports and imports were with Organisation of Islamic Conference (OIC) states.[31] At the same time Pakistan was receiving annual disbursements of $50 million and $30 million from Kuwait and the

---

30 A. Mascarenhas, *The Rape of Bangla Desh* (New Delhi, 1971). See especially Chapters 7-10.

31 J. Piscatori, 'Asian Islam: International Linkages and their Impact on International Relations' in J.L. Esposito (ed.), *Islam in Asia*, p. 242.

United Arab Emirates (UAE) respectively. Saudi generosity filled Pakistan's coffers to the annual sum of $100 million in the late 1970s. This figure represented 25 per cent of all Saudi aid.[32] Even so the United States remained the biggest single bilateral donor until October 1990, when this role fell to Japan.[33] However, culturally and not least in security terms, Pakistan could not fully free itself from its South Asia moorings even if it wanted to.

Table 1.3. PAKISTAN RELIGION BY AREA, 1982
(× *1,000*)

	Muslims	% Muslims	Ahmadi	Christian	Hindus	Other*
Punjab	46,110	98	64	1,061	29	28
Islamabad	331	97	1	8	–	–
NWFP	11,003	99	11	39	4	3
Sindh	17,557	92	21	177	1,221	52
Balochistan	4,258	98	6	20	20	–
Pakistan	79,259	97	103	1,305	1,274	83

*Parsi, Sikh, Buddhist and unspecified others.

Adapted from unpublished data, Census Organisation of Pakistan (1984), cited in C. Baxter *et al.*, *Government and Politics in South Asia*, p. 169.

The interaction between Islam and politics during the Zia era forms a principal focus of Chapter 9. Yet we must note here that intolerance and sectarian violence have become part and parcel of contemporary Pakistani culture. The restoration of democracy in 1988 intensified conflict between such extremist Sunni and Shia organisations as the Sipah-i-Sahaba-i-Pakistan (SSP) and the Tehrik-e-Nifaz-e-fiqh-e-Jafria (TNFJ). Jhang, Lahore and later Karachi were to resound to the gunfire of sectarian rivals. Seventy-eight people were killed in Jhang alone from 1990-2 as a result of such clashes.[34]

Muslim extremists' use of the legal cover provided by Section 295-C of the Penal Code[35] to persecute non-Muslims has contributed to

[32] Ibid., p. 247.

[33] Most of the foreign aid comes from the Aid to Pakistan Consortium, a grouping of Western countries and multilateral agencies including the World Bank and the Asian Development Bank. This disbursed over $1,650 million in 1992/3.

[34] Human Rights Commission of Pakistan, *State of Human Rights in Pakistan, 1992* (Lahore, 1992), p. 51.

[35] This provided for the death penalty or life imprisonment for committing blasphemy against the Holy Prophet. In October 1990 the Federal Shariat Court ruled that death was the only punishment for blasphemy.

Pakistan's continuing poor international image.[36] Indeed the new democratic dispensation saw not only highly publicised episodes of persecution of Christians and Ahmadis,[37] but attempts to forcibly convert the Kalash people of the Hindu Kush and an attempt in 1993 by the JUI to introduce legislation which would declare the heterodox Zikris as non-Muslims.[38] The stereotype of Pakistani intolerance received further credibility with the reporting of the lynching of Dr Farooq Sattar, a Deobandi *Hafiz-i-Quran* in Gujranwala, in April 1994 on groundless rumours – given credence by a Barelvi sectarian opponent – of his having burnt the Holy Quran.[39] Shortly after the February 1997 elections, thirteen churches were burnt down in Khanewal and 1,500 houses destroyed in Shantinagar following riots caused by the claim that a Quran had been destroyed.[40] Such violence, whether the result of bigotry or, as seemed more likely in the Khanewal instance, a police vendetta,[41] conflicts with Jinnah's famous address to the Pakistan Constituent Assembly of 11 August 1947 in which he articulated the equality of citizenship rights irrespective of religion. Intolerance and violence received encouragement during Zia-ul-Haq's regime, but are also rooted at least partly in the frustrations arising from the poor electoral performance of the religious parties, although more extreme groups than the JUI, JUP or JI have been behind the spiralling sectarian violence. The JI-

---

36 The most celebrated blasphemy case was the Salamat Masih and Rehmat Masih trial. This generated international attention not only because of the guilty verdict handed down by the Sessions Court and later overturned by the Lahore High Court, but because Salamat was a minor and another of the accused, Manzoor Masih, had been shot dead after an earlier court appearance. The Lahore High Court in December 1994 also acquitted another Christian who had been consigned to death row by a sessions court since November 1992.

Ahmadis as well as Christians have often been brought to court under the so-called Blasphemy Ordinance on the basis of a single complaint. The Ahmadis have also fallen foul of Ordinance XX of 1984 which added sections 298-B and 298-C to the Pakistan Penal Code. This provided for three years' imprisonment for the use of epithets and practising of rights peculiar to Islam by non-Muslims. Cases have been brought even on such issues as wearing a ring inscribed with Quranic verses. For details see Tahir Mehdi and Muddassir Rizvi, 'The Price of Faith', *Newsline*, April 1995, pp. 46-54.

37 See for example the special report in *Newsline*, April 1995, pp. 46-54.

38 See Human Rights Commission of Pakistan, *State of Human Rights in Pakistan in 1993* (Lahore, 1993), p. vi.

39 For further details of the episode see *Herald*, May 1994.

40 *Dawn* (Internet Edition), 12 February 1997.

41 A number of leading local policemen had been suspended following an earlier incident on 17 January in which a Bible had been desecrated. The extent of the damage and the use of petrol bombs and grenades confirmed the suspicion of police involvement. The minorities' marginalisation was vividly illustrated by the failure of Farooq Leghari, Punjab Governor Khwaja Ahmad, Tariq Rahim and Afzal Hayat, the caretaker Chief Minister, to express concern publicly over the incidents. *Dawn* (Internet Edition), 9 February 1997.

led Pakistan Islamic Front (PIF) garnered just 3 per cent of the votes and three out of 237 National Assembly seats in the October 1993 elections, despite entertaining hopes that it would become a third force in politics. The rival Islami Jamhoori Mohaz (IJM) which comprised largely of the JUI(F) (Fazlur Rahman faction) and JUP (Noorani) fared even worse with under 3 per cent of the vote, while bringing up the rear with two National Assembly seats was the third religious alliance which included a faction of the JUI, the Khaksars and the militant SSP.

The most prominent figure from the Islamic parties, Qazi Hussain Ahmed of the JI, failed to secure election from both the two National Assembly seats he contested. The JI boycotted the February 1997 polls ostensibly because of the caretaker Government's lack of progress with the accountability process. Those religio-political parties which did contest did no better than before. Maulana Fazlur Rahman of the JUI had not only to contend with voter apathy, but had the indignity of being opposed by a voluptuous actress, Musarrat Shaheen, in his Dera Ismail Khan constituency.

This electoral rejection of the religious parties has received much less publicity in the West than the dangers of fanaticism. Similarly, comparatively little has been written about organisations such as the Women's Action Forum (WAF) which has campaigned for minority rights. Indeed, one of its founder members, Asma Jehangir who is the present Chairperson of the Human Rights Commission of Pakistan acted as defence counsel in the celebrated Salamat Masih and Rahmat Masih blasphemy case. Violent episodes such as the retaliation for the Babri Masjid's destruction in India have instead grabbed the headlines.[42] Poverty and unequal access to civic amenities however remain a greater problem for the minorities than the threat of violence, real as this can occasionally be. The system of separate electorates[43] implemented during Zia's time has decoupled minority legislators from their constituents and thereby further reduced their avenues of redress.

Islamisation and sectarian conflict have diverted attention from the role of *pirs* in post-1971 Pakistani politics. A number of them however, not least Pir Pagaro who is reputed to have a million followers, have

---

[42] According to some reports, about 120 temples, seven churches and two gurdwaras were destroyed in Pakistan between 6-8 December 1992 in the wake of the Babri Masjid episode. Pakistan Human Rights Commission, *State of Human Rights in Pakistan 1992*, p. 44.

[43] The constituency for minority legislators in the National Assembly is the whole of the country. In Provincial Assemblies it is the whole of the province. Christians and Hindus have four seats each in the National Assembly, while other non-Muslim communities have one. Ahmadis have not contested their reserved National and Provincial Assembly seats because of the way this would compromise their religious self-identity.

been important players. Pir Pagaro was a close supporter of the PML leader Muhammad Khan Junejo. But the majority of Sindhi *pirs* were linked with the PPP and the Sindhi nationalist movement. The leading figure of the Sindhi nationalists G.M. Syed himself came from a *pir* family and founded the Bazm-e-Soofia-e-Sindh organisation which organised literary conferences and *urs* at the shrines of saints. Some followers claimed that his idea of Sindhu Desh (Sindhi homeland) was mystically inspired. At the other end of the spectrum of politics in Sindh, Altaf Hussain, the leader of the MQM, is so highly venerated by his *mohajir* followers that he is referred to as '*Pir Sahib*'.

Zulfiqar Ali Bhutto, despite his image as a modern populist leader sought support from the *pirs*. He attended the important *urs* ceremonies of leading Sufi shrines and adorned the shrine of Data Ganj Bakhsh in Lahore and Shahbaz Qalander of Sehwan in Sindh with golden gates.[44] Leading Sufi shrines in Sindh were at the forefront of the struggle against the authoritarian Zia regime, while the former Pakistan Premier was posthumously elevated to almost saintly status as the *Shaheed Baba*.[45] Significantly when Benazir Bhutto made her first visit to Lahore as Pakistan Prime Minister on 25 December 1988, she went straight from the airport to the shrine of Data Ganj Bakhsh to pay homage to Hazrat Ali Hajveri.[46]

Added to the continuing problem of Islamisation is the ongoing influence of feudal politics. Although Zulfikar Ali Bhutto promised to abolish feudalism and introduce a more comprehensive land reform than Ayub Khan, the political dominance of the landed elites has continued. Feudal power relations have persisted in Punjab's south western region and according to government records even after the 1959 and 1972 land reforms, large landholders (with farms of 50 acres and above) still owned 18 per cent of land in this area. Bhutto himself turned to the landowners in the 1977 elections. The power of the *wadero*[47] has remained a constant feature of Sindh's politics. Regional and national parties alike have drawn their leadership from this class in the Sindhi-speaking areas. When Zia undertook the civilianisation of his martial law regime, his hand-picked Prime Minister Muhammad Khan Junejo came from a prominent landed family of Sindh. Since 1988, landowners have been predominant in both the PPP and Muslim League governments.

A growing criticism of 'feudal' influence has centred around the

---

[44] A. Syed, *Pakistan: Islam, Politics and National Solidarity* (New York, 1982), p. 148.

[45] For details of Bhutto's 'veneration', see W.L. Richter, 'Pakistan' in M. Ayoob (ed.), *The Politics of Islamic Reassertion* (London, 1981), pp. 141-62.

[46] *Dawn Overseas Weekly*, Karachi, week ending 4 January, 1989.

[47] *Wadero* estates in Sindh can be anything up to 50,000 acres in extent.

exemption of direct taxes from agricultural land and income. Even after the imposition of a wealth tax in 1994, commentators pointed out that it raised only the paltry sum of Rs.22 *lakhs* (1 *lakh* = 100,000). The influential English-language monthly *Newsline*, in an issue entitled 'The Great Tax Scandal',[48] made much of the fact that the Pakistan President along with the chief ministers of Sindh and Balochistan did not pay any income tax because of their exemption as landowners. Such articulate spokesmen of the agriculturalist lobby as Shah Mehmood Qureshi retorted that the landowners were already paying huge sums in 'implicit taxation' through the agricultural support price system which fixed produce prices well below the international market level.[49] Despite the cleverness and veracity of such arguments, it is undeniable that as a result of Pakistan's narrow tax base, development activities have had to be funded through foreign capital flows rather than internal resource mobilisation.[50] The urban population has also had to bear a disproportionate tax burden. The growing disorder which undermined Benazir Bhutto's second government in the summer of 1996 was directly rooted in the swingeing tax increases of Rs.41 billion which faced the business classes and the urban consumers[51] as the Government exempted the landowners from its attempt to bring down the budget deficit. Even the nominal provincial taxation on agricultural wealth which existed in Sindh, the Frontier and Balochistan was opposed in Punjab.

Post-1971 social and economic change

The structure of the Pakistan economy has undergone tremendous change which has accelerated since 1971. The manufacturing and service sectors have grown rapidly and become major employers. In 1948 there were only 78,000 spindles and 3,000 looms in the cotton textile industry,[52] but by the end of March 1984 this had risen to 29 million spindles and 30,000 looms situated in the 181 cotton mills. The production of sugar and cement also increased dramatically. During the first four decades of independence, the number

---

[48] *Newsline* 7, no. 4 (October 1995), p. 26.

[49] *Ibid.*, p. 35.

[50] These have not only included workers' remittances but extensive borrowing. The high level of external debt – $17.3 billion by the beginning of the 1990s – has tied up export earnings in service charges. See World Bank, *World Debt Tables 1989/90* (Washington, DC, 1990), esp. Ch. 7.

[51] The General Sales Tax was increased from 15 to 18 per cent. Duties were increased on such items as beverages and cigarettes.

[52] F.K. Khan, *A Geography of Pakistan: Environment, People and Economy* (Karachi, 1991), p. 199.

of cement factories tripled, while the production of sugar increased from 10,000 tons to 1.1 million.[53] Industrialisation has enabled Pakistan to experience a rapid growth in its GDP. In Iftikhar Malik's telling phrase 'from the backwaters of the British Empire, Pakistan has reached the threshold of a middle-income country.'[54] The 1991 GNP *per capita* figure of $436 which compares favourably with India ($330) has been used by scholars such as Shahid Javed Burki to maintain that Pakistan has reached the point at which it could begin to make the transition to a middle-income country according to World Bank criteria.[55] Just three years after penning such optimism he was back in Pakistan acting as an economic advisor, as the country's debts and dwindling foreign exchange reserves of $750 million reached crisis proportions. The clouds around the silver lining of his earlier assessment included the perennial trade deficits,[56] budget deficits (Rs.20.8 billion for the year 1996/7), high defence expenditure, a low tax base[57] and low investment in human capital. Agriculture continued to act as a drag on the economy and at the mid-point of the 1990s still contributed 26 per cent of the GDP and employed 50 per cent of the labour force.[58] Even following the urban explosion in recent years, two-thirds of the population still resides in the country's 45,000 villages. As a result of poor agricultural yields, the country has been increasingly forced to import wheat and vegetables to feed its burgeoning population.

Population growth

Even after the loss of its eastern province, Pakistan's population of 120 million at the beginning of the 1990s was over 50 per cent higher than that of four decades earlier.[59] Its annual population growth rate of 3.1 per cent in 1980/1 was one of the highest in the world (in Bangladesh it was 2.8 per cent and in India 2.4 per cent) and encouraged doomsday projections that the population would

53 *Ibid.*, pp. 206, 212.

54 I.H. Malik, 'The State and Civil Society in Pakistan': From Crisis to Crisis, *Asian Survey* 36, no. 7 (July 1996), p. 675.

55 See S.J. Burki, 'Economic Policy After Zia Ul-Haq' in C.H. Kennedy (ed.), *Pakistan in 1992* (Boulder, CO, 1992), pp. 48-51.

56 These peaked at a dangerously high level in 1984/5.

57 According to one estimate, the Pakistan Government loses more than Rs. 100 billion every year because of tax exemptions and evasions.

58 *The Nation*, 2 December 1995, IV.

59 The 1951 Census enumerated the population at 73.88 million. *Census of Pakistan, 1951*, vol. 1, Table 2-F, p. 31.

double within twenty-three years.[60] Despite the fragmentary data which is available, it is clear that the natural increase in population has resulted from the birth rate declining much more slowly than the death rate. Cultural conservatism and patriarchy have hindered family planning programmes and successive Pakistani regimes have failed to reduce female illiteracy from a scandalously high rate of 79 per cent.[61] Illiterate women lack knowledge of family planning and the ability to influence their husband's decision on its use.

Rapid population growth has hindered government health and educational provision which in any case received lower budgetary allocations than defence expenditure. It has also resulted in Pakistan, like many other developing countries, possessing a high percentage of children and young adults. Indeed around half the total population is under the age of fifteen. As such it is disenfranchised, for the voting age is still twenty-one. The 'youth bulge' lies behind much of Pakistan's dynamism and violence. Ethnic riots, sectarian clashes, student fights, traffic accidents and violent tribal disputes over land and womenfolk equally attest to the Hobbesian jungle which is contemporary Pakistan. Youth underemployment has encouraged ethnic and religious extremism. Not only the rank and file but most of the leaders of the MQM in 1980s Karachi were in their twenties. Furthermore the easy availability of weapons and drugs in a youthful society has created a combustible situation.

Violence and guns have always been a part of tribal society, and the cities of Punjab were no stranger to communal clashes in the colonial era. But the development of the so-called 'kalashnikov culture' in the 1980s was a clear break with the past. The flow of modern weaponry and drugs from the war-torn Afghan frontier into an ethnically combustible Karachi turned the city of lights into a latter day Beirut. The collapse of the state's authority in Pakistan's commercial heartland posed the most serious threat to national integrity since the dark days of 1971. It was matched by the turning over of rural Sindh to a *dacoit* raj. Criminal bands established reigns of terror often with the connivance of the local authorities and leading landowners; The prudent even avoided daytime travel in many parts of rural Sindh. The growing violence in Punjab was rooted in sectarian

[60] P. Lyon, 'South Asia and the Geostrategics of the 1990s', *Contemporary South Asia*, 1, no. 1 (1992).

[61] The high level of female illiteracy depressed Pakistan's Human Development Index score in 1990 to 0.311 which compared in regional terms with India's 0.309, Bangladesh's 0.189, Afghanistan's 0.066 and Sri Lanka's 0.663. The HDI was devised in 1990 by the United Nations Development Programme as a composite index of longevity, educational attainment and 'utility derived from income.' The figures are taken from: A. Thomas *et al., Third World Atlas* (2nd edn), (Milton Keynes, 1994), Table 1, p. 74.

clashes especially in the Jhang district, in *biraderi* disputes in Gujrat
and in a rising tide of crime. In the first eleven months of 1993
alone there were officially recorded in the Punjab over 3,300 murders
and close on 4,500 abductions, mainly of children, most of whom
were never recovered and fell victim to a life of forced labour.[62]

Migration

Pakistan has been a state comprising of people on the move ever
since its creation amid the chaos of partition. Recent decades have
seen high rates of both rural-urban and overseas migration with important
political consequences.

The flood of migrants into Karachi in the 1980s as a result both
of a construction boom and of the Afghan conflict created the social
conditions in which violence and ethnic conflict were able to thrive.
The roots of the unfolding Karachi crisis lay not in Sindhi-*mohajir*
conflict, but in tension between recent lower class *mohajir* residents
and incoming Pushtun labourers. Following the December 1986 Sohrab
Goth episode and the serious ethnic rioting which followed it, Altaf
Hussain called for the repatriation of Pushtun/Afghan outsiders.[63] Elsewhere in Sindh migration established conflicts between Punjabis and
Sindhis.

Sindh did not share in the other main source of migration from
the 1970s, of Pakistani workers to the oil rich but labour poor Gulf
states. Migration to the Gulf has increased wealth and encouraged Islamisation through exposure to 'pristine' Islamic practice. Some commentators regard it as a contributory factor to the Punjab's quiescence
during the Zia era. Large numbers of Pakistanis have also packed their
bags for Britain and North America. The political impact of the establishment of these overseas Pakistani communities has been twofold:
first it has lent support to the Kashmir struggle and publicised Indian
human rights abuses since the late 1980s; second, in the 1990s, the
Urdu-speaking components of these communities provided sustenance
for the MQM struggle during the Bhutto administrations. The role of
the Pakistani diaspora in national politics possesses some parallels with
that of overseas Sikh communities during the troubled 1980s in Indian
Punjab. It is an area which requires much greater scholarly investigation
than has hitherto been accorded it.

---

[62] Human Rights Commission of Pakistan, *State of Human Rights in Pakistan 1993*, p.
15.

[63] *Dawn*, 21 January 1987.

Agricultural innovation together with population growth has released rural labour for migration to Qatar, UAE and Saudi Arabia.[64] Pakistanis have also settled more permanently in Britain and North America and from a much earlier period in the former case.[65] An 1980 estimate placed the number of Pakistanis working overseas at 1.4 million. At its peak around one in ten of Pakistan's adult male workforce was employed overseas. Indeed during the fifth plan period (1978-83) over a third of the increase in the labour force was absorbed by overseas migration.[66] The remittances which the migrants sent home aided the unfavourable balance of payments situation and indeed by the middle of the 1980s provided around 40 per cent of total foreign exchange earnings. Their effects on domestic consumption patterns and domestic demand were equally significant. The construction industry boom, and the growth in transport and consumer goods' industries can be linked with the migrants' remittances.[67] According to Jonathan Addleton, 'the Gulf migration broadened what had historically been a small middle class in Pakistan.'[68]

The Punjab was the province which gained most from the inflow of funds but the most locally concentrated impact was in the Mirpur district of Azad Kashmir. Britain's 'Islamabad' – Bradford – replaced the dockside of Bombay as the major post-Partition destination of Mirpuri migrants,[69] many of whom were 'pushed' out of the region after the flooding of 100 square miles of the best agricultural land by the construction of the Mangla dam in the early 1960s. Suzuki pick-up trucks, *pucca* dwellings and the presence of more banks *per capita* than in Karachi bear eloquent testimony to the growth of a Mirpuri remittance economy. But as Roger Ballard[70] perceptively remarked in the early 1980s, dependency rather than development has been perpetuated by

---

[64] During the period 1965 to 1989-91 the percentage of the labour force employed in agriculture fell from 60 to 44 per cent, while that in industry rose from 18 to 25 per cent. Thomas, *Third World Atlas*, Table 2, p. 76.

[65] See; P. Lewis, *Islamic Britain: Religion, Politics and Identity Among British Muslims: Bradford in the 1990s* (London, 1994); J.S. Nielsen, *Muslims in Western Europe* (Edinburgh, 1992); R.S. Williams, *Religion of Immigrants from India and Pakistan: New Threads in the American Tapestry* (New York, 1988).

[66] O. Noman, 'The impact of Migration on Pakistan's Economy and Society', p. 85.

[67] *Ibid.*, pp. 80ff.

[68] J.S. Addleton, *Undermining the Centre* (Karachi, 1992), p. 79.

[69] Around half of all Pakistani migrants to Britain come from AK. Mirpuri seamen were some of the earliest Muslim migrants. By 1991 around 29,000 of Bradford's 49,000 Pakistani-origin population were Mirpuris. See P. Lewis, *Islamic Britain*.

[70] R. Ballard, 'The Context and Consequences of Migration: Jullundur and Mirpur compared', *New Community* 11, nos 1/2 (autumn/winter 1983), p. 125.

the inflow of funds. In the intervening period, AK has experienced some development in the fields of housing and hydro-electricity. But Kashmiri resentment towards the Government of Pakistan has grown along with the continuing failure to improve communications, to pay for the utilisation of AK national resources (the Mangla Dam generates power for Punjabi industry not for local consumption and the AK Government does not receive any revenue) and the refusal to harness more effectively remittance income for development by means of an AK banking sector.[71]

Migrants to the Gulf, unlike those to Europe and North America did not permanently leave the homeland. Little is still known concerning the consequences of their reabsorption into the domestic economy. The psychological reactions arising from the frustrations of newly-enriched returnees who perhaps unsuccessfully demand an increased status has been dubbed the *Dubai chalo* (Let's go to Dubai) theme in Pakistani society.[72]

Internal migration has also dramatically increased – both seasonal agricultural migration and rural migration to Karachi and the industrial cities of the Punjab;[73] there has been an urban explosion.[74] While the overall population increased by 250 per cent in the period 1947-81, urban population growth was close on 400 per cent. This is due to both the arrival of Indian and Bangladeshi *mohajirs* and the internal migration of Punjabi, Baloch and Pushtun labourers.

Urban dwellers increased from 17.8 per cent of the total population in 1951 to 28.3 per cent at the time of the 1981 Census.[75] The most rapid growth was recorded in major cities like Karachi and Lahore. Folksongs depicted Karachi as a distant city of dreams drawing men from their native land by its promise of wealth. '*Guddi holay holay chala*' went one such song, '*lumba safar Karachi da*' (Drive the train slowly for the journey to Karachi is a long one).[76] Around a tenth

---

[71] See P. Ellis and Z. Khan, 'Partition and Kashmir: Implications Fifty Years On for the Region and the Diaspora' Paper presented to 14th European Conference on 'Modern South Asian Studies', Copenhagen, 21-24 August 1996, pp. 14ff.

[72] See Akbar S. Ahmed, 'Dubai chalo: Problems in the Ethnic Encounter between Middle Eastern and South Asian Muslim Societies', *Asian Affairs* 15, pp. 262-76.

[73] For a review of research on this theme see M.S. Karim and W.C. Robinson, 'The Migration Situation in Pakistan: Ann Analytical Review' in F. Seller and M.S. Karim, (eds), *Migration in Pakistan: Theories and Facts* (Lahore, 1986), pp. 21-39.

[74] For an early study of the urbanisation process see S.J. Burki, 'Development of Towns: The Pakistan Experience' *Asian Survey* 15, no. 8 (August 1979), pp. 751-62.

[75] Khan, *A Geography of Pakistan*, p. 77.

[76] H. Mujtaba, 'What the Other Half Thinks', *Newsline* 7, no. 6 (December 1995), p. 82.

of the total world Baloch population is squeezed into Pakistan's leading city, clustering mainly in the chronically congested environs of the Lyari district.[77] Karachi's population had risen from under half a million at independence to 12 million by the mid-1990s. It has been estimated that 250,000 Pushtuns and Punjabis settle in Karachi annually.[78] But even such small Punjabi towns at the time of partition as Sargodhad Gujranwala have mushroomed.[79] While urban migration has encouraged a construction boom, it has also placed tremendous pressure on the infrastructure[80] and created pollution and environmental degradation. It has not grabbed the international headlines like Bhopal and Lahore's Baja Line gas tragedy early in 1997,[81] but poses an even greater long-term threat to the population.

By the early 1990s, Lahore and adjoining areas discharged 200 million gallons of waste water daily into the Ravi river.[82] While the citizens of Karachi were daily generating 35,000 tonnes of waste, 300 million gallons of untreated sewage were being daily discharged by the Lyari and Malir rivers into the sea.[83] The former green belt of Malir housed the country's largest pesticide dump and was being turned into a desert as a result of illegal sand mining in the river-bed to supply Karachi's construction industry.[84] Karachi's political violence of the 1980s must be viewed against the background of the outstripping of transportation, housing and water supplies by the mushrooming population.[85] One of the MQM's early demands was for the legalisation

---

[77] See R.A. Slimbach, 'Ethnic Binds and Pedagogies of Resistance: Baloch Nationalism and Educational Innovation in Karachi' in P. Titus (ed.), *Marginality and Modernity*, pp. 139ff.

[78] F. Haq, 'Rise of the MQM in Pakistan: Politics of Ethnic Mobilisation', *Asian Survey* 35, no. 11 (November 1995), p. 994.

[79] The 1941 Census recorded the population of these Punjabi towns at 36,000 and 85,000 respectively. By 1978 their population stood at 252,000 and 486,000. Anita Weiss, *Culture, Class and Development in Pakistan: The Emergence of an Industrial Bourgeoisie in Punjab* (Boulder, CO, 1991), Table II.2, p. 43.

[80] Karachi's civic structure virtually collapsed during the 1994 monsoon rains as roads were washed away and power-cuts lasted for up to 48 hours. In response to the protests, Benazir Bhutto's government launched a 121 billion rupee 'Karachi package'.

[81] This incident, which claimed thirty lives, took place on 8 January when two cylinders of chlorine gas leaked during their transportation to Ittehad Chemicals.

[82] Human Rights Commission of Pakistan, *State of Human Rights in Pakistan in 1992*, p. 97.

[83] Human Rights Commission of Pakistan, *State of Human Rights in Pakistan in 1993*, p. 90.

[84] Nafisa Shah, 'The Browning of Malir', *Newsline* (June 1995), pp. 97-8. The same issue carried a report on the ecological hazards created by the expansion of the tanning industry in the Punjabi town of Kasur (pp. 79-82).

[85] For an introduction to the strain on infrastructure brought by the population increase

of *katchi abadis* (mud tenements) as a step towards providing them with better amenities. Piped water for example was available to less than half the homes in the unregulated slum areas at the end of the 1980s. Yet a rising proportion of the population, nine in every twenty inhabitants lived in the *katchi abadis*. Resentment at the formal state's inability to tackle socio-economic problems or provide law and order led to the rise of the informal MQM 'secondary state'. Meanwhile in Lyari the continued lack of basic amenities highlighted by the water supply problems had by the time of the 1997 elections cut into the traditional PPP domination in this predominantly Baloch area.[86]

Migration to Karachi at the time of the Afghan conflict also brought with it the presence of drug mafias and the growing problem of addiction. Criminal violence in the 'biggest Pushtun city in the world' from the mid-1980s onwards was largely drug-related. The bulldozing of the largely Pushtun/Afghan-inhabited north Karachi slum area of Sohrab Goth in December 1986 in search of illegal arms and drugs precipitated retaliatory ethnic attacks on poorer *mohajir* localities elsewhere in the city. The impact of drug-laundered money on consumer demand has never been quantified. Similarly the impact of heroin smuggling on the local economy has been even less studied than that of remittances and the return of ex-migrants. Ugo Fabietti[87] has pointed out however that the monetization of the economy of the coastal Makran region of Balochistan was greatly assisted by drug trafficking. Its controllers are now leading entrepreneurs in the building trades, agriculture and fish processing industry. They have become influential distributors of local resources and been courted by politicians.[88] Indeed Makrani society has seen considerable social mobility resulting from the influx of black drug money and remittances from the migrant worker population, who number 10 per cent of the total.

Standard accounts of Pakistan's politics frequently ignore the state's high rates of social mobility because of their focus on elites and leading personalities. In a pioneering study, Theodore Wright has seen increased inter-sectarian and inter-provincial marriage arising from social mobility

---

see United Nations, *Population Growth and Policies in Mega Cities: Karachi* (New York, 1988).

[86] Latif Baloch, 'Lyari no longer a bastion of PPP', *Dawn* (Internet Edition), 5 February 1997.

[87] U. Fabietti, 'Equality versus Hierarchy: Conceptualizing Change in Southern Balochistan' in P. Titus (ed.), *Marginality and Modernity*, pp. 3-28.

[88] Evidence for a criminalisation of politics was starkly brought home by a report published by the Qureshi caretaker government in 1993. This listed 164 former legislators as active in the drug trade. See, M. Waseem, *The 1993 Elections in Pakistan*, p. 66.

as contributing to national integration, although such alliances are confined to the elites.[89]

The growth of the middle classes

Another contemporary social change is the growth of the middle classes. This is linked with urbanisation and the burgeoning of the economy's industrial and service sectors. Another factor has been the impact of overseas' remittances on family incomes, especially during the Zia era when the GNP doubled. The term 'classes' is used advisedly however because there is no monolithic middle stratum of society; it is differentiated by occupation, income, family antecedents, language and gender. Journalists have used the term loosely to denote any elite section of society which is not 'feudal'. A younger generation of feudal families has obfuscated this terminology by adopting middle class professional occupations and lifestyles. The inchoate nature of the continued electoral dominance by the middle and landowner classes has encouraged some commentators to ignore its existence.

The growth of the middle classes can be partly assessed from the rise in consumerism set out in Table 1.4. In addition to the expenditure on durable goods, the middle classes were the main consumers of the

Table 1.4. INCREASE IN CONSUMER GOODS
(all-Pakistan figures × 100,000)

	1979-80	1984	1988	1993-4	% increase
TV ownership (estimated)	6.15	10.55	14.08	19.75	221
Newspaper/magazine readership	17.53	23.45	31.30	–	53
Visitors to cultural and historical sites	15.66	19.29	21.76	–	26
Household electricity use (Gwh)	0.02	0.05	0.08	0.10	340
Registered cars/* station wagons	2.62	3.82	5.75	8.63	228
Registered motor-cycles	5.08	7.90	10.93	15.67	208
Telephones	3.36	5.73	8.39	17.91	432

* These 'official' figures greatly underestimate the real levels of ownership.

Adapted from A. Whaites, 'The state and civil society in Pakistan', *Contemporary South Asia* 4, no. 3 (1995), Table 1: 'Indicators of Embourgeoisement', p. 237.

[89] See Theodore P. Wright Jr, 'Can There Be a Melting Pot in Pakistan? Interprovincial Marriage and National Integration', *Contemporary South Asia* 3, no. 2 (1994), pp. 131-44.

burgeoning private educational establishments and privately run polyclinics which were a growing phenomenon in the cities. More fanciful indicators might be the rise of 'Urdish' among the young listeners of the FM radio stations[90] operating in Lahore, Islamabad and Karachi and the daily crowds of up to 25,000 people who flocked to the imposing Pace departmental store which opened in Lahore in 1995.

Women have been increasingly represented in Pakistan's new professional elite.[91] Nighat Parveen for example became CEO of Wellcome-Glaxo.[92] Less seriously but equally significantly, 'Sammy' (Saman Ibrahim), a former executive secretary with the World Bank in Islamabad, became the first female disc-jockey in Pakistan at Dee Jays restaurant in Lahore.[93] Women had earlier made their mark in law and journalism, although it should be remembered that there was a journalistic tradition which dated back to the beginning of the century with such publications as *Tehrib-e-Niswan* (The Women's Reformer) and *Ismat* (Chastity).[94] Razia Bhatti,[95] Rehana Hakim and Saira Irshad Khan of the hard-hitting Karachi-based *Newsline* magazine typified female contributions to the profession. Significantly, Benazir Bhutto posted the former journalist Maleeha Lodhi to the vital Washington Embassy following the 1993 elections. She was later joined by Asma Anisa and Bilqees Qureshi in the posts of Consul-General in Los Angeles and New York respectively. Men however still outnumbered women in foreign service positions by nearly twenty to one.

As in India, the increase in opportunities for elite women has not improved the circumstances of their poorer sisters. 'Urban-based women suffer from sexual harassment, low incomes and social discrimination' Iftikhar Malik has rightly remarked, 'while in the case of rural women it is a struggle for survival on all fronts.'[96] One in fifty-four maternity cases resulted in death, producing a staggering figure of half a million fatalities in 1992 alone.[97] Violence against women, or perhaps more

---

[90] See for example, S. Akbar Zaidi, 'Radio as metaphor', *Herald Annual*, January 1996, pp. 144ff.

[91] One of the leading figures was Citibank's Saadia Khairi. See *Newsline*, January 1995 p. 87.

[92] *Herald Annual*, January 1996, p. 163.

[93] *Ibid.*

[94] *Tehrib-e-Niswan* ran from 1898 to 1948. Ismat began its long publication history in Delhi in 1908.

[95] Razia Bhatti (1943-96) was founding editor of *Newsline*. She had previously edited *Herald* for twelve years where she had established a deserved reputation for integrity and courage. She pioneered a new school of investigative reporting in Pakistan.

[96] I H. Malik, *State and Civil Society in Pakistan*, p. 165.

[97] Human Rights Commission of Pakistan, *State of Human Rights in Pakistan in 1992*, p. 88.

accurately reports of it as a result of such organisations as Women
Against Rape, increased during the 1990s. A woman was raped every
3 hours of the year in 1993 for example, every other victim being
a minor.[98] Fifty years after independence, *zamindars, waderos* and *pirs*
prey on women from tenant and share-cropper families as mercilessly
as ever. Gang rapes have increased, as have incidents in which women
are publicly humiliated by being paraded naked. In 1993 there were
forty-eight reported instances of this practice in Punjab.[99] As we
shall see, the *Hudood* Ordinances which were instituted during Zia's
Islamisation process have been abused in order to bring false charges
of adultery against women and indeed around 80 per cent of all female
prisoners were women charged under *Hudood* offences.[100] Furthermore
the police routinely rape and assault women in their lock-ups.[101] Apart
from the social costs in reporting such incidents, the difficulties in registering
cases ensure that the perpetrators of these abuses are rarely punished.

Alan Whaites has linked the rise of an urban middle class with
the strengthening of civil society, finding evidence for this in the spread
of interest groups and NGOs. One such group founded in Karachi in
July 1993 was the Concerned Citizens Association. It was soon handling
300 complaints a month regarding the activities of such organisations
as the Karachi Electricity Supply Corporation (KESC) and the Karachi
Water and Sewerage Board (KWSB). It also used judicial activism
in the superior courts to enforce implementation of civic rights enshrined
in the constitution, and it submitted a Consumer Protection Bill to the
federal government, while advertising its activities on the world wide
web.[102] The increasing number of women's associations[103] represented
both the response to the discrimination of the Zia era and the extension
of a historical tradition which dates back to Begum Muhammad Shafi's
foundation of the Anjuman-i-Khatunan-i-Islam in Lahore in 1907.

Pasban was another middle-class phenomenon. This organisation was
launched in 1990 as a youth wing of the JI, but it soon shed the conservative image of its parent organisation to campaign on such social
injustices as rape. Its rallies employed video screenings, music and

---

[98] Human Rights Commission of Pakistan, *State of Human Rights in Pakistan 1993*, p. 1.

[99] *Ibid.*, p. vii.

[100] *Ibid.*, p. 58.

[101] See, Amnesty International, *Pakistan: Reports of Torture and Death in Police Custody*,
June 1991, pp. 11ff.

[102] See http://www.Smartnet/net/khan/power.htm.

[103] By 1991 they numbered 400. A. Whaites, 'The State and Civil Society in Pakistan',
Contemporary South Asia 4, no. 3 (1995), p. 244.

laser shows to attract a new breed of young people. Such 'vulgar' displays dismayed the Jamaat leadership and caused the split which followed the 1993 elections. Pasban retained the media spotlight by successfully organising Imran Khan's fund-raising campaign for the Shaukat Khanum Memorial Hospital (SKMH).[104]

The former international cricket star's campaign struck a public chord not just because of its poignant personal circumstances, but because of the rising tide of cancer. In 1992 alone over 100,000 new cases were officially diagnosed.[105] The high levels of air pollution arising from industrial and vehicle emissions in such cities as Lahore and Karachi were unquantifiable but inevitable contributory factors in the spread of the disease. Pasban played a prominent role in the culmination of Imran Khan's fund-raising campaign – the Awami show celebration in Lahore's Fortress Stadium on 28 December 1994. However, it later shifted its ties to the PPP government.

Further evidence for the growth of civil society was provided by the 'expanded role' of the media. Ironically the charges of endemic corruption and exposures of human rights abuses which provided a rationale for the dismissal of the Benazir Bhutto and Nawaz Sharif governments under military-backed presidential decree resulted from greater press freedom and the vitality of the NGOs. Successive regimes have strictly censored Pakistan's news media.[106] This did not of course prevent recourse to both BBC World Service radio and the Indian Door-darshan television network for citizens living within range of the Amritsar transmitter. Nevertheless, the globalisation of communications with satellite television has created an unprecedented situation. The mushrooming of satellite dishes in such working-class areas of Karachi as Lyari, Lasbela and Karimabad has revealed that Star Television is not just a luxury for the rich. The copying of Western technology and the piping by cable of pictures received by a single dish to an entire tenement has spread access to those on low incomes.[107]

At the same time as post-modernist ethnic architectural and fashion styles were becoming the vogue for the educated classes, partly inspired by Imran Khan's somewhat ironic diatribes against a 'brown sahib' culture, modernist 'cultural pollution' was being beamed into Baloch villages which did not even possess access to clean water supplies.

---

104 *Herald*, February 1995, pp. 28-9. Shaukat Khanum died in Lahore on 10 February 1985. Nawaz Sharif laid the foundation stone of the memorial hospital on 25 April 1991.

105 Human Rights Commission of Pakistan, *State of Human Rights in Pakistan in 1992*, p. 88.

106 The retired journalist Zamir Niazi provides an interesting insight into control over the press, especially in the Zia era, in Z. Niazi, *The Web of Censorship* (Karachi, 1994).

107 *Herald*, May 1993, p. 62.

By the early 1990s, the '*ulama* were complaining about the 'sexual anarchy' which was encouraged by foreign media penetration.[108] The satellite revolution not only threatened Pakistani social mores, but the state's control over political and intellectual outlooks.

Furthermore Pakistan has more slowly linked itself up to the information superhighway. By the middle of 1995 the total number of networkers was estimated at little over 3,000.[109] But the problems for domestic censorship arising from cyberspace were already apparent with the posting of the MQM news bulletin on the net.[110] This provides regularly updated releases from the North London-based MQM International Secretariat. Indeed without modern technology, Altaf Husain could not have directed MQM operations in Karachi from his London exile. In an attempt to curb 'terrorism', the Bhutto administration took the controversial step in July 1995 of suspending the entire cellular telephone network and pager system in Karachi and Hyderabad.[111]

Alan Whaites has declared that following the communications revolution and the rise of associational and interest group politics, Pakistan has now reached a 'stage of significant transition' in which the state has lost its autonomy from society. The costs of suppression have increased as seen by the Zia regime's greater use of force than that wielded by its military predecessors.[112] Such an analysis is useful in reminding ourselves that Pakistan is a dynamic society.

The political influence of Pakistan's middle classes is growing and has been a factor in the success of Nawaz Sharif's Muslim League Party (PML(N)). The MQM also originally emerged in the mid-1980s as a middle class party in Karachi, although it become increasingly ethnicised in composition and outlook. The absence of strong party institutions and the distortions arising from the reliance on 1981 Census data have slowed the swing in the balance of power from the landowners to the emergent middle classes.

Socio-economic change together with the separation of East Pakistan and the international rise of Islamic reassertion have had a profound impact on Pakistan's search for political stability. The country is not only more populous, prosperous and violent than it was at its foundation,

---

[108] Munawwar Hasan. 'Our Society Is Facing Sexual Anarchy', *Newsline*, September 1992, p. 26.

[109] *Newsline*, May 1995, p. 81.

[110] *Herald*, July 1995, p. 50.

[111] *Newsline*, July 1995, p. 74

[112] Whaites, 'The state and civil society in Pakistan', p. 249.

but its society is more complex. At one end of the spectrum there is the corporate culture of Karachi, at the other the brutal feudal society of bonded labour[113] and *karo kari*[114] killings in the interior of Sindh. In between there are prosperous Punjabi industrialists and capitalist farmers, small scale traders, artisans, labourers and peasants. The booming financial sector of the early 1990s resulted from the globalisation of business and was the domain of a new generation of foreign-educated Pakistani professionals. Some also returned to set up their own hi-tech businesses.[115] Perhaps the most dramatic manifestation of the cheek by jowl existence of modernity and tradition is the presence of the modern natural gas plant at Sui, an isolated tract of Bugti tribal land in Balochistan.

Has the economic development of the past half century created a more favourable domestic environment for the functioning of a stable democracy? Optimists, taking their cue from Samuel Huntington's views,[116] would argue that urbanisation, education and the growth of a middle class will help underpin democracy by expanding civil society. A more pessimistic reading of events is that economic development in Pakistan has bolstered the power of elite groups to the masses' detriment. The best that can be hoped for in these circumstances is a formal democracy which legitimises, but does not challenge the traditional powerholders. The point has been made that the costs of electioneering, weak party organisations and emphasis on social influence in vote winning has limited the pool of candidates to the legislatures to some 400 families. Such a formal democracy dominated by 'feudal' interests has exacerbated the existing politicisation of the bureaucracy, judiciary and law enforcement agencies.

Certainly, as we shall see, the rapid economic growth of the Ayub

---

113 Although the 1992 Bonded Labour System (Abolition) Act outlawed this practice, evidence exists that many large landowners in Sindh continue to run bonded labour camps and private jails. See for example. H. Mujtaba, 'Enslaved by the System', *Newsline Annual*, 1996. pp. 121-4.

114 These are public killings of women accused of adultery. According to one source around 180 women were brutally murdered in Sindh during 1995 in *Karo Kari* cases. Police were paid up to Rs. 75,000 'hush money'. N. Shah and M. Bullo, 'War on women', *Newsline*, April 1996, pp. 91ff.

115 One of the most notable success stories was Altmash Karmal, an MIT graduate. He founded the Wavetech company which exported such products as software and satellite tracking systems. *Newsline*, January 1995, p. 60.

116 S. Huntington, *The Third Wave: Democratization in the Late Twentieth Century* (Norman, OK, 1991). The issue of development and democratisation in Pakistan has been explored in M. Monshipouri and A. Samuel, 'Development and Democracy in Pakistan: Tenuous or Plausible Nexus?', *Asian Survey* 35, no. 11 (November 1995), pp. 973-89.

era exacerbated wealth disparities. The contention that economic growth fosters democratisation, while it may hold good in some circumstances, is at best open to further investigation in the Pakistan case. Development and democracy may not go hand in hand partly because of the direction of economic change, but also because of Pakistan's geopolitical and socio-political inheritances. The colonial roots of a political culture shot through with confrontational as opposed to accommodationist attitudes and with an authoritarianism inimical to the expansion of democratic institutions will form the focus of the following two chapters.

2

COLONIAL RULE, AUTHORITARIANISM
AND REGIONAL HISTORY IN
NORTH-WEST INDIA

Although an American Embassy official was still able to uncover copies of *Punch* for 1883-4 in a Gakuch rest-house in Gilgit in June 1961,[1] many of the visible symbols of the colonial past have long since disappeared in those areas of the subcontinent which became Pakistan in August 1947. The statue of Queen Victoria which once dominated the Charing Cross intersection of the Lahore Mall has now found its final resting place in the museum where John Lockwood Kipling once worked as a curator. The Mall itself has been renamed Shahrah-e-Quaid-e-Azam, just as one of the most important remaining examples of British architecture[2] in Karachi, Frere Hall, is now known as Bagh-e-Jinnah.

Political and institutional inheritances from the Raj nevertheless continue to exert a profound influence. The words of Rajeshwari Sunder Rajan, penned in a different context ring true for Pakistan where, 'Colonialism is not simply a matter of legacy but of active, immediate and constitutive determinants'.[3] This chapter focuses on the colonial state's administrative legacy and subsequent political inheritances.

Colonial administration in the Muslim-majority areas

Many writers have emphasised the shared systems of governance which were bequeathed to the Raj's successor states. Asma Barlas for example finds the different post-colonial political trajectories of

---

[1] Murree Office of American Embassy to Department of State, 7 June 1961, 790.D.00/5-461, National Archives at College Park.

[2] Other important surviving examples are of course the famous Empress Market Tower and the Merewether Tower, which was designed in 1892 and stands at the junction of M.A. Jinnah and I.I. Chundrigar Roads. For the way in which Karachi's architecture expressed different facets of the Raj see Y. Lari and M.S. Lari, *The Dual City: Karachi During the Raj* (Karachi, 1996).

[3] R. S. Rajan, *Real and Imagined Women* (London, 1993).

India and Pakistan as striking because 'they acquired almost identical administrative structures from the Raj'. She proceeds to relate the nature of social and political forces in colonial India to the broad features of subcontinental post-colonial politics.[4] In reality however, there was no uniformity in administrative structure. Regional variations resulted from the subtleties of British interaction with Indian society and the original motives for the annexation of territory. Ayesha Jalal and Hamza Alavi are nearer to the mark than Barlas when they link Pakistan's 'overdeveloped' administrative and military institutions to the colonial practice of emphasising the requirements of law and order rather than those of popular representation.[5] This colonial legacy was first summed up in the term 'viceregalism' by Khalid bin Sayeed. There has been little detailed examination however, of either its characteristics or legacy for the future Pakistan areas. This section takes this analysis a stage further by studying what was in essence a security state in north-west India, which contrasted considerably with those areas which formed the Indian Dominion or East Pakistan after the great divide of 1947.

The British security state in North-West India

Before addressing the contrasts between north-west India and the rest of the subcontinent, it is important to note those measures of political coercion which all regions inherited from the colonial state. These included preventive detention (originating in the Bengal State Prisoners Regulation III of 1818); prohibition of political actions seen by magistrates as prejudicial to public order (Section 144 of the Criminal Code of Procedure) and control of the Press (1931 Indian Press Emergency Powers Act). The Pakistan authorities reinstituted the Emergency Powers of Section 93 (as Section 92A) of the 1935 Government of India Act, which enabled the centre to dissolve a provincial government. In addition to such legacies from the colonial state, the Public and Representatives Offices (Disqualification) Act (PRODA) was introduced in 1949.[6]

These measures arose out of the British need to combat nationalist or communal threats to their authority. They were regarded as exceptional measures only to be deployed in times of unrest. Although they harked

---

[4] A. Barlas, *Democracy, Nationalism and Communalism: The Colonial Legacy in South Asia* (Boulder, CO, 1995).

[5] A. Jalal, *Democracy and Authoritarianism in South Asia*; H. Alavi, 'Class and State' in H. Gardezi and J. Rashid (eds), *Pakistan: The Roots of Dictatorship* (London, 1983), pp. 40-93.

[6] For further details see Chapter 4.

back to the autocracy which accompanied the original British military conquest of the subcontinent, they coexisted with the progressive spread of representative institutions. The situation in the north-west corner of India was somewhat different. Political participation was far less developed there and permanent police powers existed alongside emergency coercive measures. British rule emphasised law and order rather than encouraging political participation. Why was the ethos of rule so different in the future Pakistan areas?

The answer lies partly in the timing of British annexation. With the exception of Bengal, the future Pakistan areas were acquired much later than the remainder of the subcontinent. The autocratic traditions attendant on the early period of British rule thus persisted within them well beyond the high noon of Empire. The tribal composition of these regions and the threat of Russian expansion from Central Asia and Afghanistan were further factors in reinforcing autocracy. While force had been applied to acquire territory elsewhere, it could be discarded more readily as commercial rather then strategic considerations held sway. This was never the case in much of the British security state in north-west India. In order to illustrate these arguments, a slight digression into the history of British expansion in the Pakistan areas of the subcontinent is required.

British power had already been well established in the Indian subcontinent for close on a century when the future West Pakistan regions were annexed. Charles Napier, in an act of imperial private enterprise, seized Sindh from its Baloch Talpur rulers in 1843. Six years later the British triumph in the Second Sikh War secured the remainder of the Punjab[7] and the Frontier region which had been part of Ranjit Singh's Empire. It was not until 1901 however that the settled districts of the Frontier tracts were constituted into a separate province from Punjab. British influence in the present Balochistan province increased on a piecemeal basis from 1854 onwards. Kalat and its erstwhile feudatories Makran, Kharan and Las Bela were accorded the status of protected states. A boundary commission in 1872 resolved the undefined boundary between Kalat and Persia. During the 1878-80 Afghan War the strategically important regions of Pishin and Sibi were ceded to the British and formed the Political Agency of Balochistan.

The areas which formed British Balochistan abutted the frontier with Afghanistan and had been brought under imperial sway for strategic reasons from 1876 onwards. The treaty of that year with the Khan of Kalat allowed troops to be stationed in Quetta. It became an important

---

[7] The trans-Sutlej territories had been annexed after the first Anglo-Sikh War of 1846. A Regency Council which was under the virtual control and guidance of a permanent British Resident in Lahore was established to govern the remainder of the Sikh kingdom.

centre of military operations during the Second Afghan War (1878-80) and shortly afterwards the Khan passed the whole of the Quetta district over to the British. Pishin, which had been occupied during the war, formed part of the joint district whose northern and western boundaries were demarcated by a British and Afghan commission during 1894-6.[8]

The Bolan Pass through which large quantities of arms were shipped during the Second Afghan War was similarly ceded to the British Government by the Khan of Kalat in 1883. Further agreements in 1894 and 1903 placed those areas under British jurisdiction which were traversed by the strategic Mushkaf-Bolan and Nushki railways.[9] What was to become the Zhob district[10] interested the British because of the Kakar Jogizai tribes' threat to lines of communication during the Afghan conflict. Military expeditions were sent to pacify the tribes in 1884 and 1889. The following year, the Zhob Political Agency was founded and in 1894-5 its northern boundary was demarcated by a joint Afghan-British commission.

This expansion of British power continues to exert an influence on post-colonial Balochistan. The privileging of administrative and military institutions at the expense of democratic expressions was felt more fully in the region than in any of the other 'Pakistan' areas. British Balochistan did not follow the North West Frontier in making the transition from a Chief Commissioner's to a Governor's province.

The power of the civil administration was augmented by strategic alliances with the local powerholders. Again this was by no means unique to Balochistan, but strategic imperatives and a less egalitarian society than in the Frontier enabled it to flower more fully in the region by bolstering the sardars' position through the formalisation of the tribal councils' (*jirgas*) powers. The presence of the Native States acted as a further break on democratic political development. Wayne Wilcox has shown how their consolidation with the directly administered areas evolved from the Balochistan States Union.[11] The integration of Kalat proved difficult and, especially after the October 1958 rebellion, provided the seeds for the articulation of a Baloch political identity based on hostility to the increasing intervention of the centre.

Baloch ethnic identity has also gained importance in the post-colonial era because of the competition for resources with the Pushtun. While the impact of migration and the Afghan conflict has been profound,

---

[8] *Quetta and Pishin District Gazeteer*, vol. V (Ajmer, 1907), pp. 43ff.

[9] *Bolan and Chagai District Gazeteer*, vol. IV (Karachi 1906), pp. 16ff.

[10] *Zhob District Gazeteer*, vol. I (Bombay, 1906), provides details of the administrative and political history.

[11] W. A. Wilcox, *Pakistan: The Consolidation of a Nation* (New York, 1963).

it is important to recognise the important inheritance from the colonial era. While Balochistan remained poorer than any future Pakistan region, the northern Pushtun areas achieved greater economic progress than the southern Brahui and Baloch regions. This situation reflected in part the more enlightened political and economic framework throughout the subcontinent of the directly administered areas than the Princely States. Its main cause however was the economic multiplier effects of the road and railway building programmes in the north.

The British embarked on expensive infrastructural developments to move troops more easily to pacify the local population and to meet any threat from the Afghan frontier. The railway which linked Quetta to the Bolan Pass was completed at the cost of Rs. 111 *lakh* in July 1886. The Sindh-Pishin railway in the Sibi district which opened the following year involved some of the most dangerous tunnelling work anywhere in the subcontinent. The Fort Sandeman-Chuhar Khel road which linked the Zhob district with Dera Ismail Khan in Punjab from 1895 onwards was another major engineering feat as it involved the blasting of a passage through the Dahana Tangi gorge.[12]

Trade as well as troops flowed along the new roads and railways. Within twenty years of the British occupation of the Zhob district, sixty-nine new hamlets and villages had sprung up in addition to the military and administrative centres of Fort Sandeman and Hindubagh.[13] Being a railway junction, Bostan in the Quetta district grew up as a bazaar. Sibi's thriving economy was based both on its administrative importance and the siting of the North-Western Railway workshops in the town. Quetta's population increased fourfold during the period 1883-1901 as a result of its administrative and military importance and good rail connections with the rest of India.

The British programme of road and railway construction depressed economic activity in southern Balochistan at the same time as stimulating it in the northern regions. Goods once carried by camel caravan from the coast to Afghanistan were now diverted by rail.[14] The poor communications of the southern plains and coastal areas with the remainder of India now led to their economic marginalisation. It would of course be overly simplistic to contrast backward Baloch with developing Pushtun areas. Even in the southern areas there was some economic development and new towns such as Kolpur were built along railway routes.[15]

12 *Zhob District Gazeteer*, vol. 1, p. 210.

13 *Ibid.*, p. 64.

14 F. Scholz, 'Tribal Structures and Religious Tolerance: Hindus in Pakistani Balochistan' in P. Titus (ed.), *Marginality and Modernity*, p. 201.

15 *Ibid.*, p. 216.

Moreover, many of the commercial opportunities resulting from the British opening up of the northern regions were seized by Hindu merchants rather than the Pushtuns. Indeed it was only in the aftermath of partition that they began to take up the shops and businesses which the Hindus had left behind. Nevertheless the colonial inheritance for the region was the favouring of the Pushtun population in competition with the Baloch for resources and power.

Bengal was of course an exception to the late security-driven acquisition of the Pakistan areas. The East India Company assumed the *diwani* or revenue collectorship in Bengal in 1765. European administration followed slowly thereafter and was commercially rather than strategically motivated. The British interest in harnessing the waters of Punjab and Sindh notwithstanding, their advance in Muslim north-west India was prompted by military rather than commercial considerations. They were determined initially to outflank and later to fill the vacuum created by the collapse of the dominant regional power, the Sikh Punjab kingdom of Ranjit Singh's successors. Even more significantly, their advance coincided with growing anxieties about threats to British India from Afghanistan and the expanding Russian Empire in Central Asia which lay behind it. Punjab was thus seen as a base for military operations, whilst the Frontier and Balochistan regions were buffer zones against a possible attack.

The irrigated areas of Sindh and Punjab had developed a settled agrarian lifestyle prior to the intrusion of the colonial state. But large areas of the newly-annexed regions contained volatile nomadic and semi-nomadic tribal communities.[16] Their presence, allied to the external threat to the strategic gateway to India, increased British security concerns. Cantonments, strategic roads and railways, hilltop forts and such engineering feats as the crenellated double-decker iron bridge soaring above the narrow Indus gorge at Attock, bear physical witness to these anxieties. In fact security concerns were to dominate every aspect of administration. Despite the different approaches of the 'Close Border System' and 'Forward Policy' schools,[17] the preservation of the existing social system came to be regarded as essential for the maintenance of stability in the new frontier regions.

A threefold division was created between the 'tribal' states, tribal areas and the so-called 'settled' districts. The former areas included states like Swat, Chitral and Kalat. The British exerted only advisory

---

[16] For details on the Baloch, Brahui and Pushtun tribal structure of Balochistan, see A.H. Siddiqi, *Baluchistan (Pakistan): Its Society, Resources and Development* (Lanham, MD, 1991), pp. 151ff. For a classic account of the Pushtun tribal society of the Frontier see O. Caroe, *The Pathans, 550 B.C.-A.D.1957* (Karachi, 1973).

[17] Caroe, *The Pathans*, pp. 346-9, 370-412.

power over their internal affairs which were under the exclusive jurisdiction of their hereditary rulers. As a result of this system of indirect
rule, they remained largely untouched by political, social and economic
change elsewhere in India and were amongst the most backward areas
of the subcontinent at the time of independence. The tribal areas[18] were
overseen by a British political agent and were subject to the terms
laid down in their official treaties and agreements. Control was maintained
by tribal levies in addition to the carrot of cash subsidies and the stick
of punitive expeditions and collective fines.[19] These areas were outside
British legal jurisdiction and were not subject to land revenue demands
or other taxes. Customary law, enforced through tribal *jirgas* rather
than Islamic law, was the order of the day.

The post-colonial Pakistan state has maintained the main features
of the British administration including the Frontier Crimes Regulations
in the fifteen designated tribal areas in the Frontier, Balochistan and
Dera Ghazi Khan district of Punjab. The Provincially Administered
Tribal Areas (PATA) regulations for the Malakand Agency were however
abolished by the Peshawar High Court in February 1994. The judicial
vacuum which followed encouraged the November Malakand Insurgency
of Maulana Sufi Muhammad's Tehrik-e-Nifaz-e-Shariat-e-Muhammadi
(TNSM) which fought for the replacement of the PATA tribal laws
by the *Shariat*.

The remaining tribal areas were administered directly in the Frontier,
Punjab and Sindh provinces of British India. Special considerations
for security were seen in the bureaucratic authoritarianism displayed
in the extensive powers given to deputy commissioners under the Frontier
Crimes Regulation[20] and in the tardy move towards implementing responsible government. The Punjab milieu was only marginally more
democratic given the dominating ethos of the paternalistic Punjab school
of administration.[21]

Deputy commissioners wielded extremely wide powers under the
terms of the Frontier Crimes Regulation. They could refer civil and
criminal cases to *jirgas* which they had appointed and they were also
empowered to impose collective punishments where no culprits for a
crime could be found. Trans-border tribes were sometimes 'blockaded'
and later bombed into submission. Villagers were forced to serve as

---

[18] In the Frontier region these were divided into the Malakand, Khyber, Kurram, North
Waziristan and South Waziristan Agencies.

[19] E. Jansson, *India, Pakistan or Pakhtunistan: The Nationalist Movements in the North-
West Frontier Province, 1937-47* (Uppsala,1981), p. 27.

[20] *Ibid.*, pp. 30ff.

[21] For details see P.H.M. van den Dungen, *The Punjab Tradition: Influence and Authority
in Nineteenth century India* (London, 1972).

unpaid night-watchmen in the *naubati chaukidari* system. The army stood in reserve to back up a burgeoning police force. By 1941 this stood at 7,500 and was equipped with sten guns, mortars, and motor vehicles.[22]

Consent was of course preferred to coercion and the British sought to obtain this by winning the support of the large Khans. This was obtained through the grant of 'political pensions', the awarding of honorific titles, cash and land under the *inam* scheme and allowing them local administrative and judicial powers through the *zaildari* and *lambardari* system.[23] However, the Government's neglect of a rising class of small Khans proved a major weakness by the 1930s. Indeed, the politics of the closing years of the Raj were driven both by traditional factional disputes and the intra-elite conflict between the big and small Khans.

British paternalistic rule in Punjab can be dated to the period of the three-man board of administration – dominated by the titan figures of the Lawrence brothers – which was set up after the region's final annexation in 1849.[24] An 8,000-strong military police force was deputed to keep the turbulent population in check. The British sought to govern from a position of moral as well as physical strength. The district officials, who were all invested with both administrative and judicial powers, were thus expected to win the allegiance of the rural population by their example of hard work and fair-mindedness.

The other dominant feature of British administration in the north-west security state area was the co-option of local landed elites. This not only retarded political institutionalisation, but reinforced a culture of clientelism. It also placed insuperable barriers in the way of future socio-economic reform by establishing the basis for a dominant landlord political interest. Again there are marked contrasts between Bengal and the other future Pakistan areas. The overriding consideration in Bengal was to extract revenue demands as efficiently as possible. The creation of a loyal landholding class was subordinate to this primary commercial consideration and indeed was viewed in its light. The Company did not at this time consider it necessary to shield cultivators from the effects of the commercialisation of agriculture and the introduction of private rights to ownership. The pattern and ethos of Bengal's administration was so well established that it was not unduly modified by what

[22] Sayed Wiqar Ali Shah, 'Muslim Politics in the North-West Frontier Province 1937-47', unpubl. D.Phil. thesis, University of Oxford 1997, p. 163.

[23] *Ibid.*, pp. 96-7.

[24] For details see H. Lee, 'John and Henry Lawrence and the Origins of Paternalist Rule in the Punjab 1846-1858', *International Journal of Punjab Studies* 2, no. 1 (Jan.-June 1995), pp. 65-89.

has been termed the 'conservative reaction' which followed the 1857 revolt.[25]

The present author has learned from his earlier research that the strongest alliance between the colonial state and the leading landowners existed in its Punjab bastion. This not only jeopardised the achievement of Pakistan, but was to threaten its post-colonial democratic development.[26] Indeed, the long-term influence of the British reliance on the collaboration of local rural intermediaries [27] in the future heartland of Pakistan, has been so great that a digression on the functioning of this system is required here.

The collaboration of the rural elite was secured through systems of honours, nominations to *darbars* and local boards, and involvement in administration through the posts of honorary magistrate and *zaildar*.[28] The British attached great significance to the 'steadfastness' or 'treachery' of communities during the 1857 revolt. They richly rewarded those who had stood by them in their darkest hour. Many rural Punjabi families embarked at this time on what were to prove lengthy and lucrative 'loyalist' careers. In both Punjab and the Frontier, the British abandoned economic *laissez-faire* principles to curb the predatory activity of moneylenders which threatened to undermine the colonial state's social bases of support.

The 1900 Punjab Alienation of Land Act[29] not only 'crystallised the assumptions underlying the British Imperial administration' but 'translated' them into popular politics. Henceforth both the justification of British rule and the programme of the leading men of the 'tribes' and 'clans' who banded together eventually in the Unionist Party was the 'uplift' and 'protection' of the 'backward' agriculturalist tribes. In addition to ensuring that the rural elites' political and social leadership was unaffected by the economic forces set in train by the colonial encouragement of a market-oriented agriculture, they used the resources which this provided to reward the agriculturalist population rather than

[25] See T.R. Metcalf, *The Aftermath of Revolt: India, 1857-1870* (Princeton, NJ, 1964).

[26] See I. Talbot, *Punjab and the Raj, 1849-1947* (New Delhi, 1988); *Khizr Tiwana, the Punjab Unionist Party and the Partition of India* (London, 1996).

[27] For further details see I. Talbot, *Punjab and the Raj*; S. Ansari, *Sufi Saints and State Power*.

[28] A *zail* (circle) comprised between 10-30 villages. The *zaildar* supervised the village headmen and acted as an honorary police officer. This mediatory position between government and local society was unique to the Frontier and Punjab and demonstrated clearly the role of the landowners as a pillar of British rule. For further details see I. Talbot, *Punjab and the Raj*, p. 35.

[29] This prevented the transfer of land from agriculturalists to moneylenders. It was extended to the Hazara, Bannu and Dera Ismail Khan districts of the Frontier in 1904 and later extended (1921-2) to the Peshawar and Kohat districts.

stimulate industrial development. Part and parcel of this order of priorities was the low pitch of revenue demand in both Punjab and the Frontier. This may have made political sense in the Frontier, but it did not add up economically for a province which incurred substantial law and order costs and urgently required development. As the Pakistan Government has subsequently discovered, such straitened circumstances involved reliance on external subsidy and precluded serious attempts to improve the low rate of literacy.[30] Other areas faced even greater problems. As late as 1944 Balochistan for example possessed only four government high schools and a literacy rate of under 2 per cent.[31]

The shadow side of British paternalism in north-west India was the violent repression of any perceived challenge to the *status quo*. This was meted out alike to agitators, 'terrorists' and religio-political movements like the Kukas or the Khaksars. Provincial administrations of the future West Pakistan areas all had blood on their hands and demonstrated a willingness to call for military support to aid civil power. The most infamous incident was of course the firing on an unarmed crowd in the walled area of Jallianwalla Bagh in Amritsar on 13 April 1919. It occurred within the context of mounting British repression of protests against the unpopular Rowlatt Act; these intensified rather than abated after the massacre and included the notorious crawling order and public floggings. Less dramatic but equally the subject of official and Congress investigations was the Qissa Khwani Bazaar shooting incident in Peshawar on 23 April 1930 which at the most conservative estimate resulted in thirty deaths when troops fired on an unarmed crowd. In Sindh the British introduced martial law in June 1942 in order to ruthlessly repress the Hur movement of Pir Sibghatullah Shah (Pir Pagaro).[32] The repression of the 1930 disturbances in the Frontier was almost equal in severity. Even in less exceptional times, officials wielded vast discretionary powers in maintaining public peace. Moreover, it was in the Punjab alone that direct Governor's rule was still in place on the very eve of partition.

The British desire to secure the power of their rural allies in what was the main recruiting ground of the Indian Army from the 1880s onwards had discouraged the introduction of representative institutions in the Punjab. Almost half a century of British rule had elapsed before a Punjab Legislative Council was created. Even then, the officials saw to it that its powers were severely limited. As late as 1927 the Simon Commission argued that the strategic location of the Frontier made

---

[30] The literacy rate in 1931 was only 5.6 per cent. *Census of India, 1931*, p. 156.

[31] Talbot, *Provincial Politics and the Pakistan Movement: The Growth of the Muslim League in North-West and North-East India 1937-47* (Karachi, 1988), p. 117.

[32] For details see S. Ansari, *Sufi Saints and State Power*, Chapter 6.

it unsuitable for self-government. It was only after the widespread unrest of 1930-32 that the Frontier secured the devolution of powers under the system of dyarchy as set down in the 1919 Government of India Act. At the time of the 1937 elections, Abdul Ghaffar Khan[33] was still banned from the Frontier and the Governor used his powers to prohibit all demonstrations and processions. Right up to independence, electoral politics in Balochistan were restricted to the Quetta Municipality. Balochistan's decision to join Pakistan was decided by just fifty-four members of the *shahi jirga* (tribal council) and five members of the Quetta Municipality.[34] Whenever the principle of election was conceded, the British safeguarded the position of their rural allies by linking the right to vote with property qualifications and introducing special landholders' constituencies.

In Punjab, the British had initiated a tribal idiom in representative politics by ensuring that *zails* constituted the constituencies for election to the district boards. *Zails* had been carved out to coincide as far as possible with prevailing tribal settlement patterns.[35] When from 1919 onwards wider constituencies were established, it was of course impossible to obtain a perfect fit between them and tribal blocks of land. Nevertheless, the British ensured that political power in the countryside remained the prerogative of the leading landowners. Members of non-agriculturalist tribes as defined by the 1900 Alienation of Land Act were prevented from standing for rural constituencies. These accounted for all but eleven of the Muslim block of seats in the Legislative Assembly created by the 1935 Government of India Act.

The introduction of political reforms widened the differences between Bengal and much of the future Pakistan area. Political consciousness developed much earlier in Bengal as a result of the exposure to representative institutions and the higher educational attainment of its population.[36] The Western-educated Bengali middle classes were increasingly critical of the Raj. The province was thus at the forefront of not only constitutional but also agitational and revolutionary politics from 1905 onwards.[37] Indeed the British decision to decamp to the

---

[33] See Appendix B for details of his remarkable political career.

[34] I. Talbot, *Provincial Politics and the Pakistan Movement*, p. 117.

[35] D. Gilmartin, *Empire and Islam*, p. 20.

[36] All the Presidencies were ahead of India's other provinces in the growth of education. This reflected their longer exposure to British rule and their administrative and commercial importance. For an overview see J. Brown, *Modern India: The Origins of an Asian Democracy*, 2nd edn (Oxford, 1995), pp. 123ff.

[37] G. Johnson, 'Partition, Agitation and Congress: Bengal 1904 to 1908' in J. Gallagher, G. Johnson and A. Seal (eds), *Locality, Province and Nation: Essays on Indian Politics, 1870-1914* (Cambridge 1973), pp. 213-68.

new imperial capital in Delhi reflected Bengal's emergence as the stormy petrel of Indian politics.

It is well known that the Bengali Hindu *bhadralok* (respectable middle class) dominated the province's educational and political institutions.[38] But early signs of Muslim political consciousness were provided by the establishment of such bodies as the Muhammadan Literary Society founded in Calcutta in 1863 and more importantly by the creation of the Central National Muhammadan Association in 1877. Its founder Syed Ameer Ali (1849-1928) played a leading role in the establishment of the Muslim League which of course took place in Dhaka. Equally important was the emergence by the beginning of the twentieth century of a politicised *jotedar* (sharecropper) Muslim class in such areas as Noakhali, Tippera and Mymensingh. This formed an important reservoir of support for Fazlul Haq's Krishak Praja Party (KPP) and later for the progressive wing of the Bengal Muslim League.

In sum, in much of what was to become Pakistan, a tradition of bureaucratic authoritarianism or viceregalism was deeply rooted. Its hallmarks were paternalism, wide discretionary powers and the personalisation of authority. Political institutions were weakly developed in comparison. In Punjab, the future heartland of Pakistan, a special relationship between the peasantry and the army had been established which Clive Dewey has forcefully argued holds the key to military dominance in independent Pakistan.[39] The tradition of ruthless repression of unrest and the introduction of martial law had also been established. Significantly such leading Pakistani administrative and political figures of the 1950s as Chaudhri Muhammad Ali, Ghulam Muhammad and Iskander Mirza had spent part of their formative careers in this atmosphere.

Bengal was the exception to this tradition, because it did not historically form part of the British security state. Although the region's more developed areas went to India in 1947, its political culture was more conducive to the growth of democracy and civil society than in any of the other Muslim majority areas. A future Pakistan state would face the major task of accommodating these varying colonial inheritances.

Thus a sharp contrast can be observed between the functioning of the security state in north-west India and the British administration

[38] See for example, J.H. Broomfield, *Elite Conflict in a Plural Society: Twentieth Century Bengal* (Berkeley, CA, 1968).

[39] C. Dewey, 'The rural roots of Pakistani Militarism' in D.A. Low (ed.), *The Political Inheritance of Pakistan* (Basingstoke, 1991), p. 261.

of other areas of the subcontinent. In the words of Muhammad Waseem, 'the slow growth of the elective principle in the provinces constituting Pakistan today must be taken into account in any study of electoral democracy in that country, especially when it is compared with India.'[40] This is not to suggest that Pakistani authoritarianism can be explained solely with reference to this legacy. The Pakistan struggle itself provided a countervailing tradition of mass political mobilisation. The viceregal tradition could thus have been jettisoned with the achievement of independence, especially as the bifurcation of both the civil administration and the army severely weakened these institutions. Their ability to steadily increase their power and insulate it from popular control can only be understood in terms of the character of the Pakistan movement and the chaos created by partition. The ways in which both enabled a re-establishment of viceregalism will form the focus of the following chapters.

[40] M. Waseem, *The 1993 Elections in Pakistan*, pp. 30-1.

3

THE PAKISTAN MOVEMENT: ITS
DYNAMICS AND LEGACIES

Just north of the massive Alamgiri gate of Akbar's Lahore Fort, the 1960s modernist concrete structure of the Minar-e-Pakistan rises from its flower vase like base in Iqbal Park. It marks the place where the Pakistan resolution was passed on 23 March 1940 at the Annual Session of the All-India Muslim League (AIML). Allama Iqbal, who first called for a separate state for North Indian Muslims at a League meeting ten years earlier at Allahabad, lies buried nearby within the celebrated Badshahi mosque. However, the spiritual heart of the Pakistan movement was not centred in Lahore but in the Victorian red-brick buildings of Aligarh College some 350 miles to the south-west in the Indian state of Uttar Pradesh (UP, formerly the United Provinces). Indeed, the Muslim League was a latecomer not only in Punjab, but also in the other regions which were to form Pakistan.

Writers from such varied intellectual backgrounds as Francis Robinson, Hamza Alavi and Ashok Kapur have linked the 'shallow roots' of the freedom struggle with Pakistan's subsequent problems of political development and national integration. Robinson, drawing on his specialist knowledge of UP, raises three points: first that Muslim separatist politics were primarily a phenomenon of UP; second that developments at the centre rather than the wishes of Muslim majority area politicians led to the strengthening of a Muslim-Pakistan political identity during the pre-partition decade; third that with the possible exception of Bengal, none of the provinces which came to form Pakistan possessed either a widespread positive identification with a Muslim-Pakistan political identity, or sufficiently developed political institutions to sustain it.[1]

Kapur polemically asserts that Pakistan's difficulties stem from the way it was created. Unlike the mass Indian nationalist movement with its personal sacrifice and focus on the problem of poverty, 'Pakistan's independence was a result of a combination of British India policy (1920s-1940s) and the willingness of Pakistan's 'leaders' (with no mass

---

[1] F. Robinson, 'Origins' in W. E. James and Subroto Roy (eds), *Foundations of Pakistan's Political Economy: Towards an Agenda for the 1990s.* (New Delhi, 1992), pp. 33-58.

following or ability to win elections or to form governments on their
own, i.e. without British aid) to play the British India government's
game of "divide and rule" and then "divide and quit". [...] Pakistan
got its separate status as a gift' not 'by adopting any brand of nationalism;
or through mass movement... or by conception of liberty, representative
government, or majority rule.'[2]

Hamza Alavi for his part has maintained that ethnicity has dominated
Pakistani politics in the absence of a larger concept of nationhood.
This failed to emerge during the freedom movement which was weakly
based in the 'Pakistan' areas. Alavi attributes this to the limited development within them of a Muslim salariat which was the class most committed to the ideology of Pakistani nationhood.[3]

Iftikhar Malik and Imran Ali have also linked Pakistan's post-
independence problems with the underdevelopment of a supra-regional
Pakistani identity under the conditions of colonial rule, while Yunas
Samad has pointed to the tensions between regional political identities
and Muslim nationalism arising from the ambiguities of the freedom
struggle. It is thus of supreme importance to examine the characteristics
and legacies of the Pakistan movement in the Muslim majority provinces
of British India.

Punjab

The Muslim League was a latecomer in all the future Pakistan areas.
In Punjab – termed by Jinnah the 'cornerstone' of Pakistan – it never
held power before independence. Punjab politics were dominated by
the cross-communal Unionist Party which had been founded by Mian
Fazl-i-Husain and Chaudhri Chhotu Ram in 1922. Its appeal rested
in the ability to dispense patronage and to ring-fence the interests of
the rural communities by upholding the safeguards from expropriation
provided by the 1900 Alienation of Land Act. Yet despite the popular
enthusiasm generated by the so-called 'Golden Acts' of 1938[4] which
further curbed the influence of the moneylenders, it failed to establish
a solid grassroots organisation. In such circumstances, personal influence

---

2 Ashok Kapur, *Pakistan in Crisis* (London, 1991), p. 2.

3 H. Alavi, 'Nationhood and Communal Violence in Pakistan', *Journal of Contemporary Asia* 21, no. 2 (1991), pp. 152-78. See especially pp. 153-63.

4 The key measures were the Punjab Alienation of Land Second Amendment Act which removed the loophole of the *benami* transaction, the Registration of Moneylenders Act and the Restitution of Mortgaged Lands Act. The latter enabled persons to recover all the land which they had mortgaged before 1901. In Amritsar district alone over 100 meetings were held during the course of 1938 to celebrate the passage of the 'Golden Acts'.

with the voters counted far more than the party programme in securing election. The Muslim League's pitiful showing in the 1937 Punjab elections, in which it captured just one seat, reflected its narrow social base of support. It was simply unable to garner votes through the traditional channels of political mobilisation in the countryside, the *biraderi* networks, the patron-client ties between landlords and tenants and the networks of disciples of the leading *pirs*.

The pact at Lucknow between the Unionist Premier Sikander and Jinnah following the elections ensured Muslim League Punjabi support in All-India politics, but only at the heavy cost of creating a Unionist stranglehold on its provincial organisation.[5] An AIML investigation in October 1941 worryingly discovered that in ten districts of Punjab no organisation existed at all and that the total primary League membership of the seven city and six district branches which were able to return reasonably accurate figures was only around 15,000.[6] One consequence of this was that the early work in popularising the Pakistan demand had to be left to the Punjab Muslim Students Federation. It organised a rural Pakistan Propaganda Committee after a Pakistan Conference presided over by Jinnah had met in Lahore in March 1941. During a twenty day tour it visited fifty villages, and opened a primary branch of the Muslim League in each one.[7] While this was only a drop in the ocean, it was to be a useful dress-rehearsal for the massive propaganda campaign launched by students at the time of the 1946 elections. During the peak of student activity, the 1945 Christmas vacation, there were 1,550 members of the Punjab Students Federation and 250 Aligarh students engaged in popularising the Punjab Muslim League's message.[8] This impressive contribution was nonetheless dwarfed in Bengal where 20,000 students answered the League Secretary Abul Hashim's appeal to lose if necessary one year of their studies in the greater good of the freedom struggle.[9] Works on Pakistan have frequently focused on the prevalence of student activism which, through such powerful bodies as the Baloch Students' Organisation and the All-Pakistan Mohajir Students' Organisation (APMSO), have provided militant activists and leadership cadres for ethnic parties. No links have been drawn however

[5] See Talbot, *Punjab and the Raj*, pp. 125-32.

[6] Conference of the Presidents and Secretaries of the Provincial Muslim Leagues, October 1941, vol. 326, pt. 2, p. 74, FMA.

[7] Report of Muhammad Sadiq: Sheikhupura Student Deputation, 22 July 1941, QEAP File 1099/84, NAP.

[8] I. Talbot, 'The 1946 Punjab Elections', *Modern Asian Studies* 14, no. 1 (February 1980), p. 78.

[9] Harun-or-Rashid, *The Foreshadowing of Bangladesh: Bengal Muslim League and Muslim League Politics 1936-47*, (Dhaka, 1987), p. 226.

between its contemporary and pre-independence manifestations. The question remains whether later generations of politicised students drew legitimacy for their actions from the high profile of their forbears in the creation of the state.

However, the key to the Muslim League breakthrough in Punjab lay in the new circumstances created by the Second World War. Within Punjab, the Unionist Ministry was forced to introduce the requisitioning of grain. Its supporters were also hit by inflation. The League was able to give this a communal colouring by pointing out the profiteering of Hindu and Sikh contractors. At the All-India level, the war boosted the standing of Jinnah. Many Punjabi Unionists joined the Muslim League bandwagon after the 1945 Simla Conference, although the Unionists had been under pressure from a revitalised Muslim League from the time of the 1942 Cripps mission. Jinnah cleverly exploited the 'sunshine' of official favour thereby wiping out the earlier shabby Muslim League image in the eyes of the powerbrokers in Punjab and the other Muslim majority provinces.

The untimely deaths of Sikander and the leading Hindu Jat figure Sir Chhotu Ram put pressure on the Unionist Party's fragile factional unity.[10] This emboldened Jinnah to clarify the ambiguous relationship between the Punjab League and the Unionist Party under the terms of his pact with Sikander. He journeyed to Lahore in March 1944 to resolve the matter with the inexperienced Punjab Premier Khizr, but their talks broke down because Khizr would not renege on his commitments to his non-Muslim Unionist colleagues and he was publicly expelled from the League the following May. The Muslim League seized the opportunity to launch an intensive rural propaganda campaign. For the first time ever primary branches were established in such Unionist strongholds as Sargodha and Mianwali. In July alone it was reported that 7,000 members had been enrolled in these two areas.[11] Khizr's position was further weakened by Jinnah's wrecking the July 1945 Simla Conference, when he refused to accept the inclusion of a Unionist nominee on any future Viceroy's Executive Council. Lord Wavell's capitulation to Jinnah without a fight increased still further the Quaid-e-Azam's prestige.

The entry of large numbers of landlords and *pirs* into the Muslim League's ranks is conventionally understood as the reason for its reversal in fortune in the 1946 elections. Although it had earlier criticised the Unionist Party for using 'tribalism' and the villagers' superstitious reverence for *pirs* to win political support, the Muslim League did

10 D. Gilmartin, *Empire and Islam*, p. 186.

11 Report of the Organizing Secretary, Rawalpindi Division Muslim League, vol. 162, pt. 7: Punjab Muslim League, 1943-44, pp. 74ff, FMA.

not quibble about adopting these methods when it was in a position to do so. Wherever strong *biraderis* existed, the Muslim League endeavoured to choose their leaders as its candidates. *Pirs* not only stood for election themselves, but commanded their disciples to vote for Muslim League candidates. Rallies were held at the *urs* of leading shrines and *fatwas* were issued through small leaflets, newspapers and wall-posters.[12] The *pirs'* great moral authority sanctified the Muslim League cause. They made appeals to individual Muslim voters to personally identify with the cause of Islam by supporting the Pakistan demand. 'Your vote is a trust of the community' (*qaum*) warned the *sajjada nashin* of the leading Chishti shrine at Ajmer, 'No question of someone's caste [*zat*] or conflicts of *biraderis* should at this time come before you.'[13]

Unionist attempts to rally support through the religious appeals of '*ulama* from the Jamiat-ul-Ulema-i-Hind carried much less authority amongst the rural voters. It also further undermined the confidence of the non-Muslim population. While the Muslim League squeezed out the Unionists in West Punjab, the Hindu Jat wing in the Haryana region, shorn of the inspirational Sir Chhotu Ram, was routed by the Congress.

Pressures from below caused the defection of large numbers of the Unionist party's Zamindara League field-workers. The organiser for the Rawalpindi district, Shahzada Sadiq Bukhari, frequently reported to the Unionist Party's headquarters in Lahore that he encountered hostility during his tours of the villages in the summer of 1945.[14] Chaudhri Nur Khan, the Unionist candidate for Chakwal in 1946, had to completely replace all the workers in his *tehsil* as they 'had changed colours'.[15] The problems in the Jhelum district[16] however started right at the top, as the chief worker, Muhammad Iqbal divulged secrets to the Muslim League and obstructed operations until his final dismissal. The situation was little better elsewhere. By the beginning of November 1945, the presidents of the Ludhiana, Rawalpindi and Lyallpur branches of the Zamindara League had all decamped to the Muslim League. Another tell-tale sign of demoralisation was the reluctance of some local activists to work in Muslim majority areas of their districts.[17] These difficulties

[12] Talbot, *Punjab and the Raj*, p. 211.

[13] Gilmartin, *Empire and Islam*, pp. 216-17

[14] See for example, his letters of 28 May and 18 September 1945. Personal File of Shahdaza Sadiq Bukhari, Assistant Organiser, Rawalpindi Zamindara League, Unionist Party papers.

[15] Bashir Husain, District Organiser, Jhelum Zamindara League, to Mian Sultan Ali Ranjha, 2 January 1946, file D-48, Unionist Party Papers.

[16] *Ibid.*, 16 January 1946, file D-48, Unionist Party Papers.

[17] Mian Sultan Ali Ranjha to Sufi Abdul Haq, Assistant Organiser, Sargodha District

were brought home forcibly to the Unionist Premier during his election tour of the Jhelum district. He unsuccessfully interviewed 120 people in an attempt to find someone willing to oppose the Muslim League candidate, Raja Ghazanfar Ali Khan[18] in the Pind Dadan Khan constituency.[19]

The Unionist legacy

History in Pakistan has as elsewhere been written by the victors. There is no place therefore for the Unionist era and its achievements in the official lexicon of historiography. Such figures as Khizr Tiwana are either ignored or written off as 'toadies' of the British and 'traitors' to Islam. It is therefore important to highlight two neglected but supremely important legacies of Unionism for Pakistan: the first is the laying of the foundations for Punjab's domination of Pakistan's bureaucracy; the second,[20] the establishment of a South Asian system of 'consociational democracy' which maintained communal peace for over twenty years in the 'Ulster' of India and which provides important lessons for today's strife-torn Pakistan.

As elsewhere in India, Hindus entered the new colonial educational institutions of Punjab in much greater numbers than Muslims. They consequently dominated professions such as government service which depended on Western knowledge. The devolution of responsibility for education following the introduction of dyarchy was seized upon by Mian Fazl-i-Husain as an opportunity to remedy this situation. During the period 1921-6 when he served as Education Minister he launched a vigorous drive to improve the schooling of Punjab's 'backward' communities. Since the Muslims comprised the bulk of these designated groups, they received the lion's share of free scholarships and expansion of schools. In the sphere of higher education, Fazl-i-Husain ordered a reservation of 40 per cent of places for Muslims in prestigious institutions like Government College in Lahore and the Lahore Medical College. Such centres of learning had previously been a Hindu preserve. Muslims further benefited from the opening of intermediate colleges. Within two years Muslim attendance in all institutions increased by

---

Zamindara League, 13 December 1944, file E-76, Unionist Party Papers.

18 He was not only a prominent Leaguer and powerful opponent of the Unionists in the Provincial Assembly, but more importantly the uncle of the leading Chishti revivalist, *Pir* Fazl Shah.

19 *Dawn* (Delhi), 28 October 1945.

20 See Ian Talbot, *Khizr Tiwana*, which reveals the inadequacy of such stereotypes.

42 per cent.[21] Female education lagged badly in Punjab as in other provinces, but even in this respect, the region was in advance of other future Pakistan areas. In 1932 for example, 1.6 per cent of the total Muslim female population was receiving schooling in Punjab. This was in comparison with 0.5 per cent in the Frontier and 0.4 per cent in Balochistan.[22]

Mian Fazl-i-Husain's reforms earned the censure of the Hindu elite which feared that its professional pre-eminence was under threat. Indeed, Raja Narendra Nath, the Hindu Mahasabha leader wrote to the Viceroy in 1927 and asked for the clock to be turned back from dyarchy to the pre-reform era. [23] Educationally Muslims still trailed behind the province's Hindus,[24] but they had achieved a commanding position in comparison with their brethren from the other 'Pakistan' regions. In the competitive examinations for recruitment to the All-India Services, Punjabi Muslims stood second only to candidates from UP, the traditional heartland of Indian Muslim culture and education. Significantly the most powerful bureaucratic post in the immediate post-partition period, that of Secretary-General, was held by a Punjabi, Chaudhri Muhammad Ali. Punjabi representation in the civil bureaucracy supplemented the region's predominance in the army, thereby laying the foundations for the 'Punjabisation' of Pakistan.

Mian Fazl-i-Husain also provided the spadework for the Unionist Party's system of political accommodation, although this was further refined by his successors as party leader, Sikander and Khizr. Under their leadership the Unionist Ministry bore some of the hallmarks of a grand coalition in keeping with classical consociational theory. It also successfully operated such consociational devices as proportionality in recruitment and decision-making. The 1942 pact between Sikander and Baldev Singh, the Akali Dal leader, which increased Sikh representation in government departments and endorsed Sikh 'segmental autonomy' provides a classic example of consociationalism at work. This was all to no avail in the highly charged days of community consciousness in 1946. As a Unionist worker from the Jhelum district reported, 'Wherever I went everyone kept saying,

---

[21] S. M. Ikram, *Modern Muslim India and the Birth of Pakistan*, 3rd edn (Lahore, 1977), p. 228.

[22] Government of India, *Progress of education in India*, Eleventh Quinquennial Review (Simla, 1938), p. 243.

[23] Hailey to Sir William Vincent, 8 July 1927, Hailey Collection Mss. Eur. E220/11A, IOR.

[24] According to the 1931 Census, 32 per cent of those educated in English were Punjabi Muslims, although the Muslim community comprised 52 per cent of the province's total population.

bhai, if we do not vote for the League we would have become kafir. [...] We did not vote for individuals; if we did so, it was only to vote for the Quran.'[25]

The legacy of the campaign for Pakistan

Turning away from the Unionist legacy, to that of the freedom struggle itself, three factors stand out from the narrative. First the Muslim League was in some respects the Unionist Party re-invented in that it mobilised support in 1946 through the time-honoured 'tribal' allegiances and appeal of a localised Muslim identity based on the Sufi shrines. Second there was at the same time a mass upsurge during the Pakistan movement based on Islamic idealism. Third the League was a latecomer in the future 'corner-stone' of Pakistan. Indeed it never held office there before partition. All three of these legacies were to influence post-colonial political developments.

Despite the propaganda that the 1946 elections were fought on the Pakistan issue, the Punjab Muslim League mobilised votes as the Unionists had previously done through *biraderi* and Sufi networks. The survival of the politics of mediation even at the height of the freedom struggle revealed the post-independence challenge for the Muslim League if it was to fulfil the calls for an individual commitment to an Islamic identity encouraged by Jinnah and others.[26] The Khilafat-i-Pakistan ideas of the Punjab League's most ardent student supporters were to sit uncomfortably with the outlook of the rural powerbrokers.

The Punjab Muslim League did not however achieve a breakthrough in 1946 simply because of the factional realignment of the *biraderi* leaders and landowners. The Muslim masses were not just mute by-standers as the landed magnates jockeyed for position. Far greater numbers of Muslims joined in Muslim League processions, rallies, strikes and the civil disobedience campaign in Punjab of February 1947[27] than were eligible to vote. By concentrating on legislative politics and the League's electoral breakthrough in 1946 the popular support for the freedom struggle has been obscured. It is however undeniable that there was a groundswell of rural Punjabi support for the Pakistan demand despite its previous neglect by some scholars.[28] The Punjab Muslim League's political advance in 1946 resulted from

25 Report by Ch. Shahwali of Ghumman, Zamindara League Worker, Jhelum, 20 February 1946. Unionist Party Papers D-44, Southampton University.

26 Gilmartin, *Empire and Islam*, Chapter 6.

27 See I. Talbot, 'The role of the crowd in the Muslim League Struggle for Pakistan', *Journal of Imperial and Commonwealth History* 21, no. 2 (May 1993), pp. 307-34.

28 See, for example, Gilmartin, *Empire and Islam*, p. 187

its ability to anchor this message within the substratum of local rural Islam. Not only Punjab's but Pakistan's future political development was to rest on the state's ability to reconcile this newly-emerged popular consciousness and activism with the established interests of the military and landowning elites.

Khizr shored up the Unionist citadel after the 1946 provincial elections, forming a coalition government with the Congress and the Sikh Akalis. But the tide of events both in the province and at the All-India level had turned against him. His banning of the Muslim National Guards early in 1947 prompted the launching of a mass civil disobedience campaign. This second phase of popular participation marked the final advance of the Muslim League in the 'corner-stone' of Pakistan. While the Muslim League was able to topple the Khizr Government, the cost in terms of increased communal tension rendered it unable to form one itself. The Punjab remained under Governor's rule for the remaining five months of the British Raj. This meant that of its famous 'three musketeers' (the Nawab of Mamdot, Mian Mumtaz Daultana and Shaukat Hayat) in the fight against Unionism, only the last had experienced office in the pre-independence era. Nor had his brief term as Minister of Public Works in the Khizr cabinet been a productive learning experience.[29] Such ministerial inexperience was not of course unique to the Punjab League leadership, but it was to have important repercussions in the disturbed days which followed the trauma of the province's partition.

Sindh

Few historians would quibble with the notion that the Sindh Muslim League in the early 1940s was a ramshackle organisation riddled by factionalism. This did not impede the wider progress of the freedom struggle, but it meant that the Sindh branch was in no shape to carry out the task of nation building once Pakistan was created. The League's institutional weakness was mirrored in the shallow support for the Pakistan ideal. This resulted not only from the backwardness of the overwhelmingly rural population, but also from the emergence of a Sindhi political consciousness amongst sections of the Muslim elite which coexisted uneasily with support for Pakistan. In the 1940s and indeed throughout the next four decades, Sindhi nationalism was to find its clearest articulation in the activities of

---

[29] Khizr had dismissed him on the alleged charge of corruption. Shaukat vehemently pleaded his innocence, declaring that it was a political move prompted by his support for Pakistan.

G.M. Syed and his followers. Indeed even as the most vocal proponent of Sindhu Desh lay in a coma close to death in April 1995, police commandos were posted at the entrance to his hospital room.[30]

The Sindh Muslim League had played only a peripheral role in the two formative influences on Sindhi Muslim politics during the 1920s and '30s—the Khilafat campaign and the movement to separate Sindh from the Bombay Presidency. Its parent organisation had taken up the latter issue from 1925 onwards, but more with a view to using it as a bargaining counter in any future constitutional development than out of solidarity with the Sindhi Muslims. They responded by cold-shouldering it in favour of an umbrella organisation called the Sindh Azad Conference formed in September 1932. The establishment of Sindh as a separate province on 1 April 1936 symbolically foreshadowed the larger partition of India a decade later. The leading politicians in the new province were, however, more concerned with personal rivalries than with larger issues. The Sindh Muslim League was consequently ill-disciplined and its ministers pursued policies designed to keep themselves in power, even if they conflicted with the long-term aims of the parent organisation. A classic example of this was the passage of the Joint Electorates Bill in April 1940.[31] Fortunately for Jinnah the League did not face an organised opposition. Otherwise determined opponents might have buried 'Pakistan in Sindh'.

The Hindu community[32] played a disproportionately important part in Sindh's legislative politics, because of its high socio-economic status and the favourable weightage which it received under the 1932 Communal Award.[33] This ensured it at least one seat in every cabinet. The Hindus' wealth rested on their dominance of trade, commerce and the professions (they also began to acquire large landholdings as a result of Muslim indebtedness), but the community was not split along urban-rural lines as in neighbouring Punjab. The Hindu business classes did however come into conflict with the Muslim Memon, Khoja and Bohra traders. These Muslim 'immigrants' accounted for the bulk of the non-Hindu middle class. Significantly they were more responsive than the rural Sindhis to the Muslim League's appeal.

30 Hassan Mujtaba, 'Death of a Nationalist', *Newsline*, May 1995, pp. 73–6.

31 The agreement to introduce joint electorates for local bodies had been part of a 21-point programme accepted between Mir Bandeh Ali and Hindu Independents before the formation of the Muslim League government in the wake of the Sukkur riots.

32 The Hindus formed 28 per cent of the population, but there were no Hindu majority districts as in neighbouring Punjab, although they had a virtual equality with the Muslims in Tharparkar.

33 Although the Muslims made up 70 per cent of the total population, they had a bare majority (34/60 seats) in the Assembly.

Indeed it was largely funded by these groups who also provided it with many of its leading figures.[34] Perhaps because they were aware of growing sentiment against them, the Punjabi cultivators who had settled permanently in Sindh were also early and ardent supporters of the League. The key to its impact however, in the restricted and largely rural electorate lay with the support of the Baloch and Sindhi landowners and the leading *pirs*.[35] Jinnah's inability to convince them to contest the 1937 provincial elections on the League ticket resulted in its failure to win a single seat.[36]

The Sindh United Party emerged victorious securing a clear majority in the Muslim constituencies (21 out of 34 seats). It had been founded in June 1936 with the express purpose of bridging the gap between Hindu and Muslim Sindhis [37] by stressing the importance of economic rather than religious interests. This inspiration was clearly derived from the success of the Unionist Party in neighbouring Punjab,[38] as the Unionist leader Mian Fazl-i-Husain had been consulted shortly before the decision to launch the Sind United Party. Its early leadership was drawn from such leading Muslim landowners as Sir Shah Nawaz Bhutto, Allah Baksh, Umar Soomro and Yar Muhammad Junejo. Urban Muslim interests were represented by Abdullah Haroon, the prominent Karachi Memon sugar merchant. In his inaugural speech, Haroon declared that the Sindh United Party would make Sindh 'safe' from communal strife[39] such as that in 1927 in Larkana caused by the campaign to separate Sind from the Bombay Presidency, and would ensure that 'the communities would work and live in' peace.'[40]

The party was weakened by the defeat of its leading figure, Sir Shah Nawaz Bhutto, in Larkana. The campaign in the Larkana North constituency had been fought on religious lines with Bhutto's opponent,

---

[34] These included Abdullah Haroon; Hatim Alavi, a Bohra businessman who was at one time Mayor of Karachi; and Muhammad Hashim Gazdar who was a Karachi contractor.

[35] Tribal chiefs, large landholders and *pirs* won 27 out of 34 Muslim seats.

[36] I. Talbot, *Provincial Politics and the Pakistan Movement*, p. 39.

[37] In sharp contrast to contemporary Sindh, during the colonial era the Hindu population was an overwhelmingly urban and wealthy community. It controlled trade and commerce and the middle class professions of law and medicine.

[38] Historians have failed to recognise the importance of the Unionist Party as a role model in the Muslim majority provinces. Significantly, Abdullah Haroon had consulted with the Unionist leader Mian Fazl-i-Husain shortly before the decision to launch the Sindh United Party.

[39] Up till the modern era Sindh had a tradition of tolerance and syncretism partly derived from Sufi influence. The first serious riots occurred as late as 1927 in Larkana against the background of the separation campaign of Sindh from the Bombay Presidency.

[40] A.K. Jones, 'Muslim Politics and the Growth of the Muslim League in Sindh', unpubl. Ph.D. thesis, Duke University, 1977, p. 84.

Sheikh Abdul Majid Sindhi employing mullahs and attempting to evoke sympathy by playing on his conversion from Hinduism. [41] Bhutto was portrayed as anti-Islamic and as one who would levy taxes on beards and graveyards. [42] His defeat had wider repercussions, for it encouraged the British Governor Graham to pass over the Sindh United Party in favour of the Sindh Muslim Party of Sir Ghulam Hussain Hidayatullah which had captured just three seats. Hidayatullah's differences with Bhutto were more personal than ideological, dating to their days on the Bombay Council. Moreover, he found it expedient to include members of the Hindu Mahasabha in his coalition ministry. Nevertheless, the future of Sindhi politics seemed destined thereafter to follow not only a highly factionalised and unstable course, but also one in which communal solidarity counted for more than accommodation.

A flurry of Muslim League activity early in 1938 led by Sheikh Abdul Majid Sindhi saw the establishment of branches in such districts as Tharparkar, Nawabshah, Sukkur, Jacobabad and Larkana.[43] Progress depended to a large extent on the support of influential landowners such as Muhammad Ayub Khuhro; the Muslim League remained unable to convert the enthusiasm which greeted Jinnah's visit to the province in October 1938 into a disciplined mass base of support.[44] Legislative politics were marked by a bewildering array of floor-crossings and shifting factional alignments in which, as in today's Pakistan, party loyalties counted for nothing. The only constant factors were the importance of the solid blocs of *Mir* and *Sayed* members [45] and Hidayatullah's determination to hang on to the reins of power. By March 1938 however he had run out of allies and was forced to resign in favour of Allah Baksh. His coalition government included Hindu Independents, Muslim members of the Sindh United Party and three Europeans.[46]

The pro-Congress leanings of the Baksh ministry led to an upturn in Muslim League fortunes. Abdullah Haroon, Hidayatullah and G.M.

---

[41] After being disowned by his family he had moved to Hyderabad from Thatta where he began a career as a journalist. He rose to political prominence as the Secretary of the Khilafat Conference of Sindh.

[42] For further details see Jones, 'Muslim Politics', p. 108.

[43] I. Talbot, *Provincial Politics and the Pakistan Movement*, p. 41.

[44] Jinnah had journeyed to Karachi to preside over the first Sindh provincial Muslim League Conference. He was conveyed through the streets in a three-mile procession in a manner 'befitting a King'. For the significance of such 'regal' displays see I. Talbot, 'The role of the Crowd in the Muslim League Struggle for Pakistan'.

[45] For details see I. Talbot, *Provincial Politics and the Pakistan Movement*, pp. 36ff.

[46] Governor of Sindh to Linlithgow, 19 March 1938, Linlithgow Papers, IOR MSS Eur F 125/93.

Syed all joined the party at this juncture. Hidayatullah's subsequent defection in January 1939 on being offered a cabinet post revealed his opportunism. But both Haroon and Syed were prompted by more genuine motives. The latter, who throughout this period posed as the upholder of the *haris'* (peasants) interests, had been angered by a proposed increase in land revenue assessments in the Sukkur Barrage area. His inclusion in the League brought it the valuable support of the *Sayed* grouping within the Assembly. The final blow to the Allah Baksh ministry was dealt by the 1939 Manzilgarh agitation. As early as 1920, Muslims in Sukkur had demanded that the ancient domed building at the Manzilgarh site (meaning a place of rest) be declared a mosque and handed over to them by the Government. The Muslim League, like the BJP decades later at Ayodhya, seized on the dispute over sacred space at Manzilgarh to solidify support on a communal platform.

On 3 October 1939, following five months of agitation, Muslim volunteers pushed past a police cordon and forcibly occupied the site. Communal rioting spread throughout the surrounding districts when government forces re-entered the building some forty-eight days later.[47] The resulting collapse in law and order toppled the Baksh government as it robbed it of its Hindu support. The Muslim League, although now in government, still faced problems because of its intense factionalism.[48] Nor was the 'ethnic cleansing' of urban Hindus from Sindh henceforth an inevitability. This in fact only happened after Muslim refugees had arrived from India. Nevertheless, the Manzilgarh agitation undoubtedly marked an important watershed in Sindh's modern history.

The labyrinthian details of Sindh's sordid politics from 1940-7 need not detain us here.[49] Suffice it to say that such events as the arrest of the leading Muslim Leaguer Muhammad Ayub Khuhro in connection with Allah Baksh's murder in December 1944[50] should dispel any inclination to view the freedom struggle era through rose-coloured glasses. It has hardly been a case of 'paradise lost' in the post-independence period.[51] The British Governor's summing-up of the situation in 1942 could have been made at any time during the following four decades: 'I have an uneasy feeling', he reported shortly after the formation of

---

[47] Jones, 'Muslim Politics', p. 197.

[48] See I. Talbot, *Provincial Politics and the Pakistan Movement*, pp. 42-55.

[49] *Ibid.*, Chapter 2.

[50] The fact that Khuhro was a leading suspect speaks volumes. He was acquitted, although hardly exonerated. On his release, Yusuf Haroon garlanded him with gold sovereigns.

[51] This point was clearly recognised by the late Khalid Shamsul Hasan who devoted much of his spare time to bringing out the reality of the freedom struggle as it was revealed in his father's Muslim League records. See K. S. Hasan, *Sindh's Fight For Pakistan* (Karachi, 1992), p. xiii.

a second Muslim League ministry headed by Ghulam Hussain Hidayatullah, 'that almost any member would be able to form a government
with...12 well-paid ministerships and parliamentary secretaryships in
his gift. [...] The only sensible question which one can ask any politician
is whether he is in office or out, and if he is out, his only study [*sic*]
is how he can get in.'[52] While the Muslim League leaders in Punjab
entered the post-independence era with little experience of office, their
counterparts in Sindh were already well versed in using power to feather
their own nests through the manipulation of wartime contracts and the
control of rationed and requisitioned goods.[53] The establishment of a
track record of financial probity, party discipline and reforming zeal
was however a different matter.

The Sindh Muslim League of course contained idealists as well as
opportunists. Nor should the popular enthusiasm generated by the Pakistan campaign be overlooked. In April 1940 for example, a 10,000-
strong procession wended its way through Karachi's streets as part of
Pakistan Day celebrations.[54] Even amid the gloom of the Hidayatullah
ministry, progress was being made in enrolling members in local Muslim
League branches. During 1943-4, the branches rose from 474 to 547
with an increase in membership from 122,623 to 177,118.[55] Nevertheless,
as the League's *Annual Report* for this period acknowledged, 'We should
require years to create political consciousness among [the] Muslim masses in the province, where on account of long distances, scattered villages,
illiteracy and local influence it is rather difficult to easily approach
the people.'[56]

The Muslim League therefore had to adapt to these realities as it
sought to expand in the region. Its dilemma was especially acute at
the time of the 1946 elections. The *waderos* alone possessed the money
and influence to secure election in the interior of Sindh. But they were
primarily concerned with winning power for themselves, rather than
piling up votes for Pakistan. By September 1945 a bitter three-way
struggle for League tickets had broken out between G. M. Syed, Khuhro
and Ghulam Hussain Hidayatullah. 'I wish people thought less of Premier
and Ministers and thought more of the paramount and vital issue con-
fronting us,' Jinnah admonished Khuhro. 'I do hope the seriousness
of the situation will be fully realised. [...] The only issue before us

52 Dow to Linlithgow, 5 November 1942, L/P&J/5/258, IOR..

53 S. F. Kucchi, member of the Working Committee Sindh Provincial Muslim League
to G. M. Syed, SHC, Sindh, 11:37.

54 Sindh FR, Second Half of April 1940, L/P&J/5/255, IOR..

55 *Annual Report of the Sindh Provincial Muslim League for 1943-4*, SHC Sindh 1:24.

56 *Ibid.*

is Pakistan *versus* Akhand Hindustan, and if Sindh falls God help you.'[57] Such appeals fell on deaf ears. The Governor Sir Hugh Dow sympathised. 'Jinnah dislikes them all', he wrote to the Viceroy; 'he once told me he could buy the lot of them for five *lakhs* of rupees, to which I replied I could do it a lot cheaper.'[58] The clash between the President of the Sindh Muslim League (G.M. Syed) and the Province's Premier climaxed in the former's expulsion from the organisation in January 1946.

The Syed group nevertheless triumphed in the Assembly elections against official Muslim League candidates mainly because of the support which it received from the influential *pirs* and *sajjada nashins* of Hala, Jhando and the shrine of Shah Abdul Latif Bhit.[59] Far from giving an overwhelming mandate for Pakistan, the elections had thus even put the limited objective of forming a Muslim League government in Sindh in extreme jeopardy. Jinnah had to turn elsewhere in Muslim India to demonstrate backing for Pakistan. The power of the Syed group was not broken until a further round of provincial elections in December 1946. These took place when communalism was rising elsewhere in India following the collapse of the Cabinet Mission proposals. Even so the success of official League candidates had depended on desertions from the Syed camp. The victory had been won in the name of Pakistan, but had rested on the same local loyalties and outlooks which Jinnah had opposed for so long.

The Muslim League's troubled state was not however simply the result of personal rivalries and opportunism, although there was no love lost between G.M. Syed and Hidayatullah. The League President from 1943 onwards had presented his case in terms of the clash of interests between the large landholders of Sindh and their labourers and tenants. G.M. Syed complained that the Ministers' support of the landed elite's interests was unpopular and was retarding the Pakistan cause.[60] When it became clear that Jinnah would not back him in his tussle with Hidayatullah, he became increasingly critical of the AIML leadership, linking its 'interference' in Sindh with the domination of the 'corrupt' Ministers and '*jagirdars*'. As the British departure loomed ever nearer, G.M. Syed increasingly talked of the need for a 'Sindhi Pakistan'. This was cast more in terms of a hands-off Sindh by the central League leadership than the idea of Sindhi nationalism which he was to develop after independence. Nevertheless, he played

---

[57] Jinnah to Khuhro, 13 October 1945, SHC Sind VI:10.

[58] Dow to Wavell, 20 September 1945, L/P&J/5/261, IOR..

[59] Muhammad Shah Saleh to President of Sindh Muslim League, n.d., SHC Sindh 8:33.

[60] G. M. Sayed to Jinnah, 8 July 1944, SHC Sindh 1:44.

up the existing anti-Punjabi sentiment as for example in his attack on the Cabinet Mission proposals for the grouping of the Muslim majority provinces in north-west India.[61] Through the columns of his Sindhi newspaper, *Qurbani* (Sacrifice), G.M. Syed inveighed against the possible subordination of Sindh to Punjab.[62] Sindhi separatism fuelled by anti-Punjabi sentiment thus found a favourable environment in which to flourish even before the massive post-partition migration of 'outsiders' into the province.

The North-West Frontier Province

The shallow roots of the freedom movement were evidenced in the Frontier Province both by the institutional weakness of the Muslim League and the abiding strength of a Pushtun political identity which coexisted uneasily with the Pakistan demand. Although a Muslim League ministry held office from October 1943 to March 1945, the League, in stark contrast to its showing elsewhere, won a mere seventeen seats to the Congress's thirty in the 1946 provincial elections. In the June 1947 referendum, however, the province's Muslims voted overwhelmingly for Pakistan, but it was nevertheless clear that the new state would have to tread carefully in order to reconcile Pakhtun sentiments with the requirements of nation building.

In order to fully understand the clash between Pushtun loyalties and Pakistan nationalism it is necessary to briefly examine the Frontier's social structure and historical development in the closing decades of British rule. This will then be followed by an account of the Muslim League's development in the region, before an attempt is made to consider the legacies of the pre-independence era.

The main ethnic division in the Frontier Province existed between the Pushtuns and other social groups. Although the Pushtuns formed less than two-fifths of the population[63] they were socially and politically dominant. Non-Pushtuns did not own land, nor did they have the right to participate in the tribal councils – *jirgas*. Among the non-Pushtuns only *pirs* were traditionally allowed to own land. Both their spiritual status and their standing as impartial brokers in a society divided

[61] Mudie to Wavell, 24 March 1946, L/P&J/5/262, IOR.

[62] See, for example, the issue for 11 June 1946. Sindh Muslim League, Part IX, 1944-6, vol. 386, FMA.

[63] While the Pushtuns predominated in the surrounding tribal areas, they were in a minority in the British province. Non-Pushtun Muslims formed 55 per cent of the population, Hindus and Sikhs 8 per cent and the Pakhtuns 37 per cent. Non-Pushtun Muslims predominated in the Hazara and Dera Ismail Khan districts, while in Peshawar, Kohat and Bannu, Pakhtuns formed a clear majority.

by lineage rivalries enabled them to acquire political influence. The ascendancy of the predominantly rural Pushtun community meant that political parties which failed to appeal to its interests were inevitably confined to the margins. It also ensured that traditional Pushtun '*tabur-wali*'[64] political alignments would structure the operation of modern parties in the rural areas. The penalty of intermingling *taburwali* with party politics was that if one local faction joined the Muslim League its traditional rival would join the Congress and vice versa. The British patronage of the large Khans and the growing aspirations of smaller Khans also structured political developments. The latter provided the leadership of the Congress-Khudai Khidmatgar (Servant of God) movement, while many of the larger Khans turned to the Muslim League in the 1940s to safeguard their interests. The Khan brothers, Abdul Ghaffar Khan and Dr Khan Sahib, who for a generation were the outstanding political leaders of the Frontier Province, based their power around the factions of the smaller Khans. Important political repercussions also flowed from the few Hindu and Sikh residents and their virtual invisibility in the rural centres of Pushtun culture,[65] for while other Muslims might view them as a threat to their religious and material interests, as far as Pushtuns were concerned it was inconceivable that they might be ruled by non-Muslims.

The philosophy of Pushtun nationalism was articulated by Abdul Ghaffar Khan in the monthly Pushto journal, the *Pakhtun*, which he launched in May 1928. The following year he embodied these ideals in a new grassroots party called the Afghan Jirga. This was rapidly overshadowed by a parallel organisation, the Khudai Khidmatgars, which was established in November 1929 on quasi-military lines. Its members wore uniforms dyed with red brick dust since their ordinary white clothing showed the dirt too easily. The British thereafter dubbed them the 'Red Shirts'. Just as in Sindh, the politicisation of ethnic consciousness was linked with hostility towards the Punjabi 'other.' In November 1931, Abdul Ghaffar Khan outraged non-Pushtun audiences in Hazara by denigrating the Punjabi language and Punjabi culture and declaring: 'When we have self-government we will have everything in Pashto.'[66]

---

[64] Pushtun politics revolved around factional rivalry among landholders – *parajamba*. Its most vital aspect was competition among patrilineal cousins, '*taburwali*' (*tabur* in Pushtu means first cousin). *Taburs* organised factions (*gundis*) consisting of their lineage segment and clients in their struggle for political prominence or land.

[65] Three-quarters of all non-Muslims lived in urban areas. The Hindus and Sikhs together accounted for a third of the Frontier's town dwellers.

[66] S. Rittenburg, 'The Independence Movement in India's North-West Frontier Province, 1901-1947', unpubl. Ph.D. thesis, Columbia University, p. 176.

Abdul Ghaffar Khan toured the Frontier to enrol Khudai Khidmatgars. He called on the people to reform their social and religious condition, and articulated the poorer classes' grievances against the pro-British large Khans. The alliance between Abdul Ghaffar Khan's organisations and the Congress was cemented by the 1930 Civil Disobedience campaign. The April riots in Peshawar created the martyrs and myths of the Khudai Khidmatgar movement which were to sustain it until the eve of independence. The Congress national leaders eagerly sought the Pushtuns' support because it strengthened their organisation's claim to be secular and cross-communal. For his part, Abdul Ghaffar Khan allied with them in the freedom struggle and the quest for Hindu-Muslim unity, but specifically Pushtun interests remained his first priority.

The Frontier Muslim League

The Frontier Muslim League had experienced a chequered existence since its formation in 1912. Its support was limited to urban lawyers and to the non-Pushtun Muslims residing in the Hazara region. The 1937 provincial elections starkly revealed the League's marginality. The only two elected members, P.R. Bakhsh and Malik Khuda Bakhsh, had actually stood as Azad Party candidates. The League's fortunes were ironically revived during the course of the Congress ministry of Dr Khan Sahib (September 1937-November 1939). Such measures as the abolition of the honorary magistrate and *zaildar* system and of rights to revenue remission in return for government service struck directly at the interests of the large Khans. Finally, the Government encouraged tenants in their refusal to pay rent. This drove most of the large Khans into the Muslim League's arms. Just as in neighbouring Punjab, tensions arose between long-time urban activists and the new rural entrants. The Khans were no more assiduous in organising the League than the Unionist landlords of 1938-9. Indeed, opponents termed it a 'drawing-room' and 'Motor League' as the main task of the leaders seemed to be 'travelling by car to the places where the meetings are convened, taking tea, and returning to their houses.'[67]

The Frontier Muslim League profited sufficiently from the imprisonment of many of the Congress MLAs to form its first government in May 1943. Aurangzeb Khan's ministry, however, undermined rather than enhanced the League's fortunes. In order to scrape together a majority, the Muslim League had secured the support of a number of independent Assembly members. Their new found allegiance rested on the prospect of rich pickings, not on any loyalty to the party's ideals.

---

[67] Cited in Sayed Wiqar Ali Shah, 'Muslim Politics in the North-West Frontier province' p. 124.

'The whole Khanite class flocked into the Muslim League like vultures over a corpse', a local worker wrote despairingly to Jinnah, 'The Ministers got salaries and bribes, and members of the League Party got permits [while] the masses groaned under war conditions.'[68] Another Leaguer lamented that the ministry 'had dragged the name of the Frontier [branch] in the dust' in the way it handled 'contracts, permits and membership of syndicates for the distribution of wheat'.[69] The loyal *Khyber Mail* bluntly protested: 'Corruption with a capital C is writ large on the face of the Frontier administration and almost everybody who has anything to do with the administrative machinery there bothers about just one thing – how best to feather his own nest.'[70]

Clashes between the organisational and ministerial wings of the Frontier League compounded these problems. As in Sindh such rivalry was rooted partly in ideological considerations and in the inevitable resentment the 'outs' felt towards the political 'ins'. The personal enmity between the Premier and former League President Saadullah Khan however gave it an especially bitter twist.[71] The hostilities reached a climax at the Frontier League Council meeting of 25 March 1945 when the well-armed rival groups of supporters attempted to shout each other down.[72] The All-India leadership responded to the developing crisis by instituting an enquiry led by the Committee of Action.[73] It uncovered widespread corruption and infighting and gloomily concluded that there was 'no organisation worth the name in the Frontier'.[74]

It was however much easier to diagnose the problems than treat them. Qazi Isa, a Pushtun from Balochistan, was entrusted with the arduous task of overhauling the League organisation. The attempts at reorganisation through a series of *ad hoc* committees only intensified factionalism. Jinnah was bombarded by complaints from activists that these committees were being captured by the ministerialists who discouraged genuine workers 'whose only interest was to make the Muslim League strong for the attainment of Pakistan' because they saw the

---

68 Asadul Haq to Jinnah, 20 December 1945, SHC, NWFP 1:90.

69 Saadullah Khan to Jinnah, 1 September 1945, SHC, NWFP 1:59.

70 *Khyber Mail*, 21 April 1944.

71 The rivalry had taken on the form of a vendetta after Aurangzeb Khan had arranged for criminal proceedings to be brought against his rival and had him subjected to the dishonour of having his house searched for allegedly hoarding unlicensed weapons.

72 Abdur Rahman to Liaquat Ali Khan, 28 March 1944, FMA vol. 344.

73 This important standing committee of the All-India Muslim League had been appointed in December 1943 with the powers to suspend, dissolve or disaffiliate any provincial Muslim League.

74 Proceedings of the visit of the Committee of Action to the North-West Frontier Province, FMA vol. 343, NWFP ML Part III, 1944.

death of their vested interests in 'such mass work'.[75] Another writer asserted that Qazi Isa was misleading the Quaid-e-Azam about the League's standing in the Frontier and had hardly stirred from the luxury of Deans Hotel in Peshawar when he was supposed to be organising the League.[76] The desperation of the situation was underlined by the suggestion that the Frontier League should be given over to the neighbouring Punjab branch and 'enthusiastic workers like Shaukat Hayat and Maulana Zafar Ali Khan'.[77] The All-India leadership was in such circumstances relieved to postpone further reorganisation in the summer of 1945 in order to concentrate its energies on the forthcoming provincial elections.

The Frontier Muslim League approached the polls poorly organised and internally divided. The Finance and Election Boards failed to co-ordinate their activities.[78] The allocation of tickets caused so much dissension in Peshawar that the local activists ceased campaigning.[79] There was similar disquiet elsewhere at the number of tickets given to Aurangzeb Khan's followers. Asadul Haq, a League leader from Abbotabad, complained that this demonstrated absolute disregard for elementary principles of justice and fair play. 'People ask, is this the type of Pakistan that is come to?', he lamented to Jinnah, 'and we in shame have no answer to give.'[80]

When Jinnah toured the Frontier late in November 1945 he attempted to transcend such squabbles by an appeal to the wider aims of the freedom struggle. He summed this up by declaring: 'Every vote in favour of the Muslim League candidates means Pakistan. Every vote against the Muslim League candidates means Hindu Raj.'[81] The rural Pakhtun voters however did not fear Hindu domination. Nor were they convinced that the Khudai Khidmatgar movement was against Islam and a tool of the Hindus. Its anti-British propaganda and attacks on the privileges of the large Khans still carried weight. The Congress emerged from the elections not only as the major party, but with a majority (19) of the 36 seats reserved for Muslims. The Muslim League had barely broken out of its urban stronghold and the non-Pushtun base of the Hazara district.

---

75 Asadul Haq to Jinnah, 20 October 1945, SHC NWFP 1:90.

76 Ghulam Rab Khan to Jinnah, 29 August 1945, SHC NWFP 1:58.

77 Akhter to Liaquat Ali Khan, 3 April 1945, FMA vol. 344.

78 M. Ziauddin to Liaquat Ali Khan, 2 November 1945, FMA vol. 344.

79 A.B. Yusufi to Jinnah, 19 December 1945, SHC NWFP 1:89.

80 Asadul Haq to Jinnah, 20 October 1945, SHC NWFP 1:90.

81 *Dawn* (Delhi), 29 November 1945.

We have seen elsewhere the reasons for the transformation in the Muslim League's fortunes in the period between the elections and the June 1947 referendum.[82] It is important to grasp that while there was a genuine mass mobilisation during the League's civil disobedience campaign in the spring of 1947, this period also saw the raising of the slogan for an autonomous Pushtun state. This was the logical conclusion to the Congress's earlier championing of Pushtun interests and culture. It contained within it the powerful Pushtun fear of Punjabi domination 'in the name of religion.'[83] Three weeks before the referendum was due to be held, Abdul Ghaffar Khan declared in a public meeting at Bannu that the Congress would boycott it and continue to work peacefully for its Pakhtunistan demand; his attempts to do so in post-independence Pakistan cost him lengthy periods of imprisonment. His son Wali Khan nevertheless continued to press for Pushtun interests which were further institutionalised in the National Awami Party (NAP) in 1957. It called for the dissolution of the One Unit Scheme[84] and demanded federal reorganisation which would give greater regional autonomy. The NAP's successful passage of a bill through the West Pakistan Assembly which provided for the dissolution of the One Unit precipitated Pakistan's headlong descent to military takeover and the abrogation of the 1956 Constitution.

It is also important to note another colonial inheritance, namely the factionalised nature of the Frontier Muslim League. There was a further reorganisation of the League during the second half of 1946. This was given new impetus by a series of Pakistan Conferences organised by *Pir* Manki. It was further assisted by the almost daily influx of former Congress leaders including its former Frontier President Ghulam Muhammad Khan and Arbab Abdul Ghaffar, one of the Afghan *Jirga's* main organisers in Peshawar.[85] Nevertheless, the All-India leadership left nothing to chance and ensured that two of the three organisers of the referendum campaign, namely the Punjabi Leaguer Firoz Khan Noon and I.I. Chundrigar, the Commerce Minister in the Interim Government, were aloof from any provincial factional groupings.[86] Such caution was well-advised for factional infighting re-emerged once success in the referendum had been assured. It was thus hardly surprising that within a year of independence the Frontier League had split amid recriminations

[82] See I. Talbot, *Freedom's Cry*, esp. Chapter 1; *Provincial Politics and the Pakistan Movement*, Chapter 1.

[83] *Tribune* (Ambala), 15 May 1947.

[84] This involved a merging of the West Pakistan provinces.

[85] Talbot, *Provincial Politics and the Pakistan Movement*, p. 24.

[86] The trio was completed by Abdul Qaiyum, the leader of the Frontier Muslim League Assembly Party.

between *Pir* Manki and Abdul Qaiyum. The latter, armed with the coercive administrative powers bequeathed by the Raj, clamped his authority so tightly over the Frontier League that *Pir* Manki had to voice his opposition outside of its ranks.

Bengal

At the time of Partition, one in three Indian Muslims (33 million) lived within Bengal's borders. Although the province's distinctive cultural and linguistic traditions marked it off from the Muslim areas of north-west India, historically it had been closely connected with the cause of Muslim separatism. Indeed, the AIML had been inaugurated in Dhaka in 1906.

The freedom struggle in Bengal shared some of the features already examined, such as clashes between the ministers and party organisers and intrigues between factional rivals in the scramble for power and patronage. Khwaja Nazimuddin's ministry from March 1943 onwards was no more adept at dealing with the acute problems brought by the war than was Aurangzeb Khan's in the Frontier or Ghulam Hussain's in Sindh. Before focusing on Pakistan's political inheritance from this era, it is necessary to point out the significant differences between the Muslim League's position in Bengal and the other majority provinces.

The Muslim League's performance in the 1937 Bengal elections was markedly superior to that in any other of the 'Pakistan' areas. It captured 39 of the 82 seats contested and emerged with three more victories than its main Muslim rival, the KPP, although it polled fewer votes.[87] The Bengal League shared power in a coalition government headed by Fazlul Haq from the 1937 elections until December 1941. During this period it greatly consolidated its power at the expense of the Premier and his KPP.[88] Thus even before the period of Abul Hashim's dynamic secretaryship of the League organisation, it was a much more influential force than elsewhere in Muslim India.

Abul Hashim became the Secretary of the Bengal Muslim League in November 1943. He aimed to build it up as a broad democratic institution, based on 'clarity of purpose' capable of 'fighting for liberation from all forms of oppression'.[89] In addition to extensively touring the *mofussil*, he employed full-time workers who received training and ac-

---

[87] It secured 27 per cent of the Muslim vote compared with the KPP's 31 per cent.

[88] For details see Harun-or-Rashid, *The Foreshadowing of Bangladesh*, Chapter 3. See also H. Momen, *Muslim Politics in Bengal: A Study of the Krishak Praja Party and the Elections of 1937* (Dhaka, 1972).

[89] Harun-or-Rashid, *The Foreshadowing of Bangladesh*, p. 164.

commodation at party houses. Among those based at the Calcutta centre was Sheikh Mujibur Rahman the later chief of the Awami League and architect of Bangladesh. These activities brought a rapid increase in membership in the districts of Tippera, Barisal and Dhaka during 1944. Enthusiasts hailed this rising tide of support as 'revolutionary' and rejoiced in the fact that the League had become a 'really mass movement'.[90] The League old guard of the Nawab of Dhaka's family (Khwaja faction)[91] looked askance at these activities, which threatened its traditional domination. What was especially damaging to its interests was the League Secretary's insistence on elections at all levels of the organisation and his reduction of the President's powers of nomination to the League Council and Working Committee. Hashim and his supporters were dubbed as communists in such papers as *Azad* (Free) which were controlled by the Khwaja group. Unlike in Sindh, the 'progressive' organisational wing of the Muslim League triumphed over the ministerialists to such an extent that Khwaja Nazimuddin, the former Premier (March 1943-March 1945), did not stand for election in 1946. Power was passed over to the Calcutta-based politician Hussain Shaheed Suhrawardy[92] who was Hashim's patron. By the eve of the 1946 elections, the Bengal League boasted the largest grassroots support of any provincial branch of the AIML with a membership of over 1 million.[93] Over a decade and a half later, Ayub Khan was to turn to Abul Hashim's organising genius to establish the Convention Muslim League in East Pakistan. The efforts of the 1940s could not however be reproduced in a much more politically hostile environment and with an increasingly frail Abul Hashim deputing the work to Shamsul Huda.[94]

The mass support for the Bengal Muslim League was demonstrated in its sweeping election successes in 1946. It polled so heavily that three-quarters of its opponents forfeited their deposits. The League had entrenched itself so strongly in the rural areas by 1946 that it captured 104 out of 111 seats. The popular enthusiasm its campaign generated

[90] Raghib Ahsan to Jinnah, 15 November 1944, SHC Bengal 1:43.

[91] Ten members of the family had been elected in the 1937 elections.

[92] Suhrawardy had first come to prominence during the Khilafat movement. He then went on to organise trade unions in Calcutta. It was also during this period that he built up his notorious links with the Calcutta underworld. For a sanitised version of the Suhrawardy family's history see Begum Shaista Ikramullah, *From Purdah to Parliament* (London, 1963).

[93] Harun-or-Rashid, *The Foreshadowing of Bangladesh*, p. 194.

[94] Hashim optimistically claimed in October 1963 that the Convention Muslim League was organised in 3,500-4,000 unions in the East Pakistan province. American Consul Dacca to Department of State 7, October 1963. Central Foreign Political Files, 1963, Pol 6-14. National Archives, College Park.

amongst the seven out of eight Muslims ineligible to vote was evidenced by the massive crowds at its meetings and the active part played by the poor. Visiting a village, a volunteer wrote:

> It was a new experience for me that the poor peasants and day labourers of the village engaged themselves in building up the League. [...] While selling treacle, Khowaz Bepari, one of the village headmen, used to realise subscriptions from the customers at the rate of two *pies* per (*maund*) of treacle. [...] Mamtaz (a very poor League worker) and his friends collected Rs. 2/- from the Muslim shopkeepers and customers in the village bazaar at the rate of one *pie* to four *annas* and deposited it in the League fund.[95]

Such accounts completely contradict the generalisations of Hamza Alavi, Ashok Kapur and others concerning the Muslim League's elitism. Even remote villages in Bengal possessed primary Muslim League branches. Its rapid decline after independence should not be allowed to blind us to this reality. The later demise, as we shall see in Chapter 4, was rooted partly in the inability to meet the revolution of rising expectations for social and economic reform which the freedom struggle had generated. The partition cut away the ground from the West Bengal leadership of the Hashim-Suhrawardy group and allowed the Khawaja old guard to make a comeback. Nazimuddin became Chief Minister although he had no mass base of support. 50,000 supporters of Suhrawardy and Hashim were expelled along with their leaders from the party.[96] This situation underlined the political and cultural tensions between the Bengali- and Urdu-speaking Muslim worlds which were rooted in the freedom struggle. Significantly, Harun-or-Rashid's excellently researched study of the pre-partition decade is entitled *The Foreshadowing of Bangladesh*.

Rashid maintains that Abul Hashim's activists fought for the ideal of a sovereign East Pakistan state. Indeed Hashim prophetically warned that a united Pakistan would result in the imposition both of Urdu and an alien bureaucracy and reduce East Bengal to a stagnant backwater.[97] The vision of a sovereign Bengal was based both on the reference of the 1940 Lahore Resolution to Muslim states[98] and on the distinctiveness of Bengali cultural identity. The United Bengal scheme raised by Suhrawardy in April 1947 which was supported by the Congressmen

---

95 Harun-or-Rashid, *The Foreshadowing of Bangladesh*, p. 215.

96 Y. Samad, *A Nation in Turmoil: Nationalism and Ethnicity in Pakistan, 1937-58* (New Delhi, 1995), p. 107.

97 *Ibid.*, p. 106.

98 Harun-or-Rashid, *The Foreshadowing of Bangladesh*, pp. 177ff.

Surat Bose and Kiran Shankar Roy should thus be viewed not as a belated response to the threat of the province's partition, but as emerging from these long-held ideals. Rashid, unlike Joya Chatterji,[99] sees the hostility of the Congress High Command as being the primary cause of the United Bengal scheme's failure.

Crucial to future developments in East Bengal however, was the incipient conflict between the Urdu- and Bengali-speaking elites and the marginalisation of Bengali interests in the councils of the AIML. The Urdu-speaking business classes of Calcutta along with the Khwajas of Dhaka remained loyal to Jinnah's conception of an East Pakistan zone within a single Pakistan state. They also subscribed to the belief expressed as early as July 1933 by the All-Bengal Urdu Association that 'Bengali is a Hinduised and Sanskritised language' and that 'in the interests of the Muslims themselves it is necessary that they should try to have one language which cannot be but Urdu.'[100] This was of course firmly in step with the AIML's official two nation theory ideology. Diametrically opposed to this were the views of Bengali-speaking Muslim League members active in the East Pakistan Renaissance Society, formed in 1942 to articulate intellectually and culturally the 'ideal of Pakistan in general and Eastern Pakistan in particular'. In his May 1944 Presidential address the Muslim League journalist-cum-politician, Abul Mansur Ahmed, maintained that Bengali Muslims were not only different from Hindus, but from Muslims of other provinces. 'Religion and culture are not the same thing,' he maintained; 'religion transgresses the geographical boundary but *tamaddum* (culture) cannot go beyond the geographical boundary. [...] Here only lies the differences between *Purba* (Eastern) Pakistan and Pakistan. For this reason the people of *Purba* Pakistan are a different nation from the people of other provinces of India and from the "religious brothers" of Pakistan.'[101]

It was however the Urdu speaking elite which had a direct line to Jinnah in Bombay and New Delhi. The Quaid-e-Azam never nominated Abul Hashim or Suhrawardy to the AIML Working Committee despite their tremendous organisational achievements. He preferred to deal with such trusted lieutenants as Hasan and Ahmed Ispahani[102] who knew little of Bengal outside of Calcutta, or with the Dhaka Nawab family

[99] J. Chatterji, *Bengal Divided: Hindu Communalism and Partition, 1932-1947* (Cambridge, 1994). Chatterji devotes more attention to the communalisation of the Bengal Congress's *bhadralok* supporters in the wake of the political and economic challenges to their former supremacy from the 1930s onwards.

[100] Harun-or-Rashid, *The Foreshadowing of Bangladesh*, p. 45.

[101] *Ibid.*, p. 181.

[102] The Ispahani family originated in Persia. It moved to Calcutta from its earlier Madras and Bombay trading centres at the turn of the twentieth century.

which was bitterly opposed to the Muslim League roots being put down in the countryside by the Hashim-Suhrawardy group. Both the language issue and the marginalisation of Bengali political influence were to subsequently dominate East-West Pakistan relations and contribute to the Bangladesh breakaway of 1971. An indication of the disregard for the Bengali Muslims' interests which awaited in a future Pakistan state was provided by the AIML's decision in October 1946 to fill the province's quota on the Interim Government with a scheduled caste representative, Jogendra Nath Mondal.

The All-India Muslim League and Pakistan's future political development

The achievement of Pakistan just a decade after the trouncing of the AIML in the 1937 provincial elections remains one of the major reversals of political fortune in the modern era. Without Jinnah's adroit leadership, history would have taken a very different course. The centralisation of power in the hands of the Quaid-i-Azam and his allies on the AIML Working Committee nevertheless set a dangerous precedent. The more 'representative' institutions of the Muslim League, the Council of the AIML and the provincial branches were increasingly subject to the authority of bodies nominated by the President, such as the Working Committee and, from December 1943, the Committee of Action. It could be argued that the tightening of the organisation was necessary in view of the factional intrigues in the provinces. Moreover, Jinnah always maintained that his authority was not dictatorial but rested on the AIML Constitution. Nevertheless, the Working Committee always rubber-stamped his behest and the centralising powers conferred by the AIML Constitution provided a model for Pakistan's future political development. A tradition of looking to a great leader was also established which could have dangerous consequences in the hands of less honest leaders than Jinnah.

Future centre-province problems were presaged by the fact that the Muslim majority areas (especially Bengal) which were to form Pakistan counted for little in the AIML's counsels. Bengal with its 33 million population possessed just ten more members on the AIML Council than UP with its 7 million Muslims. This reflected the historical role of UP and Aligarh in the foundation of Muslim separatism in India. For most of its existence the focal point of the Muslim League had lain not in the future Pakistan areas but in the Muslim minority centres of population. The dominance of politicians from Bombay and UP even after the introduction of the new constitution in February 1938[103] on

---

[103] This increased Punjabi and Bengali membership of the AIML Council to 90 and

such powerful Muslim League bodies as the Council and the Working Committee not only gave the Muslim League organisation a top heavy look, but meant that many of Pakistan's future leaders would lack a popular power base. The future Premier Liaquat Ali Khan was a good case in point. He was eventually nominated a place in the Constituent Assembly from an East Bengal constituency. As Yunas Samad has perceptively pointed out, 'the establishment of a strong centre was a lifeline' for many *mohajir* politicians who lacked electoral support in the country.[104] The historical role which politicians from UP had played in both the emergence of Muslim separatism and in the subsequent counsels of the AIML, was by the 1980s feeding directly into the rhetoric of the MQM. The claim that the *mohajir* community from UP represented the true Pakistanis and had made the most sacrifices for the achievement of the state has formed an important component of *mohajir* political identity.[105]

The freedom struggle also saw the glimmerings of Pakistan's post-independence political culture of intolerance. In order to justify its claim to be the sole representative of the Indian Muslims, the AIML had adopted a strident approach in which its Muslim Nationalist, Unionist or Red Shirt rivals were denounced as both traitors to Islam and the Indian Muslim community. The Congress, because it was not making such exclusivist claims, could afford to be more tolerant. Significantly, while the Congress in the early years of India's independence sought to accommodate and absorb opposition under its umbrella, the Muslim League retained its rigidity. At its December 1947 Karachi Council meeting, for example, Suhrawardy unsuccessfully attempted to open its membership to all communities. This would have enabled the large Hindu minority in East Bengal to have entered mainstream politics. But ideology took precedence over the task of nation-building. Such a move 'would finish the League', Sardar Abdur Rab Nishtar explained; 'I say if the League exists, Islam exists, Musalmans exist.'[106]

While the Congress integrated diverse groupings into an Indian participant democracy, the Muslim League crushed those who contested its hegemonic claims. It set about this task through such legislation as the PRODA of 1949 and the later Security of Pakistan Act (1952).

---

100 members respectively. They still only had 40 per cent of the votes however. UP had 70 members and Bombay 30.

104 Yunas Samad, *A Nation in Turmoil*, p. 127.

105 For further details see Julian Richards, 'Mohajir Subnationalism and the Mohajir Qaumi Movement in Sindh Province, Pakistan', unpubl. Ph.D thesis, University of Cambridge 1993, pp. 199ff.

106 H. Zaheer, *The Separation of East Pakistan*, p. 18.

In addition the central government intervened in provincial affairs. The recourse to such measures was not simply a response to Pakistan's pressing problems. This attitude to dissent had also been conditioned by the freedom struggle itself. Thereafter, it was all too easy to identify the national interest with that of the Muslim League and to regard opposition as illegitimate. Symptomatic of this attitude was the bald statement by Liaquat Ali Khan in October 1950 that 'the formation of new political parties in opposition to the Muslim League is against the interest of Pakistan.'[107]

Four important inheritances from the freedom struggle can be identified as exerting a profound influence on post-colonial political developments. The first was the poor institutionalisation of the Muslim League with the exception of a few districts in Bengal. Many branches existed only on paper or were weakened by factional infighting. The pyramid of branches stretching from the localities to the All-India level which was the hallmark of the Congress was noticeably absent. The League was thus far less able to form a democratic pillar of the post-colonial state than its Congress counterpart. Institutional weakness was compounded by the centralisation of power within the AIML and its exclusivist claims. Together all these features militated against the establishment of a participant democracy.

A second important inheritance was the incipient clash between regional and 'Pakistani' identities. Within Bengal for example the Muslim League's popular base of support rested on regional interests and identities which were difficult to harmonise with Jinnah's All-India understanding of the Pakistan demand. Similar difficulties were present in Sindh, Punjab and the Frontier. In these circumstances it was hardly surprising that provincialism as it was termed became a barrier to nation building almost immediately after independence.

The third legacy was the low level of political culture in the Muslim majority areas. Even at the height of the Pakistan struggle, many landlords had revealed that their primary occupation was the cynical pursuit of power. Factionalism, corruption and violence formed part of the League's everyday experience. Its more highminded activists had to live with this, for they had no alternative but to accommodate themselves with the realities of rural power, as they sought to expand the Muslim League's influence from the traditional narrow urban confines. Of equal concern was the inexperience of its provincial League leaderships – many of the most able Muslim politicians in the majority areas had favoured its rivals.

---

107 *The Statesman* (Calcutta), 28 October 1950.

Finally, the freedom struggle had gained its popular support by being deliberately vague about the nature of a future Pakistan state. Was Islamisation to be the goal, or as Jinnah seemed to indicate in his speech of 11 August 1947, a plural secular society? Ambiguity concerning future national aims rested in part in the fact that the Pakistan movement was simultaneously a 'movement of Islam' and of Muslims. Later generations of Pakistani leaders have however ignored the complexities and ambiguities of the freedom struggle. For instance the acting Prime Minister Ghulam Mustafa Jatoi declared early in October 1990 that 'it was imperative to constantly keep an eye on the objective behind the creation of Pakistan which was *nothing but seeking the glory of Islam*'[108] (emphasis added).

Given the exigencies which faced the All-India leadership in the early 1940s, it could hardly be blamed for attempting to be all things to all men. But by presenting Pakistan as a panacea for all social and personal ills, the seeds were sown for the disenchantment which has been so palpable in the post-colonial era. It could be argued that none of this was unique to Pakistan's situation. European decolonisation usually brought in its wake the problems of transforming nationalist movements into political parties and meeting the demands of a revolution of rising expectations. However the tendencies towards authoritarianism were stronger in Pakistan than in some new states because of the inherited tradition of the British security state and the myriad problems which faced Pakistan in the chaotic aftermath of partition. It is to these and the governmental strategies for their management that we now turn.

[108] *Dawn*, 5 October 1990.

4

PICKING UP THE PIECES:
PAKISTAN, 1947-49

Pakistan's birth was a difficult one which involved the immense suffering of thousands of its citizens. Its British midwife had abandoned it to a chaotic environment in which an elder Indian sibling looked on with scarcely disguised hostility. In such circumstances, historians appear slightly perverse in directing more attention to how Pakistan was conceived, rather than to why it was not stillborn. Furthermore the question arises whether the medicine administered to the fledgling state carried long-term side-effects which stunted its democratic development.[1] Before addressing these questions it is necessary both to delineate the features of the new-born state and to describe the traumas which surrounded its arrival into the world.

The economic and geographical inheritance

From a political standpoint, the most significant features of Pakistan's geography in 1947 were its relatively small share of the Indian sub-continent and the contrasts and distance both within and between its western and eastern wings. Pakistan was by no means a small country, with a combined area almost four times that of the United Kingdom, or equal to that of Texas and Arizona in the United States, but it was dwarfed by its Indian neighbour. It had in fact inherited 23 per cent of the landmass of undivided India and 18 per cent of the population.[2] The disputes over Kashmir, the division of assets and water at the time of Partition, increased anxieties about Pakistan's precarious geopolitical situation in relation to its much larger neighbour.[3] Furthermore, the Pakistani sense of inferiority and insecurity was

---

[1] A. Jalal, *Democracy and Authoritarianism in South Asia*, p. 23.

[2] *Ibid.*

[3] Indian force levels not only outstrip those of Pakistan, but they are backed up by an indigenous arms-manufacturing capability which Pakistan lacks. The country's topography and main lines of communication further increase its vulnerability to Indian attack.

psychologically rooted in the country's status as a seceding state
rather than inheritor of the Raj. Membership of international organisations
such as the United Nations had devolved upon India, whereas Pakistan
had to go cap-in-hand to apply for membership.

Diplomatic and defence policies have been decisively influenced
by the need to counteract this Indian regional preponderance. As we
shall see in later chapters, external alliances with the United States[4]
in the CENTO (1955) and SEATO Pacts (1954) and friendship with
China[5] were successively called into play to help offset a strategic imbalance which worsened dramatically following the secession of East
Pakistan. The emphasis on building an effective army and bureaucracy
rather than representative institutions in the early years after independence
was also rooted in this geopolitical situation. Wayne Wilcox and Stephen
Cohen have linked the military's central role in the political decision-
making process with Pakistan's unfavourable security environment,
which has seen domestic policy much more influenced by defence and
foreign policy than is usual.[6]

The Dominion of Pakistan started life not only with a strategic deficit,
but also with an industrial one. At its outset it had an overwhelmingly
agrarian society in which new definitions of land rights and the needs
of imperial rule had strengthened the existing powers of elite groups.
Capitalist farming had been unevenly limited to the irrigated areas in
Punjab, Sindh and the Peshawar Valley of the Frontier. Elsewhere age-old
nomadism and subsistence farming remained unaltered.

North-west India's status as what has been termed an 'agrarian
appendix' to the subcontinent is revealed in the low rate of urbanisation
and industrialisation. The 1931 Frontier Census for example enumerated
the urban population at just 16 per cent, a figure which was itself
inflated by the listing of large agricultural villages as towns.[7] Sindh
recorded an urban population just 2 per cent higher[8] and even the

---

[4] Before joining SEATO and CENTO, Pakistan signed a mutual defence assistance pact
with the United States in 1954.

[5] Close ties with China date back to the early 1960s. They were symbolically cemented
with the opening of the Karakoram highway linking the two countries in 1982. Four
years later the countries signed an agreement for cooperation in the peaceful use of
nuclear energy.

[6] W. Wilcox, 'Political Role of the Army in Pakistan: Some Reflections' in S. P. Varma
and V. Narain (eds), *Pakistan Political System in Crisis: Emergence of Bangladesh* (Jaipur,
1972), p. 35; S. Cohen, 'Pakistan' in E. A. Kolodziej and R. E. Harkavy (eds), *Security
Policies of Developing Countries* (Lexington, MA, 1982), pp. 93-118.

[7] *Census of India 1931*, vol XV, part 1, pp. 40-1.

[8] *Census of India 1941*, vol XII, p. 2.

more developed Punjab province remained essentially rural in character.[9]
Colonial industrial development had clustered around Bombay, Ahmedabad, Calcutta and the West Bengal/Bihar coal belt. These areas all formed part of the new Indian dominion leaving Pakistan with just 10 per cent of the subcontinent's industrial base. Significantly, in the areas which went to Pakistan in 1947, there was no equivalent of the giant TATA steelworks at Jameshedpur or of the concentrated industrial belts to the west of Calcutta. Indeed on the eve of partition just one of the top fifty-seven Indian companies was owned by a Muslim.[10] Hindus in fact owned the majority of the industrial enterprises which were in existence in the Muslim majority regions. This, together with the traditional Hindu domination of trade and the professions, explains the disproportionately high non-Muslim urban populations[11] in the future Pakistan areas. The urban imbalance of the Hindus and Sikhs was especially pronounced in the southern towns of the Frontier and in the Thar Parkar and Hyderabad districts of Sindh. Karachi, which was the second largest urban centre in the future West Pakistan with a population just under 400,000, possessed a substantial Hindu population of over 130,000.[12] Cities such as Lahore and Peshawar had always been inhabited by substantial non-Muslim populations, but British rule enhanced the differences between them and their rural hinterland by creating administrative and professional opportunities for employment in addition to the traditional commercial and trading pursuits. Non-Muslims eagerly seized them because of their greater proficiency in English. The impact on Muslim separatism of this educational and socio-economic 'gap' is explored in a later chapter. *Mohajirs* mainly took over the running of Hindu-owned shops and businesses after 1947, although in some instances, former artisan employees or local entrepreneurs stepped into the gap.

Partition not only left most industrial development in India, but separated Pakistani raw materials from their markets. The main cotton producing areas of what became West Pakistan for example had supplied the raw materials to mills in Bombay and Ahmedabad. Just fourteen of the subcontinent's 394 cotton mills were located in Pakistan at the

[9] In 1921 60.5 per cent of the population was directly dependent on agriculture. *Census of India 1921*, vol XV, p. 9.

[10] Claude Markovits, *Indian Business and Nationalist Politics, 1931-1939: The Indigenous Capitalist Class and the Rise of the Congress Party* (Cambridge, 1985), Appendix 1.

[11] In the Frontier, 74.5 per cent of the Hindus and 71.5 per cent of the Sikhs lived in urban areas in 1941. *Census of India 1941*, vol. X, p. 20. In Sindh, there were 129 Hindus to every 100 Muslims living in urban areas, although they were outnumbered by 4:1 in the countryside. *Census of India 1931*, vol. VIII, part 1, Ch. 11, Statement 24, p. 51.

[12] This population largely comprised Gujarati-speakers from the Bombay region.

time of partition.[13] It also emphasised the uneven capitalist development between the western and eastern wings of Pakistan. Punjab possessed two-thirds of all the organised industrial units situated in the Pakistan areas.[14] East Pakistan, which produced the bulk of the world's raw jute supply, did not in fact boast a single mill since all the crop was sent in undivided India to Calcutta where it was made into hessian and exported. As British officials acknowledged before the partition of Bengal, East Bengal without Calcutta would be reduced to a 'rural slum'. During the 1950s and '60s East Pakistan was unable to overcome its relative backwardness at the time of Partition – with increasingly dangerous political consequences.

From this low starting base Pakistan's industrial development as a whole has been impressive,[15] as has been the exploitation of power potential, which was very limited at independence.[16] Despite the advance of both Karachi and Hyderabad, the greatest provincial concentration of manufacturing is today firmly established in Punjab. Within the province, Lahore and Faisalabad (formerly Lyallpur) retain their position as the major industrial locations, although there has been considerable growth in Multan (cotton ginning) and Gujranwala (metal engineering, electrical goods and textiles). There are still a large number of bazaar workshops, but the size of unit has increased. Manufacturing has also diversified from the colonial era, in which it was largely agro-related with the exception of the Sialkot sports goods industry, the Lyallpur textile industry and foundries like the Ittefaq concern which was jointly established by Nawaz Sharif's father in 1940. Nevertheless the shortage in electricity generation remains a major infrastructural weakness. While the poor economic inheritance at the time of Partition did not inhibit Pakistan's subsequent industrial development, the democratic deficit resulting from the legacy of a large feudal agrarian sector has proved more difficult to overcome.

Furthermore, Pakistan received but a meagre share of the Raj's material inheritance. In principle it was entitled to 17.5 per cent of the assets of undivided India, but the growing mistrust between the two governments prevented a smooth division of the spoils. It was not until December 1947 that an agreement was reached on Pakistan's share of the cash balances. The bulk of these (Rs.550 million) were held back by the Government of India as a result

---

[13] Muhammad Ali, *The Emergence of Pakistan* (New York, 1967), p. 334.

[14] A. Weiss, *Culture, Class and Development in Pakistan*, p. 33.

[15] As a result of an industrial growth-rate of 10 per cent per annum throughout much of the 1950s and '60s the industrial sector today contributes around 18 per cent of the GDP.

[16] Natural gas was discovered at Sui in Sindh in 1955 and has become a major source of power.

of the hostilities in Kashmir, and only paid on 15 January 1948 following Gandhi's intervention and fasting. Pakistan's military equipment was also delivered tardily by the Indians. Just over 23,000 of the 160,000 tons of ordnance stores allotted to Pakistan by the Joint Defence Council were actually delivered.[17] Most of the defence-production facilities and military stores in fact remained on the Indian side of the border.

Strategic and institutional inheritances

Strategically and institutionally Pakistan faced harsh challenges from its inception. Its eastern wing was separated from West Pakistan by 1,000 miles of Indian territory. This bred not only a sense of isolation from the centres of power but reinforced the existence of different world outlooks in the two wings with West Pakistan turning its face to the Middle East, East Pakistan to South-east Asia.[18]

Pakistan's north-western borders not only contained potentially troublesome tribal populations but were vulnerable to incursions from an unfriendly Afghan neighbour. The government in Kabul refused to accept nineteenth-century Anglo-Afghan treaties[19] which now demarcated its country's boundaries with Pakistan. It also expressed support for the Khudai-Khidmatgars' Pakhtunistan demands and voted against Pakistan's admission to the United Nations. Armed tribal incursions from Afghanistan into Pakistan's border areas began with the transfer of power and became a continual irritant. Afghan-Pakistan relations were to reach their nadir in 1955 when diplomatic relations were severed following the ransacking of the Pakistan embassy in Kabul, and again in 1961 when the Pakistan Army had to repel major Afghan incursions at Bajaur. By then the army had been greatly expanded, but at the time of partition it was too weak simultaneously to face an Indian and Afghan threat. This reality was immediately brought home by the necessity of employing almost 500 British officers because of the shortfall of qualified Pakistanis in the technical branches and at senior army rank. In the bifurcation of the Indian Army, Pakistan received just six armoured regiments to India's forty, and eight artillery and infantry regiments to India's forty and twenty-one

17 R. LaPorte, *Power and Privilege: Influence and Decision-making in Pakistan* (Berkeley, CA, 1975), p. 36.

18 A. McGrath, *The Destruction of Pakistan's Democracy* (Karachi, 1996), p. 4.

19 The most important of these followed the November 1893 negotiations between Sir Mortimer Durand and Amir Abdurrahman, and established what became known as the Durand Line boundary between British India and Afghanistan.

respectively.[20] The Pakistan Army was greatly expanded from its modest beginnings, but only at the cost of dependency on foreign aid and by siphoning funds from development activities.

The organisational atrophy of the Muslim League outside Bengal, as we have already noted, was a major feature of the freedom struggle. This institutional weakness contrasted with the pyramidal Congress organisation which stretched from New Delhi down to the villages. It was thus better placed to articulate local aspirations and implement policies than its Pakistani counterpart. Most importantly of all, as Ayesha Jalal has pointed out, the League's weakness meant that Pakistani politicians had to concede much 'greater autonomy to the administrative bureaucracy' to consolidate state authority than did their Indian counterparts.[21]

India had inherited both the colonial state's central apparatus in the former imperial capital New Delhi and the Bengal provincial secretariat in Calcutta. Pakistan on the other hand had to improvise its federal government in the provisional capital at Karachi. The Constituent Assembly was housed in the Sindh Assembly building. Far more important than locating officials to Karachi and finding space to house them however, was the shaping of a new federal structure and coordinating the administration of the provinces and princely states. A new provincial government also had to be created at Dhaka in East Pakistan. This task was especially difficult as the majority of the officials were Hindus and had opted for service in India. Indeed, of the 133 Muslim Indian Civil Service (ICS) and Indian Political Service (IPS) officials who opted for Pakistan at the time of partition, just one came from Bengal.[22] Muslims from other areas of Pakistan were despatched to East Pakistan, although this remedy was to evoke later claims of internal colonisation.

At the same time as establishing a system of government literally from scratch, with ministers using wooden boxes as their tables,[23] the Pakistan authorities were faced with the serious refugee problem which accompanied the partition of Punjab. The two-way mass migrations of August-November 1947 occurred against a background of horrific massacres, administrative chaos and mounting conflict between the two dominions over the division of assets, water ownership and water use and the political future of the northern princely state of Jammu and Kashmir. Most of these problems remained unresolved at the time when

---

[20] S.P. Cohen, *The Pakistan Army*, p. 7.

[21] Jalal, *Democracy and Authoritarianism*, p. 22.

[22] R. Braibanti, *Research on the Bureaucracy of Pakistan* (Durham, NC, 1966), p. 49.

[23] K.B. Sayeed, *Pakistan The Formative Phase 1857-1948* (London, 1968), p. 261.

Pakistan received the shattering blow of the death of its architect Muhammad Ali Jinnah in September 1948. Indeed as late as May 1960 the joint Indo-Pakistan Punjab Partition Implementation Committee was still grinding its way through various financial disputes, relating to government revenues, pensions of the victims of the 1947 disturbances, third party claims and public investments.[24]

Massacres and migrations

The magnitude of the refugee problem is brought home by the stark fact that Pakistan's 1951 Census enumerated one in ten of the population, some 7 million people, as of refugee origin.[25] While most refugees went to West Pakistan, the influx into the eastern wing should not be overlooked. At the time of the 1951 Census some 700,000 refugees were reported as residing in East Bengal.[26] Two-thirds of these had originated in West Bengal and Assam, while the remainder were Urdu-speaking migrants from Bihar and UP. Most refugees[27] had arrived between August and November 1947; at the same time, an almost equal number of Hindus and Sikhs had departed for India.

In the three and a half months which followed independence, 4.6 million Muslims were evacuated from the East Punjab alone.[28] The migrations were accompanied by horrific massacres which at the most conservative estimate claimed 200,000 lives.[29] The worst violence occurred in Punjab which had been partitioned along a line passing between Lahore and Amritsar. The other disturbed areas were the Punjab princely

---

[24] American Consul Lahore to Department of State, 25 May 1960. 790D.00(W)6-162-790D 1/2-1060, National Archives at College Park.

[25] Cited in K.R. Sipe, 'Karachi's Refugee Crisis: The Political, Economic and Social Consequences of Partition-Related Migration', unpubl. Ph.D. thesis, Duke University, 1976, p. 73.

[26] T. P. Wright, 'Indian Muslim Refugees in the Politics of Pakistan', *Journal of Commonwealth and Comparative Politics* XII, (1975), p. 194.

[27] The 1951 Census defined a refugee as a 'person who had moved into Pakistan as a result of partition or for fear of disturbances connected therewith.' The term *mohajir* is narrower in meaning and can only be understood in the Islamic context of religious flight (*hijra*). Such flight is central to Islam and indeed the Muslim calendar is dated from the Prophet's flight from Mecca to Medina in AD 622. The term *mohajir* was applied to the faithful who followed him. It has since been applied to Muslims who have fled to preserve their faith and is encouraged by the Quran, Surah 4, Women, 'He who emigrates in the path of God will find frequent refuge and abundance.'

[28] The exact figure given by Brigadier F.H. Stevens, commander of the Pakistan Military Evacuation Organisation, was 4,680,000. Quoted in *Eastern Times* (Lahore), 25 Dec. 1947.

[29] Sir Penderel Moon cited this figure in his work *Divide and Quit* (London, 1961). The controversy concerning it has recently been reopened in A. Roberts, *Eminent Churchillians* (London, 1994), pp. 128-9.

states and western UP. Bengal remained largely peaceful despite the 'great Calcutta killings' and subsequent rural Noakhali violence and the uncertainties created by its own partition. Even such a prominent Muslim League politician as Hussain Shaheed Suhrawardy continued to reside in Calcutta until 1949. Large minority populations remained in both East and West Bengal. The existence of a considerable Hindu minority in East Pakistan was another factor giving its politics a different flavour from that of West Pakistan. A further important legacy for East Pakistan of the Partition era was the presence of refugees from Bihar and UP who had fled the communal violence in their Indian homeland. Their attachment to North Indian culture led to increasing conflict with the indigenous Bengali elite. Those who were able, embarked on the second migration of their life in 1971. Many remained 'stranded' in refugee camps and the issue of their repatriation emerged as a major demand of the *mohajir* movement in Sindh in the late 1980s. Indeed the MQM-PPP Accord collapsed over the repatriation issue in October 1989 with dramatic consequences for both national and provincial politics.

The new Pakistan government was totally unprepared for the mass migrations and had not anticipated the violence which precipitated the flood of refugees. The demand for a separate Muslim homeland had not been linked with a call for movements of population. This was discouraged by the uncertainties over the exact boundary demarcation. Moreover, the so-called 'hostage' theory propounded the benefits of large minority populations in both India and Pakistan as a guarantee of communal stability. The only anticipatory migration which Jinnah had encouraged was the establishment of some 'nation-building' enterprises in the Pakistan areas. The future problems might however have been forseen from the stockpiling of weapons in Punjab and its surrounding princely states from the spring of 1947 onwards. Private Sikh armies[30] had sprung up often under the leadership of ex-INA (Indian National Army) soldiers in the wake of the attacks on the scattered Sikh communities of north-west Punjab in March 1947.[31] During the final days before the publication of the Radcliffe Boundary Award, Sikh raiding parties launched heavy attacks on Muslim villages in disputed 'border' areas of Punjab.[32] Shortly before independence, 5,000 Muslim refugees reached Lahore from the disturbed Amritsar district.

---

[30] Such as the Akal Fauj and *shahidi jathas.*

[31] See I. Talbot, *Punjab and the Raj*, p. 228. 40,000 Sikhs had taken refuge in hurriedly established camps before being transported to the safety of Amritsar following the disturbances in the Mianwali, Jhelum, Attock and Rawalpindi districts.

[32] Punjab FR, 30 July 1947; 13 August 1947. L/P&J/5/250, IOR.

They arrived in a city already abandoned by its Hindu and Sikh inhabitants following weeks of communal disturbances.

The causes of the Partition-related violence are complex and have evoked considerable controversy. Authors have debated whether Mountbatten should be held at least partly responsible because of his bringing forward the British departure from June 1948 to August 1947 and making inadequate security arrangements in the Punjab border areas.[33] The West Punjab Government apportioned the blame to the Sikhs,[34] while non-Muslims pointed accusingly at the role of the Muslim National Guards.[35]

Boundary demarcation certainly played a part in Sikh violence as did the need for revenge following the earlier assaults in West Punjab. The publication of the Boundary Award added desperation to this desire for it involved the loss to Pakistan of the rich Sikh farmlands of Lyallpur[36] and the shrine of Nankana Sahib.[37] Indeed, shortly before the British departure the Akali leader, Master Tara Singh, called for funds 'for the forthcoming struggle'. He particularly emphasised that territory full of Sikh religious places and properties should not be included in Pakistan at any cost and that Sikhs should enlist in *shahidi jathas* (martyrs' military detachments).[38] They not only attacked Muslim villages in the Jullundur and Amritsar districts, but also the packed refugee trains heading for Pakistan. Many of the *jathas* operated from the safety of the neighbouring Sikh princely states. The situation became so chaotic following the collapse of the civil administration in the East Punjab[39] that Master Tara Singh was forced to admit to India's first Chief of General Staff that he could not guarantee Muslim refugees safe passage through Amritsar.[40] Reports of atrocities such as when Sita Ram, the

---

[33] For a trenchant criticism of Mountbatten's role see A. Roberts, *Eminent Churchillians* (London, 1994), pp. 80ff.

[34] See such publications as *The Sikhs in Action* and *The Sikh Plan* which were both published from Lahore in 1948.

[35] See G.S. Talib, *Muslim League Attack on Sikhs and Hindus in the Punjab 1947* (Allahabad, 1950).

[36] Sikhs had acquired lands in the Canal Colonies which they had helped develop. On 13 September 1947, a convoy of 40,000 Sikhs left the Lyallpur Colony taking with them all they could load on bullock carts. *Civil and Military Gazette* (Lahore), 19 September 1947.

[37] This was the birthplace of the founder of Sikhism, Guru Nanak. The village of Nankana Sahib lies some 40 miles west-south-west of Lahore.

[38] *The Sikh Plan*, pp. 26-7.

[39] The British Governor of West Punjab wrote to Jinnah on 23 September 1947, 'that the East Punjab Government has ceased to exist as a Government.' In such districts as Jullundur power subsequently lay not with the Deputy Commissioner, but with Sikh Committees of Action. Mudie to Jinnah, 23 September 1947, Mudie Papers Mss.Eur.F 164/15, IOR.

Deputy Superintendent of Police, Ambala, supervised an assault on a refugee train on 1 September which claimed 1,000 lives[41] created a cycle of revenge killings.

Punjabi Muslims launched reprisals against Hindu and Sikhs residents and also attacked those who were travelling to India. The worst violence was in Sheikhupura[42] where looting, killing and burning lasted twenty-four hours on 25-26 August. Two wells in the Namdhari Gurdwara were filled with the bodies of Hindu and Sikh women who had committed suicide to save themselves from assault.[43] Elsewhere in the district, Sangla Hill and Sharakpur suffered much loss of life and physical destruction. Refugee trains passing through Wazirabad, Narowal and Raiwind were frequently attacked. Indeed, the railway track between Sialkot and Amritsar was strewn with Sikh corpses.[44] The mounting disturbances sparked a massive exodus across the new international boundaries in the Punjab region. Within just ten days of Pakistan's creation, an estimated 25,000 Muslims were streaming over from East Punjab each day.[45] On 5 September alone, 50,000 Muslim refugees arrived in Kasur on foot from the Ferozepore district and the neighbouring Sikh states.[46] Three weeks later, 80,000 Muslims reached the Wagah border safely from Amritsar.[47] Caravans were visible from miles away because of the clouds of dust thrown up by the thousands of bullock carts. In the evenings their camp fires pierced the darkness. They were thus easily recognisable targets. Eye-witness accounts recall the bodies heaped on either side of the road from Amritsar to Lahore, converting the whole area into a massive graveyard.

In such cities as Delhi and Karachi the arrival of refugees sparked off disturbances against the local minority population. Riots in Karachi in January 1948 led to a belated departure of over 11,000 Hindus from the city. Events followed a similar course, though on a much larger scale, in Delhi where trouble began in and around the city early in

---

[40] H.V. Hodson, *The Great Divide: Britain-India-Pakistan* (London, 1969), p. 411.

[41] *The Sikhs in Action*, p. 29.

[42] Non-Muslims formed around a third of the population of the Sheikhupura district. The Sikhs had played an important role in its agricultural development and the district of course contained the Nankana Sahib birthplace of Guru Nanak. The resistance put up by the Hindu and Sikh villagers of Bhullair has been commemorated in folk songs and stories. M. S. Randhawa, *Out of The Ashes – an Account of the Rehabilitation of Refugees from West Pakistan in Rural Areas of East Punjab* (Chandigarh, 1954), p. 15.

[43] G. S. Talib, *Muslim League Attacks on Sikhs and Hindus in the Punjab 1947*, p. 170.

[44] *Ibid.*, p. 191.

[45] *Eastern Times* (Lahore), 26 August 1947.

[46] *Ibid.*, 9 September 1947.

[47] *Ibid.*, 2 October 1947.

September soon after the advent of the first fugitives from Pakistan. They instigated attacks on Muslim localities and in some instances forcibly seized property. As the native progressive novelist Shahid Ahmad, a wealthy native of Delhi, recalls in his autobiography *Dilhi ki Bipta* (The Sad Tale of Delhi), Muslim houses in such suburbs as Karol Bagh were marked so that they could be identified by assailants. He also details the defence systems of gates on streets, guard groups and coloured lights – red if riots threatened, green as an all-clear signal – which the Muslims designed for their protection. When they had been evacuated, Muslims were herded into camps in places like Purana Qila and Humayan's Tomb. The latter camp was bulging with over 30,000 refugees by December 1947.[48] Shahid Ahmad provides graphic details of the squalid conditions there.

The migration from Delhi and UP was, however, by no means the final chapter in Muslim refugee history. The Indian 'police action' in the princely state of Hyderabad in September 1948 led to a further influx of refugees to Pakistan. According to the 1951 Census there were 95,000 Hyderabadi refugees.[49] Muslims have in fact continued to leave India at times of communal tension, as for instance after the January 1964 Calcutta riots[50] and particularly in the wake of the wars of 1965 and 1971. Bouts of communal violence in East Pakistan caused a similar Hindu exodus. Violence in the Noakhali district in July 1962 was prompted by the arrival of Muslims expelled by the Indian authorities from Tripura state.[51]

The poor physical state of many of the migrants added to the Pakistan Government's problems of resettlement. In the confusion, families had been split up, their womenfolk kidnapped and disgraced. Many refugees had been robbed of all their possessions by the East Punjab police. The Sub-Inspector of Police at Sarhali, for example, extorted Rs.10,000 from the villagers of Kot Muhammad Khan as the price for a military escort.[52] The police looted trains to such an extent that the East Punjab Governor,

---

[48] Report of A.S. Bhatnagar, Secretary to the Chief Commissioner, Delhi, 4 December 1947. MB1/D276 Mountbatten Papers, University of Southampton.

[49] Sipe, *Karachi's Refugee Crisis*, pp. 109ff.

[50] Communal tensions were high in the subcontinent at this time over the Hazratbal episode. The violence in Calcutta had been preceeded by conflict in Khulna and Jessore in East Pakistan. Within a few days of the violence in Calcutta, 20,000 Muslims had crossed into East Pakistan. American Embassy Karachi to Department of State 17 January 1964, Central Foreign Policy Files 1964-6 Political and Defence Pol 27-2, National Archives at College Park.

[51] American Consul Dacca to Department of State 12 July 1962, 790D/007/-1162, National Archives at College Park.

[52] *The Sikhs in Action*, pp. 31-2.

Sir Chandulal Trivedi, exclaimed at a conference on 17 September that he would 'not be sorry if the army shot...those [police]...including their officers.'[53]

The squalid conditions in the refugee transit camps resulted in the spread of cholera and other diseases. The smell emanating from one of the biggest of these just outside Ludhiana was so bad 'that it continued for almost a mile down the road'.[54] According to K.C. Neogy, the Indian Minister for Relief and Rehabilitation, there were between 100 and 250 deaths from cholera in one Muslim foot convoy from Rohtak alone, besides another 200 serious cases.[55] When the Pakistan Government complained about the lack of sanitation and low rations in such camps, Nehru was forced to concede privately that these criticisms were justified.[56]

The dramatic displacement of population in north west India and the tensions generated by the Kashmir dispute should not be allowed to obscure the much slower but continuous migration in the north-east. A close reading of the British Deputy High Commissioner's reports for East Bengal during 1948 immediately dispels the view that problems were non-existent in this region. In addition to surges of Hindu migration despite repeated reassurances to the minorities, there were serious tensions between the West Bengal and East Bengal governments. Sporadic armed clashes erupted in the riveraine area between Rajshahi and Murshidabad throughout October and November 1948,[57] and the Pakistan border with Tripura was another flashpoint area.[58]

The political inheritance from the refugee situation

The influx of refugees during the partition period was to possess long-term political consequences for Pakistan. The *mohajir*-Sindhi conflict in such cities as Karachi and Hyderabad forms the focus of later chapters, as does the transition from a *mohajir*-Punjabi-run state to what has been termed by the minorities 'Punjabistan'. It is necessary

---

[53] Report of Colonel Sher Khan, Administrative Headquarters, Military Evacuation Organisation Amritsar, 24 September 1947, Mudie Papers Eur.F 164/15, IOR.

[54] *Ibid.*

[55] Extract, Minutes 27th Meeting Emergency Cabinet Committee, MB1/D276, Mountbatten Papers, University of Southampton.

[56] Indian High Commissioner to Commonwealth Relations Office Cypher, 27 October 1947. East Punjab Affairs 1947-8, Weekly Reports G 2275/14 Do. 35 3159, Dominions and Commonwealth Relations Office, PRO.

[57] Deputy High Commissioner's Report for East Bengal for the Period Ending 31 October 1948; 20 November 1948; 27 November 1948, L?P&J/5/323, IOR.

[58] *Ibid.*

to note here three immediate consequences of the refugee situation: namely the politicisation of the resettlement issue caused by the need for refugee politicians to establish a vote bank in Pakistan; the tension between the Sindh and central authorities; and the differing experiences of *mohajirs* from Punjab and UP.

Refugee politicians from East Punjab were allowed to take up their seats in the new West Punjab Assembly but they needed to reassemble their former vote banks in order to survive in the long term. From July 1948 onwards Chaudhri Muhammad Hasan led them in a vociferous campaign for district-wise resettlement. The East Punjab MLA Rao Khurshid Ali took matters into his own hands and collected 50,000 of his followers in Montgomery from as far afield as Sindh and Bahawalpur.[59] The British Governor of the West Punjab sternly warned of the unthinkable consequences of making refugees who had only just settled move all over again. But the refugee Premier the Nawab of Mamdot, supported by his Education Minister Sheikh Karamat Ali, vacillated on the issue of district-wise settlement. Two important consequences stemmed from this. First the earlier spontaneous clashes between refugees and officials became more overtly political. In August 1948 for example police had to *lathi*-charge 500 refugees who had blocked the road near the Police Superintendent's residence in Multan and had raised anti-Pakistan slogans in a procession carrying effigies of the Deputy Commissioner and Camp Commander.[60] In another incident in Lahore 2,000 irate refugees had marched to the Municipal Office and smashed cars parked outside it before vandalising the office itself.[61] Second, these disturbances, along with the problems in Sindh, led Jinnah in one of his last actions to authorise the declaration of a state of emergency regarding the rehabilitation of refugees. This was issued under Section 102 of the 1935 Government of India Act which served as Pakistan's constitution. The centre had previously shied away from what was a provincial responsibility, and this summary action was to be one of a number of occasions early in Pakistan's history when a precedent was established for overriding provincial politicians.

The situation facing UP refugee politicians was of course even more difficult than that of their East Punjab counterparts. They had dominated the central organs of the All-India Muslim League but had no Pakistani base, or large numbers of tenants and labourers who could be relocated so as to provide them with one. In such circumstances they were reluctant

---

[59] Mudie to Jinnah, 5 August 1948, Mudie Papers Eur. F 164/15, IOR.

[60] Mudie to Jinnah, 20 August 1948, Mudie Papers Eur. F 164/15, IOR.

[61] *Ibid.*

to hold elections which would pitch them into obscurity. This in part explains the delay in holding national elections which would have revamped the Constituent Assembly. This delay, which was also rooted in the tensions between West and East Pakistan, was to provide an opening for the establishment of a non-elected bureaucratic authority.

The uneasy relations between the Sindh government and the central authorities were another consequence of the refugee situation. The province's Premier, Muhammad Ayub Khuhro strongly opposed the demand that Sindh should accept those refugees who could not be absorbed in West Punjab. By December 1947 Sindh had only resettled 244,000 displaced persons, while West Punjab had resettled over 4 million.[62] Its government that month agreed to take another 500,000 refugees provided that they were relocated in the Sukkur, Shikarpur and Mirpurkhas districts as Karachi was 'super-saturated'. Within a month Khuhro had reneged on this promise, declaring that Sindh would be unable to rehabilitate more than 150,000 refugees during the first half of 1948. This 'uncooperative' attitude was criticised by the West Punjab Governor. In a letter to Jinnah early in 1948 he cited census figures to demonstrate that Sindh had a net loss of 600,000 Hindu and Sikh agriculturalists and therefore should have no difficulty in meeting its responsibilities.[63]

Khuhro was severely upbraided by Raja Ghazanfar Ali, the Pakistan Minister for Refugees and Rehabilitation, at a sub-committee meeting of the Pakistan Muslim League Council held on 23 February 1948. His defence that the local populace was suffering from the burdens imposed by the refugee influx was dismissed by Ghazanfar Ali as raising 'the virus of provincialism'. 'This is not only against the teachings of Islam and in direct contravention to the principle on which we fought for the achievement of Pakistan,' Ghazanfar Ali added, 'but is a deadly weapon which if allowed to operate unchecked will destroy the foundations of our newly-born state.'[64] Khuhro's stance on the refugee issue was a contributory factor in his eventual downfall. It was to exert a much wider negative impact on Pakistani politics, for it not only strengthened Sindhi sentiment against the centre, but also encouraged the precedent of executive action against elected representatives. This boded ill for the future.

The differing experiences of *mohajirs* from UP to those from East Punjab and Gujarat is of crucial importance to an understanding of post-independence political developments. Linked with this is their self-

[62] *Dawn*, 12 December 1947.

[63] Mudie to Jinnah 4 February 1948, Mudie Papers Eur. F 164/15, IOR.

[64] *The Statesman* (Calcutta), 25 February 1948.

image that they had sacrificed for Pakistan and were engaged on a true *hijrat* rather than being 'acute' migrants. The *mohajirs* from UP were in fact just a minority of the refugees who had left India at the time of partition. Three quarters of all the *mohajirs* were Punjabis (4.7 million). They were able to settle quickly in Pakistan and rapidly abandoned the *mohajir* label. They did not have to make the linguistic and social adjustments which usually face refugees because they spoke the Punjabi language of the indigenous West Punjab population and entered an environment which was both climatically and culturally similar to that of their natal East Punjab villages. They settled on land vacated by the Sikh Jats and were thus enabled to continue their traditional agricultural pursuits.

Similarly Khoja and Memon migrants from Bombay entered a familiar environment. Karachi had formed part of the Gujarati-speaking coastal belt as a result of its administrative attachment to the Bombay Presidency. Some of the migrants had previously established business and family links. Even when this was not the case, they were able to step into the shoes of the former Hindu business class. Many Karachi enterprises which had been run by Gujarati-speaking Hindus before partition, were controlled by Gujarati-speaking Muslim migrants afterwards.

Mohajirs from UP did not share the advantages of Punjabis and Gujaratis. There was no cultural region in the Pakistan areas similar to their North Indian home. Around 60 per cent of the 464,000 *mohajirs* from UP[65] resettled in Sindh. The greatest concentration was in Karachi and Hyderabad, but a small proportion were dispersed in the towns of the interior. Some stayed in Karachi simply because they had been routed there by rail. On a less mundane note, Karachi was seen as an attractive destination because it was Pakistan's leading commercial centre and the initial headquarters of the Pakistan Government. It thus afforded better employment prospects for the mainly middle class North Indian *mohajirs* than the rural West Punjab. Finally, it is possible that the *mohajirs* were discouraged from settling in Punjabi cities like Lahore and Multan because of their domination by the traditional landed elites, although this did not discourage settlement by refugees from East Punjab areas such as Jullundur and Amritsar. Whatever their motives, the North Indian refugees who came to settle in Sindh almost four decades ago have impacted dramatically on the 'local' culture, whilst retaining their own strong cultural distinctions. Intizar Hussain's short stories reveal the melancholy attachment to a lost UP world which is felt by *mohajir* intellectuals. Emphasis on Urdu and its protection has remained a strong political element in community identity. The transformation of the dominant urban centres into Urdu-speaking enclaves within Sindh has

[65] Sipe, *Karachi's Refugee Crisis*, p. 75.

created acute tensions. By the time of the 1951 Census, *mohajirs* accounted for 58 per cent of the population of Karachi, 66 per cent of Hyderabad, 54 per cent of Sukkur, 68 per cent of Mirpurkhas and 35 per cent of Larkana.[66] The continued historical links with the role of UP in the freedom struggle are seen in the veneration accorded to Liaquat Ali Khan by some *mohajir* groups. The 1988 MQM-sponsored biography of Altaf Hussain quotes him as saying that 'Every Government which came to power after Liaquat Ali Khan discriminated against the *mohajirs*.'[67] The *mohajir* leader has also claimed that he and his supporters are the 'heirs' of the 'two million' minority province Muslims who sacrificed their lives: 'We have a right to Pakistan, and it is a right of blood, we gave blood for it.'[68] Rather than abandoning their *mohajir* status, the Urdu-speaking refugees have adopted it as a source of ethnic political allegiance with wide-ranging implications. The cultural dissonance lying behind the politics of the MQM is starkly revealed by the depiction of its red, green and white tricolour in the shape of a *patang* (kite) – a reminder of a common north Indian pastime which is alien to Sindh.[69]

Five additional points regarding the legacy of migration need to be made. The first is that concern with the *mohajir* Karachi crisis should not be allowed to obscure the importance of East Punjabi migrants in shaping the political development of the Pakistan state. As Muhammad Waseem has pointed out, the 5 million migrants have both provided a major support for Islamist parties and shaped the Punjab province's strong anti-Indian and pro-Kashmiri leanings. Support for centralist martial law regimes has also come from this quarter. The politics of Punjabi cities like Lahore, Sialkot, Multan and Gujranwala, of whose population around half were enumerated as migrants at the time of the 1951 Census, cannot be understood without reference to the refugee dimension. Delhi's politics have been similarly influenced by the presence of a large Punjabi Hindu migrant population.

The rising Punjabi industrial elite of the 1980s came largely from the migrant trading communities which had originated from Ambala, Batala, Jullundur, and Hoshiarpur. They prospered during the Zia era and provided an urban support base for Nawaz Sharif's Muslim League. 'Himself belonging to a Kashmiri migrant family', Muhammad Waseem

---

[66] T. Rahman, 'Language and Politics in a Pakistan Province: The Sindhi Language Movement', *Asian Survey* 35, no. 11 (November 1995), p. 1008.

[67] F. Haq, 'Rise of the MQM in Pakistan: Politics of Ethnic Mobilisation', *Asian Survey* 35, no. 11 (November 1995), p. 997.

[68] A. Jalal, 'Conjuring Pakistan', p. 83.

[69] Julian Richards, 'Mohajir Subnationalism and the Mohajir Qaumi Movement in Sindh Province, Pakistan', p. 414.

has declared, ' Nawaz Sharif reflected a migrant ethos [and] his natural constituency lay with migrants from East Punjab and Kashmir.'[70]

The second point is that in the realm of comparative politics little attention has been drawn to Pakistan's emergence as a settler/refugee-dominated state. Surprisingly little has been made of this characteristic, although parallels are there to be drawn for example with the state of Israel.

Thirdly it should be noted that although Punjab as a whole did not suffer ethnic conflicts arising from refugee resettlement, where cultural differences coincided with economic resentment concerning the migrants, as in the south-western Siraiki-speaking areas, a similar political pattern emerged as in Sindh.

The fourth point concerns the migration experience and the establishment of a tradition of bureaucratic as opposed to parliamentary rule. Muhammad Waseem has maintained that the undercutting of parliament resulted both from the *mohajir* presence in the civil service and the loss of its political base. 'Recourse to elections', he states, 'was considered suicidal by the migrant-led government at Karachi because there was no way it could win elections and return to power in the centre. Elections were considered dysfunctional for the political system of Pakistan in the immediate post-independence period.'[71]

Finally, concerns with the uneven economic inheritances at the All-India level and their political consequences should not be allowed to obscure the regional dimension. Within the Punjab region, Hindus and Sikhs left behind not only more urban property than their Muslim refugee counterparts, but some 2 million acres of excess cultivable land. The East Punjab Government thus adopted a sliding-scale formula for allocating land to refugees.[72] Shinder Thandi has argued forcefully that this encouraged new forms of risk-taking and more progressive farming methods as well as strengthening the political economy of owner-cultivation which has lain behind the greater agricultural productivity of Indian Punjab. As we have already noted, the legacy of the partition for the structure of land ownership in West Punjab was to sustain an agrarian system in which land was 'perceived to be a political rather than a commercial commodity.'[73]

[70] M. Waseem, *The 1993 Elections in Pakistan*, p. 163.

[71] *Ibid.*, p. 32.

[72] See M. Randhawa, *Out of the Ashes*, p. 99.

[73] S. S. Thandi, 'The Unidentical Punjab Twins: Some Explanations of Comparative Agricultural Performance Since Partition', *International Journal of Punjab Studies*, 4, 1 (Jan.-June 1997), p. 72.

The crisis in Indo-Pakistan relations

The refugee situation formed part of a wider deterioration in Indo-Pakistan relations. Indeed, it played an important role – many Pakistani officials were convinced that the Indians were intent on making things impossible for them by pushing as many Muslims out of their country as possible. Certainly, Pakistani attitudes towards the increasingly serious situation in the princely state of Jammu and Kashmir were influenced by the migration issue. Before turning to Kashmir we must refer to another area of Indo-Pakistan conflict, the Indus Waters dispute.

The dispute over water management and water-sharing between the two dominions reveals both the insecurity of Pakistan and the importance of administrative as opposed to political initiatives in solving its post-Partition problems. The British had never anticipated that it would be necessary to disentangle the intensive network of canals which drew water from Punjab's famous five rivers (Sutlej, Beas, Ravi, Chenab, Jhelum) and also from the Indus. The massive irrigation schemes which they had constructed from the end of the nineteenth century had transformed the desert of the West Punjab into one of the most prosperous farming regions in Asia. Pakistan's economic survival depended on the continued availability of water from these irrigation systems.

The Punjab Partition Council which met in Lahore from the end of June 1947 agreed that the existing apportionment of water resources from the canal systems should be maintained intact after independence. However, the Radcliffe Boundary Award which was not announced until 17 August placed the Madhopur and Ferozepur control points of the Upper Bari Doab canals, the Pipalpur canal and the Eastern Grey canal – all vital for Pakistan – on the Indian side of the border. Andrew Roberts has recently reopened the controversy concerning Mountbatten's role in the award of the Muslim majority tehsils of Ferozepur and Zira to India with the consequent control of the Sutlej river canal headworks.[74]

On 1 April 1948[75] the East Punjab Government shut off water supplies to the Dipalpur canal from the Ferozepur headworks. This not only deprived Lahore of its main water supply, but put at risk 5.5 per cent of the sown area of West Pakistan at a crucial time in the agricultural year – the sowing of the *kharif* (autumn harvest crop).[76] The Indian

---

[74] Andrew Roberts, *Eminent Churchillians*, pp. 93ff.

[75] Although the apportionment of water supplies had not been referred to the Inter-Dominion Arbitral Tribunal, it was no coincidence that the water dispute began the day after it had been wound up.

[76] S.S. Thandi, 'The Unidentical Punjab Twins: Some Explanations of Comparative Agricultural Performance Since Partition', pp. 63-85.

action was based on the claim that Pakistan had no right to the waters and would have to pay a seigniorage charge if the canals were to be reopened. Direct negotiations between the two dominions in May 1948 led to the restoration of the flow of water to the Dipalpur but not to the Bahawalpur canals. Supplies to Pakistan's canals were increasingly reduced by Indian construction of new canals and the raising of the capacity of the Bhakra dam.[77] Moreover, it proved impossible to resolve the impasse created by the contention that proprietary rights in the waters of the East Punjab rivers were vested wholly in the East Punjab Government. India refused Pakistan's offer to refer the legal dispute to the International Court of Justice.[78]

The tension between India and Pakistan over the Kashmir issue prevented a political breakthrough over the legal arguments concerning water ownership. The initiative thus fell to administrators such as Muhammad Ali[79] and S.S. Kirmani[80] to find a technical solution to provide insurance against the cessation of supplies from India. This both proved to be costly and marked a further shift towards Pakistan's transformation into an 'administrative state'. The Balloki-Suleimanki, Bambanwali-Ravi-Bedian and Marala-Ravi link canals were sanctioned as was the Mangla Dam on which preliminary access work began in 1959. By the time of its completion it was the longest (11,000 feet) earth-filled dam in the world.

The Indus Waters dispute was only finally resolved in September 1960 partly as a result of the initiative taken by the World Bank. The Indus Waters Treaty created a permanent Indus Waters Commission and assigned the waters of the Indus, Jhelum and Chenab to Pakistan. Internationally-financed link canals nearly 400 miles long transferred water from the above three rivers to areas previously irrigated by the water supplied from India by the eastern Ravi, Sutlej and Beas rivers. The scheme included in addition the construction of the Mangla and Tarbella dams.

The Kashmir conflict

Indo-Pakistan relations during the fifty years since independence have been dominated by the dispute over Kashmir. This has provoked two

[77] For details see Michel, cited above.

[78] The Indian government made the counter offer in September 1950 of submitting the issues to a court of two Indian and two Pakistani judges.

[79] For an insight into Muhammad Ali's role and approach see Ali, *The Emergence of Pakistan*, Chapter 15.

[80] Kirmani was Director of Central Designs in the West Punjab Irrigation Department. For his role see Michel, *The Indus Rivers*, pp. 284ff.

wars (1948 and 1965), threatened war in 1987 and led to sporadic fighting from 1984 onwards on the Siachen glacier in northern Kashmir. The danger of nuclear conflict as a result of an escalation of hostilities over Kashmir has existed throughout the 1990s. Almost as damaging to the Indian subcontinent's future is the threat to its material well-being arising from the dispute. The distrust this has generated continues to fuel a regional arms race which diverts scarce resources from infrastructural investment and human development. Furthermore the hindrance it provides to Indo-Pakistan economic cooperation seems likely to marginalise the region in a world dominated by trading blocs.

Vital strategic interests were at stake in Kashmir in 1947. Moreover, their continued presence helps in part to explain the conflict's bitterness and longevity. The headwaters of the Indus, Jhelum and Chenab rivers which were crucial to West Pakistan's agriculture were all situated in Kashmir. Its borders met with Tibet and China and were only a few miles distant from the Soviet Union. Control of Kashmir was thus of exceptional economic and military importance.

In addition the fate of Kashmir in 1947 was (and indeed remains) symbolically significant for both Pakistan and India. Kashmir formed the 'K' in the term 'Pakistan' which was first coined by Chaudhri Rahmat Ali in 1933. As a Muslim majority princely state it was expected, in keeping with the two-nation theory, to form part of Pakistan on the lapse of British paramountcy. Indeed its non-inclusion was a threat to the ideological basis of Pakistan's existence. However, the decision concerning accession in 1947 lay with the ruler and not the subjects of a princely state although, as Pakistanis noted, this did not seem to be the case in circumstances where Indian interests were threatened, as in the Kathiawar state of Junagadh.[81]

For Nehru, whose family originally hailed from Kashmir, and for the Indian National Congress the accession of Kashmir was of course symbolically important as a guarantor of the ideals of a 'secular' composite Indian nationalism. The self-identity of both India and Pakistan thus became linked with Kashmir. In such circumstances, conciliation and compromise have been almost impossible. It is indeed very difficult for the 'outsider' to appreciate the emotions aroused in Pakistan by the Kashmiri cause. As we shall see, the new phase in the conflict which unfolded in the 1980s strengthened rather than diminished its salience in the internal politics of both countries.

---

[81] In what was the opposite situation to Kashmir, Junagadh was a Hindu majority state with a Muslim ruler. He acceded to Pakistan, but a rebellion led to the intervention of the Indian Army. Shortly afterwards a plebescite recorded a 90 per cent vote in favour of accession to India. This verdict ensured Junagadh's annexation, despite Pakistan's protests to the UN Security Council.

The Kashmir conflict remains the most maleficent inheritance from the climacteric of the British departure from the subcontinent. Beyond this fact, its origins are clouded in controversy. Pakistani writers claim that the Muslim majority[82] princely state's accession to India on 26 October 1947 was 'fraudulent' and indeed had been planned by Nehru and Mountbatten.[83] The debate indeed continues over whether or not the Instrument of Accession had been signed before Indian troops were sent to Jammu and Kashmir.[84] While the legality of the Instrument of Accession in particular continues to exercise historians, the former Foreign Secretary of the Government of India, J.N. Dixit, expressed the *realpolitik* of the situation to the British author Victoria Schofield in April 1994 when he declared: 'Everybody who has a sense of history knows that legality only has a relevance up to the threshold of transcending political realities. And especially in inter-state relations... so to quibble about points of law and hope that by proving a legal point you can reverse the process of history is living in a somewhat contrived utopia. It won't work.'[85]

The traditional Indian riposte to claims of a 'fraudulent' accession has been that the invasion of Pakhtun tribesmen in mid-October which precipitated the Hindu Maharajah Hari Singh's accession to India was encouraged and aided by the Pakistan Government.[86] Less well known is the impact of the arrival of Sikh evacuees on communal relations in Jammu province from March 1947 onwards.[87] Indian authors are generally reticent concerning both the indigenous roots of the revolt

[82] At the time of the 1941 Census, Muslims comprised 78 per cent of the 4 million population. They held a clear majority in all three of its provinces, including Jammu province (60 per cent), which was the ancestral home of the Dogra rulers.

[83] Subsequent events in Kashmir encouraged Pakistanis to regard with suspicion the award to India of the Muslim majority district of Gurdaspur in Punjab by the Radcliffe Boundary Commission. This district was contiguous to Jammu and Kashmir and without it the Indian Union would not have possessed a viable access route.

[84] The issue can be followed in V. Schofield, *Kashmir in the Crossfire* (London, 1996), pp. 146ff.

[85] *Ibid.*, p. 291.

[86] The balance of evidence seems to indicate that the Pakistan Government did not instigate the tribal incursion which was a spontaneous *jihad*. Nevertheless, provincial officials and politicians in NWFP and West Punjab sympathised with the action and on occasion assisted the transit of the tribesmen. British officials' testimonies tend to support the 'official' Pakistani line that attempts to halt the tribesmen would have resulted in widespread violence. See Diary of Sir George Cunningham, Governor NWFP, Mss. Eur.D 670/6, IOR.

[87] This influx followed the Muslim League civil disobedience campaigns in Punjab and NWFP. The Sikh evacuees were joined by armed groups from Patiala, Faridkot and Nabha States. The period from 1946 onwards witnessed a dramatic rise in RSS support and activity in Kashmir.

of the Muslim inhabitants of Poonch[88] in August 1947[89] and the orgy of communal violence in Jammu province which was orchestrated by the state police and Dogra armed forces.[90]

The September 1947 communal massacres in Jammu province created a flood of over 80,000 Muslim refugees to neighbouring Sialkot in West Punjab. Their miserable conditions undoubtedly encouraged support for the subsequent Pakhtun incursion among some Pakistani officials. They saw the *jihad* as not only avenging the Muslim victims, but as the best means of preventing further mass migrations into Pakistan. They quite rightly saw that the killings were not random but formed a policy of 'ethnic cleansing'. The Pakhtun invaders' indiscriminate plunder and violence not only alienated many Kashmiri Muslims but also led the Maharajah to accede to India in return for the airlifting of troops to Srinagar. The regular Indian forces drove the tribesmen back up the valley to Uri.

Mountbatten, who as Governor-General of India had officially accepted the accession of Kashmir, had promised that this action by the Maharajah would be confirmed by a referendum. The 1948-9 Indo-Pakistan war, India's failed attempt to indict Pakistan before the United Nations Security Council for violating her sovereignty and the continued Pakistani military occupation of Azad Kashmir (AK) led Nehru to conclude that the circumstances were not right for a plebiscite to be held, despite the passage of a United Nations resolution calling for a plebiscite to be conducted by its nominee administrator. Following the 1954 vote by the Kashmiri Constituent Assembly in favour of the accession of Jammu and Kashmir to the Indian Union, New Delhi has seen no need for a plebiscite. The Pakistan Government however has attempted to secure international support for its conduct in the name of Kashmiri self-determination. Significantly, it followed the line of the original United Nations resolution in limiting the choice in any referendum to accession either to India or itself. This restriction as we shall see

---

88 Poonch was ruled indirectly as a *jagir* of the Dogras by a Hindu Raja. The poverty of the barren and mountainous western districts of Poonch was partly alleviated by large-scale recruitment into the Indian Army.

89 The revolt began in August as a 'no-tax' campaign. This was prompted by the introduction of a number of unpopular taxes following the assumption of direct rule by Hari Singh in the wake of the dispossession during the Second World War of the Raja. The unpopularity of the new dispensation was compounded by the billeting of Dogra troops in Poonch to enforce tax collection.

90 The attacks on Muslim villages in Jammu province began in the middle of October. Thousands of Muslims were killed at the hands of the Dogra troops, members of the RSS and Sikh *jathas*. The Pakistan Government's slant on these massacres can be found in Government of Pakistan, *Kashmir Before Accession* (Lahore, 1948), pp. 34ff.

was increasingly called into question with the rise of Kashmiri separatist feelings in the 1980s.

The uprising in Poonch which had initiated the crisis saw no quarter given by either side, but the large number of Muslim ex-servicemen[91] in the region tipped the balance firmly against the Kashmir state army. Poonch was thereafter to become the first base of the Pakistan-controlled AK Government. By the time that the United Nations brokered ceasefire came into operation in January 1949, the AK boundary had been extended into parts of western Jammu province and covered an area of over 30,000 square kilometres of rugged terrain with the exception of the more cultivable Mirpur district. Aside from this, the only other prosperous area was Muzaffarabad which had been an important pre-1947 point of entry into the Kashmir Valley. To the south and east, the Kashmir Valley and most of Jammu province now formed the territory of the Indian Union. Both states have continued to claim the territory held by their rivals. India refers to the Pakistan-administered area as 'Pakis-tan-occupied Kashmir' or POK.

The other regions of the former Kashmir princely state which are administered by Pakistan but are not fully integrated in it are the so-called Northern Areas. These comprise Gilgit and its related territories. The rebellion in the far-flung western Kashmiri suzerainty of Gilgit by a platoon of the Gilgit Scouts commanded by a British officer remains as contentious as anything else concerning Kashmir. Indian writers regard it as a coup;[92] Pakistani commentators portray it as a popularly-backed rebellion. Since the 'revolution' night of 31 October 1947, Gilgit along with Baltistan, Hunza and Nagar have formed the Northern Areas. This area with a population of around a million is not fully integrated with Pakistan, nor, despite a 1993 ruling of the High Court of Azad Jammu and Kashmir which was quashed by the Supreme Court, is it integrated with that authority.[93] Pakistan's official stand on the UN resolutions precludes the Northern Areas' full integration, while their strategic access to China obstructs the so-called 'third option' of independence for the entire Kashmir state as it existed in 1947.

The administrative framework for the Northern Areas with political agents in Gilgit and Baltistan reporting to residents situated initially in Rawalpindi and a mix of tribal sub-agencies (*chilas*), political sub-divisions (Gilgit, Astor), districts (Punial, Gupis, Yasin, Ishkuman)

[91] Over 60,000 Muslims served from Poonch and Mirpur during the Second World War. Cited in Schofield, *Kashmir in the Crossfire*, p. 133.

[92] See for example, B.L. Kak, *The Fall of Gilgit: The Untold Story of Indo-Pak Affairs from Jinnah to Bhutto* (New Delhi, 1977).

[93] Schofield, *Kashmir in the Crossfire*, p. 275.

and states (Hunza, Nagir) was based on the British system. The Political Agent in Gilgit also handled the relations of the semi-autonomous states of Hunza and Nagir with the Pakistan Government. Aside from the relatively fertile Punial district, the Northern Areas were food-deficit regions which had to be supplied during the winter months in the 1960s by airlifts employing C-47 Dakotas which made 2-3 sorties every day in good weather.[94] Little has been written either about the Northern Areas or about AK,[95] whose status has never been defined in international law: it is neither a province of Pakistan nor a sovereign state, but is rather a 'local authority' with responsibility for administering the territory held by Pakistan under the 1949 cease-fire agreement. During the period 1950-71, under the 'rules of business of the Azad Kashmir Government', full executive powers were vested in the 'Supreme Head of State' (i.e. leadership of the Muslim Conference), but supervision and the ultimate source of authority in fact lay with the Pakistan government's Ministry of Kashmir Affairs Joint Secretary (after 1958 'Chief Adviser'). Even after the introduction of an elective principle with Ayub Khan's Basic Democracy system, the Chairman of the AK Council (and *ex-officio* President) was to be nominated by the Chief Adviser.[96]

Events in Kashmir in 1947-9 provided a defining moment both in Indo-Pakistan relations and for Pakistan's domestic priorities. Any lingering hopes of the two dominions' economic or military interdependence were snuffed out in Jammu's killing fields. Although the military conflict between the two dominions was confined to Kashmir, it brought home the strategic dangers facing Pakistan, the weaker of the protagonists. The priority of building up the armed forces was spelled out by Liaquat Ali Khan in a broadcast to the nation on 8 October 1948: 'The defence of the State is our foremost consideration ... and has dominated all other governmental activities. We will not grudge any amount on the defence of our country.'[97]

Pakistan thus embarked on the establishment of a 'political economy of defence'. The years 1947-50 saw up to 70 per cent of the national budget being allocated for defence.[98] This sum could only be made

---

94 Muree Office American Consul to Department of State 7 June 1961, 790D.00/5-461, National Archives at College Park.

95 The material in this paragraph has been taken from the one exception to this: Leo.E. Rose, 'The Politics of Azad Kashmir' in Raju. G.C. Thomas (ed), *Perspectives on Kashmir: The Roots of Conflict in South Asia* (Boulder, 1992), pp. 235-53.

96 The Council was to be elected indirectly from local bodies and to comprise 12 members elected by AK Basic Democrats and 12 by Kashmiri refugees in Pakistan. *Ibid.*, p. 239.

97 Ali, *Emergence of Pakistan*, p. 376.

98 Samad, *A Nation in Turmoil*, p. 128.

available by diverting resources from 'nation-building' activities and expanding the state's administrative machinery to ensure the centre's control over the provinces' finances. The long-term repercussions were a strengthening of the unelected institutions of the state – the bureaucracy and the Army – at the expense of political accountability. This process contributed incalculably to the sense of alienation in East Pakistan, where priorities were of a different order and did not involve sacrificing democratic politics on the altar of the Kashmiri Muslim cause. Moreover, the Army increasingly acquired an almost insatiable appetite for new technology, and which became ever more expensive. By 1958 an American intelligence report attested that the 'Pakistani army had developed as a pressure group' and would 'continue to have priority over economic development for appropriations', irrespective of the Indian factor.[99]

However much Pakistan skewed its economy and politics to meet its strategic defence requirements,[100] it could not match unaided the resources of its Indian neighbour. This fact was recognised from the outset. Indeed as early as October 1947 Pakistan unsuccessfully requested a \$2 billion loan from the United States.[101] Britain lacked the financial resources to provide major assistance and also needed to appear even-handed in its dealings with the Indians and Pakistanis. The Americans thus appeared a better bet especially in the light of their requirement for regional Cold War allies as part of their policy of containment towards the Soviet Union and China. When external US military and economic assistance eventually arrived in 1954, it inevitably came with the strings of membership of SEATO and the Baghdad Pact attached. In the wake of the Kashmir conflict, the Pakistan authorities thus eschewed ties with the Muslim world which would have commanded popular support[102] and became increasingly locked into a dependent relationship with the United States. It provided the bureaucrats and their military allies at the centre with both the motives – the exclusion of political interference on foreign policy issues and increasing resources – to tilt the balance of power away from representative parties and politicians. A full five years before the military takeover of October 1958, the Governor-General

---

[99] A. Jalal, *The State of Martial Rule*, p. 238.

[100] In 1953 the Economic Appraisal Committee conceded that Pakistan's annual expenditure on defence and civil administration was wholly out of line with available resources. Ibid., p. 237.

[101] Ibid., p. 55.

[102] Liaquat Ali Khan was toying with alternatives to a pro-Western foreign policy shortly before his assassination on 16 October 1951. Popular opposition to the pro-Western stance of the establishment was especially evident during the July 1956 Suez crisis.

had appointed a political nonentity, Muhammad Ali Bogra, as Prime Minister because of his pro-American stance.[103]

The survival of Pakistan

How did Pakistan survive the social turmoil, economic dislocation and hostility with India which accompanied its birth? The answer lies as much in the courage and resilience of the ordinary people as in government initiatives. Standard 'top-down' accounts of Pakistan's politics have ignored this dimension, as have subsequent prognostications concerning the collapse of the Pakistan state. In an earlier study[104] the present author discussed the way in which many of the refugees regarded their journey to Pakistan as a true *hijrat*, an opportunity for a renewal of their faith. Individual acts of heroism and sacrifice amid the sadism and inhumanity of the Partition-related massacres have also been pointed out.

Some politicians and officials got rich on the pickings of evacuee property or through the exploitation of refugees themselves. Amir Abdullah Khan Rokri in his autobiographical account even recalls one incident in the main Muslim transit camp in Pathankot in which Muslim officers in connivance with local Muslim and Hindu businessmen sold on to the black market rationed goods which had been provided by the Indians for the refugees.[105] But many ordinary Muslims acted as true *ansars*, feeding and clothing the *mohajirs* and taking them into their own homes. They acted in this way, as Rokri records for the Mianwali district, 'because they knew that these people were being driven out of India simply because they were Muslims'.[106] The author moved his entire family to one small room to accommodate refugees and paid for their needs out of his own pocket. A similar idealism was displayed by the women who came out of *purdah* to work for the Red Crescent or who pawned their jewellery for the emergency loan raised to cover Pakistan's 'missing' share of the cash balances.

Those who have grown cynical over the passage of time in Pakistan will be surprised by the widespread manifestations of social solidarity and improvisation, reminiscent of Britain during the Blitz in the Second World War, which marked the early days of the state's existence. Auxiliary nurses worked in the hospitals, and bank clerks were trained in evening classes to fill the gaps left by the Hindu clerks and accountants. In

---

103 Bogra had previously been Pakistan's Ambassador in Washington.

104 Talbot, *Freedom's Cry*.

105 A. A. K. Rokri, *May aur mera Pakistan* (Me and my Pakistan), 2nd edn (Lahore, 1989), p. 76.

106 *Ibid.*, p.72.

the countryside, cooperative societies provided the credit formerly supplied by the departed moneylenders. They also opened stores, handled the distribution of essential commodities, and ran abandoned cotton-ginning mills. The cooperative banks initially replaced the joint stock banks and acted as treasuries for the Government.[107]

Further evidence of the people helping themselves can be seen in the establishment of small-scale manufacturing units in the Sialkot sports goods industry by the Muslim craftsmen who had formerly sold their products to Hindu and Sikh middlemen. By 1951 the export of tennis racquets, hockey sticks and footballs was worth Rs.7 million annually.[108] This was not however the usual pattern for recovery from the economic dislocation brought by Partition, which mainly took the form of refugees reacting to the business opportunities created by the departure of the Hindus and Sikhs. The process was most marked in the cities of Sindh, where *mohajirs* filled the shoes of the non-Muslim commercial elite as the native Sindhis lacked the skills or capital to compete with them. But even in Punjab many industrial enterprises were run by refugees from India.[109]

While *mohajirs* from UP and Bombay stepped into the shoes of the commercial castes, refugees from East Punjab[110] occupied land in the West Punjab Canal Colonies which had been vacated by Sikh landowners. The Lyallpur district's population rose by over 40 per cent, Multan's, Montgomery's and Sheikhupura's by 20 per cent.[111] In the Jaranwala tehsil of the Lyallpur district the ratio of refugees to former landholders was 3:1.[112] The first arrivals found the fields almost ready for harvesting; millet and rice crops provided them with food, while cotton could be sold for cash.

Not all refugees were so fortunate. Many could not fend for themselves but had to rely on government efforts for resettlement and rehabilitation. As with the Indus Waters dispute, technical and executive solutions were preferred to political initiatives with the similar consequence of underscoring the bureaucracy's influence in comparison with democratic processes. Mian Iftikharuddin,[113] the Minister of Refugees and Rehabilita-

107 R. Symonds, *The Making of Pakistan* (Islamabad, 1976) p. 135.

108 Anita M. Weiss, *Culture, Class and Development in Pakistan*, p. 124.

109 Anita Weiss provides evidence of this process at work, for example in Lahore's pharmaceutical and steel re-rolling industries. *Ibid.*, pp. 58-90, pp. 98-107.

110 Around three quarters of all *mohajirs* were Punjabis (4.7 million), of whom two-thirds were agriculturalists. K. Sipe, 'Karachi's Refugee Crisis', p. 86.

111 Summary of the Migrations of 1947-8, n.d., Mudie Papers Mss.Eur.F. 164/47, IOR.

112 *Ibid.*

113 Mian Iftikharuddin (1907-62) came from the wealthy Arain Mian family of Bagh-

tion in the West Punjab Cabinet, in fact pressed for the kind of policies of tenancy reform and redistribution of land which were to be pursued in the resettlement programme in East Punjab. This was only to be expected from a former President of the Punjab Congress who had also been associated at one stage with the Congress Socialist Party. But Iftikharuddin was no maverick. He represented a radical tradition within the Muslim League which was displayed in the November 1944 manifesto of its Punjab branch,[114] in Abul Hashim's rural radicalism in Bengal and in the socialistic slant of the 1945 draft plan of the AIML Planning Committee.[115]

Iftikharuddin called for a 50-acre ceiling on landholdings, the nationalisation of basic industries, the provision of Rs.5 a month for the unemployed and the exchange of refugee property through officially appointed trustees.[116] When the Punjab Premier the Nawab of Mamdot, himself a refugee from East Punjab, refused to countenance these demands, Iftikharuddin sensationally quit his post. His departure brought the organisational and ministerial wings of the Punjab Muslim League virtually to blows.

In the absence of a political lead, the British Governor of the West Punjab, Sir Francis Mudie, left the responsibility for the settlement of refugees on the land with the overworked deputy commissioners and *tehsildars* who acted as Assistant Rehabilitation Commissioners for the areas under their jurisdiction. The deputy commissioners were also responsible for furnishing each refugee camp within their jurisdiction with medical, food and sanitary requirements.[117] Agriculturalist Muslim refugees were rehabilitated on Crown Land in the West Punjab Canal Colonies as well as on land vacated by Hindus and Sikhs.[118]

---

banpura, Lahore. He founded Progressive Papers Ltd, which published the *Pakistan Times*. Following his expulsion from the Muslim League in 1951, he founded the Pakistan National Party which was later merged into the National Awami Party.

[114] D. Gilmartin, *Empire and Islam*, p. 196-7.

[115] See I. Talbot, 'Planning for Pakistan: The Planning Committee of the All-India Muslim League 1943-46,' *Modern Asian Studies*, 28, no. 4 (1994), pp. 875-89.

[116] *Eastern Times* (Lahore), 29 September 1947.

[117] In reality administrative oversight lay with the District Refugee and Evacuee Officer. Each camp possessed its own commandant who was ordered to keep a strict account of numbers, *purdah* considerations notwithstanding.

[118] The governments of East and West Punjab initially agreed on a common response to the problem of abandoned property early in September 1947. They refused to recognise the illegal seizure of property and appointed custodians to oversee evacuees' possessions. They reversed this approach however when it became apparent that the massive transfer of population was permanent. Both governments then introduced ordinances to limit the evacuees' rights to transfer or repossess their property in order to ease the task of rehabilitating the refugees.

Iftikharuddin's radical views were reflected in the June 1949 Report of the Agrarian Committee of the Pakistan Muslim League. This took its cue from a speech by Muhammad Ali Jinnah to the All-India Planning Committee in November 1944 in which he linked the redistribution of wealth with the Islamic concept of justice.[119] The committee urged a ceiling on landownership of 450 acres for unirrigated land and 150 acres for irrigated land as a step towards the 'elimination from our economy of landlordism and all superior but idle interests in land above the actual cultivator'.[120] Such recommendations were naturally regarded as unacceptable by the dominant landholding interests, and the Report was quietly shelved after its acceptance by the Pakistan Muslim League Council.[121] Four and a half decades later, the landholding interests are still able to block the call which the Report made for agricultural income tax.

The failure to introduce tenancy and land reforms in the period 1947-9 ensured that West Punjab followed a vastly different socio-economic and political trajectory than its Indian neighbour. Indeed the unsettled conditions in the aftermath of partition enabled landlords to tighten their grip in Pakistan Punjab. They acquired additional land which they either purchased at rock bottom prices from fleeing Hindus and Sikhs or by 'unlawfully' possessing state evacuee property. In many areas they also replaced the *banias* as the main source of agricultural credit. The important implications for public policy and agricultural performance arising from the continued domination of landlordism in West Punjab is considered in later chapters.

An important key to understanding both the survival of the infant Pakistan state and its democratic growing pains can be found in its early months of existence. On the face of it, those members of the Indian National Congress who expected Pakistan to be still-born had good cause. Few states have sprung into existence with as many material disadvantages, institutional weaknesses and uncertain national loyalty. The refugee problem alone could have suffocated Pakistan at birth. This fate was avoided

---

[119] Talbot, 'Planning for Pakistan', p. 881.

[120] Muhammad Hasan Khan, *Underdevelopment and Agrarian Structure in Pakistan* (Boulder, 1981), p. 139.

[121] It is true that in 1950 and 1952 the Punjab government passed legislation which met the Agrarian Committee's call for greater security for tenants and uncompensated abolition of *jagirs*. But these measures had only a limited scope as, for example, military and religious revenue free grants were exempted in the 1952 Act. Moreover, landlords were able to exploit loopholes in the Punjab Protection and Restoration of Tenancy Rights Act to evict tenants.

thanks to both the resilience of innumerable ordinary men and women and to the organisational capabilities of the civil bureaucracy. Herein however lay the seeds of future problems.

If Pakistan meant anything at all to the masses during the freedom struggle, it had been understood in terms of social and economic transformation and a diffusion of political power. In order for the state to survive its painful delivery its rulers had to draw on another tradition inherited from the colonial era. This emphasised bureaucratic control and the maintenance of the local elites' power, which was seen most clearly in the great missed opportunity for land reform at the time of refugee rehabilitation in West Punjab, an episode which has, remarkably, been overlooked in most standard histories.

The immediate post-Partition era also provides an important key to the future course of Indo-Pakistan relations and the subcontinent's international links. Negative stereotypes of Muslim 'fanaticism' and Hindu 'chauvinism' which developed during the freedom struggle appeared to be borne out to Pakistani and Indian elites during the traumas of 1947-8. The refugee crisis and disputes over the division of assets and the Indus Waters confirmed the view soon to be expressed by Liaquat Ali Khan that the Government of India had never 'wholeheartedly accepted the Partition scheme' and 'was out to destroy' the Pakistan state.[122]

The Kashmir conflict and war with India in 1948-9 provided the defining moment. The armed conflict coming in the wake of Indian military intervention in Junagadh (later confirmed by intervention in Hyderabad and Goa) established an apprehension of an Indian security threat to the Pakistan state which subsequently coloured not only its foreign but domestic policy. Pakistan sought to counterbalance India's greater material resources first by calling on British and later American assistance. But the latter possessed its own agenda for intervention in the South Asia region, leading to eventual strains in its relationship with Pakistan.

Domestically, Pakistan's suspicions of India supported the need for a strong central authority even if this flew in the face of the loose federal structure envisaged by the Lahore Resolution. This in itself took the country further away from the direction of democracy, given the likely effects of centralisation on an ethnically plural society. Moreover, Pakistan was set on the course of dependence on foreign aid and of the diversion of scarce resources to military expenditure in order to overcome its strategic weakness. The growing ascendancy of the civil bureaucracy and the Army over the elected representatives during the 1950s which accompanied this course of action is addressed in the next chapter.

[122] R. Sisson and Leo E. Rose, *War and Secession: Pakistan, India, and the Creation of Bangladesh* (Berkeley, CA, 1990), p. 44.

Part II

THE DESTRUCTION OF PAKISTAN'S DEMOCRACY AND UNITY

5

THE DESTRUCTION OF DEMOCRACY IN PAKISTAN

Why did democracy fail in Pakistan during the period 1947-58? Was it because of the poor institutionalisation of the Muslim League? Did the state's inherited political culture, with its class, regional and gender-related inequalities, present an insuperable barrier to the establishment of a participatory political process? How significant were the country's geopolitical weaknesses in encouraging authoritarianism? These questions have preoccupied all who have studied Pakistan's politics during its turbulent early years.

This chapter attempts to address these complex issues through holding in creative tension the knowledge that the colonial legacy is crucial for understanding Pakistani politics with the belief, as Eduardo Galeano put it, that history 'is each morning born anew.'[1] Before addressing the interplay between both colonial inheritances and post-independence transformations, and national and provincial political frameworks, we should first be aware of the course of events which led to the breakdown of democracy and their various scholarly interpretations.

---

[1] E. Galeano, *Days and Nights of Love and War*, trans. by Judith Brister (New York, 1983), p. 113.

Pakistani politics: processes and perceptions

The first decade of Pakistan's parliamentary politics was marked by abject failure. Interminable constitutional wrangling meant that the state was governed under the 1935 Government of India Act until 1956. By the time the first Pakistani Constitution was ratified in March of that year, the Pakistan Muslim League, the only nation-wide political organisation, had disintegrated and a tradition been established of executive dissolution of both provincial and national governments. Indeed in a judgement with subsequent wide-ranging implications, the Supreme Court legitimised the Governor-General Ghulam Muhammad's dismissal of the first Constituent Assembly in October 1954.[2] In the absence of a nation-wide general election – Pakistan had to wait until 1970 for this democratic landmark – the parliamentary system was unable to put down roots. Prime Ministers moved through the revolving doors of office with increasing rapidity as power slipped from Karachi to army headquarters in Rawalpindi. One of these, the former Bombay businessman I.I. Chundrigar, was to survive scarcely two months from October 1957.

The political and constitutional crises exacerbated the tensions between the provinces and the centre. The latter became increasingly identified with Punjab because of the region's dominance of the two main institutional structures of the state – the Army and the civil bureaucracy. Their senior echelons cast around for ways to deprive the East Bengalis of their democratic majority which, if effectively deployed, would threaten both the foreign policy orientations of Pakistan's 'guardians' and their domestic priorities. The latter placed expenditure on defence and civil administration before social programmes and developmentalist activities. Punjabi landlords, although on occasion at odds with the military-bureaucratic combine, shared its hostility to such Bengali populist parties as the Awami League and Ganatantri Dal with their implied threat of implementing land reform.

The 1956 consolidation of West Pakistan into a One Unit province and its parity with East Pakistan in the National Assembly could thus be understood as an attempt to safeguard the centre from a populist Bengali challenge. Indeed one reading of the causes of Pakistan's first military coup in October 1958 is the need to postpone elections which would have endangered Punjabi class and institutional interests. Such an explanation of the onset of military rule is helpful in that it switches attention away from weaknesses in the political party system, for example factionalism and corruption, and instead focuses attention on the state.

[2] This ruling on the grounds of legal necessity was given following the appeal to the Sindh High Court of the President of the Constituent Assembly, Maulvi Tamizuddin Ahmad that the Governor-General's action be declared unconstitutional.

This is a requirement which, as we shall see below, has been persuasively advocated by Ayesha Jalal. Where it falls down, however, is in its depiction of a monolithic Punjabi interest. Both at this juncture and in more recent times, opponents have been quick to spot a Punjabi conspiracy and to cry foul. While Punjab's political predominance cannot be gainsaid, it is also important to recognise its internal class and regional differentiation. Not all Punjabis shared the military and bureaucratic elites' interests and supported its actions in 1958, nor were all, as is sometimes asserted, to benefit from the Ayub and Zia martial law dispensations.

There exist a variety of purported explanations of Pakistan's democratic failure during this period. The simplest is that put forward by the Ayub regime to justify the 1958 coup, which depicts the politicians as bringing the country to its knees through their misuse of power, corruption and factional intrigue. As illustrated later, the Army as an institution had its own motives for intervention. Nevertheless such a characterisation of the civilian politicians was not merely special pleading. Majid Lahori's poetical satire published in the columns of the Karachi-based daily *Jang* (War) during the 1950s would reveal a similar litany of political corruption. The lack of a popular challenge to the coup is further evidence of the discredited character of parliamentary politics.

Khalid B. Sayeed traces Pakistan's democratic failure back to the early days of Jinnah's Governor-Generalship and his perpetuation of the viceregal system inherited from the Raj.[3] The lively debate concerning his assumption of the role of Governor-General along with that of President of the Constituent Assembly need not detain us here[4] other than to note that it was motivated by a desire to underscore Pakistan's sovereignty and not by vanity.[5] The threat that Mountbatten might pose to this as a joint Governor-General was real rather than imagined. Indeed in a cabinet meeting shortly before Partition he had expressed the opinion that a speedy division of the subcontinent was in India's best interest, because a truncated Pakistan 'if conceded now was bound to come back later'.[6] The fragility of Pakistan's sovereignty was indicated by

[3] K. B. Sayeed, *Pakistan: The Formative Phase*, esp. Chapters 7-10.

[4] See for example, A. Jalal, 'Inheriting the Raj: Jinnah and the Governor-Generalship Issue', *Modern Asian Studies*, 19, no. 1 (February 1985), pp. 29-53. More recently Allen McGrath has commented on the precedent set by the fact that Jinnah's assumption of the office constituted a departure from the dominion practice that the Governor-General should be non-political. McGrath, *The Destruction of Pakistan's Democracy*, pp. 35ff.

[5] The latter claim has been made by Jinnah's detractors especially those close to Mountbatten, who was personally affronted by Jinnah's action. The Quaid-i-Azam no longer trusted the Viceroy and correctly calculated that a common Governor-Generalship in Mountbatten's hands would be inimical to Pakistan's sovereignty.

[6] Cited in McGrath, *The Destruction of Pakistan's Democracy*, pp. 27 and 35ff.

an announcement made as late as March 1948 that Indian banknotes would be legal tender until the coming September and coins until September 1949, although Pakistani currency would not have reciprocal status in India.[7]

By assuming the position, Jinnah undoubtedly created a tradition in which the holder of the highest office in the land would not merely be a constitutional figurehead. A precedent for the dismissal of elected governments was also established, when the Governors of the Frontier and Sindh dismissed the Ministries of Dr Khan Sahib and M.A. Khuhro on 22 August 1947 and 26 April 1948 under Jinnah's express directions. Nevertheless it could be argued that despite his immense prestige as Pakistan's founding father Jinnah never exceeded the limits of his authority as Governor-General laid down by the India Independence Act. Moreover, the strengthening of executive authority in the early months of Pakistan's independence by Jinnah keeping the Evacuation and Refugee Rehabilitation and State and Frontier Regions portfolios under his direct control could be justified as necessary if the state was to function at all.

More adverse criticism has however been directed at the wielding of executive authority by Ghulam Muhammad (Governor-General 1951-5) and Iskander Mirza (President 1956-8).[8] Indeed such writers as M.M. Syed attach the bulk of the responsibility for Pakistan's democratic failure to the 'misfortune' of having such 'seasoned bureaucrats' elevated to positions of authority.[9] Both men certainly possessed profound anti-democratic instincts and by their dismissal of elected governments paved the way, in Mirza's case directly, for the military assumption of power. Allen McGrath has recently added Chief Justice Muhammad Munir to the rogues' gallery.[10] He depicts Munir as possessing an authoritarian

[7] Deputy High Commissioner's Report for East Bengal For the Period Ending 15 March 1948, L/P&J/5/322, IOR.

[8] Mirza was a direct descendant of the 'traitor' of the Battle of Plassey, Mir Jafar. He was the first Indian to graduate from Sandhurst. Iskander Mirza's son Humayn, a retired World Bank executive, is currently attempting to rehabilitate his historical standing. Iskander has rightly been blamed for undermining Pakistan's fragile democracy but he is not solely culpable in this and his reputation was deliberately blackened by Ayub in his autobiography *Friends Not Masters*. Ayub destroyed Iskander's papers and diaries, which helps to account for the absence of a serious study of his career. In Iskander's favour it may be said that he was neither a religious bigot nor corrupt. Unlike Ayub, he did not use public office to accumulate a personal fortune for his family members. See 'Memoirs of a President' I and II (previously unpublished interview of 23 September 1967 between Iskander and M.A.H. Ispahani), *Newsline* (May and June 1996).

[9] M.M. Syed, 'Pakistan: Struggle for Power 1947-58', *Pakistan Journal of History and Culture*, XV, no. 2 (July-December 1994), pp. 85ff.

[10] See especially Chapter 8 of A. McGrath, *The Destruction of Pakistan's Democracy*.

outlook which he had inculcated during the colonial era. This prompted him to provide legitimacy to Ghulam Muhammad's October 1954 dissolution of the Constituent Assembly and to Ayub's later military rule. According to McGrath neither the people of Pakistan through their lack of education, nor the politicians through their alleged ill-discipline and corruption were to blame for the demise of Pakistan's democracy.[11] The responsibility lay with Mirza, Ghulam Muhammad and Munir who provided a legal smokescreen for their authoritarian activities. McGrath brings to light a number of important new insights to the key Tamizuddin Khan case arising from the dissolution of the Constituent Assembly – not least the subterfuge required to bring the petition to court which involved a junior attorney disguising himself as a *burqa* clad woman[12] and the extent to which the case revolved around British legal discussion and precedent.[13] Nevertheless, by focusing on the role of individuals, McGrath like Syed and others has ignored the wider failings of the political system.

Safdar Mahmood has linked Pakistan's weak parliamentary politics directly with the decline of the Muslim League.[14] He cites among other factors the League's corruption, institutional weakness and the dominance of landlord interests. As we have already noted these features can all be traced back to the freedom struggle. The League's failure to evolve as an institutional pillar of the Pakistan state contrasts dramatically with the role played by Congress in Indian politics in the early post-independence era. A number of writers would have us believe that the absence of mass Muslim League support during the freedom struggle is at the root of the different experiences in the two states, but the historical reality is somewhat more complex. Similarly, it is not just a case of executive encroachment on legislative authority as a result of the filling of a 'power vacuum' created by the weak institutional moorings of the Muslim League and other political parties.

Ayesha Jalal has convincingly depicted the contradictions between the requirements of state consolidation and political participation in Pakistan's early years.[15] The state's pressing financial problems and

[11] *Ibid.*, pp. 218ff.

[12] *Ibid.*, p. 158.

[13] Much of the legal argument centred around the issue of the presence of a Crown prerogative and whether this gave the Governor-General the right to assent to all of the Constituent Assembly's legislation. McGrath has emphasised the previously ignored role of the British constitutional expert Sir Ivor Jennings in preparing the federal government's case. *Ibid.*, pp. 160ff.

[14] S. Mahmood, 'Decline of the Pakistan Muslim League and Its Implications (1947-54)', *Pakistan Journal of History and Culture* 15, no. 2 (July-December 1994), pp. 63-84.

[15] This is the major theme of *The State of Martial Rule*.

strategic insecurities are portrayed as working against the decentralisation of resources and authority which would have enabled the Pakistan Muslim League to secure popular bases of support. In these circumstances it suffered from 'benign neglect', its decay further strengthning the state's reliance on the Army and bureaucracy for the exercise of authority. Another consequence was the intensification of conflict between the centre and the provinces, as with the demise of the League went the 'only potential political vehicle linking the central leadership and the provincial, district and local levels of society'.[16] Jalal concludes her analysis of the background to the 1958 coup by maintaining that the political processes in the provinces had been curbed, but not entirely crushed during the consolidation of state authority around its non-elected institutions. The Army stepped in to counter the threats which still remained on the eve of national elections.[17] In other words, while the politicians' chaotic behaviour, ill-discipline and corruption may have brought the patient into a state of parlous health, the bureaucrats and generals assisted the death of Pakistan's democracy.

Yunas Samad explains the political failures of the post-independence decade not so much in terms of the decay of the Pakistan Muslim League as the resurgence of 'centrifugal' forces following the temporary unity at the closing stages of the freedom struggle. Heavy-handed attempts at centralisation by the state encouraged their re-emergence, although they were rooted in the encouragement of 'provincialism' by the colonial state. Samad, like Jalal, draws attention to the boost which the bureaucracy and army axis received from US support. This he believes was 'crucial' when Ghulam Muhammad dissolved the Constituent Assembly on 24 October 1954, and 'provided...the necessary means to subdue the op- position and tilt the equilibrium in the centre's favour'.[18] Ashok Kapur similarly links domestic political developments with Pakistan's external relations. He claims that immediately after independence Jinnah cast around for an international patron to provide the same kind of protection as the British had offered the Indian Muslims against Congress in domes- tic politics.[19] Far nearer the truth than this jaundiced view of the Muslim League as a 'creature' party is an analysis rooted in Pakistan's strategic imperatives and in the fact that the United States appeared to be the only source of military assistance following the cooling of Anglo-Pakistani relations over the Kashmir issue.[20] This formed part of the background

---

16 *Ibid.*, p. 297.

17 *Ibid.*, pp. 299ff.

18 Samad, *A Nation in Turmoil*, p. 169.

19 Ashok Kapur, *Pakistan in Crisis*, p. 27.

20 This was rooted both in criticisms of Britain's 'even-handedness' in the dispute and

to the campaign in 1949 to oust Sir Francis Mudie as Governor of Punjab.

Samad, Jalal and M. Rafique Afzal[21] all point to the existence of Punjabi and Bengali factions within the cabinet ever since Liaquat's Premiership. The Bengalis who were led successively by Khwaja Shahabuddin and Khwaja Nazimuddin were religiously more conservative and at best ambivalent towards the pro-US foreign policy advocated by the Punjabi coterie which included the Ahmadi Foreign Secretary Zafrullah Khan and the Governor-General Ghulam Muhammad. The dismissal of Nazimuddin's cabinet in the wake of the 1954 Punjab disturbances marked an important stage on the road to direct military rule. Afzal and Samad point out that the thunder of the anti-Ahmadi disturbances should not detract attention from the foreign policy disputes within the Cabinet and the significant fact that before Nazimuddin was dumped both the Governor-General and the Commander-in-Chief, General Ayub Khan, had entered into discussions with high-ranking US officials concerning military assistance and security arrangements.[22]

Whatever the explanation for the Pakistan Muslim League's demise, authors are agreed on its major signposts: the February 1948 Pakistan Muslim League Council decision to separate the party from the government by debarring ministers from holding any office within it;[23] the assassination of Liaquat Ali Khan in October 1951 as he was on the point of reactivating the party;[24] the defeat of the Muslim League in Pakistan's first general elections in East Pakistan in the spring of 1954;[25] the influx of its West Punjab landlord supporters to the Republican Party following its establishment as a 'pet' of the bureaucracy in May 1956;[26] and finally the resignation of the bureaucrat turned Prime Min-

---

the unwillingness of the British Commander-in-Chief General Gracey to carry out Jinnah's orders and commit troops to the Kashmir Valley in October 1947.

21 M. Rafique Afzal, 'Nazimuddin Ministry: Reasons for its Dismissal', *Pakistan Journal of History and Culture*, 15, no. 2 (July-December 1994), pp. 47-62.

22 *Ibid.*, p. 57.

23 Jalal maintains that Jinnah's decision not to wear the hats of both Governor-General and President of the Pakistan Muslim League left the 'one party capable of claiming a nationwide basis of support out...in the cold'. Jalal, *The State of Martial Rule*, p. 61.

24 Liaquat reactivated the links between the party and government symbolising this move by his election as Muslim League President in October 1950.

25 Muslim League representation was reduced to a mere 10/309 Assembly seats. It never recovered from this blow to its prestige not only in East Pakistan but at the centre.

26 The party was built on the shifting sands of factionalism and intrigue. West Punjab landlords like Firoz Khan Noon deserted the Muslim League to join the Republican bandwagon, just as they had earlier ditched the Unionists.

ister, Chaudhri Muhammad Ali the following September as it signalled the end of a Muslim League government presence at both the centre and the provinces.

Recent research thus underlines the importance of understanding the decline of Pakistan's parliamentary system not just in terms of corruption, chaos and social disorder. It was in fact rooted far more complexly in the bureaucratic traditions[27] and political culture inherited from the colonial era and in the centralising solutions which accompanied the construction of the state in a context of financial constraint and strategic insecurity. In these circumstances the Punjabi prescription for domestic and foreign policy orientation triumphed over the more populist Bengali initiatives. The new dispensation had not however secured a hegemonic control on the eve of promised national elections. The army moved into power to safeguard its institutional interests which it had long projected as being identical to the nation's. It is important to keep this analytical framework clearly in view as we turn in the following sections to the complex and confused interplay of events in the arenas of national and provincial politics. While the focus is on developments at the national level it is also important to recognise that the provinces remained the liveliest political arenas throughout the post-independence decade.

The bewildering switches in their governments reflected the predominance of opportunist landlord groups in West Pakistan and the ideological flux in the eastern wing. Another cause of the incoherence was the intervention by the centre as it sought to exert some semblance of control by bolstering groups amenable to its interests. The influence was not simply one-way as political changes in the provinces could undermine weak national governments in Karachi. Similarly, politicians with strong provincial power bases such as Suhrawardy and Abdul Qaiyum sought to cash in on this by attempting to establish themselves at the centre. Increasingly the provinces' ability to act as checks on the growth of the latter's power was eroded. The emergency powers in the 1935 Government of India Act (Section 93) which made possible the suppression of provincial ministries were re-enacted from Liaquat's time onwards under Section 92A. This was first deployed against the Mamdot Ministry in Punjab.[28]

In addition to this viceregal legacy, it is important to note the continuities with the colonial era. Not only are many of the *dramatis personae*

---

[27] I. A. Rehman has argued that Mirza's attitudes were forged for example during his years as a political agent in the tribal areas of the NWFP during the Raj. He thereafter viewed the population as 'half-subjects who had to be kept away from mischief' and treated their political leaders as 'tribal maliks'. I. A. Rehman, 'Damned by History', *Newsline* (May 1996), p. 129.

[28] A. McGrath, *The Destruction of Pakistan's Democracy*, pp. 147ff.

the same, for example, Nazimuddin, Suhrawardy, Daultana, Mamdot, but politics tended to run along the tracks laid down in this period. There was a continuation for example of the tensions between the organisational and ministerial wings of the Muslim League. Following the mass mobilisations of 1946-7, Punjab politics reverted to the traditional pattern of landlord dominance. The factional rivalries amongst the rural elite which had split asunder the Unionist Party re-emerged in its Muslim League successor shortly after independence. The personal rivalries between Mian Mumtaz Daultana, the Finance Minister, and Nawab Iftikhar Hussain of Mamdot, the Prime Minister, dominated the early months of freedom and paved the way, along with the need to resolve the refugee problem, for the centre's intervention in Punjab affairs. Mamdot increasingly cultivated the religious groups and posed as the upholder of Punjabi autonomy, while the more progressive Daultana became known as the centre's man. This was demonstrated most clearly in the support which he received from Liaquat at the time of the 1951 provincial elections.

Other persisting provincial political features include the faction-ridden politics of Sindh and the tensions in East Bengal between the conservative Urdu-speaking Khwaja group and populist Bengali-speaking rivals. The British Deputy High Commissioner, who had been following the Muslim League struggle, closely depicted this in terms of personalised rivalries. In reality the outcome represented a much more profound shift in power from the Bengali-speaking leaders who were rooted in the countryside to the urban *ashraf* (gentry) Urdu-speaking elite, who had close ties with the national leadership in Karachi and shared its attachment to a one nation, one culture policy.

The centre was anxious to have what it saw as loyal allies controlling the East Bengal Muslim League because of the mounting public controversy over the language issue. The Constituent Assembly's rejection of Bengali as a state language coupled with the refusal to hold sessions in Dhaka led to growing protests. Another source of discontent involved the posting of large numbers of Punjabi officials to East Pakistan. At street level the economic dislocation arising from the cessation of trade with West Bengal was another source of anti-centre sentiment.

The national political elite refused from the outset to accord any legitimacy to Bengali grievances. They were at best dismissed as inspired by misguided provincialism, at worst they were seen as evidence of the existence of an Indian fifth column in Dhaka. These sentiments were expressed as early as January 1948, during a tour by the Federal Communications Minister Abdur Rab Nishtar. 'Regional patriotism [is] simply repugnant to Islam,' he declared to a gathering at Parbatipar; 'Pakistan was established on the basis that Muslims were one nation and the tendency to think in terms of Bengali,

Punjabi and Bihari would undermine the very foundations of Pakistan. [...] These disruptive ideas (are) being spread by enemies of Pakistan who [are] working as fifth columnists amongst the Muslims.'[29] The pursuit of this Pakistanisation programme was however to continuously undermine the process of nation building it was designed to serve. A minor example was provided in July 1948 when protests forced the Director of Broadcasting to end the highly unpopular practice of introducing Arabic and Persian words and phrases into the Bengali news bulletins of Radio Pakistan Dhaka.[30]

The One Unit Scheme (the merging of Punjab, Sindh, Balochistan and the Frontier in the West Pakistan province) invariably created centre-province tensions. These were most acute in Sindh where opposition was led by Hyder Baksh Jatoi. There was surprisingly less opposition in the Frontier despite the colonial legacy of a well-developed Pakhtun political consciousness. An important reason for this was the co-option of Dr Khan Sahib at the centre, which muted the opposition of Abdul Ghaffar Khan and his followers. Moreover, the so-called Daultana Memorandum falsely held out the prospect that the capital of a West Pakistan Province would be situated in the Frontier.

The formative phase, 1947-51

The Constituent Assembly was in theory a crucial cog in the political process at the centre. The national cabinet was responsible to it and it was empowered to act as both a legislature and constitution-making body. It also possessed the authority to restrict the Governor-General's powers. In reality authority lay in descending order with the Governor-General, the Prime Minister and the central cabinet. The Assembly's muted legislative role was seen in the frequent recourse to rule by ordinance. This procedure had its legitimisation in the 1935 Government of India Act which served in an amended form as Pakistan's constitution. The Constituent Assembly's delay in coming up with a replacement[31] because of conflicting interpretations of the role of Islam and the conflicting political interests of the eastern and western wings of the country[32] further undermined its standing. This was also diminished by its un-

---

[29] Deputy High Commissioner's Report for East Bengal, 12-18 January 1948, L/P&J/5/322, IOR.

[30] Deputy High Commissioner's Report for East Bengal, Period Ending 11 July 1948, L/P&J/5/322, IOR.

[31] Its Indian counterpart had adopted a constitution by November 1949 which came into operation the following January.

[32] Bengalis sought a majority in both the proposed Upper and Lower Houses. There was considerable opposition in East Pakistan to the proposals of the Interim Report which denied this power.

representative character – its members were not directly elected but had gained their seats by way of the 1946 provincial Indian elections.[33] The deference of the Assembly members to Jinnah as Pakistan's founding father was witnessed in their voting him the title of Legal Guide to the constitution-making process in addition to his role as President of the Legislature.

Many of the pressing problems which enabled the executive to establish its supremacy over the legislature have already been examined in this and the preceding chapter. What is of note here is that the ailing Jinnah was the mainstay of the new state throughout its first year of existence. Just as during the freedom struggle factional disputes in the local Leagues were referred to him for arbitration. Moreover, even though the Constituent Assembly in May 1948 had resolved that Karachi should be made the federal capital, the Sindh Muslim League Party only accepted it after a deputation had journeyed to Ziarat to seek Jinnah's views.[34] The central cabinet was even more docile than the Working Committee of the AIML had formerly been. Its members were not only hand-picked by the *Quaid*, but he chaired their meetings and was authorised to overrule their decisions.

One should not, however, blame Jinnah for Pakistan's subsequent authoritarianism. In numerous speeches and statements he always insisted that Pakistan should be a progressive democracy based on the concepts of brotherhood, fraternity and equality. 'Pakistan is now a sovereign state, absolute and unfettered, and the Government of Pakistan is in the hands of the people,' he declared to a gathering of civil bureaucrats at Sibi in Balochistan on 14 February 1948. 'Until we finally frame our constitution, which of course can only be done by the Constituent Assembly, our present provisional constitution based on the fundamental principles of democracy not bureaucracy or autocracy or dictatorship, must be worked.'[35] In a similar vein, when addressing East Pakistan officers at Chittagong the following month he declared: 'Those days have gone when the country was ruled by the bureaucracy. It is people's government, responsible to the people more or less on democratic lines and parliamentary practices.'[36]

---

[33] In addition there were 6 refugee seats. At the provincial level, 7 refugee seats were added for Sindh. MLAs from East Punjab took up their seats in the West Punjab Assembly.

[34] Sayeed, *Pakistan: The Formative Phase, 1857-1948*, p. 269.

[35] 'High or Low – We are all Servants of the State', address to a gathering of the Civil Officers of Balochistan of the rank of Naib-Tehsildars and above at Sibi, February 14, 1948. *Quaid-i-Azam Muhammad Ali Jinnah: Speeches and Statements, 1947-48* (Karachi 1989), p. 143.

[36] 'Do Your Duty as Servants: Advice to Officers', address to the Gazetted Officers at Chittagong, March 25, 1948. *Ibid.*, p. 198.

Not only would the people be sovereign, but Jinnah also expressed the belief that there should be equal citizenship rights for all regardless of religion. This sentiment, which has proved so uncomfortable for those seeking to transform Pakistan into a theocracy, was stated unequivocally in Jinnah's inaugural address to the Constituent Assembly:

> 'We are starting with this fundamental principle that we are all citizens and equal citizens of one State. [...] Now I think we should keep that in front of us as our ideal and you will find that in course of time Hindus would cease to be Hindus and Muslims would cease to be Muslims, not in the religious sense, because that is the personal faith of each individual, but in the political sense as citizens of the State.'[37]

Jinnah's death at the age of seventy-one on 12 September 1948 shocked the nation and marked the passing of an epoch in Indian Muslim history. The day after the *Quaid's* burial, India invaded the Muslim-ruled princely state of Hyderabad, heaping yet another problem on his successors. The post of Governor-General fell to the East Bengal Chief Minister, Khwaja Nazimuddin. Liaquat continued as Prime Minster, while Tamizuddin Khan became President of the Constituent Assembly.

Liaquat was a respected if uncharismatic Prime Minister who was to stand head and shoulders above most of his successors. While he continued the centralisation of power which had begun in Pakistan's early months of independence, he also made some moves in the direction of reinvigorating the Muslim League organisation. It could be argued however that in the long run, by simultaneously holding the offices of Prime Minister and Muslim League President, he encouraged the League to be seen as nothing more than a handmaiden of the government.[38] Liaquat's legacy was damaging for democracy also because he reinforced the intolerant attitudes, seen in the attacks on the Punjab Unionists, which had grown up in the political culture of the Pakistan movement. He denounced such political opponents as H.S. Suhrawardy and Maulana Abdul Hamid Khan Bhashani as 'dogs let loose by the enemies of Pakistan.'[39] Opposition to the Muslim League continued to be equated with hostility to Pakistan.[40]

Liaquat's low estimation of Pakistan's politicians was revealed in the introduction early in 1949 of the PRODA. It laid down a penalty

---

[37] Presidential Address to the Constituent Assembly of Pakistan at Karachi: August 11, 1947. *Ibid.*, pp. 46-7.

[38] McGrath, *The Destruction of Pakistan's Democracy*, p. 67.

[39] Cited in T. M. Murshid, *The Sacred and the Secular: Bengal Muslim Discourses, 1871-1977* (Calcutta, 1995), p. 346.

[40] McGrath, *The Destruction of Pakistan's Democracy*, p. 67.

of ten years disqualification from public office for such offences as nepotism, bribery and corruption. Charges could be initiated against ministers and ordinary Assembly members not only by the Governor-General and provincial Governors, but by any citizen who could afford the Rs. 5,000 security.[41] By creating categories of political crimes which would be tried by tribunals whose judges would be appointed at the Governor-General's or provincial Governor's discretion, the PRODA statute contributed to the Pakistan state's creeping authoritarianism. Moreover, it was a further distraction from the pressing tasks of constitution making and socio-economic reform legislation. In the bear-pit of provincial political life, factional rivals frequently filed false PRODA charges against their opponents.

More positively, Liaquat oversaw the Pakistanisation of the higher echelons of the army, although Ayub Khan's taking over the mantle of Commander-in-Chief in January 1951 was to have unforeseen long-term consequences. He also underscored Pakistan's independence when he sanctioned the decision[42] to refuse to join other members of the Sterling Area, including India, in devaluing their currencies against the US dollar in September 1949.[43] As the Indian rupee floated downwards against Pakistan's currency, New Delhi retaliated by ceasing all trade and thus ending the common market which had existed between the two dominions since August 1947. Pakistan was faced with the twin problems of finding new sources for many of its consumer goods and paying for them with foreign exchange. The onset of the Korean war induced a commodity boom for Pakistan's exports[44] of jute, cotton and leather goods which provided the wherewithal for the new imports until the bubble burst in 1953.

With the exception of Ayesha Jalal, few scholars have written about the impact of non-devaluation on the eastern wing. The jute trade which until 1949 was still closely tied to India was adversely affected, despite the establishment of a Jute Board in October to support the growers' prices. The resulting recession in East Pakistan fed into existing political discontent and further embittered the relations between the two wings. The economic disparity between them at the time of independence[45]

---

41 *Ibid.*, pp. 149ff.

42 This course of action was advocated by Fazlur Rahman, the Minister of Commerce.

43 The rupee was eventually devalued in 1955.

44 The value of exports soared from $171 million in 1949-50 to $406 million in 1950-1. S.J. Burki, 'The Management of Crises' in W. E. James and S. Roy (eds), *Foundations of Pakistan's Political Economy*, p. 122.

45 This can be gauged from levels of per capita income which stood at Rs.330 in West Pakistan to Rs.305 in the eastern wing. Other indicators were rates of urbanisation and the number of factory units where the gap was considerably larger. *Ibid.*, p. 30.

widened during the first decade as industrial production and infrastructural development in West Pakistan outpaced that in the east. Manufacturing output for example grew at an annual rate of 21 per cent in East Pakistan during the period 1949-50 to 1954-5 compared with 34 per cent in West Pakistan.[46] There were a number of complex factors behind this, including the effects of placing the federal capital in the western wing, the dynamism brought to its economy by migrant entrepreneurs and the greater foreign capital investment in West Pakistan. But far more obvious to Bengali critics were the disparities in the governmental loans and grants between East and West Pakistan. Central government developmental outlay stood at Rs.172 *crore* (ten million) for East Pakistan during the period 1947-8 to 1960-1 compared with Rs.430 *crore* for the western wing.[47] The greatest criticism, however, was reserved for the transfer of resources from east to west through the diversion of foreign exchange earnings.[48] This evidence for internal colonialism was to feed into demands for political autonomy and, ultimately, separatism.

Indo-Pakistan relations were bedevilled not only by the trade issue but also the ongoing Kashmir dispute. On the first of what were to be a number of occasions, the two countries appeared on the brink of war in July 1951. In a celebrated gesture, Liaquat appeared before a huge procession in Karachi and raised his fist in the air in what became a symbol of national defiance. The Kashmir impasse was a key factor behind the attempted coup of Major-General Akbar Khan a few months earlier.[49] Members of the Central Committee of the Communist Party of Pakistan (CPP)[50] were also implicated in what became known as the Rawalpindi Conspiracy Case. The secrecy surrounding the tribunal which tried the eleven accused and the subsequent crackdown not just on the CPP but on trade unions and prominent writers such as Faiz Ahmad Faiz has led Ayesha Jalal to declare that the episode marked an important landmark in the 'metamorphosis' of Pakistan into 'a veritable intellectual wasteland'.[51]

The Objectives Resolution was another 'legacy' of Liaquat's Premiership. He had moved the resolution in the Constituent Assembly on

[46] G. F. Papanek, *Pakistan's Development: Social Goals and Private Incentives* (Cambridge, MA, 1967), p. 20.

[47] R. Jahan, *Pakistan: Failure in National Integration* (New York, 1972), p. 34.

[48] *Ibid.*, pp. 35ff.

[49] He had earlier fought in Kashmir and believed that a military government would be able to resolve the deadlock by the use of force.

[50] The CPP had been set up the year before following a decision by the Communist Party of India.

[51] Jalal, *The State of Martial Rule*, p. 123.

7 March 1949 and it had been adopted five days later after one of the few outstanding debates in the chamber's history. It embodied the main principles on which a future constitution should be based and was to subsequently form its preamble. The principles laid down in the resolution included democracy, independence of the judiciary, freedom, equality, tolerance, Islamic social justice and the rights of minorities to practise their religion and develop their culture. Many have subsequently been honoured more in the breach than the observance. The next stage in constitution making, the publication of the basic principles committee's report in October 1950, became mired in controversy mainly because of Bengali opposition to the denial of their demographic majority. No further progress had been made by the time Liaquat was assassinated while addressing a Muslim League meeting at Rawalpindi on 16 October 1951.

As with the fateful occurrence in Dallas a decade later, a series of official investigations have not dispelled the conspiracy theses which surround the assassination. These have been fuelled by the fact that the Afghan assailant Said Akbar was a former intelligence agent. His earlier British paymasters have been implicated, as have Pakistan's own intelligence agencies. The alleged motive is Liaquat's consideration of a shift away from a pro-Western foreign policy orientation in the Middle East. Earlier in October, Raja Ghazanfar Ali Khan, Pakistan's ambassador in Iran had received instructions to sound out the possibility of cooperation with both Iran and Egypt.[52]

Liaquat's reported final words, 'God shall protect Pakistan',[53] were in keeping with his lifetime's devotion to the Indian Muslim cause. Appropriately the *mohajir*-dominated northern Karachi suburb of Laluk-het was renamed Liaquatabad in 1951. Like Jinnah he compensated for the lack of a local power-base in Pakistan by his moral authority. This was reflected in the title *Quaid-i-Millat* which was based on a reputation for honesty and duty. These characteristics were conspicuously absent in many of his political successors. Liaquat's reputation has subsequently grown with the passage of time. With his removal from the stage, Pakistan's national politics entered a chaotic period during which the bureaucrats were increasingly transformed from the state's servants to its masters.

The collapse of democracy, 1951-58

In the highly secretive game of 'musical chairs' which followed Liaquat's death, disregarding all constitutional convention, the music stopped

---

[52] Syed Nur Ahmad, *From Martial Law to Martial Law: Politics in the Punjab, 1919-1958* (Boulder, CO, 1985), p. 310.

[53] *Ibid.*, 311.

with Khwaja Nazimuddin transferred from the Governor-General's seat to Prime Minister's. In a portentous move for the future, the former bureaucrat and Finance Minister, the ailing Ghulam Muhammad became Pakistan's third Governor-General. He was an intelligent, ruthless and highly ambitious individual who had established his bureaucratic reputation through financial expertise. Like Jinnah he was to use the office of Governor-General to assume an active political role. However the exceptional circumstances which could have justified such a course of action no longer existed.

Khwaja Nazimuddin was a pious but vacillating and indolent figure. During his two-year tenure of office the Muslim League further atrophied, and although he was a Bengali, tensions between the eastern and western wings of the country intensified. To make matters worse the divisions between the so-called Punjabi and Bengali groups at the centre widened at a time of growing disorder in the provinces. This unrest was the product both of heavy handed centralisation and the widespread economic discontent arising from the collapse of the Korean war export boom. Ghulam Muhammad was thus able to cite the Nazimuddin ministry's inadequacy in grappling 'with the difficulties facing the country' when he summarily dismissed his Premier on 17 April 1953. Just a few days earlier Nazimuddin had confirmed that he still commanded a majority in the legislature by successfully steering the budget through the Constituent Assembly.

Khwaja Nazimuddin was so eager to become the President of the Pakistan Muslim League that he secured an amendment to its constitution which would have disqualified his seeking election to the office.[54] Once installed he failed dismally in his duties. Given his pre-independence record of hostility to Abul Hashim's efforts to breathe life into the Bengal Muslim League, it was of course hardly to be expected that he would galvanise the organisation into action. As things turned out, he was never able to establish a properly functioning Working Committee, nor to impose his will in the factional disputes of the provincial branches. Indeed, Muhammad Ayub Khuhro the Sindh President openly flouted his authority and obtained restraining orders from the Sindh High Court when the party President attempted to expel him.[55] The institutional basis of the League was further undermined when at its October 1952 Dhaka meeting over which Khwaja Nazimuddin presided, an amendment removed the constitutional provision for the annual election of office bearers. Unsurprisingly

---

[54] The constitution laid down that a candidate seeking election as President should be a member of least a year's standing. Nazimuddin as Governor-General had not been a member of the party.

[55] M. Rafique Afzal, 'Nazimuddin Ministry', p. 59.

when Nazimuddin needed the League's political support against Ghulam Muhammad's executive action, it was supine.

Although he owed office in part to his Bengali background, Khwaja Nazimuddin distanced himself from those groups in the country's eastern wing who were campaigning on the platform of greater autonomy. It will be recalled that during the freedom struggle he had been associated with the Urdu-speaking *ashraf* elite against whom Fazlul Haq had pitched the interests of the Bengali speaking *jotedars*. Nazimuddin's cavalier handling of the sensitive language issue during a visit to Dacca in January 1952 provoked a province-wide strike in which a number of demonstrators were killed. The episode consigned the Muslim League to oblivion in Pakistan's most populous province.

Despite Nazimuddin's reputation in his home province for being in the vanguard of those who wanted to 'de-Bengalise' the Bengalis, in the federal cabinet he led the Bengali faction. By the time of his Premiership, however, the rival Punjabi grouping could call on the increasingly powerful triumvirate of Ghulam Muhammad, General Ayub Khan (Commander-in-Chief) and Iskander Mirza (Defence Secretary). The fact that neither Ayub nor Mirza was a Punjabi highlights the point that the factions were rooted far more in foreign policy differences than in ethnic allegiances. Their divisions increasingly crystallised around whether Pakistan should pursue a pan-Islamic foreign policy or enter a Cold War driven regional defence organisation sponsored by the USA. Nazimuddin's reluctance to embrace the latter course of action undoubtedly played a part in his dismissal.

His position was further undermined by the growing disorder in the provinces. This occurred to the background of food shortages, unemployment and inflation which accompanied the petering out of the Korean war boom. As we shall see later in this chapter, there is strong evidence that the Punjab Prime Minister Mian Mumtaz Daultana viewed the anti-Ahmadi movement as a useful distraction from this deteriorating economic situation. Although his masterly inactivity created the circumstances in which martial law had to be imposed in March 1953, Nazimuddin's opponents at the centre, led by Ghulam Muhammad, seized on the crisis as a pretext for his dismissal. Nazimuddin had certainly acted indecisively concerning the anti-Ahmadi movement, no doubt because of his close association with the '*ulama*. His predecessor Liaquat would have responded differently, but given Nazimuddin's diminished authority and his obstruction of the Punjabi group's foreign policy orientations, it is in any case unlikely that his ministry would have continued much longer.

Nazimuddin's lack of guile was evident to the end: on his dismissal he sought to telephone the Queen in London to advise the removal of Ghulam Muhammad as Pakistan's Governor-General. He was then shocked to find that his telephone was cut off and the official residence was surrounded by police.[56] Nazimuddin's status and the diminished authority of the Muslim League were brutally demonstrated by the deafening silence which greeted the Governor-General's action. The American Ambassador inexactly but portentously described it as 'one of the most popular coups in history'.[57]

The facade of a parliamentary system was to survive for five more years, but its heart had already been cut out. Real power now lay with Iskander Mirza, Ayub Khan and an increasingly ill Ghulam Muhammad. Pakistan's next Prime Minister, Muhammad Ali Bogra, was also a Bengali, thereby continuing the fiction that the eastern wing wielded influence at the centre. Unlike Nazimuddin, he had played little part in pre-independence politics and was generally regarded as a nonentity – this was probably a recommendation as far as Ghulam Muhammad was concerned. More importantly however, Bogra had been selected because of the pro-American sympathies which he had displayed during his successful tenure as Ambassador in Washington. He in fact immediately came up trumps in securing wheat aid from the US. Army headquarters now looked to military assistance but, by the time this arrived in April 1954, the Muslim League had been routed in the East Bengal elections and its old opponent Fazlul Haq was in the ministerial saddle. The ensuing labour unrest and observation of an 'anti-US-Pakistan Military Pact day' by the United Front Government brought the expected riposte from Ghulam Muhammad. Mirza was now appointed as Governor to directly rule East Bengal. This turn of events undermined Bogra's authority, particularly as he had controversially agreed to the status of Bengali as a national language in a futile attempt to shore up the Muslim League's position in advance of the elections. The Prime Minister's stock had in fact already fallen after his August 1953 minuet with Nehru around the Kashmir issue. The final stages of the constitution making process however provided one more opportunity to escape the noose which was tightening around his neck.

Bogra accepted the amendments produced by Nazimuddin, Fazlur Rahman and other East Bengali leaders which if enacted would have stripped the Governor-General of his power to dismiss the cabinet and nullified the use of PRODA proceedings against politicians. Punjabi politicians however rallied behind the Governor-General who, after consultation with the Chief Justice of the Supreme Court on 24 October 1954, declared an emergency and simultaneously dismissed the cabinet

---

56 McGrath, *The Destruction of Pakistan's Democracy*, p. 95.

57 *Ibid.*, p. 97.

and the Constituent Assembly. Bogra was retained as Prime Minister, after he had consented to the dissolution of the Constituent Assembly, in the new 'cabinet of talents' which barely served as a fig leaf for the 'constitutional dictatorship'. Ayub Khan and Mirza respectively held the important defence and interior posts, while the trusted administrator Chaudhri Muhammad Ali continued as Finance Minister. The only surprise was that Dr Khan Sahib, the pre-independence Congress Premier of the Frontier, entered the cabinet.

In advance of the creation of a second Constituent Assembly through indirect election by the provincial legislatures, Bogra lifted the imposition of Governor's rule in East Bengal. He also lent his support to the growing chorus for the merging of the West Pakistan provinces in the One Unit Scheme. This idea had been mooted for a number of years, despite opposition in the non-Punjabi provinces. The proposal was now to be steam-rolled into existence[58] with the primary aim of forestalling any future Bengali domination at the centre in the wake of nation-wide elections. Dr Khan Sahib whose career had been rehabilitated by his uncompromising support for the One Unit Scheme became the first Prime Minister of the new West Pakistan province on 14 August 1955. When the Muslim League displayed unwillingness to cooperate with a former opponent, Mirza encouraged the formation of the Republican Party as an official supporters club.[59] Just two months later Bogra was unseated at the centre not as a result of the tensions arising from the final lap of constitution making, but because he opposed Mirza's replacing the ailing Ghulam Muhammad as interim Governor-General.

If Bogra was a political nonentity, Chaudri Muhammad Ali was a civil servant who became Prime Minister in October 1955 without any political pretensions. His elevation thus marked, in the words of the British High Commissioner, a 'deplorable' departure from the established parliamentary norms.[60] It fell to Chaudhri Muhammad Ali to oversee the protracted negotiations which culminated in the approval of the Constitution Bill on 29 February 1956. When the new Islamic Republic of Pakistan came into existence shortly afterwards, Iskandar Mirza took the post of President. The office's wide-ranging executive

---

[58] There was such widespread opposition in Balochistan that the central government had to send in troops to maintain order. See Fayyaz Ahmad Hussain, 'The Problem of Federalism and Regional Autonomy in Pakistan', unpubl. M.Phil. thesis, London School of Economics, 1989, p. 101.

[59] Mirza's later version of events however was that Dr Khan Sahib had taken the initiative on Nawab Gurmani's prompting and that he had no hand in this and was personally against the fragmentation of the Muslim League. 'Memoirs of a President, I', *Newsline* (May 1996), p. 132.

[60] Cited in Jalal, *The State of Martial Rule*, p. 227.

authority[61] contradicted those elements in the constitution which reflected the Westminster model with its emphasis on the requirement of the Prime Minister to command a majority of the 310 strong National Assembly, elected on the basis of parity between the western and eastern provinces. Mirza had already proven that he would not hesitate to use such executive authority to enforce his will on the political process. Similarly the latitude given to the President in the use of his emergency powers under Articles 191, 193 and 194 conflicted with the constitution's federal principles. These were further undermined by the financial and administrative arrangements.[62]

The promised elections to the National Assembly were in fact never to take place, partly because of the delays concerning the issue of whether or not there were to be joint or separate electorates – the former were the preferred option of the eastern wing. The Constituent Assembly limped along instead for two years as an interim National Assembly. Mirza put it out of its misery on 7 October 1958 when he abrogated the constitution and proclaimed martial law throughout Pakistan.

The prospects for democratic stabilisation had looked uncertain from the outset of the new constitution given Chaudhri Muhammad Ali's reluctant approach to politics. The formation of an Awami League government in Dhaka in August 1956 was the immediate cause of his undermining. But his Republican, Muslim League and United Front government had been teetering on the brink of collapse for some time. Its demise in September following Chaudhri Muhammad Ali's breakdown paved the way for the assumption to power of democracy's last best hope, the experienced Bengali leader Husain Shaheed Suhrawardy. He was a cultivated, subtle and resilient politician whose cosmopolitan interests extended to ballroom dancing. Although much more clearly 'provincialist' than his Bengali predecessors as national Premier, the responsibilities of office forced him into compromises which undermined his regional power base. This ultimately rendered him dispensable in the minds of the centrists in the bureaucracy.

Indicative of the tightrope which Suhrawardy had to walk was the vexed issue of separate versus joint electorates. His eventual compromise that in the western wing separate electorates should be implemented, but in the east, joint electorates could be operated pleased no one, except Mirza who had helped pull the irons out of the fire for him.[63]

61 The President could appoint and dismiss the cabinet and the Prime Minister remained in office at 'his pleasure'. The budget was only to be placed before the National Assembly after the President's approval. Other executive powers included the appointment of provincial governors and of the three commanders-in-chief.

62 Jalal, *The State of Martial Rule*, p. 220.

63 *Ibid.*, p. 255.

Suhrawardy's hold over his supporters in East Pakistan was further weakened by the hostility to the state's pro-western foreign policy following the July 1956 Suez crisis. There were angry anti-British demonstrations in Dhaka and Karachi early in November and with President Mirza absent in Tehran, Suhrawardy temporarily threatened to withdraw Pakistan from the Commonwealth in protest at the Anglo-French military intervention in Egypt. Emergency British diplomacy ensured that Mirza thwacked Suhrawardy back into line[64] to the Premier's cost. The United States had of course by this time long replaced British influence. But hostility towards an albeit junior partner in the western alliance still perturbed the bureaucrat and military establishment which had seen Pakistan's pro-Western stance fill the coffers with $500 million of military aid and $750 million of economic aid by this juncture.[65]

Suhrawardy's popularity with his East Pakistan constituency further dipped when he backed down over the Awami League's call for land reforms because of the resistance of the West Punjab rural elite. He was now in the dangerous business of disappointing friends and creating enemies. He evoked the ire of the western province's business class, for example, by having the temerity to tinker with the longstanding regional economic imbalances in distributing the lion's share of American aid to East Pakistani industrialists.[66] The West Pakistanis now decided that it was time to pull the carpet from under his feet. The withdrawal of Republican support from the coalition sealed Suhrawardy's fate[67] and ushered in the farce of Chundrigar's two month ministry. Brief though it was, Chundrigar stayed sufficiently long enough to further widen the gulf between the eastern and western wings by reversing Suhrawardy's decision on the allocation of the US $10 million aid package.

The fall of Chundrigar's government in December 1957 ushered in the final ministry before the coup of the following October. The Republican coalition Government led by the veteran West Punjab politician Firoz Khan Noon was inherently unstable from the outset. The rivalries between Noon and his erstwhile Muslim League colleagues prevented cooperation between them, despite the fact that they shared common landlord interests. The Byzantine goings-on in Karachi were positively gentlemanly compared to the bear-pit in Dhaka where the physical violence during a debate on 21 September 1958 resulted in

---

[64] For details see Sir Morrice James, *Pakistan Chronicle* (London, 1993), Chapter 4.

[65] Samad, *A Nation in Turmoil*, p. 169.

[66] Jalal, *The state of Martial Rule*, p. 262.

[67] Mirza's previously unpublished memoir claims that he exerted great efforts to patch up the differences between Suhrawardy and Dr Khan Sahib. *Newsline* (May 1996), p. 137.

the death of the Deputy Speaker Shahid. This episode would not alone have guaranteed army intervention, but it occurred against a background of growing industrial unrest fuelled by inflation. Opposition parties noisily demanded early elections, while stridently lacing such calls with vituperative denunciations of the regime's pro-Western foreign policy. As early as 19 May 1958, Mirza and Ayub had separately conveyed their opinion to the US ambassador that 'only a dictatorship would work in Pakistan.'[68] The whistle had to be blown before any democratic successes might be scored in the promised national elections. It was the end of the beginning of Pakistan's experiment with democracy.

Mirza, in a 1,400-word statement justifying the introduction of martial law, made specific reference to the 'disgraceful scenes' in East Pakistan's Provincial Assembly. He also castigated the politicians' 'ruthless struggle for power', corruption and 'prostitution of Islam for political ends'.[69] Two days before the Supreme Court judgement of 27 October which legalised the new regime, President Mirza announced the formation of a twelve-man cabinet. The youthful Zulfikar Ali Bhutto was appointed as Commerce Minister, and Ayub Khan, the Chief Martial Law Administrator, was named as Prime Minister. Just four of the members were from East Pakistan.[70]

The first public strains in the Ayub-Mirza duumvirate were already apparent in their contradictory statements concerning the timing of the lifting of martial law. The President wanted this to continue no longer than 7 or 8 November. Mirza also disagreed with Ayub over the need for land reform. There may also have been friction resulting from his promotion of Lieutenant-General Musa to Commander-in-Chief of the army, although Ayub continued as Supreme Commander. The catalyst for Mirza's dismissal however was his reported meddling in army affairs[71] and attempt to instigate a counter-coup.[72] At around 10 o'clock on 27 October a startled Mirza was summoned in his dressing-gown to receive a delegation consisting of General Burki, General Azam and General Khalid Shaikh. They declared that 'in the interests of the country we want you to leave Pakistan.'[73] The bridge loving President had lost his final rubber. Mirza and his Iranian wife Khanum Naheed were given

68 Jalal, *The State of Martial Rule*, p. 273.

69 *Dawn* (Karachi), 8 October 1958.

70 H. Feldman, *Revolution in Pakistan: A Study of the Martial Law Administration* (London, 1967), p. 13.

71 Mirza in his memoir claims that this was an absurd charge which had been fabricated to justify Ayub's action against him. *Newsline* (May 1996), p. 139.

72 F.M. Khan, *Story of the Pakistan Army* (Lahore, 1963), p. 202.

73 Feldman, *Revolution in Pakistan*, p. 14.

little more than an hour to pack and were informed that they would have to buy their own airline tickets and pay for their passports.[74] They were then shunted into a London exile with almost indecent haste. The post of Prime Minister was abolished, but the cabinet which had been sworn in earlier that day now agreed to serve under President Ayub Khan as Pakistan entered a new era.

[74] *Newsline* (May 1996), p. 141.

6

SOLON AMONG THE SUBALTERNS

The publication of Samuel P. Huntingdon's seminal study *Political Order in Changing Societies* coincided with the tenth anniversary of the coup d'état which had brought Muhammad Ayub Khan to power. Huntingdon was fulsome in his praise of the Field-Marshall, declaring: 'More than any other political leader in a modernising country after World War II, Ayub came close to filling the role of a Solon or Lycurgus, or "Great Legislator" on the Platonic or Rousseauian model.'[1] However, hard on the heels of a month's celebrations of the regime's not inconsiderable economic achievements, disturbances broke out in Punjab's north-western towns which had spread by January 1969 to the whole of the country. In the western wing they were directed at the overthrow of the regime, while in the east they increasingly took on a separatist character. By March the system of Basic Democracies, which Huntingdon and others had vaunted, had collapsed like a mud fort in a monsoon.

A disillusioned and humiliated Ayub handed over power to General Yahya Khan. The 1962 Constitution, which was the cornerstone of Ayub's Pakistan, was abrogated and the country reverted once more to martial law. Ironically the political system designed to bring order to Pakistan ended in chaos, the protests against it led by the very journalists, lawyers, teachers and students who Ayub might have expected to support his modernisation programme. Furthermore, a regime committed to eradicating the economic disparity between East and West Pakistan ended with a graver sense of alienation between the two wings.

Why did the Ayub era end in such abject failure? Was its economic and political experiment doomed from the outset? Why did economic and social modernisation bring political chaos rather than stability? A ready response to these questions is that the regime collapsed both because it lacked political legitimacy and failed to ensure that all sections of the population shared in the economic growth. Part of this chapter seeks to analyse these two failures. Nevertheless, it is also important to view the Ayub era in relation to the longer-term historical inheritances of 'viceregalism', urban-rural social and political dichotomy and the continual interweaving of regional, national and international politics.

[1] S. P. Huntingdon, *Political Order in Changing Societies* (New Haven, 1968), pp. 250-1.

Before turning to these themes it is important to examine the formative influences on Ayub's political philosophy.

The making of a leader

Ayub Khan was born on 14 May 1907 in the village of Rehana which lies some 50 miles north of Rawalpindi. The Tarin tribe from which he came were 'lowland' Pakhtuns who had imbued Punjabi culture and values. Ayub's native tongue was thus Hindko, not Pashto.[2] He was thus during his youth culturally insulated from the Pushtun nationalism of the Khan brothers' Khudai Khidmatgar movement. Indeed, his native Hazara district was for many years the Muslim League's only toehold in Frontier politics.[3] Ayub's military training naturally reinforced this cultural predisposition towards Muslim (i.e. Pakistani) as opposed to Pushtun nationalism. Although ethnically a Pushtun, he rested easy with the project of a centralised Punjabi-dominated state as epitomised by the One Unit scheme. His contribution to 'nation-building' was to lie not by the way of Pushtun autonomy, but rather by co-opting Pushtuns to the centre through encouraging their presence in the main institutions of the state.

Ayub's family background shaped his social as well as his cultural outlook. He came from a comfortable but by no means wealthy family. The middling income derived from his father's army pension and landholdings had to provide for a large family in which Ayub was the fifth child. They could only make ends meet by 'working the lands well'. Here we can see the seeds of the attitude which Ayub was to later bring to his land reform programme, which was conceived of not as a 'punitive measure' but to 'remove social imbalance' and to 'enable a family to live reasonably well on the land by working hard'.[4]

Although his father, Risaldar Major Mir Dad Khan, had served in Hodson's Horse, it was not inevitable that Ayub should embark on a military career. Indeed, the deeply pious Mir Dad Khan had originally intended his son to become a *Hafiz-e-Quran*. These hopes were ended when Ayub slapped the village *maulvi* in retaliation for a beating. The young Ayub preferred riding to scholastic pursuits, but Mir Dad Khan insisted that he be sent to Aligarh College because he wanted Ayub to 'learn to feel like a Muslim'.[5]

---

[2] Pashto predominated in the Peshawar, Kohat and Bannu districts of the Frontier, but 9 out of 10 inhabitants of Hazara spoke the Punjabi derived Hindko language.

[3] For details see E. Jansson, *India, Pakistan or Pakhtunistan?*

[4] Muhammad Ayub Khan, *Friends Not Masters: A Political Autobiography* (London, 1967), p. 83

[5] *Ibid.*, p. 5.

Aligarh from its foundation in 1877 had however been more concerned with enabling students to make their way in the modern world than with Islamic training. It provided not only a bridge between Islam and the modern world, but a meeting ground for Muslims drawn from different regions of India. Ayub noted in his autobiography how the Aligarh experience taught him 'to live with people of differing origins and backgrounds and how to understand their point of view', He also gradually improved his Urdu pronunciation.[6] In addition to imbibing a Muslim nationalist outlook at Aligarh, Ayub also acquired the modernist approach to Islam which was to shape the social and religious policy of his regime. In a speech to an audience of leading Deobandi *'ulama* in May 1959, Ayub most clearly articulated this Aligarh inheritance. He opined that Islam was originally

....a dynamic and progressive movement...but with the passage of time, the Muslims at large sought to concentrate more on the dogmatic aspects of Islam.[...] Those who looked forward to progress and advancement came to be regarded as disbelievers and those who looked backward were considered devout Muslims. It is a great injustice to both life and religion to impose on twentieth century man the condition that he must go back several centuries in order to prove his bona fides as a true Muslim.'[7]

Throughout the remainder of his career, Ayub made little attempt to hide his detestation of the *mullahs* who he declared had, no less than the politicians, been covetous of 'wealth' and power and did not stop short of any mischief'.[8]

Ayub sailed for England in July 1926 to take up his scholarship at Sandhurst. The beginnings of a distinguished military career were already visible when he became the first overseas cadet to be promoted to corporal. Ayub served initially in the 1st/14th Punjab Regiment before being posted to army headquarters in Delhi as a staff officer. During the Second World War he saw active service in Burma as Second-in-Command of the 1st Assam Regiment. His subsequent transfer to the more familiar terrain of the Khyber Pass was his first command position. While stationed at Landi Kotal he heard that his old battalion of the 1st/14th Punjab Regiment had been captured by the Japanese. At the end of the war he was involved in its re-raising at the regimental training centre at Ferozepur.[9]

---

6 *Ibid.*, p. 6.

7 Muhammad Ayub Khan, *Speeches and Statements*, vol. 1 (Karachi, 1961), pp. 110-11.

8 Cited in Anwar Hussain Syed, *Pakistan: Islam, Politics and National Solidarity*, p. 106.

9 Khan, *Friends Not Masters*, p. 14.

There had been nothing in Ayub's career to this juncture to cause him to question the Sandhurst dictum that a professional soldier should not intervene in politics. But this changed following his appointment as an advisory officer to Major-General Rees's ill-fated Punjab Boundary Force, which had been constituted to protect the population of the twelve border areas of partitioned Punjab during the transfer of power. The force was hopelessly inadequate to cover this vast area of over 29,000 square miles. This situation was exacerbated by the collapse of the civilian administration and the poisonous communal atmosphere which infected the police and the Boundary Force itself. The mayhem attendant on the mass migrations was so uncontrollable that the Boundary Force had to be ignominiously disbanded by the Joint Defence Council which met in Lahore on Friday 29 August 1947.

Ayub later recorded: 'This was the unhappiest period of my life. [...] My faith in human nature was shaken and I used to ask myself, "what can one do to stop this madness?" '[10] A dislike for politicians was bred by their constant sniping at his role in ignorance of the problems actually being faced on the ground.[11] From the outset of Pakistan's creation, Ayub recalled, 'I was certain of one thing: Pakistan's survival was vitally linked with the establishment of a well-trained, well-equipped, and well-led army.'[12] Subsequent developments in the period 1948-51 reinforced this early sentiment. In January 1948 Ayub had been posted to serve as General Commanding Officer in East Pakistan. He experienced Dhaka's turbulent politics at first hand when called upon to ring the Assembly Building with troops to prevent students from attacking it.[13] Before his recall to the General Headquarters at Rawalpindi, he had come to the conclusion that 'little constructive work was being done by the government and ... all energies were getting diverted into political channels.'[14]

Shortly after Ayub's return to West Pakistan, General Gracey's term as Pakistan's Commander-in-Chief expired. His hopes of an extension had been dashed by his controversial refusal in October 1947 to obey Jinnah's order to send troops into Kashmir. Henceforth the army was to have a Pakistani commander. Ayub took over this role on 17 January 1951. The Rawalpindi Conspiracy[15] and the assassination of Liaquat

---

[10] *Ibid.*, p. 17.

[11] *Ibid.*, p. 15; See also, S. A. Pataudi, *The Story of Soldiering and Politics in India and Pakistan* (Lahore, 1983), p. 114.

[12] Khan, *Friends Not Masters*, p. 21.

[13] *Ibid.*, pp. 29-30.

[14] *Ibid.*, p. 25.

[15] The events surrounding the coup plotted by Major-General Akbar Khan remain shrouded in mystery to this day. Fourteen persons were convicted by a special tribunal held in Hyderabad. They were all released within four years.

Ali Khan followed soon afterwards. Both events reinforced Ayub's distrust of politicians. 'I would come back from my visits to Karachi depressed and distressed,' he recalled, 'wondering what was happening to the country. Why were people not attending to their work with some honesty of purpose and why could they not evolve some team spirit?'[16] He was 'disgusted and revolted' at the matter-of-fact way in which the new cabinet responded to Liaquat's assassination:

> I wondered at how callous, cold-blooded, and selfish people could be. It seemed that everyone of them had got himself promoted in one way or another. [...] I got the distinct impression that they were all feeling relieved that the only person who might have kept them under control had disappeared from the scene. The political arena was now available to them for a free-for-all.[17]

Ayub Khan had an even closer vantage-point to view the political disarray following his entry into the cabinet as Minister of Defence after Ghulam Muhammad's dismissal of the Constituent Assembly in October 1954. Although he relinquished the office after a year, he viewed with distaste the intrigues and bargaining which accompanied the promulgation of the constitution. 'Yesterday's "traitors" ', Ayub wearily noted, were 'today's Chief Ministers, indistinguishable as Tweedledum and Tweedledee!'[18] These sentiments which were made public in 1968 could be dismissed as a *post hoc* justification for the introduction of martial law. Even if taken at face value they do not indicate an inevitable process leading to the October 1958 coup. However, they are historically important for two reasons: first and foremost, the sense that the country was sliding into chaos because of the actions of self-seeking politicians was widely held among the officer corps; second, and leading on from this, there was a growing feeling within the Army that it was the only properly functioning institution and that its responsibility was to protect the state from both external and internal dangers. Given this mindset there was a strong likelihood that while the Army might not actively seek occasion to intervene in the political process, it would step in if it believed that civil authority could no longer cope. The strange event of the Khan of Kalat's attempted secession from Pakistan[19] fol-

---

16 *Ibid.*, p. 39.

17 *Ibid.*, p. 41.

18 *Ibid.*, p. 55.

19 The Khan had reluctantly acceded to Pakistan in March 1948, and in 1951 his state became part of the Balochistan States Union. In September 1958 he briefly offered armed defiance which was only terminated by the use of the Pakistan Army.

lowing hard on the heels of the disturbances in the East Punjab Provincial Assembly provided such an occasion.

Political developments, 1958-65

Ayub laid Pakistan's ills at the door of the politicians and sought to establish a new constitutional order more suited to 'the genius of the people' than the 'failed' parliamentary democracy. As we have seen this reading of events was based partly on his experience. It also reflected the mindset of Pakistan's inherited viceregal tradition. Ayub's demonising[20] of the professional politicians and paternalistic solicitude for the 'real' people – the rural classes[21] – could have been culled from any Punjab School of Administration handbook. In its time-honoured tradition, governance was privileged to the detriment of political participation. Like his predecessors, Ayub found that the short-term benefits of stability were offset in the long run by a lack of legitimacy.

Despite Ayub's depiction by Huntingdon as an innovator who through the device of the Basic Democracies sought to transform the institutional basis of Pakistan's politics, he was a paternalist in the tradition of the Raj's non-regulation provinces. He reintroduced the nineteenth-century ideas of political tutelage through indirect elections and official nomination of representatives. However, like the paternalistic Punjabi colonial officials, Ayub discovered that while this model of governance would work in a static society, it was found wanting in a period of rapid socio-economic change. Just as the development of the Canal Colonies in colonial Punjab threatened bureaucratic governance, as was seen in the 1907 disturbances,[22] so the processes of migration and urbanisation unleashed by the Green Revolution and industrialisation put an increasing strain on the Ayub system in the post-1965 period. Development which, in Muhammad Waseem's words, unleashed 'hitherto

---

[20] In his first broadcast as Chief Martial Law Administrator on 8 October, Ayub had declared that the politicians had 'waged a ceaseless and bitter war against each other regardless of the ill effects on the country, just to whet their appetites and satisfy their base demands'. There had been 'no limit to the depth of their baseness, chicanery, deceit and degredation.' Ayub Khan, *Speeches and Statements*, vol. 1, p. 2.

[21] This was reflected in the Basic Democracies scheme and the rural public works programme. Many of his speeches echoed British paternalism. For example, he declared that the rural people were 'by nature patriotic and good people' who were 'tolerant and patient and can rise to great heights when well led'. Cited in R. Jahan, *Pakistan: Failure in National Integration*, p. 64.

[22] For details see, N.G. Barrier, 'The Punjab Disturbances of 1907: the response of the British Government in India to Agrarian Unrest', *Modern Asian Studies* 1, no. 4 (1967), pp. 353-83.

relatively immobile social and economic forces' and 'led to increased impoverishment of the masses as it was concentrated in a few hands',[23] ultimately undermined a system which had deliberately closed off channels of political participation. The mass mobilisation Ayub had sought to deny the people ultimately swept him away.

At the same time as promising to introduce a democratic system the 'people could understand' the early actions of the Ayub era were to ban political parties and lock up such perennial 'troublemakers' as Abdul Ghaffar Khan and G. M. Sayed. Ayub sought to clip the politicians' wings further by the introduction in March and August 1959 respectively of the Public Offices (Disqualification) Order (PODO) and the Elective Bodies (Disqualification) Order (EBDO). These established the concept of 'accountability' and gave former politicians the option of trial by a tribunal for 'misconduct' or voluntary withdrawal from public life. Persons found guilty under EBDO were to be automatically disqualified from membership of any elective body until after 31 December 1966. The roll-call of 'Ebdoed' politicians included Mian Mumtaz Daultana, Firoz Khan Noon, M.A. Khuhro, Abdul Qayyum Khan and Mian Iftikharuddin. Muhammad Waseem has maintained that EBDO 'turned out to be one of the strongest arms in the hand of the Ayub Government' and that its stifling of meaningful opposition helps to explain the longevity of the Ayub system.[24]

The most constructive measures during the early period of martial law included the clampdown on hoarding, black-marketing and smuggling. In a single day in Karachi, 10,000 bags of grain, bales of cloth and imported luxury goods were seized. Other signs of the new discipline included fixing the prices of milk, vegetables and *ghee* (clarified butter) and introducing a penalty of one year's rigorous imprisonment for urinating in public places in the Karachi Federal Area.[25] The energetic Minister for Rehabilitation, Lieutenant-General Azam Khan pushed through the new housing development of Korangi in a six-month period in order to relieve the housing shortage in Karachi where thousands of refugees still lived in makeshift slum accommodation.

Ayub in his role as President promulgated the Basic Democracies Order on the first anniversary of the coup. Although the urban population

---

[23] Waseem shows how mechanisation forced landless labourers to migrate to cities in search of employment. Small farmers who could not compete with the large landowners moved into agro-based industry. The increased disparities arising from the Green Revolution are seen in the fact that the percentage of the rural population living below the poverty line rose from 64 to 74 percent in the 1966-7 to 1971-2 periods. M. Waseem, *Politics and the State in Pakistan* (Lahore, 1989), pp. 227-38.

[24] *Ibid.*, p. 155.

[25] H. Feldman, *Revolution in Pakistan*, p. 8.

was included in the newly-instituted union committees, the scheme was primarily designed both to promote rural development and to create a rural power-base for the regime by establishing a new class of collaborators in the countryside. Ayub naturally refuted this intention and claimed on numerous occasions that the Basic Democracies system was a training ground for citizenship. The system initially involved a five-tier[26] structure stretching from its base in the rural union councils and urban union committees, through the *thana* or *tehsil* committee, to the district and divisional councils, finally to two Provincial Development Advisory Councils. These were replaced in 1962 with the opening of new provincial legislatures, reducing the pyramid to four tiers. Direct elections under universal franchise were only to take place at the lowest tier; thereafter representation was to proceed by indirect election. Even at the union council or committee level the government could nominate as voting members up to one-third of the elected members. In a direct echo of British nineteenth-century practice, provision was made for official supervision of the bodies from the *thana* level upwards by *ex-officio* membership. Moreover, an equal number of nominated members could take their places alongside the indirectly elected Basic Democrats.

Basic Democrats were elected to the union councils and committees which were demarcated on a population basis of between 10,000-15,000 people. In all there were 80,000 Basic Democrats (later rising to 120,000) equally divided between the two wings of the country. The union councils and committees were permitted to raise local taxes and to concern themselves with a list of thirty-seven types of activity which included responsibility for such items as sanitation, water supply and the upkeep of cemeteries, gardens and public thoroughfares.[27] More extensive functions were given to the District Council which was presided over by the District Magistrate and was more an executive than representative body. Further funds for the Basic Democracies scheme were released following the October 1961 $621 million Agricultural Commodities Agreement with the United States although the bulk of this was earmarked for the Rural Works Programme.[28] It was piloted in East Pakistan in 1961, before being extended to the whole of the country two years later. The Basic Democracies system itself had been introduced first in AK before Pakistan itself. AK also witnessed vigorous presidential and State

[26] In the Tribal areas of the Frontier and Balochistan, there was a three-tier structure of Agency Councils, Divisional Councils and and Provincial Advisory Committees. American Consul Peshawar to Department of State 21 January 1960, 790.D.00/1-460, National Archives at College Park.

[27] H. Feldman, *Revolution in Pakistan*, p. 105.

[28] L. Ziring, *The Ayub Era: Politics in Pakistan, 1958-1969* (Syracuse, NJ, 1971), p. 20.

Council elections in October/November 1961.[29] The AK President K.H. Khurshid and his supporters[30] triumphed over their Muslim Conference opponents, despite some Pakistan Government disquiet about Khurshid's public espousal of the idea of an 'independent Azad Kashmir'.[31]

Even in the suffocating atmosphere of martial law criticism was voiced over the official stranglehold clamped on the Basic Democrats system. This was popularly expressed in the derisive term *Bekas* (Helpless) Democrats. Rather than establishing a popular base for the regime, the Basic Democrats were increasingly ridiculed and at the height of the 1969 agitation they simply faded away. Ayub did everything in his power to popularise the scheme. He took the train – the celebrated 'Pak Jamhuriat Special' (Pakistan Republican Special) – to meet the people and explain his proposals. A one-week tour of West Pakistan was followed in January 1960 by a similar expedition in East Pakistan. Despite such novel steps, it was impossible to hide the democratic shortcomings of his scheme from a politically sophisticated yet increasingly alienated East Pakistan populace. They had already expressed their verdict in that less than one in two of those eligible had cast their vote in the election of Basic Democrats.[32]

The Basic Democrats collectively formed the electoral college which affirmed Ayub Khan as President in January 1960. The ballot showed 75,084 votes for and only 2,829 against.[33] They similarly re-elected him as President in 1965 following his contested election with Miss Fatima Jinnah. The Basic Democrats also chose the members of the National and Provincial Assemblies in the partyless elections of April 1962. Just as in Zia's later experiment this ensured that a parliament emerged which was dominated by landowners and *biraderi* leaders. On 8 June 1962 the National Assembly held its first session in Ayub Hall at Rawalpindi. The President took this opportunity to announce the termination of forty-four months of martial law.[34]

---

[29] There were 2,400 Basic Democrat voters for the presidential elections.

[30] Khurshid did not institutionalise his support into a new party, until September 1962 with the formation of the Jammu and Kashmir Liberation Front.

[31] For a full coverage of the controversial elections, see the following State Department Central Files 1960-3 which were forwarded to Washington from the Murree office of the American Embassy: 20 February 1961 790.D.00/6-1261;8 October 1961 790.D.00/10-361; 20 February 1962 790.D.00/6-1261.Further information is found in telegrams of 11 and 13 October 1961. National Archives at College Park.

[32] Ziring, *The Ayub Era*, p. 17.

[33] Feldman, *Revolution in Pakistan*, p. 109.

[34] Opinion in the officer corps was in fact divided over this decision. American Embassy Karachi to Department of State 21 June 1962, 790.D.00/6-2062, National Archives at College Park.

The troops had in fact been ordered back to their barracks as early as November 1958. By the end of the following year, only fifty-three army officers held civilian administrative positions.[35] Unlike his later successor as Chief Martial Law Administrator, General Zia-ul-Haq, Ayub relied on the civil bureaucracy to provide the backbone of his regime.[36] He made some attempt to purge it of 'corrupt' elements, but the screening process initiated under Martial Law Regulation no. 61 was only half-hearted.[37] A number of officials were demoted and around 500 were compelled to retire, but the purge was much smaller than that carried out subsequently by Zulfiqar Ali Bhutto. Ayub's concern for stability again limited his room for innovation. While he relied on such bureaucrats as Akhter Husain, S.M. Yusuf, Fida Hasan and Altaf Gauhar for advice,[38] he made his own decisions and remained throughout his tenure of power a somewhat remote figure.

With the formal termination of martial law, the 1962 Constitution came into operation. As might be expected this heavily bore Ayub's imprint. He had in fact overridden the advisory recommendations of the Constitution Commission's report which had been presented on 6 May 1961. This argued against the inclusion of the Basic Democracies as an electoral college for the election of the President. It had also expressed its opposition to the banning of political parties. But Ayub would not be brooked on either issue. He was also unable to accept its recommendation for a bicameral legislature and a Vice-President.[39] Ayub's modernist approach to Islam was also reflected in the dropping of the title Islamic from the country's name. Another subtle but significant change was the rewording of the Repugnancy Clause. This dropped the earlier direct reference to the Quran and Sunnah and merely stated that no law should be enacted which was repugnant to Islam, Thus encouraging the modernist conception of *ijtihad*.[40] The *'ulama* opposed

[35] S. J. Burki, 'Twenty Years of the Civil Service of Pakistan: A Reevaluation' *Asian Survey* 9, no. 4 (April 1969), p. 248.

[36] General Azam Khan formed a notable exception to this. He played a leading role in the resettlement of Karachi's refugees as Minister of Rehabilitation before going on to serve as Governor of East Pakistan.

[37] Ziring, *The Ayub Era*, p. 12.

[38] Akhter Husain as well as chairing the Land Reforms Commission for example, served in a number of ministerial posts including Minister of Information and Broadcasting and Minister for Education. Altaf Gauhar played an important role in developing the Basic Democrats scheme.

[39] He did however approve of its suggestions regarding a presidential system of government and its advocacy for the need of a strong centre. Muhammad Ayub Khan, *Friends Not Masters*, p. 212ff.

[40] This refers to the extension of the legal code contained in the Quran and the Sunnah (Prophet's example) by analytical extrapolation and consideration of the public good.

these changes and were also unhappy with the composition of the Islamic Advisory Committee which was established by Ayub to assist the Legis-lature in framing laws based on the concepts of Islam. They also attacked the anti-democratic features of the constitution. Leading East Pakistani parties such as the Awami League, National Awami Party (NAP) and the Krishak Sramik Party (KSP) also entered the lists against the con-stitution in a joint statement issued on 24 June 1962.[41]

Ayub was forced to retreat both on the name of the country and on the banning of political parties. The First Constitutional Amendment Act of 1963 restored the name 'Islamic Republic of Pakistan'. The Political Parties Act of July 1962 legalised party organisations. This was intended to regularise a situation in which political activity had already been unofficially resumed outside the Legislature. While the measure made pragmatic sense, it shifted the initiative to Ayub's op-ponents. The President found himself increasingly on the defensive. Almost immediately the JI reorganised itself. Its leader Maulana Maududi fired off volleys of criticism at the anti-Islamic and anti-democratic features of the regime from his Zaildar Park Lahore headquarters. The Markazi Majlis-i-Shura (Central Council), which met in Lahore during the first week of August 1962, passed resolutions which condemned among other things the official Advisory Council of Islamic Ideology, the Muslim Family Laws, the Pakistan Arts Council, the Girl Guides and the Blue Birds, the construction of cinemas and the importation of books critical of Islam.[42] The JI joined the National Democratic Front which the former Pakistan Prime Minister Suhrawardy launched on 4 October, although its bedfellows included the Awami League, the NAP and the KSP along with more congenial former Republican Party members and the Council Muslim League.[43]

Ayub viewed the re-emergence of party politics with disquiet as he remained convinced that a partyless system was best suited to Pakistan. The course of events now inexorably led him to reinvent himself as a party political leader, although he wisely spurned the quixotic offer of leadership of the Khaksar movement which was proffered in late August 1962.[44] Ayub was never happy with this role for he remained in essence a hardheaded administrator. The cut and thrust of political

41 American Consul Dacca to Department of State, 25 June 1962, 790.D.00/6-2062, National Archives at College Park.

42 American Consul Lahore to Department of State, 13 August 1962, 790.D.00/18-1062, National Archives at College Park.

43 American Consul Lahore to Department of State, 8 October 1962, 790.D.00/10-1062, National Archives at Colllege Park.

44 American Embassy Karachi to Department of Airforce, 4 September 1962, 790.D.00(W)/8-362, National Archives at College Park.

debate was unattractive to him, and he and the intelligentsia regarded each other with contempt. He was as much a philistine as his later military successor Zia-ul-Haq, although he conspicuously lacked Zia's cruelty and vindictiveness.

By September 1962 the pro-government politicians in the legislatures, many of whom had only come into public life in the Ayub era, were formed into the Convention Muslim League. On 5 September its constitution was established in a meeting in Karachi. It drew largely on the Muslim League's 1956 Constitution, although significantly the Working Committee was increased in size from twenty-two to thirty members, while the representation on the Council from the provinces of East and West Pakistan was reduced from 180 to 100 members each. The Working Committee's quorum was reduced from six to five members in a further step to increase its executive influence.[45] Clearly the party's prospects were from its inception closely linked with the regime's fortunes. They were also hindered by the tensions between its leading figure Chaudhri Khaliquzzaman and Nawab Yamin Khan who had sponsored its foundational convention. At the beginning of 1963, the former UP Muslim League leader and Governor of East Pakistan accused Yamin Khan of forming a 'pocket' Muslim League in Karachi. The Nawab retorted by charging Khaliquzzaman with intrigues and misappropriation of funds. Each dismissed the other from their respective party post.[46] Not surprisingly, Ayub hesitated until May before joining the party. He agreed to become its President in December 1963.

Old-style Muslim Leaguers who objected to this government hijacking of the Muslim League nomenclature formed a rival Council Muslim League. They were led by the former Prime Minister Khwaja Nazimuddin who was highly critical of the presidential system of government.[47] He emerged from retirement to rally support for the Council Muslim League in West Pakistan in January 1963. 'The receptions accorded him at Lahore and along the route from Rawalpindi to Peshawar', an American official reported, 'were characterised by scenes reminiscent of the days immediately preceding independence, when the Muslim League's popularity was at its height.'[48] Khwaja Nazimuddin held the

---

[45] American Embassy Karachi to Department of State, 9 September 1962, 790.D.00/3-1362, National Archives at College Park.

[46] American Embassy Karachi to Department of State, 26 January 1963, 790.D.00/1-1663, National Archives at College Park.

[47] The last Muslim League President Abdul Qayyum Khan was restricted under EBDO regulations until February 1967.

[48] American Embassy Karachi to Department of State, 5 January 1963, 790.D.00/1-363, National Archives at College Park.

post of Council Muslim League President until his death in 1964, when Nurul Amin took control.

The 1965 presidential elections marked a major turning-point in Ayub's fortunes. This was not because he was ever in danger of defeat; his control of the machinery of government and the restriction of the electorate to the Basic Democrats who were his creatures ensured a by no means sweeping victory with 65 per cent of the votes cast. The opposition cause had also been weakened by the deaths of Suhrawardy (5 December 1963) and Fazlul Haq (27 April 1962),[49] and in these circumstances the mantle fell to the seventy-one-year-old Miss Fatima Jinnah. Tumultuous crowds had gathered to greet her during a visit to Peshawar from Rawalpindi in October 1962 even before she had publicly manifested support for the anti-regime Council Muslim League. The crush of the crowds was so great that her motorcade took two hours to cover the 6 miles from the heart of the city to her Dean's Hotel destination.[50] In scenes reminiscent of her late brother's public acclamations,[51] crowds thronged the streets and balconies along the route in the city, while triumphal arches had been erected on the Attock highway at such places as Pirpai, Pabbi and Nasarpur.

Nevertheless, despite such manifestations of support and her veneration by some as *Khatoon-i-Pakistan* (First Lady of Pakistan) and *Madar-i-Millat* (Mother of the Nation) the prospect of a female head of state was anathema to leading members of the *'ulama*. Maududi and the JI expediently agreed to support her as did leading Deobandis such as Mufti Muhammad Shafi, but most Barelvis threw in their lot with Ayub. He was also supported by Pir Dewal Sharif and many of the prominent *sajjada nashins*.

During the campaign, Fatima Jinnah attracted large crowds and took full advantage of the opportunity to deride the authoritarianism of the Ayub regime in her slogan 'Democracy versus dictatorship'. The 200-mile journey by rail from Dhaka to Chittagong during her week-long tour of East Pakistan lasted twenty-eight hours, such were the tumultuous receptions accorded her. The spontaneous enthusiasm

---

49 Suhrawardy had been far more politically active than the octogenarian Haq. His efforts to forge a National Democratic Front had been hampered by the regime's repression and failing health. Haq nevertheless remained a potent symbol of Bengali aspirations as was evidenced by the unseemly row between the government and the 'Tiger' of Bengal's supporters over the organisation of a condolence meeting. American Consul Dacca to Department of State, 3 May 1962, 790.D.00/5-162, National Archives at College Park. Haq's public memorial became the first calling point for the batches of political prisoners who were released soon afterwards in June 1962.

50 American Consul Peshawar to Department of State, 31 October 1962, 790.D.00/10-3162, National Archives at College Park.

51 For their symbolic significance see, I. Talbot, *Freedom's Cry*, pp. 29-40.

her campaign generated throughout the country was to have longer-term significance than her respectable poll result. Ayub trumpeted his victory as a 'clear and final verdict on the Constitution'. In reality however it was a shallow triumph. He may have won the election, but he lost the people. The polls had directed the glare of publicity towards a system which denied participation to the masses and stacked the odds in favour of the candidate who controlled the government apparatus. Ayub's acquisition of legitimacy remained as elusive as ever. Attempts at building a political structure from the bottom up had foundered because the Basic Democrats had been tied too tightly to the leading strings of the bureaucracy. One report into their working discovered that 85 per cent of the items for discussion at union council meetings were initiated by government officials.[52] The alternative top down experiment with the Convention Muslim League was equally unsuccessful. Like the earlier Republican Party it amounted to little more than a coterie of sycophants and scarcely existed outside the legislatures. It was even largely bypassed in Ayub's 1965 presidential election campaign when he preferred to mobilise support through the bureaucracy than its rudimentary organisation.

The lack of legitimacy however threatened not only the regime, but national integration. The period from 1958 onwards witnessed the increasing alienation of the Sindhi and Bengali populations. This was rooted in part in their historic marginalisation in what were the preeminent institutions of the state, the Army and the elite cadre of the Civil Service of Pakistan (CSP). This is brought out starkly in Tables 6.1 and 6.2 overleaf.

The CSP became an increasingly important partner in Ayub's ruling coalition as a result of the central role accorded Commissioners and Deputy Commissioners in the Basic Democracies scheme and the control over development funds which they acquired under the Rural Works Programme. In 1963 East Pakistanis comprised just 5 per cent of the Army Officer Corps. They fared much better in the CSP accounting for 139 out of 467 officers in 1967, but this was still considerably below the Bengalis' demographic majority in Pakistan. In a classic case of too little too late, the recruitment system was changed to redress this imbalance, so that ten of the sixteen probationers in 1968 were drawn from the eastern wing.[53] Moreover, Bengalis were under-represented not only at the Central Secretariat level but in the numerous commissions of inquiry which were instituted in such varied fields as land reform, franchise and constitutional recommendations, and the press.

[52] A.T. Rahman, *Basic Democracies at the Grass Roots* (Comilla, 1962), p. 95.

[53] Burki, 'Twenty Years of the Civil Service of Pakistan', p. 253.

Table 6.1. THE MILITARY ELITE IN PAKISTAN, 1955

	East Bengal	West Pakistan
Lt.-General	0	3
Major-General	0	20
Brigadier	1	34
Colonel	1	49
Lt.-Colonel	2	198
Major	10	590
Navy officers	7	593
Air Force officers	40	640

Source: Dawn, 9 January 1956. Cited in Mizanur Rahman, 'The Emergence of Bangladesh as a Sovereign State', Ph.D thesis, Institute of Commonwealth Studies, 1975, p. 67.

Table 6.2. CENTRAL SECRETARIAT ELITE POSTS, 1955

	East Bengal	West Pakistan
Secretary	0	19
Joint Secretary	3	38
Deputy Secretary	10	123
Under Secretary	38	510

Source: Pakistan Constituent Assembly Debates, vol. 1, 7 January 1956, p. 1844. Cited in Mizanur Rahman 'The Emergence of Bangladesh as a Sovereign State', p. 68.

Just seventy-five out of 280 members of the commissions of inquiry were from East Pakistan.[54] None of Ayub's key aides were Bengalis. He thus 'had no one around him to advise him adequately or intelligently', as a high-ranking army officer informed the American Consul-General in January 1963, 'East Pakistanis in the Cabinet are men of no particular stature and competence and are only trying to please Ayub and say what they think he might like to hear.'[55]

The centre in fact took back more than it conceded in the 1962 Constitution in terms of decentralisation of powers. While important subjects of administration such as industries and railways were devolved to the two provinces, they were not under their exclusive jurisdiction as the centre could intervene in the name of 'co-ordination and uniformity of policy.' Moreover, any provincial scheme which cost more than Rs.5 million in foreign exchange required central approval.[56]

[54] Jahan, *Pakistan: Failure in National Integration,* p. 98.

[55] American Consul-General Lahore to Department of State, 22 January 1963, 790.D.00/1-1663, National Archives at College Park.

[56] Jahan, *Pakistan: Failure in National Integration,* pp. 101ff.

The Bengali elite's access to power had of course traditionally lain through political mobilisation not the bureaucracy. The EBDO restrictions and banning of political parties left its urban section literally without a voice. Students in Dhaka promptly responded to the 1962 Constitution by going on strike and burning copies of it. Suhrawardy's arrest under the Security of Pakistan Act on 30 January 1962 sparked especially violent student protests. Ayub, in Dhaka to chair a Governor's Conference, was a virtual prisoner in the President's House for the last three days of his visit.[57] Order was only restored after units of the Punjab Regiment were despatched to the Dhaka University campus. In addition to rioting, students more positively put forward a three-point programme for the 1962 Constitution's repeal, the reintroduction of democracy and the release of all political prisoners. Sheikh Mujibur Rahman was in fact released on 18 June from the Dhaka Central Jail where he had been held under the East Pakistan Public Security Act.

The Bengali elite's alienation was intensified by the fact that the economic development of the Ayub era largely passed them by. The demand for regional autonomy and for a two-economy policy[58] became increasingly linked. Ayub steadfastly rejected the claim that Pakistan possessed two distinct economies with different interests and requirements as he saw this approach as a prelude to political disintegration.

Sindhis also did not figure in the famous twenty-two families who came to dominate the industrial and commercial sectors of the economy. Industrial development continued apace in the *mohajir* dominated urban areas. The Sindhi political elite continued to chafe under the One Unit Scheme. Its claim that this was providing the cover for the 'Punjabisation' of Sindh appeared justified by the increasing allocation of land made available through the construction of the Ghulam Muhammad Barrage near Hyderabad to army officers and bureaucrats.[59]

The fate of the Sindhi language increasingly became both a symbol of the population's sense of economic and political deprivation and of internal colonialism. The Bengali pattern appeared to be repeating itself in the subcontinent's 'gateway' of Islam. The proposal by the 1959 Report on National Education to reduce the educational importance of Sindhi by introducing Urdu as the medium of instruction from class 6 upwards evoked a storm of protest. Following a Sindhi day of protest,

---

[57] Consul-General Dacca to Department of State, 8 February 1962, 790.D.00/2-162, National Archives at College Park.

[58] For further details see Muhammad Anisur Rahman, *East and West Pakistan: A Problem in Political Economy of Regional Planning*, Occasional Paper no. 20, Harvard University Centre for International Affairs, 1968.

[59] See S. Ansari, 'Punjabis in Sind-Identity and Power', *International Journal of Punjab Studies* 2, no. 1 (January-June 1995), pp. 12ff.

Ayub suspended the orders. Sindhi nationalists nevertheless maintained that the decline in Sindhi medium schools and the replacement of Sindhi by Urdu on such official buildings as railway stations was part, of a general conspiracy. Bitter disputes accompanied the decision in June 1965 of the Hyderabad Municipal Corporation to make Urdu its official working language. The following year another agitation was unleashed in the city by the efforts of Sindhi students to persuade the University of Sindh to adopt Sindhi as the medium of instruction and examination. Blood was not spilled as in Dhaka in February 1952, but the arrest of the student leaders by the Urdu-speaking Commissioner of the Hyderabad Division, Masroor Hasan Khan, provided a focus for the increasing alienation of Sindhis from Ayub's regime.[60]

This period also saw the first glimmerings of *mohajir* disquiet. Martial law shifted the balance of power in the ruling coalition firmly in the Punjabis' favour. This was symbolised by the shifting of the seat of national government from Karachi to the Punjab. The cabinet had decided in February 1960 that the new capital city which would be constructed on the site of the villages of Saidpur and Nurpur with the backdrop of the Margalla Hills would be called Islamabad.[61] By September of that year, the second phase of the movement of Central Government personnel had been completed. Seven special trains had taken government officials and their families from Karachi to the cantonment town of Chaklala (near Rawalpindi) which temporarily housed them while the construction work on Islamabad was carried out. As early as September 1960, below policy-making level only the Ministries of Foreign Affairs and Commonwealth Relations and of Law remained intact in Karachi.[62]

Economic and social reform

Ayub justified his system of guided democracy not just in terms of cleaning out the Augean stables of the politicians, but also maintained that it could deliver reforms which were essential for the modernisation of Pakistan. Indeed Mirza had fallen from grace largely because he wished to backtrack on the issue of land reform. Ayub linked this with his Basic Democracies scheme – institutional agrarian and political reform would together establish a new middle class leadership in the

[60] T. Rahman, 'Language and Politics in a Pakistan Province: The Sindhi Language Movement', *Asian Survey* 35, no. 11 (November 1995), pp. 1010-11.

[61] The decision was taken on 24 February 1960. American Embassy Karachi to Secretary of State, 25 February 1960, 790.D.001/7-2860, National Archives at College Park.

[62] American Embassy Karachi to Department of State, 16 September 1960, 790.D.001/7-2860, National Archives at College park.

countryside, a development which would possess wide ranging social and economic implications.

On 31 October 1958 the Land Reform Commission was established. It provided a rather rough and ready set of data on landownership[63] which revealed for example that 10 per cent of the cultivated area in Punjab was owned by large landholders (500 acres or over). 24 per cent of the total area was owned by farmers of 100 acres or more.[64] Its recommendations were embodied in the West Pakistan Land Reforms Regulation on 7 February 1959. This was the first serious reform measure in the landlord-dominated western wing of the country. It was hailed at the time as a major landmark which abolished feudalism. Subsequently such writers as S.J. Burki have depicted it along with the introduction of the Basic Democracies system as embodying a shift in political power from the feudalists to a new dynamic middle class of capitalist farmers. These 'economic maximisers' who according to Burki owned from 50-100 acres of land created the Green Revolution of the 1960s and were its main beneficiaries.[65]

In reality the reform was far from being radical. It set a notably high ceiling of 500 acres irrigated or 1,000 acres unirrigated per person.[66] Holdings in excess of these ceilings were to be resumed to the Government which was to pay compensation to the former owners on a sliding scale in the form of interest-bearing bonds. Part of the resumed land was to be sold directly to its cultivating tenants, and the remainder disposed of in public auction. In either case its new owners were to pay back the government in annual instalments at a fixed rate of interest.

Did the reforms, as their supporters claimed, create a new class of capitalist farmers? Scholars such as Mahmood Hasan Khan maintain that on the contrary landlordism remained virtually unchanged;[67] Khan has declared that the results were unimpressive in terms of the extent of the resumed area, the quality of its land and the number of new owners.[68] Certainly landlords were able to hang on to their property

---

63 The incomplete data related to the mid-1950s for Punjab but used pre-Partition figures for Sindh.

64 The average area per owner in Punjab was 8 acres.

65 R.D. Stevens, H. Alavi and P.J. Bertocci (eds), *Rural Development in Bangladesh and Pakistan* (Honolulu, 1976), Chapter 15.

66 Strictly speaking the individual ceiling was set in terms of Produce Index Units, a measure of the gross value of produce on each acre of land by soil type. The allowance was thus set at 36,000 PIUs which was calculated at 500 acres irrigated, 1000 acres unirrigated.

67 Mahmood Hasan Khan, *Underdevelopment*, p. 7.

68 *Ibid.*, Only 1.045 million acres were resumed in Punjab of which only 277,134 acres

by taking advantage of the provision for transferring land to their heirs and female dependants. The effects of the reform could also be mitigated by leasing back horse- and cattle-breeding land from the Government and by repurchasing at auction land which had been resumed in the names of selected family members and trusted retainers.[69] Moreover, implementation of the reforms was the responsibility of the local revenue administration which was in the pocket of the landlords: this rendered useless the regulation that intra-family transfers after 8 October 1958 would be excluded from the ceiling on land. There were numerous irregularities concerning the resumption of land to tenants – local officials cancelled sales to tenants and landlords still charged rent on land which the tenants had purchased!

A consensus is not only lacking concerning the impact of Ayub's land reforms. There is a similar debate regarding the effects of the reforms which he introduced into the administration of Sufi shrines. The 1959 West Pakistan Auqaf Properties Ordinance created a department entrusted to manage the endowed properties attached to mosques and shrines. Katherine Ewing[70] echoing in part Ayub's own justification of the measure[71] has seen this as a 'modernising' endeavour which aimed both to provide a cultural underpinning of the state and to loosen the traditional hold of the *pir* over the 'unwary' masses. Saifur Rahman Sherani on the other hand has maintained that the reforms actually strengthened the influence of the *pirs* and *sajjada nashins* by recognising their practices and appointing staff to organise practices like the *nazar*.[72] Whatever Ayub's intentions he was forced to turn to the *pirs* for support in the face of mounting opposition from the '*ulama*.[73] This was directed

---

were cultivated. Thus large landholders not only retained the most valuable part of their estates, but received generous government compensation for unproductive land.

[69] 'Requiem for a provincialist: Sir Khizr Hayat Tiwana, 1900-1975', *Friday Times*, special supplement I-IV, 19-25 January 1995.

[70] K. Ewing, 'The Politics of Sufism: Redefining the Saints of Pakistan', *Journal of Asian Studies* 42, (1984), pp. 106-14.

[71] Ayub provided a preface for a work which expressed the 'official' view that the Department of Aufaq was 'the remedy for the paralysing influence of the Mulla and the Pir over the rural and urban visions of Islam. [...] Unless and until the Mulla and Pir are excluded from our religious life, there is no likelihood of the successful dissemination of enlightenment, liberalism and a meaningful and vital faith among the people of Pakistan.' Javed Iqbal, *Ideology of Pakistan* (2nd edn Lahore, 1971), p. 58. Cited in Akhtar, 'Pakistan Since Independence', p. 381.

[72] S. R. Sherani, 'Ulema and Pir in Pakistani Politics' in H. Donnan and Pnina Werbner (eds), *Economy and Culture in Pakistan: Migrants and Cities in a Muslim Society* (Basingstoke, 1991), pp. 232ff.

[73] In 1965 Mufti Muhammad Shafi for example established a Council for Preaching and Reforms to challenge the views of the government-sponsored Islamic Research Institute

not just, as we have seen earlier, at his attempts to secularise the constitution. Even greater hostility arose from the Muslim Family Laws Ordinance (MFLO) which was promulgated on 15 July 1961. This measure marked the high-point of Islamic modernism in Pakistan, and was arguably the greatest innovation of the Ayub era. In order to fully appreciate its significance, it is important to consider both its background and the traditional Islamic teaching on the four issues of divorce, polygamy, child marriage and inheritance.

The MFLO was based in part on the recommendations of a Commission on Marriage and Family Laws which had been appointed in somewhat controversial circumstances[74] on 4 August 1955 during the Premiership of Muhammad Ali Bogra. The adverse response to the publication of the Commission's report the following year ensured that it lay unadopted. Ayub however felt both politically secure enough and sufficiently committed to its 'secular' recommendations to utilise its findings for reform purposes.

Islamic law on divorce (*talaq*) distinguishes between what is morally approved and what is permissible but morally reprehensible. In this latter category is *talaq al-bid'a* whereby a husband can unilaterally dissolve his marriage by three verbal pronouncements of divorce (*talaq*) at one time. The morally approved form of divorce is *talaq ahsan* in which the husband pronounces a single *talaq* and thereafter enters into a celibate relationship with his wife for three months during which a reconciliation is possible. The divorce only becomes final at the end of the three-month period. A variant on this which enjoys less approval on moral grounds is known as *talaq hasan* which involves a series of three *talaq* pronouncements at monthly intervals, after the third of which divorce is final. *Talaq al-bid'a* was the most common form of divorce among Pakistani Sunni Muslims, although it was unrecognised in Shia law. The MFLO set out to remove the abuses involved in this practice.

In this as in other matters relating to marriage, the Ordinance decreed that reference should made to an Arbitration Council which would comprise representatives of each of the spouses and the Chairman of the Union Council in which they resided. In order for a divorce to be legalised it had to be notified to the Arbitration Council and a period of three months would then elapse before it became final. During this

---

which was headed by the leading modernist Fazlur Rahman. The greatest opposition to Ayub however came from the JI.

[74] Bogra had entered into a polygamous marriage while in office, much to the outrage of the All Pakistan Women's Association (APWA). He agreed to the establishment of the Commission to mitigate the embarrassment arising from his own matrimonial affairs.

period the arbitration would attempt a reconciliation. In effect this meant that divorce had now to comply with the *talaq ahsan* form.[75]

Sunni law allows a husband to have up to four wives at one time subject to the provision that each receives just and equal treatment. Within the Shia community the system of *mut'ah* marriage is also practised, which allows an unlimited number of marriages of a fixed term only. When the term expires, which could be as little as a day, the marriage is immediately dissolved. Sunni scholars have criticised the *mut'ah* marriage contract as a form of legalised prostitution. Ayub was equally scathing in his criticism of Sunni and Shia polygamous practices which, he declared, had caused 'immense misery to innumerable tongue-tied women and innocent children. Thousands of families have been ruined because of the degenerate manner in which men have misused this permission [to have more than one wife] to suit their convenience.'[76] This disapproval was reflected in the MFLO requirement that the permission of the Arbitration Council would have to be sought if a husband wished to contract a polygamous marriage. The Council would be able to inquire both into the husband's motives and whether he had the consent of his existing wife. Remarriage without consent would provide grounds for a wife's judicial divorce. The Arbitration Council was empowered to enact a penalty of up to a year's imprisonment or a fine of Rs. 5,000 for a man who had married without its prior permission.

A more limited social reform introduced by the MFLO concerned the practice of child marriage. This had been restrained during the British era by a 1929 Act which placed the minimum ages for marriage at fourteen years for a female and eighteen for a male.[77] Arranged Child marriages were still contracted despite this legislation. The MFLO sought to discourage this practice further by raising the minimum age for a girl's marriage to sixteen.

Far more radical were the MFLO's provisions relating to inheritance. Both Sunni and Shia law excluded orphan grandchildren from inheriting a share of their grandfather's estate. The Ordinance however guaranteed to grandchildren of both sexes the share equal to that which would have passed to their father or mother had they been alive at the time of their grandparent's death.

Conservative Muslim opinion regarded the MFLO reform's regarding marriage and inheritance as contrary to Islamic law. A meeting of fifty

[75] Lucy Carroll, 'Nizam-i-Islam: Processes and Conflicts in Pakistan's Programme of Islamisation, with Special reference to the Position of Women', *Journal of Commonwealth and Comparative Politics* 20, no. 1 (March 1982), p. 59.

[76] Ayub Khan, *Friends Not Masters*, p. 106.

[77] Carroll, 'Women and Islamisation in Pakistan', p. 60.

'*ulama* from both East and West Pakistan met in Lahore on 13 March 1961 and backed Maududi's condemnation of the measure.[78] As soon as martial law was lifted, a bill was introduced into the National Assembly designed to repeal the Ordinance.[79] To counter this, Ayub ensured that the Constitution contained provisions which protected it from judicial scrutiny. Similar safeguards were built in at the time of the 1973 Constitution by which the MFLO had become totem for women's rights on the one hand and the *bête noir* of the Islamists on the other.

Economic development

The importance which Ayub attached to economic development can be seen in the fact that he assumed the Chairmanship of the Planning Commission[80] in 1961 and elevated the post of his deputy to Central Cabinet rank. This centralisation of planning however reduced the representation of Bengali views. This was because it abolished the East Pakistani Planning Board which had previously formulated plans for the eastern wing. Ironically, Ayub saw economic development as achieving both the aims of modernisation and of aiding east-west national integration.

In order to reduce east-west economic disparities, East Pakistan was given a greater share in central taxes. In comparison with the 1947-58 period, there was also a significant increase in public sector developmental expenditure.[81] This had little impact since it was the private sector which provided the motor for Pakistan's significant economic achievements during the so-called 'Golden Decade' of development during the Ayub era. These included a rise in *per capita* income of 14 per cent during the period of the second Five Year Plan (1960-5), which was achieved as a result of stepped up agricultural and manufacturing output. The average annual growth of manufacturing output during the Plan period was around 11.5 per cent. Private sector advances in the latter field had been encouraged through tax holidays and the expansion of credit facilities by means of the Industrial Development Bank of Pakistan (IDBP) and the Pakistan Industrial and Credit and Investment Corporation (PICIC). West Pakistani entrepreneurs received the bulk of this state sponsorship.

From 1961/2 to 1966/7 only 22 per cent of the PICIC loans went

78 Akhtar, 'Pakistan Since Independence', p. 392.

79 Feldman, *Revolution in Pakistan*, p. 149.

80 This replaced the Central Planning Board which had been established in 1953 and which had drafted Pakistan's first Five Year Plan (1955-60).

81 Jahan, *Pakistan: Failure in National Integration*, pp. 75ff.

to East Pakistan.[82] Therefore, although the province's annual growth rate increased from 1.7 per cent in 1954/5 to 1959/60 to 5.2 per cent for 1959/60 to 1964/5 it lagged considerably behind the western wing which recorded figures of 3.2 per cent and 7.2 per cent respectively.[83] The economic developments of the Ayub era thus added to Bengali alienation from the centre, despite such window dressing as establishing a separate Pakistan Industrial Development Corporation for each wing. There were however not only inter-wing but intra-wing disparities in development. Punjab with its military connections was not only the politically predominant region in West Pakistan, but possessed growing economic strength. Table 6.3 below provides a snapshot of the Punjabisation process at work in the years 1969-70.

Table 6.3. INDUSTRIAL DEVELOPMENT IN
WEST PAKISTAN, 1969-70

Region	Reporting (est.)	Value fixed assets (× 1,000 Rs.)
West Pakistan	3,587	4,852,949
Punjab	2,052	2,178,582
Sindh	1,419	2,099,535
NWFP	98	554,208
Balochistan	18	19,624

Source: Adapted from Pakistan Ministry of Finance Planning and Development, *Census of Manufacturing Industries, 1969-70* (Karachi, 1973) p. 5. Cited in M. Waseem, *Politics and the State in Pakistan* (Lahore, 1989), p. 203.

The emphasis on a private sector led development stood in stark contrast with that of many other 'third world' countries. It reflected the preferences of the United States, Japan and West Germany which were Pakistan's major aid donors and whose economic largesse was crucial to the aim of bringing about rapid industrialisation.[84] It was also in keeping with the ideology of the World Bank which provided loans for the PICIC and IDBP. Moreover the Planning Commission, which played a key role in coordinating the state's import substitution and export promotion policies, was assisted by the Development Advisory Service of Harvard University. In a real sense therefore Pakistan was a laboratory for modernisation theory's prescription for a 'take-

[82] *Ibid.*, p. 74 and 75.

[83] G.F. Papanek, *Pakistan's Development: Social Goals and Private Incentives* (Cambridge, MA, 1967) p. 20.

[84] During the period 1960-65 Pakistan received $2,365 million in total foreign assistance nearly 80 per cent of which took the form of loans. Anita M. Weiss, *Culture, Class and Development in Pakistan*, p. 35.

off'[85] into sustained economic growth through massive infusions of capital directed to industry by government and the establishment of a cultural, political and economic environment conducive to the releasing of entrepreneurial abilities.

The Pakistan economy made rapid strides during the Ayub era. Large-scale manufacturing grew at almost 17 per cent and economic growth rates averaged 5.5 per cent each year.[86] But development involves more than high rates of economic growth: wealth trickles down slowly if at all, and a policy based on the 'social utility of greed' is likely to threaten the fabric of society. Ayub's strategy of channelling resources to an entrepreneurial elite increased still further the inequalities in Pakistani society. In a staggering concentration of capital, a private entrepreneurial class emerged comprising Gujarati-speaking Khojas and Memons leavened with a sprinkling of Punjabi Chiniotis which controlled two-thirds of all industrial assets, and around three-quarters of insurance company and bank assets.[87] This class hardly required co-opting, dependent as it was on the government for credits, permits and licences. Nevertheless it became increasingly linked with the military, bureaucratic and landlord elites through strategic marriages.

While a small elite reaped the advantages of the rapid economic growth, the bulk of the population had to bear its burdens. These consisted of rising prices, especially for manufactured goods, which hit the rural poor hard. Real wages for industrial labour also declined because of the rise in food prices. Rapid urbanisation added to the misery as housing, health and transport services lagged hopelessly behind. Despite the high levels of growth, maldistribution of wealth meant that the absolute number of impoverished people rose from 8.65 to 9.33 million people in 1963-8.[88] The disenchantment increased as the economy slowed down[89] in the wake of the decline of foreign investment following the 1965 war with India. Drought also hit the agricultural sector which despite the industrial development still accounted for just under half of the total GNP in the mid-1960s.

Freed from the political constraints of his predecessors, Ayub had

---

85 This phrase was coined in the seminal study by W.W. Rostow, *The Stages of Economic Growth: a Non-Communist Model* (Cambridge, 1960).

86 M. Monshipouri and A. Samuel, 'Development and Democracy In Pakistan', p. 977.

87 Weiss, *Culture, Class and Development*, p. 34.

88 *Ibid.*, p. 35.

89 The growth in GNP in 1966/7 and 1967/8 declined from its pre-war annual average of 7.8 per cent to 5.5 per cent. Manufacturing output increased at 6 per cent compared with the annual average of 11.5 per cent of the second Five Year Plan (1960-5). S. J. Burki, 'The Management of Crises' in W. E. James and S. Roy (eds), *Foundations of Pakistan's Political Economy*, pp. 122-3.

hoped to achieve an economic breakthrough in the development decade.
Due to the emphasis on growth at the expense of income distribution,
the existing inequalities in Pakistani society had been exacerbated. The
regime was to reap the whirlwind of both growing social tensions and
regional conflicts as the imbalances increased between the eastern and
western wings. Foreign policy 'failures' provided a further focus for
the growing discontent.

Foreign affairs

Ayub's military training made him acutely aware of Pakistan's geostrategic vulnerability. Indeed he had played an important role, not
least during his visit in 1953, in the establishment of close defence
and diplomatic ties with the United States. Eight years later, this
time on a state visit, he earned ringing applause when he declared
in a speech to the Joint Session of the Congress: 'The only people
who will stand by you are the people of Pakistan.' President Kennedy
in his address of welcome the previous day at Andrews Air Force
Base had fulsomely described Pakistan as 'a friend of immediacy
and constancy'.[90] It was therefore no surprise when Ayub appointed
the pro-American Muhammad Ali Bogra as Foreign Minister in the
new cabinet which followed the promulgation of the 1962 Constitution.
Bogra's sudden death on 23 January 1963 opened the way, however,
for Zulfiqar Ali Bhutto to be appointed in his place.

Bhutto had made his debut on the international stage as early
as September 1957 when he addressed the United Nations General
Assembly. The following year he represented Pakistan at the Law
of the Sea Conference in Geneva, before holding a number of domestic
portfolios in Ayub's cabinets. Then, from 1963 until his resignation
in June 1966, he brought an unaccustomed glare of publicity to
the post of Foreign Minister. Bhutto cut a dynamic figure as a champion
of Pakistani rights which increasingly contrasted with the tired and
defeatist image of the President. Many Punjabis thrilled to his call
for a 'thousand-year war' with India in order to secure justice over
the Kashmir issue. His anti-Indian image was honed to perfection
by his 1965 United Nations Security Council address. Bhutto was
also lionised by the Pakistani left for his tilt away from the United
States and rapprochement with the Soviet Union and China. While
he earned the credit as the architect of this new foreign policy,
Ayub had in fact initiated the process before Bhutto became Foreign
Minister.

Ayub had reconsidered his long-established foreign policy doctrine

[90] Ayub Khan, *Friends Not Masters*, p. 136.

because of two important developments which cast their shadow over US-Pakistan relations. The celebrated U-2 spy plane episode of May 1960 brought home to Pakistan the dangers it faced if it incurred the wrath of its mighty Soviet neighbour. Gary Powers's plane had begun its ill-fated flight of 5 May from a base near Peshawar. Thirteen days later Khrushchev warned the world that not only would future flights be shot down, but the foreign bases from which they had taken off would 'receive shattering blows'.[91] Such an outburst was grist to the mill of those sections of Pakistani society which had always opposed the links with the United States. Ayub moreover must have been privately troubled by the fact that the Pakistanis had been kept in the dark about Powers's mission.[92] Significantly in the wake of the U-2 incident, Pakistan came to an agreement with the Soviet Union for technical assistance in oil exploitation in the Attock region.[93]

Pakistan-US relations were further strained in the autumn of 1961, when hostilities briefly erupted with Afghanistan in the disputed Bajaur region. Pakistan was criticised by sections of the American press and Congress for driving Afghanistan into the Soviet Union's arms by threatening its trade relations in retaliation for the violence in the Bajaur tribal area. The border with Afghanistan was not in fact reopened until July 1963. Pakistan was also censured for using US weapons in the conflict which had been provided only to deter communist aggression.[94]

This issue of US arms shipments to the subcontinent and the purpose of their deployment became more acrimonious following the war between India and China in October 1962. In the wake of India's defeat, the United States for the first time supplied weapons on a large scale to Pakistan's rival. The expansion of the Indian armed forces was viewed in Rawalpindi however as being directed at Pakistan rather than China. There was unanimous condemnation of the 'large-scale' Western arms sales to India during an emergency session of the National Assembly which met on 21 November-8 December 1962.[95] The session had followed a series of popular protests which had seen an invasion of the USIS library grounds in Karachi[96] and the stoning of government and army

[91] L.J. Halle, *The Cold War As History* (London, 1971), p. 374.

[92] See American Embassy Karachi to Department of the Airforce, 16 May 1960, 790.D.00(W) 15-1260, National Archives at College Park.

[93] This was signed in Moscow in January 1961 by Zulfikar Ali Bhutto who was at this time Pakistan's Minister for Fuel, Power and Natural Resources.

[94] Ziring, *The Ayub Era*, p. 21.

[95] American Embassy Karachi to Department of State, 3 January 1963, 790.D.00/1-363, National Archives at College Park.

[96] American Embassy Karachi to Department of State, 16 November 1962, 790.D.00/10-2762, National Archives at College Park.

vehicles in Rawalpindi, along with Flashman's Hotel which was well-known for its Western clientele.[97] In the wake of these popular out-pourings, Section 144 orders prohibiting meetings of more than five persons were imposed in Karachi, Lahore, Peshawar and Rawalpindi. Even more disquieting for the Americans however were reports forwarded to the State Department of a growing hostility towards them among the junior officer ranks of the Pakistan Army.[98]

Pakistan had begun negotiations with China earlier in 1961 over the demarcation of their borders. These were to bear fruit in the agreement of 2 March 1963. There was however growing Sino-Indian tension on the disputed McMahon Line[99] on the Tibet-North East Frontier Agency (NEFA) border and in the strategic Aksai Chin plain of eastern Ladakh in Kashmir. The halcyon days of the Panchsheel agreement had long since departed.[100] The Chinese invasion of the NEFA began on 20 October 1962. After a month of hostilities in which they roundly defeated the Indians, the Chinese declared a unilateral ceasefire and withdrew to the 1959 'line of actual control'.

The Indian military débâcle cost the stylish and irascible Krishna Menon his post as Defence Minister and cast a pall over the remainder of Nehru's Premiership. The much-vaunted policy on non-alignment was now made sufficiently flexible to allow the acceptance of Western military hardware. In December, Britain and America agreed at Nassau to supply Nehru with up to $120 million of emergency military aid. Within Pakistan, the hawks criticised Ayub for eschewing the opportunity to march troops into Kashmir. The growing anti-Americanism among Pakistan's intelligentsia was also given a clear focus with the dispatch of every new shipment of arms to New Delhi. The perceptible shift in American strategic interests from Pakistan to India prompted a reappraisal in Rawalpindi. The response was the development of a 'trilateral' policy in which Pakistan sought equidistant relationships with the United States, the Soviet Union and China.[101]

---

[97] American Embassy Karachi to Secretary of State, 21 November 1962, 790.D.00/11-2062, National Archives at College Park.

[98] Embassy Karachi to Department of State, 8 January 1963, 790.D.00/1-363, National Archives at College Park.

[99] China disputed the legitimacy of the McMahon Line, which had been drawn up in the 1914 Simla Convention. Similarly It did not accept the British Indian frontier imposed in Ladakh. Tensions had increased in the North East Frontier Agency following the 1959 revolt in Tibet and the Dalai Lama's exile in India.

[100] The five principles of mutuality negotiated between India and China in 1954 had included: respect for each other's territorial integrity and sovereignty; non-aggression; non-interference in each other's internal affairs; equality and mutual benefit; peaceful co-existence.

[101] The Americans displayed their displeasure at the Air Agreement Pakistan signed with China in August 1963, which introduced regular commercial services, by suspending

In March 1965 Ayub was greeted enthusiastically during a visit to Beijing. Joint statements were issued on such 'Third World' subjects as colonialism, Afro-Asian solidarity and, most important, Kashmir.[102] More substantially, Pakistan enjoyed the fruits of its new relationship with China in the form of a $60 million interest-free loan. The Soviet Union in the wake of its more balanced post-Tashkent South Asia policy vied with China in its economic[103] and military aid programme to Pakistan. For example, an arms agreement in July 1968 provided Rawalpindi with $30 million worth of equipment.[104] This assistance was important following the American termination of military aid to both India and Pakistan in the wake of the 1965 war.[105] Ayub's earlier pro-American image however meant that he personally gained few plaudits for this foreign policy shift. Bhutto was seen as its architect and became the main beneficiary of its popularity.

The atmosphere in the subcontinent after the autumn 1962 Chinese-Indian border conflict was not conducive to a continuation of Pakistan's constructive diplomacy with India which had culminated in the Indus Waters Treaty of 19 September 1960. This notable achievement was increasingly overshadowed by the Kashmir issue, which continued not only to bedevil bilateral relations but to form the principal interface between Pakistan's international and domestic politics.

The dismissal of Sheikh Abdullah's government in August 1953[106] marked the beginning of the strengthening of constitutional ties between Srinagar and New Delhi which threatened Pakistan's hopes for a plebiscite. The new Jammu and Kashmir Constitution which came into operation in January 1957 had declared that the state was an 'integral part of the Union of India'. The elections of the following March, in which the National Front triumphed, were indeed viewed in New Delhi as a popular confirmation of the state's accession to India. Pakistani opinion held however that both these and the subsequent elections of 1962 were rigged.

Two developments in 1963 led to a further deterioration in Indo-

---

a $4.3 million loan which had been agreed to help renovate Dhaka airport. Sir Morrice James, *Pakistan Chronicle*, p. 111.

102 Ayub followed this up the next month with a visit to Moscow.

103 This included aid towards the construction of Pakistan's first modern steel mill.

104 R. Sisson and Leo. E. Rose, *War and Secession*, p. 238.

105 The boycott was not total in that both countries could still purchase American equipment under a 'one-time exception' ruling.

106 Abdullah's attempts to extend the autonomy granted to the state of Jammu and Kashmir under Article 370 of the Indian Constitution had raised fears that he was really seeking independence. The immediate cause of his dismissal was the deteriorating situation in the Hindu-majority district of Jammu as a result of the agitation by the Praja Parishad.

Pakistan relations. In October the outgoing Prime Minister of Jammu and Kashmir, Bakshi Ghulam Muhammad, announced further constitutional changes which would bring the state more in line with the rest of the Indian Union.[107] A month or so later there was the major crisis of the mysterious disappearance and reappearance of the sacred relic of the Prophet Muhammad's hair from the Hazratbal shrine on the banks of the Upper Dal lake in Srinagar where it had been displayed since the time of Aurangzeb.[108] Kashmiri refugee groups led a day of protests and processions in Karachi on 1 January 1964. The largest demonstrations were in Srinagar itself. Communal disturbances rippled out from the state as far afield as Calcutta and the Khulna and Jessore districts of East Pakistan.

Internal developments in Jammu and Kashmir took another turn however with the release of Sheikh Abdullah from Jammu central jail on 8 April 1964. Hopes for a thaw in Indo-Pakistan relations were raised when Abdullah followed discussions with Indian leaders by being granted permission to meet Ayub in Rawalpindi the following month. Half a million people greeted the Lion of Kashmir's arrival. The talks ended with a public announcement that Ayub would visit India in June to discuss the Kashmir issue with the Indian Prime Minister, but Nehru's sudden death on 27 May brought this promising chapter to an end; his successor Lal Bahadur Shastri was in a much weaker position to bring about a rapprochement, even if he had wanted to. On 4 December his government announced that Articles 356 and 357 of the Indian Constitution, which laid down the provision for the introduction of direct presidential rule, would henceforth apply to Jammu and Kashmir to bring it in line with the other states. Thereafter relations deteriorated both within Kashmir and between India and Pakistan. Sheikh Abdullah's arrest on his return to India on 8 May 1965 following his departure on *hajj* and a controversial meeting on 31 March with the Chinese Prime Minister Chou En-Lai sparked off disturbances in Srinagar. These were to be overshadowed by a wider Indo-Pakistan conflict which marked a major turning-point in Pakistan's international and domestic politics.

The crisis began early in 1965 not in the mountains of Kashmir but on the tidal mud flats of the desolate Rann of Kutch which had formed a disputed frontier between Sindh and India since 1947. Clashes between border police escalated into full-scale fighting in which the

---

[107] These included changing the title of the head of the state, the *Sadar-i-Riyasat*, to Governor and the title of Prime Minister to Chief Minister. The state's representatives in the Indian parliament were henceforth to be directly elected rather than nominated by the Jammu and Kasmir Legislative Assembly.

[108] For further details see A. Lamb, *Kashmir: A Disputed Legacy, 1846-1990* (Hertingfordbury, 1991), pp. 205-6.

Pakistanis had the upper hand because they controlled the dry ground to the north of the Rann. Both sides agreed on 30 June, following British-led mediation,[109] that the *status quo* of 1 January 1965 would be restored. The reasons for the conflict still remain obscure, although it may well have been a testing-ground of both country's resolve and its equipment.

Even less transparent is the background to the infiltration of armed volunteers from Pakistan to Kashmir in what was code named Operation Gibraltar.[110] This attempt to resolve the Kashmir issue by force was probably planned as early as 1964, and it is apparent that Zulfiqar Ali Bhutto, whom Ayub had increasingly come to trust, played a leading role in its advocacy.[111] The disturbances in Kashmir following the Hazratbal episode seemed to indicate that the dislike of Indian rule was now overcoming the Kashmiri Muslims' stereotypical docility. Further encouragement was lent to the plan by India's poor military showing in 1962 and more recently in the Rann of Kutch. Operation Gibraltar however contained two basic flaws which were to cost Pakistan and the Ayub regime dear. It wrongly assumed that the mass of the Kashmiri Muslims were willing to engage in a general uprising at this juncture. The flawed intelligence-gathering which rationalised this assessment was to be repeated with even more catastrophic results on the eve of the army crackdown in East Pakistan some nine years later. Equally disastrously, Operation Gibraltar misread Indian intentions in assuming that New Delhi would seek to limit the conflict to Kashmir.[112] The normally cautious Ayub, perhaps because he wanted success in Kashmir to bolster his generally failing fortunes, nevertheless gambled on the Operation Gibraltar proposal.

The fighting in August escalated in Jammu and soon involved regular units of the Pakistan Army as well as the *mujahadin* irregulars. In response to the Pakistani thrusts south towards Chhamb and Akhnur in the additional operation known as Grand Slam,[113] the Indians attacked at dawn on 6 September across the Punjab frontier towards Lahore and Sialkot. The element of surprise was so great that many Pakistani soldiers stumbled to the front line in their pyjamas. The following days saw fierce engagements between the Pakistani M-48s and the Indian Centurion tanks near Sialkot and to the south of Lahore. The citizens

---

109 For details see Sir Morrice James, *Pakistan Chronicle*, pp. 124ff.

110 See R. Brines, *The Indo-Pakistani Conflict* (New York, 1968); for a personal account see Mohammad Musa, *My Version: Indo-Pakistan War 1965* (Lahore, 1983).

111 James, *Pakistan Chronicle*, p. 128.

112 Bhutto appears to have specifically assured Ayub that India would not attack Pakistan across the Punjab frontier. *Ibid.*, p. 132.

113 For details of this operation see Altaf Gauhar, *Ayub Khan, Pakistan's First Military Ruler* (Lahore, 1994), pp. 330ff.

of both Lahore and Rawalpindi grew accustomed to air raid warnings and sporadic raids. The tank battles, though highly destructive, were indecisive. The run-down of equipment which could not be replenished following the US arms ban of 8 September exerted far more influence on Ayub's thinking than the unanimous United Nations Security Resolutions of 4 and 6 September calling for an immediate cease-fire.

Altaf Gauhar has revealed in his autobiography, from the Pakistan President's own verbatim account, that Ayub took the Chinese card sufficiently seriously at this time to make a clandestine visit to Beijing on the night of 19/20 September. In order to maintain secrecy, the daily routine was continued in the President's House with the bearer taking morning tea to Ayub's bedroom. Even the security guards did not suspect his absence. Neither Ayub nor Bhutto, who accompanied him, was prepared however to accept an offer of unconditional support from Chou En-lai dependent on the Pakistanis' preparedness to fight a long guerrilla-type war in 'which cities like Lahore might be lost' but the 'Indian forces would be sucked into a quagmire of popular resistance'.[114]

Ayub's decision to accept the ceasefire on 22 September shocked a populace fed on a diet of victory reports. It infuriated Bhutto, who had garnered support from Indonesia, Turkey and Saudi Arabia for the Pakistan cause and set great store by the Chinese stance which had been openly hostile to India. Indeed, by raising Sino-Indian differences over Sikkim, Chou En-lai appeared to pave the way for military intervention. Bhutto's anti-Western attitudes were certainly strengthened by the knowledge that Britain and America had leaned heavily on Ayub to agree a ceasefire. The seeds of his breach with Ayub which was to be so damaging to his erstwhile patron, were also sown at this time.

Ayub's action had been prompted not so much by the loss of heart which Bhutto later claimed as by the reality of declining ammunition stocks and other essential supplies. The US freeze on military shipments dealt a savage blow to the Pakistan Air Force, despite its low ratio of losses compared to the Indian Air Force. The absence of spare parts jeopardised not only its fighting ability but also such routine tasks as the shipment of food to the Gilgit Agency in C-130 Transports.[115] There is some truth however in the claim that his fear of annoying Pakistan's Western allies prevented him from taking full advantage of the leverage provided by China. Significantly Ayub embarked

114 *Ibid.*, pp. 352-3.

115 American Embassy Karachi to Secretary of State, 16 October 1965, Central Policy Files 1964-6 Pol 27 Military Operations India-Pakistan, National Archives at College Park.

on a damage limitation excursion to Washington the month before his January 1966 meeting with the ill-fated Shastri at Tashkent. Kosygin had offered the Soviet Union's diplomatic good offices in the negotiation of a settlement in the hope of checking Chinese influence in Pakistan.

The preliminary discussions began on 4 January and were led on the Pakistan side by Bhutto and on the Indian by Swaran Singh, but Ayub kept Bhutto out of the talks with Shastri. Within hours of the signing ceremony, Shastri suffered a fatal heart attack. This tragedy stilled criticism of the agreement in India. The sullen response in Pakistan turned within forty-eight hours to rioting in Lahore, led by students of the Punjab University who denounced Ayub for selling out Kashmir to India. The violence was confined mainly to the University area and the Mall[116] and was brought rapidly under control, but the Tashkent Declaration dealt a mortal blow to Ayub's reputation. At a press conference in Lahore on 13 January 1966, Maulana Maududi (JI), Chaudhri Muhammad Ali (Nizam-i-Islam), Nawabazada Nasrullah Khan (Awami League) and Shaukat Hayat (Council Muslim League) denounced Ayub's 'unpardonable weakness' in purchasing peace at the cost of national honour and betraying the 'just cause' of Kashmir.[117] The future lay with Bhutto who in stark contrast to his President was hailed as the champion of Pakistan's rights.

The descent from power

Ayub's final years in power, like those of Anthony Eden who had launched a similarly ill-conceived secret invasion plan a decade earlier, were dogged by ill-health[118] and dissension. Zulfiqar Ali Bhutto, following a lengthy leave, finally resigned in June 1966. He was fêted by crowds at every stopping place on the train journey home from Rawalpindi to his native Larkana. Such an acclamation sowed the seeds

116 American Embassy Karachi to Secretary of State, 15 January 1966, Central Policy Files 1964-6, Political and Defense Files Pol 27 Military Operations India-Pakistan, National Archives at College Park.

117 American Embassy Karachi to Secretary of State, 31 January 1966, Central Policy Files 1964-6, Political and Defense Files Pol 27 Military Operations India-Pakistan, National Archives at College Park.

118 Ayub was seriously ill at the beginning of 1968 and took some time to recuperate. According to Altaf Gauhar's account, the Commander-in-Chief, General Yahya Khan, responded to the crisis by staging what amounted to an unofficial coup in which Ayub's contact with his political and civilian associates 'was terminated'. Ayub's illness, he maintains, 'changed the domestic situation drastically. [...] Ayub was never the same man again...the generals did not quite forget the taste of power they had briefly savoured. They also knew that Ayub would not be able to go through the strain of another election in 1969-70.' A. Gauhar, 'Pakistan: Ayub Khan's Abdication', *Third World Quarterly* 7, no. 1 (January 1985), p. 117.

for his decision fifteen months later to form a new opposition party dedicated to 'democracy, independent foreign policy and a socialist pattern of economy'. Such a new force was clearly required in the wake of the dismal showing of the opposition National Conference which was held in Lahore early in February 1967. The small contingent of East Pakistani delegates quit when the gathering failed to support a demand for more autonomy in the eastern wing as expressed by the 6-Point Programme of Sheikh Mujibur Rahman, the leader of the East Pakistan Awami League. It was also impossible to establish a consensus for the launching of a civil disobedience campaign to revoke the Tashkent Declaration. Protests were limited to the actions of individuals like Shaukat Hayat who were promptly arrested for their pains.

The first convention of the Pakistan People's Party was held in Lahore at the end of November 1967. In order to circumvent the Government's prohibition of assembly in public places it took place at the private residence of the left-wing intellectual Mubashar Hasan.[119] The assembled gathering including a handful of women, but significantly no delegates from East Pakistan. The Foundation Meeting Document set out the party's progressive credo, declaring that 'the people...are not willing to tolerate the present conditions much longer. They want a new system based on justice and attached to the essential interests of the toiling millions. Only a new party can discharge this responsibility.'[120] These ideas were later to be given fuller expression in the concept of Islamic *musawaat* (egalitarianism/socialism) and to be popularised by such writers as Hanif Ramay.

The formation of the PPP was a major blow for the Ayub regime as it enabled the mounting labour and student unrest to be channelled against it. In its early years the party attracted support from radical union and student leaders such as Mukhtar Rana, Ziauddin Butt, Mahmud Babur, Mairaj Muhammad Khan, Raja Anwar and Amanullah Khan.[121] The students were attracted by Bhutto's patriotic stand in 1965 and by the fact that the PPP was sympathetic to such interests as the repeal of the University Ordinance.[122] Labour unrest was rooted in the restrictions on union activity and the failure of wages to keep pace with

[119] Maleeha Lodhi, 'The Pakistan People's Party', p. 118.

[120] *Ibid.*, p. 124

[121] Mukhtar Rana was a labour activist in the leading Punjabi industrial city of Lyallpur. Ziauddin Butt and Mahmud Babur were involved with unions in Lahore and Multan respectively. Mairaj Muhammad Khan was a former President of the National Students Federation. Raja Anwar and Amanullah Khan were student activists from Rawalpindi and Lahore.

[122] This restricted student political activity and held the Damocles Sword of the forfeiture of their degrees over the heads of students accused of subversive activities.

inflation or to share in the profits which were accruing to the business class. The PPP provided an important rallying point for the mounting opposition.

Ayub was dealt almost as grievous a blow by his former chief economist of the Planning Commission, Dr Mahbubul Haq, as by his former Foreign Minister. In April 1968 Haq raised serious questions about the thrust of economic development during the previous decade which had encouraged economic growth without reference to social justice and redistribution. Inequalities had multiplied as the benefits of the increased production had accrued to the 'twenty-two families' who controlled 66 per cent of all industrial assets, 79 per cent of insurance funds and 80 per cent of bank assets.[123] Such a critique chimed in with the opposition's long-held views and was particularly devastating coming from one so close to the regime. The JI fulminated against the 'un-Islamic' outlook of the Government which had fostered the ostentatious display of wealth amid squalor and poverty. Workers, students and professionals increasingly took to the streets. A further crack in the regime's support was revealed on 17 November when Air Marshal Muhammad Asghar Khan, the retired former chief of the Pakistan Air Force, threw in his lot with the opposition.

Pakistan was wracked with popular disturbances from November 1968 until Ayub's resignation on 25 March 1969.[124] Clashes between students and the police in Rawalpindi in which one demonstrator was killed sparked the countrywide violence. On 10 November a student attempted to assassinate Ayub when he was addressing a public meeting in Peshawar. Bhutto threw his considerable weight behind the student-led disturbances which now spread like wildfire in the towns and cities of the north-west Punjab. He even turned his unpolished Urdu to advantage by declaring:

> There are only two languages in Pakistan – the language of the exploited and the language of the exploiters. Today I am going to speak to you in the language of the exploited.[125]

Bhutto was arrested on 13 November, but even then the PPP was able to play a leading role in the agitation because of its close links with the main protesting groups – the students, lawyers and organised labour. It was not of course alone in orchestrating protests, both the NAP and the JI also played a significant role. In December the disturbances spread to East Pakistan where they reflected the widespread

123 Harun-or-Rashid, 'The Ayub Regime and the Alienation of East Bengal', *Indo-British Review* 17, nos 1. and 2 (September 1989 and December 1989), p. 181.

124 For a detailed examination see S. J. Burki, 'Socio-economic determinants of political violence'.

125 M. Lodhi, 'The Pakistan People's Party', p. 152.

enthusiasm for the radical autonomy claims contained in Sheikh Mujibur Rahman's 6-Point demand.[126] The significance of the different bases of agitation in the two wings is examined in the next chapter. It is important to note here however that the simultaneous political breakdown raised the spectre of the reintroduction of martial law if Ayub could not come to an agreement with his opponents. Eight opposition parties including the PPP joined the Democratic Action Committee which was convened by Nawabzada Nasrullah Khan. The notable absentees were the East Pakistan Awami League and the NAP. In an attempt to establish a dialogue with the Democratic Action Committee, Ayub agreed to lift the three-year-old state of emergency and to the release of Bhutto and other detainees. The PPP leader received tumultuous welcomes both in his native Larkana and in Karachi. He accused Ayub of 'playing cat-and-mouse games' and boycotted the talks with the Government which were to take place in Rawalpindi. The die was now cast. The PPP would not accept any reform proposed by the regime which fell short of Ayub's ousting from power. The President who was now faced with his political system collapsing like a pack of cards was not anxious to hang on to power, but 'could not leave the field to extremists'.[127] Moreover, the army commanders were becoming impatient with the mounting chaos which had already led them to be called to maintain law and order in a number of cities.

Ayub nevertheless felt the necessity to have a final attempt to establish a dialogue with the opposition. In order to seize the initiative he announced on 21 February that he would not be a candidate in the forthcoming elections. Shortly afterwards he released Sheikh Mujibur who attended the opening of the Round Table Talks in Rawalpindi, but eventually walked out as the issue of autonomy for East Pakistan and representation on the basis of population in the National Assembly (which would give East Pakistan a majority) was unresolved. Bhutto had also boycotted the parleys which began on 10 March as did the NAP, leaving the field open to the more moderate opposition groups. Even they demanded what in effect was the complete dismantling of Ayub's political edifice with a return to direct elections, and a federal parliamentary system which included the dismantling of the One Unit Scheme. 'They thought I was God Almighty,' Ayub disclosed to his advisers; 'each one of them presented his demands thinking I could grant them. If all their demands were met we would be left with no Pakistan.'[128] While he was speaking, strikes and demonstrations were

---

[126] See Chapter 7 for details.

[127] Gauhar, 'Pakistan: Ayub Khan's Abdication', p. 121.

[128] *Ibid.*, p. 123.

paralysing East Pakistan and the administration virtually collapsed. The
disorder which had preceded the 1958 coup appeared like child's play
in comparison with the anarchy which now prevailed in some towns
and rural areas of East Pakistan.

By 17 March Ayub decided that martial law should be promulgated.
Mindful perhaps that this was an admission of personal defeat, he began
to waver in this conviction, before finally resigning from office on
25 March. In his last address he reiterated the West Pakistan elite's
long-held contention that 'the secret of the continued existence of Pakistan
is in a strong centre.'[129] The mounting evidence from his regime pointed
to the opposite conclusion. The non-participation of the Bengali elite
in the tightly-controlled political process and in the centralised administration had accelerated the process of alienation historically rooted
in economic disparity and in the ethnocentrism of the West Pakistan
establishment. The key to Pakistan's survival lay not in maintaining
a strong centre, but in developing consociational-type arrangements of
power-sharing based on the acceptance of cultural pluralism. The inherited traditions of viceregalism and political intolerance precluded
such a course of action, with tragic consequences.

The Army Chief of Staff, General Agha Muhammad Yahya Khan,
took up the reins of power at Ayub's invitation. The 'handover' was
without any legal foundation – according to the 1962 Constitution, the
Speaker of the National Assembly would take over in the event of
the President's resignation. Yahya like his predecessor had received
his training in the pre-independence Indian Army[130] and seen active
service during the Second World War. He shared the West Pakistani
military elite's prejudices towards the non-martial castes. In a replay
of the events ten years earlier, the constitution was abrogated, the national
and the provincial legislatures were dissolved, and political activities
were banned, prompting *The Economist* editorial headline 'Tweedle
Khan Takes Over'.[131]

Ayub saw the answer to Pakistan's search for stability in modernisation
and depoliticisation. While the achievement of the MFLO cannot be
gainsaid, Pakistan's first military ruler institutionalised the muzzling
of the press through the National Press Trust and manipulation of the
electoral process was also developed as a fine art. The Ayub era looked

129 R. Jahan, *Pakistan: Failure in National Integration*, p. 175.

130 He was however a product not of Sandhurst, but of the Dehra Dun Indian Military
Academy.

131 *The Economist* (London), 29 March 1969. In reality Yahya differed considerably in
temperament and personality from Ayub – He was much more outgoing and less puritanical.

backwards to the guardian state of the British Raj at the same time as witnessing a state-sponsored Green Revolution and industrialisation process. Rapid socio-economic change without an increase in political participation and Interest articulation culminated in the regime's collapse.

The Ayub system ended by exacerbating regional and class inequalities and failed to address the state's longstanding identity and legitimisation problems. Ayub's inability to establish 'a genuine participatory political process' ensured for example that his anti-disparity measures failed to placate Bengali grievances. The regime, which had been expected by Western 'neo-realists'[132] to demonstrate a superior ability to its civilian predecessors in initiating 'development', instead provided empirical support for the contention that Third World military governments are as bound by economic, social and political constraints as are democracies. The man on horseback has no more proved to be a national saviour in the subcontinent than in Africa or Latin America.

---

[132] This school of thought depicted military regimes as more rational in decision making and more institutionalised than civilian counterparts. The military were thus better equipped to implement modernisation than other types of government in developing countries. See for example the work of H. Daadler, *The Role of the Military in Developing Countries* (The Hague, 1962); J.J. Johnson, *The Military and Society in Latin America* (Stanford, CA, 1964).

7

THINGS FALL APART

Yahya Khan ruled Pakistan as President[1] from March 1969 until December 1971. This momentous period witnessed the dissolution of the One Unit Scheme and the holding of Pakistan's first national elections based on universal suffrage in December 1970. The success of Bhutto, the *Quaid-i-Awam* (Leader of the Masses), in West Pakistan and of Mujibur Rahman, *Bangla Bandho* (Brother of Bengal), in the eastern wing confirmed the different political trajectories and aspirations in the two parts of the country. Yahya's decision to launch a pre-emptive military operation in East Pakistan set in train the course of events which culminated in the break-up of Pakistan and the emergence of Zulfiqar Ali Bhutto as leader of the truncated country. Thereby Pakistan achieved two unwanted historical firsts, boasting both a civilian Martial Law Administrator in Bhutto and being the first new state to experience a successful secessionist movement. In Tariq Ali's masterful words, 'the "two nations" theory, formulated in the middle-class living rooms of Uttar Pradesh, was buried in the Bengali countryside.'[2]

Inevitably a passionate debate has raged concerning the traumatic events of this era. Writings on the role of India, Mujib and Bhutto[3] in the break-up of Pakistan are especially polemical.[4] The reasons for Yahya's action in March 1971 are equally contested, as is the number of casualties which resulted from the Pakistan Army's genocidal massacre in the eastern wing.[5] Before turning to the tumultuous tide of events, it is necessary to reflect both on this literature and on the longer-term causes of the alienation of the East Pakistan political leadership. For while Yahya's mishandling of the situation created the final dénouement, in Herbert Feldman's words he received into his hands a political *haereditas*

---

[1] He assumed the office of President on 31 March 1969, 6 days after taking over power as Chief Martial Law Administrator.

[2] T. Ali, *Can Pakistan Survive? The Death of a State* (Harmondsworth, 1983) p. 96.

[3] For Bhutto's interpretation of events see *The Great Tragedy* (Karachi, 1971).

[4] Bhutto's opponents especially in the JUI and NAP claimed that his lust for power had resulted in the collapse of Pakistan.

[5] For a detailed account see A. Mascarenhas, 'Genocide: Why the Refugees Fled', *Sunday Times* (London), 13 June 1971.

damnosa in terms of inter-wing relations.[6] Bhutto was equally gloomy when he compared Pakistan at the time of Yahya Khan's assumption of the powers of Chief Martial Law Administrator to 'a patient in the last stages of tuberculosis'.[7]

Various explanations, many of which are polemical in content, have been offered for the break-up of Pakistan. Bangladeshi writers have naturally understood developments in terms of Bengali nationalism rooted both in the perception of the western wing's constitutional, economic and social discrimination and in attachment to Bengali culture and language.[8] Primordialist explanations however are faced with the problem of both explaining the gap between the language movement of the early 1950s and the nationalist struggle a decade later on the one hand and, on the other, the apparent plasticity of Bengali political identity, which was moored in Islam in 1947 and linguistically centred just twenty-four years later.

Harun-or-Rashid has attempted to synthesise primordialist and instrumentalist understandings of the emergence of Bangladesh. On the one hand he acknowledges that 'it was not simply geography that separated the two wings' but that the people 'had different ethnicity, history, tradition, language and culture.' But on the other, he sees as highly significant the 'near total elimination of East Bengal's dominant and expanding petit-bourgeoisie by the Ayub system.' This class in its competition with the West Pakistan power elite developed its 'self-image as the preserver of Bengali culture',[9] a comment which seems to go against the evidence from elsewhere that Ayub in his last years was trying to develop a Bengali class of entrepreneurs.

In sharp contrast to Harun-or-Rashid's analysis are the conspiracy theses of West Pakistani writers. Qutbuddin Aziz for example points the finger of accusation at India and blames the loss of the eastern wing on the Indian intervention on behalf of the 'rebellious' Mukti Bahini forces.[10] This type of analysis took its cue from the official Pakistani version of events contained in the White Paper on *The Crisis in East Pakistan.* It pointed to Indian 'collusion' with 'anti-State' elements in East Pakistan from the time of the Agartala Conspiracy and maintained that the Indian military intervention in 1971 was rooted in the fact

---

[6] H. Feldman, *The End and the Beginning: Pakistan, 1969-1971* (Karachi, 1976) p. 6.

[7] Bhutto, *The Great Tragedy* p. 9.

[8] See, M. Ahmed, *Bangladesh: Constitutional Quest for Autonomy, 1950-1971* (Dhaka, 1971); Talukder Maniruzzaman, *The Bangladesh Revolution and its Aftermath* (Dhaka, 1980); R. Jahan, *Pakistan. Failure in National Intergration* (New York, 1972).

[9] Harun-Or-Rashid, 'The Ayub Regime and the Alienation of East Bengal' *Indo-British Review* XVII, nos 1 and 2 (September and December 1989) p. 187-8.

[10] Q. Aziz, *Blood and Tears* (Karachi, 1974).

that India had never accepted the creation of Pakistan.[11] Sheikh Mujib's contact with the Indian authorities cannot be denied, but it is too convenient to blame India for the outcome which was rooted in the widespread cultural and political alienation of the Bengali people.

Indeed, the most fruitful approach is to link the cultural and historical dimension with a state centred analysis.[12] The events of 1971 firstly cannot be fully understood without reference to the ambiguities surrounding Bengali Muslim support for the Pakistan movement. A Bengali as distinct from Pakistani identity was further strengthened by the language movement of the 1948-52 era. By the time the language issue was addressed, a serious psychological rift had been created. But the shift from linguistic regionalism to nationalism only occurred because of the Pakistan state's rejection of the principle of unity in diversity in favour of a highly centralised political system. This philosophy rested on the inherited viceregal tradition and on the domestic and foreign policy interests of the West Pakistani power elites. The bureaucratic-military oligarchy felt threatened by the demands for political participation and decentralisation of power made by the articulate sections of Bengali society. Executive action was resorted to in both 1954 and 1958 to defuse this threat. This misguided political strategy was at the root of Bengali alienation.

Such a policy did not command the soldiers' universal support. Major-General Khwaja Wasid-ud-Din, Commander of the 10th Division at Lahore, opined to the American Consul-General early in 1963:

'The only thing for the Central Government to do is to recognise and admit the mistakes it has made in the Eastern Wing since Partition and through sympathy and understanding' try to deal with the East Wing problems. Forceful or repressive measures will not only fail, *but will only contribute to a further deterioration in the political situation there* [emphasis added].'[13]

Such sane counsels unfortunately did not prevail. In the words of Aijaz Ahmad, 'full-scale military terror [was deployed] in defence of a unitary state and a vice-regal tradition on the part of a regime that preferred, in the long run to lose half the country than to come to terms with the democratic aspirations of the [Bengali] majority of the Pakistani population.'[14]

[11] Government of Pakistan, *The Crisis in East Pakistan* (Islamabad, 1971).

[12] This understanding is sketched out in A. Jalal, *Democracy and Authoritarianism in South Asia: A Comparative and Historical Perspective* (Cambridge, 1995) p. 186-7.

[13] American Consul General Lahore to the Department of State, 22 January 1963, 790D.00/1-1663 Box 2116 National Archives at College Park.

[14] A. Ahmad, 'The Rebellion of 1983: A Balance Sheet', *South Asia Bulletin* 4, 1 (spring

Despite both the cultural suppression highlighted by Ayub's playing down of the 100th anniversary celebrations of the birth of the great Bengali poet Rabindranath Tagore (1861-1941)[15] followed by the later ban on the broadcasting of Tagore's poetry and the internal economic colonisation of the eastern wing, a process of political accommodation could have ensured Pakistan's unity. Instead the easier option of repression was adopted which only radicalised Bengali opinion. The consequences for example of the dismissal of the United Front Government were evidenced in the Awami League's replacement of its 21-Point Programme with the 6-Point Programme (May 1966).[16] While the demand for the recognition of Bengali as one of the national languages formed the centre piece of the former, the latter called for the establishment of full provincial autonomy in East Pakistan on the basis of the Lahore Resolution. Fiscal autonomy which had not been included in the original 21 Points was now added with the provision that the eastern wing should not only raise its own taxes but mint its own currency and operate its own separate foreign exchange account. The centre would be left only with responsibility for defence and foreign affairs. Significantly, with regard to defence the 21 Points' call for the movement of the Pakistan naval headquarters to the eastern wing was beefed up in 1966 with the demand for a separate militia or paramilitary force.

Yahya's inheritance from Ayub

It should be unnecessary to labour any further the point that the economic policies and depoliticisation of the Ayub decade exerted a counter-productive impact on inter-wing relations. The aim of this section is rather to emphasise two specific legacies, namely the impact of the 1965 Indo-Pakistan War and of the celebrated Agartala Conspiracy Case.

The conventional wisdom is that the 1965 conflict was unpopular in East Pakistan because the Kashmir issue had always possessed much less emotional appeal for Bengalis than for their West Pakistani brethren. While this latter fact is undeniable,[17] declassified State Department docu-

---

1984) p. 43.

[15] The East Pakistan hierarchy was conspicuously absent from all the Tagore centenary celebrations in April-May 1961. This contrasted with the Government's enthusiasm for the counter-celebration of the Muslim poet Nazrul Islam on 25 May. American Consul Dacca to Department of State, 1 June 1961, 790D 00/5-2261.

[16] For complete details of the 6 Point Programme see: M. Rashiduzzaman, 'The Awami League in the Political Development of Pakistan' *Asian Survey* 10, 7 (July 1970) p. 583.

[17] Nurul Amin, the East Pakistan Council Muslim League leader, privately remarked to the US Ambassador in January 1966 for example, that the 'West Wing is infected with

ments reveal that East Pakistani attitudes to the 1965 war were in reality
surprisingly enthusiastic. A perplexed Consul-General attempted to explain this state of affairs to Washington in terms of the 'exciting change
from the usual boredom which characterises life in the East Wing',
and the 'shaky personalities' of the Bengali intellectuals who 'seek
to externalise their problems into fervent cataclysmic struggles between
good and evil' while the enthusiasm among large elements of the traditional peasantry stemmed from the 'issue being presented to them as
Islam in danger from attack'. He ended his unconvincing explanation
with the revealing comment that 'reactions to War have shown an almost
unusual lack of interest in its effects...on economic development.
Economic development [was] *brushed aside by people from all walks
of life as something definitely unimportant* [emphasis added].'[18]

The reality was thus not as clear-cut as some writers would have
us believe. Nevertheless, in three other important respects the 1965
War did mark a watershed. Most important, it underscored the geographical isolation and vulnerability of the eastern wing. During the seventeen
days of the conflict it was left to fend for itself in defence and economic
matters. There was just one infantry division, elements of a tank regiment
and a squadron of Korean war vintage US-built F-86 Sabre jets stationed
in the province to face a potentially vastly superior Indian force.[19] No
clearer lesson could have been provided in the need for self-reliance.
One immediate response was the demand for an independent defence
capability. The war secondly undermined the myth of the of the West
Pakistan martial castes' military prowess. The realisation that the generals
possessed feet of clay (though impossible to demonstrate) must have
emboldened Bengali activists in their struggle for provincial autonomy.
Finally, the depression which followed the war, together with the further
diversion of resources to the West Pakistan military, fuelled the regional
economic disparities.

Sheikh Mujib had been in prison since May 1966 when on 18 January
1968 he was named as a leading figure in a conspiracy to bring about

---

a kind of madness over Kashmir. We have a good case on Kashmir, but we can only
get the substance of what we want through agreement with India.. Even if we could
(impose our will) we would destroy ourselves in the process. We must cultivate good
will with India if we really want freedom for the people of Kashmir.' American Embassy
Karachi to Department of State, 17 January 1966, Central Policy File 1964-6 (Political
and Defense) Pol. 27 Military Operations India-Pakistan. National Archives at College
Park.

[18] American Embassy Karachi to Secretary of State, 3 October 1965, Central Policy
File 1964-6 (Political and Defense) Pol. 27 Military Operations India-Pakistan. National
Archives at College Park.

[19] Mizanur Rahman, 'The Emergence of Bangladesh as a Sovereign State', unpubl. Ph.D.
thesis, Institute of Commonwealth Studies, 1975, London, p. 100.

the secession of East Pakistan with Indian help[20]. The list of thirty-five conspirators included three high-ranking East Pakistan civil servants. The case against them became known as the Agartala Conspiracy since it was at Agartala that the accused were alleged to have met Indian army officers. It is now clear that Mujib did hold secret discussions with local Indian leaders there in July 1962. Moreover, following the 1965 war there were meetings between Awami League leaders and representatives of the Indian Government at a number of secret locations.[21] The Ayub regime thus had some grounds to believe that bringing the case would take the wind out of the sails of the 6-Point movement. The Agartala contacts however did not provide solid evidence of a Mujib-India secessionist conspiracy in East Pakistan, and in its absence the accusations were to prove extremely counterproductive given the prevailing political atmosphere.

Bengali resentment was already at a peak when the case was brought to court. Sheikh Mujib and his co-defendants took on the role of martyrs as evidence emerged of police torture. Moreover, the hearing in open court presented Sheikh Mujib with the perfect platform to argue the Awami League cause. The prosecution's bungling undermined the credibility of the case so that it increasingly appeared that the conspiracy was against the Bengali autonomists rather than against the Ayub regime. The popular hostility evoked by the case peaked when one of the defendants, Sergeant Zahurul Haq, was murdered while in custody. In a by now familiar pattern, students led the protests forming an Action Committee with its own 11-Point Programme. Ayub attempted to placate the rising tide of anger by dropping the case and convening a Round Table Conference. Sheikh Mujib triumphantly emerged from prison to represent the Awami League at the Conference, but he walked out when its demands for full provincial autonomy were ignored. The continuing disturbances in the eastern wing played an important role in the toppling of the Ayub regime.

Administrative and constitutional developments

The early period of Yahya Khan's administration was reminiscent of Ayub's with its publication of a stream of regulations designed to curb corruption and improve public discipline. A stiff penalty of up to fourteen

[20] The same day that Mujibur was publicly named in the case, Mr Ojha, the First Secretary of the Indian High Commission in Dhaka, was declared *persona non grata*.

[21] Md. Abdul Wadud Bhuiyan, 'The Movement for Regional Autonomy in East Pakistan and the Agartala Conspiracy Case', *Indo-British Review* XVII, nos 1 and 2 (September and December 1989), p. 200.

years' rigorous imprisonment was introduced for the adulteration of foodstuffs, whjle publications offensive to Islam or 'disrespectful' to the Quaid-i-Azam were punishable by seven years' imprisonment.[22] The Fundamental Rights enshrined in the 1962 Constitution were suspended and the military courts' judgements could not be challenged by civil courts.

Martial Law Regulation no. 58 established a system of accountability for civil servants, who could be dismissed for inefficiency, corruption, misconduct or subversive activities; 303 persons in all were dealt with under this regulation.[23] In contrast with Ayub, the second military regime in its early stages kept the bureaucrats at arm's length from the decision-making process. Its 'parade ground' style has been dissected by Hasan Zaheer in his authoritative study of the separation of East Pakistan.[24] The most influential positions were held by soldiers who acted as martial law administrators, governors and advisers. Within the Secretariat of the Chief Martial Law Administrator, Lieutenant-General S.G.M. Peerzada acted as the Principal Staff Officer to the President, assuming the status of a *de facto* Prime Minister. Beneath him were a number of army officers dealing with martial law and civil affairs. The Secretariat's legal expert was Colonel Hasan.[25] The only two civilians in Yahya's inner coterie of eight decision-makers were M.M. Ahmad, his Economic Adviser, and the Director of the Civil Intelligence Bureau. In another departure, Yahya operated a much more collective leadership. This reflected in part his personal style but, more important, stemmed from the fact that he lacked Ayub's authority *vis-à-vis* his fellow-officers. The 'inner cabinet' was to become increasingly divided as a result of the conflicts between the former Air Force Commander-in-Chief Nur Khan and the more conservative army generals.

Yahya announced on 5 August the appointment of a Council of Ministers. Power however still lay firmly with the military despite the establishment of a civilian cabinet. While there were equal numbers of members from the two wings, the most powerful portfolios were reserved for West Pakistanis. These included Defence, Foreign Affairs, Economic Affairs and Planning which were all personally held by Yahya. His kinsman Nawab Muzaffar Qizilbash, who had begun life as a Punjabi Unionist, held the Finance Portfolio. Three of the East Pakistani representatives were mediocre placemen who had accepted positions during

---

[22] Feldman, *The End and the Beginning,* p. 24.

[23] *Ibid.,* p. 26.

[24] H. Zaheer, *The Separation of East Pakistan: The Rise and Realization of Bengali Muslim Nationalism* (Karachi, 1995), pp. 109ff.

[25] *Ibid.,* p. 111.

Ayub's martial law administration. Symptomatic of the atmosphere in the eastern wing were the ostentatious celebrations on 7 August which marked the twenty-eighth anniversary of Rabindranath Tagore's death. More disquieting still for the regime was Mujib's attempt to build bridges with West Pakistani opposition politicians. Early in the month he had visited Karachi and established contacts with G.M. Syed's Sindh United Front. The following October he visited London where he met Mian Mumtaz Daultana, the leader of the Council Muslim League.[26]

Yahya's announcement on 28 November that he intended to dissolve the One Unit scheme in West Pakistan was undoubtedly a response to these overtures. It was not however until July 1971 that the four former provinces of West Pakistan were resurrected. Despite the removal of the longstanding grievances which the One Unit scheme had generated in Balochistan and Sindh, little historical credit has redounded to the Yahya regime because things went so badly wrong in East Bengal afterwards.

Opponents were equally sceptical about Yahya's intentions concerning the restoration of democracy. Within a day of assuming power he had declared the intention to hold 'fair and free' elections. Ayub had earlier held out similar promises, but while he had qualified these by referring to the need for a type of democracy 'suitable for Pakistan', Yahya had specifically spoken of 'direct adult franchise'. He repeated this pledge in important speeches on 10 April and 28 July, following which he appointed a Bengali Judge of the Supreme Court of Pakistan, Justice Abdus Sattar, as Chief Election Commissioner. His task was to prepare electoral rolls and delimit constituencies. Both were based on the 1961 Census. In a number of Punjab Constituencies, tribal and *biraderi* networks played an important role in the delineation of boundaries, establishing what were in effect 'pocket boroughs.'[27] By the middle of June 1970 the Election Commission had completed its task. In all there were 56.94 million registered voters. These included for the first time the population of Azad Kashmir which was to elect a President and Legislative Assembly.[28]

In an address on 28 November 1969, Yahya went a stage further by promising to hold direct elections on the following 5th of October. Most importantly the principle of parity of representation between the two wings in the National Assembly was to be abandoned, giving East

---

[26] Feldman, *The End and the Beginning*, p. 41.

[27] M. Lodhi, 'The Pakistan Peoples Party', p. 188.

[28] The Assembly comprised 48 members, 28 of whom were popularly elected in Azad Kashmir and 12 (6 for Jammu and 6 for Kashmir valley refugees) elected by Kashmiris in Pakistan. The President could be removed by a two-thirds vote in the Assembly. Leo. E. Rose, 'The Politics of Azad Kashmir' in Raju G.C. Thomas (ed.), *Perspectives on Kashmir: The Roots of Conflict in South Asia* (Boulder, CO, 1992) p. 240.

Pakistan its long-cherished majority of seats. In the context of Pakistan's earlier constitutional development this was a truly revolutionary step. Further in keeping with the full restoration of democracy, it was announced that as from 1 January 1970 party politics would be allowed although martial law remained enforced. These moves represented a considerable gamble as far as the political establishment was concerned. Ayub's coup of 1958 had indeed been prompted precisely by the desire to head off elections which would deliver a populist challenge to the dominant elites' domestic and foreign policy interests. The perils were surely greater in 1969 with the radicalisation of opinion in East Pakistan and the scrapping of parity between the wings.

Yahya's action was prompted in part by his regime's lack of a political agenda. After his first broadcast to the nation he reportedly 'sat down holding his head in dismay...woefully remark[ing] "What should we do now?" '[29] On another occasion he reportedly declared, 'I made no particular attempt to know how to run a government...for 32 years I had been in the army...and so I thought running the country was no different from running the army.'[30] While Ayub had sought to modernise Pakistan and Zia later wielded power in order to Islamicise it, Yahya regarded the introduction of martial law in March 1969 merely as an interim measure. He had been totally sincere when he declared during his first press conference of 10 April that he had not come to stay and that there would be a restoration of political activity as soon as possible. However he lacked not only vision but political acumen, a trait exacerbated by his vanity. From November 1969 until the announcement of the national election results, he discounted the possibility of an Awami League landslide in East Pakistan. When this duly arrived, the western wing's nightmare scenario materialised: either a constitutional deadlock, or the imposition in the whole of the country of the Bengalis' longstanding commitment to unfettered democracy and provincial autonomy.

Yahya had made some provision to safeguard the constitutional outcome through the promulgation of the Legal Framework Order (LFO) on 30 March 1970. It set a deadline of 120 days for the framing of a constitution by the National Assembly and reserved to the President the right to authenticate it. G.W. Choudhury, who played a major role in framing the LFO, has left a valuable account of the discussions which took place in Yahya's inner circle before its announcement. General Tikka Khan, who was to later carry out the military operations in East Pakistan along with Major-General Omar and General Hamid,

---

[29] F.M. Khan, *Pakistan's Crisis in Leadership* (Islamabad, 1973) p. 16.

[30] Zaheer, *The Separation of East Pakistan* p. 113.

the Chief of Staff, opposed the 'one man, one vote' principle which enshrined Bengali domination of a future National/Constituent Assembly [31] But Yahya stood firm on the issue as was essential for retaining Bengali confidence. Talks which he, and Vice-Admiral Ahsan, the Governor of East Pakistan had earlier had with Mujib encouraged the belief that the Awami League leader would modify the 6-Point demands once the elections were over. [32]

The LFO laid down that the future National Assembly which would also frame the constitution should comprise of 313 members of whom 169 would be from East Pakistan. The constitution it produced could only pass into law if it was authenticated by the President. It would also have to enshrine the following five principles: an Islamic ideology in which the Head of State should be a Muslim; free periodical federal and provincial elections based on population and on universal adult franchise; the independence of the judiciary along with the guarantee of the fundamental rights of the citizens; the provision of maximum provincial autonomy in a federal system which would provide adequate powers to the Central Government to enable it to discharge its responsibilities in relation to external and internal affairs and the preservation of the territorial integrity of the country; full opportunities to the people of all regions to participate in national affairs together with the removal by statutory and other measures in a specified period of economic and other disparities between provinces and regions. [33]

The President's power of authentication was criticised in East Pakistan, but Yahya sought to allay fears during a visit to Dhaka early in April. He dismissed this as a 'procedural formality' and maintained that he was 'not doing all this for fun' but was earnest in his pledge to restore democracy. [34] He also refused to countenance intelligence service reports both of Mujib's aim to tear up the LFO after the elections and establish Bangladesh and of India's growing involvement in the affairs of East Pakistan. [35]

The 1970 elections

Severe monsoon flooding in East Pakistan in August 1970, followed by the terrible disaster of the November cyclone which claimed an

[31] G.W. Choudhury, *The Last Days of United Pakistan* (London, 1974), pp. 92-3.

[32] *Ibid.*, p. 92.

[33] Feldman, *The End and the Beginning*, pp. 65-6.

[34] Choudhury, *The Last Days of United Pakistan*, p. 96.

[35] *Ibid.*, pp. 98-9.

estimated million lives, delayed the elections from October to December. The polling days for the National and Provincial Assemblies – the 7th and 17th – were declared public holidays. Almost a year had elapsed since the restoration of political activities. While Pakistan had suffered a dearth of elections, just four provincial elections on adult franchise in the early 1950s and Ayub's two 'indirect' national elections, it was now to experience a surfeit of electioneering. In the heat of a sustained electoral battle, attitudes were forged and expectations raised which imperilled future compromises. The most strident Bengali criticism of West Pakistan had in fact emanated not from Mujib's Awami League, but from the veteran radical leader Maulana Bhashani who headed the NAP.[36]

It appears that throughout the campaign, Yahya clung to the belief that there would be no decisive victors and that his regime would play the role of a political broker.[37] With hindsight such a misreading of the outcome beggars belief, but it did possess a rational basis in that it was based on the projections of the intelligence agencies. Just a week before the Awami League landslide, government agents were projecting the following results:

Awami League	80
Qayyum Muslim League	70
Muslim League (Daultana)	40
National Awami Party (Wali)	35
PPP	25

[38]It is still a mystery how this Himalayan miscalculation could have come about, whether it was an unforgivable but genuine blunder, or whether it possessed more sinister implications. It could of course be reasonably expected that the large number of contesting parties (twenty-five in all) and independent candidates (319) would split the vote. In Karachi alone there were seventy-three candidates for the seven National Assembly seats.[39] Moreover, Yahya expected a better showing from the parties favoured by his regime than eventually transpired.

36 R. Sisson and Leo E. Rose, *War and Secession: Pakistan, India and the Creation of Bangladesh* (Berkeley, CA, 1990) p. 30.

37 This generally accepted interpretation is challenged by G.W. Choudhury, who maintains that Yahya acknowledged that the Awami league would triumph in East Pakistan, but was assured as a result of secret discussions that Mujib would modify his six-point plan. Choudhury, *The Last Days of United Pakistan*, p. 128.

38 Cited in A. Mascarenhas, *The Rape of Bangla Desh* (New Delhi, 1971), p. 56.

39 Feldman, *The End and the Beginning*, p. 91.

One such party was the Muslim League which had been formed by the former Chief Minister of the Frontier, Abdul Qayyum Khan, in May 1969. In a dress-rehearsal for the intervention of the intelligence agencies in the political process during the 1980s and '90s, the Intelligence Bureau patronised the Qayyum League.[40] The official support and funds, allegedly some Rs. 4 million which it received could not however, compensate for either the opposition from the rival Convention[41] and Council Muslim Leagues, or most importantly for the absence of a mass base of support. The regime also increasingly favoured the *Islam pasand*[42] (Islam loving) parties because of their conservatism and attachment to the ideal of a strong central government. In April 1970, the former Chief Justice and JI sympathiser, S.A. Rahim became Chairman of the National Press Trust. Sher Ali Khan, the Minister of Information also influenced the press and was known as an active supporter of the JI. During the electioneering, he became embroiled in increasingly bitter disputes with Bhutto.[43] The JI itself warned that an Awami League victory would mean the disintegration of Pakistan.

In the event the Islamic parties fared poorly in this as in most Pakistani elections.[44] The JI, the Deobandi JUI[45] and JUP of Khwaja Qamaruddin Sialvi together won just eighteen seats in the National Assembly. A third of these were owed to the support of the *mohajir* voters in urban Karachi and Hyderabad. Their performance was little better in the provincial elections in which they captured twenty-three constituencies. A number of factors lay behind their rejection by the voters. The Islamic parties' failure to capture a single National or Provincial Assembly seat in East Pakistan was rooted in their close identification with a North Indian Urdu culture which Bengalis regarded as alien and oppressive. The social and economic conservatism of the *'ulama*-based parties also carried little appeal for Bengali voters. Significantly, within

---

[40] Zaheer, *The Separation of East Pakistan,* pp. 124-5.

[41] A.K.M. Fazlul Quader Chaudhury had succeeded Ayub as its President.

[42] These groups believe that Pakistan remains unfulfilled until it has been Islamicised. The *'ulama* based parties adhere to this ideal.

[43] Bhutto claimed he was trying to derail the election process. One of their disputes involved a government ban on the flying of party flags from rooftops.

[44] This may partly stem from the negative stereotype of the *mullah* held by sections of the population as being greedy, hypocritical and ignorant. For a satirical attack on the *mullahocracy* see Majid Lahori, *Kan-e-Nimak* (Salt Mine) (Karachi, 1958), pp.46-8, cited in A.H. Syed, *Pakistan. Islam, Politics and National Solidarity* (New York, 1982), p. 189.

[45] From 1969 this had slit into conservative faction led by Maulana Eteshamul Haq (JU(T)) and a leftist faction led by Maulana Ghulam Ghaus Hazarvi (JU(H)). For further details see C. Baxter, 'Pakistan Votes – 1970', *Asian Survey* 11, 3 (March 1971), p. 206.

West Pakistan their best showing, aside from the *mohajir* constituencies of urban Sindh, was in the more conservative Frontier[46] and Balochistan regions.[47] Elsewhere, the PPP's projection of them as a reactionary force opposed to the Family Laws[48] and in the pockets of the landlords carried weight with the electorate. As Craig Baxter's and Shahid Javed Burki's studies have revealed, the PPP's greatest success was in the urban and rural areas of the Punjab which had been undergoing modernisation.[49] Bhutto's victory can be regarded among other things as an indication that voters in West Pakistan no less than in the East were more concerned with the issues of democracy and social egalitarianism than being told by the state how they should practise Islam.

The religious parties' depiction of the election as being a contest between Islam and socialism was evidenced in such slogans as '*Socialism kufr hai. Muslim millat ek ho*' (Socialism is heresy. Let the Muslim people remain one) But these backfired as they confirmed in the mind of the voter the PPP's projection of itself as the only party concerned with relieving the poverty of the masses. This was summed up in the ringing PPP cry '*Roti, Kapra aur Makan*' ('Food, Clothes and Shelter') – a slogan which contained as much populist appeal as Indira Gandhi's cry in the Indian 1971 parliamentary elections '*Garibi Hatao*' (Abolish poverty). Moreover, Bhutto deftly avoided criticism that socialism was antagonistic to Islam by equating 'Islamic Socialism' with '*musawat*' (egalitarianism) and by maintaining that the equality and brotherhood enjoined by Islam could not be attained in an exploitive capitalist system.

Bhutto relied on the support in the elections from the groups of students, lawyers and other professionals who had been at the forefront of the anti-Ayub campaign. He also received the backing of organised

---

46 JU(H) won 6/25 NWFP National Assembly seats.

47 The PPP's single victory in the National Assembly elections in the Frontier was in the more developed Mardan region. It was not just social conservatism which influenced the voting however in Balochistan and the Frontier, as in earlier contests, tribal allegiances were very much to the forefront. The NAP's success in Balochistan rested largely on thesupport it received from the major, Marris, Bizenjos and Mengals tribes, while in NWFP its support came from the Yusufzai.

48 This alienated many of the 26 million women voters as did JI's segregationist policies in education and the workplace.

49 These included such areas as Lahore, Lyallpur and Sheikhupura. For a detailed analysis of the 1970 elections see C. Baxter, 'Pakistan Votes – 1970', *Asian Survey* XI (March 1971), pp. 197-218; S.J. Burki and C. Baxter, 'Socio-Economic Indicators of the People's Party Vote in the Punjab: A Study at the Tehsil Level', *Journal of Asian Studies* XXXIV (August 1975), pp. 913-30. They classified *tehsils* according to socio-economic indicators, before examining the relation between votes cast for the PPP in National Assembly contests and these indicators. In the 'advanced rural' *tehsils* they uncovered a strong relationship between the level of development and modernisation and the vote for the PPP. See pp. 922ff.

labour including the Pakistan Labour Party of Bashir Bakhtiar, and the Pakistan Press Workers Union and Tonga and Taxi Drivers Union. Such groups responded eagerly to his call for social justice.

Another source of the PPP's popularity especially among *mohajirs* and Punjabi voters was Bhutto's uncompromising attitude towards India. Early in the campaign he talked of 'a thousand years war with India'. He also returned to the earlier theme of Ayub's 'betrayal' of Pakistan's interests at Tashkent in order to remind voters of his patriotism. This was vital in overcoming the handicaps of his Sindhi and Shia background in the key Punjab region.

There are a number of parallels between the PPP's electioneering and that of the Muslim League's in 1945-6.[50] Both parties benefited from a groundswell of popular support which transcended more traditional *biraderi* based politics. They also both relied heavily on the charismatic appeal of their leaders who drew huge crowds to their rallies. Bhutto travelled as extensively as Jinnah had done and was similarly seen as the physical embodiment of his party's message. The PPP was however no better organised than its Muslim League predecessor and thus had to compromise with existing power structures in order to maximise its victory. Despite its socialist ideology, it enlisted the support of *pirs* and *waderos* in its electioneering in Sindh. Support came from the Pir of Hala, Pir Rasool Shah of Tharparkar and the landed Talpurs, Jatois and Jam Sadiq Ali. In the Punjab, leading landlords such as the Noons, Gilanis and Qureshis accommodated themselves to the PPP just as they had once deserted the Unionists for the Muslim League bandwagon. Just as the League in 1946 passed over loyal workers to give election tickets to such opportunists, so Bhutto repeated the process a generation later. The twin-track approach of securing the feudals' support in the less developed Punjab regions and in the interior of Sindh and in appealing to the small cultivators, tenants and landless in central Punjab and the Canal Colony districts ensured the PPP's electoral success. It nevertheless disconcerted such leftist activists as Ziauddin Butt, Mairaj Muhammad Khan and Tariq Aziz and cast a pall of doubt over the party's future implementation of agrarian reform.

In East Pakistan, Sheikh Mujib towered over his Awami League party and symbolised its aspirations every bit as much as Bhutto did the PPP. The two rivals did not however lock horns during the campaign, as the PPP put up no candidates in East Pakistan, and the Awami

---

[50] A major difference of course was that television and radio played an important role in the 1970 election campaign. Political broadcasts ran from 28 October to 14 November and in all the leaders of fourteen parties were given air time. Choudhury, *The Last Days of United Pakistan*, p. 124.

League ran just seven in the western wing. This course of action enabled both parties to maximise their influence in their major centres of support, but was to create problems after the elections. The Awami League's hopes of gaining a foothold in West Pakistan through an alliance with Wali Khan's Frontier and Balochistan based NAP had been dashed when their negotiations broke down in late September.

The Awami League contested the elections on the 6-Point programme and on the history of the western wing's treatment of East Bengal as a 'colony'. The by now traditional charges were repeated of West Pakistan's monopolisation of foreign investment, dumping of manufactured goods in the eastern wing and misuse of the foreign exchange raised by its jute exports. Just as the Muslim League in 1946 had presented Pakistan as a panacea for social ills, the Awami League depicted the prospect of a *Sonar* (Golden) Bengal if the autonomy programme was implemented.

The Awami League's attitudes hardened during the course of the prolonged election campaign. Tensions were increased following the police action at a 14 August Independence Day football match riot in Dhaka. They intensified shortly afterwards with the claims of government inaction during the November 1970 cyclone and its aftermath. The latter was denounced by Mujib for its slow response to the emergency, while the former was depicted as inciting hatred towards non-Bengalis by its exploitation of the natural disaster. Increasingly, the candidates of western based parties such as the JI and the three Muslim Leagues were likened by the Awami League to Mir Jafar who had treacherously assisted the East India Company's ascendancy in Bengal in 1756. Two persons were killed during a JI meeting and rallies of other parties were broken up by crowds chanting '*Joy Bangla*' (Victory to Bengal).[51]

Iftikhar Ahmad's and J.K. Bashir's work provide detailed studies[52] of the polling which proceeded in a peaceful and orderly manner throughout Pakistan. Around 60 per cent of those who were registered cast their votes. The most striking feature of the results was the Awami League's total eclipse of its rivals in East Pakistan. It secured complete control of the Provincial Assembly. Out of the 162 seats allotted for East Pakistan in the National Assembly it won 160 and secured three-quarters of the total votes polled in the eastern wing. Although it failed to win a single seat in the four provinces of West Pakistan, its landslide victory ensured a majority in the National Assembly.

51 Sharif al Mujahid, 'Pakistan: First General Elections', *Asian Survey* 11 (January 1971), p. 166.
52 Iftikhar Ahmad, *Pakistan General Elections 1970* (Lahore, 1976); J.K. Bashir, *NWFP Elections, 1970* (Lahore, 1973).

The PPP formed the second major party in the National Assembly. Contrary to official expectations it had beaten off the challenge of the religious parties to capture 81 out of 138 West Pakistan seats. This performance, according to one PPP leader was, 'greater than even Bhutto's wildest dreams would have ever allowed.'[53] Most victories (62) had been secured in the Punjab and all but one of the remainder were seats in Bhutto's native Sindh. Indeed in Balochistan's first ever direct elections, the PPP failed to return a member in either the National Assembly or Provincial Assembly elections.[54] The latter confirmed the PPP's emergence as a major power in the Punjab heartland of West Pakistan where it won 113 out of 180 seats. The use of smaller constituencies in these elections enabled *biraderi* solidarity to play a greater role in voting. In the relatively backward Dera Ghazi Khan and Jhang districts, the PPP had fared poorly when it had been unable to field the right type of *biraderi* candidates.[55]

The results confirmed the provincialisation of Pakistani politics (see Tables 7.1 and 7.2 below). The long-established political cleavages between East and West Pakistan were now laid bare. The first national

Table 7.1. NATIONAL ASSEMBLY
ELECTION RESULTS, 1970-1

Party	Punjab	Sindh	NWFP	Bal.	(West) Total	(East) Total	(Undivided Pakistan) Total
AL	–	–	–	–	–	160	160
PPP	62	18	1	–	81	–	81
PML (Q)	1	1	7	–	9	–	9
CML	7	–	–	–	7	–	7
JU (H)	–	–	6	1	7	–	7
JUP	4	3	–	–	7	–	7
NAP (W)	–	–	3	3	6	–	6
JI	1	2	1	–	4	–	4
PML (C)	2	–	–	–	2	–	2
PDP*	–	–	–	–	–	1	1
Independent	5	3	7	–	15	1	16
Total	82	27	25	4	138	162	300

* PDP (Pakistan Democratic Party).

[53] Sisson and Rose, *War and Secession* p. 33.

[54] The most successful party in the Balochistan National Assembly elections had been Wali Khan's National Awami Party. The turnout in the province had been much lower than elsewhere in Pakistan.

[55] Burki and Baxter, 'Socio-Economic Indicators of the People's Party Vote in the Punjab', p. 923.

elections since independence had been fought almost in two separate countries, each with their own agendas and political organisations. The split was such that no party could boast representation in both of the wings. The Bengalis had responded to years of exclusion from the decision-making process by propelling to national power a party which stood diametrically opposed to the economic and political interests of the civil-military establishment. The future of Pakistan now rested on the complex negotiations which were to be held between Bhutto, Mujib and Yahya.

Table 7.2. PROVINCIAL ASSEMBLY
ELECTION RESULTS, 1970-1

Party	Punjab	Sindh	NWFP	Bal.	(West) Total	(East) Total	(Undivided Pakistan) Total
AL	–	–	–	–	–	288	288
PPP	113	28	3	–	144	–	144
PML (Q)	6	5	10	3	24	–	24
NAP (W)	–	–	13	8	21	1	22
CML	15	4	1	–	20	–	20
JUP	4	7	–	–	11	–	11
JU (H)	2	–	4	2	8	–	8
PML (C)	6	–	2	–	8	–	8
PDP	4	–	–	–	4	2	6
JI	1	1	1	–	3	1	4
Others	1	1	–	2	4	1	5
Independent	28	14	6	5	53	7	60
Total	180	60	40	20	300	300	600

Source: C. Baxter, 'Pakistan Votes-1970', *Asian Survey* 11, no. 3 (March 1971), p. 211.

The drift to civil war and the creation of Bangladesh

Sisson and Rose in their authoritative study *War and Secession: Pakistan, India and the Creation of Bangladesh* examine the drift to civil war and the Indo-Pakistan conflict in the period after the December 1970 elections. In contrast with Choudhury, they depict these events as surprising all the protagonists, not least the military regime which had expected to play a mediating role among a large number of equally balanced parties. In the absence of a contingency plan, it thereafter followed rather than moulded events. Even more damaging for the negotiations, 'instead of remaining a neutral umpire or arbiter, the government became a partisan participant.'[56] Efforts to tough out the situation and make Mujib 'see sense' were also highly counterproductive as the Awami

---

[56] Sisson and Rose, *War and Secession*, p. 272.

League inevitably questioned Yahya's sincerity concerning the transfer of power into civilian hands.

Sisson and Rose also link the failure of the negotiations with the participants' mutual mistrust. Consequently, 'possibilities of accommodation were not explored; instead the probability of intent to do harm became the basis of inference, planning and decision making.'[57] Mujib's refusal to go to West Pakistan for negotiations during the first week of February 1971 was thus seen as evidence of the Bengalis' disaffection towards a United Pakistan and their secessionist tendencies, when there was in reality an innocent explanation.[58] Similarly, the Awami League leaders too readily accepted that Bhutto's discussions with Yahya at Larkana on 17-18 January evidenced collusion between the military and the PPP. It was nevertheless 'impolitic' of Yahya to accept Bhutto's hospitality for highly sensitive constitutional discussions.

The Pakistan regime's reading of events was further distorted by a collapse of information gathering which resulted in 'Political advocacy [being] treated as technical advice'.[59] From December 1970 onwards, the Pakistan Government continuously underestimated the intensity of popular support for the Awami League. The establishment of a parallel government in East Pakistan in the wake of the decision to postpone the calling of the National Assembly in early March thus came as a violent shock to the military authorities. Their sense of impotence and fear of internal division over the issue, 'caused a swing in preference from uncomfortable political negotiation to command and a drastic application of force.'[60]

During the period from the 25 March military crackdown onwards, Sisson and Rose depict the Pakistan Government as becoming increasingly incoherent and driven by events. Yahya retreated from the President's House to the more 'congenial' atmosphere of the army general headquarters and was thus 'sequestered' from civilian advice. Just as in the drift to civil war, the regime foundered because it lacked clarity of vision. It was ultimately misled by the precedent that the superpowers 'had never...allowed conflicts between India and Pakistan...to get out of hand before.'[61] While Pakistan thus sleepwalked to war with India, decision making in New Delhi was undertaken professionally and deter-

---

57 *Ibid.*, p. 275.

58 For Zaheer's reflections on this 'extraordinary behaviour' see *The Separation of East Pakistan*, p. 132.

59 Sisson and Rose, *War and Secession*, p. 272.

60 *Ibid.*, p. 274.

61 *Ibid.*, pp. 279-80.

minedly. Sisson and Rose argue that Indian policy was driven by the refugee crisis. By June nearly 4 million Bengalis had arrived from East Pakistan. This influx was judged as 'unacceptable' not only because of its volume, but because its destination was 'the politically volatile' north-eastern hill states of Tripura and Meghalaya and Naxalite ridden West Bengal.[62] Support for the Bangladeshi 'freedom fighters' was thus motivated, according to Sisson and Rose, as much by the desire to 'quarantine' and control them, as by a long held desire to destroy Pakistan. Such an analysis is at variance with many Pakistani accounts, although there would be little dispute with the North American scholars' contention that the Indian decision to 'go to war was deliberate, not taken under duress, or with a sense that immediate action was needed to stave off disaster.'[63]

Sisson and Rose's assessment of Bhutto's role in the events leading to the break-up of Pakistan is equally controversial. They explain his confrontational attitude towards the Awami League in terms both of an elemental drive for power and the anxiety that the PPP would 'unravel' if it was denied the fruits of national power. They thus report that Bhutto confided to Yahya that he 'had to accede to power "now" for his family "died young" ', and that a senior minister observed to Yahya that if Bhutto 'did not assume power within a year he would literally go mad.'[64] Earlier on the same page, they declare: 'Bhutto...feared that the party (PPP) would become...divided in a National Assembly in which the Awami League could extend positions and favours to selected groups in the opposition. [...] Thus the top leadership of the PPP early on decided that it could not participate in the National Assembly without a guarantee of the share of governmental power.'[65] The reader is thus left with the strong impression that if Bhutto had not existed, the military regime would have been forced to invent him, as his reluctance to enter an Awami League-dominated National Assembly strengthened its objectives of 'tempering extremist demands in terms of both constitutional design and policy-making'.[66] The army's principal concern in the former area was the maintenance of a strong central government;

---

62 The Naxalites were Maoists committed to armed revolution. They took their name from Naxalbari, the site of a peasant uprising in the Darjeeling district of West Bengal. In 1969 the various Naxalite groups founded the Communist Party of India (Marxist-Leninist). See Biplap Dasgupta, *The Naxalite Movement* (Bombay, 1974); M. F. Franda, *Radical Politics in West Bengal* (Cambridge, 1971).

63 Sisson and Rose, *War and Secession*, p. 278.

64 *Ibid.*, p. 57.

65 *Ibid.*

66 *Ibid.*, p. 55.

in the latter it sought to safeguard military expenditure and ring-fence matters of promotion and recruitment from political interference.

Bhutto maintained throughout that his stance was reasonable and the PPP was not therefore responsible for the deepening crisis. He was loyally representing West Pakistani interests in the attempt to evolve a national consensus on the constitution. The way in which the Awami League responded however threatened disaster and put 'the future of our country...in the balance'.[67] In a number of public addresses in March 1971 for example, Bhutto maintained that it was a 'lie' that he was only interested in power and that this explained the postponement of the National Assembly. All he had wanted was his voice to be heard and to speak for the integrity of Pakistan. The Awami League's demands however would mean 'more or less independence' and hinder the PPP confrontation with India over Kashmir. [68]

Until archival material has been made available, a definitive history cannot be written of the final days of United Pakistan. In the interim, the Yahya regime's attempt to pin the blame on Bhutto for its own folly has partly succeeded, as can be seen in Sisson and Rose's account of the delay in calling the National Assembly. The reality in all probability was much closer to Ayesha Jalal's assessment. She follows Sisson and Rose in seeing the PPP's insecure power base as limiting room for political accommodation, but goes on to declare that 'the institutional stakes of the military and the bureaucracy within the existing state structure were [great]... even if they had wanted to, Mujib and Bhutto could not palpably arrive at any formula to share power without the implicit approval of the praetorian guard and the mandarins.'[69] Hasan Zaheer, who has reconstructed some of the key developments through interviews and conversations, opines: 'It would not be fair to blame Bhutto for the postponement of the National Assembly session unless it is conceded that the 6 Points were acceptable to the Army, the establishment and to West Pakistan in general. If the 6 Points were acceptable to Yahya then he need not have postponed the Assembly Session.[...] In fact Yahya seems to have used Bhutto to get out of the situation created by his thoughtless decisions.'[70]

While the interpretation of the roles of the main actors remains contested, it is nevertheless possible to identify the key events in the denouement. Shortly after the elections, Bhutto in a speech in Lahore laid

---

[67] Radio Pakistan Newscast of 11 March 1971, cited in Sisson and Rose, *War and Secession*, p. 105.

[68] For a further development of these arguments see Bhutto, *The Great Tragedy*.

[69] A. Jalal, *The State of Martial Rule: The Origins of Pakistan's Political Economy of Defence* (Cambridge, 1992), p. 310.

[70] Zaheer, *The Separation of East Pakistan*, p. 147.

down the principle which was to remain his constant refrain. He argued that 'a majority alone doesn't count in national politics' and that the PPP's historic role in opposing the Ayub regime entitled it to participate in a parliamentary government.[71] Sheikh Mujib's riposte came shortly afterwards in his famous Ramna Race Course speech of 3 January 1971. The Awami League leader maintained that his party was the majority party for the whole of Pakistan. It would act responsibly in the framing of the constitution and cooperate with West Pakistan parties, but the constitution would be based on the 6 Points.[72]

Yahya responded to this growing acrimony by visiting Dhaka in mid-January 1971. His talks apparently went well with Mujib, but they raised doubts in the minds of some of his officials who recoiled at the prospect of military interests henceforth becoming dependent on the goodwill of an Awami League government. Once these misgivings had surfaced, they were never to be completely dispelled, despite Mujib's string of reassurances. On his return to West Pakistan, Yahya journeyed to the Bhutto estate at Larkana for his celebrated duck shoot. Bhutto argued for the establishment of a consensus on the constitution before the National Assembly was convened. He also reportedly expressed the opinion that Mujib was 'a clever bastard' who wanted an early Assembly meeting in order to 'bulldoze' through the constitution.[73] The fact that Yahya had taken the trouble to journey all the way to Larkana convinced some Awami Leaguers that Bhutto was the catspaw of the military.

Bhutto held talks with Mujib in Dhaka on 27-30 January, but no progress was made largely because the PPP leader, to Mujib's annoyance, concentrated on the issue of ministerial posts, rather than constitutional discussions. Despite this impasse, Yahya shortly afterwards announced that the National Assembly would meet in Dhaka on 3 March. Bhutto took up most of February in consultation with his PPP members in order to solidify the West Pakistani viewpoint. The hijacking of an Indian Airlines flight from Srinagar to Jammu also provided him with the opportunity to return to his pro-Kashmiri stance, to the embarrassment of Mujib. [74] When the 14 February announcement about the convening of the National Assembly was made, Bhutto said he would stay away, as he could not risk his party members becoming a 'double hostage' in Dhaka to Indian hostility and Awami League intransigence.[75] When

71 Sisson and Rose, *War and Secession.* p. 60.

72 *Ibid.*, p. 62.

73 *Ibid.*, p. 67.

74 *Ibid.*, p. 76.

75 *Ibid.*, p. 79.

Yahya summoned him to Rawalpindi for a meeting, Bhutto declared that framing a constitution without PPP participation would be 'like staging Hamlet without the Prince of Denmark'.[76] The PPP National Assembly members on 21 February swore an oath on the Quran that they would support his stance in negotiations with the Awami League and promised to resign *en bloc* if it was convened without them. Nevertheless, at in a mass rally at Lahore a week later Bhutto felt moved to issue the warning that he would 'break the legs' of any party member who went to Dhaka.[77]

From the third week of February onwards, the military began considering the possibility of making a show of force to make Mujib 'see sense'. In order to clear the decks for this possibility, the Council of Ministers which had been appointed in August 1969 was instructed to resign. Thus free of its 'nuisance' value, Yahya consulted with his governors and martial law administrators over his future course of action. Conflicting opinions were presented by those stationed in the two wings over the likely consequences of a postponement of the National Assembly. Momentously, Yahya ignored the misgivings of those on the spot in Dhaka.[78] Vice-Admiral Ahsan's attempts to urge the President to reconsider this course of action cost him his job as Governor of East Pakistan. Far more importantly, Yahya's decision imperilled the unity of the Pakistan state whose integrity he was pledged to uphold. After the 1 March announcement of the postponement of the National Assembly meeting was made, the drift towards civil war continued inexorably.

A province-wide *hartal* (strike) paralysed East Pakistan on 3 March the day which had been set for the abortive convening of the National Assembly. The days which followed were marked by clashes between demonstrators and troops and the establishment of what amounted to a parallel Awami League government. It was in this radically changed atmosphere that Yahya backtracked and announced on 6 March that the inaugural session of the National Assembly would be held on 25 March. Mujib gave his response at a mass Ramna Race Course rally the following day. He did not announce the independence of Bangladesh as many people had thought, but rather laid down four conditions for participation in the National Assembly. They were: immediate withdrawal of martial law; the return of the troops to their barracks; a judicial enquiry into the loss of life caused by military shootings since 1 March; and the immediate transfer of power to elected representatives before the Assembly would meet. The agenda had now shifted sharply from

[76] *Ibid.*, p. 80.

[77] *Ibid.*, p. 88.

[78] *Ibid.*, pp. 84-5.

the original 6 Points and prospects of accommodation by the Awami League had diminished following the further radicalisation of opinion in East Pakistan. This was soon to be reflected in Mujib's refusal of Bhutto's overture for talks in a telegram of 10 March.

Five days later Yahya arrived in Dhaka and, escorted by a company of heavily armed Punjabi troops, made his way from an eerily quiet airport to the confines of the President's House. This final bid to maintain Pakistan's integrity has been likened to 'giving oxygen to a dying patient when the doctors have declared him a lost case'.[79] The level of mistrust between Yahya and Mujib was so great that their first meeting had to take place in the bathroom off the main bedroom – as the Awami League leader would not hold discussions in the Presidential House's drawing-room in case it was bugged. Some progress was nevertheless made on the four issues Mujib had raised in his Ramna Race Course speech. The announcement on 18 March of the composition of the commission of enquiry into the police and army firings bitterly disappointed the Awami League negotiators as it betokened a whitewash. The Government and the Awami League were nonetheless inching towards a settlement when Bhutto and his aides arrived in Dhaka on 21 March. Mujib resented the PPP leader's presence, but at Yahya's behest held discussions with him.

While steady progress was being made in the meetings inside the President's House, the mood outside boded ill. The anniversary of the passage of the Lahore Resolution, 23 March, was celebrated as usual as Independence Day in West Pakistan. In the eastern wing however it was renamed Resistance Day. Student militias paraded under the Bangladesh flag and were ceremonially saluted by the Awami League leader at his residence. Support for the Bangladesh movement was urged during an ex-serviceman's rally. The Awami League negotiating team arrived at the President's House flying the Bangladesh flag on their vehicles. This confirmed in the eyes of the West Pakistani military elite that they had been right all along when they had suspected Mujib of secessionist tendencies. Not surprisingly, the Awami League draft document's use of the term 'Constituent Conventions' for the earlier agreed 'Constituent Committees'[80] and its substitution of the term 'Confederation of Pakistan' for 'Federation of Pakistan' appeared to take on a sinister character in the light of events outside the President's House. By teatime on 23 March the army command had recommended to Yahya that military action was now essential to suppress the Awami

[79] Choudhury, *The Last Days of United Pakistan*, p.161.

[80] These were to meet in the two wings of the country instead of at a convocation of the National Assembly to initially discuss the constitution.

League 'rebellion'.[81] The crackdown, code-named 'Operation Searchlight', which sealed the fate of national unity was launched at midnight on 25 March. Yahya later justified it because of the threats to non-Bengali Muslims, the murders committed by the Awami League and its insults to the Army,[82] the Pakistan flag and the Quaid-e-Azam.[83]

The subsequent brutal army assault on the Iqbal and Jaganath Halls of Residence in Dhaka University killed hundreds of students. 'Two days later bodies still smouldered in burnt out rooms, others were scattered outside, more floated in a nearby lake.'[84] The Army had also turned its firepower on the headquarters of the police and East Pakistan Rifles, ensuring that it brought the peace of the grave to Dhaka. These massacres ensured the 'mutiny' of the East Bengal regiment under Major Zia-ur-Rahman. By the end of April however, the Pakistan Army had 'cleared' the urban areas of rebels throughout the whole of the eastern wing. The human cost had been high. Many of the atrocities the Army committed on its own population were the unspeakable outpourings of racial hatreds and stereotyping.

Strict censorship[85] kept West Pakistanis largely in the dark about the actions carried out in the name of national unity. 'Those of us who were serving in East Pakistan', Hasan Zaheer records, 'on our visits to the West found its Press and people totally out of touch with the ground realities in the East Wing and apparently they could not have cared less. [...] No one questioned the aims and objectives of the army action.'[86]

As in other instances of state terrorism in South Asia, the violence was totally counterproductive. The Bengali population's desire for self-determination was reinforced rather than diminished. The likelihood of an independent Bangladesh was increased as around 7 million people fled to India, thereby internationalising the crisis in East Pakistan; 900,000 Bengalis crowded into the hill state of Tripura alone, where the indigenous population numbered only 1.5 million. As early as 17 April a Bangladesh Government-in-exile was established in Calcutta following the decla-

---

[81] The hardline army commander General Tikka Khan reportedly declared to Yahya, 'Give me enough force and I will crush them in forty eight hours.' Majharul Islam, *Ami Smriti Ami Itihas* (Dacca, 1974), p. 544, cited in T. Banerjee and Md. Habibur Rahman, 'The Election of 1970: A Prelude to the Break-up of Pakistan', *Indo-British Review*, XVII, nos 1 and 2 (September and December 1989), pp. 207.

[82] During the civil disobedience movement, army units had been denied foodstuffs and spat on and jeered by the local populace.

[83] Sisson and Rose, *War and Secession*, p. 155.

[84] Cited in Choudhury, *The Last Days of United Pakistan*, p. 185.

[85] Mascarenhas, *The Rape of Bangla Desh*, see Ch. 10.

[86] Zaheer, *The Separation of East Pakistan*, p. 326.

ration of independence on 26 March. Radio Free Bangla transmitted broadcasts to the 'Sovereign People's Republic' from Kalurghat. Most of the Awami League leadership had made good its escape to the new party headquarters in India named Mujibnagar, although Mujib himself had been arrested. Yahya's refusal to countenance his release served as an insuperable barrier to any new political settlement. Rather than take up the Pakistan President's invitation to return to their homes in May, the younger elements turned to armed struggle. Training camps were set up in the border areas where former servicemen, policemen and students were recruited into the *Mukti Bahini* (liberation force) and trained by the Indian Army. The serious rivalries within the *Mukti Bahini* between nationalists and leftists, themselves divided into pro-Beijing and pro-Moscow groupings, were in fact barely kept in check.

While the army action re-established a semblance of order in East Pakistan, it was almost impossible to reconstitute the civil administration. Where it did function, it took on an 'alien' non-Bengali character. Hasan Zaheer was one of fifteen West Pakistan officers ordered to Dhaka, arriving at a deserted airport on 17 May 'as if we had come to a foreign country.'[87] The police force relied entirely on Punjabis for secondment and non-Bengali 'Bihari' Muslims for its personnel. The Government also sought to counter guerrilla activities by raising paramilitary forces of Razakars. Most recruits were drawn from the Urdu-speaking Bihari population. The Razakars' state-sponsored terrorism completed the social, political and cultural divide between the Biharis and the Bengali majority. Nearly a tenth of the million strong Bihari population was relocated to the west after the war and three times their number became stranded in refugee camps in Bangladesh, eking out a miserable existence which became an increasingly important symbol for the politics of *mohajir* ethnic mobilisation within Pakistan.

Yahya's attempts to restart the political process were equally ineffectual. He sought to split Awami League moderates from the radicals by a system of investigation and disqualification of those who were to be 'cleansed' – a move reminiscent of the early Ayub era. Disqualifications freed 78 and 105 East Pakistan seats for re-election in the National and Provincial Assemblies respectively. The rightist parties which had fared badly in the 1970 elections jostled to obtain the spoils without questioning their role as the 'B' team of the martial law regime and intelligence agencies. In the event the threat to law and order ensured that the bulk were filled without a contest. This sideshow occurred amid gathering war clouds. Yahya's riposte to the signing of an Indo-Soviet Treaty of Peace and Friendship on 7 August was to begin Mujib's trial before a special military court. Henry Kissinger termed the trial

[87] *Ibid.*, p. 173.

a 'truculent move' by a desperate man.[88] It completed a catalogue of actions by the Yahya regime which totally alienated world opinion. The trial had still not run its course by the time that war was declared on 3 December.[89]

The prelude to war between India and Pakistan was an escalation of *Mukhti Bahini* guerrilla activity in the post-monsoon (post-September) season. There were attacks on key installations in Dhaka and vessels moored in Chittagong harbour, whose cargo-handling was less than half the normal average from May onwards. The railway system was virtually inoperative because of the destruction of key bridges. Dhaka itself became a ghost city. 'Bomb blasts, automatic weapons, and stray firing', Hasan Zaheer recalls, 'were the only sounds heard from early evening throughout the night.'[90] On 6 June, Tikka Khan hosted a dinner for a World Bank mission in the Governor's House to the accompaniment of explosions and gunfire. The guests departed early at 10pm to 'a cacophony' of bomb explosions and 'rapid firing of machine-guns' unconvinced that there had been a return to 'normalcy'.[91] In the absence of IMF and World Bank support for debt rescheduling, Pakistan had to negotiate short-term loans to tide over the foreign exchange problems brought by the collapse of earnings from jute. Other economic problems arising from the crisis included mounting insurance claims, shortages of essential goods, dwindling revenue receipts at a time of rising defence expenditure and, inevitably, inflation. The economic strength built up during the previous two decades was being 'frittered away in the swamps of East Pakistan'.[92] A morally bankrupt regime was on the verge of economic bankruptcy.

The guerrilla attacks coincided with increased direct Indian intervention in the fighting. The use of tanks, artillery and occasionally airpower marked a new phase in the military campaign. The Pakistani response was confused because of uncertainties about the Indian objectives.[93] Indeed there could not be a greater contrast between Yahya blundering into civil war without considering the implications of the March crackdown and Indira Gandhi's calculated response to an unprecedented opportunity to achieve, in the words of K. Subrahmanyam, Director of the Indian Institute for Defence Studies and Analysis, the

---

[88] *Ibid.*, p. 310.

[89] Sisson and Rose, *War and Secession*, p.172.

[90] Zaheer, *The Separation of East Pakistan*, p.177.

[91] *Ibid.*, p. 201.

[92] *Ibid.*, p. 234.

[93] There was debate as to whether this was the prelude to a full-scale attack, or merely an attempt to secure a liberated zone in the border area.

'break-up of Pakistan'. International opinion was carefully prepared for an Indian military intervention by stressing the humanitarian problems arising from the refugee influx.[94]

From 21 November onwards there was a build up of Indian military activity along the key border areas. It appears that this was the prelude to an all-out offensive to capture Dhaka, which was scheduled for 6 December.[95] In the event full-scale war was brought forward by 3 days as a result of the Pakistani air attacks in North-west India. The Pakistani decision to open up a western front, in keeping with all that had proceeded it, was taken without the knowledge of the Governor of East Pakistan, although it gave India a free hand to invade. Because of intelligence failure the air attacks did not destroy a single Indian Air Force plane on the ground. They did however enable Pakistan to be 'blamed' for starting the war. Air supremacy[96] was to play a part in the humiliating defeat of the Pakistan Army in East Pakistan, although its major handicap was its lack of mobility and the hostility of the Bengali population.

The war from the Indian viewpoint went almost exactly to plan, although the strained relations it brought with the United States caused some disquiet in New Delhi. The United States for geostrategic reasons did not want to see West Pakistan destroyed and became concerned as the Pakistan Army in the east began rapidly to collapse. During the last week of the conflict the Seventh Fleet was despatched to the Indian Ocean both as a warning to the Soviet Union[97] and to mollify Pakistan's Islamic sympathisers. But there was never any real possibility of a confrontation with India. Congressional opinion was hostile to the Nixon administration's alleged 'tilt' to Pakistan, especially because arms shipments still in the 'pipeline' were reaching Pakistan after the State Department's 6 April embargo on military aid. $75 million of economic aid was also suspended in July 1971 following Congress's pressure. Within the Government itself there were sharp differences between the White House and the State Department concerning the issue of whether there should be public criticism of Yahya's repression. Here the *realpolitik* of Kissinger triumphed over more moralistic posturing. However, Washington did discreetly advise on the need for a political solution in East Pakistan. When the third Indo-Pakistan war

---

94 Zaheer, *The Separation of East Pakistan,* Chapter 9.

95 Sisson and Rose, *War and Secession,* p. 213.

96 India had a two-to-one numerical advantage in war planes.

97 Soviet naval forces in the Indian Ocean had been heavily reinforced following the outbreak of war. Tass denied reports that Soviet servicemen took part in Indian naval and airforce combat operations.

broke out, the Nixon administration suspended licences for military sales to India along with $87.6 million economic aid.[98]

The Pakistan Government's greatest disappointment concerned China's limited diplomatic support which came only in response to Yahya's letter of 30 March to Zhou Enlai and belated economic and military assistance. The delivery of military aircraft which it promised only arrived after the fighting had ceased. In reality the Chinese did all that could be expected of them in the very different circumstances to the 1965 conflict with India. Their rhetorical support for the Pakistani cause inevitably lacked material substance, although Bhutto sought to muddy the waters following the Pakistani delegation's visit to Beijing on 7 November by publicly stating that China had assured Islamabad of its support in the event of an Indian attack. The Chinese did not contradict this claim, but had no intention of militarily engaging India.[99]

During the course of the two-week war,[100] Pakistan lost half its navy, a third of its army and a quarter of its air force.[101] General Manekshaw, the Indian Chief of Army Staff, rejected pleas for a cease-fire which would enable the Pakistan Army to be repatriated to the western wing complete with its weapons. Yahya, under intense diplomatic pressure from America, agreed to accept the offered Indian cease-fire terms. The Pakistani commander General Niazi had no choice but to surrender unconditionally on 16 December along with his 93,000 troops who had een surrounded at Dhaka. While Mujib returned in triumph to Bangladesh, the West Pakistan military establishment faced the humiliation of seeing an important section of its forces languishing as Indian prisoners-of-war. With Indian forbearance Mukhti Bahini militants took revenge on civilian collaborators.

The united Pakistan born of the exigencies of 1945–7, but not of the Lahore Resolution, had survived a mere twenty-three years. Islam had proved an insufficient bond to hold the two wings together. Pakistan had not fallen apart because of Bengali primordialism or Indian machinations. The primary responsibility lay in Islamabad – chauvinism had compounded folly in the dangerous denial of Bengali democratic urges.

Crowds spilled on to the streets of West Pakistan's cities calling for Yahya and his advisors to be tried as traitors. Almost to the end they had been fed a diet of military successes. The banner headline of one Urdu paper published in Lahore screamed '*Aik awaz, aik elan: Qaum*

[98] Sisson and Rose, *War and Secession*, p. 261.

[99] The possible reasons for this are set out in Sisson and Rose, *War and Secession*, p. 251.

[100] The best account remains R. V. Jackson, *South Asia Crisis: India, Pakistan and Bangladesh: A Political and Historical Analysis of the 1971 War* (New York, 1975).

[101] T. Ali, *Can Pakistan Survive? The Death of a State* (Harmondsworth, 1983), p. 95.

ka katil Yahya Khan' (One voice, one declaration: Yahya Khan is the murderer of the nation).[102] It was inconceivable in these circumstances that Yahya could continue in office. He nevertheless had to be persuaded by Gul Hassan, the Chief of General Staff, before agreeing to step down. The blow to the Army's collective pride and the growing hostility of the junior officers to the high command[103] ruled out the elevation of another military man to the position of President, although Gul Hassan jockeyed for power. Instead, Bhutto was hurried home from New York where he had been representing Pakistan in the United Nations debates. On 20 December, at the military high command's behest, he assumed the post of President and Chief Martial Law Administrator.

---

102 *Daily Javadan* (Lahore), 19 December 1971. The previous issue had boldly declared: '*Pakistan ki Shikast ka zimmadar Yahya Khan hain*' (Yahya Khan is responsible for Pakistan's defeat). Cited in Hasan-Askari Rizvi, *The Military and Politics in Pakistan, 1947-86* (Delhi, 1988), p. 195.

103 A delegation of junior officers led by Colonel Aleem Afridi demanded Yahya's removal in a meeting with the Army Chief of Staff, Lt.-General Gul Hassan.

Part III

FROM BHUTTO TO ZIA

8

PEOPLE'S POWER: HOPES
AND IMPEDIMENTS

Zulfiqar Ali Bhutto was the outstanding political figure of his generation. No Pakistani leader since Jinnah had possessed his vision or authority. Bhutto's charisma was rooted in his embodiment of popular aspirations for social justice and for the attainment of Kashmiri self-determination. He projected himself as a man of the people in contrast with the 'drawing-room' politicians and maintained that 'his voice was the people's voice, his speeches their speeches.'[1] He was not merely a demagogue, however, despite his earthy language and theatrical style at his *jalsas* (public meetings), but possessed the lawyer's[2] attention to detail along with a fertile imagination. His experience and competence in foreign policy for example was always an important part of his self-characterisation.

Bhutto was no plaster saint. He could be arrogant and ruthless and would give no quarter to his opponent. He wrote: 'Politics is movement *per se* – a politician should be mobile. 'He should sway now to right now to left; he should come up with contradictions, doubts. He should change continually, test things, attack from every side so as to single out his opponent's weak point and strike at it.'[3] Idolised by his friends, he was despised by his foes who claimed that he never outgrew the arbitrariness and cruelty (*zulm*) of his feudal background.[4] Detractors

[1] A.H. Syed, 'Z.A. Bhutto's Self-Characterisations and Pakistani Political Culture', *Asian Survey* 18, no.12 (December 1978), p. 1258.

[2] Bhutto had been called to the Bar at Lincolns Inn in 1953 had lectured in international law at Southampton University before his return to Pakistan. In 1954-8 he practised as a barrister at the Sindh High Court in Karachi.

[3] Sisson and Rose, *War and Secession*, p. 59.

[4] The Bhutto's landholdings in the Larkana district of Sindh were so extensive that they

also point to the megalomaniac tendencies lying behind his imagined affinity with Napoleon and see them as being directly responsible for the dismemberment of Pakistan through his inability to share power with Mujibur Rahman.[5] Lieutenant-General Gul Hassan Khan maintained in his memoirs[6] that Bhutto was a mendacious, vindictive 'showman of high calibre' and that his engineering of the downfall of the NAP-JUI coalition ministries in the Frontier and Balochistan displayed an authoritarianism equal to that of any martial law era. While Balochistan subsequently became the scene of a tribal insurgency which required massive military intervention, events were set in train in the Frontier which culminated in the arrest of Wali Khan and other leading members of the NAP and the banning of the party.[7]

Executed as a criminal by the Zia regime, Bhutto came to be seen by many as a martyr (*shaheed*) and *pir*, with hundreds of thousands of ordinary people flocking annually to his tomb. Even before his death he had on occasion spoken in mystical terms, declaring to his audiences that there were 'two Bhuttos', one of which resided in each of his hearers in an inseparable bond.[8]

Bhutto's political style was combative and confrontational. The exercise of power not only fascinated him, but fed his ego. On one occasion he declared that politics was the milk he had received at birth and that the political vocation inspired him and kindled in him 'the flame of a lasting romance'.[9] He ultimately rejected the leftists and party workers who had propelled the PPP to power and regarded all opposition as illegitimate. Although still only in early middle age when he took over the reins of office, he had been a close observer of the workings of the Pakistan political establishment for more than a decade. He also

---

were measured in square miles rather than acres.

[5] Anthony Mascarenhas argues for example that Bhutto astutely realised that his interests and those of the military coincided after the December 1970 elections and that he colluded with Yahya Khan in order to forestall Sheikh Mujibur Rahman so that he could become Prime Minister. A. Mascarenhas, *The Rape of Bangla Desh*, pp. 70-81.

[6] The author, who took over as Commander-in-Chief after the Bangladesh débâcle, had a rocky relationship with Bhutto until he was replaced by Tikka Khan and sent into 'exile' as Ambassador to Austria. Inevitably a jaundiced view of Bhutto emerges from his memoirs. Interestingly he is equally scathing about Zia. *Memoirs of Lt.-General Gul Hassan Khan* (Karachi, 1993).

[7] This followed the assassination of the Frontier PPP leader Hayat Muhammad Khan in a bomb blast in Peshawar in 1975. At the time a minority PPP Qaiyum Muslim League coalition government was ruling the province.

[8] A.H. Syed, 'The Pakistan People's Party: Phases One and Two' in L. Ziring, R. Braibanti, and W. Howard Wriggins, *Pakistan: The Long View* (Durham, NC, 1977), p. 75.

[9] Syed, 'Bhutto's Self-Characterizations', p. 1255.

possessed the experience of representing Pakistan on the wider world stage. Aside from his own sense of destiny, no Pakistani politician was in fact better placed to rebuild the machinery of government and national morale shattered by the Bangladesh débâcle. Its tangible consequences were equally serious and involved the loss of the foreign exchange brought by jute and tea exports and of an assured market for up to 40 per cent of the products of West Pakistan's manufacturing base.

Despite Bhutto's immense influence, his definitive biography is still awaited. Stanley Wolpert's work *Zulfi Bhutto of Pakistan* (Oxford, 1993) is well-known, but has rightly been regarded by critics[10] as a missed opportunity. It eschews a detailed study of Bhutto's contribution to Pakistani politics in favour of psychobabble and an almost prurient concern with the subject's sexual proclivities. Wolpert follows the earlier study of S. Taheer[11] in depicting his contradictory actions in terms of the 'two faces of Bhutto', the Western-educated progressive and the despotic feudal chief. Unfortunately, Wolpert's work has established a trend and there have been other psychoanalytical studies of Bhutto's career[12] which, despite their ingenuity, have shed little fresh light on an important episode in Pakistan's history. Equally unhelpful are the large number of adulatory works in Urdu which appeared in the early 1970s.[13]

Although the breakaway of the eastern wing dramatically altered the context of Pakistan's politics, Bhutto faced the same dilemmas which had defeated his predecessors, namely how to assert the authority of the elected institutions of the state over the military and bureaucracy, establish a functioning federal system and resolve the role of Islam in constitutional theory and practice. These problems were all rooted in the imperial past and in the traumatic period which immediately followed Partition. Equally pressing was the need to tackle the accumulated grievances of the rural and urban poor whose expectations had soared since the PPP's populist campaigns against Ayub. Bhutto

---

10 See the review article by Leslie Wolf-Phillips in *Third World Quarterly* 15, no. 4 (December, 1994), pp. 723-30.

11 S. Taheer, *Bhutto: A Political Biography* (London, 1979).

12 S. Zulfiqar Gilani, 'Z.A. Bhutto's leadership: A Psycho-social View', *Contemporary South Asia* 3, no.3 (1994), pp. 217-37.

13 Representative works include: Mahmood Sham, *Larkana Se Peking* ('From Larkana to Peking'), Karachi, 1972; Khalid Kashmiri, *Awam Ka Sadar* ('President of the Masses'), Lahore, 1972; Yunus Adeeb, *Quaid-e-Awam* ('Leader of the Masses'), Lahore, 1972; Qazi Zulfiqar Ahmad and Rana Mahmood-ul-Ahsan, *Zulfikar Ali Bhutto* (Lahore, 1973); Rana Rahman Zafar, *Zulfikar Ali Bhutto* (Lahore, 1973).

rose to these historic challenges by reforming the non-elected state institutions and by clipping the wings of their landlord allies. Land reform was accompanied by labour reform and by an extensive nationalisation programme. The 1973 Constitution was intended once and for all to lay the foundations of the place of Islam in the governance of the country and to resolve the issue of autonomy for the provinces. Before turning to Bhutto's major endeavours to resolve the dilemmas which had defeated his predecessors, it is necessary to examine the functioning of the PPP in power.

The PPP in power

Like the Muslim League a generation earlier, the PPP had emerged as a broad-based opposition movement held together by a single, dominating figure. Once in power, it faced the problem which had defeated its predecessor, namely how to make the transition from a movement to a well-structured party of government. Far more was at stake than its own well-being, for the problem of weak party organisation was a major factor in Pakistan's institutional crisis which paved the way for praetorianism.

In the event, the PPP failed to break with past patterns of political organisation in Pakistan. Party-building, instead of proceeding along the lines of elected institutions and formal structures, revolved around the utilisation of patronage. The result was growing factionalism, dependence on Bhutto's personal support for authority, and an increasing rift between Bhutto and the leftist groups who attached more importance to organisation. They were also increasingly disillusioned by the entry of rural notables into the party. The situation might have been different if the party had been more strongly institutionalised before it came to power, although a number of writers have claimed that its characteristics suited Bhutto's patrimonialist style, hence the party chairman's tardiness in acting. It was not until 1976 that he began to undertake provincial 'reorganisation tours', which were followed by conventions organised on a divisional basis.

The comprehensive reorganisation which finally took place in December 1976 still emphasised personal loyalties over effective institutionalisation. Bhutto himself selected the higher office-holders, his secretariat, and those at the district level and below. Indeed by this juncture decision-making had become entirely centralised, and Bhutto had personalised the PPP much as Indira Gandhi stood for the Congress in India. Symptomatic of the refashioning of the PPP according to Bhutto's personal dictates was the marginalisation of its founding members one by one: sycophancy replaced creative thought as the key to influence in the higher echelons of the party. Even J. A. Rahim,[14] who had drafted the PPP Foundation Documents, found himself out in the cold in July 1974 after he had the temerity publicly to disagree with Bhutto's handling of affairs.[15]

Factional divisions went hand in hand with the PPP's increasingly clientelist politics. This was illustrated most clearly by the clash in the Punjab between Sheikh Rashid and Ghulam Mustafa Khar.[16] Before the 1970 elections, Khar and Rashid had held the posts of Secretary-General and President respectively of the Punjab PPP and had clashed over the allocation of tickets. The former had utilised his membership of the PPP Central Parliamentary Review Board to reverse some of Rashid's decisions which had gone against the landholders. By the beginning of 1973 many of Rashid's supporters had been purged from the party; others had false income tax cases brought against them.[17] Later similar cases were instituted against rival landlord faction leaders such as Yaqub Maan and Raja Munnawar Khakwani. Even more worrying were reports of abductions and political murders of Khar's opponents. The Khar-dominated PPP Government became known as a *danda* (stick) *raj* rather than an *awami* (people's) *raj*. Khar's hatchet-man, Iftikhar Ahmed Tari, was reputed to have underworld connections and became an especially disliked figure.

Corresponding to Rashid and Khar in Punjab were Jam Sadiq Ali and Rasul Baksh Talpur in Sindh, or in the Frontier Humayan Saifullah and Habibullah Khan in Bannu, and Abdul Samad Khan and Abdul Razik Khan in Mardan. Such personal rivalries increasingly spilled over into violence[18] causing Bhutto to note in a memo of 16 August 1973: 'Pistols to the right of us, pistols to the left of us, pistols all around us. This seems to be the motto of the party. For

---

[14] Mubashir Hasan replaced him as PPP General Secretary. He too was a party stalwart, but this had not protected him from earlier demotion from the post of Minister of Finance.

[15] For background on the Rahim-Bhutto clash see L. Ziring, 'Pakistan: A Political Perspective', *Asian Survey* 15, no.7 (July, 1975), pp. 630-3.

[16] Khar came from a branch of the Kharral tribe who were large landowners from Kot Addu in the Muzaffargarh district of the Punjab. He was one of a family of seven brothers.

[17] Khar used this well-established technique of harassment not only on personal rivals but on ideological opponents such as Mahmud Ali Kasuri, who had formed the 'Manifesto Group' within the PPP on 28 March 1973 to protest against the party's growing authoritarianism at both national and provincial levels.

[18] The rising tide of violence was seen in the assassinations and attacks on opposition and PPP figures alike. Those who died by the bullet included Maulvi Shamsuddin, Khwaja Rafique and Abdus Samad Achakzai. Wali Khan and Asghar Khan narrowly cheated death on a number of occasions.

the most trivial of things pistols are drawn and flashed.'[19] Between February and May 1972 alone there were serious factional clashes between PPP rivals in Lahore, Gujjar Khan, Wazirabad, Gujranwala and Vehari in the Punjab, while the party secretariat offices in Karachi were occupied by disgruntled workers.[20]

Some of the differences within the PPP were ideological, as for example the clash between the conservative Information Minister Kauser Niazi and his radical ministerial colleague Mairaj Muhammad Khan. But most factional conflict was based on *biraderi* rivalries. Like the Muslim League in the 1940s, the PPP expanded into the rural areas of the Frontier and Punjab by securing support from local landowners and tribal leaders. While this approach provided a secure power-base, it also intensified the existing organisational weaknesses created by Bhutto's patrimonialism by importing 'particularistic cleavages' into the party.

Preferential politics

Sindhis were disproportionately under-represented in the main institutions of the Pakistan state and among its business elite, but before 1971 ethnicisation of the province's politics was much less developed than in East Bengal. This was seen clearly in the failure of G. M. Syed to win any seats in the 1970 election. Politicisation of a *mohajir* identity was even more remote as the community formed a core part of the ruling national elite[21] and predominated within the commercial and economic life of Sindh.

Tensions were increased between the Sindhis and *mohajirs* were heightened by the Teaching, Promotion and Use of Sindhi Language Bill which was introduced in the Sindh Assembly on 3 July 1972[22] and by the nationalisation of large industrial houses owned by *mohajirs*. The situation was further exacerbated by the national government's introduction in 1973 of a new quota system for federal employment.

---

[19] A.H. Syed, 'The Pakistan Peoples' Party', p. 111.

[20] *Ibid.*, pp. 94, 109.

[21] *Mohajirs* held a third of the gazetted posts in the civilian bureaucracy, although their share of the total population by the early 1970s was less than 10 per cent. In 1968 eleven out of the forty-eight officers in ranks senior to brigadier in the Pakistan Army were held by *mohajirs*. T. Amin, *Ethno-national Movements of Pakistan: Domestic and International Factors* (Islamabad, 1988), p. 82.

[22] Its most controversial clauses were those that stipulated that Sindhi should be a compulsory subject from school classes 4 to 9 and that arrangements should be made for its progressive introduction in government offices, departments, the courts and the legislature. This would have endangered the Urdu-speaking *mohajirs'* employment prospects.

Table 8.1 sets out the details of the system. Its most controversial element was to split Sindh's overall provincial quota of 19 per cent 60:40 between rural and urban areas (i.e. cities over 100,000 population). Given the rural-urban split between Sindhi and *mohajir* populations this meant that the highly-educated urban *mohajir* community had reserved for itself just 7.6 per cent of the total quota of federal jobs. This was in addition to the 10 per cent reserved for national competition, but was well below both the proportion of the total population residing in urban Sindh and the *mohajirs'* previous representation. Under the 1949 federal quota, they could compete for Sindh's 17 per cent reservation in addition to the 20 per cent reserved for merit.

The resentment caused by this 'discrimination' in favour of rural Sindhis was intensified by the extension of the application of the quota to educational institutions and by the domicile issue. Domicile documents enabled the enforcement of the quota, but their existence encouraged forgeries and corruption. Connections, as ever in Pakistan, counted for everything, with the result that wealthy Sindhi students encroached on the already limited urban quota. These events lay behind the decision by Altaf Hussain, Azim Ahmed Tariq, Saleem Haider, Imran Farooq and ten other Karachi University students to found the All Pakistan Mohajir Student Organisation (APMSO) in 1978. This was the direct precursor of the MQM, which came into existence some eight years later.[23]

Table 8.1. THE QUOTA SYSTEM IN
PUBLIC SECTOR EMPLOYMENT

Area of domicile	Quota (%)
Punjab/Islamabad	50.0
NWFP	11.5
Rural Sindh	11.4
Urban Sindh	7.6
Northern Areas/FATA	4.0
Balochistan	2.5
Azad Kashmir	2.0
Merit	10.0

Source: Government of Pakistan, Establishment Division, Memo. no. F.8/9/72 (TRV), 31 August 1973. Islamabad. Cited in J. Richards, 'Mohajir Subnationalism and the Mohajir Qaumi Movement in Sindh Province. Pakistan', unpubl. Ph.D. thesis, University of Cambridge, 1993, p. 214.

[23] For a brief introduction to the MQM's history see F. Haq, 'Rise of the MQM in Pakistan: Politics of Ethic Mobilisation', *Asian Survey* 35, no. 11 (November 1995), pp. 990-1004.

Bhutto, the Army and the bureaucracy

Bhutto sought to curb the power of the bureaucracy and the military, those unelected institutions of the Pakistan state which both inherited and upheld the pre-independence tradition of viceregalism. Their disarray and the public disillusionment in the wake of the secession of Bangladesh provided him with an unparalleled opportunity for breaking with the past. But in the event hopes for radical change to the traditional civil-military configuration of power were to be cruelly disappointed. Ironically, rather than securing autonomy of action, Bhutto became increasingly reliant on both the Army and the civil service.

The Army. Hasan-Askari Rizvi has detailed the steps which Bhutto took in order to establish control over an army whose myth of military invincibility had been shattered in the swamps of East Bengal. Twenty-nine senior officers were relieved of their duties within the first four months of Bhutto's assumption of power,[24] including the Chief of Army Staff, Lieutenant-General Gul Hassan Khan who was replaced by General Tikka Khan. The seemingly pliant General Zia-ul-Haq was to succeed him on his retirement in March 1976. A commission chaired by Hamudar Rehman, Chief Justice of Pakistan, was convened to inquire into the military catastrophe in East Pakistan. Its findings have never been made public.

In addition to taking full political advantage of the military's post-Bangladesh disarray and unpopularity, Bhutto instituted a number of measures to reduce its longer-term influence. They included the restructuring of the military high command in order to disperse power, and the reduction of the tenure of the Chiefs of Staff to three years. The most controversial reform was the creation of the Federal Security Force (FSF) in October 1972.[25] This was a well-equipped task force under the control of the Federal Government which was designed to assist the police in the maintenance of law and order. Opponents criticised it as an oppressive private army, and its existence along with the People's Guards (a PPP organisation) reminded serving army officers of Bhutto's earlier calls for the replacement of a conventional force by a 'People's Army'.[26] Such anxieties were not allayed when, on returning from an overseas visit, Bhutto inspected a guard of honour of the People's Guards

---

[24] Including naval and air force chiefs, 43 senior military officers in all were relieved from service during this period. Hasan-Askari Rizvi, *The Military and Politics in Pakistan, 1947-86* (Delhi, 1988), Table XXV, pp. 198-9.

[25] By the beginning of 1977 it was a force of 18,500 men..

[26] Hasan-Askari Rizvi, *The Military and Politics in Pakistan*, p. 197.

rather than an army contingent.[27] Military resentment at the creation
of a parallel force was expressed in the refusal to train FSF recruits.
Significantly one of the first actions of the Zia regime was to disband
the force.

A number of clauses in the 1973 Constitution were specifically
designed to discourage future military intervention. Its third schedule
contained an oath which serving members of the military were to take
forswearing political activities of any kind. Article 245 defined high
treason as any attempt to abrogate or subvert the constitution 'by the
use of force or show of force or by other unconstitutional means'.
Within a month of the Constitution being enforced, a law was passed
enforcing the death sentence or life imprisonment for those found guilty
of attempting to subvert it. These clauses strengthened the legal cover
provided by the 1972 Supreme Court judgement in the Asma Jilani
case, which ruled that Yahya Khan's assumption of power on 25 March
1969 was 'illegal and unconstitutional'. This judgement reversed the
1958 Dosso case which had legitimised the Ayub Khan regime in terms
of the doctrine of 'revolutionary legality'.

Despite this favourable background, Bhutto always remained uneasy
in his relations with the generals. He was prepared to risk the wrath
of left-wing supporters when he exempted army officers' holdings from
the March 1972 land reforms, and made strenuous efforts to dispel
any notion of a Tashkent-'sell-out' following the July 1972 Simla Agreement with Mrs Gandhi. Bhutto's caution resulted from the awareness
that while it was easy on paper to clip the military's wings, the reality
was somewhat different. A People's Army could not provide security
in a regional context shaped by the resurrection of the Pakhtunistan
issue by the Afghan Government of Sardar Muhammad Daud following
the overthrow of King Zahir Shah on 17 July 1973[28] and by the Indian
nuclear explosion in the Rajasthan desert in May 1974. There was also
the requirement to replace the equipment which had been lost in the
Bangladesh war. Pakistan's defence expenditure rose by over 200 per
cent during the Bhutto era. Throughout this period $8 for every Pakistani
citizen was being spent on the armed forces.[29] Yet despite spending
almost twice as great a percentage of its GNP on defence as India,
the military balance between them widened throughout the 1980s as
India's defence expenditure in absolute terms was nearly four times

---

[27] *Ibid.*

[28] For further details see L. Ziring, 'Bhutto's Foreign Policy, 1972-73' in H. Korson
(ed.), *Contemporary Problems of Pakistan* (Leiden, 1974), pp. 64-8.

[29] S.J. Burki, *Pakistan Under Bhutto 1971-1977* (London, 1980), Table 5.2, p. 105.

greater.[30] For the period 1971-80, India's weapons imports stood at $3.76 billion against Pakistan's $1.54 billion.[31] The United States once again became a major source of military hardware following the lifting of its arms embargo in 1975. By then Pakistan had become heavily dependent on China as an arms supplier: in the 1970s it provided some 500 T-59 tanks, twenty-five naval vessels and 300 F-6 combat aircraft in a $600 million programme.[32] The Chinese also constructed a tank repair factory at Taxila and an Air Force repair facility at nearby Kamra. Yet every dollar Pakistan spent on weaponry reduced funding where it was desperately needed – education, healthcare and housing – and created budget deficits. As in April 1974, attempts to reduce these by curbing food subsidies cost the government support among its natural constituency, the urban poor.

The re-equipment of the Pakistan Army marked its post-Bangladesh rehabilitation. Even more important, however, was Bhutto's reliance on it to maintain internal security. This enabled the men in uniform to renew their taste for power and drew them back into politics. The Army was called into action as early as July 1972 to restore law and order following the language riots in Sindh. The civil government called it out again shortly afterwards following labour disturbances in the Landi and Korangi areas of Karachi.[33]

It was the Army's involvement in Balochistan from 1973-7 which most undermined the attempt to establish civilian supremacy. Bhutto's handling of political developments there has been regarded by a number of writers as representing the Achilles' heel of his regime. His despatch of around 80,000 troops into the sparsely populated province of under 5 million people to deal with the tribal/autonomist insurrection of 1973-6 returned the Army to a political role. The use of force carried echoes of Yahya's ill-conceived actions in East Pakistan and depressingly repeated the pattern of the state hampering national integration by provoking regional opposition through its violent suppression of legitimate demands.

The Pakistan Army had previously intervened in the region in both March 1948 and October 1958. The first episode followed on immediately from the accession of Kalat State to Pakistan and quelled the opposition of Prince Abdul Karim. The Army had been employed a decade later in hostilities with the Zehri tribe. Skirmishes continued during the Ayub

---

[30] R.G. Wirsing, 'The Arms race in South Asia: Implications for the United States', *Asian Survey* 25 , no.3 (March 1985), p. 269.

[31] *Ibid.*, p. 270.

[32] *Ibid.*, p. 276.

[33] For details see T. Ali, *Can Pakistan Survie?*, pp. 109-10.

era, and at its close there were also numerous clashes with the Bugti tribe. Ayub's regime was also marked by an attempt to wean the tiny Baloch intelligentsia to the state's side by patronage of cultural and literary societies. A Balochi Academy was established in Quetta in 1961 which shifted the heart of the literary renaissance[34] from its previous base in Karachi.

The attempt at co-option was not entirely successful as the nascent professional class provided a support-base for Prince Abdul Karim's Ustaman Gall (People's Party), which was eventually absorbed into the NAP. Balochistan's ethnic and linguistic mix meant that with the ending of One Unit in 1971, a political identity based on language did not emerge. Balochistan's multilingualism was the product not only of a sizeable Pushto-speaking Pakhtun population in the districts of Sibi, Zhob, Loralai and Pishin[35] but also of the prevalence of Brahvi among groups which claimed Balochi ethnicity.[36] Indeed the Khan of Kalat's family was Brahvi-speaking, but in spite of this, Balochi nationalists looked to Mir Nisar Khan, who had forged the Kalat State in the second half of the eighteenth century, as an inspiration for in-dependent statehood in much the same way as Sikh ethno-nationalists harked back to the achievements of his contemporary Ranjit Singh.

Baloch long-term grievances were in some respects similar to those of Bhutto's native Sindhis. They included a sense of status displacement as a result of the migration of Pakhtuns and Punjabis into the province. Baloch intellectuals also pointed to the under-representation of their community in the structures of the Pakistani state,[37] and argued that development was exploitative of local resources such as natural gas, while road-building also served strategic rather than Balochi interests.

The tensions between the Federal Government and the NAP-JUI administration in Quetta were kept in check until the July 1972 passage of the Simla Accord. Thereafter they escalated. The hostility between the Bugti and Marri tribes gave Bhutto further leeway to intervene

[34] For material on this consult T. Rahman, 'The Balochi/Brahvi Language Movements in Pakistan', *Journal of South Asian and Middle Eastern Studies* 19, no.3 (spring 1996), pp. 77-8.

[35] *Ibid.*, p. 72.

[36] There has been considerable controversy concerning the origins of the Brahvi-speaking population. Some writers claim that they have a Dravidian origin because of the similarities between their language and the Dravidian language of southern India. Others refute this and maintain a common ethnic origin for the Brahvis and Balochis.

[37] Only 4 of the 179 central cabinet members in Pakistan's opening three decades were Baloch. According to one study only 2,000 out of 40,000 civil employees in Balochistan were Baloch, most of them in low-ranking positions. R.G. Wirsing, *The Baluchis and Pathans* (London, 1987), p. 9.

in the situation. Finally, repression could be justified in terms of the NAP's alleged anti-state activities. The pretext for the dismissal of the Mengal Government, which sparked off the tribal insurgency, was provided by the controversial 10 February 1973 arms discovery in the Iraqi Embassy. The writing had been on the wall, however, following the earlier clashes between the provincially-controlled Dehi Muhafiz (a civil armed force) and the Jamote tribe of Lasbella. The Jamotes along with the Bugtis and Zehris were traditional opponents of the Mengal-led NAP-JUI Government. There is considerable controversy concerning the background to these clashes, which can variously be explained in terms of the Jamotes' opposition to the Government's reforms, or as being cynically engineered by Bhutto.[38] If the latter is true, it represented a grave miscalculation.

The tribal uprising escalated into a major military confrontation. The Balochistan People's Liberation Front, which drew support from both students and the Marri tribe, numbered around 60,000 supporters and established bases in Kandahar under the command of Mir Hazar Khan and in Baghdad as well as in Balochistan.[39] At the height of the struggle, the Pakistan Air Force received assistance from the Shah of Iran[40] who had his own 'Baloch problem'.[41] Although such US analysts as Selig Harrison[42] over-estimated the Soviet security threat, the conflict claimed at least 9,000 lives and gravely undermined the Bhutto regime. Indeed in his testament from his 'stinking death cell' Bhutto claimed that the army overrode his plans for a withdrawal because the generals wanted to 'spread their tentacles throughout Baluchistan.'[43] The revival of the Balochistan Assembly[44] in the run-up to the national elections

---

[38] S.A. Qureshi, 'An Analysis of Contemporary Pakistani Politics: Bhutto versus the Military', *Asian Survey* 19, no.9 (September, 1979), p. 913.

[39] See Inayatullah Baloch, 'Afghanistan-Pashtunistan-Baluchistan', *Aussenpolitik*, 31, (3rd quarter, 1980), pp. 298ff.

[40] S. Harrison, 'Baluch Nationalism and Superpower Rivalry', *International Security*, 5, no.3 (1980/81), p. 154. Robert Wirsing has questioned the accuracy of this depiction by Harrison and maintained that Iranian piloted Chinook helicopters played a very minor role in the fighting. R.G. Wirsing, *Pakistan's Security under Zia: The Policy Imperatives of a Peripheral Asian State* (Basingstoke, 1991), pp. 105-6.

[41] His father Reza Khan had successfully crushed the Baloch tribes who made up less than 2 per cent of Iran's population. But their home in the remote south-eastern part of the country had taken on a new strategic significance with the construction of the air and naval base at Chah Bahar and the movement of oil in large quantities through the Strait of Hormuz and the Gulf of Oman.

[42] *Ibid.*, pp. 152-63.

[43] Bhutto, *If I Am Assassinated* (New Delhi, 1979), p. 19.

[44] Federal rule had been imposed on 31 December 1975.

could not put the military genie back in the bottle. Bhutto had shown his future executors the way forward in reducing unrest in Pakistan's troubled tribal frontiers by instituting a major programme of electrification, roads and other infrastructural development. By the time martial law was lifted in 1985 the 'economic balm' of development had restored the province to 'normalcy'.

The bureaucracy. The compartmentalisation of the bureaucracy between its central and provincial services and the elitism of the CSP cadre, which accounted for under 1 per cent of the entire personnel, had drawn adverse comment in government reports from the 1950s onwards. But such was the influence of the CSP, variously called by critics the 'Sultans of Pakistan' and 'the best organised political party in Pakistan' that these had been shelved. Radical opinion hoped that Bhutto would make good earlier gestures towards reform, especially in the light of the animosity towards the bureaucracy during the 1968-9 anti-Ayub campaign. Two of the ringing slogans of this era had been '*Naukershahi Murdabad*' (Death to the servant-kings) and '*Rishwat sitani Khatum Karo*' (End corruption).[45] On assuming power Bhutto dismissed leading civil servants associated with the military era, which he dubbed as one of *naukarshahi* (rule by civil servants)[46] and jailed Ayub's former right-hand man, Altaf Gauhar.[47] The purge of public servants on grounds of corruption and inefficiency was by no means unique, but had been a feature of the early days of all martial law administrations.

Full details of Bhutto's reform of the bureaucracy can be found in Charles Kennedy's work *Bureaucracy in Pakistan*.[48] It is sufficient to note here that despite the abolition of the CSP and the introduction of a unified grade structure, key positions in the Central Secretariat continued to be headed by members of the former elite cadre and the functions of civil servants were never usurped by the PPP bureaucracy.

Bhutto's personal control of the administrative system was nevertheless secured through the creation of special posts and the establishment

---

45 Quoted in M. Lodhi, 'The Pakistan People's Party', p. 594.

46 At the announcement of his civil service reforms, Bhutto forcefully declared: 'No institution in the country has so lowered the quality of our national life as what is called "Naukarshahi" It has done so by imposing a caste system on our society. It has created a class of Brahmins or mandarins, unrivalled in its snobbery and arrogance, insulated from the life of the people and incapable of identifying itself with them.' W. Eric Gustafson, 'Economic Reforms under the Bhutto regime' in H. Korson (ed.), *Contemporary Problems of Pakistan*, p. 96.

47 Burki, *Pakistan Under Bhutto*, p. 100.

48 C. Kennedy, *Bureaucracy in Pakistan* (Karachi, 1987).

of a lateral entry scheme administered not by the Federal Service Commission but by a politicised Establishment Division. Critics claimed that this raised an 'army of stooges' who were the sycophantic appointees, relatives and hangers-on of federal ministers.[49]

In the latter period of his regime, Bhutto came increasingly to rely on the bureaucrats just as he did on the Army. This was the unintended consequence of his institutional and socio-economic reforms. The nationalisation of banks, industries and educational establishments all contributed to a burgeoning public sector which required administrative oversight. Land reforms, labour legislation and the implementation of the People's Works Programme further added to the tasks of the civil servants. In the case of such 'Bhuttocrats' as Rao Abdur Rashid and Afzal Saeed Khan these even extended to mediating PPP factional disputes. For all his attempts to break with the past, Bhutto was ultimately as dependent on the bureaucracy for the maintenance of his rule as had been any of his predecessors.

Constitutional developments

The period of civilian martial law lasted just four months from Bhutto's assumption of office until 21 April 1972, when an Interim Constitution was introduced. Its 290 clauses and seven schedules had been approved by those delegates elected to West Pakistan's four provinces in the 1970 elections and now acted as a National Assembly. The Interim Constitution provided for a centralised government with a presidential system at the centre and a parliamentary system in the provinces.

By the time the National Assembly, acting as a Constituent Assembly, began a clause by clause examination of the new permanent constitution, there was increasing tension between the PPP and the opposition parties arising from the deteriorating situation in Balochistan. On 2 March 1973 the main opposition parties grouped together in Islamabad to form the United Democratic Front (UDF) under Pir Pagaro's leadership. He headed a reunified Muslim League. The opposition groups argued for the inclusion of Islamic principles in any constitution and for regional autonomy. The UDF in melodramatic fashion[50] voted on 10 April in favour of the new constitution, despite its earlier walkout from the National Assembly. In marked contrast with Pakistan's first constitution, its adoption had taken just a year and had the consent of the main

---

[49] Burki, *Pakistan Under Bhutto*, p. 102.

[50] The opposition members returned to the Chamber half an hour before the Constitution Bill was passed.

opposition parties. In contrast with the second, it offered the hope of genuine democratic development.

The 1973 Constitution came into operation on 14 August. It provided for a parliamentary system of government in which power resided with the Prime Minister not the President. Article 48 stipulated that he should be bound by the Prime Minister's advice and that his ordinances would not have legal sanction unless they were countersigned by the Prime Minister. The latter[51] was to be elected by a majority of the 200-member National Assembly in which also resided initiatory powers of legislation. The Senate Upper House could delay but not veto a bill passed by the National Assembly. Its members were to be divided equally among the four provinces[52] and would be elected by a combined sitting of the National and Provincial Assemblies. The 1973 Constitution also provided for an independent judiciary, guaranteed fundamental rights and granted more autonomy to the provinces than any previous constitution. Article 153 for example created a Council of Common Interest to resolve economic disputes between the federating units. The very long list of concurrent subjects and the powers of the centre to intervene in the provinces nevertheless remained considerable. The claim that the 1973 Constitution had finally resolved Pakistan's longstanding problem of composing differences between the provinces and the centre appeared increasingly chimerical. Bhutto, despite his often expressed sentiments in favour of federalism, was no more willing to shift power from the centre to the provinces than any of his predecessors.

The Islamic provisions included the declaration that Islam was the state religion and only Muslims could hold the offices of President and Prime Minister.[53] The state was also enjoined to provide facilities to the Muslims of Pakistan to fashion their lives, individually as well as collectively, to the teachings of Islam and to promote the teaching of the Quran and Sunnah. All steps would be taken by the Government to teach Islamiyat and the Holy Quran. In order to ensure that laws were in agreement with the teachings of Islam, a Council of Islamic Ideology was to be appointed by the President as an advisory body. Simultaneously Article 34 for the first time introduced the new principle that 'Steps shall be taken to ensure full participation of women in all

---

51 The Prime Minister could be removed by a vote of no confidence in the National Assembly provided that a successor was named in the motion. A no-confidence motion could not however be tabled while the annual budget was being discussed in the National Assembly.

52 In addition to fourteen members from each of the provinces, the Senate contains two members from the minorities and five from the FATA area.

53 The constitution for the first time provided a definition of a Muslim.

spheres of national life.' Initial protection was also provided against the repeal of the MFLO of 1961.[54]

Despite its mutilation by Zia's Eighth Amendment, the 1973 Constitution has proved more durable than any of its predecessors in pointing the way to a democratic future. As with its 1950 Indian counterpart however safeguards for the rights of minorities on paper do not ensure their existence in practice. Similarly civil liberties as well as provincial autonomy have been legally overridden by extraordinary powers accorded to rulers for reasons of state. Such measures during the Bhutto era included the Prevention of Anti-National Activities Ordinance (1973) and the Suppression of Terrorist Activities Act (1975). Opponents were also detained under the Defence of Pakistan Rules.

Economic and social reforms

Bhutto sought to consolidate the PPP's support among the rural and urban poor by policies of land and labour reform and by the nationalisation of industries, financial institutions and schools. Such reforms were condemned as half-hearted by leftist groups associated with the PPP who were already disconcerted by the opportunist entry of landlords into its ranks and by Bhutto's increasing personalisation of power. At the same time the reforms created powerful enemies among the propertied classes. The economy, already buffeted by the worldwide inflationary pressures generated by the 1973 Arab-Israeli war, suffered as capital took flight from the country. Rates of savings, investment and output all declined. The devaluation of the rupee[55] on 11 May 1972 stoked inflationary pressures. Dependence on foreign aid from the OPEC countries to tide over the deteriorating balance of payments situation from 1974 onwards was a mixed blessing, as aid also found its way into the pockets of the regime's Islamic opponents. For the man in the street, the rhetoric of egalitarianism sounded increasingly hollow when confronted with annual price rises of 20 per cent.

Land reforms. In his 1970 election campaign Bhutto had called for the removal of the 'remaining vestiges of feudalism'.[56] The land reforms which he introduced two years later were certainly more radical than

---

[54] F. Rahman, 'Islam and the New Constitution of Pakistan' in H. Korson (ed.), *Contemporary Problems of Pakistan*, p. 37.

[55] It was devalued from Rs.4.76 to the dollar to a new official rate of Rs.11 to the dollar.

[56] S.J. Burki, *Pakistan Under Bhutto*, p. 138.

Ayub's. The maximum land ceilings were reduced to 150 acres of irrigated land and 300 acres of un-irrigated land. Orchards and stud,
livestock and game farms were no longer exempted. Moreover land
was to be resumed by the state without compensation and distributed
free of cost to landless tenants and small peasant owners. But behind
the rhetoric the *status quo* was largely unshaken. Intra-family land transfer
was still allowed[57] and owners of tractors and tubewells could also
claim allowances which would increase their individual land ceiling.
As in 1959 only a limited amount of land was ultimately made available
for redistribution. This consisted of even poorer-quality land than before
as the absence of compensation predictably encouraged owners to retain
their most fertile holdings.

The Bhutto reforms suffered from the same irregularities in their
implementation as the 1959 land reforms. In numerous instances the
landless were made owners of resumed areas in name only, or fictitious
transfers were entered. Ironically the reforms, rather than signalling
a shift in the balance of power in the favour of tenants, encouraged
Punjabi landlords to enter the PPP's ranks in order to safeguard their
position. The success with which large numbers of landlords concealed
their lands owed as much to official patronage as administrative inefficiency. Craig Baxter has pointed out the remarkable ability of the
leading landlord families to accommodate themselves to successive
regimes.[58] Despite his populist rhetoric Bhutto liberally dispensed PPP
election tickets to the landlords in 1977. Those individuals who lost
heavily under the land reform legislation almost invariably came from
families politically opposed to Bhutto.[59]

In an admission of the failure of earlier measures, Bhutto announced
more stringent land reforms on the eve of the 1977 elections. Ceilings
were lowered to 100 acres of irrigated land and 200 acres of un-irrigated
land. The loophole of defining land ownership by the individual rather
than the family was retained from the earlier 1972 reforms. Compensation
was also provided for the resumption of land in the form of ten year
interest-bearing bonds. The PPP also announced in January 1977 that
the Land Revenue would be replaced by an agricultural income tax
system. This was a long-overdue reform which sought to increase
revenues and reduce tax evasion by individuals whose wealth was in
reality urban-rather than rural-based. These measures were suspended
with the introduction of martial law on 5 July.

[57] Up to a maximum of 14,000 PIUs (Produce Index Units).

[58] Craig Baxter, 'The People's Party versus the Punjab Feudalists', *Journal of Asian
and African Studies*, 8, nos 3-4 (July-October 1973), pp. 166-89.

[59] Interview with Saqib Hayat Khan, Islamabad, 17 December 1994.

Labour reforms. On 10 February 1972, Bhutto announced a far-reaching set of labour reforms which revealed the radical influence of Muhammad Hanif, the Minister for Labour. Union power was increased with the establishment of Works Councils and special Labour Courts for the adjudication of industrial disputes. A compulsory system of elected shop stewards was established in factories. The workers' lot was also to be improved by increasing profit-sharing arrangements in larger industries from 2-4 per cent. Employers were also called on to provide cheap housing and education to matriculation level for at least one child of every worker. The state also held out the promise of old age pensions and insurance against injury.[60]

As with other reforms the regime faced the opprobrium of vested interests and met with unforeseen consequences which diminished the gratitude of their beneficiaries. Emboldened by the reforms, workers flexed their muscles in a series of strikes and *gheraos* (lock-ins) which hit production in the poorly-managed newly-nationalised heavy industries. A bloody confrontation ensued between the Army and strikers in Karachi which precipitated the radical labour-based Mairaj group's break with Bhutto. The fact that the new labour laws did not apply to pieceworkers further alienated PPP leftist activists, as did the failure to introduce a minimum wage. The extension of the definition of 'registered enterprises' to small-scale units of five workers presented many lower-middle-class PPP supporters with the cost of pension, medical and welfare benefits and of workers' participation in management decisions as they were brought under the purview of the reforms. The regime found itself caught between two constituencies of support and was unable to please either.

Many small-scale enterprises were located in Punjab in such towns as Gujrat, Wazirabad and Kamoke. Part of the collapse of the PPP 'citadel' in the Punjab in the 1977 elections is attributable to the alienation of the small entrepreneurs. Those in the Sialkot-based sporting goods industry sought to circumvent the reforms by going back to a homework based decentralised production.[61] The erosion of business confidence hit investment which declined across the industrial sector leading to rising unemployment for workers whose lives were already being made miserable by the spiralling prices of foodstuffs. Ironically, the improved conditions which some sections of the working class experienced owed far more to the government's encouragement of the export of labour to the Gulf than to its vaunted reform programme.

[60] For details see Gustafson, 'Economic Reforms under the Bhutto Regime', pp. 85ff.

[61] A.M. Weiss, *Culture, Class and Development in Pakistan*, p. 134.

The Bhutto regime and nationalisation

In January 1972, the Bhutto regime introduced the nationalisation of over thirty large firms in ten basic industries.[62] This measure, which kept the promise of PPP manifesto undertakings, was intended to 'eliminate, once for all, poverty and discrimination in Pakistan.'[63] In reality it was far more important in clipping the wings of the 'twenty-two families' than in achieving the latter goal, as the heavy industrial sector did not possess a dominating economic influence.[64] S. J. Burki has maintained that the subsequent mismanagement of these newly nationalised industries by the Board of Management chaired by Dr Mubashir Hasan not only depressed production, but weakened the standing of leftist groups in the PPP.[65] Two months later, nationalisation was extended to the financial sector with the takeover of the life insurance companies. The following November the Government set up a State Life Insurance Corporation of Pakistan.

The next burst of nationalisation occurred in August 1973 and involved the *ghee* (clarified butter) industry. Unlike the earlier measure this affected the interests of small-sized entrepreneurs who had supported the PPP in 1970. It was justified by the 'profiteering' which had occurred in the wake of the severe monsoon flooding. The confidence of small businessmen in the regime was further undermined by the subsequent nationalisation in July 1976 of the rice husking and cotton trading industries. Significantly small traders and merchants were at the forefront of the 1977 anti-Bhutto movement. In a 'New Year present' to the people of Pakistan, Bhutto had announced the nationalisation of all privately owned banks at the beginning of 1974. Indira Gandhi, motivated by similar populist ideals had adopted this policy some five years earlier.

The nationalisation of private colleges was introduced in September 1972. The following month this was extended to schools, the process being phased in over a two-year period. Up to this point the private school sector, fed by middle-class demand, was growing rapidly in the main urban centres. No provision for compensation was made for the owners of colleges and schools. There was opposition to this policy

---

62 The industries affected included: iron and steel, basic metal industries, heavy engineering, heavy electrical machinery, motor vehicle assembly and manufacture, tractor plants, heavy and basic chemicals, petro-chemical industries, cement, and public utilities.

63 Z.A. Bhutto, 'Address to the Nation Announcing Nationalisation of Ten categories of Industries', 12 January 1972, *Speeches and Statements (20 December 1971 – 31 March 1972)* (Karachi, 1972), p. 33.

64 According to S.J. Burki it accounted for 12.8 per cent of the GDP and employed only 3.4 per cent of the labour force. Burki, *Pakistan Under Bhutto*, p. 114.

65 *Ibid.*, p. 115.

from missionary-run institutions which had traditionally maintained high academic standards and feared that these would fall in the absence of sufficient financial support. Deteriorating educational standards was indeed one further factor which encouraged urban middle-class opposition to the regime in 1977.

In common with the labour reforms, support from the poorer groups did not outweigh the opposition from vested interests which the government's policies generated. However, the nationalisation policy was accompanied by the provision of free education for children up to the age of thirteen. This was a significant achievement, but the goal of universal education still remained distant. While poor parents no longer had to afford fees, there was still the need for their children's labour. Added to this there was the cultural resistance to sending girls to school in the more conservative rural areas. Enrolment rates consequently did not improve dramatically, but the regime's emphasis on educational development continued to win support even from its critics.

Before moving on from this brief examination of Bhutto's nationalisation programmes, it is important to draw attention to the frequently neglected fact that they secured government control of financial and industrial assets of over Rs. 2 billion ($200 million). This vastly increased resource-base bankrolled the clientelist politics, which we have already noted was a marked feature of the operation of the PPP in government. The support of the large landholders was also facilitated by the provision of cheap credit from the newly-nationalised banks. A precedent was set in which successive governments were to use loans from government-controlled financial institutions to buy political support. By the mid-1990s the scale of loan defaults had reached the staggering level of Rs. 108 billion. The bad loans threatened the liquidity ratios of the nationalised banks, undermined Pakistan's credibility with international financial institutions and fed into a culture of endemic corruption.

Foreign policy

Zulfiqar Ali Bhutto's forte had, since the 1960s, lain in the conduct of foreign policy, and he was to deploy his diplomatic skills to good effect when in power. Foreign affairs occasioned his greatest triumph in the 1972 Simla Summit meeting with Indira Gandhi. In Bhutto's own mind his pursuit of Pakistan's independent interests with regard to nuclear policy by going ahead with plans for a plutonium reprocessing plant ultimately presented an opportunity for an 'external hand' to secure his downfall.

Bhutto's policy centred around the need to repair the physical and psychological scars left by the Bangladesh breakaway. The emphasis on close ties with China and the Middle East and the nuclearisation of Pakistan must all be understood in this light. China, as we have already seen, had become an indispensable arms supplier by the end of the 1970s. The most spectacular example of Sino-Pakistan cooperation was the construction of the strategic Karakoram Highway, which on its completion in 1978 connected Pakistan's Northern Areas with Xinjiang Province through the Kunjerab Pass.[66]

Shortly after Bhutto came to office he embarked on a morale-boosting tour of the Middle East and North Africa. The need for Pakistan to develop closer links with the Islamic world and to look westwards towards the Middle East rather than elsewhere in Asia was a constant theme of his regime. He also sought to boost Pakistan's self-esteem by emphasising the break with the pre-1947 era and its earlier reliance on the United States. Pakistan thus left the Commonwealth (30 January 1972) and the SEATO security pact (8 November 1972). Bhutto hoped that these steps would help pave the way for his country to become more acceptable in the counsels of the Third World. Indeed, he aspired to play a leading role in this emerging international grouping by hosting the first Third World Summit.

Bhutto had to pick up the pieces left by the Bangladesh conflict. These included the tricky issues of whether or not to recognise the new state, the need to secure the release of 93,000 prisoners of war of whom 195 were claimed to be war criminals, and the Indian occupation of almost 6,000 square miles of Pakistani territory. Behind these problems lay the necessity for bilateral talks with India, which had greatly strengthened its strategic position *vis-à-vis* Pakistan. Preliminary talks in the spring of 1972 between Indian and Pakistani officials[67] at the Murree hill-station outside Rawalpindi paved the way for a summit meeting at the former viceregal summer capital, Simla, between Bhutto and Indira Gandhi. The Pakistan President realised the high risks these entailed as the Indian Premier held all the strong cards, yet any sign of concession on his part could prove as fatally wounding as had the Tashkent summit for Ayub. In the event Bhutto was so adept at negotiating from a position of weakness in this first meeting of the subcontinent's leaders since Tashkent that the agreement signed in the early hours of 3 July was acclaimed in Pakistan as a great triumph. The subsequent attempts by his opponents at the time of his 1978 trial to claim that

---

66 For further details of the strategic significance of this magnificent engineering feat see Mahnaz Z. Ispahani, *Roads and Rivals: The Political Uses of Access in the Borderlands of Asia* (Ithaca, NY, 1989), esp. pp. 185-213.

67 The suave Kashmiri D.P. Dhar led the Indian team and his Pakistani counterpart was the veteran diplomat Aziz Ahmed.

a 'secret clause' agreed to the permanent acceptance of the *status quo* on Kashmir failed to remove the gloss from this achievement.[68]

Bhutto had departed for Simla from Lahore a week earlier accompanied by a large entourage which included his nineteen-year-old daughter Benazir who was on her Harvard summer vacation. For an insight into the personal dynamics of the summit her account[69] should be read alongside that of her father's former Bombay school companion Piloo Mody.[70] Bhutto was prepared to leave the former 'Abode of the Little Tin Gods' without an agreement rather than acquiesce in Indian demands for an explicit no-war pact,[71] or the recognition of Bangladesh by Pakistan.[72] The talks accordingly dragged on for a number of days without any prospect of success. The eleventh-hour agreement was so unexpected that neither a typewriter nor official seals were at hand. Bhutto in fact signed the treaty with a borrowed pen.[73] Mrs Gandhi had apparently acquiesced in the Simla Accord on the assumption that any agreement was better than none.

From Bhutto's point of view, the fact that the agreement did not include a no-war pact or Pakistani recognition of Bangladesh, yet secured Indian withdrawal from the occupied territory was a major cause for celebration. Despite Indian hopes, there was also no 'final' solution to the Kashmir issue, although Indira Gandhi claimed that the agreement of both sides to settle their differences by peaceful means through 'bilateral negotiations' buried the dispute as an international issue which could be brought before the United Nations. This interpretation was however later disputed by Bhutto in a speech to Pakistan's Institute of International Affairs in which he quoted Article 103 of the United Nations Charter which privileged its obligations over obligations of its members under any other agreement in the event of their conflict.[74] In practical terms the agreement saw both sides accept the 17 December 1971 cease-fire line as the new line of control in Kashmir. Finally, the Simla Accord allowed the resumption of trade and communications, including overflights, and called for the promotion of scientific and

---

[68] For Bhutto's vigorous rebuttal of this canard see Z.A. Bhutto, *If I am Assassinated*, pp. 130-1.

[69] B. Bhutto, *Daughter of the East: An Autobiography* (London, 1988), pp. 55ff.

[70] P. Mody, *Zulfi, My Friend* (Delhi, 1973), pp. 141ff.

[71] The last no-war pact had been signed by Liaquat in 1950 and had been followed by the Rawalpindi Conspiracy. Bhutto had no intention of risking military opposition by accepting a similar agreement.

[72] Such a diplomatic move would have incurred the wrath of the Islamic parties.

[73] S. Taseer, *Bhutto: A Political Biography*, p.141.

[74] *Ibid.*, p. 142.

cultural exchanges. Bhutto did not however secure the release of the prisoners of war from India.

A large crowd greeted the Pakistani delegation on its return to Rawal-pindi airport. A jubilant Bhutto declared to the onlookers: 'This is not my victory. Nor is it a victory of Mrs Gandhi's. It is a victory for the people of Pakistan and India who have won the peace after three wars.'[75] Twelve days later the National Assembly almost unanimously supported the Simla Accord, thanks in part to Bhutto's successful presen-tation. The contrast to the reception accorded to Ayub on his return from Tashkent could not have been greater.

Bhutto further displayed his adroitness with respect to the outstanding issues left over from Simla. He bided his time on the recognition of Bangladesh until the euphoria and sense of Muslim solidarity evoked by the February 1974 Islamic Summit in Lahore removed all possibility that recognition would arouse charges of a 'sell-out'. Up to this juncture the JI had orchestrated a vigorous '*Bangladesh-Na-Manzur*' (No recog-nition for Bangladesh) campaign. Mujib reciprocated by dropping the war criminal cases against the remaining 195 prisoners of war.[76] The summit, which focused on the Arab-Israeli conflict in the wake of the October war, was in other ways an outstanding success. It was better attended than its predecessor in Rabat; indeed the only notable absentee was the Shah of Iran. By bringing together on the same platform Yasser Arafat, King Faisal of Saudi Arabia, Colonel Qaddafi, and Presidents Assad, Sadat and Boumedienne, Bhutto ensured that the world spotlight was turned on Pakistan. Lahore, with its Mughal splendours and special place in the history of the Pakistan movement, formed the perfect back-drop. The euphoria of the crowd which packed the new Qaddafi stadium to hear the Libyan leader declaim that Pakistan was the 'citadel of Islam in Asia' and 'our resources are your resources'[77] contrasted dramati-cally with the gloom of December 1971. The summit was not only to bolster national pride, but to boost the economy with oil and monetary support. It also strengthened the Prime Minister's hand against his Islamic opponents, but this only had a short-term impact. Within two months of the conference's ending, an eight-party coalition of the '*ulama* led by Maulana Muhammad Yusuf Binnawri was to launch a hundred-day campaign against the Ahmadi community. Unlike its predecessor in 1953, it achieved the goal of legally stripping the Ahmadis of their

---

[75] B. Bhutto, *Daughter of the East*, p. 58.

[76] The bulk of the 93,000 prisoners had been returned following negotiations between India and Pakistan in August 1973. The India position up to this date had been to link their return with the recognition of Bangladesh.

[77] Wolpert, *Zulfi Bhutto of Pakistan* (Oxford, 1993), p. 234.

personal status as Muslims. This opened the way for further persecution. It was also to be the first of a number of concessions which Bhutto made to the religious parties. He found that while closer ties with the Islamic world were all well and good for strengthening Pakistan's diplomatic position, money from the oil-rich Middle East also flowed freely into the coffers of his would-be political opponents. The export of labour to the Middle East further encouraged the spread of Islamist ideas.

Arab money (Libyan and Saudi) was vital for Bhutto's quest to secure a Pakistani bomb. From the mid-1960s onwards, he argued that Pakistan should secure a nuclear weapons capability, even if the people had to eat 'grass or leaves' or 'even go hungry' (in his detailed study of Pakistan's nuclear development Ashok Kapur has demonstrated that Ayub Khan did not share this view, even after the 1965 war[78]). It was not until January 1972 that Bhutto made the decision to produce a nuclear weapon. This preceded India's nuclear test by over two years. According to Kapur, Bhutto's decision was motivated by the need both to deter India's military superiority after the Bangladesh war and to restore Pakistan's place in the world after the defeat. Its 'hidden domestic agenda' included the need to strengthen Bhutto's hand against the military (the bomb programme was to be independent of military control) and it would also cement the President's populist, anti-Indian credentials.[79]

According to one version of events, including that propounded by Bhutto in his death-cell memoirs *If I am Assassinated*, his decision to obtain a nuclear military capability[80] despite the existence of the Nuclear Non-Proliferation Treaty may have led to his ouster from power.[81] Bhutto claimed that he was warned by his Minister of Production, Rafi Raza,[82] in January 1977 not to proceed with the nuclear reprocessing plans and that external funding for the opposition's March election campaign and the motive for the subsequent military coup was the

[78] A. Kapur, *Pakistan's Nuclear Development* (London, 1987), p. 74.

[79] Ibid., p. 150.

[80] Official diplomacy throughout the post-1972 period stressed that Pakistan's nuclear programme was entirely peaceful in character.

[81] Dr Henry Kissinger is reported to have threatened to make a 'horrible example of him' if he did not abandon his plans to reprocess plutonium. *Ibid.*, p. 145.

[82] During the course of an interview on 2 January 1997, Rafi Raza maintained to me that he had warned Bhutto about sabre-rattling on the nuclear issue because of its impact on American opinion. While he believed that the United States was happy about Bhutto's fall, it had not engineered the PNA campaign which Bhutto had to a large extent brought upon himself.

desire to dislocate and destroy Pakistan's nuclear programme.[83] Certainly the Carter administration viewed with disquiet the CHASHMA agreement Pakistan signed with France for the supply of both a nuclear power station and a reprocessing plant. The French finally suspended the deal under US pressure in 1978, but not before 95 per cent of the blueprints had been transferred by the French company SGN. Canada had earlier in 1976 cut off its supply of heavy water, fuel fabrication plant and spare parts for the KANUPP nuclear reactor at Karachi.[84] This decision had been prompted by fears[85] that spent fuel might be diverted for clandestine reprocessing in contravention of International Atomic Energy Agency (IAEA) safeguards.

In the aftermath of these setbacks, Kapur has shown how attention was diverted from a plutonium to uranium[86] bomb route and a process began of clandestine acquisition of such equipment as centrifuges and yellowcake (semi-refined uranium ore). The enrichment uranium bomb option lent itself to a more covert development.[87] It was masterminded by Dr A.Q. Khan[88] who had returned to Pakistan in 1975. Centrifuge plants were established at Sihala and Kahuta. It was not however until after Bhutto's fall from power that Pakistan acquired its 'bomb in the basement' nuclear weapon option.[89] In the wake of the Soviet invasion of Afghanistan, the Reagan administration adopted a much softer attitude towards non-proliferation in Pakistan's case than its predecessor had done.

The March 1977 elections

Although Bhutto had decided to hold elections in June 1976, when Rafi Raza was made his campaign manager,[90] the announcement on

83 Z.A. Bhutto, *If I am Assassinated*, pp. 106-7, 135-8.

84 Canada had provided the plant following an agreement with the Pakistan authorities in 1969.

85 These had been raised in the mid-1970s following the failure of IAEA surveillance cameras and the 'loss' of the inventory of spent fuel. A subsequent enquiry by the IAEA did not reveal any diversion of materials. Kapur, *Pakistan's Nuclear Development*, p. 6.

86 *Ibid.*, p. 139.

87 *Ibid.*, p. 205.

88 Up to this juncture the leading role had been played by Professor Abdus Salam and Munir Ahmad Khan who chaired the Pakistan Atomic Energy Commission. The latter's failure to make a plutonium bomb paved the way for the entry of his later rival, Dr A.Q. Khan.

89 Kapur quotes Indian press reports that by 1985, Pakistan possessed sufficient weapon grade uranium for a single bomb, *Ibid.*, p. 209.

90 Private communication to the author from Leslie Wolf-Phillips, 1 September 1996.

7 January 1977 concerning the holding of national and provincial polls was as unexpected for the public as Mrs Gandhi's some eleven days later. Like his Indian neighbour Bhutto was surprised by the ability of the opposition to unite. The Pakistan National Alliance (PNA), founded on 11 January, comprised nine political parties embracing a range of secular, leftist and Islamist outlooks.[91] Not surprisingly its electioneering focused mainly on the grievances arising from inflation, government arbitrariness and unemployment. The more positive aspects of its programme were unconvincingly vague, as over the issue of denationalisation, although a commitment to Islamisation was given.[92]

Marvin Weinbaum's contemporary examination remains the most authoritative analysis of the campaign.[93] It brings out clearly the in-fighting within the PPP resulting from the influx of many of the Punjabi landlords which the party had successfully opposed just seven years earlier.[94] It also reveals the defensiveness of the government campaign on Islamic issues. Finally it emphasises that despite the PPP's control of the media, use of the machinery of government and intimidatory tactics, large crowds spontaneously flocked to PNA rallies.[95] This feature of the campaign led most observers to anticipate a strong showing for the opposition, although no one doubted a PPP victory. The announcement of the results on 7 March thus caused general astonishment and led to immediate claims that the election had been rigged. As Table 8.2 sets out, the PPP had apparently trounced its opponents, capturing in all 155 out of 200 National Assembly seats. The PNA's immediate response was to boycott the provincial polls and stage a nationwide strike on 11 March. Three days later the PNA campaign got into full swing which was to end in the introduction of martial law. After the coup of 5 July a series of White Papers were issued listing Bhutto's misdeeds, which included the rigging of the elections. The deposed Prime Minister's refutation of this charge and his counter-claim of army and 'external' support for the PNA campaign is set down at length in *If I am Assassinated* (Chapters 3-8). The reality seems to be that a certain PPP

---

[91] The component groups of the PNA were: Tehrik-i-Istaqlal (TI); JI; JUI; JUP; Pakistan Muslim League-Pagaro (PML(P)); National Democratic Party (NDP); Pakistan Democratic Party (PDP); Khaksat Tehrik (KT); Azad Kashmir Muslim Conference (AKMC).

[92] The familiar targets were alcohol, obscenity and co-education.

[93] M.G. Weinbaum, 'The March 1977 Elections in Pakistan: Where Everyone Lost', *Asian Survey* 17, no.7 (July, 1977), pp. 599-618.

[94] *Ibid.*, p.608.

[95] *Ibid.*, pp. 608-10.

victory was inflated by malpractices committed by local officials, which may have affected 30-40 seats. According to the PPP election campaign manager and manifesto architect Rafi Raza who resigned as Production Minister after the polls, Bhutto was unprepared for the furore which accompanied the rigging episode and had not authorised it as some opponents alleged in order to secure the two-thirds majority necessary to bring in constitutional change.[96]

Table 8.2. NATIONAL ASSEMBLY ELECTION
RESULTS, MARCH 1977

Party	Candidates	Seats won	% vote
PPP	191	155	58.1
PNA	168	36	35.4
PML-Qayyum	37	1	
Independent	324	8	
Minor parties	21	0	
Total	741	200	

Source: Hasan Askari-Rizvi, *The Military and Politics in Pakistan* (Delhi, 1988), p. 219.

The PNA agitation

There are parallels between the PNA agitation and the earlier movement which Bhutto had led against Ayub in 1968-9. On both occasions, students and small businessmen played leading roles in the street demonstrations which occurred not just in big urban centres but in the small towns of Punjab. At least 200 people were killed in violent clashes between demonstrators and the security forces. Bhutto found it no easier to come to a successful dialogue with the opposition leaders than Ayub had done, despite the good offices of Sheikh Riad al-Khatib, the Saudi ambassador and the PLO leader Yasser Arafat's Organisation Chief, Hani al Hassan. A still earlier parallel is provided by the Muslim League direct action campaign against the Unionist Ministry of Khizr Tiwana early in 1947. On that occasion police excesses leading to the death of a demonstrator in Lahore marked a major turning-point.[97] Similarly firing by police in Lahore on 9 April 1977 gave new vigour to the campaign of *hartals*. Within a fortnight, martial law had been declared not only in the Lahore district but also in the Karachi division and Hyderabad district.[98]

[96] Interview, 2 January 1997.

[97] I. Talbot, *Freedom's Cry*, p. 41.

[98] Hasan Askari-Rizvi, *The Military and Politics in Pakistan*, p. 222.

Bhutto made a number of compromises in an attempt to halt the agitation. On 17 April at a press conference he announced the introduction of Islamic measures such as the prohibition of gambling and the closing of wine shops and night clubs. Earlier the Attorney-General, Yahya Bakhtiar, had promised that the National Assembly would be dissolved if the PNA participated and secured a majority in Provincial Assembly elections. Opponents merely seized on this as an admission of guilt. While some PNA leaders like the unassuming Mufti Mahmood displayed a willingness to come to terms, the more resolute approach of retired Air Marshal Muhammad Asghar Khan carried the day. He argued in a letter early in May to his former military colleagues that as the Bhutto regime was no longer lawful they were not obliged to obey its orders.[99] Such an appeal reinforced the growing reluctance of the army to turn its firepower on its Punjabi brethren following the introduction of quasi martial law. The deadlock in talks between the government and opposition which began on 3 June further reduced the armed forces' patience with the Bhutto regime. It appears that mistrust on both sides finally aborted an agreement which appeared well within reach.

General Khalid Mahmud Arif, Zia's Chief of Staff after the coup, has provided a vivid account[100] of the background to army intervention in the operation code-named Fair Play. He cites the politicising of the corps commanders[101] as a result of their frequent meetings with General Zia and the Prime Minister.[102] His claim that the threat of army disunity was another powerful factor is borne out by reports of the refusal of three brigadiers – Ishtiaq Ali Khan, Said Muhammad and Niaz Ahmad – to fire on those protesting in Lahore against 'election riggers and cheats'.[103] Arif concludes his assessment of the prelude to intervention by citing the time-honoured justification for the staging of a coup in Pakistan, 'reconciliation, accommodation and tolerance among the quarrelling politicians could have saved yet another setback to the process of democracy.'[104] In addition to Arif's justifications it is important to note the Islamic dimension. The introduction of a more middle-class pattern of recruitment in the officer corps (a process greatly increased

---

[99] *Ibid.*, 223.

[100] General Khalid Mahmud Arif, *Working with Zia: Pakistan's Power Politics, 1977-1988* (Karachi, 1995).

[101] These were Lt.-General Muhammad Iqbal Khan, Lt.-General Sawar Khan, Lt.-General Faiz Ali Chishti, Lt.-General Ghulam Hassan Khan, Major-General Jahanzeb Arbab and Major-General Ghulam Muhammad.

[102] Arif, *Working with Zia*, 80.

[103] *Ibid.*, 73.

[104] *Ibid.*, 88.

during the Zia era) made it more sympathetic to the PNA's call for the establishment of *Nizam-i-Mustafa* (demand for an Islamic system). Nevertheless, it was not apparent at the time of the bloodless coup of 5 July that Pakistan had entered a new era. The army Commander-in Chief-General Zia-ul-Haq, in his maiden national address delivered in Urdu, promised fresh elections within ninety days. Bhutto and the PPP leaders – as they played cards and discussed politics in the comfort of their Murree and Abbotabad captivity – could confidently look forward to the wheel of political fortune once more turning in their direction. The PPP and PNA[105] leaders were released after three weeks of detention. Justice Mushtaq Hussain, the Chief Election Commissioner announced the schedule for polling on 2 August. The response of the crowds when Bhutto was released from protective custody evoked echoes of the glorious early days of the PPP's existence. Such was the crush of people that the journey from Karachi railway station to his Clifton residence took 10 hours.[106] This and similar massive crowds in such places as Lahore, Multan and Rawalpindi convinced Zia that he had gravely mis-calculated. The release of the PPP leader was only to prove a temporary respite as Pakistan was about to be consigned to a decade of unenlightened rule whose doleful legacy was to be increased sectarianism and ethnic tensions.

What lay behind the failure and ultimate tragedy of the Bhutto era? With hindsight it is easy to pinpoint turning-points such as the in-volvement of the Army in Balochistan from 1973 onwards and the later introduction of concessions to the Islamic parties. Character defects, a half-hearted commitment to the abolition of feudalism, the opposition of vested interests and the alienation of Pakistan's erstwhile Western allies have all been cited as explanations for Bhutto's failure to create a new Pakistan. Of greater importance was the loss of support of two key groups that had brought the *Quaid-i-Awam* to power. The first comprised the professional elites and students who were alienated by the increased stifling of political expression through the banning of the NAP and the use of Section 144 of the Penal Code, the High Treason Act, Prevention of Anti-National Activities Ordinance and the Press and Publications Ordinance. The regime of their former hero seemed identical in these respects to those of his predecessors, Ayub and Yahya

---

105 Asghar Khan, Mufti Mahmood, Pir Pagaro, Nawabzada Nasrullah Khan, Professor Ghafoor Ahmad, Maulana Shah Ahmed Noorani and Sherbaz Mazari had all been taken into custody.

106 Bhutto, *Daughter of the East*, p. 89.

Khan. Hindsight has reinforced the view that Bhutto's greatest personal weakness in office was his failure to regard political opposition as legitimate.

The lower middle class formed the second key support group which defected to the opposition. Once again Punjab held the key to power in Pakistani politics and it was the loss of support among the small traders, merchants and shopkeepers of this province which proved crucial. Many of these groups came from the Sheikh and Ansari communities originally from East Punjab. On arrival in Pakistan, they replaced the Punjabi Hindu commercial classes. They had been badly hit by the labour reforms and by the nationalisation of *ghee*, cotton and rice husking trades. Their *mohajir* background also made them susceptible to the religious appeals of the Islamic parties which remained inveterately opposed to the regime, despite its increasing wrongheaded attempts to placate them as in the anti-Ahmadi issue.

Moreover, just as rapid socio-economic change undermined Ayub's experiment in controlled democracy, the oil shock which saw the fuel import bill soar from $85 million in 1973-4 to $385 million in 1974-5 dealt a blow to Bhutto's populist experiment. In Muhammad Waseem's words, 'the regime's failure to check the price-hike was one of its most important political liabilities'[107] because of its impact on the PPP's lower-class constituency.

This chapter has argued that Bhutto ultimately failed to transform Pakistan because he was unable to institutionalise his authority by restructuring the PPP itself: when in power, its incipient right-left ideological tensions and factional rivalries came to the surface. Like the Muslim League it proved unable to make the transition from a popular movement to a modern party of government. Opportunist landlords flocked to its bandwagon and replaced loyal party workers. Patronage counted for more than organisational structures. The resulting weak institutionalisation of the PPP was a crucial factor in the regime's inability to provide a counterweight to the military and bureaucracy. Bhutto remained immensely popular with the urban and rural poor to the end, but in the absence of viable independent political institutions was vulnerable to renewed army intervention on behalf of those interests which had been affronted by his populism. For his supporters Bhutto's fate was comparable to that of Salvador Allende in Chile, but his critics found more parallels with Argentina's Juan Peron.

[107] M. Waseem, *Politics and the State in Pakistan*, p. 322.

9

ISLAM CHANGES EVERYTHING?

The coup of 5 July 1977 ushered in the longest period of military rule in Pakistan's history. Even when it was withdrawn on 30 December 1985, Zia, unlike Ayub, retained his post as Chief of Army Staff [1] and continued to exert power over the civilian Government through the office of President.[2] Indeed on 29 May 1988, he dismissed his hand-picked Prime Minister Muhammad Khan Junejo.

Pakistan during the period 1977-88 was not only authoritarian in political structure; it also aspired to be an ideological state. The official discourse swept to one side the ambiguities of the freedom struggle because the goal of an Islamic state was deemed to be its main basis. Jinnah, the secularist became Jinnah the upholder of Islam in such writings as Karam Hydri's *Millat ka pasban* (The Nation's Sentinel – Karachi, 1981), while the *'ulama* whose influence had been marginal in the creation of Pakistan were elevated to a vanguard role. By making a hegemonic Islamic ideology the pillar of the state, Zia sought to solve at a stroke the identity problems which had beset it since 1947. The enterprise failed, partly because of the persistence of regional counternarratives based on plural, linguistic and ethnic loyalties and histories. In 1985 the Sindh-Balochistan-Pushtu Front under the leadership of Mumtaz Bhutto came together to advocate a confederation of Pakistan.[3] Sindhi nationalists went a step further than confederalism and demanded total independence. Mir Ghaus Bakhsh Bizenjo, the Baloch leader of the Pakistan National Party (PNP), argued less radically for a 'loose' federation reflecting the existence of the four nationalities in Pakistan. Zia's attempt at nation-building was also doomed because the state-sponsored Islamisation opened up sectarian fissures within a far from monolithic Pakistani Islam.

Zia's longevity in power thus rested ultimately not on a hegemonic

---

[1] This followed an amendment to Article 47 of the 1973 Constitution which ruled that the President could not hold any other office of profit.

[2] He assumed this office following the December 1984 referendum.

[3] The four confederating states of Sindh, Balochistan, Punjab and the Frontier would enter into a treaty to establish a Republic of Pakistan to which would be assigned the five subjects of defence, foreign affairs, currency, communications, and interstate transportation.

Islamic discourse but on the skill with which he both wrong-footed opponents, and managed senior military officers through rotation and fixed appointments.[4] Their career opportunities were greatly expanded both within Pakistan and overseas through postings in Saudi Arabia, Jordan, Libya, Oman and the UAE.[5] The main welfare associations for ex-servicemen, the Fauji Foundation (Army), the Shaheen Foundation (Air Force) and the Bahria Foundation (Navy) all greatly expanded their operations during this era. Furthermore, the period of rapid economic growth during the 1980s[6] also dampened threats to Zia's power, although it was based more on the bounty of remittances from overseas' workers than on economic policies. Significantly Pakistan's long-term problems of poor infrastructural development and weak domestic resource mobilisation remained unresolved.

Finally and most important, Zia profited from the redrawing of the geopolitical map in West Asia in the wake of the overthrow of the pro-American Shah Muhammad Reza Pahlavi of Iran (1941-79) and the Soviet occupation of Afghanistan on 28 December 1979. This later dramatic development which ushered in the Second Cold War followed the violent internecine conflict between the Parchami and Khalqi factions of the People's Democratic Party (PDP) of Afghanistan which had originally seized power in a coup in April 1978. Zia was transformed overnight from an international pariah to America's front-line ally in the fight against communism.

Zia was in many ways Bhutto's antithesis as well as his nemesis. While his predecessor was flamboyant, excitable and sophisticated, Zia was homespun, cautious and down-to-earth. Bhutto's brilliance and charisma had been both his strength and undoing; Zia compensated for their absence through his meticulousness and most notably his native cunning. His other overriding characteristic was his cold and calculating ruthlessness. This streak was demonstrated most clearly in his dealings with the deposed Prime Minister before his execution.

Zia remains as controversial a figure in Pakistan politics as Zulfiqar Ali Bhutto. Admirers such as Shahid Javed Burki have stressed his personal traits of humility, courtesy and piety.[7] In the realm of public affairs, conservative Western scholars and their Pakistani counterparts

[4] See S.J. Burki, 'Zia's Eleven Years' in S.J. Burki and Craig Baxter (eds), *Pakistan under the Military: Eleven Years of Zia ul-Haq* (Boulder, CO, 1991).

[5] Up to 30,000 soldiers and airmen were contracted out in this way.

[6] For details see J. Adams, 'Pakistan's Economic Performance in the 1980s: Implications for Political Balance' in C. Baxter (ed.), *Zia's Pakistan: Politics and Stability in a Front-Line State* (Boulder, CO, 1985), pp. 47-62.

[7] S.J. Burki, 'Pakistan Under Zia, 1977-88', *Asian Survey* 28, no.10 (October 1988), pp. 1085ff.

have praised his bold Afghan policy[8] which contributed to the collapse of the Soviet Empire, his halting of the country's moral decay and the economic progress which occurred during his decade in power. Between 1977-8 and 1985-6 for example Pakistan's GNP increased by 76 per cent and *per capita* income by 34 per cent,[9] but the economy also benefited in this period from overseas remittances of $25 billion.[10] To his detractors Zia will always appear an intolerant and vindictive ruler who illegally hanged the country's Prime Minister, cynically manipulated Islam[11] and during the eleven and a half years of his repressive rule opened the floodgates to drug trafficking[12] and the widespread ethnic and sectarian violence which are the hallmarks of the so-called 'Kalashnikov culture'. Indeed by the time his protégé Nawaz Sharif designated 1993 a year of *jihad* against drug addiction, one in every sixteen Pakistani males was an addict. In some jails the figure rose to one in every five inmates.[13] On one occasion in March 1986, Government attempts to halt poppy planting met with armed resistance led by a National Assembly member.[14]

There are a number of striking contrasts between Zia and Ayub. Pakistan's first military ruler encouraged modernising impulses and attached great importance to economic development. Zia eschewed Ayub's Islamic modernism for his Deobandi personal piety and scripturalism. He had no interest in economics or development and was happy to delegate the management of the economy to such technocrats as Ghulam Ishaq Khan, Aftab Qazi and Vaseem Jaffrey.[15] Despite his initial purge, Ayub's regime remained highly dependent on the bureaucracy and never acquired political legitimacy. In contrast Zia inducted army officers

8 The US Secretary of State George Shultz praised Zia at the time of his funeral as 'a defender of Pakistan's freedom and independence and a steadfast champion of the Afghan cause'. *Washington Post,* 20 August 1988.

9 Burki, 'Pakistan Under Zia, 1977-88', p. 1093.

10 S.J. Burki, 'Pakistan's Economy under Zia' in Burki and Baxter (eds), *Pakistan Under the Military*, Table 3, p. 107.

11 See, for example, M. Ayoob, 'Two faces of Political Islam: Iran and Pakistan Compared', *Asian Survey* 19, no. 6 (June 1979), p. 539.

12 According to a United Nations Drug Control Programme report there were 1.5 million heroin addicts in Pakistan by the mid-1990s, over three-quarters of whom were under thirty; if unchecked this figure would rise to 2.5 million by the year 2000. *The News* (Islamabad), 3 December 1995.

13 Human Rights Commission of Pakistan, *State of Human Rights in Pakistan, 1993,* pp. 84-5.

14 Eliza Van Hollen, 'Pakistan in 1986: Trials of Transition', *Asian Survey* 27, no. 2 (February 1987), p. 150.

15 Burki, 'Pakistan Under Zia 1977-88', p. 1092.

into many civilian bureaucratic posts by means of the introduction of a military preference in the federal quota system, as well as giving them lucrative assignments in the autonomous corporations.[16] General Fazle Raziq for example became the Chairman of the Water and Power Development Authority (WAPDA). In the period 1980–5, no less than ninety-six Army officers entered the Central Superior Services on a permanent basis, while another 115 were on contracts.[17] Until Muhammad Khan Junejo was sworn in as Prime Minister on 23 March 1985, all the powerful provincial governors had been military men.[18]

Zia, unlike Ayub, bent both the politicians and the bureaucrats to his will. He retained much greater authority than his predecessor when he made the transition from military to civilian rule. The Army remained the pillar of his regime,[19] and while Ayub was hounded from office, Zia was still firmly in the saddle at the time of his death.[20] His popularity with certain sections of the population was demonstrated by the huge crowds of mourners at his burial on 20 August 1988 at the Faisal Mosque in Islamabad.

Despite Zia's desire for a break with the past—symbolised by his unavailing wish to change the celebration of independence from 14 August to 27 Ramadan[21] in the Islamic calendar—it is important, as with the preceding Bhutto era, not to lose sight of the historical continuities. One of these was Punjab's continued importance in national political life. If the province had been disturbed during the 1983 Movement for the Restoration of Democracy (MRD) agitation, the regime would have been severely threatened.[22] Large sections of its population

---

[16] Another General Zahid Ali Akbar was also head of the Water and Power Development Authority (WAPDA).

[17] Hasan-Askari Rizvi, *The Military and Politics in Pakistan*, p. 243.

[18] R. LaPorte, 'Administrative Restructuring during the Zia Period' in Burki and Baxter (eds), *Pakistan Under The Military*, p. 129.

[19] There were only isolated signs of disaffection most notably at the time of an alleged plot to overthrow the government in 1985. Seven officers, all junior in rank were convicted in July after their trial in camera before military courts.

[20] Both Craig Baxter and Rasul Rais have argued however that he had run out of political cards following his dismissal of the hand-picked Prime Minister Muhammad Khan Junejo on 29 May 1988. C. Baxter, 'A New Pakistan under a Revised Bhuttoism', *Middle East Insight* 6, no. 4 (winter 1989), p. 24; R. B. Rais, 'Pakistan in 1988: From Command to Conciliation Politics', *Asian Survey* 29, no. 2 (February 1989), p. 201.

[21] In 1947 Independence Day coincided with 27 Ramadan in the Islamic lunar calendar, i.e. the day following *laylatal-qadr*, the night during which Muhammad received the first revelation. At the beginning of the month of fasting in 1978, Zia suggested a change in the future celebration of Independence Day.

[22] Another reason why the Punjabis did not heed Nusrat Bhutto's appeals to join the campaign was their traditional animosity towards India. Mrs Gandhi's statement supporting

profited both from military rule and the expansion of employment opportunities in the oil-rich Middle East. During the 1970s and '80s half of all Pakistan's migrants to the Gulf region came from Punjab. At its peak in 1982 skilled workers sent remittances home of $3.2 billion. Thus while the Punjab's Western-educated elite chafed under the social and political restrictions of the Zia regime, the lower middle class and the emerging industrial class provided a solid backbone of support. Many members of these classes came from Zia's native East Punjab and were especially receptive to his Islamic and anti-Indian discourse. In addition there was all-round support for the regime's receptivity to Punjabi interests, as seen for example in the 1983 Haleem Commission recommendations on the apportionment of Indus water shares on the basis of 37 per cent each for Punjab and Sindh and 12 per cent each for the Frontier and Balochistan. Such patronage of Punjabi interests increased the antipathy of the smaller provinces to what they saw as the long-term 'Punjabisation' of Pakistan.

An even more striking continuity was the interplay between domestic and international politics. Whether or not one agrees with the contention that a foreign hand wrenched power from Bhutto, it is undeniable that the longevity of Zia's regime was linked with the entry of Soviet forces into neighbouring Afghanistan. At this juncture, Pakistan's relations with the United States were at a low ebb. The Carter administration was strongly wedded to both human rights and nuclear non-proliferation, and on both counts Pakistan seemed unworthy of assistance. Under the terms of the Symington Amendment[23] (Section 669 of the Foreign Assistance Act), economic and military aid was suspended in April 1979. Relations reached their nadir on 21 November 1980 when the American Embassy in Islamabad was attacked following rumours of US involvement in an assault on the Holy Kaaba in Mecca which, according to Lieutenant-General Faiz Ali Chishti,[24] were personally inflamed by Zia during his bizarre cycling tour of neighbouring Rawalpindi on the same day.

Within weeks of the Soviet occupation of Afghanistan Carter despatched his National Security Adviser, Zbigniew Brzezinski, to Pakistan. This was the prelude to an offer of a $400 million economic and military aid package. Zia disdainfully rejected this as 'peanuts' but eagerly accepted the incoming Reagan administration's offer of $3.2

---

all democratic movements in Pakistan created a bad impression.

23 This barred military aid to non-nuclear states which imported enrichment technology or equipment and whose nuclear installations were not subject to international safeguards.

24 For further details see Lt.-General Faiz Ali Chishti, *Betrayals of Another Kind: Islam, Democracy and the Army in Pakistan* (London, 1989), pp. 102 ff.

billion which was to be spread over a six-year period.[25] As during the 1950s the resulting American military and economic largesse bolstered the unelected institutions of state power to the detriment of democratic forces.

Reagan's preoccupation with Pakistan's status as a front-line state in the struggle against the 'evil empire' ensured that his administration did not raise too many embarrassing questions either on the nuclear front or on the human rights issue. Robert Wirsing[26] among others has chronicled the mounting 'scorecard' of Pakistan's violations of non-proliferation policy during this period, which included some spectacular smuggling of nuclear components vital for its uranium enrichment capability.[27] On 17 December 1987 Arshad Parvez, a Canadian citizen of Pakistani origin, was found guilty by a Philadelphia jury of seeking to supply Pakistan with sensitive materials for uranium enrichment. According to the Carnegie Task Force report on non-proliferation and South Asian security of July 1986, Pakistan had stockpiled sufficient material to make from one to four nuclear weapons annually. India at the same time was estimated to have sufficient plutonium-producing capacity to make from fifteen to thirty weapons annually.[28]

Early in January 1982, Amnesty International charged the Pakistan authorities with torture, imprisonment and other human rights abuses. The public flogging of political prisoners being carried out by bare-chested wrestlers remains one of the starkest images of the martial law era.[29] The Pakistan Human Rights Society in August 1983 registered its protest against the flogging of women as an Islamic punishment. In one reported case a woman, Lal Mai was lashed by a man in front of a 5,000-strong crowd at Liaqatpur, Bahawalpur, as a punishment for *zina* (adultery).[30] Despite Congressional opposition, the Reagan White House turned a blind eye to both human rights and non-proliferation violations on the grounds of the Soviet threat. However, once this had lifted at the beginning of the 1990s, Congress was to strike back with a vengeance.

Zia faced the same problems of reconciling regional political and

---

[25] This was followed up by a $4.02 billion programme which was negotiated in 1987.

[26] R.G. Wirsing, *Pakistan's Security Under Zia*, pp. 110ff.

[27] Under Zia the enrichment route was favoured over reprocessing in the race to achieve a nuclear weapon capability. See A. Kapur, *Pakistan's Nuclear Development*, ch. 7.

[28] Wirsing, *Pakistan's Security Under Zia*, p. 123

[29] Martial Law Regulation no. 48 of October 1979 invoked a maximum penalty of twenty-five lashes for taking part in political activities, all of which had been banned.

[30] *Al-Mushir*, 26, no.1 (1984), p. 172.

cultural aspirations with the imperatives of nation-building as had all his predecessors. In his first televised speech he declared that 'Pakistan, which was created in the name of Islam, will continue to survive only if it sticks to Islam. That is why I consider the introduction of [an] Islamic system as an essential prerequisite for the country.'[31] Islam was however less effective in providing a national cohesive force than Zia anticipated. The state-sponsored process of Islamisation dramatically increased sectarian divisions not only between Sunnis and Shias over the issue of the 1979 *zakat* Ordinance but also between Deobandis and Barelvis. Sunni-Shia clashes in Karachi were no longer confined to the traditional tension-filled month of Muharram and also intensified in violence. Riots between 22 February and 19 March 1983 claimed twelve lives.[32] There were further serious clashes in October 1984. Disputes over the department of Auqaf's management of mosques and shrines led to a major confrontation between Deobandis and Barelvis at the Badshahi mosque in Lahore on 21 May 1984.[33] The greatest tension of all was between the state's legalistic imposition of Islam and the humanist traditions of Sufism. This was particularly explosive in Sindh where Sufism had always been an integral component of regional cultural identity. Significantly the *pirs* of Sindh played a leading role in the MRD[34] agitation of August and September 1983. 50,000 disciples of the Makhdum of Hala successfully blocked the national highway on one occasion.[35]

Less serious but nevertheless highly suggestive of the different conceptions of Islam was the legal challenge by the *sajjada nashin* (custodian) of Baba Farid's famous Chishti shrine at Pakpattan to the ban on pigeon-flying in Lahore early in 1981. This practice, along with kite-flying, had been banned in the district under Section 144 of the Criminal Procedure Code on the grounds that they violated the sanctity and privacy of women. Not only were these favourite Pakistani pastimes, but the keeping of pigeons was associated with many great Sufi saints and was a familiar feature of the leading shrines. Following the challenge the authorities withdrew their ban.[36]

---

[31] W.L. Richter, 'The Political Dynamics of Islamic Resurgence in Pakistan', *Asian Survey* 19, no.6 (June 1979), p. 555.

[32] *Al-Mushir* 25, nos 1 and 2 (1983), p. 146.

[33] *Al-Mushir* 26, nos 3 and 4 (1984), p. 202.

[34] The MRD was a broadly based party coalition dominated by the PPP, set up in February 1981 to demand the ending of martial law and the holding of elections under the terms of the 1973 Constitution. For further details see Appendix C.

[35] Sufism in Sindh had traditionally underpinned a Sindhi cultural identity. Its humanist traditions were directly opposed to Zia's state-sponsored Islam based on the implementation of the *Shariat*.

[36] *Al-Mushir* 23, no.3 (1981), p. 57.

The need for stability in the strategic region of Balochistan during the Afghan war led Zia to distance himself from the sectarian conflict between the heterodox Zikri community and the *'ulama*. The Zikris, who form a large proportion of the population of Makran, are the followers of Syed Muhammad (b. 1443) whom they consider to be a Mahdi. They regard themselves as Muslims although their doctrines are heterodox.[37] In their drive to implement *Shariat* law the *'ulama* founded the Tehrik Khatm-e-Nabuat (Movement for the Finality of the Prophethood) in Balochistan in 1978. Their intention was to demand that the state should declare the Zikris to be non-Muslims, like the Ahmadis earlier. Significantly standing aside from the issue, Zia lent credence to critics' claims that his call for Islamisation was just a cover for his undemocratic regime rather than a genuine desire.

Baloch and Pushtun political opposition to the centre was muted during the Zia era. The Chief Martial Law Administrator began a process of co-opting Baloch nationalists by releasing as many as 9,000 prisoners who had been incarcerated during the Bhutto period. As in Sindh, energies were increasingly turned inwards in growing ethnic clashes. Quetta for example saw escalating Baloch-Pushtun violence in October 1986.[38] The immediate catalyst was a transportation dispute, but the longer-term causes reflected the relative economic predominance of the Pushtuns. They prospered not only in Balochistan but also in their native Frontier which experienced considerable economic development.[39] The co-option of the Pushtun elite through the Army into national power was also a marked feature of this period. Along with the government's support for the Afghan *jihad* it played a major part in damping down the Pushtunistan movement.

However, Sindh could not be reconciled. The province missed out on the prosperity brought by both government-sponsored development programmes and the export of labour to the Gulf. Army rule increased the traditional hostility towards Punjabi domination. The sense of alienation was completed by Zia's hanging of Pakistan's first Sindhi Prime Minister. The strong sense of Sindhi identity which fuelled the opposition's struggle in 1983 can be glimpsed in such poems as Niaz

[37] The Zikris possess no mosques or prescribed prayers. Their places of worship are known as *Zikrana* where they recite *zikr* (remembrance of the various names of Allah). Their greatest affronts to the orthodox are the belief that Syed Muhammad Mahdi was the interpreter of the Quran and the practice of *haj* at the Koh-e-Murad in the city of Turbat in Makran.

[38] For details see P. Titus, 'Routes to Ethnicity: Roads, Buses and Differential Ethnic Relations in Pakistani Balochistan' in P. Titus (ed.), *Marginality and Modernity: Ethnicity and Change in Post-Colonial Balochistan* (Karachi, 1996), pp. 288ff.

[39] K. Bin Sayeed, 'Pakistan in 1983', *Asian Survey* 24, no.2 (February 1984), p. 224.

Hamayooni's 'Love for Homeland'.[40] Massive repression was required to crush the MRD agitations in the Sukkur, Larkana, Jacobabad and Khairpur districts.[41] The Sindh Governor was forced to admit that in the opening three weeks of the struggle, 1,999 people had been arrested, 189 killed and 126 injured.[42]

Resistance took literary and cultural forms. Writers and poets like Rehmatullah Manjothi, Naseer Mirza, Tariq Alam and Adal Soomro challenged Zia's ideological state. Atiya Dawood opposed the oppression of women in her writings. The words of the poet Manzoor Solangi were frequently chanted at MRD rallies: '*Manban, chhapran, ghar ghar mein golioon, fouji police chaway dharial paya goliyun*' (There are bullets over homes and huts, but the Army and the police say they are searching for dacoits).[43]

Unlike the mass movement against Ayub in 1968-9 or against Bhutto in 1977, the 1983 agitation in Sindh was not just an affair of the urban middle class and workers. The rural population of such districts as Thatta, Dadu, Larkana, and Sanghar were heavily involved. Leadership was provided by the PPP and the 'peasant'-based Sindhi Awam Tehrik[44]

---

[40] It had been translated from Sindhi by Anwer Pirzado as follows:

> *The Makli graveyard is shedding tears*
> *the battlefield of Miyani is crying:*
> *Will anyone rid us of these sympathisers?*
> *We have decided*
> *Not to retreat*
> *Against any impediment.*
> *We are armed with the slogan of Hooshoo:*
> *'We may die but not give up Sindh'*
> *Love for the homeland*
> *Is our only creed.*
> *We'll pronounce it even on the gallows*
> *None dare teach us any other lesson.*
> *O, Sindh, I swear upon Samoi*
> *To fight those*
> *Who hurt the hearts*
> *Of my countrymen.*
> *Either we'll die*
> *Or the aliens will perish.*
> *Truth will triumph*
> *Against the falsehood of the day.*

H. Rahman (ed.), *Resistance Literature* (Islamabad 1995), pp. 384-5.

[41] *Ibid.*, p. 223.

[42] *Al-Mushir* 26, no.1 (1984), p. 166.

[43] H. Mujtaba, 'The Desert's Legacy', *Newsline* 7, no.11 (May 1996), p. 98.

[44] For further details of its role see A. Ahmad, 'The Rebellion of 1983', pp. 28ff.

of Rasul Bux Palejo. The rural insurrection was only finally quelled following the deployment of three army divisions backed up with helicopter gunships.

The later 1980s also saw the emergence within Sindh of a *mohajir* ethnic identity. The controversy surrounding this and its legacy will be examined in greater detail later. It is enough to say here that it reflected in part the general ethnicisation of Pakistani politics in the wake of the banning of party organisations. However, it also reflected the alienation of *mohajirs* from power at the centre by the Punjabi-Pushtun combine. Its economic consequences were felt as Chiniotis, Arains and other Punjabi industrialists gained a march on their Memon and Khoja rivals through access to generous loans from government-controlled financial institutions.

Before turning to an assessment of the major political developments and legacies of this period, it is necessary to examine briefly the background of Pakistan's military ruler. What were his ideals and values? What was his attitude to the Pakistan political system?

The world of a dictator

Zia was born on 12 August 1924 into a modest middle-class Arain family from Jullundur. This upbringing allowed him in later years to articulate the values and Islamic outlook of what is known as the *shurafaa* (the respectable citizens). It provided him with a source of popular support alongside his main strength derived from the Army. His father's salary as a junior official of the Raj was just sufficient to pay for his son's education at St Stephen's College, Delhi. The opening up of military service during the Second World War enabled Zia, like a number of his generation, to obtain a commission in the 13th Lancers, although he was neither a landowner nor a member of the 'martial castes'. He served in Burma, Malaya and Java at the end of the Second World War, and following Partition was posted to the Armoured Corps Centre at Nowshera.

Zia was profoundly influenced by his family's uprooting from Jullundur to Peshawar. Years later when he was Pakistan's President he declared at an International Islamic Conference in Islamabad: 'I will tell you what Islam and Pakistan means to me. It is a vision of my mother struggling on, tired, with all her worldly possessions in her hands, when she crossed the border into Pakistan.'[45] Significantly, Zia picked as his Vice-Chief of Army Staff General Arif, who came from East Punjab, while General Akhtar Abdur Rahman from Jullundur com-

[45] Sayeed, *Pakistan in 1983*, p. 1084.

manded the powerful ISI 1984-8. Operation Fairplay, which terminated
the Bhutto regime, was carried out by Zia's fellow Arain from Jullundur,
Lieutenant-General Faiz Ali Chishti.

Shortly after his marriage to his cousin Shafiqa in August 1950,
Zia joined the Guides Cavalry.[46] What had up to this point been
a fairly humdrum military career was transformed by his performance
at the Command and Staff College, Quetta, in 1955, after which
he was given a number of important staff assignments. Following
his promotion to brigadier in 1969, Zia was seconded to Jordan
where he helped King Hussein's forces in their operations against
the PLO.[47] On his return home he commanded the first Armoured
Division for three years. He was still relatively unknown when Bhutto
called on him in the spring of 1976 to head the Pakistan Army.
Indeed the Prime Minister promoted him over the heads of half
a dozen more senior generals. Ironically the very characteristics of
the new Chief of Army Staff which appealed to Bhutto – his piety,
patriotism and professionalism – turned him in the circumstances of
the 1977 PNA *Nizam-e-Mustafa* agitation from an apolitical soldier
into a successful coup-maker.

Zia's background and beliefs led him to extend much further the
concept of the Army's role in domestic politics than that put forward
by Pakistan's earlier military leaders. Under Ayub the Army was
seen as the ultimate guarantor of the country's internal stability and
territorial integrity. Zia went further than this and saw it as indispensable
for the maintenance of Pakistan as an ideological state. In May 1982
for example he declared that the 'preservation of that Pakistan Ideology
and the Islamic character of the country was... as important as the
security of the country's geographical boundaries.'[48] This sentiment
lay behind the attempt to rewrite the history of Jinnah's intentions
in the creation of Pakistan. Newspaper articles on the occasion of
Jinnah's birth anniversary in December 1981 omitted the words from
his speech to the Constituent Assembly that 'Hindus would cease
to be Hindus and Muslims would cease to be Muslims, not in the
religious sense, because that is the personal faith of each individual,
but in the political sense as citizens of the state.' When the veteran
Muslim Leaguer Shaukat Hayat objected to such puerile attempts
to show Jinnah favouring the establishment of an Islamic state (as
did the former Chief Justice Muhammad Munir in his book *From
Jinnah to Zia*), a resolution was moved in the Majlis-i-Shura that

46 General Khalid Mahmud Arif, *Working with Zia*, p. 117.

47 *Ibid.*, p. 118.

48 Hasan-Askari Rizvi, *The Military and Politics in Pakistan, 1947-86*, p. 242.

sought to ban any verbal or written comment that 'would in any
way, directly or indirectly, detract from, or derogate (Jinnah's) high
status, position and achievements'.[49]

Political and constitutional change, 1977-85

Immediately after the launching of Operation Fairplay, Zia declared:
'My sole aim is to organise free and fair elections which would be
held in October this year. Soon after the polls, power will be transferred
to the elected representatives of the people. I give a solemn assurance
that I will not deviate from this schedule.'[50] The martial law era was
to be punctuated by such promises of national elections[51] which never
materialised and by discussion of the relevance of democracy for an
Islamic state. Zia was of the opinion that a Western-style democracy
was unsuitable for Pakistan. The advisory Council of Islamic Ideology
(CCI)[52] in August 1983 made the pronouncement that a presidential
form of government was the 'nearest to Islam'. It was later to rule
that political parties were non-Islamic.

The execution or, as opponents of the regime called it, the judicial
murder of Zulfiqar Ali Bhutto cast a dark pall over politics. The
die was now irrevocably cast between Zia and the PPP. There is
truth in the assertion that the Chief Martial Law Administrator's
sense of self-preservation now stood in the way of the restoration
of democracy. In the words of his former ministerial colleague Lieutenant-
General Faiz Ali Chishti, 'General Zia's "mission" was dignified with
many fine-sounding descriptions, but in reality his mission was to
save his own life, which necessarily involved his staying in power
until his death.'[53] The regime survived the major challenge of the
MRD campaign in 1983, but even the Islamist parties which had
been close to it during the 1978-9 PNA Cabinet began to distance

---

[49] *Al-Mushir* 24, no.2 (1982), p. 93.

[50] Hasan-Askari Rizvi, 'The Paradox of Military Rule in Pakistan', *Asian Survey*, 24,
no.5 (May 1984), p. 538.

[51] As early as 1983, Zia established a system of local government institutions which
bore many similarities to Ayub's Basic Democracies. They too were dominated by the
landowners and tied closely to the bureaucratic structure.

[52] This body was originally set up under the 1956 Constitution with the task of bringing
'all existing laws of the country in conformity with the Quran and the Sunnah.' Zia
reformed it in September 1977 and transformed it from a desultory organisation which
met spasmodically to an interventionist body. During the period 1981-4, for example, it
reviewed over 300 federal laws, drafted fifteen Islamic ordinances and prepared extensive
reports on the Islamisation of the economy.

[53] Lt.-General Faiz Ali Chishti, *Betrayals of Another Kind*, p. 101.

themselves. There was also mounting international disquiet at the growing evidence of widespread human rights abuses. Zia was thus eventually to recognise the need for reintroducing some semblance of political participation, albeit strictly controlled.

Zulfiqar Ali Bhutto was re-arrested on 3 September 1977, charged with conspiracy to murder Nawab Muhammad Ahmad Khan, the father of a maverick PPP politician, Ahmed Raza Kasuri. He had been the alleged target in an assault on his car on 11 November 1974, but unlike his father survived this as he had fifteen earlier attempts on his life. A High Court inquiry headed by Justice Shafi ur-Rahman had exonerated Bhutto, but Kasuri, who had failed to be adopted as a PPP candidate in the 1977 elections, refiled the case shortly after the coup. Zia's use of this old charge against Bhutto to re-arrest him has been variously viewed as part of a vendetta against the deposed Prime Minister, or as a result of new information which had come to light concerning his government. In Bhutto's absence, the PPP election campaign was now led by Nusrat who at her husband's express wish had assumed the chairmanship of the party. Huge crowds attended the rallies addressed by Nusrat and her daughter Benazir.[54] The PPP bandwagon rolled on despite Zia's launching of an accountability process and propaganda campaign directed against Bhutto's supporters.[55] A PPP victory would have ensured that Zia rather than Bhutto would be in the dock for violating the constitution. The Chief Martial Law Administrator thus went back on his public statement of 5 July – it was in fact to be ninety months rather than ninety days before elections were held.

While her husband's case was being heard in the Lahore High Court, Begum Bhutto tested in the Supreme Court the validity of his and other PPP leaders' detention under Martial Law Order 12 of 1977. A ruling in her favour would in effect have made Zia liable to a charge of high treason. Just as the Dosso case legalised the 1958 coup, so the Supreme Court, by rejecting Begum Bhutto's petition on the basis of the doctrine of state necessity, legitimised Zia's extra-constitutional assumption of power. While the judgement referred to 'the earliest possible holding of free and fair elections', it empowered the Chief Martial Law Administrator in the pursuit of the aim to restore law and order and normalcy to the country to 'promulgate legislative measures' and to amend the 1973 Constitution.[56]

---

54 Benazir Bhutto, *Daughter of the East,* p. 58.

55 S.A. Qureshi, 'An Analysis of Contemporary Pakistani Politics', pp. 912-13.

56 This is taken from the judgement of Chief Justice Anwaral Haq cited in Kamal Afzar, 'Constitutional Dilemmas in Pakistan', in Burki and Baxter (eds), *Pakistan under the*

The Lahore High Court found Bhutto guilty on 18 March 1978 and sentenced him to death. The prosecution case had been insecurely based on the confession of Masood Mahmood, Director-General of the FSF. Witnesses were briefed on what they should say, and the presiding judge, acting Chief Justice Maulvi Mushtaq Hussein, was a Zia appointee who hailed from his home Jullundur district.[57] The Supreme Court upheld the conviction and sentence on 6 February 1979, although three of the seven sitting justices, Muhammad Halim, G. Safdar Shah and Dorab Patel, issued dissenting opinions. This situation, together with the fact that the death sentence[58] was unprecedented in cases of conspiracy to murder, should have provided grounds for mercy, aside from the international appeals which were made by heads of state and political leaders from both the Western and Islamic worlds. However, the haste with which the mercy petition was processed[59] reveals that Zia was set on Zulfiqar Ali Bhutto's 'judicial murder'. Bhutto's wife and daughter were released from their detention at Sihala to visit him on 3 April 1979. In the early hours of the following day, Pakistan's former Prime Minister was hanged in the district jail at Rawalpindi. His body was secretly airlifted for burial at the family gravesite at Garhi Khuda Bakhsh. Neither Nusrat nor Benazir Bhutto was released to attend the committal.

The ongoing Bhutto legal case had encouraged Zia to broaden the basis of his regime by including civilian personnel in the Federal Cabinet. The initial sixteen-member Council of Advisers which had been formed on 14 January 1978 was dominated by bureaucrats and Army officers. These were retained in the Cabinet announced on the first anniversary of the coup, but Muslim League politicians, most notably Muhammad Khan Junejo as Railways Minister, also found a place. Their presence threatened the unity of the PNA, some of whose component members refused to join the Government. Indeed as early as 10 November 1977 Asghar Khan's Tehrik-i-Istiqlal (TI) had quit the alliance.[60] Relations between the parties and the martial law authorities were conducted through the election cell headed by Lieutenant-General Faiz Ali Chishti who, by the time of his retirement from military service in March 1980, had become estranged from Zia.

Military, p. 84, note 13.

[57] See Benazir Bhutto, *Daughter of the East*, pp. 104-8.

[58] Leslie Wolf-Phillips, feature review of S. Wolpert's *Zulfi Bhutto of Pakistan: His life and Times* in *Third World Quarterly* 15, no. 4 (December 1994), p. 729.

[59] Chishti, *Betrayals of Another Kind*, p. 81.

[60] Arif, *Working With Zia*, p. 156.

Zia, who became Pakistan's President following the end of the five-year tenure of Fazal Elahi Chaudhry in September 1978, once again promised elections, to be held in November 1979. The civilian members of the Federal Cabinet who wished to participate in them were obliged to tender their resignations in April. Registration rules were introduced governing political parties, which the PPP refused to accept; it nevertheless decided to fight the elections with its members standing as independents. On 16 October, however, Zia postponed the polls and announced a ban on all political parties and meetings. Rigid censorship was also introduced, and editors of 'defamatory' publications could now be punished by ten lashes and twenty-five years of rigorous imprisonment. Zia had once again got cold feet over the prospect of a PPP victory. Moreover, as Lieutenant-General Chishti records, he was also increasingly surrounded by 'opportunists and sycophants' who fed his appetite for power by suggesting that he was Allah's chosen instrument to transform Pakistani society.[61]

The alleged[62] hijacking of a Pakistan International Airlines (PIA) plane in March 1981 by the Al-Zulfikar organisation headed by Bhutto's exiled son Mir Murtaza undermined the broad political alliance of the MRD which had been established the previous month.[63] A further crackdown on opponents of the regime ensued. The torture and human rights abuses of this period have been immortalised in Urdu short stories such as Afzal Tauseef's 'Testimony'; the Sindhi writings of Badar Abro, 'Furnace Days' and Siraj's 'The Eighth Man'; also Rashid Hasan Rana's Punjabi poem 'Faceless People'.[64]

At the end of 1981, Zia announced the formation of a 350-member nominated assembly, the Majlis-i-Shura. Its fourfold task was to accelerate the process of Islamisation, suggest plans of action for the establishment of an Islamic democracy, offer 'opinion and wisdom' on important national and international matters, and assist in economic and social reform.[65] However, this body possessed only consultative

61 Chishti, *Betrayals of Another Kind*, p. xi. Chishti had argued continuously for early elections and the ending of martial law with the formation of a national government, including the PPP (p. 153).

62 There were claims that Zia had stage-managed the hijacking to discredit the PPP and undermine the MRD. Tehmina Durrani in *My Feudal Lord* (London, 1994) states that 'the hijacking was an ISI plot created by Zia to malign and isolate Mir and Shah [Bhutto]', p. 153.

63 The MRD included the PPP, NDP, PDP, TI, JUI, PML (Khairuddin-Qasim Group), the PNP (Pakistan National Party), NAP (Pushtunkhwa), the Awami Tehrik and finally the Quami Mahaz-i-Azadi.

64 These are all available in translation in H. Rahman, *Resistance Literature*.

65 J. Henry Korson and M. Maskiell, 'Islamization and Social Policy in Pakistan: The

powers, so it was in effect nothing more than a talking shop. Zia justified its unrepresentative character in terms of the broader process of Islamisation in which he was engaged at this juncture. This did not win favour with the JUP leader Sattar Niazi who maintained that a shura as prescribed in the Quran would have made decisions through mutual consultation; all that the Majlis-i-Shura did was to endorse the decisions already taken by the Government.[66]

The impotence of the Majlis-i-Shura was vividly demonstrated at the time of the 1982 Budget when the Finance Minister read his speech on television immediately before the Majlis session devoted to its discussion. The second and third Majlis sessions did however witness some serious debates on Islamisation measures such as the implementation of the 1980 ordinances on *ushr* and *zakat* (Islamic charity taxes). Two main bodies of opinion emerged – the *'ulama* and the relatively more liberal lawyers' group. The *'ulama* associated with the JI[67] had been closest to the martial law authorities, but with the continuing postponement of elections and slowness in implementing Islamisation they began to distance themselves from the regime. Yet it was in fact the deep-rooted differences among the *'ulama* themselves which delayed Islamisation.

Zia's pledge to the Majlis-i-Shura on 12 August 1983 that national and provincial elections would be held within eighteen months failed to head off the eleven-party MRD's campaign. The disturbances in Sindh continued into November and Zia thereafter extended the ban on political activity by PPP members to ten years. In the first quarter of 1984, Zia reiterated his promise to hold elections, although he made it clear that they should be held on an Islamic basis. This meant that separate electorates would be re-introduced for the non-Muslim minorities. The most vexed issue remained whether they should be fought on a party basis. Zia preferred non-party elections and was armed by the publication in December 1984 of the findings of the commission of Maulana Zafar Ahmed Ansari. The Federal Shariat Court had in December 1980 dismissed retired Justice B.Z. Kaikaus's petition based on the claim that political parties were repugnant to Islam.[68] After much testing of the water Zia also made it clear in the autumn of 1984 that

---

Constitutional Crisis and the Status of Women', *Asian Survey* 25, no. 6 (June 1985), p. 590.

66 *Al-Mushir* 24, no. 2 (1982), p. 85.

67 The rift further widened early in 1984 when the party's powerful student wing, Islami Jamiat-i-Tulaba (IJT) was banned along with all other student political organisations. W.L. Richter, 'Pakistan in 1984: Digging In', *Asian Survey* 25, no. 2 (February 1985), p. 184.

68 *Al-Mushir* 26, no. 1 (1984), p. 164.

he would continue as President after the holding of national elections. The referendum hastily arranged in December was designed to provide him with the semblance of a popular mandate before general elections. The wording of the referendum proposition[69] made it difficult for voters to oppose Zia without giving the appearance of voting against Islam. This was reinforced by the fact that the 'Yes' column was printed in green and the 'No' in white.[70] When the MRD called for a boycott, Zia effectively silenced their campaign by making such appeals a criminal offence. The deserted polling stations on 19 December indicated a considerably lower turnout than the official figure of 62.15 per cent with 97.71 per cent voting 'Yes'.

Fortified by this 'endorsement' of his Presidency, Zia announced that National Assembly elections would be held on a non-party basis in February 1985. The MRD decided to boycott[71] the polls which were dubbed the 'deaf and dumb' elections because of the stringent ban on public meetings, processions and public address systems.[72] In the absence of party organisations, *biraderi* loyalties, *piri-muridi* ties and the economic wealth of candidates were even more important than in previous elections in deciding the outcome.[73] Alongside the feudal powerholders, members of the emerging industrial and commercial elite also secured election to the 217-strong National Assembly and to the four Provincial Assemblies. Zia took the oath of office as elected President at the first joint session of the parliament on 23 March. Two days later his appointee as Prime Minister, Muhammad Khan Junejo, received a unanimous vote of confidence. Despite Junejo's formation of a thirteen-member central cabinet and the installation of civilian chief ministers in the provinces, martial law was not lifted until 30 December. By that time the President had armed himself with wide discretionary powers which emphasised the power of the

69 This read as follows: 'Whether the people of Pakistan endorse the process initiated by General Zia-ul-Haq, the President of Pakistan, to bring the laws of Pakistan in conformity with the injunctions of Islam as laid down in the Holy Quran and the Sunnah of the Holy Prophet (peace be upon him) and for the preservation of ideology of Pakistan, for the continuation and consolidation of that process for the smooth and orderly transfer of power to the elected representatives of the people.'

70 Richter, 'Pakistan in 1984', p. 147.

71 This had less impact than during the referendum and there was a genuinely good turnout especially for the National Assembly and the Punjab Provincial Assembly. See Hasan-Askari Rizvi, *The Military and Politics in Pakistan*, Table XXXII, p. 248.

72 Hasan-Askari Rizvi, 'The Civilianization of Military Rule in Pakistan', *Asian Survey* 26, no.10 (October 1986), p. 1069.

73 For a detailed study see Muhammad Waseem, 'Election Politics 1985', *The Muslim* 9, nos 10, 11, 21 and 22 (April 1985).

executive over the legislature. The Senate had also passed the Eighth
Constitutional Amendment which gave the President the power to
dismiss the Prime Minister and dissolve the National Assembly as
well as the prerogative to appoint provincial governors and the chief
of the armed forces. These powers were to be used by Zia and
his successors to fetter the democratic process.

Political developments, 1985-88

The lifting of martial law saw the formal emergence of the Muslim
League under Muhammad Khan Junejo as the ruling party in Pakistan.
It also encouraged the return from their London exile of leading
members of the PPP. Benazir Bhutto returned to a tumultuous reception
in April 1986, and Ghulam Mustafa Khar[74] to imprisonment the following
August. Benazir campaigned for free and fair elections and was briefly
re-arrested the same month. President Zia's relations with the increasingly
self-confident Junejo, whose tenure of office was marked by increasing
Indo-Pakistan tension and by a rising tide of ethnic violence in urban
Sindh, deteriorated. Zia demonstrated where power still lay in Pakistan
through his unexpected dismissal of the Prime Minister and dissolution
of the Assemblies on 29 May 1988. He himself headed the caretaker
Government and once again promised to hold fresh polls in ninety
days. In a repetition of the past which was part farce and part tragedy,
he also reverted to plans for the Islamisation of the economy and
for partyless elections. His dramatic death on 17 August unexpectedly
released Pakistan from this political *cul de sac.*

Muhammad Khan Junejo's political experience in office and with
the Muslim League dated back to the 1960s and he had served
as Railways Minister in Zia's Cabinet. His main qualification for
the post of Prime Minister however was that he was a Sindhi. Ilahi
Buksh Soomro from Sindh had also been nominated as a candidate
by the members of the National Assembly, but the strong support
which Junejo received from the Pir of Pagaro convinced Zia that
he was the most suitable choice.[75] Relations between Zia and Junejo
were to move from cordiality and courtesy to coolness, as the soft-
ly-spoken and unassuming Prime Minister developed an unexpectedly
independent attitude. Zia found it temperamentally difficult to share

---

[74] Khar had left Pakistan in October 1977 by promising to return from London in a
month with documents which incriminated Bhutto. While in Britain he is alleged to have
plotted with the Indian authorities to overthrow the Zia regime and to have made several
clandestine visits to India and met with Indira Gandhi. For details see Tehmina Durrani,
My Feudal Lord, pp. 94, 135-6, 139, 161-71.

[75] Arif, *Working With Zia,* p. 234.

power and had therefore not followed Ayub's example and the urging of the Pir of Pagaro to don full political garb as President of the Muslim League. Junejo for his part did not want to appear a mere puppet. He differed with Zia over the speed in formally ending martial law and the formation of political parties within the National Assembly. Equally irksome for the President was Junejo's responses to military promotions and to the issue of the return to the Army of officers who had served for three years or more in the civil bureaucracy.[76] Even on apparently trivial matters of protocol, Junejo sought to do everything possible to raise the dignity of the Prime Minister's office.

Despite these endeavours, Junejo totally lacked credibility with the opposition outside the Assembly. In the colourful phrase of Sheikh Rashid, most of the MLAs were so intimidated by Zia's power that they preferred to sit and freeze rather than to muster up the courage to ask for the air-conditioning in the hall to be turned down.[77] In order to strengthen his position, Junejo sought to organise a government party. Political parties could be officially registered from February 1986 onwards, but Junejo jumped the gun and reconstituted the Muslim League a month earlier.[78] He simultaneously expanded his cabinet. The rapturous response accorded Benazir Bhutto during her ten-hour procession from Lahore airport to the Minar-i-Pakistan on 10 April[79] convinced Junejo that the Muslim League would have to put down populist roots. Its eleven-resolution manifesto issued on 2 July promised social and economic reforms for the rural and urban poor,[80] even though Junejo lacked the political base to implement such an ambitious programme. He did however secure support in the legislature by allowing members of the National Assembly to disburse development funds and residential plots to their own constituents. This style of patronage politics, which reinforced its participants' self image as petty rajas rather than serious legislators, was perfected to a fine art by Junejo's successors in the post-1988 democratic dispensation.

Yet all was not plain sailing for the PPP as fissures emerged between the old guard and Benazir's younger supporters. In August the veteran Sindhi landlord leader Ghulam Mustafa Jatoi announced the formation

---

76 *Ibid.*, p. 240.

77 Cited in Muhammed Hanif's review of Sheikh Rashid's autobiography, *Farzand-e-Pakistan* (Lahore 1995), in *Newsline,* December 1995, p. 212.

78 Fakhr Imam, the Speaker of the National Assembly had called for an investigation into this action which cost him his post in a no-confidence motion on 26 May. Thereafter he led the opposition in the Assembly.

79 For details see Benazir Bhutto, *Daughter of the East,* pp. 279-81.

80 Eliza Van Hollen, 'Pakistan in 1986', p. 145.

of the National People's Party.[81] It was never to add up to much more than one of Pakistan's many personality-based parties, although Ghulam Mustafa Khar was to join it after his release from prison in November 1988 and Jatoi was to serve as caretaker Prime Minister in August-October 1990 following President Ghulam Ishaq Khan's dismissal of the first Bhutto government.

Divisions within the PPP increased after confrontation with the Government over the 14 August Independence Day celebrations. Benazir was briefly detained and by the time of her release in September the agitation had died down. She was warned that the PPP might be better served cooperating with other members of the MRD rather than going it alone against the Government. Junejo also did not emerge untarnished. His decision to abandon a rival rally in Lahore smacked of fear that the PPP would draw a larger crowd, while the use of civil code detention provisions to round up opponents belied his democratic pretensions.[82] Zia, who was on *hajj* at the time of the August crisis, continued to remain in the background but retained the constitutional authority to end at any moment the experiment with parliamentary rule. A ready-made reason for intervention was provided by the deteriorating law and order situation in Sindh. The agitation during August/September 1986 revealed the simmering resentment in the interior at what was still seen as Punjabi domination despite Junejo's status as Prime Minister. Anti-state activities took both the form of political opposition in the PPP, the Sindh Awami Tehrik of Rasul Bux Palejo and Mumtaz Bhutto's Sindh-Baloch-Pushtun Front and a general lawlessness in which *dacoits* held sway in vast rural tracts. But it was the escalation of ethnic conflict in urban Sindh which increasingly threatened the stability of Junejo's government.

We have noted in an earlier chapter how the *mohajir* community of urban Sindh regarded itself as victimised during the Bhutto era following the introduction of the provincial quota arrangements for federal public sector employment and the support which Bhutto gave to the Sindhi language issue. The MQM emerged in March 1984 out of the cadres of the APMSO most of whom had come to prominence in Karachi student politics in the late 1970s. The controversy surrounding the alleged role of the military regime in sponsoring the MQM should not detain us here;[83] it is more important to understand its socio-economic background and the impact of the movement on community relations.

---

[81] B. Bhutto, *Daughter of the East*, p. 147.

[82] *Ibid.*

[83] A number of writers have claimed that the ISI sponsored the MQM to weaken the PPP and the MRD in Sindh. Altaf Hussain, who soon emerged as the dominant figure

The MQM was very much a product of the socio-economic changes of the Zia era in Karachi. These saw an acceleration of Punjabi migration and of an increasing Punjabi role in the expanding bureaucracy at the expense of the *mohajirs* at the elite level.[84] Simultaneously, Pushtuns increased their stranglehold on the city's transport, labouring and construction industries. Baloch settlers also formed another important component of the labour force. *Mohajirs* found themselves squeezed out of employment and were angered by the ostentatious display of 'new money' which accompanied the flood of guns and heroin from the areas adjacent to the Afghan war zone. Significantly, the MQM initially allied itself with the native Sindhis against Pushtun/Afghan, Baloch and Punjabi 'outsiders'. It was also no coincidence that the first major riot in April 1985 followed the death of a *mohajir* schoolgirl, Bushra Zaidi, under the wheels of a Pushtun-driven minibus. The violence spread to large areas of the cities, especially to Orangi where Pushtuns and Biharis engaged in a series of ethnic attacks. Days of curfew ensued in selected districts of Karachi.

The partyless elections of 1985 further encouraged ethnic and *biraderi* loyalties. The political responses to this situation were seen in the *mohajirs'* claims that they should be recognised as a fifth 'nationality'[85] and in the formation of the Punjabi-Pushtun Ittehad (Union) in March 1987. In December 1986 Pushtuns sought reprisals on the street for *mohajir* assaults in April 1985 at the time of the slum clearance operation launched by the Army and police in the north Karachi Pushtun locality of Sohrab Goth. A more cynical interpretation would see this not just as motivated by the need for *badla* (revenge) but an attempt by 'drug traffickers and land developers... to get the law-enforcing agencies off their back by initiating an ethnic riot'.[86] The use of machine-guns indicates that this was no spontaneous riot; equally sinister was the careful targeting of non-Pushtun businesses and homes for arson in scenes reminiscent of the 1984 Delhi riots.

The brittleness of state power demonstrated at the time of the 1986 unrest encouraged the rise of the MQM. However, its political breakthrough

---

in the MQM has always denied these charges. For an examination of the background see I. Malik, 'Ethno-Nationalism in Pakistan: A Commentary on Muhajir Qaumi Mahaz (MQM) in Sindhi, *South Asia* 18, no. 2 (1995), pp. 60-1. Altaf Hussain was in fact jailed twice during the Zia era and moved to Civil Hospital, Karachi, for kidney treatment. While in jail he continued to issue press statements.

84 See Feroz Ahmed, 'Ethnicity and Politics: The Rise of Muhajir Separatism', *South Asia Bulletin* 8 (1988), p. 50.

85 *Mohajirs* had always previously identified with Pakistan and Islam rather than with community. This was demonstrated in their traditional support for the JI.

86 Malik, 'Ethno-Nationalism in Pakistan', p. 61.

in the 1987 local government elections in both Karachi and Hyderabad impacted on its relations with the Sindhi community which had previously been cooperative. Indeed its foundation document, the *Charter of Resolutions*, had talked of *mohajirs* and Sindhis as 'real' Sindhis and sought to limit the franchise and the ability to buy property to them. By 1988 Pushtun-*mohajir* violence was being replaced by a pattern of Sindhi-*mohajir* conflict which was to intensify with the restoration of democracy. By the mid-1990s *mohajir* audiences were chanting, '*Sindh mein hoga kaise guzara, adha hamara adha tumhara.*' (How can we co-exist in Sindh? Half is ours, half yours.)[87]

There is insufficient space here to detail the shifting pattern of violence. Interested readers should consult Julian Richards' excellent thesis for a detailed examination.[88] Three points should be noted: first that the switch reflected the MQM's flexing of its muscles as it sought to dominate the local political scene and thereby secure national leverage; second that Sindhi politics had become more nationalist and anti-*mohajir* in outlook, as seen in the rise of Dr Qadir Magsi's Jiye Sindh Progressive Party; third that Sindhi-*Mohajir* civil disorder spread from Hyderabad to Karachi. As Richards demonstrates[89] the spatial organisation of the former city both reflected and encouraged a much more direct competition for resources between the communities. The tension finally spilled over in the violence of 30 September 1988, which in its turn prompted the *mohajir* backlash in Karachi.

While the law and order situation in Sindh provided a pretext for Junejo's dismissal, major precipitating factors, as we shall see later, were his attempts to investigate the Ojhri blast and his stepping out of line on the Afghanistan issue. New domestic priorities impelled Mikhail Gorbachev to work towards an agreed withdrawal. In the rounds of negotiations which preceded the Geneva Accords of 14 April 1988, there was increasing tension between the stances advocated by Zia and Junejo.[90] The latter, in order to facilitate a rapid Soviet pull-out, was prepared to accept an agreement which left Najibullah's People's Democratic Party of Afghanistan still in power in Kabul. Zia wanted to see an interim *mujahideen* coalition government in power in advance of any settlement. In the words of the US Ambassador Arnold Raphel, 'Zia and the ISI were... concerned about what they called "strategic realignment" and about establishing a pan-Islamic

---

[87] *Newsline* (Karachi), 28 March 1994, p. 27.

[88] See J. Richards, 'Mohajir Subnationalism and the Mohajir Qaumi Movement in Sindh Province, Pakistan', esp. pp. 433ff.

[89] *Ibid.*, pp. 267-8.

[90] For details see R.G. Wirsing, *Pakistan's Security under Zia*, pp. 66ff.

confederation of Pakistan and Afghanistan. They felt that after eight years Pakistan was entitled to its own show in Kabul. They didn't want an Afghanistan that had fifteen hundred Indian advisers as it did in the days of the King.'[91] This desire was eventually to be thwarted by pressures from both Washington and Moscow and by Junejo's unexpected mobilisation of political opinion in favour of signing the Accords at the Round Table Conference of 5-6 March.[92] While this made the Soviet disengagement possible, the failure to broaden the basis of the Kabul regime and the continuation of both Soviet and US arms supplies after General Boris Gromov's historic final walk across the Friendship Bridge to neighbouring Uzbekistan on 15 February 1989, ensured that Afghanistan's agony continued for years after Moscow's withdrawal. Moreover, while Zia failed to reconstitute the government in Kabul, he could shuffle the pack in Islamabad. Junejo paid the price for the regime's inability to capitalise on its considerable investment in the Afghan conflict. This commitment to the *mujahideen* cause forms the focus of our next section.

Pakistan and the war in Afghanistan

This section aims to draw out the intersection between the strategic threat posed by the Soviet occupation and domestic politics rather than to fully chronicle all the developments. We look at the motives for Pakistan's support for the *mujahideen*, the dangers which this course of policy created, and its consequences for political developments within Pakistan.

We have already noted how the outbreak of the conflict ended the Zia regime's diplomatic isolation and forced the Americans to reappraise their security arrangements with Pakistan, and the cynical reading of Zia's decision to support the cause of the Afghan resistance advanced by his left-wing National Awami Party (ANP) opponents was that it had been prompted solely by the desire to bolster his power through securing military and economic aid from the West. At the other end of the ideological spectrum the JI portrayed support for the *mujahideen* as a *jihad* which might eventually spread the Islamic revolution to the Central Asian republics. Both explanations are facile and fail to appreciate the complexity of motivations which existed. These included a traditional *realpolitik* concern about Afghan-Pakistan relations in the light of the Pushtunistan issue, and the long-established need to secure

91 D. Cordovez and S. Harrison, *Out of Afghanistan: The Inside Story of the Soviet Withdrawal* (Oxford, 1995), p. 259.
92 *Ibid.*

arms and alliances to offset Indian predominance in the subcontinent. Fears of a Soviet invasion did not figure in Pakistani minds to the extent that they did in Washington, and India was still perceived as the principal threat. Significantly, Indira Gandhi's government had refused to condemn the Soviet action on coming to office, a hardly surprising course given the growing Indo-Soviet trade links and Indian reliance on Soviet weapons.

Zia's attempts to bring about a normalisation of relations with New Delhi met with repeated rebuffs. In the autumn of 1981 for example he offered a 'no war' pact with India and proposed the establishment of a nuclear-free zone.[93] India protested at the sale of F-16 fighters to Islamabad and at the arms and aid package agreed by the Reagan administration. From June 1984 onwards there were bitter Indo-Pakistan military clashes in the area of the remote Siachen glacier.[94] Tensions were further increased by the major military exercise codenamed Operation Brass Tacks, which the Indian Army conducted on the Pakistan border during the winter of 1986-7.

The pragmatism which undergirded the Zia regime's response to the Afghan crisis was reflected in the low-profile support it gave to the *mujahideen* and its attempt to influence the outcome by encouraging the formation of the seven-party Peshawar-based alliance as well as by channelling weapons to favoured groups. The main beneficiary was the Hezb-i-Islami Afghanistan (Afghanistan Islamic Party) of Gulbuddin Hekmatyar. Yet Islamabad was unable to achieve a Kabul regime owing fealty to Pakistan following the withdrawal of the last Soviet forces in February 1989.

Even covert support risked a military escalation with the Soviet Union. Although this never happened, there was a price to pay in the border incursions[95] and numerous terrorist outrages engineered by the Afghan KHAD or Soviet secret services which maimed and killed over 4,000 people.[96] The introduction of the drug/Kalashnikov culture into Pakistan following the Afghan crisis has become a cliché in political analysis. Edward Girardet[97] has pointed out that resistance leaders themselves connived at the diversion of arms shipments. Pakistani authorities sought not only to appropriate arms illicitly for their own use, but also to

---

[93] W. Howard Wriggins, 'Pakistan's Search for a Foreign Policy after the Invasion of Afghanistan', *Pacific Affairs* 57, no. 2 (summer 1984), p. 297.

[94] Wirsing, *Pakistan's Security under Zia*, Chapter 4.

[95] There were over 5,000 ground/air violations in the period 1980-9, causing 2,362 casualties. Arif, *Working with Zia*, Annexure 1, p. 329.

[96] *Ibid.*, Annexure 2, p. 330.

[97] See E. Girardet, *Afghanistan: The Soviet War* (London, 1985), p. 67.

maintain the resistance at a low intensity to avoid the risk of escalation. A less commented-upon legacy of the conflict was the immense growth in the ISI's power which both shaped Afghan policy and funnelled Western largesse to the *mujahideen*. Its Director-General, Lieutenant-General Akhtar, was eventually promoted to the Chairmanship of the Joint Chief of Staff Committee, thereby ensuring his presence on the fateful flight of the C-130 aircraft on 17 August 1988. As Iftikhar Malik's pioneering work[98] has revealed, the ISI has destabilised Pakistan's fragile democracy through its unchecked interventions, unaccounted for funds and uncompromising rivalry with other intelligence-gathering agencies. Both Junejo and Benazir Bhutto turned to the civilian Intelligence Bureau to counteract the ISI's power.

Much has been written about the most visible consequence of Pakistan's involvement in the Afghanistan conflict – the influx of over 3 million Afghan refugees.[99] This had begun with the Communist takeover of April 1978 but dramatically increased after the Soviet invasion. By the early 1980s it formed the largest displaced population in the contemporary world, although it was smaller than the migration which accompanied Pakistan's inception. Marvin Weinbaum is by no means alone in pointing out the burdens and blessings of this huge population.[100] Among the former were the resentment felt by Pakistanis facing competition for jobs from the refugees, and the drain on the national budget in maintaining them, although Robert Wirsing has claimed that this was exaggerated.[101] The refugees were also blamed for the ethnic civil disorder in Karachi during 1985-6. It was widely acknowledged, however, that their enterprise boosted the economies of the Frontier and Balochistan which had received between them all but 200,000 of the total Afghan influx.[102] Rather than creating new political strains, the refugee presence exacerbated long-established problems such as the ethnic tensions both in urban Sindh[103] and between the Pushtuns and Baloch

98 I.H. Malik, *State and Civil Society in Pakistan*, Chapter 5.

99 See, for example, Grant M. Farr, 'The Effect of the Afghan Refugees on Pakistan' in C. Baxter (ed.), *Zia's Pakistan*, pp. 93-110.

100 M.G. Weinbaum, 'The Politics of Afghan Resettlement and Rehabilitation', *Asian Survey* 29, no.3 (March 1989), p. 299.

101 He has pointed out that the great bulk of relief came from the World Food Programme and the UN High Commission for Refugees. Moreover the Pakistan Government did not always pay out its monthly maintenance allowance. Wirsing, *Pakistan's Security Under Zia*, pp. 43-4.

102 One reason why the dispersal of the refugees throughout Pakistan was officially discouraged was the belief that this would make their eventual repatriation more difficult.

103 Indeed, as we have seen earlier the MQM directed much of its early rhetoric against the Afghans. In January 1987 it demanded the repatriation of those living in Sindh. On

in Balochistan.[104] The traditional resentment which the smaller provinces felt towards Punjab also increased. The lion's share of military and economic aid was claimed by the province which faced neither the burden of refugee rehabilitation nor the casualties brought by terrorist bombings and Soviet cross-border incursions. Criticism of Punjab was summed up by the ANP leader Wali Khan's comment in which he likened the refugees to a giant cow, with the Frontier holding its horns and the Punjab its teats.[105]

Islamisation

The Islamisation process became the most identifiable feature of the Zia regime and increasingly its main *raison d'être*. But it never provided the ideological cohesion for Pakistani society that its protagonists anticipated – partly because of the unresolved argument dating from the British era between modernists and reformists concerning the desirability of incorporating Islamic laws into the framework of a modern state, but mainly because state-sponsored Islamisation intensified sectarian divisions within Pakistani Islam. A correspondent of the *Pakistan Times* perceptively remarked on 3 May 1983:

> When we say that the country's laws will be brought into conformity with the Holy Quran every Muslim knows the book referred to, but when we say *sunnah* [the example of the Prophet and the first two – or for some the first four – Caliphs] we cannot point out any book acceptable to the *ummah* (community as a safe, secure and current authority. So far as the matter remains up to an individual's faith it does not affect others but when a faith is converted into a law, that will affect the *ummah* as a whole.[...] The situation will continue ... [until] the government [can] provide a universally accepted book of *sunnah*.[106]

This lack of consensus was exacerbated by the Government's inconsistency in applying Hanafi interpretations to Islamic *fiqh* (law).[107] Eventually

---

his release from prison Altaf Hussain declared that if Pakistan could keep and 'feed' Afghans, then it should bring 'its own people' from Bangladesh. Richards, 'Mohajir Subnationalism'. p. 264.

[104] See Pervaiz Iqbal Cheema, 'The Afghanistan Crisis and Pakistan's Security Dilemma', *Asian Survey* 23, no. 3 (March 1983), p. 235.

[105] Wirsing, *Pakistan's Security under Zia*, p. 52.

[106] Cited in *Al-Mushir* 25, nos 3 and 4 (1983), pp. 150-1.

[107] There are four Sunni schools of legal interpretation and the Shia *fiqh* Jafaria. Differences over the compulsory deduction of *zakat* by the Government led to major Sunni-Shia

different laws were introduced for different sects following the Sunni-Shia furore over the *Zakat* Ordinance. Although Zia's sentiment was summed up in the phrase '*apna maslak mat chhoro, dusre ke maslak ko mat chhero*' (Do not give up your own creed, but also do not interfere in someone else's creed), the expectation that this would resolve the dissensions was hopelessly naive. Indeed in 1985, two JI members unsuccessfully introduced a *Shariat* Bill in the Senate which would have required all laws in Pakistan to be in accordance with Hanafi jurisprudence.[108] The Tehrik-e-Nifaz-e-Fiqh-e-Jafria (INFJ – Movement for the Establishment of the Shia *Fiqh*), which had been founded in April 1979, led Shia opposition to the passage of this bill and the Junejo Government's compromise version. In addition to differences over *zakat*, Shia jurisprudence parts company with the Sunni over such matters as marriage and divorce (especially temporary marriage), inheritance and wills and the imposition of *hadd* punishments. Differences between the *fiqh-e-Jafria* and the Hanafi *fiqh* became increasingly politicised, not only because of the Sunni state-sponsored Islamisation process, but also due to the impact of the Khomeini revolution in Iran. The new leader of the TNFJ from February 1984 onwards was Allama Arif Hussain al-Husaini[109] who had imbibed many of Khomeini's teachings while studying in seminaries in Iran and Iraq.[110] Following Husaini's assassination, the TNFJ spawned the militant splinter group Sipah-e-Muhammad which in the early 1990s was engaged in an increasingly violent struggle with its Sunni rivals, the Sipah-i-Sabha-i-Pakistan (SSP) and the Sunni Tehrik.[111]

Another factor which undermined the impact of Islamisation was, in the words of Hasan-Askari Rizvi, its emphasis on the 'regulative, punitive and extractive' aspects of Islam, rather than on its 'social and

---

clashes. The Hanafi *fiqh* is the dominant school in Pakistan.

108 C. Baxter, 'Restructuring the Pakistan Political System' in S.J. Burki and C. Baxter (eds), *Pakistan Under the Military*, p. 38.

109 Following Allama Arif Hussain al-Husaini's murder, the former Governor of the Frontier, Lt.-General Fazle Haq was arrested and jailed on charges relating to the crime in July 1989. Haq was himself assassinated in October 1991 amid claims of Iranian involvement in the murder.

110 See A. Hayder, 'The Politicization of the Shias and the Development of the Tehrik-e-Nifaz-e-Fiqh-e-Jafaria in Pakistan' in C.H. Kennedy (ed.), *Pakistan in 1992*, pp. 83ff.

111 The SSP emerged in the mid-1980s as a militant breakaway group from the Deobandi JUI. It agitated for Pakistan to become a Sunni state in which all other sects would be declared non-Muslim minorities. Its first two leaders were both assassinated in bitter struggles with rival Shia organisations. The movement's headquarters are in Jhang.

economic egalitarianism'.[112] The introduction of *zakat* was intended to be an important step towards the creation of an Islamic welfare society, but there were in fact numerous complaints to the office of the CII[113] about the administration and distribution of *zakat*, only meagre amounts of which went to the needy poor (*mustahiqqin*) – there were instances of fake *zakat* committees. Even Grace Clark, who was favourably disposed, had to admit at the conclusion of a study that, 'viewed as a public welfare system', Pakistan's *zakat* programme had been only 'modestly' successful.[114]

The Islamisation programme faced even greater difficulties when it set itself the goal of enforcing laws and rules to bring about the vaguely defined *nizam-i-mustafa* (rule of the Prophet) and encouraging the moral uplift of the individual. Steps in this direction included the 1981 Ramadan Ordinance which made eating, drinking and smoking in public a crime liable to a Rs. 500 fine or two months' imprisonment and the establishment of *nazim-i-namaz* (prayer wardens). In August 1984 a presidential directive introduced a national plan for the appointment of prayer wardens to persuade and inspire persons to perform *namaz* five times daily. This measure raised chilling visions of a thought police, but also demonstrated the futility and impracticality of a government's attempts to bring about individual as well as collective moral transformation. The CII in fact recognised that an Islamic order could not be established simply through public legal enactment and in August 1982 the Islah-i-Mu'ashra Committee was established to encourage the strengthening of moral values.

The *'ulama* who might have provided guidance were more concerned with sectarian disputes and symbolic gestures. The latter preoccupation involved attempts to impose dress codes on women and unsuccessful appeals to the government to issue a martial law ordinance to make beards compulsory. Energies were also expended in debates on whether blood transfusion and eye donation were against the teaching of Islam. Symbolic exhortations to honesty as on banknotes which were printed with the inscription '*rizq-i-halal 'ayn 'ibadat hai*' (Earning your livelihood in an honest way is the true act of worship) did not of themselves create in Pakistan a society of truthful and pious Muslims. A correspondent to *The Muslim* at the time of the prayer warden initiative summed up the reality:

112 The Sunni Tehrik is a Barelvi organisation with its greatest support in the Faisalabad and Jhang areas. It has been at the forefront of anti-Christian agitation.

113 Hasan-Askari-Rizvi, 'The Paradox of Military Rule in Pakistan', p. 545.

114 G. Clark, 'Pakistan's Zakat and Ushr as a Welfare System' in A.M. Weiss (ed.), *Islamic Reassertion in Pakistan: The Application of Islamic Laws in a Modern State* (New York, 1986), p. 93.

Many instances may be quoted to show that a person who says his prayers regularly is involved in smuggling or profiteering or other immoral practices. As long as an attempt is not made to create objective conditions necessary for a balance between the urges of the body and the spiritual self, i.e. social justice, rule of law, fair distribution of wealth and equality, the growth of greed, avarice and cupidity cannot be checked.[115]

The Islamisation programme began in February 1979 and covered the four areas of judicial reform, implementation of the Islamic Penal Code, economic activity and a new educational policy. Following a successive examination of each of these areas, we will reflect on the impact of Islamisation on women and the minorities. When discussing Islamisation it is important not to overlook Richard Kurin's[116] highly significant finding based on fieldwork at 'Chakpur' that this was primarily an urban phenomenon, and that its impact on the village populace was limited.

Judicial reform. Before one turns to the impact of Islamic reform, it is necessary to note from the outset that Zia had undermined the judiciary by his Provisional Constitution Order of 1981 which required all judges to take a new oath of allegiance. This state of affairs left some out in the cold, while others felt obliged to tender their resignations. Two years earlier, Presidential Order 3 of 1979 established *Shariat* benches of the four provincial High Courts with the power to strike down any law found 'repugnant' to Islam; such a law would be invalid from the date set by the court. The great quantity of often intricate petitions created a serious backlog. By early 1980, it was obvious that the *Shariat* benches were not performing their functions adequately. In May they were replaced by a Federal Shariat Court, which sat full-time and broke new ground in May 1981 with the appointment of *'ulama* as judges. This was the first time in Pakistan's history that *'ulama* had been appointed to a court;[117] until the reorganisation of May 1981 they had only acted in an advisory capacity. During the period from May 1980 until its reorganisation, the court had made a number of controversial rulings, not least its dismissal of a petition that political parties were un-Islamic and its declaration that stoning to death for adultery was

115 Cited in *Al-Mushir* 26, nos. 3 and 4 (1984), p. 204.

116 R. Kurin, 'Islamisation in Pakistan: A View from the Countryside', *Asian Survey* 25, no. 8 (August 1985), pp. 852-62.

117 The three appointees were Maulana Pir Muhammad Karamullah of Sargodha, Maulana Muhammad Taqi Usmani of Karachi and Maulana Malik Ghulam Ali of Lahore. *Al-Mushir* 23, no. 2 (1981), p. 42.

not a *hadd* punishment and therefore un-Islamic too. The Government had to appeal to the Shariat Appellate bench of the Supreme Court regarding the latter judgement as it questioned the *Hudood* (singular *hadd*) Ordinance which had been introduced in February 1979.[118] Significantly, following the reconstitution of the Federal Shariat Court with *'ulama* membership, it reversed its earlier decision on stoning. From August 1982 onwards *'ulama* were also represented on the three-man Shariat Appellate Bench of the Supreme Court. Significantly no Shia judges were appointed to the Federal Shariat Court, a state of affairs which led the community to refuse to accept any of its judgements.

From 1982 onwards the Federal Shariat Court was empowered to examine laws for their repugnancy to Islam *suo moto* (of its own motion) as well as on petition. This resulted in an overlapping jurisdiction between the Court and the CCI. The latter's recommendations were only advisory, unlike the mandatory nature of the Court's rulings. One important respect in which the court's powers of judicial review were circumscribed was the exclusion of its jurisdiction from the Constitution, any fiscal review and Muslim personal law.[119] The latter limitation excluded from scrutiny Ayub's controversial MFLO, which was a prime target for challenge before the Shariat courts.

The piecemeal construction of an Islamic judicial system continued in 1984 with the creation of Qazi courts in which cases could be tried according to the *Shariat*. The Qazi courts were intended to operate in the locality like the old magistrates' courts. *'Ulama* with a *sanad* (madrassah degree) in jurisprudence were eligible for appointment as *qazis* (judges). By this juncture, Pakistan thus possessed federal and lower Shariat courts, civil courts and summary military courts.

There were many courts, but there was little justice. Cases brought before the Shariat benches were slow to resolve because of the number of frivolous petitions and lack of understanding of the new Islamic laws. The Shariat bench of the Sindh High Court for example had to respond to a petition that women's hockey and cricket matches were repugnant to Islam because they allegedly violated *purdah* rules. Moreover, access to justice still depended on wealth and power in a society of rampant police corruption. 'The [police] official who records the first report is socially so depressed that he is easily influenced in favour of the parties wielding...wealth,' an editorial of the *Pakistan Times* noted early in 1983. 'The curse of false testimony is today the biggest impediment in the process of adjudication.'[120]

[118] *Ibid.*

[119] Lucy Carroll, 'Nizam-Islam', p. 65.

[120] *Al-Mushir* 25, nos 1 and 2 (1983), p. 134.

The Islamic penal code. One of the tasks of the Federal Shariat Court was to decide on appeals from lower courts concerning verdicts under the *Hudood* Ordinances of 1979. This endorsed punishments ordained by the Quran and the *Sunnah*. On 29 June 1982 for example the Federal Shariat Court confirmed for the first time a sentence of amputation of the right hand of a young man, Ghulam Ali, convicted by the Additional Sessions Judge, Sahiwal, for stealing a clock from a mosque in Okara.[121] This conviction was later overturned by the Supreme Court. Other crimes subject to the Islamic Penal Code included murder, adultery, perjury and intoxication. The severity of the punishments which could be meted out made this the most notorious aspect of the Islamisation process. However, very strict Islamic rules of evidence were required, which greatly reduced the likelihood of conviction. Theft, for example, could only be proved by confession or the testimony of two 'unimpeachable' adult Muslim males[122] (other than the owner), each of whom had to actually to have witnessed the crime. Another condition before *hadd* punishments could be imposed was that the value of the stolen property had to be above a minimum value which was fixed by the 1979 Ordinance at the equivalent of 4.457 grams of gold. At the time of the theft of the clock this *nisab* was reckoned at Rs.511.46 while the stolen item was worth around Rs.2000.[123] The *Hudood* Ordinance also provided for proper medical supervision of such punishments as amputation and flogging.[124] Human rights activists and doctors remained opposed to their implementation even on a restricted basis. The Executive Committee of the Karachi branch of the Pakistan Medical Association called on the Government early in September 1983 not to involve the medical profession in the process of flogging and to 'stop such punishments on humanitarian and medical grounds'.[125]

The enforcement of an Islamic code with respect to sexual crimes was especially controversial. We have already referred to the controversy over whether the punishment for adultery was to be death by stoning as contained in the collections of *Hadith* of the Prophet, or 100 lashes as laid down in the Quran, Sura 24, verse 2. Cases of rape (*zina-bil-jabr*) called for a lesser punishment of flogging and imprisonment. Such penalties were roundly denounced by groups like the Women's Action Forum

---

121 *Al-Mushir* 24, no. 3 (1982), p. 102.

122 If the accused was non-Muslim, evidence from non-Muslim witnesses was admissible.

123 *Al-Mushir* 24, no. 3 (1982), p. 102.

124 Section 5 (F) of the Execution of the Punishment of Whipping Ordinance (1979) laid down that the 'punishment shall be executed in the presence of an authorised medical officer.'

125 *Al-Mushir* 26, no.1 (1983), p. 172.

276   Islam Changes Everything?

(WAF) as 'brutal' and 'degrading'. The *Zina* Ordinance, in line with the Quran (24:2), prescribed whipping as a punishment which was to take place in a public place. It was also discriminatory: in many cases female rape victims were not only 'doubly' punished, but saw their violators go free. The law of evidence in all sexual crimes required either self-confession or the testimony of four upright (*salah*) Muslim males. In the case of a man, self-confession involved a verbal confession. For women however medical examinations and pregnancy arising from rape were admissible as proof of self-guilt. The conviction of the blind servant girl Safia Bibi in these circumstances was particularly notorious. She was sentenced to fifteen lashes after becoming pregnant following a multiple rape, while the perpetrators, unlike the victim, went unpunished because of lack of evidence.[126]

Charles Kennedy has argued that Anita Weiss and other scholars who have claimed that the *Hudood* Ordinances were discriminatory are mistaken.[127] He bases this claim on a sample of cases drawn from the files of the Federal Shariat Court, which revealed that 70 per cent of those convicted for *zina* crimes during the period 1980-4 were men. 'One may have legitimate quarrels with the implementation of the Hudood Ordinances,' Kennedy maintains, 'but gender bias against women is not one of them.'[128] This comment seems disingenuous as just a few pages later he notes the widespread use of the *Zina* Ordinance in nuisance suits against 'disobedient daughters' or 'estranged wives' and the great monetary and social costs faced by those accused of *zina*-related crimes.[129]

The introduction of the *hadd* punishments was followed by the Islamisation of the sections of the Pakistan Penal Code pertaining to murder – provision for the punishment of *qisas* (retaliation on the principle of 'a life for a life and an eye for an eye') and of *diyat* (blood money). This was a protracted process in which the CII drafted an ordinance which, after soliciting public opinion, was placed before the President and then examined by committees of the Majlis-e-Shura over a two-year period in an endeavour to arrive at a consensus. Controversy was generated by the practicality of regarding assaults and murder as compoundable, that is subject to the substitution of prosecution by monetary compensation. Equally divisive was the fixing of *diyat* for a female victim as half that for a man. If the *Zina* Ordinance laid

---

[126] Anita M. Weiss, 'Women's Position in Pakistan: Sociocultural Effects of Islamization', *Asian Survey* 25, no.8 (August 1985), p. 870.

[127] C. Kennedy, "Islamization in Pakistan: Implementation of the Hudood Ordinance', *Asian Survey* 28, no.3 (March 1988), pp. 312-3.

[128] *Ibid.*, p. 313.

[129] *Ibid.*, pp. 314-5.

bare the problem of an authoritative definition of Islamic law, the draft law of *qisas* and *diyat* revealed the difficulties of applying legislation designed for a tribal society to the late twentieth century.

The *hadd* punishments did not deter robbery, rape, murder, theft or drug abuse. If anything they encouraged the brutalisation of society. Pictures of public whippings sustained Western misapprehensions and misconceptions concerning Islam. Pakistan's own image plummeted with the spectacle of its government 'appealing to the highest court in the land in an attempt to secure the right to stone adulterers to death'.[130]

The economy and Islamisation. Islamisation in the economic sphere included policies such as the abolition of *riba* (interest), prohibited in the Quran (2:275),[131] and the introduction of the charity taxes *zakat* and *ushr*. The elimination of *riba* had been called for in the 1956 Constitution, and throughout the following decade the CCI made recommendations to this effect, but the political will to tackle the issue was lacking. The abolition of interest on domestic transactions but not on Pakistan's foreign debts was put into operation in 1979. In that year, following the submission of an interim report by the CII, three government financial institutions, the National Investment Trust, the Investment Corporation of Pakistan and the Small Business Finance Corporation, adopted interest-free operations.[132] Capital was provided on the basis of profit and loss sharing (*modaraba*)[133] or mark-up (*murahaba*)[134] contracts which replaced interest. In January 1981 profit and loss sharing accounts were opened alongside interest-bearing accounts in savings banks. Within three years they accounted for almost a quarter of all deposits. Their popularity stemmed partly from the Government's having ensured returns higher than on interest-bearing accounts by restricting their use to safe projects in the public sector, especially the financing of export and import operations.

While bankers questioned how the practices of early Islam could fit a complex modern economy, some of the *'ulama* did not believe

---

130 Carroll, 'Nizam-i-Islam', p. 73.

131 This *ayat* (verse) is again subject to conflicting interpretations. One reading is that it refers to all types of interest. A more liberal interpretation is that it forbids 'usury' but not regulated banking practice.

132 *Al-Mushir* 26, no.2 (1984), p. 184.

133 Funds are raised from the public in the form of certificates which provide investment. Profits are distributed among the *modaraba* managers and certificate holders.

134 In this procedure the bank finances a customer's trade by purchasing specified goods. The customer promises to re-purchase them from the bank at a price which includes a pre-arranged mark-up or profit margin.

that Islamisation had gone far enough and that profit and loss trading was just another name for *riba*. This view was increasingly held by Islamic economic experts in other countries who had initially followed Pakistan's pioneering steps with great interest. At an International Seminar on Islamic Banking held at Islamabad in March 1984, the Finance Minister Ghulam Ishaq Khan conceded the 'inadequacy' of an 'approach to Islamisation which features only the replacement of interest by profits in the modern banking system.[...] We have to do away with profiteering, hoarding and unlawful pressures on the market, which are also sources of exploitation in a no less despicable way than the charging of interest and usury.'[135] Despite this clear statement that interest was not the only villain of the piece, the seminar and the remainder of the Islamisation process were henceforth dominated by a discussion of 'Islamically acceptable alternatives' for modern banking practices. Pakistan's strong economic performance during the early 1980s merely coincided with Islamisation, owing much of its progress to remittances and rising exports.

The *Zakat* Ordinance came into effect on 20 June 1980. Despite fourteen months of consultations and drafting by the Ministry of Finance and the CII, it was one of the most controversial Islamisation measures. The compulsory deduction of 2.5 per cent *zakat* as a charity tax from all bank savings accounts aroused the objection that it was not in keeping with *zakat*'s original concept as a voluntary donation to be given with the right intention (*niyya*). The establishment of a state-run administration of *zakat* inevitably led to Shia protests over being forced to follow a Sunni Hanafi system of jurisprudence. This delayed the introduction of *ushr* on crops until the 1982-3 fiscal year. Shias were exempted from *ushr* (also from *zakat*), as were non-Muslims from the compulsory levy of 5 per cent of the crop. Poorer tenant-farmers would also be excluded if their crop did not exceed the *nisab* minimum. Despite the rhetoric surrounding their implementation, the *ushr* and *zakat* taxes did not eliminate rural and urban poverty or reduce the massive inequalities in wealth which had become a traditional feature of Pakistani society.

Islam and educational reform. Educational reforms were in keeping with the Government's understanding of Pakistan as an ideological state. Quranic, Islamic and Pakistan studies were thus made compulsory and textbooks were revised to conform to the official discourse. Urdu, as might be expected, was emphasised as the language of instruction. Further measures included the establishment in 1980 of an Islamic University in Islamabad and the proposal for a women's university. The latter – delayed due to financial constraints – was not intended to bar female

[135] *Al-Mushir* 26, no.2 (1984), p. 186.

students from co-educational universities. Moreover, the Islamic University's own statutes explicitly declared that it would be open to both sexes.[136] In 1982 the University Grants Commission recognised the *asnad* (certificates) awarded by Islamic seminaries as equivalent to the MA university degree in Arabic/Islamayat. Students of the seminaries were eligible for government financial support; indeed provincial *zakat* councils disbursed substantial sums to the seminaries.

At primary level, the Government sought to tackle the problem of mass illiteracy through patronage of mosque schools. In 1983-4 nearly 12,000 mosque schools[137] were opened, which in return for government support were obliged to adopt an expanded curriculum introducing modern scientific disciplines. These were also introduced in the secondary Islamic educational institutions. The inclusion of 'some worldly subjects' was intended to encourage greater uniformity between Islamic and other schools. However, the mosque schools' and seminaries' expansion and pattern of socialisation, closed off from the general society, bear startling similarities to their Jewish counterparts, the *yeshivot* seminaries in Israel. The products of both can only function intellectually and emotionally in a relatively closed world.[138]

Women, the minorities and Islamisation

The dramatic impact of Islamisation on Pakistani women, together with the burgeoning academic interest in women's studies in the West, ensured the growth of a rich literature around this theme. Alongside the work of foreign scholars like Lucy Carroll, Anita Weiss and Michelle Maskiell, an important account of the resistance by the WAF and the Pakistan Women Lawyers Association was contained in the collection *Women of Pakistan: One Step Forward Two Steps Back*, edited by Khawar Mumtaz and Farida Shaheed.[139]

This is an area of study which requires great sensitivity, since it is easy to fall into the trap of cultural relativism. It should be acknowledged that Islamic law would increase the rights of women living in the tribal areas, in the areas of divorce and inheritance, and end such un-Islamic practices as bride-price. Low social status

---

136 Carroll, 'Nizam-i-Islam', p. 76.

137 For details of the harsh conditions in many of the madrassahs and the second Bhutto administration's attempts to stop military training and ban funding from foreign sources in the wake of increased sectarian violence see *Newsline* (Karachi), February 1995, pp. 34ff.

138 I am grateful to Philip Lewis for this comparative insight.

139 K. Mumtaz and F. Shaheed (eds), *Women of Pakistan: One Step Forward Two Steps Back* (London, 1987).

and poor access to education in rural areas resulted from the absence rather than presence of Islamisation. There is also some truth in the Islamist criticism of the women's organisations' claim to speak on behalf of all women when they were really the preserve of the small professional and upper-class urban elites. Moreover some women agitated in favour of Islamisation as well as against it, especially those in the female wing of the JI's student organisation and members of the Majlis-e-Khawatin-i-Pakistan. Furthermore, it is simplistic to portray the Zia regime as irremediably misogynistic, concerned only with confining women to the boudoir and kitchen. Zia not only appointed the first female Cabinet Secretary in Pakistan's history, but also set up a Women's Division at cabinet level. This preceded the establishment of a Pakistan Commission on the Status of Women whose investigations provided a catalogue of intolerance and of mental and physical abuse.[140] In 1980 Zia appointed a National Council on Population Planning,[141] headed by a female expert Dr Attiya Inayatullah, which called for expanded family planning services. This decision incurred the ire of the *'ulama* and indicated how far Zia had by now parted company with the JI.[142] In 1984, following the notorious Nawabpur incident,[143] a Crimes Ordinance was introduced which made it a penalty punishable by death or life imprisonment to assault a woman, 'strip her naked and in that condition expose her to the public'. Such informal 'punishments', along with illiteracy, poverty and conservative customs like marriage to the Quran of female heirs to prevent land loss, were far more restrictive than the state-sponsored Islamisation programme.

None of the foregoing should obscure the fact that women's rights were severely restricted by the Islamisation process and the resulting climate of discrimination. The Ansari Commission, which from 1982 onwards advised the President on un-Islamic social conventions, recommended that women should be prohibited from leaving the country without a male escort and that unmarried, unaccompanied women should not be allowed to serve overseas in the diplomatic corps. An Islamic dress code was imposed on women in the public eye such as newsreaders and air stewardesses but not on their male counterparts. Equally dis-

---

[140] See Malik, *State and Civil Society in Pakistan*, pp. 150ff.

[141] There are conflicting Islamic interpretations on the permissibility of family planning. It can be justified in terms of protecting the health of the mother, although many *'ulama* regard it as forbidden. Quranic teaching, which encourages late weaning helps the spacing of pregnancies as well as reducing the problems concerning infant formula diets.

[142] The breach was to be widened still further when its Karachi Corporation political stronghold was dissolved by ordinance in 1986.

[143] See Malik, *State and Civil Society in Pakistan*, p. 148.

criminatory was an attempt to ban female models from appearing in commercial advertisements.[144]

As already noted, the greatest furore was aroused by the *hadd* punishments, the issues of *diyat* and the Law of Evidence. Women's groups opposed the *Diyat* Ordinance which set the blood money compensation for a female victim at half that for a male, as it moved from its draft stage to acceptance by the Majlis-i-Shura. Their protests were co-ordinated by Liaquat Ali Khan's widow, Begum Raana Liaquat Ali Khan, the founder of the All Pakistan Women's Association (APWA). Even stronger protests greeted the proposed Law of Evidence which literally interpreted a verse in the Quran (2:282) requiring two women to testify in the place of one man. Shortly after a leak from Mufti Idree's select committee of the Majlis-i-Shura, which revealed hostility to the CCI's draft, a public protest was organised in Lahore on 12 February 1983 by a number of women's organisations including APWA and the WAF.

The women protesters were subjected to tear-gassing and were *lathi*-charged by the police outside the High Court building on the Mall. The episode polarised opinion, with *'ulama* describing the protest as an act of apostasy which challenged Quranic injunctions, while the Lahore High Court Bar Association condemned the 'barbarity' of the police. Significantly the protesters argued in Islamic categories to oppose the proposed Law of Evidence, offering an alternative interpretation of the Sura al-Baqr *Ayat* 282 and emphasising that in other *ayats* (verses) men and women are assumed to be equal as witnesses. They also pointed out the importance of the testimony of the Prophet's wives, Hazrat Khadija and Hazrat Aisha, in early Muslim history. When the *'ulama* denied the competence of women trained in Western law to interpret the Quran, the Islamabad branch of the WAF started classes in Quranic and Islamic studies.[145]

The Law of Evidence (*Qanoon-i-Shahadat*) was finally decreed by a presidential order in October 1984. By way of compromise it laid down that the testimony of two women was equal to one man only with respect to financial transactions, otherwise women had equal voice in giving legal evidence. This represented a minor victory for the women's organisations, although the Punjab Women Lawyers' Association and a splinter group of the WAF still called for a boycott of government functions.[146]

Much less attention has been given to the impact of Islamisation

---

144 Carroll, 'Nizam-i-Islam', p. 83.

145 J.H. Korson and M. Maskiell, 'Islamization and Social Policy in Pakistan', p. 607.

146 *Ibid.*

on the non-Muslim minorities, although they were as much victims of discrimination as women. President Zia in a speech on 12 August 1983 maintained: 'In Islam minorities are not regarded as suppressed classes, rather they are the most privileged ones. In fact in a Muslim society their rights are more than Muslim populations. In Islamic system of Government their rights will be fully protected.'[147] The impact of the Law of Evidence and the introduction of separate electorates for the minorities[148] conflicted with this reassurance and led some minority leaders to fear that their position would be reduced from that of citizens with full rights to the protected *dhimmi* (non-Muslim taxpayers) status and thus repudiate Jinnah's famous foundational statement in the Constituent Assembly. Cases concerning the abduction of Hindu women and forcible conversions were increasingly reported from the Sukkur, Larkana and Mirpurkhas districts of Sindh. The greatest fears however were aroused by amendments to the 1860 British Indian Penal Code dealing with religious offences. The vaguely-worded Blasphemy Law Section 295-C PPP[149] was open to malicious abuse and arbitrary enforcement. This was to be demonstrated later in the celebrated Manzoor Masih and Salamat Masih case. Moreover, following the judicial amendment of the Federal Shariat Court in February 1990, it carried with it a mandatory death penalty.

The most vulnerable of the minority communities, the Ahmadis, suffered most from the amendment of the Pakistan Penal Code. Although from 1980 onwards Zia distanced himself from the *'ulama* over a number of issues, he was too mindful of the events of 1953 to halt the clamour against the Ahmadis. This took a personally dangerous turn in 1983, when religious opponents to the slowness of the Islamisation process spread the rumour that Zia was an Ahmadi. The President was forced to deny this allegation publicly and denounce the Ahmadis as *kafirs* (infidels).[150]

The following year the *'ulama* stepped up their campaign in a series of conferences defending the doctrine of the finality of Prophethood. At one such gathering on 1 January 1984 resolutions were passed declaring

---

[147] *Al-Mushir* 26, no.1 (1984), p. 173.

[148] The minorities were marginalised from the political mainstream. In all 10 out of 237 seats in the lower house of the Majlis-i-Shura was reserved for them.

[149] It read: 'Use of derogatory remarks etc. in respect of the Holy Prophet: Whether by words, either spoken or written, or by visible representations, or by any imputation, innuendo or insinuation, directly or indirectly, defiles the sacred name of the Holy Prophet (peace be upon him) shall be punished wih death, or imprisonment for life, and shall also be liable to fine.' Cited in Amnesty International, *Pakistan: Use and Abuse of Blasphemy Laws* (New York, 1994), pp. 6-7.

[150] *Al-Mushir* 26, no.2 (1984), p. 182.

that any Muslim becoming an Ahmadi would face the death penalty;
that the Ahmadis should be prevented from using such Islamic terminology as *masjid* (mosque); that their literature should be confiscated
and their newspaper *al-Fazl* closed; and they should be removed from
all military and civil positions.[151] In April some '*ulama* threatened to
launch a direct action campaign if the Government did not act on these
demands. Zia was now faced with the task of pacifying the tiger of
Islamisation that he himself had unleashed. He at first tried soothing
words, declaring at a seminar in Lahore on national integration that
'non-Muslims, particularly Qadianis [i.e. Ahmadis] could not be permitted to preach their religion among Muslims in an ideological state
like Pakistan.'[152] Actions were required to cage the beast, and on 26
April he issued an ordinance which inserted sections 298-B and 298-C
in the Pakistan Penal Code. These made it a criminal offence for Ahmadis
to 'pose' as Muslims, to 'preach or propagate by words either spoken
or written', and to use Islamic terminology or Muslim practices of
worship. The ordinance served its short-term purpose in defusing the
opposition campaign. However it placed the religious sensitivities of
the majority at a higher premium than the universal human right to
freedom of 'thought, conscience and religion' and its expression.[153] It
also rode roughshod over the freedom to profess religion (Article 20),
freedom of speech (Article 19) and equality of citizens (Article 25)
provisions in Pakistan's own constitution. Militant Islamists were henceforth encouraged to bring charges against Ahmadis for simply exercising
their religious beliefs. A number of these cases have been investigated
by the Human Rights Commission of Pakistan and Amnesty International.
Symptomatic of the atmosphere of hatred which had been engendered
was the October 1994 shooting of a mild-mannered physics professor,
Nasim Babar, on the Quaid-e-Azam University Campus in Islamabad,
due apparently to his Ahmadi religious faith.

A stormy summer

The title of this section is taken from Chapter 15 of General Arif's
memoir *Working with Zia*, and sums up the atmosphere which pervaded
the closing months of Zia's rule. The foreboding was brought on

---

[151] *Ibid.*

[152] *Ibid.*, p. 183.

[153] Article 18 of the *Universal Declaration of Human Rights* thus lays down the right
to freedom of religion. 'Everyone has the right to freedom of thought, conscience and
religion; this right includes freedom to change his religion or belief, and freedom, either
alone or in community with others and in public or private, to manifest his religion or
belief in teaching, practice, worship and observance.'

by the massive explosion at Ojhri camp on 10 April 1988. This arms depot, situated in a heavily populated area midway between Islamabad and Rawalpindi, had been used by the ISI as a transit facility during the Afghan conflict. The tragedy occurred on the eve of the signing of the Geneva Accords and intensified the turf wars between Junejo, Zia and the ISI. The Imran Commission report on the explosion uncovered not sabotage but a chronicle of incompetence and mismanagement. According to Arif,[154] Zia's desire to⸱ exonerate the former ISI director, General Akhtar Abdur Rahman, was a factor in his unexpected dismissal of Junejo under Article 58(2)(b) of the constitution. Zia himself led the caretaker government which replaced Junejo's cabinet. In what seemed to be a case of 'back to the future', the new political dispensation wrapped itself in the cloak of Islam by successively announcing the *Shariat*'s legislative supremacy in Pakistan[155] and the introduction of an Islamic economic system. The national and provincial elections scheduled for 16 November were to be held on a non-party basis.

On 17 August, Zia travelled to the Tamewali firing range to witness the US-made M1 Abrams tank being put through its paces. He was accompanied by the Ambassador Arnold Raphel and the Chief of the US military mission in Pakistan, Brigadier-General Herbert Wassom. Just a couple of minutes after its take-off from Bahawalpur on the return journey to Islamabad, the four-engined Hercules C-130 carrying the VIP party plummeted to the ground, and burned with such intensity on impact that the remains of the passengers and crew were barely identifiable.

The causes of the crash remain shrouded in mystery. Disciples of Pir Pagaro who had predicted Zia's demise regard it as a 'miracle' wrought by their *pir*.[156] A more mundane explanation put forward by the Pakistan Air Force Board of Enquiry found that 'the most probable cause' was sabotage. A long list of possible perpetrators was speculated upon in the press, including the Soviet and Afghan security services. The American line of inquiry pursued by an Air Force accident investigator team concluded that mechanical failure had caused the Pak One flight to drop from the skies. Robert B. Oakley, who replaced

---

[154] General Khalid Mahmud Arif, *Working with Zia*, p. 390.

[155] Zia had become impatient at the Junejo Government's inability to promulgate a *Shariat* Bill, but his ordinance lapsed after the election of the PPP government. It had in any case been regarded as flawed by Islamists as it exempted the constitution from Islamic judicial review.

[156] For this and further details on the pir and his *hurs* disciples see *Newsline* (Karachi), February 1995, pp. 66-71.

Raphel as US Ambassador, reiterated this interpretation during an interview with the present author in Washington, DC, in November 1996.

Oakley also confirmed the important role General Mirza Aslam Beg, the new Army Chief of Staff, played in ensuring that the Army did not act unconstitutionally and move into the power vacuum created by Zia's sudden death. Beg, along with senior Army, Air Force and Navy commanders, met at General Headquarters before Zia's death had been made public. They decided to ask Ghulam Ishaq Khan, Chairman of the Senate, to assume the post of Acting President in line with constitutional procedures. Beg subsequently made a number of public declarations that the Army would keep out of politics and that its 'sole objective' was the preservation of the 'security and integrity of the nation'. Hasan-Askari Rizvi has speculated that a combination of the belief among senior officers that political power had undermined the Army's reputation and professionalism, along with Beg's own insecurity as a *mohajir* among a high command dominated by Punjabis and Pushtuns, ensured that the Army remained in the background.[157]

In his first address to the nation Ghulam Ishaq Khan confirmed that the elections scheduled for 16 November would go ahead. Further justification for the belief that a new era was about to begin was provided by two court rulings. First, the Lahore High Court ruled that Zia's dismissal of the National and Provincial assemblies on 29 May was *ultra vires*. Its recommendation that they be reconvened was however waived by the Supreme Court in the light of the impending elections. In the second ruling the Supreme Court decided that 'partyless' elections were contrary to the free assembly provisions of the constitution.[158] This raised the possibility that the recently married Benazir Bhutto[159] would return the PPP to power eleven years after the coup which had toppled her father's regime.

Zia-ul-Haq's prescription for Pakistan's political ills was a hefty dose of depoliticisation and Islamisation. Such medicine, rather than acting as a palliative exacerbated the underlying malady. Partyless elections encouraged sectarian and ethnic mobilisation to the detriment of national integration. C. Rakisits points out that 'by failing to respond to the demands from the non-Punjabi ethnic groups, who erroneously see the

---

157 Hasan-Askari Rizvi, 'The Legacy of Military Rule in Pakistan', *Survival* 31, no.3 (May-June 1989), pp. 256-7.

158 C. Baxter, 'A New Pakistan Under a Revised Bhuttoism', *Middle East Insight* 6, no.4 (winter 1989), p. 24.

159 Benazir married Asif Ali Zardari on 6 December 1987.

Punjab as being monolithic, and increasing the centre's powers, the present administration has caused an increase in the centrifugal pulls of the smaller provinces.[...] Ethnic identification has increasingly replaced the Pakistan "nation" as a symbol of emotional loyalty.'[160] Finally, depoliticisation further strengthened the power of the army and bureaucracy while perpetuating the weak institutionalisation of parties, trade unions and other representative bodies. In the words of another scholar, 'Pakistan was in its worst time, nationalism lay bruised, people turned to earlier identities and the state was triumphant in its ascendancy over its own people and institutions.'[161]

Islamisation, which may be variously viewed as the legitimisation of a repressive, un-representative martial law regime or as an attempt to fulfil Pakistan's *raison d'être*, fanned sectarian divisions and revealed the difficulties in achieving a consensus on scholarly interpretation of the Quran and *Sunnah*. Cultural pluralism and the rich inheritance of South Asian Islam could not be forced into the straitjacket of a self-proclaimed ideological state. In the words of the opposition Baloch leader, Mir Ghaus Bakhsh Bizenjo, 'You can occupy, suppress but not create a nationality.'[162] The regime's attempt to sponsor individual moral reform was self-defeating. Zia increasingly realised that a return to the medieval prescriptions of some of the *'ulama* could not serve the needs of a modern state. After 1980 he distanced himself from them, although not with respect to the persecution of the Ahmadis. To foreigners and Pakistanis alike, Islamisation appeared to have reduced a great faith tradition, rich in humanity, culture and a sense of social justice, to a system of punishments and persecution of minority groups. Zia left behind not only a political process distorted by the Eighth Amendment, which enabled his successors to dismiss elected Prime Ministers with impunity, but an atmosphere of bigotry, fanaticism and distorted values.

---

[160] C.G.P. Rakisits, 'Centre-Province Relations in Pakistan under President Zia: The Government's and the Opposition's Approaches', *Pacific Affairs* 61, no. 1 (spring 1988), pp. 96.

[161] Malik, *State and Civil Society in Pakistan*, p. 74.

[162] Rakisits, 'Centre-Province Relations', p. 92.

Part IV

EVER-DECREASING CIRCLES: PAKISTAN POLITICS SINCE 1988

10

DEMOCRACY RESTORED? PAKISTAN POLITICS, 1988-93

The restoration of democracy and the victory of the PPP, led by Benazir Bhutto in the 1988 elections, raised immense expectations of a new era in Pakistan politics. There were hopes of establishing a modern party system which would increase governmental legitimacy. Simultaneously, the inequalities born of gender and religious minority status would be addressed along with the long-standing alienation of the smaller provinces from the centre. It was also hoped that the presence of two subcontinental leaders, Benazir and Rajiv Gandhi, born after the Partition, would improve bilateral relations. Commentators outside South Asia were if anything even more optimistic as they saw Pakistan's progress in terms of a third wave of democracy which was sweeping the globe following the ending of the Cold War and the trend of intensified communication and economic interaction.

Optimism was blunted, however, by President Ghulam Ishaq Khan's dismissal of Benazir Bhutto in 1990 and of Nawaz Sharif on 18 April 1993. The use of presidential power to dismiss elected governments was depressing enough in itself, but an even greater pall was cast on the restoration of democracy by the circumstances which had enabled this action to be taken. Instead of a modern two-party system, Pakistani politics had become a zero-sum game in which oppositions denied ruling parties any legitimacy and governments used selective accountability to harry and intimidate their opponents. Parliament was at worst a bear-pit, at best the fountainhead of patronage politics, with legislation being restricted to presidential ordinance.

The standing of politicians was lower than it had been even in the

1950s, with constant charges and counter-charges of corruption, and regular rounds of financial scandals such as the 1991 Punjab Cooperative Societies affair. The *Hudood* Ordinances remained unchallenged and the persecution of Christian and Ahmadi minorities besmirched Pakistan's human rights record in international eyes.[1] Democratisation had not improved relations with India, but had coincided with a mounting arms race involving the deployment of medium and short-range missiles. In 1990 the two countries had stood on the brink of war over Kashmir. The UN and the United States appealed for calm early in April of that year as both countries put their troops on alert and fire was exchanged across the Poonch sector of the line of control.[2] From 1994 talks even at Foreign Secretary level were in abeyance. Pakistan's relations with the United States had also nose-dived in the wake of the ending of the Cold War and of the Afghan conflict. From 1 October 1990 the United States suspended all economic and military aid excepting counter-narcotics assistance and disaster relief because of the inability to certify under the Pressler Amendment that Pakistan did not possess a nuclear weapons programme. The catalogue of woe in a democratic Pakistan was completed by the spiralling ethnic conflict in the country's main commercial centre, Karachi; this in turn limited the gains derived from the privatisation process which was a response to globalisation.

The deceleration in economic growth in the 1990s coincided with mounting budgetary and external balance of payments deficits which reached crisis proportions. Despite charges of rampant corruption and inexcusable mismanagement directed against the Bhutto and Nawaz Sharif Governments by their opponents, the roots of Pakistan's 1990s economic crisis lay in such long-term structural weaknesses as low savings rates, a weak tax-base, low agricultural productivity, failure to diversify the range of exports, and a chronic underdevelopment of human capital. In such human development indicators as literacy, Pakistan in the mid-1990s ranked 161 out of 174 states in UN statistics. The historically low investment in the social sector despite good GDP *per capita* growth rates until the 1990s, also played a major part in the failure to defuse the country's demographic time-bomb. In sum, many long-term economic problems came to a head in the 1990s. The

---

[1] In 1992 alone some ten blasphemy cases were instituted against Ahmadis. Two years later the Archbishop of Karachi said that twenty-five Christians had been charged with blasphemy. Economic or professional rivalry lay behind a number of these cases, as for example that of Chand Barkat, a small Karachi merchant who was arrested in October 1991 on unsubstantiated accusations by a rival. For details of religious persecution see Amnesty International, *Pakistan: Violations of Human Rights of Ahmadis* (ASA 33/15/91); and *Pakistan: Use and Abuse of the Blasphemy Laws* (ASA 33/08/94).

[2] *Dawn*, 13 April 1990.

scene was set for the crises which beset both Benazir Bhutto and Nawaz Sharif as the Pakistan economy became especially dependent on foreign resources for capital formation, and vulnerable to shocks on its supply management.

The highly controversial nature of these political and economic developments, the absence of reliable sources and the prevalence of misinformation compounds the problems of lack of distance from events which always accompanies the writing of contemporary history. Inevitably it is impossible at this juncture to provide a definitive account. What is offered is an interpretative narrative drawn on newspaper and periodical sources supported by interview material. In order to move beyond a 'journalistic' approach, there is an attempt to set the events within the context provided both by political science and the historical approach of the earlier parts of this work. As might be expected, strong elements of continuity can be discerned with earlier periods in Pakistan's history. The legacy of the Zia era for example can be clearly discerned not only in the debilitating effects of the Eighth Amendment, but also in the heightened Islamic sectarian sentiment and the continuing political influence of the Army and intelligence services. This raises the question of whether democratisation was just a façade for international consumption, with real power still lying with the unelected pillars of the state.

It is however too easy to blame all of Pakistan's contemporary ills on the Zia inheritance. The problems of weak political institutionalisation and legitimacy, the prevalence of ethnic politics and the inability to address glaring social inequalities have existed since the country's emergence. They were rooted as we have seen in the pre-independence security state and in the ambiguities which surrounded the Pakistan movement. Successive regimes have intensified them by seeking to coerce plural societies into an ill-fitting absolutist political and ideological framework. Another constant from Liaquat through to Bhutto, Zia and hence to the contemporary era has been the refusal to regard political opposition as legitimate. In its absence, elected as well as authoritarian rulers have resorted to intimidation. Although the Punjabi Unionist tradition means that Pakistan, unlike many other developing countries, does not have to invent consociational and power-sharing devices, there has been a marked lack of constructive dialogue at crucial junctures in its history – Dhaka 1970-1 and Karachi 1988 onwards.

Alongside these continuities, the contemporary Pakistan crisis has been intensified by the dynamic external environment and internal social transformation. To cite just three examples, Islamic militancy has been heightened both by Zia's sectarian legacy and by the impact of the

Afghan conflict with its *jihad* mentality and huge supplies of weapons; rapid urbanisation has exacerbated ethnic tensions in Sindh;[3] and nationally the failure to redraw constituencies in the light of demographic change has added to the political tensions between the middle class and the 'feudals'. The 1981 Census figure for urbanisation was by the mid-1990s well below the true level, which was estimated to be as much as 40 per cent.

Finally, it should be noted that increased concern with corruption and religious bigotry in the national discourse is in part rooted in the strengthening of the institutions of civil society through urbanisation. Corruption charges, along with selective accountability processes, have been weapons to beat opponents since the introduction of PRODA. Certainly, the resources available to 'corrupt' politicians have increased in recent years with the inflow of foreign funds in the Zia era and the process of privatisation since the late 1980s. Another factor has been the total eclipse of the politics of ideology by that of patronage, an offshoot of the limitations on representative democracy imposed by the 'troika' system. Shorn of real powers and influence, the legislatures have been reduced to a '*lota*-cracy'. But greater public scrutiny, as much as these increased temptations, has led the wielding of political power and corruption to become synonymous in Pakistan's public mind. This perception is itself injurious to the democratic process. Just as in the 1950s the civil-military bureaucracy was to cite corruption on the charge-sheet against politicians, so the successive dismissals of Benazir Bhutto and Nawaz Sharif were justified in this way. This chapter will examine these themes in further detail through an analytical narrative of developments in the 1988-93 period. Before turning to this, however, it is necessary to define what is meant by democracy and to set its restoration in Pakistan within a theoretical context.

Democratisation, democracy and Pakistan: some theoretical contexts

The democratisation of Pakistan formed part of the 'third wave' global democratic revolution. Its centrality to world politics in the late twentieth century has produced a vast comparative literature. Much of this is theoretically elegant, but abstract and ahistorical in approach; the 'strategic choice' model of democratic transition employed by such influential authors as Adam Prezeworski is a case in point. It is extremely debatable whether the strategic choices of political actors

[3] See for example Arif Hasan's hard-hitting article 'What is Karachi really fighting for?', *Herald* 26, no.9 (September 1995), pp.59ff.

during democratic transition are unaffected by the historical legacies of the *ancien régime* from which they are departing. The very nature of transitional periods itself requires historical analysis with its emphasis on change through time. Most of the literature on recent political processes is in fact dominated by disembodied North American paradigms which betray limitations when individual cases depart from ideal types. In order to carry forward the research agenda it is important to understand particularities and allow for the unfolding of unexpected developments. History can play an all-important role in allowing for a more open-ended understanding.

There are conflicting 'prerequisites'[4] and 'process' approaches to the origins of democratic transition: while the former emphasises the context within which transitions were initiated and allows some room for historical and cultural factors as explanatory preconditions, the latter focuses on the schisms within the *ancien régimes* (between adherents of the *status quo*, and liberal and democratic reformers) and the pattern of state elite and opposition bargaining. Democratic transition itself has been conceptualised in terms of 'transformation', 'transplacement' and 'replacement'.[5] Although early studies did not always define clearly the distinction between it and democratic consolidation, subsequent works have linked the nature of the original transition with the prospects for democratic consolidation. A recurring argument is that the more consensual and less violent the transition, the better the prospects for consolidating democracy.

Democracy itself has not always been clearly defined. The term has been used loosely, but there is a world of difference between what may be called 'procedural' and 'social' democracy. The former means little more than the holding of regular ballots, while the latter implies a participatory element in the exercise of power and the removal of social inequalities. In its absence, only lip-service to democracy can be paid. Pakistan may be seen as having made the transition from authoritarianism to procedural democracy, but as lacking any of the characteristics of a consolidated democracy.

The democratic transition in Pakistan can be best conceptualised as a 'transformation'. Despite the formation of the multi-party MRD in 1981, democracy 'emerged' following the voluntary withdrawal of the military after Zia's sudden death in August 1988. The post-Zia military elite was thus able to exert power behind the scenes by brokering a deal which ensured the unity of anti-PPP political forces

---

4 This approach is reflected in the work of such theorists as Share, Karl and Prezeworski, while Huntingdon favours a 'process' analysis.

5 Huntingdon has developed this methodologial insight.

under the leadership of Nawaz Sharif. Thus, the PPP could not sweep the polls. It also enabled the military to dictate the terms under which Benazir Bhutto took office. These 'understandings' rested on the assurance that the defence budget was sacrosanct and the Army retained a veto in vital foreign policy and security matters. The armed forces were able to enforce this veto through their allies in the bureaucracy led by Ghulam Ishaq Khan, Zia's successor in the office of President, whose powers had been appreciably augmented by the Eighth Amendment to the Constitution. The PPP's enforced enfeeblement was compounded by economic crisis and the ethnic conflict in Sindh, a legacy of the Zia era. The weakness of the Government was laid bare by its inability to bring forward any meaningful legislation during a two-year period. Indeed Pakistan's experience in 1988-90 lends weight to those understandings which maintain that transitions unilaterally imposed by armed forces are at best likely to result in fragile democracies which eschew the improvement in economic equity while maintaining guarantees of political freedom, but which are more likely to produce a hybrid mix of electoral forms and authoritarianism. The latter has been dubbed 'electocratic rule.'

Ironically, given his questionable democratic credentials, Nawaz Sharif was in a stronger position than his PPP predecessor to tilt the balance of power in favour of the elected institutions over the state structure. This resulted from both his power-base in the politically crucial Punjab region and his greater acceptability to the Islamic parties. Nevertheless, although the civil-military bureaucracy had engineered Nawaz Sharif's rise to power in 1990, relations between the new Premier and the establishment became increasingly uneasy as he sought to carve out an independent political agenda. This formed the background to Ghulam Ishaq Khan's second dismissal of an elected leader.

The President's subsequent resignation in a deal brokered by the Army to end the constitutional crisis was sparked off by the Supreme Court's restoration of Nawaz Sharif, but it did not mark the breakthrough many hoped for. Democratic transformation was too easily elided into consolidation in this analysis. Pakistani democracy has in reality remained extremely fragile and is still in the early stages of the unfolding sequence from transition to consolidation. Two critical tasks await Pakistani democratisers: first to further loyal opposition and responsible government through processes of institutionalisation and consociation; second to encourage wider political participation and re-establish civilian supremacy over the armed forces. Only after these formidable tasks have been achieved can the Herculean toil be begun of ensuring that governmental and administrative structures reflect the reality of Pakistani pluralism, and that they are responsive to the needs of disadvantaged sections of society.

Benazir and the PPP are back

Even after the relatively short lapse of time since Benazir Bhutto first assumed power as the youngest Prime Minister in Pakistan's history, it is almost impossible to exaggerate the weight of expectation which her return aroused, not only among party activists who bore the physical and mental scars of the Zia era but also among large sections of the population.[6] Benazir's imprisonment during the early 1980s had converted her into a symbol of resistance to an oppressive regime. In addition she could draw on the mystique of her father and the PPP's traditional populist appeal to the poor. Women, who had seen their rights reduced by Zia's Islamisation programme, sought redress from the first woman to head the government of a Muslim nation. The failure to fulfil the enormous expectations placed upon her, as much as mounting charges of corruption, incompetence and intimidation, explains the palpable growth of disillusionment. The limited achievements of her 1988-90 government[7] compounded allegations concerning her alleged authoritarian *wadero* mentality and the activities of her increasingly controversial spouse, 'Mr Ten per cent' Asif Ali Zardari.

Any criticism of Benazir Bhutto's leadership must accommodate the difficulties which she confronted. Foremost among these was the post-Zia political entrenchment of the Army and intelligence services. Their power was largely unobtrusive and informal, but was capable of being directly utilised by their ally President Ghulam Ishaq Khan by means of the Eighth Amendment. Over such matters as Afghanistan, defence expenditure and service conditions, the Army exerted a veto on government policy. Public admissions of the Army's continuing influence were provided by the retention of Zia's foreign minister Yakub Ali Khan in Benazir's Cabinet and her support for Ghulam Ishaq Khan's appointment as President for five years. Ishaq Khan had been very tardy

6 *Dawn* for example floridly recorded that 'the long night of authoritarianism is over and the warm sunshine of a new dawn of democratic renewal bathes the national horizon and lights the path ahead.' *Dawn Overseas Weekly*, week ending 14 December 1988.

7 These included in the foreign field Benazir Bhutto's successful visit to Washington in June 1989 which led to a promise of over $400 million in economic assistance and Pakistan's re-entry into the Commonwealth the following October. In domestic politics the main achievements were the lifting of restrictions on trade union activity in key public-sector enterprises and the inauguration on 1 December 1989 of Pakistan's first Women's Bank

in calling on her to form a government.[8] This had increased her vulnerability arising from the PPP's failure to capture more than 92 out of 207 National Assembly seats. Coalition partners at the centre included the MQM (it held 13 National Assembly seats) with which the PPP had an increasingly troubled relationship because of developments within Sindh. Two other consequences of the absence of a strong parliamentary power-base were an inability either to remove the Eighth Amendment or to sweep aside the *Hudood* Ordinances and a reliance on patronage politics to maintain a coalition government.

A number of explanations have been provided for the PPP's disappointing electoral performance which from the outset undermined Benazir's government. Syed Vali Reza Nasr has maintained that the Zia era's legacy of the 'gradual sacralization of the national political discourse... did not favour the PPP whose myopic emphasis on secular politics and the polemic of democracy restricted its manoeuvrability in a religiously charged polity.'[9] Andew Wilder has demonstrated that in the 1988 Punjab National and Provincial Assembly elections, and even more so in 1990 and 1993, the PPP suffered from the fact that 'voters are increasingly voting for those who will provide them with tangible benefits rather than empty slogans.' It has found itself unable to compete in the game of 'patronage/development politics' with its Muslim League opponents who first perfected this during the Zia era.[10] Wilder's lack of historical 'feel' causes him to exaggerate the shift from 'ideological politics' to 'patronage/development politics'. Patronage has always been the stuff of Punjab politics, no less for the PPP than for other parties. Party structures and ideology were weak well before the depoliticisation of the Zia era. He is also strangely quiet about the role of *biraderi*, tribal and *piri-muridi* allegiances in political mobilisation, although he breaks down the election results along class, gender and regional lines. In many of the central Punjab constituencies *biraderi* contests played a crucial role in the outcome. In Lahore itself rivalries between Kashmiris and Arains lay beneath party affiliations. In Jhang, where the formidable Islami Jamhuri Ittehad (IJI) figure Syeda Abida Hussain was elected, politics was dominated by the factional rivalries of the Pir Jewana and Sultan Bahu *pir* families. Similarly in Multan the pattern of Qureshi-Gilani rivalry,

---

[8] For details of the tense intervening period between the polls and her swearing–in see A. Puri, 'Benazir: The Price of Power', pp. 154 and 162 in M.D. Dharamdasani (ed.), *Pakistan under Democratic Regime* (Varanasi, 1994).

[9] Syed Vali Reza Nasr, 'Democracy and the Crisis of Governability in Pakistan', *Asian Survey* 32, no. 6, p. 523.

[10] A. R. Wilder, 'Changing Patterns of Punjab Politics in Pakistan: National Assembly Election Results 1988 and 1993', *Asian Survey* 35, no. 4 (April 1995), p. 393.

which had first emerged before independence, still continued. Nevertheless, despite these lacunae Wilder's findings on the shifting patterns of PPP support are important, for Punjab continues to hold the key to political power in Pakistan. If the PPP had reproduced within the region its results in Sindh, where it captured 31 out of 46 National Assembly seats, Benazir's hand against Ishaq Khan and his Army backers would have been greatly strengthened.

Punjab provided the main power-base of the IJI or Islamic Democratic Alliance opposition to the PPP. It comprised both the Nawaz Sharif and Junejo Muslim Leagues and eight other parties.[11] Like the PNA coalition in 1977, it was held together by little more than hostility to the PPP. As Syed Vali Reza Nasr has shown, the ISI was instrumental in bringing the opposition coalition into existence.[12] According to Muhammad Waseem,[13] the incumbent caretaker Chief Ministers used public funds to finance its candidates. In all probability the IJI also benefited from the requirement that voters produce identity cards. This ruling disenfranchised many of the PPP's traditional lower-class voters and contributed to the low (42 per cent) turnout. In all, the IJI was to secure 55 National Assembly seats (45 of which were from Punjab) and some 30 per cent of the vote. Moreover, drawing on Nawaz Sharif's long-established influence in the province it won office in the Punjab provincial elections.[14] By-election successes strengthened the IJI majority. It also benefited from the traditional opportunism of the Punjabi landholding elite. Such landholders as Malik Khuda Bakhsh Tiwana secured election as independents and then promptly allied themselves with the winning party.

The IJI ministry in the Punjab set the stage for Nawaz Sharif to pitch the Punjab Government against the federal authorities in a bitter power struggle following his decision not to lead the opposition in the National Assembly.[15] The struggle was symbolised by the transformation of the fiftieth anniversary of the passing of the Pakistan Resolution

11 These were the National People's Party (NPP), the JI, JUI (Darkhwasti group), Jamiat-e-Mashaikh, Jamiat-e-Ahle Hadith, Nizam-e-Mustafa, Hizb-e-Jehad and the independent group led by the former speaker of the National Assembly, Fakhr Imam.

12 Nasr, 'Democracy and the Crisis of Governability', p. 523.

13 M. Waseem, 'Punjab's Inconclusive Mandate', *Muslim*, 10 December 1988. Cited in R. B. Rais, 'Pakistan in 1988: From Command to Conciliation Politics', *Asian Survey* 29, no. 2 (February 1989), p. 203.

14 The IJI captured 108 out of 240 seats, the PPP won 94. 32 seats were held by independents.

15 The leaders of almost all opposition groups in the National Assembly finally came together on 4 June 1989 in the Combined Opposition Parliamentary Front (COP). This was headed by the NPP leader Ghulam Mustafa Jatoi.

Table 10.1. PROVINCIAL ASSEMBLY ELECTION RESULTS, 1988
(% of vote by party)

Punjab

PPP	IJI	JUI(F)	ANP	NPP(K)	BNA	PAI	JUI(D)
34.1	34.98	0.53	0.11	1.14	–	4.86	0.06

PML(Q)	PDP	WP	TNJF	PPIS	PMAI	Other	Indep
0.02	0.5	0.01	0.14	–	–	0.56	22.85

Sindh

PPP	IJI	JUI(F)	ANP	NPP(K)	BNA	PAI	JUI(D)
45.23	7.12	0.76	1.14	–	–	0.42	0.17

PML(Q)	PDP	WP	TNJF	PPIS	PMAI	Other	Indep.
0.02	0.01	–	–	1.82	–	1.05	42.26

NWFP

PPP	IJI	JUI(F)	ANP	NPP(K)	BNA	PAI	JUI(D)
19.87	25.78	7.84	15.41	–	–	1.12	0.16

PML(Q)	PDP	WP	TNJF	PPIS	PMAI	Other	Indep.
–	0.06	–	–	–	0.20	0.23	29.33

Balochistan

PPP	IJI	JUI(F)	ANP	NPP(K)	BNA	PAI	JUI(D)
10.99	23.19	13.23	3.30	–	10.91	0.75	0.65

PML(Q)	PDP	WP	TNJF	PPIS	PMAI	Other	Indep.
–	–	0.84	–	–	3.74	8.06	25.14

Party Abbreviations. PPP Pakistan People's Party; IJI Islami Jamhoori Ittehad; JUI(F) Jamiat-ul-Ulema-i-Islam (Fazlar-ur-Rahmam group); ANP Awami National Party; NPP(K) National People's Party (Khar Group); BNA Balochistan National Alliance; PAI Pakistan Awami Ittehad; JUI(D) Jamiat-ul-Ulema-i-Islam (Darkhasti group); PML(Q) Pakistan Muslim League (Qasim group); PDP Pakistan Democratic Party; WP Wattan Party; TNJF Tehreek-e-Nafaz-e-fiqh-e-Jafaria; PPIS Punjabi Pakhtoon Ittehad Sind; PMAI Pakistan Milli Awami Ittehad (Pushtoon Khaw).

Source: Election Commission of Pakistan, *Report on the General Elections 1988*, vol. 2 (Islamabad 1988). Adapted from table 8, pp. 172-3.

into a rally competition despite the efforts of the veteran Muslim Leaguer Sardar Shaukat Hayat to evolve a formula for a joint meeting.[16] The Punjab administration blocked a PPP rally at the Minar-i-Pakistan on 23 March so that a rival Muslim League rally could go ahead. The thwarted Pakistan Prime Minister had to settle for a premature celebration some three days earlier.[17]

[16] *Dawn*, 2 February 1990.
[17] *Herald*, 21, no. 6 (April 1990), p. 65.

It would of course be tendentious to portray Benazir as a hapless daughter of destiny who in no way contributed to her downfall, aside from the contentious corruption charges concerning her husband. Bridges might have been built with Nawaz Sharif to end the confrontation with the centre. This was certainly not entirely one-sided, although Benazir could be forgiven for harbouring suspicions arising from the Punjab Chief Minister's connections with the erstwhile Zia regime and security services. Even the PPP's election result might have been improved with a more flexible approach. Despite her immense personal popularity, it is clear with hindsight that the failure to enter into an electoral alliance with the other MRD parties was a mistake. Although it subsequently freed the PPP from such MRD commitments as the August 1986 Declaration on Provincial Autonomy[18] and 'to have the armed forces restructured to reflect a truly federal structure', it would in probability have precluded Benazir from being invited to form any government. Rather than goad the military, she in fact risked demoralising traditional supporters by promising to build a strong and professional army. While she reviled Zia as an individual she was careful to avoid criticism of the Army as an institution.

Even before the elections, many party activists had been elbowed aside, and the stampede for PPP tickets reinforced this process. Just like her father Benazir undermined the PPP's institutionalixation by increasingly regarding it as an extension of her own persona. After her triumphant return to Pakistan on 10 April 1986 many of the surviving old guard such as Mumtaz Ali Bhutto and Abdul Hafeez Peerzada, who possessed their own power-bases, were replaced by newcomers whose attachment was to Benazir rather than the party. Asif Ali Zardari, who has become the main subject of Pakistan's numerous rumour factories, has been blamed for his wife's estrangement from the PPP old guard and subsequently from her mother Nusrat and her late brother Mir Murtaza. There is certainly evidence that he was instrumental in distributing 1988 election tickets to opportunist entrants to the party rather than to loyal activists.[19] Even before her marriage to Zardari, however, Benazir displayed little interest in strengthening and

18 The PPP agreement to the MRD declaration marked a departure from its traditionally centralist approach. The declaration called for a limitation of the centre's purview to the four areas of currency, communications, defence and foreign policy. It also put strict limits on the dissolution of provincial governments by the centre. After six months of emergency rule, the President would have to call a referendum if he wished to extend the state of emergency.

19 The investigative journalist Hasan Mujtaba has alleged that 'the only criteria or credentials for securing a PPP election ticket were either to be associated with Zardari or pay anywhere from two million to five million rupees to the party fund.' *Newsline*, November 1996, p. 34.

democratising her own party, while simultaneously leading the national crusade for democratisation of Pakistan's politics.[20]

The consequences of the election results and of the Army's continued influence in the background were summed up by Benazir Bhutto herself when she declared that her government's freedom of action was 'institutionally, economically, politically (and) structurally' constrained.[21] From this weak position she had to face both a bitter confrontation with the opposition and mounting ethnic violence in Karachi, while also having to ensure economic progress and deliver on the promise she made when taking the oath of office on 2 December to eradicate illiteracy and poverty, restore student unions, liberate political prisoners, provide equal rights to women[22] and free the media. Benazir Bhutto's unceremonious removal from office in August 1990 and her subsequent reinvention of herself in opposition[23] glossed over her own contribution to the failure successfully to achieve these tasks. The repetition of many of the problems of her first ministry during the second 1993-96 spell in office raised serious doubts as to whether she possessed the managerial skills and ability to promote the political accommodation necessary to begin to tackle the persistent problems of weak governmental efficiency and legitimacy.

The politics of confrontation and regional identity

We have repeatedly pointed to two predominant features of Pakistani politics: the absence of accommodationist attitudes and the uneasy relationship between the centre and the provinces. The election of the Bhutto Government intensified both these trends but, in a striking discontinuity arising from the electorally split mandate, Punjab found itself at the forefront of the struggle between the provinces and the centre.

The running battle between the PPP and the IJI administration in Punjab sapped much of the energy of Benazir Bhutto's government.

---

[20] Saeed Shafqat, 'Pakistan Under Benazir Bhutto', *Asian Survey*, 36, no. 7 (July 1996), p. 656.

[21] Hasan-Askari Rizvi, 'The Legacy of Military Rule in Pakistan', p. 266.

[22] Benazir reiterated the promise to repeal all laws 'that are discriminatory to the women of Pakistan' when she addressed the fortieth anniversary meeting of APWA on 1 March 1989. *Dawn Overseas Weekly*, week ending 15 March 1989.

[23] Benazir sought to re-establish her liberal, progressive credentials. In a press conference at Lahore on 29 August 1991 she set out a four-point agenda to salvage the country from a 'serious crisis.' This called for a breakaway from the 'impure' legacy of the Zia era, the establishment of a modern liberal and egalitarian Pakistan as envisaged by the Quaid-e-Azam, a clear definition of the civil-military relationship and of the relationship between the provinces and the centre, and strict fiscal discipline. *Dawn*, 30 August 1991.

The tone was set as early as 7 December 1988 when the PPP Punjab parliamentary leader Farooq Leghari led an opposition walkout as the Chief Minister Nawaz Sharif presented the supplementary budget for 1987-8 in the Punjab Assembly.[24] There were undoubtedly provocations on both sides. The Federal Government's appointment of General Tikka Khan as Punjab Governor helped inflame passions, as did the refusal to accede to the request to call a meeting of the Council of Common Interests (CCI) to resolve financial issues between the centre and the provinces.[25] The return of Zulfiqar Ali Bhutto's hatchet-man Ghulam Mustafa Khar[26] into the Punjab PPP fold, following the merger of his faction of the National People's Party (NPP)[27] with the PPP in October 1989[28] and despite his earlier hostility and role in securing the success in the Kot Addu (Muzaffargarh) by-election of Benazir's Sindhi rival Ghulam Mustafa Jatoi,[29] also did little to lower the temperature. The IJI Government in the Punjab kept the confrontation at boiling-point by refusing to send back senior government officials recalled to Islamabad by the Federal Government. In September 1989 three Federal Investigation Agency officials were arrested by the Punjab police while they were working on a case of suspected tax evasion at a factory owned by a Punjab provincial minister.[30]

The use of rival governmental institutions by the PPP and IJI was most conspicuous during the by-elections on 28 January 1989. Indeed in the preceding weeks, there were almost two parallel administrations in Punjab. The PPP sought to mobilise support by promising electrification to far-flung voters through its control of WAPDA.[31] In the words of one journalist, 'ambitious [electrification] plans were announced by roving federal ministers even in areas where the provision of the services

24 *Dawn Overseas Weekly*, week ending 21 December 1988.

25 Benazir Bhutto refused to convene the CCI following deadlock at the 23 May 1989 National Economic Council, maintaining that there was no constitutional link between them.

26 Khar's skill in the politics of *biraderi*, and of *thana* (police station) and *kutchery* (court) immediately benefited the PPP when it defeated the IJI in the February 1990 Raiwind by-election.

27 This was a breakaway faction from the party formed by Ghulam Mustafa Jatoi, the former Chief Minister of Sindh and leader of the PPP.

28 *Dawn*, 20 October 1989.

29 Jatoi on 4 June 1989 became leader of the Combined Opposition Parties (COP) in the National Assembly.

30 *Herald*, 20, no. 10 (October 1989), p. 78.

31 WAPDA was set up in 1958 to maintain and implement irrigation schemes and generate and distribute electricity. It rapidly became the largest employer in the public sector.

was impractical, or, as in the case of the labyrinthine maze of narrow streets in Lahore's walled city, a potential fire hazard.'[32] Nawaz Sharif responded by taking on 'the mantle of a latter-day Sher Shah Suri' and promising to the voters provincial government support for road-building schemes.[33] More dangerous than the use of rival institutions for patronage politics was the polling day showdown between the police and the federally-controlled rangers.

The by-election results[34] were favourable for the PPP and its coalition partners in other parts of Pakistan, but in Punjab they appeared to justify the IJI's policy of confrontation. The prestigious NA-94 seat in Lahore, which had been vacated by Benazir Bhutto and had once been held by her father, was won by the IJI candidate Mian Umar Hayat by a margin of nearly 5,000 votes. Rather than marking the end of the PPP-IJI tussle, the by-elections were the prelude to further bitter in-fighting, which became increasingly personalised.[35]

On the evening of 11 September 1989 during an IJI rally at Lahore's historic Mochi Gate, Nawaz Sharif and other speakers such as Sheikh Rasheed launched blistering attacks both on the Federal Government and on Benazir Bhutto. The latter was declared to be the enemy of Pakistan, seeking to 'establish Indian hegemony', but its days were numbered: 'We will hold [them] accountable and dump the Bhuttos' remains in the Arabian Sea.'[36] This vitriol from Punjab's Chief Minister was occasioned in part by the ongoing dispute between the federally-controlled Pakistan Railways and his family's Ittefaq Foundries over the non-availability of wagons to deliver scrap-iron from Karachi to Lahore. The dispute, which eventually lasted seven months, was seen by the IJI leader as victimisation for his stance against Islamabad. On 21 September 1989, the National Assembly Speaker Malik Meraj Khalid ruled out of order an adjournment motion sought by 16 IJI members to discuss this issue.[37]

The image of the IJI as a protector of Punjabi interests increasingly emerged in its party propaganda. This was also laced with anti-Sindhi and anti-Indian sentiments. Some commentators saw these as simply

---

[32] Talat Aslam, 'Punjab: Clash of the Titans', *Herald* 20, no. 2 (February 1989), p. 48.

[33] *Ibid.*, p. 49.

[34] In all there were twenty national and provincial by-election seats. The PPP and its coalition partners captured seven out of fourteen National Assembly seats.

[35] The PML President Junejo whose own relations with the Punjab Chief Minister were strained was significantly much less intemperate in his criticisms of the PPP during this period.

[36] *Herald* 20, no. 10 (October 1989), p. 78.

[37] *Dawn*, 22 September 1989.

playing to the gallery. Their catalyst was the PPP's decision to release prisoners from the martial law era in Sindh, which the IJI claimed would undermine law and order in the province, and the thaw in relations with India which it depicted as a sell-out of Pakistan's interests. This study however has sought to reveal the profound historical roots of these sentiments among the anxious Punjabi settlers in Sindh and the psychologically scarred East Punjab migrant community. Both groups provided a natural support-base for the Muslim League and its religious allies. The IJI's anti-Indian rhetoric prevented the cordiality between Benazir Bhutto and Rajiv Gandhi at the time of the December 1988 Islamabad SAARC summit[38] leading to a major long-term improvement in bilateral relations. The summit did however yield one of the foreign policy successes of the Bhutto administration with the agreements not to attack each others' nuclear facilities and to enhance cultural cooperation.

While the IJI's strident anti-Sindhi and anti-Indian sentiments were grounded in reality, its pose as the upholder of provincial autonomy was much less convincing. The comment of the federal Interior Minister Aitzaz Ahsan that 'had Nawaz Sharif been in the Centre, he would have been the greatest opponent of provincial autonomy'[39] was based not just on Nawaz Sharif's martial law antecedents, but on the fact that his government had made no attempt to introduce Punjabi as a medium of instruction in the schools. The attempt by Punjabi intellectuals to promote the region's culture and heritage, which had been given up to 'embrace the amorphous concept of Pakistani nationalism', coincided with but owed little to the politically-motivated tussle between Punjab and the centre. Symbolic of this latter struggle was Nawaz Sharif's inauguration of the Bank of Punjab on 15 November 1989 with its own paid-up capital of Rs.100 million.[40] Significantly it adopted as its logo the rising sun royal insignia of Maharaja Ranjit Singh, the last ruler of an independent Punjab.[41] Within two months, seven branches of the bank had been opened. On 30 November the Punjab Revenue Minister, Arshad Khan Lodhi, announced plans for setting up a provincial

[38] This was the fourth annual session of the heads of state and government of the SAARC which brings together Bangladesh, Bhutan, India, the Maldives, Nepal, Pakistan and Sri Lanka.

[39] *Herald* 20, no. 10, p. 89.

[40] The PPP opposition had vigorously opposed the Bank of Punjab Bill in the Assembly on 3 July 1989 declaring it unconstitutional and a 'treason against the Federation'. *Dawn Overseas Weekly*, week ending 19 July 1989. The bank was in fact set up under Item 28 of the Federal Legislative List given in the fourth Schedule of the Constitution which allows the provinces to establish corporations owned or controlled by them provided they only do business within their own geographical boundaries.

[41] *Newsline*, May 1994, p. 21.

television station because 'Pakistan Television, under instruction from the Federal Government, was not projecting Punjab's point of view on various issues.'[42]

Still wearing the turban of Punjab, Nawaz Sharif declared at the annual dinner of the Punjab Civil Service Association early in January 1990 that he would do his best to stop the implementation of the People's Works Programme and that the assembled bureaucrats were not answerable to any federal authority.[43] The Rs.2 billion People's Work's Programme had been launched by the PPP Federal Minister for Local Government and Rural Development, Faisal Saleh Hayat, on 8 February 1989 to meet human development needs. But it had already been denounced by opponents as designed to undermine non-PPP governments. Indeed the Balochistan Chief Minister Nawab Akbar Bugti had already maintained that it infringed provincial autonomy.

Nawaz Sharif's stance on Punjabi interests was undermined from within by the formation of the Saraiki Qaumi Movement in October 1989. Its call for a new province comprising Bahawalpur, Multan, Dera Ghazi Khan, Dera Ismail Khan and the Jhang divisions[44] revealed once again that there was no monolithic Punjabi entity. Feudal power relations were to restrict the Saraiki movement's electoral chances. But it represented a deep Saraiki discontent with the IJI which was closely identified with East Punjabi settlers' interests.

While Punjab grabbed the limelight, regional Sindhi movements were active, despite the presence of a Sindhi Prime Minister in Islamabad. G.M. Syed attributed his opposition to the PPP to its agreement with the MQM, the allocation of funds for the Kalabagh dam and the agreement to build more cantonments in the province. He explained to *Dawn* late in September 1989 that his concept of Sindhu Desh meant 'an independent and sovereign state' which would be a member of the United Nations.[45] The following month the octogenarian leader was placed under house-arrest after a demonstration of his Jiye Sindh supporters at Sukkur airport during which the Pakistan flag was burned. Mumtaz Ali Bhutto, who had formed the Sindh National Front the previous March, stopped short of separatism but talked of 'Sindh for the Sindhis' in a 15-point manifesto.[46]

In spite of all of these problems, why did the Bhutto government

[42] *Dawn*, 1 December 1989.

[43] *Herald* 21, no. 1 (January 1990), p. 68.

[44] L. Ziring, 'Pakistan in 1989: The Politics of Stalemate', *Asian Survey* 30, no. 2 (February 1990), p. 130.

[45] *Dawn*, 29 September 1989.

[46] Ziring, 'Pakistan in 1989', p. 131.

not seek accommodation with the IJI? The answer may be variously sought in the country's ingrained culture of political confrontation, in the need to stand up to the IJI's deliberate attempt to undermine it, and in the pressures which the Federal Government faced from the Punjab branch of the PPP. In July 1990 for example Benazir had to reject demands from her own supporters for a suspension of conciliation talks with the Punjab Government made in the light of its 'increasing victimisation' of PPP workers.[47] Many PPP partymen had in any case little stomach for a deal with Nawaz Sharif, who was seen as the protégé of the despised Zia regime. In some respects the PPP-IJI tussle may be viewed as an action replay of Zulfiqar Ali Bhutto's struggle with the PNA in 1977. Significantly IJI criticism, which caused pandemonium in the Punjab Assembly on 27 December 1988, of a proposed special television programme on Zulfikar Ali Bhutto's sixty-first birth anniversary was followed the next day by the IJI's Maulana Ahmed Chinioti's attempt to introduce a motion offering *fateha* (prayer for the dead) for General Zia.[48]

Whatever the reasons for the confrontation, the only beneficiaries were those members of the Army and civil bureaucracy who were highly sceptical of the democratisation process. As early as July 1989, Ghulam Ishaq Khan was calling on both leaderships to end their bickering. A former Chief Minister of the Punjab during the Zulfikar Ali Bhutto era, Muhammad Hanif Ramay, came up with a novel suggestion some three months later – namely, that the centre-Punjab row might be resolved by forming national governments both in the centre and in the Punjab with no opposition in the two houses.[49]

The PPP and the crisis in Sindh

If the absence of power in Punjab provided Benazir's government with its greatest problem, not far behind it was the need to achieve a workable relation with the MQM in Sindh in order to curb the mounting violence there. The large-scale riots of the mid-1980s were giving way to much more targeted shootings and bombings. These were increasingly taking on a Sindhi-*mohajir* complexion as evidenced by the bombing campaign in Hyderabad on 30 September 1988 which claimed around 200 mainly *mohajir* victims,[50] and in which the extremist Jiye Sindh Progressive Party was believed to be involved. The bitter rivalry between the MQM

[47] *Dawn*, 20 July 1990.

[48] *Dawn Overseas Weekly*, week ending 11 January 1989.

[49] *Dawn*, 13 October 1989.

[50] *Dawn*, 2 October 1988.

and JI, going back to their turf wars in Karachi in the early 1980s, ensured however that Altaf Hussain looked first to a political agreement with the PPP rather than to Nawaz Sharif's IJI in the wake of the October elections which confirmed the PPP as the predominant party of the Sindhi community.

On 2 December the PPP and MQM signed the Karachi Declaration which both sides called 'a charter of peace, love and rights' designed to 'reunite the rural and urban populations of Sindh as the destiny of Pakistan rests on a united and unstratified society'.[51] The APSMO origins of the MQM were reflected in the fact that ten of the fifty-nine points concerned educational matters.[52] Points 32 and 47 addressed the longstanding grievance of job quotas and domicile certificates. The penultimate point called for compensation for the victims of the Hyderabad bombings. The overall impression given by the declaration is that the MQM had adopted an instrumentalist rather than primordialist approach to ethnic political identity. Significantly, nowhere within the document is there the demand for *mohajirs* to be recognised as a nationality.

The speed with which the accord unravelled encourages a questioning of its signatories' motivations. Had the MQM merely been buying time, signing the accord to secure the release of its activists? Did the PPP really intend to risk alienating its Sindhi supporters by acquiescing in *mohajir* economic and political demands? The MQM's public explanation for the growing rift concerned non-implementation of the innocuous-sounding Point 34: 'Those Pakistanis living abroad by choice or compulsion will have all the privileges accorded to citizens of Pakistan.' What lay behind this was of course the demand for the repatriation of the 250,000 or more Biharis living in camps in Bangladesh. Their fate had long become a central element of MQM rhetoric and community identity. Its counterpoint was the Sindhis' fear of being reduced to a minority in their home province. Hawks within the Sindh PPP organisation led by the Makhdums of Hala attacked any sign of weakness towards the MQM. In such circumstances Benazir Bhutto's room for manoeuvre was greatly constrained.

The beginning of March 1989 saw an escalation of unexplained shooting incidents in Karachi. On 10 March a pedestrian was killed and scores were injured by shooting from speeding cars in the Gulshan-i-Iqbal, Quaidabad and Nazimabad *mohajir* localities of the city. The following week similar attacks by masked men led to ten deaths in the Malir and Khokrapar colonies.[53] Altaf Hussain, in a speech at

[51] *Dawn Overseas Weekly*, week ending 14 December 1988.
[52] *Ibid.*
[53] *Dawn Overseas Weekly*, week ending 29 March 1989.

Landi on Pakistan Day (23 March), maintained that the killings were designed to spark off riots. He also claimed that conspiracies were being hatched against the MQM 'by elements who feared that MQM might unite all oppressed classes in the country and challenge their system of exploitation.'[54] MQM speakers joined the IJI in condemning the deteriorating law and order situation in Karachi during an adjournment motion in the National Assembly, although the three MQM ministers, Muhammad Juwaid Akhtar (Health), Syed Altaf Hussain Kazmi (Local Government) and Shamsul Arfeen (Public Health), remained in the Sindh Cabinet.

A less dramatic development but nonetheless one which was to have profound consequences was the arrival at Karachi airport of Jam Sadiq Ali following twelve years of self-imposed exile. The controversial PPP leader was greeted by an enthusiastic if somewhat unruly crowd as soon as his PIA Boeing 747 from London touched down. One supporter painted 'Long Live PPP' on the VIP lounge wall with his own blood.[55] No one could have predicted that within eighteen months the blood of numerous PPP activists would have been shed by the returning hero.

Coincidentally Jam Sadiq Ali's first appearance in court on 3 May in one of the few cases still pending against him was overshadowed by the furore surrounding the resignation of the three MQM ministers from the Sindh Cabinet. Their action had been prompted by the Hyderabad administration's alleged three-hour detention of Altaf Hussain during his visit to the troubled city. The PPP Chief Minister Qaim Ali Shah had at first refused to accept their resignations. In distant Rawalpindi, Benazir Bhutto described the situation in Sindh as a 'mini-insurgency'. She blamed the crisis on the legacy of the previous eleven years, declaring; 'The tree of martial law does not let anything grow in its shade. It will take some time for this situation to change.'[56]

The departure of the MQM ministers did not signal an immediate termination of the Karachi Declaration, and indeed the MQM Joint Secretary Badar Iqbal provided public assurance on this the next day. Nevertheless the MQM increasingly criticised the PPP for its failure to maintain law and order and to keep its bargains. In a conciliatory step the Federal Government reversed its decision to cut the urban quota of places in Dawood Engineering College admissions. This did not however prevent the MQM from observing a 'black day' of protests on 26 May. Although this passed off peacefully, the following weeks

54 *Dawn Overseas Weekly*, week ending 5 April 1989.
55 *Dawn Overseas Weekly*, week ending 17 May 1989.
56 *Ibid.*

were marked by an upturn in violence[57] which included a shoot-out at Karachi University on 8 July between PSF (People's Students Federation) and APMSO student supporters which left three dead.[58] After an incident on 14 July in which gunmen had sprayed bullets on two roadside MQM charity collection camps, seventeen MQM Provincial Assembly members publicly expressed their grave concern at the 'wave of terror'. To the PPP's outrage, they also revealed that Altaf Hussain had spoken to Ghulam Ishaq Khan and sought his intervention in Sindh affairs.[59]

Despite these warning signs, the PPP was shocked when Altaf Hussain appeared at a joint press conference with Nawaz Sharif the day after the opposition had tabled a no confidence motion. The defection of the fourteen MQM National Assembly members threatened to overturn the Government's majority. According to some reports, President Ghulam Ishaq Khan had been instrumental in the MQM move which followed a new 17 point accord with the IJI in which the repatriation of Biharis figured prominently. During the tension-filled week which followed the tabling of the motion both the Government and the opposition sequestered their supporters in an endeavour to prevent defections. In the event the Government carried the day by twelve votes, but the democratic process had been badly damaged by charges and counter-charges of political harassment and attempts to buy votes. Indeed following her dismissal, Benazir was charged with having used Rs.20 million of secret service funds to buy votes.[60] In the wake of the no-confidence motion, the frosty relations between Benazir Bhutto and Nawaz Sharif became glacial.

During the months which followed, the MQM was at the forefront of the anti-Bhutto movement. Altaf Hussain, the MQM *quaid* and *pir*, was at the height of his popularity. Female supporters were especially devoted, showering him with rose petals when he visited MQM free field hospitals, fundraising bazaars and cleanliness campaigns. The COP rally in the grounds of the Quaid-e-Azam's mausoleum on 26 January 1990 was a personal triumph and displayed to the full the MQM leader's charisma and oratorical skills. Although Altaf's claim that the rally numbered over 6 million people was an exaggeration, this was undoubtedly the largest political gathering in Pakistan's history. Just under

---

[57] These incidents not only involved *mohajirs* and Sindhis, but armed clashes throughout 10 July in the Baloch Lyari locality.

[58] *Dawn Overseas Weekly*, week ending 19 July 1989.

[59] *Dawn Overseas Weekly*, week ending 26 July 1989.

[60] K.B. Sayeed, 'The Three Worlds of democracy in Pakistan', *Contemporary South Asia*, 1, no. 1 (1992), p. 62.

a fortnight later, however, the dark side of the MQM's mass mobilisation strategy was seen when a call for a peaceful strike unleashed a day of violence which left fifty-seven dead, a number of whom were innocent victims caught in the crossfire between police and 'unknown persons'.[61] Ishaq Khan reportedly 'summoned' the PPP Federal Interior Minister, Aitzaz Ahsan, to explain the gravely deteriorating situation in the country's commercial capital.[62] The Sindh Chief Minister Qaim Ali Shah was subsequently replaced by Aftab Shaban Mirani in the Karachi hot-seat.

In protest at the 'killing of *mohajirs*' Altaf began a hunger-strike on Sunday, 8 April. The following Thursday a panel of doctors examined him for an hour and came to the conclusion that his life was in danger.[63] It was only after an appeal by a number of top COP leaders who had come to Karachi that the MQM *quaid* broke his fast. He was being treated for kidney problems at the Princess Grace Hospital in London when the tide of violence reached its peak.

Despite a continuing depressing round of curfews and killings in Karachi, the crisis in Sindh came to a climax in Hyderabad with the Pucca Qila incident of 27 May 1990. This episode, which has been likened by *mohajir* leaders to the Jallianwala Bagh massacre,[64] remains shrouded in controversy. The Pucca Qila area in the centre of Hyderabad is a *mohajir* locality, and on the day of the massacre a Sindhi police party entered it to recover suspected illegal arms. It opened fire, allegedly killing over forty people and wounding many more. While the police version of events explains the firing as retaliation to sniping, the MQM maintains that it was indiscriminate. Many of the victims were women and children, and in the MQM account the women were carrying copies of the Quran over their heads and pleading for the police to stop the massacre. Whatever the truth of the matter, the event and the wave of violence which followed in Karachi, including the Qayyum bus massacre of 31 May,[65] was cited by President Ghulam Ishaq Khan as part of his justification for the dismissal of the Bhutto Government.

---

61 *Dawn*, 9 February 1990.

62 *Ibid.*

63 *Dawn*, 13 April 1990.

64 For example the Secretary-General of the MQM, Dr Imran Farooq, declared on 23 August 1990 that, 'The Pucca Qila firing in Hyderabad has superseded the Jallianwala Bagh, Amritsar tragedy and Ms. Benazir Bhutto has gone one step ahead of General Dyer.' *Dawn*, 24 August 1990.

65 Twenty-four people were killed and another thirty-three injured in the attack on the KTC bus. *Dawn*, 1 June 1990.

Azad Kashmir

The events in Sindh overshadowed an ongoing crisis in Azad Kashmir which further demonstrated the Pakistanisation of its politics and diverted domestic attention from the grim struggle which was being waged in the Indian state of Jammu and Kashmir and its attendant human rights abuses. Indeed the Kashmiri '*intifada*' brought India and Pakistan close to war in 1990. The May Assembly Elections in AK revealed the conflict between the Muslim Conference in Muzaffarabad and the PPP government in Islamabad. PPP workers and ministers were despatched from Pakistan to boost the AKPP's chances against the AKMC incumbents, who responded by turning to the IJI for external assistance.

The AKMC emerged with more seats than the AKPP, but the latter – after a period of horse-trading in which the Federal Ministry of Kashmir Affairs played a questionable role – was able to secure the support of sufficient independents and such other groups as the J&K Liberation League and the Tehrik-i-Amal Party to form a government. The waters were further muddied when Sardar Abdul Qayyum Khan of the AKMC was returned to office as AK President during an interregnum with a pro-IJI interim government. He was thus pitched against the AKPP Prime Minister, Mumtaz Hussain Rathore. The bickering was confined not just to PP-MC rivalries, but was also rife within the latter party where there were rival aspirants for power in the shape of Sardar Sikander Hayat the former Prime Minister, Chaudhri Muhammad Yousaf the Deputy Leader of the Opposition, and M. Attique Khan the AK President's son. The '*pajero*' politics which accompanied the see-saw for power was reported as 'disgraceful and even disgusting' in light of the 'heroic struggle for freedom under way across the border'.[66]

While the AKPP and AKMC tussle was proceeding in Azad Kashmir, there was continued agitation in the northern areas of Gilgit and Baltistan for an end to direct rule by the Federal Ministry of Kashmir Affairs. The PPP Government was however no more prepared than its predecessors to restore the region's constitutional status as an integral part of the Kashmir state. The clamour for representation in the AK Legislative Assembly remained unabated.[67]

The PPP and the military-bureaucratic establishment

Throughout much of her office as Prime Minister, Benazir Bhutto was the least powerful of a *troika* which also included the President

---

[66] *Dawn*, 25 January 1991.

[67] See 'AJK Diary 1990: an eventful year', *Dawn*, 11 January 1991.

and the Chief of the Army Staff. She not only had her hands tied in key policy areas regarding the nuclear programme and Afghanistan, but faced attempts by the security agencies to subvert her government. The most notorious of these which has come to light involved a clandestine 'night jackals' meeting of 6 October 1989 in Rawalpindi between two leading ISI officials Major Aamer and Brigadier Imtiaz, opposition National Assembly members and Sindhi PPP members.[68] What was extraordinary about this meeting was not the ISI involvement in 'horse-trading' to unseat the Bhutto Government – such actions dated back at least to the previous spring – but that the government had got wind of the activities and set a trap to record the conspirators in the hope that the Punjab Chief Minister Nawaz Sharif might himself be implicated. In the event Nawaz Sharif stayed away from the meeting, which marked a further escalation in the tussle between the Government, its Intelligence Bureau 'ally' and the ISI. Earlier that summer, Benazir Bhutto had taken advantage of the failed ISI-backed Afghan *mujahadin* assault on Jalalabad to replace General Hamid Gul as ISI head.[69] His replacement, the retired General Shamsur Rahman Kallue, was virtually boycotted by the ISI. The Prime Minister also appointed a committee under the chairmanship of retired Air Marshal Zulfikar Ali Khan to investigate the intelligence agencies. These steps created further enemies without securing civilian control of the secret state.

Benazir Bhutto's vulnerable position with the Army and President as a result of the ethnic polarisation in Sindh and the stand-off with the IJI was further weakened by her attempts to extend civilian jurisdiction. Here parallels can be seen with Junejo's earlier fate and with the later situation which faced her successor Nawaz Sharif. Prime Minister and President initially clashed over who had the right to appoint and retire the chairman of the Joint Chiefs of Staff Committee (JCSC). The so-called Sirohi affair (Admiral Sirohi held the chairmanship of JCSC) undermined Benazir Bhutto's relations not only with Ghulam Ishaq Khan but with the military top brass. The recriminations arising from the Pucca Qila incident further damaged personal and professional relations between Bhutto and Aslam Beg. Indeed Prime Minister and Chief of Army Staff did not meet throughout the period 27 May-24 July. During these weeks the gulf widened because of Benazir's attempt to influence the Army's selection board to extend the term of Lieutenant-General Alam Jan Mehsud, Corps Commander in Lahore. Equally contentious was the Government's refusal to accede to the

---

68 See *Dawn Magazine*, 11 September 1992.

69 See Shaheen Sehbai, 'The Day of the Night Jackals', *Dawn Overseas Weekly*, week ending 14 June 1989.

Army's demands for increased powers governing its deployment in Sindh. It was not prepared to agree to the imposition of virtual Martial Law in order to increase operational effectiveness.

The Army jealously guarded its professional domain. Significantly, following this episode, the Corps Commanders conveyed to Ghulam Ishaq Khan their dissatisfaction with the Bhutto Government.[70] Within a month, the President used the powers given him by the Eighth Amendment to dismiss Benazir Bhutto and dissolve the National Assembly and the Frontier and Sindh Provincial Assemblies. This action might have evoked even greater criticism from Benazir's Western admirers had it not been overshadowed by Iraq's invasion of Kuwait on 2 August. Ishaq justified his action by citing charges of corruption and political horse-trading, and failure to discharge legislative functions and enforce law and order. In accordance with the constitution, national and provincial elections were scheduled for 24 and 27 October respectively.

The Bhutto Government had comprehensively failed to live up to expectations during its twenty months in office. This resulted in part from the unrealistic hopes built around it, given the economic and institutional constraints which hedged about the restoration of democracy. Moreover its demise owed far more to the fact that it 'had stepped on the Army's toes' than to the charges the President raised against it. Nevertheless, the Government had in many respects dug its own grave. The new democratic era had ushered in the politics of patronage and confrontation rather than of principle and consensus. Activists reared on the radical rhetoric of Zulfiqar Ali Bhutto were disappointed by the Benazir Government's privatisation and pro-US policies, which were barely distinguishable from those of their Muslim League rivals.

The 1990 elections and Nawaz Sharif's rise to power

The caretaker Prime Minister, Ghulam Mustafa Jatoi, harboured hopes of a more permanent preferment, but these were shattered by the refusal of both the JUI and MQM to join his Government. Relations with his Muslim League partners were also rocky following the cynical inclusion of Ghulam Mustafa Khar as the caretaker Federal Minister for Water and Power. Meanwhile, the maintenance of law and order in Karachi remained a continuing problem as became clear on 22 August when unknown terrorists pumped Kalashnikov fire into the camps set

---

[70] Shafqat, 'Pakistan Under Benazir Bhutto', p. 663.

up to welcome Altaf Hussain on his return from London the following day.[71] This claimed more than thirty lives.

The caretakers' image as non-partisan was sullied by their attitudes to the PPP[72] and the manifestly selective accountability process, with the time-frame for investigations into corruption limited to the Bhutto administration. Benazir Bhutto had cases pending against her during the electioneering, while Asif Ali Zardari who was contesting the Karachi Lyari seat was arrested on 11 October in connection with the kidnapping case of Murtaza Hussain Bukhari, a Pakistani philanthropist living in Britain. The former Prime Minister fainted amid scenes of pandemonium in the Lahore High Court on 2 October and subsequently alleged that the Punjab caretaker administration had engineered an attempt on her life.[73]

No new themes or visions for making Pakistan's democracy more workable emerged during the elections, as politicians concentrated on winning power rather than considering the issues which would confront them afterwards. The campaign's backward-looking nature was exemplified by the approaches made by prominent IJI leaders and candidates to Begum Zia-ul-Haq to address public meetings in their constituencies.[74] Public debate swirled around conflicting interpretations of the record of the Bhutto administration and the President's decision to dissolve the National Assembly. Benazir Bhutto traded insults with Ghulam Mustafa Jatoi, calling the caretakers 'a clique of usurpers, thieves, thugs, robbers and looters',[75] while he retorted that the nation's wealth had been 'looted' during the previous PPP regime.[76]

The heat of the campaign ensured that the issues of ethnicity and centre-province relations were not treated constructively. Syeda Abida Hussain, the Federal Minister for Information and Broadcasting and future Washington Ambassador, picked up on the theme of '*Punjabiat*' and played on anti-Sindhi sentiments in a series of speeches. Addressing a large public rally at Haq Bahu Colony in Jhang on 18 October, for example, she declared that Punjab had been deprived of its share in the River Indus by Zulfikar Ali Bhutto and that his daughter had made the Punjabi settlers in Sindh 'flee their hearths and homes'. 'Those who turn to the Punjab for votes and work against it', she said, 'forfeit

---

[71] *Ibid.*

[72] *Dawn*, 24 August 1990.

[73] Benazir Bhutto had wanted to address the court even though she had not received a show cause notice. She had not recognised the jurisdiction of the special tribunals. For details of the Lahore High Court episode see *Dawn*, 5 October 1990.

[74] *Dawn*, 12 October 1990.

[75] *Dawn*, 5 October 1990.

[76] *Dawn*, 12 October 1990.

their right to be elected from here.'[77] A few days earlier she had maintained that Punjab 'had always given sacrifices for others' but had been 'deprived' of its right of leadership in the country for the last forty-two years, which resulted in 'political confusion...besides creating chaos and promoting provincialism, regionalism and factionalism in the country.'[78] The MQM chief Altaf Hussain banged the drum just as vigorously on behalf of *mohajir* interests. In an emergency news conference at his Azizabad residence, he expressed the need for recruiting the police from the 'urban areas' in Sindh in order to make them more effective.[79]

The PPP constructed a Pakistan Democratic Alliance (PDA) comprising the TI, the Malik Qasim faction of the Muslim League and the TNJF. The IJI was ranged against this and, as in 1988, its major component was the PML. The MQM and JUI(F) contested independently of these coalitions. The real loser even before polling began, however, was the caretaker Prime Minister Jatoi. He had hoped that the IJI would contest under the COP umbrella ensuring him the prize of premiership in the event of victory. This expectation was dashed when his electoral base was effectively reduced to his insignificant NPP by the IJI's decision to contest outside of the COP. Women also lost out before polling because the provision to reserve twenty seats in the National Assembly and 5 per cent of the seats in each Provincial Assembly for them had expired. This meant that they had to compete with men for votes from a conservative and patriarchal electorate. The Bhutto ladies unsurprisingly were the only successful female candidates to enter a male-dominated National Assembly.

The elections took place against the background of the US cessation on 1 October of economic and military aid to Pakistan, following President Bush's failure to certify under the Pressler Amendment that Pakistan did not possess a nuclear weapons programme. It meant not only the loss of $564 million of economic and military aid, but also prevented the delivery of seventy-one F-16 fighters and spare parts to the Pakistan Air Force. Benazir Bhutto's opponents claimed that she had prevailed on her friends on Capitol Hill to cut off aid in order to influence the polls in the PPP's favour. In an interview with the present author in 1996 Robert Oakley denied that the timing of the decision had anything to do with the impending Pakistan elections.[80] Such an intentional step would in any case have proved counterproductive, since the beneficiaries

---

[77] .*Dawn*, 19 October 1990.

[78] *Dawn*, 12 October 1990.

[79] *Ibid.*

[80] Interview, 8 November 1996.

of the news were not the PPP but rather the resolutely anti-Western JI.

The national results confirmed a number of well-established trends in Pakistan politics; first that Punjab held the key to national power; second that despite national issues and manifestos in many constituencies the elections still revolved around landed influence and *biraderi* allegiances; third that the MQM had become the dominant political force in urban Sindh; fourth that politics in Balochistan continued to be dominated by the tribal leaders of regional parties and by the Pushtun-Baloch divide with the JUI(F) dominant in the Pushtun areas; and fifth that the religious parties and the nationalist parties in Sindh remain unable to convert 'moral' influence into electoral success. They also demonstrated the distortions arising from the first-past-the-post system, with a difference in vote share between the PDA and IJI of less than 1 per cent (36.65-37.27 per cent), resulting in the IJI capturing seventy more seats in the 207 member National Assembly.

The PDA's much weaker performance than anticipated, in terms of seats[81] led to immediate claims of rigging. The PDA Secretary-General, Mian Khurshid Mahmood Kasuri, maintained that the national results were as 'bogus' as General Zia's referendum and that they had come into being 'because of votes cast by Angels'.[82] Election-rigging, like selective accountability, is a tradition deeply rooted in Pakistan's history. Indeed the Muslim League claimed that the 1946 Punjab polls on which the Pakistan demand hinged had been rigged by the Unionists. The Leghari report in the early 1950s on district board elections in Punjab uncovered a catalogue of rigging including such devices as gerrymandering, arresting of rival candidates, rejection of nomination papers and pressurising of voters.[83] Electoral malpractice is thus a venerable Pakistani tradition. 'Rigging is now a part of the electoral contest itself', Muhammad Waseem maintains, 'in terms of the rival candidates' ability to cast bogus votes and get away with it.'[84] The trick of not being caught has been made more complicated by the fact that since 1988 all general elections have been closely monitored by international observers.

The PDA 'White Paper' publication *How An Election Was Stolen* (Islamabad, 1991) was refuted by the report of a forty-member in-

---

81 It was generally acknowledged that the one-sided accountability process and the inability of the eleven special tribunals to make charges stick had increased sympathy for Benazir Bhutto and her party.

82 *Dawn*, 26 October 1990.

83 Cited in M. Waseem, *The 1993 Elections in Pakistan*, p. 39.

84 *Ibid.*, p. 41.

ternational delegation sponsored by the Washington-based National Democratic Institute for International Affairs. It recognised that the election process 'was not without problems' and had taken place in a highly-charged atmosphere, but despite malpractices in certain constituencies, it had received no evidence of systematic fraud on a 'national scale'.[85] The danger that the election observer teams themselves might become part of the political conflict was raised when PDA charges of a 'whitewash' received support from a more critical assessment of the polls by a four-member team from the International Federation for Human Rights.[86] With hindsight it seems clear that rigging did occur which inflated the IJI victory but did not significantly effect the outcome. What seems more important in a broader perspective is that the polls represented yet another occasion for cynicism regarding electoral processes. This was reflected in the low turnout of 45 per cent of voters.

Table 10.2. NATIONAL ASSEMBLY ELECTION RESULTS, 1990

	PDA	IJI	MQM	ANP	JUI/F	Indep.	Other	Total
Punjab	14	92	–	–	–	6	3	115
NWFP	5	8	–	6	4	3	–	26
Sindh	24	3	15	–	–	4	–	46
Balochistan	2	2	–	–	2	–	5	11
Total	45	105	15	6	6	13	8	198

Source: National Democratic Institute, *The October 1990 Elections in Pakistan* (Washington, DC, 1991) p. 196.

On 7 November, amid desk-thumping by IJI members, Nawaz Sharif was confirmed as Prime Minister following a crushing victory in a vote of confidence in the National Assembly. 'We are embarking on a journey to deliver the goods for our labourers and the poor,' the Prime Minister declared. 'The oppressed of the country have been waiting for the last 44 years to have their grievances removed. [...] They genuinely want the removal of poverty for which we have already worked out a big plan.'[87] Despite these fine words, the tone of confrontation which was to mark his first term of office was set by the PDA members' absence from the proceedings. Hopes of a government-opposition

[85] See National Democratic Institute of International Affairs, *The October 1990 Elections in Pakistan* (Washington, DC, 1991).

[86] See W. L. Richter, 'The 1990 General Elections in Pakistan' in C. H. Kennedy (ed.), *Pakistan in 1992* (Boulder, CO, 1993), pp.33ff.

[87] *Dawn*, 9 November 1990.

dialogue early in 1991 were dashed following the removal of the Rathore AKPP administration in Azad Kashmir.

Nawaz Sharif in power, 1990-93

Nawaz Sharif's tenure saw a continuation of confrontational politics, a crisis in Sindh and claims of corruption which had dogged his predecessor. Despite his close association with the Zia regime, he was discomfited by its legacies in the fields of Islamisation and civil-military relations. Economic management was constrained by the country's continued reliance on IMF and World Bank assistance, following the setbacks arising from the cut-off of US aid and a decline in migrant remittances from the Gulf. Corruption was also draining the national exchequer, with state-owned banks reporting a loan recovery rate of less than 8 per cent in the first quarter of 1990.[88]

As befitted his background, Nawaz Sharif embraced economic liberalisation more enthusiastically than the PPP had done. Early in February 1991, he announced the lifting of all controls on foreign currency entering the country along with other policies to encourage foreign investment.[89] By October eighty-nine state enterprises had been put up for sale. In the field of foreign policy, the new Prime Minister faced the same limitations posed by the more powerful members of the troika as Benazir Bhutto, without the advantage of her sympathisers in Washington. Moreover, the Gulf crisis threatened not only political but economic repercussions for Pakistan. Indeed, within days of taking office, the IJI Government had to announce a rise in oil prices of over 40 per cent.[90] Added to these problems was the disparate character of the IJI coalition itself with the incompatibilities between such members as the PML and ANP, the JI and both the MQM and the and JUP. Ultimately Nawaz Sharif found that there were too many circles to square and suffered the same fate of dismissal as his predecessor, although with a dramatically different outcome.

The Gulf War

Nawaz Sharif possessed three distinct advantages over those of his predecessor at the outset of her term of office: his finesse in the art of patronage politics, his clear electoral victory, and a secure power-base in Punjab. This was centred around those middle-class groups

88 See *Newsline*, August 1990, p. 20.

89 For details see *Dawn*, 8 February 1991.

90 *Dawn*, 16 November 1990.

who had profited during the Zia era. His family most spectacularly symbolised this process with the Ittefaq business group diversifying into sugar, cement and textiles and increasing its turnover in a decade from $10 million to $400 million.[91] Ironically, however, events conspired to highlight his comparative disadvantages to the Daughter of the East, namely inexperience in dealing with the media and a lack of expertise in foreign affairs. The caretaker administration had linked Pakistan with the anti-Iraq coalition by despatching 11,000 troops to Saudi Arabia to guard the holy places of Islam. The mounting tension in the Gulf, culminating in the launch of Operation Desert Storm, threw this policy into the spotlight. To his discomfort Nawaz Sharif found that the Chief of Army Staff, General Aslam Beg, smarting under the cessation of US economic and military aid from 1 October onwards began to question the foreign office coalition line and hinted that Pakistan might adopt a posture of 'strategic defiance' like Iraq's.[92] Simultaneously popular sympathy for Saddam Hussain threatened to unravel the IJI coalition almost as soon as it had taken office.

Maulana Shah Ahmad Noorani, head of the JUP, urged Muslims on 27 December to pray for Saddam Hussein's victory and maintained that both Jews and Christians were scheming against Islam. The JUP's criticisms were to increase following Operation Desert Storm. On 7 February Noorani discussed the opposition PDA's call for a strike with Asghar Khan. The JUP's Secretary, General Maulana Abdul Sattar Khan Niazi, eventually resigned from Nawaz Sharif's cabinet in March over the Gulf War issue. The JI, the second largest group in the IJI, was similarly at odds with the Prime Minister. Its student wing, IJT, organised a number of demonstrations in support of Saddam Hussein, and dummy Scud missiles were taken out.[93] The pro-Saddam wave of sympathy was further demonstrated by the flying of Iraqi flags and the display of pictures of the Iraqi leader. The most vivid illustration of support was the registration of thousands of volunteers to join the *jihad* against the allies by such organisations as the Anjuman-i-Tuleba-i-Islam.[94] Processions in numerous cities burnt US flags and effigies of President Bush and condemned the 'dictation' of Pakistan's foreign policy by US Ambassador Robert Oakley.[95]

Mumtaz Ahmad's excellent study has revealed how Nawaz Sharif's unpopular stand over the Gulf War opened up the first cracks in

[91] J. Bray, 'Nawaz Sharif's New Order in Pakistan', *Round Table* 318 (1991), p. 180.

[92] *Dawn*, 7 December 1990.

[93] *Dawn*, 25 January 1991.

[94] *Dawn*, 18 January 1991.

[95] *Ibid.*

the alliance between the Muslim League and the religious parties.[96] The JI did not withdraw until May 1992, and even then it was over the 'unsatisfactory' Islamisation process and Nawaz Sharif's refusal to back the JI's favourite, Gulbuddin Hekmatyar, in the Afghan power struggle. Domestic difficulties were not compensated by improved ties with the Americans. There was no resumption of Washington's economic and military aid in the wake of the Gulf War. Indeed, by the close of Nawaz Sharif's time in office, relations had plunged to an all-time low. In January 1993 Pakistan was placed on the watch-list of potential terrorist states for six months.[97] The following August the United States imposed trade sanctions on both China and Pakistan for alleged violation of the Missile Technology Control regime in the supply of M-11 missiles to Pakistan from China.[98] Such a turn of events was a shock both to the civilian politicians and the military leadership of a state which for most of its history had prided itself on being the most 'allied' of US Cold War allies and as recently as 1981 had received a tranche of $3,000 million in economic and military aid.[99]

Islamisation and the IJI Government

The support of IJI senators for a Shariat Bill in the closing months of Benazir Bhutto's government, together with the presence of religious parties in the subsequent IJI Government, meant that Islamisation which had been in abeyance since 1988 would re-emerge during Nawaz Sharif's premiership. Like his former patron Zia, Nawaz Sharif found that necessary governmental pragmatism inevitably disappointed the ideologically motivated *'ulama*.

His attempt to reconcile the twin goals of economic liberalisation and Islamisation trapped him 'between a rock and a hard place' when the Federal Shariat Court in its Faisal ruling of November 1991 declared twenty federal and provincial laws dealing with *riba* to be repugnant to Islam.[100] This injunction could not have come at a more embarrassing time, since it imperilled foreign investment in the ambitious $1.3 billion

---

[96] M. Ahmad, 'The Politics of War: Islamic Fundamentalism in Pakistan' in J. Piscatori (ed.), *Islamic Fundamentalisms and the Gulf Crisis* (Chicago, 1991), pp. 155-87.

[97] The dismissal of Brigadier Imtiaz, the Army Intelligence Chief who was suspected of having links with terrorist groups, contributed to Pakistan's removal from the list.

[98] Tahir Amin, 'Pakistan in 1993: Some Dramatic Changes', *Asian Survey* 34, no. 2 (February 1994), pp. 197-8.

[99] World Bank loans have in part compensated Pakistan for the loss of US bilateral aid.

[100] See C.H. Kennedy, 'Judicial Activism and Islamization After Zia: Toward the Prohibition of Riba' in C.H. Kennedy (ed.), *Pakistan in 1992*, pp. 67ff.

power generation project at Hub near Karachi. Rather than directly compromise the Government's Islamic credentials, the back door route of challenging the injunction in the Supreme Court was used by encouraging the semi-independent Agricultural Development Bank to file an appeal. This action was regarded as self-serving by many of the *'ulama* who were already discontented with the Government's Shariat Act.

This measure had been piloted through the National Assembly in May 1991. Nawaz Sharif hailed its passage as 'historic' and declared that 'the objective of the creation of Pakistan had been realised'. Farooq Leghari, the deputy leader of the opposition termed it a 'Zionist conspiracy against Muslims' and maintained that it did not embody the 'true' *Shariat*.[101] It was not only the PDA opposition that voiced dissent; the MQM also expressed reservations and the JUI pointedly stayed away from the proceedings. This was because the Bill did not amend the constitutional provisions which limit the scope of the Shariat courts' jurisdiction. In an attempt to limit Shia recriminations, it also laid down that the interpretations of personal law of Muslim sects would be respected. To avoid contentious issues regarding economic and educational Islamisation, special commissions were established to report back at a later date. Such fudging led the JUI's Maulana Fazlur Rahman to make the bitter comment that the measure was *Aab-i-zamzan* (holy water) in a bottle of whisky.[102] Nawaz Sharif compounded the religious parties' disappointment with his government by supporting United Nations proposals for a broad-based interim government in Afghanistan early in 1992. This, together with the Gulf War policy and the Shariat Bill issue, proved to be too much for the JI which left the alliance.

Successes and setbacks

Nawaz Sharif is generally credited as being more successful than Benazir in bringing forward legislation and in working Pakistan's federal system of government. The IJI's secure power-base at both the national and Punjab levels enabled the impasse of the Bhutto era in the latter field to be overcome. The CCI actually met and divided financial assets between the provinces. Progress was also made in March 1991 on the contentious issue of the division of the Indus Waters.[103] The harmonious functioning of relations between

---

[101] *Dawn*, 17 May 1991.

[102] Sayeed, 'The Three Worlds of Democracy', p. 64.

[103] M. Waseem, 'Pakistan's Lingering Crisis of Dyarchy', *Asian Survey* 32, no. 7 (July 1992), p. 626.

the provinces and the centre was undoubtedly a stabilising factor at the time of the Gulf War. Defence and foreign policy however were never fully under the Prime Minister's control, and the decision to send the Army into Sindh was not his.

Nawaz Sharif introduced a number of populist measures to address poverty and social inequality. They brought the Muslim League considerable popularity, although opponents denounced them as ineffectual gimmicks. In July 1992 for example the Government fixed a monthly minimum wage of Rs.1,500 for unskilled workers. Earlier in February 1991 it had announced that 3.75 lakh acres of land in the Sukkur and Ghulam Muhammad Barrage areas of Sindh would be distributed to landless *haris*, each having 15 acres.[104] The best-known and most controversial of Nawaz Sharif's populist measures was of course the Self-Employment Scheme, popularly known as the Yellow Taxi scheme. This was announced in April 1992, and loans of up to Rs.300,000 were promised to the unemployed to finance schemes for self-employment. The seriousness of the proposal was immediately called into question by the confusion over whether Rs.2 billion or Rs.20 billion was to be made available.[105] The Federal Finance Minister Sartaj Aziz also had to clarify that the loan would not be paid in cash. Nevertheless, by 1993 around 40,000 households had benefited from the loans which had been sanctioned for 95,000 taxis, buses, coaches and trucks.[106]

Shafik Hashmi has examined the privatisation programme which is seen by some as another success of the Nawaz Sharif administration.[107] This included the creation of a private airline and the transfer of the Muslim Commercial Bank into private hands by the Privatisation Commission of General Saeed Qadir. Hashmi however raises a number of criticisms of the programme including the lack of accountability, private entrepreneurs' absence of concern with social obligations, and the contention that 'changing the locus of the ownership of industries is by itself neither a necessary nor a sufficient condition for an efficient operation of specific industrial enterprises.'[108] Less remarked-upon is the impact of privatisation on attitudes towards the Punjabisation of Pakistan. Stanley Kochanek has revealed that the failure of the

---

[104] *Dawn*, 8 February 1991.

[105] *Dawn*, 10 April 1992.

[106] Waseem, *The 1993 Elections in Pakistan*, p. 122.

[107] Shafik H. Hashmi, 'Privatization Policy' in C.H. Kennedy and R.B. Rais (eds), *Pakistan in 1995*, pp. 31-47.

[108] *Ibid.*, pp. 42-3.

Memon Adamjee family to regain control of the privatised Muslim Commercial Bank, although they outbid the Chinoti-Punjabi Mansha-Saphire group, aroused precisely these feelings among the Gujarati business community.[109] Political connections could count for more than commercial considerations during the denationalisation process.

Nawaz Sharif's government came under increasing attack in 1991 for alleged financial mismanagement. It was implicated in the misappropriation of public funds which led to the collapse of co-operative societies in the Punjab in which depositors lost Rs.20 billion. A number of the major societies which had incurred huge bad debts, including the National Industrial Credit and Finance Corporation (NICFC) and the Services Co-operative Credit Corporation, were owned by IJI Provincial Assembly members. The Ittefaq group repaid its loans to the NICFC when it was in crisis, but this did not limit the political damage: nor did the probe into the scandal by the Commission of Justice Muhammad Afzal Lone of the Supreme Court. During a press conference on 31 October Benazir Bhutto attacked the IJI's policies, which she maintained would 'turn Pakistan into a banana republic'.[110]

The Latin American theme re-emerged in another financial context the following spring. On 17 March the Government had placed Foreign Currency Bearer Certificate advertisements in US, Japanese and European newspapers for the sale of high-interest five-year bonds that could be purchased without the identity of the purchaser or the source of the funds being disclosed. This was immediately denounced as a charter for the laundering of drug money. The Deputy Governor of the State Bank of Pakistan was despatched post-haste to Washington to mend fences and prevent a boycott of the Pakistan banking system because of this violation of US banking laws.[111] The threat was only lifted when the offer was withdrawn.

Confrontation with the PPP

When the PDA was not boycotting the National Assembly, it was hurling charges and counter-charges at the Nawaz Sharif Government. Following the collapse of the Cooperative Societies, the PDA sent a telegram to President Ghulam Ishaq Khan asking him to sack the Prime Minister and requesting an interview with him.[112] A year later in November

---

[109] S. A. Kochanek, 'Ethnic Conflict and the Politicization of Business' in Kennedy and Rais (eds), *Pakistan in 1995*, p. 149.

[110] *Dawn*, 1 November 1991.

[111] *Dawn*, 10 April 1992.

[112] *Dawn*, 8 November 1991.

1992, Benazir Bhutto organised a long march on Islamabad, followed by a 'train' march, to dislodge Nawaz Sharif. The next year she sided with the President who had earlier dismissed her to bring down the elected government, promising in secret talks that she, unlike the Prime Minister, would support Ghulam Ishaq Khan's bid for a second term of office.

How do we explain this strange turn of affairs? The answer lies partly in the 'win at all costs' Pakistani political mentality resulting from a long tradition of confrontation rather than accommodation. Linked with this is the culture of political intolerance of opposition. The PPP leader could argue that it was impossible to act as loyal opposition when the Minister for Religious Affairs termed her a '*kafir*' and the Prime Minister's principal Sindhi ally called her a 'terrorist'. The Government's victimisation of PPP activists and of the Bhuttos and their immediate entourage severely limited the scope for constitutional niceties. Moreover, Benazir Bhutto believed that the Government was illegitimate because it had only secured office following extensive electoral rigging.

The tussle between the IJI and PPP took on much of the character of a personal vendetta between Benazir Bhutto and Nawaz Sharif. This was rooted, as we have seen, in the original nationalisation of the Ittefaq Foundries by Zulfikar Ali Bhutto and in the Sharif family's alleged victimisation during the 1988-90 Bhutto administration. Soon after being acquitted on charges of fraudulently obtaining a bank loan, Asif Ali Zardari was charged on 12 May 1991 with the murder of political opponents. Benazir also faced charges at this time for the misuse of secret service funds. According to Lord Gifford, a member of the UK Parliamentary Human Rights Group who had attended earlier proceedings against her in October 1990, the charges had been brought for political motives; the proceedings were 'misconceived and partisan' and seemed to 'compromise the judiciary.'[113]

The politics of malice reached their height in the Veena Hayat affair. At around 7.30 p.m. on 27 November 1991, five masked men broke into the Karachi residence of Veena Hayat, a close friend of Benazir Bhutto and daughter of the veteran Muslim Leaguer Sardar Shaukat Hayat. She subsequently brought a charge of gang rape and claimed that the men had been sent by Irfanullah Marwat, the son-in-law of President Ghulam Ishaq Khan and Adviser on Home Affairs to the Sindh Chief Minister Jam Sadiq Ali. Much to the embarrassment of the President, the PPP and other opposition parties led by Nawabzada

113 Amnesty International, *Pakistan : Arrest of Political Opponents in Sindh Province August 1990-early 1992* (London, 1992), p. 7.

Nasrullah Khan 'politicised' the event in rallies across the country. Children wielded placards with the emotive slogan 'It could be your daughter next'. On 12 December, the police baton-charged female protesters on Aiwan-i-Sadr Road in Karachi and eight women required hospital treatment.[114]

A *jirga* of the Hayats' Khattar tribe promised retribution following the failure of the Sindh Tribunal of Justice, headed by Abdul Rahim Kazi, to find any evidence. The accusations against Irfanullah Marwat are not as incredible as they may seem: the President's son-in-law held operational responsibility for the activities of the notorious Central Intelligence Agency which had been established to assist the police in the investigation of crime and the conduct of surveillance activities. Investigative journalism of the highest order, courageously published[115] by the monthly *Herald* in October 1991, revealed a catalogue of torture and murder within its precincts and showed that CIA operatives were engaged in such crimes as car theft, kidnapping and gang rape. These reports were given international publicity by Amnesty International.

The activities of the CIA reflected both the collapse of law and order within Karachi and the victimisation of the PPP by the Jam Sadiq Ali Government. The former PPP leader had secured election as an independent in 1990 and headed a coalition comprising anti-Bhutto Sindhi politicians and the MQM. Until his death on 4 March 1992 Jam Sadiq Ali presided over a calculated attempt to destroy the PPP's power-base in the province, and this repression was carried out with the knowledge and undoubted support of President Ghulam Ishaq Khan. A report published by Amnesty International in June 1992 provided details of the mass arrests of hundreds of PPP workers who were allegedly linked with the Al-Zulfikar organisation; on 19 November 1991, the Chief Minister claimed that both Nusrat and Benazir Bhutto were its heads and were 'no friends of the people'.[116] The Amnesty report catalogues cases of unacknowledged detention of political prisoners, including the former PPP Minister of Transport and Youth Affairs, Manzoor Hussain Hassan; short-term abductions by the police of such PPP Provincial Assembly members as Mir Hayat Talpur to prevent them voting in the Assembly; torture of prisoners in police custody, most notably in the Rahila Tiwana case;

114 *Dawn*, 13 December 1991

115 The magazine was confiscated from news-stands in a heavyhanded attempt at censorship. Later the editor, Ms Sherry Rehman, had a criminal defamation suit filed against her by a Deputy Superintendent of the CIA, Ayaz Khan. See *Dawn*, 18 October and 29 November 1991.

116 *Dawn*, 29 November 1991.

and extra-judicial murder in the context of so-called 'encounter' killings.[117]

Although the Jam Sadiq Ali regime reduced overt ethnic violence, criminal lawlessness became almost endemic. Much of the interior of Sindh was under the control of *dacoits*. Within Karachi increasing clashes between rival MQM factions and Sunni and Shia militants added to the violence waged by warring drug barons. In June 1991 the spotlight shifted temporarily from Sindh to Punjab with two especially gruesome mass murders in Sheikhupura and Lahore. Nawaz Sharif responded to the increased lawlessness in Punjab by cancelling a projected visit to Japan. However, it was the serious situation in Sindh which posed the greatest threat to his continued tenure in office.

Sindh

The word '*dacoits*' was on the lips of everyone following the kidnapping early in 1991 of Japanese students and Chinese engineers. Indeed the Friday *Dawn* magazine ran a series of articles in July/August on 'Dacoity in Sind'. Sindh possessed a long history of banditry, although as late as 1979 only cattle were being lifted, rather than individuals being kidnapped for ransom. The *dacoits* were traditionally part of the rural social order and indeed were protected and encouraged by the large landowners who could use them against rivals. There was also an element of social banditry in the *dacoits*' actions. The legacy of the 1983 MRD movement and of rising rural unemployment greatly increased the ranks of the *dacoits*, who infested the riverain jungles on both sides of the Indus and the mountain ranges adjacent to Balochistan. By 1991 the 2,000 or so *dacoits* had gained such an influence that travel was restricted to daylight in much of rural Sindh. Those who ventured out at night risked the fate of a Lahore-bound coach early in May 1991: it was stopped on the National Highway near Moro and its passengers were relieved of their valuables. Other incidents at this time included attacks on villages in Dadu and Naushero districts.[118] It was the kidnapping of Mashoq Ali, who had close ties with the Agha Khan, the following May which finally tilted the balance in favour of an Army-led 'clean-up' operation in Sindh.

During the intervening year the *dacoits* had become bolder in the interior and Karachi had been wracked by crime and violence. Car theft and bank raids became a daily occurrence. During the period 24-25 December 1991, for example, Karachi witnessed a million rupee bank

117 Amnesty International, *Arrests of Political Opponents*, pp. 29-30, 17, 34-5 and 48.
118 *Dawn*, 10 and 24 May 1991.

robbery, two shot dead in a police encounter, a hit-and-run case inside a graveyard, three deaths by shooting, and a shooting during an operation in the Emergency Ward of the Jinnah Postgraduate Medical Centre.[119] Just three days earlier an assassination attempt on the MQM leader Altaf Hussain had narrowly failed. His unknown assailants were almost certainly dissidents within his party.

The split within the organisation earlier in the year fuelled much of the violence in Karachi. It arose from the decision to broaden the MQM from a *mohajir* organisation to a Pakistan-wide movement of the *gharibon* (downtrodden) to be known as the Muttaheda Qaumi Movement. This was opposed by a 'gang of three' which included a MQM provincial minister, Badar Iqbal, and the MQM's joint secretaries, Aamir Khan and Afaq Ahmed. They were expelled and fled the country. The purge included other zonal leaders including Rashid Ahmad and Mujtaba Khan and the whole of the Zone 'A' committee which represented Landhi, Korangi, Malir and Shah Faisal Colony.[120] The dissensions were accompanied by Altaf Hussain's retreat to a hospital bed in the Abbasi Shaheed hospital[121] and violence and boycotts against such newspapers and journals as *Dawn, Takbeer, Herald* and *Newsline* which had reported on the MQM's difficulties. On 22 March, in an unprecedented step, the Karachi edition of *Dawn* was suspended following threats against its journalists, distributors and hawkers.

The death of Jam Sadiq Ali and the replacement of the *mohajir* Army chief General Aslam Beg by General Asif Nawaz Janjua paved the way for the May 1992 military crackdown within Sindh. It seems that the Prime Minister was much more uneasy about the launching of Operation Clean-up than the other members of the troika. Despite the setback of the Tando Bahawal incident in which innocent villagers were killed by the Army, its actions temporarily curbed the rural *dacoit* menace. By the middle of 1995 traffic was plying not only the highway but the link roads of such previously forbidden areas as Dadu, Larkana, Naushero Feroz, Sukkur and Tando Allahyar.[122]

It was in Karachi that intervention by the Army had its greatest impact, as its deployment in the city took the MQM completely by surprise. In the confusion many of its activists went underground and MQM legislators resigned from the Provincial and National As-

[119] *Dawn*, 27 December 1991.

[120] *Dawn*, 8 March 1991.

[121] This for a time replaced 90 Azizabad as MQM headquarters. Altaf Hussain received well-wishers and supplicants there under heavy guard in what amounted to a state within a state.

[122] *Herald*, May 1995, pp. 28ff.

semblies. The military's uncovering of arms caches and *khels* (torture cells) dealt the organisation a major propaganda blow. The greatest long-term impact came about with the return of the dissidents on the Army's coat-tails in July 1992. With the support of the Army and the intelligence services, the MQM Haqiqi ('Genuine') Group re-established itself in large areas of the city. What was left of the MQM was headed by Azim Tariq, although all crucial decisions remained in the hands of Altaf Hussain who had taken up a self-imposed exile in London. In subsequent years he was to issue a string of exhortations and instructions to his followers through satellite link-ups. The MQM *Quaid* could rest easy in the knowledge that there was no extradition treaty between Britain and Pakistan.

The IJI and the military-bureaucratic establishment

The launching of Operation Clean-up further strained an increasingly fragile relationship between Nawaz Sharif and the President and Army chiefs. He had started out in office with a much greater fund of goodwill in these quarters than Benazir Bhutto had ever possessed. However, the Gulf War, dissensions over the Shariat Bill, mounting economic problems and claims of corruption had all diminished his stock. The unravelling of the IJI alliance had also been carefully noted in Islamabad but, like Junejo and Bhutto before him, it was Nawaz Sharif's efforts to extend the Prime Minister's powers which led to a parting of the ways.

Nawaz Sharif's independent initiatives included the development of policies in the highly sensitive Kashmir and Afghan situations as well as the issue of a restoration of American economic and military assistance.[123] He also differed with the President in the choice of Army Chief following both General Beg's retirement and General Janjua's sudden death in January 1993. Ghulam Ishaq Khan's resentment increased still further with the signs of a rapprochement between the Prime Minister and Benazir Bhutto. This was signalled by the PPP leader's agreement to chair the Parliamentary Committee on Foreign Affairs and by the release of her husband on bail after two years in prison. These moves coincided with Nawaz Sharif's decision to review the Eighth Amendment and his silence on the issue of the government's support for Ishaq's re-election as President. Ghulam Ishaq Khan took the latter two stances as a personal insult.

---

123 S. Yasmeen, 'Democracy in Pakistan: The Third Dismissal', *Asian Survey* 34, no. 6 (June 1994), p. 577.

Pressure began to mount on Nawaz Sharif at the beginning of 1993, orchestrated at the Aiwan-e-Sadr President House. The Prime Minister faced a split in his cabinet and in the Muslim League following the establishment of the Junejo faction. Islamabad was also rocked by the claims that General Asif Nawaz Janjua had been poisoned. Benazir Bhutto returned from London after the birth of her third child and immediately plunged into the fray. Despite the advice of Iftikhar Gilani, Yahya Bakhtiar and others who wanted to see her support Nawaz Sharif in order to trim the power of the President, she decided to pay back the Punjabi Prime Minister 'in his own coin'.[124] She allowed herself to be wooed by the President and exacted a delicious personal revenge when he was pressurised into inducting her previously vilified husband into the caretaker Government formed after Nawaz Sharif's dismissal. It is debatable, however, whether such personal satisfaction justified a dangerous liaison for the future of Pakistani democracy.

The Nawaz Sharif Government went the way of its predecessor on similar charges of corruption, nepotism and maladministration. Just as a former PPP leader had been inducted as caretaker Prime Minister in August 1990, that honour now fell to a former Muslim League loyalist, Balkh Sher Mazari. The inclusion in the caretaker Government of a number of PPP leaders including Farooq Leghari and, almost ludicrously, Asif Ali Zardari[125] held out as little hope for impartial elections within the ninety-day timetable as had the composition of caretakers in 1990. However, as we shall see in Chapter 11, it was here that the similarities between the 1990 and 1993 dismissals ended.

---

[124] *Herald*, May 1993.

[125] 'The size and composition of the cabinet became a subject of public ridicule,' Moham-mad Waseem has written. 'It was compared with the Qissa Khwani Bazar at peak business, with its ministers remembered as wheeler-dealers, smugglers of drugs and arms, and a variety of sycophants, agents, "Saints and Sinners" led by an acting Prime Minister, "every inch an elegant hair dresser".' M. Waseem, *The 1993 Elections in Pakistan* (Lahore, 1994) p. 47.

11

DEMOCRACY IN CRISIS:
PAKISTAN POLITICS, 1993-98

The years 1993-7 were filled with almost continuous crisis. Civil war
in Karachi carried overtones of the earlier breakdown in Dhaka which
had cost the state half its territory. Meanwhile economic collapse loomed
in the background, darkened by a further use of presidential authority
to dismiss an elected government and by mounting sectarian violence.
American analysts were moved to question whether Pakistan was a
'failed state', another Somalia or Rwanda in the making. To the historian
the rush of contemporary crises can be viewed with a little more
equanimity: Pakistan has, after all, survived earlier reports of its death
and its most 'dangerous decade.' The continuities with the past again
appear striking, as does the persistent viceregalism of the CDNS introduced during the caretaker administration which followed Benazir
Bhutto's second dismissal from power. Moreover the country continues
to pay a high cost for its weak political institutionalisation and a culture
of confrontation. More widely the subcontinent continues to suffer from
the loss of trade opportunities and high military expenditure resulting
from the fifty-year-old Indo-Pakistan tensions surrounding the issue of
Kashmir. Despite the resumption of Foreign Secretary-level talks following the installation of a United Front Government in Delhi and
the return of Nawaz Sharif to power in 1997, the weeks which followed
the golden jubilee of independence were marked by shelling and renewed
tension along the Kashmir border.

Constitutional crisis

Nawaz Sharif's bold televised address of 17 April 1993, in which
he directly accused President Ghulam Ishaq Khan of conspiring to
overthrow him, finally sealed his fate, but it presaged a defiant public
stance by the dismissed Prime Minister. Crowds of supporters thronged
the route of his train journey from Rawalpindi back to Lahore. Sheikh
Rashid beat the drum of Punjabi chauvinism, declaring: 'The people
of the Punjab had been genuinely hurt and they have reason to

believe that this act has been against their province.'[1] Nawaz Sharif was transformed overnight from a 'cowardly businessman' to a 'fighter politician'. The PML(N), once regarded as a 'King's party' confection of the President and Army chiefs, was also established as a genuine political force in the public mind.

On 19 April Nawaz Sharif filed a petition against the dismissal of his government.[2] The Supreme Court some twenty-one days later historically reversed the trend of the courts[3] siding with executive authority by declaring in a 10-1 verdict that the dissolution was 'not within the ambit of powers conferred' on the President by the constitution.[4] The Government and National Assembly were reinstated. The decision sent shock waves through the political establishment.

Nawaz Sharif may have struck a blow for democracy, but the position of the reinstated Prime Minister was much weaker than it had been before 18 April. The rug had been pulled from under his feet in the Punjab with the installation of a PML(J) coalition ministry under the leadership of the former Speaker, Mian Manzoor Wattoo. Nawaz Sharif once again successfully turned to the courts and secured a ruling from the Punjab High Court on 26 June which restored the Punjab Assembly. The President, supported by Acting Chief Minister Wattoo, responded by instantaneously dissolving it. The constitutional crisis intensified when, during a joint parliamentary session boycotted by the opposition, the Prime Minister responded by passing a proclamation under Article 234 which brought Punjab under federal rule. He then appointed a fresh Governor and Chief Secretary. Ghulam Ishaq Khan supported Wattoo's contention that the proclamation was 'null and void' as he had not approved or signed it. This in effect left two parallel governments operating in Punjab with all the potential this carried for anarchy and bloodshed. The struggle between President and Prime Minister for control of the province could not have illustrated more graphically the region's crucial position in Pakistani political life. From the time that Liaquat set up shop on the eve of the 1951 provincial elections, the region had been the fulcrum of Pakistani politics. Ghulam Ishaq Khan's and Nawaz Sharif's turf wars invariably alarmed the Pakistan Army, which shared the same power-base. In less trying economic and diplomatic times Martial Law would have resulted.

---

[1] *Herald*, May 1993.

[2] The National Assembly Speaker Gohar Ayub had earlier challenged the dissolution in the Lahore High Court.

[3] Indeed six of the judges in the 1990 Tariq Rahim case had upheld the President's earlier dissolution of the Bhutto government.

[4] S. Yasmeen, 'Democracy in Pakistan: The Third Dismissal', *Asian Survey* 34, no. 6, p. 581.

The men in khaki did not however want to assume responsibility for a plummeting economy, the aftermath of devastating floods and political instability. Nor did they wish to alienate US opinion further at a time when relations with Washington had reached a nadir and when, in the wake of the 6 December 1992 destruction of Ayodhya's Babri Masjid and the Kashmir *'intifada'*, Indo-Pakistan hostility was at boiling-point.[5] Although Nawaz Sharif could still count on the support of the former ISI chief General Hameed Gul, pressure on him mounted following an emergency meeting of the Corps Commanders on 1 July.[6] The Army's 'formula' for resolving the crisis at first appeared to be the calling of mid-term elections. On 18 July however the Chief of Army Staff General Abdul Waheed brokered an unprecedented deal in which both Ghulam Ishaq Khan and Nawaz Sharif stepped down. The Senate Chairman Wasim Sajjad was appointed as acting President and Moeen Qureshi became the second caretaker Prime Minister of 1993. His administration however was to be very different to that of the thirty-eight-day tenure of Balkh Sher Mazari.

Rule by the IMF?

How many Prime Ministers at their first press conference have had to insist that they never relinquished their national passport or held one from a foreign country?[7] It had certainly never happened before even in Pakistan's turbulent history. But then there have not been many Prime Ministers without prior political involvement and who, like Moeen Qureshi, had spent over a quarter of a century working abroad. He was far more at home in English than in Urdu, and used it in his national radio and television addresses. It was therefore not surprising that the former Vice-President of the World Bank was unable to rebut convincingly the charge that he was 'an imported Prime Minister'. His ministers shared two things in common, first a lack of political involvement and ambition and secondly expertise in the fields of business.[8]

---

5 Communal tension arose increased dramatically throughout the subcontinent in the wake of the mosque's destruction in December 1992. The Indian Government blamed the ISI for the subsequent bomb blasts in Bombay on 12 March 1993. Tensions also continued over the Kashmir insurgency and both countries deployed troops along the border. India continuously claimed that Pakistan was waging a proxy war in Kashmir.

6 Zaffar Abbas, 'Enter the Army', *Herald*, July 1993, pp. 19ff.

7 A legal case was in fact brought in Multan to establish that Moeen Qureshi could not be appointed Prime Minister because he was not a Pakistani citizen.

8 The Finance Minister was a leading industrialist and the Information Minister was the Pakistan head of IBM.

Qureshi had been accepted as a compromise caretaker leader by both Nawaz Sharif and Benazir Bhutto. However, it was clear from the outset that his primary role was not to oversee fresh elections, but rather to introduce major economic reforms under cover of army support. The professional politicians were prepared to accept this turn of events as it absolved them from the responsibility for unpopular measures.

As befitted his career background, Qureshi sought to apply the kind of economic policies which form part of the standard structural adjustment package which the World Bank and IMF have prescribed for failing Third World economies. The economic reforms which he drew up, assisted by the US-based economist Shahid Javed Burki, were designed to restore Pakistan's credibility with Western lending agencies in order to secure further IMF and World Bank financial flows. They included the establishment of operational autonomy for the State Bank of Pakistan, the introduction of a long-awaited agricultural income tax, a 6 per cent devaluation of the rupee and the removal of subsidies on such items as fertilisers, flour and *ghee*. The policies were designed to boost exports and start bringing the huge budgetary deficit under control. The resulting price rises were of course deeply unpopular. The JI, which had reconstituted itself as the Pakistan Islamic Front (PIF), led the protests, including a successful strike which paralysed Karachi on 18 September.[9] Even those politicians who acknowledged the gravity of the economic situation questioned whether a caretaker administration possessed the mandate for such far-reaching reforms.

Moeen Qureshi's most controversial and dramatic action was the release on 27 August of a list of over 5,000 bank loan defaulters and beneficiaries of loan write-offs.[10] Publication was made possible by the removal of the secrecy clause in the 1974 Banking Nationalisation Act. The World Bank had been calling for disclosure ever since a December 1987 mission, but this had proved politically impossible for successive governments. The enormity of the loan defaults and write-offs can be seen in that a total of some Rs.62 billion was involved. This massive amount of bad loans deterred prospects of overseas investment and undermined the domestic banking system. The list of defaulters read like a political and industrial *Who's Who*[11] and indicated political and bureaucratic interference on a massive scale regarding banking operations. Legal loopholes and lack of professional banking expertise ensured

---

[9] For further details on the Moeen Qureshi caretaker administration and its critics see Z. Abbas, 'Moeen Qureshi and Associates', *Herald*, September 1993, pp. 22ff.

[10] He also prepared a list, apparently with CIA help, which disclosed the names of a number of prominent politicians who had been involved in drug dealing.

[11] See M. Sahibuddin Ghausi, 'The Great Bank Robbery', *Herald*, September 1993 pp. 28ff.

that there was no check on the culture of patronage and easy access to bank loans for the well-connected.

While it was clear that incoming elected politicians would accept some of the reforms as a *fait accompli* under constraint of army pressure and the requirements of international lenders, withdrawal of the agricultural income tax was a strong possibility. Moreover, would two months disclosure of loan defaulters change the realities which lay behind the decades-long misuse of the country's banking system?

The 1993 elections

Muhammad Waseem[12] has provided the most comprehensive study of the National Assembly and Provincial Assembly polls which took place on 6 and 8 October respectively. He not only interprets the results and uncovers the dynamics of the campaign, but provides a good historical background to the contemporary electoral process. Parallels can be seen with earlier elections in the role of the *biraderi* in mobilising voters,[13] the importance of local political influence compared to party organisation and manifestos, especially in the smaller Provincial Assembly constituencies,[14] and the poor electoral showing of the Islamic parties' rival PIF, IJM and MQM alliances[15] which, despite fielding just under 200 National Assembly candidates between them, captured only nine seats.[16] Internal dissension, sectarian rivalries and their reputation as 'Martial Law's B Team' all contributed to their unpopularity outside their narrow lower-middle-class support-base. Just as the ethnic-based MQM had earlier pushed the JI out of urban Sind, so there was evidence of the JUI(F)'s traditional hold in the Pushtun-dominated areas of Balochistan being wrested from it by the ethnic PKMP. The results in Balochistan once again revealed the regional character of its politics, with the Jamhoori Watan Party and PKMAP[17] confined respectively to the Baloch and Pushtun ethnic areas. Weak party institutionalisation was also evidenced by the presence of ten parties and nine independents in its Provincial Assembly.[18]

In the absence of the restoration of women's reserved seats, female

---

12 Waseem, *The 1993 Elections in Pakistan.*

13 *Ibid.*, pp. 141-2

14 Independents were elected for example in 17 out of 240 Punjab Assembly seats.

15 See Waseem, *The 1993 Elections in Pakistan*, pp. 90-3, 105-7, 112-13, 175-9, 233-5.

16 The JI-led PIF achieved its best performance in the Frontier. Even here it won only 10 per cent of the vote, despite its long-term commitment to the Afghan *jihad.*

17 Details on these parties can be found in the Appendix.

18 Waseem, *The 1993 Elections in Pakistan*, p. 180.

candidates for both National and Provincial Assembly seats, with the notable exception of the MQM's Feroza Begum, were restricted to a handful of elite family members.[19] Another continuity was present in the PPP's dominance in rural Sindh where it won twenty-six National Assembly seats, despite the inroads of the PML(N)which won over a quarter of the rural votes and the distraction provided by the emergence of the still exiled Murtaza Bhutto on the electoral scene.[20]

Table 11.1 sets out the national results. The MQM(A)'s decision to boycott the national polls provided a bonus of six seats for both the PML(N) and PPP, although it triumphantly contested the Sindh

Table 11.1.
NATIONAL ASSEMBLY ELECTION RESULTS, 1993

Party	% of total votes	Punjab	Sindh	NWFP	Balch	Islbd	FATA	Total
PPP	38.1	47	33	5	1	–	–	86
PML(N)	39.7	52	10	10	–	1	–	73
PML(J)	n.a.	6	--	--	–	–	–	6
PIF	3.1	–	1	2	–	–	–	3
ANP	1.7	–	–	3	–	–	–	3
Other	8.8	2	1	4	9	–	–	16
Indep.	7.4	5	1	1	1	–	7	15
Total		112	6	25	11	1	7	202

Source: Adapted from 'People's Verdict', *Newsline* October 1993, and *Dawn*, 8 October 1993

provincial elections, pushing the MQM(H) to one side. In contrast to 1990, charges of rigging were muted. Indeed the elections were acknowledged as being the fairest since 1988, despite the continuing deficiencies in the voters' lists.[21]

Once again Punjab held the key to national power, although there were striking regional voting variations. Nawaz Sharif's Muslim League increased its influence in the more developed central areas of the Lahore, Gujranwala and Faisalabad divisions and in the Rawalpindi division which contained the major army recruitment areas of north-west Punjab. The PPP power-base was in the more 'feudal' southern regions of the Multan and Bahawalpur divisions. The rural-urban divide was

[19] *Ibid.*, p. 144.

[20] *Ibid*, pp. 173-4. See Appendix for biographical details. He was regarded by Benazir Bhutto as a challenger for her father's charisma, although Nusrat Bhutto campaigned enthusiastically for her exiled son. In the event, Murtaza captured a Provincial Assembly seat as an independent, although he failed in three National Assembly constituencies

[21] *Ibid.*, pp. 147-51.

most strikingly demonstrated by the PPP's failure to capture a single seat in the Punjab's seven largest cities;[22] in fact it won just four out of thirty-seven urban seats. This contrasted dramatically with its performance in 1970, when it had been the victor in the urban areas and more 'developed' rural regions. Poor organisation and the absence of a Punjabi leadership figure to match Nawaz Sharif, despite the re-entry once more into its ranks of the redoubtable Ghulam Mustafa Khar, partly explain the PPP's weak showing in its former Punjabi heartlands. Growing urban prosperity since 1970 has undoubtedly increased the Muslim League's constituency. It has also cut into the PPP's traditional lower-class vote banks,[23] in part because of poor PPP policy implementation. Moreover, Nawaz Sharif's Yellow Taxi scheme was immensely popular and, as Muhammad Waseem has revealed, the PML(N) vote also grew in the villages and towns whose economic activity had increased with the much-vaunted construction of the Lahore-Islamabad motorway.[24] The PPP-PML(N) tussle in the Punjab squeezed out other parties with the exception of the PML(J), which captured six seats in the national polls and eighteen in the Provincial Assembly elections. Its support enabled the PPP to form a coalition government in the province, although its activists were increasingly angered by the extent to which the PML(J) tail of Manzoor Wattoo wagged the PPP dog.

Benazir Bhutto's second administration, 1993-96

Despite worrying electoral trends in both Punjab and Sindh, Benazir Bhutto took office in a much stronger position after the 1993 elections than she had done five years earlier. Her position in the National Assembly was bolstered by control of the most important province, Punjab. Moreover, in the presidential election of 13 November her close confidant and PPP loyalist, the nominee Foreign Minister Farooq Leghari, had trounced the PML(N) candidate, Acting President Wasim Sajjad, by 274 to 168 votes.[25] Ironically in the light of subsequent

[22] These are Lahore, Faisalabad, Rawalpindi, Multan, Gujranwala, Sialkot and Sargodha.

[23] A. R. Wilder, 'Changing Patterns of Punjab Politics in Pakistan: National Assembly Election Results, 1988 and 1993', *Asian Survey* 35, no. 4 (April 1995), p. 383.

[24] Waseem, *The 1993 Elections in Pakistan*, pp. 168-9.

[25] Leghari had not been the PPP's automatic candidate, nor was a PPP victory guaranteed given the PML(N) support in the Senate which comprised 87 out of 476 electoral college votes in a Presidential election. The remaining votes were divided between the National Assembly (217) and the four Provincial Assemblies which had 43 votes each. For further details of the Presidential election see Waseem, *The 1993 Elections in Pakistan*, pp. 191-204.

events, Asif Ali Zardari had lobbied vigorously for Leghari as the 'Mr Clean' candidate for President. Leghari promised that he would be 'neutral and non-interventionist' when elected, and it thus seemed likely that Benazir Bhutto might become the first Prime Minister since 1985 to see through a full term in office. Within three years, however, Leghari had dismissed her amid bitter recriminations, paving the way for Nawaz Sharif's eventual return to power. Where had it all gone wrong? Why did the 'political' President use his powers under the Eighth Amendment with the same impunity as his bureaucratic predecessor, Ghulam Ishaq Khan?

There are strong parallels between Benazir Bhutto's two tenures of office. Parliament continued to have little standing as a law-making body, with most bills being enacted through presidential ordinance.[26] As in the period 1988-90, foreign policy successes were overshadowed by mounting mayhem in Karachi and debilitating confrontation with the Nawaz Sharif-led opposition. While the Army and presidential strait-jacket had loosened a little during the second tenure, the constraints imposed by the IMF's conditions had tightened. Debt repayments and sacrosanct military expenditure conspired to place the burden of reducing the budget deficit on both consumers and business groups. The resulting unpopularity could not be alleviated by rewarding lower-class PPP supporters with long-awaited reforms because of the budgetary constraints. Unemployment caused by privatisation policies hit organised labour, which had formed another traditional PPP vote-bank. Party activists who had suffered at the military's hands during the Zia era were also disquieted by Benazir's penchant for appointing ex-officers as Governors, a good case in point being the elevation of one of Zia's associates, retired Lieutenant-General (retd.) Raja Muhammad Saroop Khan, as Governor of Punjab in June 1995. Finally, weak party institutionalisation and the 'death of ideology' forced the PPP to rely brazenly on patronage to sustain itself in power. It was less practised at this art than the PML(N), and by adopting this approach inevitably laid itself open to corruption charges.

A short-term response to the question of why the Bhutto administration was dismissed would focus on such issues as the deteriorating relations between Prime Minister and President in the wake of Murtaza Bhutto's killing; alleged charges of corruption and extra-judicial killings in Karachi; economic mismanagement; and massive corruption leading to financial ruin. A number of Pakistan's long-term post-independence dilemmas were writ large during the Bhutto administration. The religious

---

[26] Over 200 ordinances were promulgated during the three years of the Bhutto administration.

parties' electoral débâcle, rather than closing the issue of Islam's role in politics, led it to take on the dangerous forms of insurrection and military adventurism. Sectarian conflict intensified both in Karachi and parts of Punjab. The centre's long-established tendency to treat ethnic mobilisation as a law and order rather than a political issue resulted in a mini-civil war raging in Karachi. The counter insurgency measures which quelled the violence further brutalised the state. It also reduced respect for the rule of law, as did the Government's long-running dispute with the judges over the age-old issue of their independence from the executive.

Foreign policy

Benazir Bhutto's 'charm offensive' ensured an improvement in relations with the United States, which had been further jeopardised by Nawaz Sharif's statement of 23 August 1994 that Pakistan possessed nuclear weapons. To many this was the major achievement of her government. There was no breakthrough in Indo-Pakistan relations, which alone held the key to a reduction in military expenditure and to improved trade relations, both of which would be of immense benefit to the majority of Pakistan's population.

Benazir Bhutto was at her most effective when addressing Western audiences. She projected an image of Pakistan as a moderate Islamic state, open for business and willing to assist the West in its international struggle against drugs and terrorism. Diplomacy was linked to the encouragement of foreign investment, and considerable progress was made in this, especially in the energy sector following the visit to Pakistan of US Energy Secretary Hazel O'Leary in October 1994.[27]

By far the most important overseas journey by Benazir Bhutto was the one she made to Washington at cherry blossom time in April 1995.[28] This followed a pre-visit publicity blitz. A favourable impression had also been created by Pakistani participation in UN peacekeeping activities in Somalia, Haiti and Bosnia and in the extradition of terrorists[29] and drug-traffickers. While the nuclear issue and the continued sanctions under the terms of the Pressler Amendment remained high on the agenda, considerable attention was devoted to investment

[27] A large number of memoranda of understanding amounting to $4 billion were signed with foreign investors in the energy field.

[28] See *Newsline*, April 1995, pp. 24-32.

[29] Ramzi Yusuf, who was wanted by police in connection with the World Trade Centre bombing in New York, was arrested in Islamabad and extradited to the United States shortly before Benazir's visit.

opportunities. Maleeha Lodhi, the extremely able Pakistan Ambassador[30] and assiduous lobbyist, built on the favourable impression created by the visit. Indeed this former journalist was able to run rings round her Indian counterpart Siddhartha Shankar Ray. This bore fruit on 21 September when the Senate voted in favour of the Brown Amendment. This proposed a waiver of the August 1990 Pressler Amendment which had cut off aid and halted arms sales until Pakistan agreed to a verifiable capping of its nuclear programme. Under the terms of the Brown Amendment, over $350 million worth of military equipment would be released which Pakistan had paid for but not received. Equally important, however, was the paving of the way for economic aid to Pakistan, as the Brown Amendment deleted the Pressler Amendment requirements for economic sanctions. President Clinton ratified the Brown Amendment on 27 January 1996.

While Pakistan's relations with the United States had thus improved from the low-point they had reached in 1993, the cold war with India continued. The two countries accused each other of fishing in the troubled waters of Sindh and Kashmir. The Indian consulate in Karachi was closed amid claims that RAW agents were attempting to destabilise the country in retaliation for Pakistani involvement with Kashmiri separatists.[31] Earlier the fire which severely damaged the Parliament building in Islamabad in November 1993 was blamed on RAW agents. However Kashmir continued to be the major obstacle to the normalisation of economic and political relations. Following fruitless talks early in 1994 and continued clashes between the security forces and Kashmiri militants, the Pakistan Government unsuccessfully attempted to move resolutions on Kashmir in the United Nations Human Rights Commission (March 1994) and later in the General Assembly (November). The Casablanca meeting of the OIC did however pass a condemnatory resolution and established an OIC contact group on Kashmir.

Clashes between the Pakistan and Indian armies continued in 1995 along the Line of Control during the usually quiet winter period. On 26 January 1996 two Indian rockets hit a village in Azad Kashmir, killing nineteen people and destroying a mosque. The following day, India provocatively carried out the fifteenth test firing of its 'Pakistan-specific' Prithvi short-range missile.[32] The depth to which relations had plunged is reflected in the fact that on 30 January the Pakistan President

[30] She relinquished her post on 31 January 1997 and was replaced by the Pakistan Ambassador to India, Riaz Khokhar. The government of Meraj Khalid had in fact asked her to stay on another year.

[31] For a comment on this development see I. A. Rehman, 'Unholy Acrimony', *Newsline*, January 1995, pp. 125-6.

[32] *Herald*, February 1996, pp. 70-1.

Farooq Leghari had to reassure the public that there was no possibility of war between the two countries.

On the eve of Benazir Bhutto's dismissal, the outlook for Indo-Pakistan relations remained decidedly uncertain. At the beginning of 1996 Indian and Pakistani forces had exchanged heavy fire along the Line of Control. The election of H.D. Deve Gowda's coalition Government raised hopes of a thaw in relations. India's decision to hold State Assembly polls in Kashmir and its refusal to sign the Comprehensive Test Ban Treaty did nothing to encourage this. The replacement of Gowda in April by his former Foreign Minister, I.K. Gujral, who had grown up in West Punjab before Partition, appeared to open another window of opportunity. The golden jubilee of the subcontinent's independence was also looked to as an opportunity to build bridges. Hopes of a new era were raised by the meeting between the Indian and Pakistani Prime Ministers at the Male (Maldives) SAARC summit. Meetings at Foreign Secretary level in June 1997 identified Kashmir as one of eight outstanding issues in bilateral relations. However, the Indian deployment of medium-range Prithvi missiles in the border areas cast a shadow shortly afterwards, as did the increased shelling along the Kashmir border in late August.

Political problems and confrontations

Murtaza Bhutto returned to Pakistan from his exile in Damascus on 4 November 1993. True to his bravado image, the story circulated that when his plane was first refused permission to land he asked to be provided with a parachute.[33] He was jailed for seven months before being finally released on bail. He received a rapturous welcome from his activists and supporters, but the loyalty he reciprocated to such diehards as Ali Muhammad Sonara[34] was to cost him his life. Murtaza's arrival on the scene sparked off infighting in the PPP as brother and sister sought to 'appropriate' Zulfiqar Ali Bhutto's charisma. He increasingly posed as the guardian of the party's old-time radicalism and gained powerful support from his mother. The breach between Nusrat and Benazir Bhutto was made painfully public when Nusrat was dislodged from her longstanding position as co-chair of the PPP early in December

---

[33] For a colourful portrayal of Mir Murtaza Bhutto's life see Hasan Mujtaba, 'The Eternal Rebel', *Newsline*, October 1996, pp. 39-45.

[34] Sonara came from the Kharadar neighbourhood of Karachi. He was a leading figure in the Al-Zulfiqar Organisation during Murtaza's years of exile. His base was in the Lyari Baloch neighbourhood, although he was a Kacchi Memon. He organised the Shaheed Bhutto Committee of the PPP from 70 Clifton shortly before Murtaza's return from exile.

1993. The following month there was a major clash between Murtaza Bhutto's supporters and the police at the family's Larkana estate.

Murtaza bitterly criticised Asif Ali Zardari's influence over his sister and the PPP. This hostility formed the background to subsequent claims that Zardari was behind Murtaza's death in a hail of bullets during a police encounter outside the new Clifton Gardens in Karachi on the evening of 20 September 1996. Just three days earlier, Ali Muhammad Sonara had been arrested on terrorist charges, and rumours circulated that he and other members of Murtaza's entourage were RAW agents.[35] Murtaza with typical boldness went to great lengths to secure Sonara's release, clashing violently with the local police in the process. On the morning of 20 September he had thrown the Station House Officer, Haq Nawaz Sial, out of his 70 Clifton residence when he came to arrest him. The same officer was a witness to the later shoot-out and apparently committed suicide (his family claim he was murdered) just a week later.

Ghinwa Bhutto, Murtaza's Lebanese-born second wife, filed a petition in the Sindh High Court accusing senior police and intelligence officials of murdering her husband. An emotional Benazir Bhutto claimed that her brother was murdered in a conspiracy aimed at eliminating the Bhutto family, and widened the breach between herself and President Leghari by appearing to implicate him. The court case continued during the electioneering which followed Benazir's dismissal. By this juncture, Nusrat had become reconciled with her daughter and supported Benazir in the struggle with Ghinwa who, on 30 November (the twenty-ninth anniversary of the PPP's foundation), had become chair of the Shaheed Bhutto faction (PPP(SB)) of the party at the famous 70 Clifton residence. The Bhutto family feuds not only made excellent journalistic copy, but undermined the PPP's position in its Sindhi heartland, revealing the extent to which the party had fallen prey to dynastic politics.

Benazir also faced a challenge from another unexpected quarter, the Pakistani hearthrob and former cricket star Imran Khan. As we noted earlier, he had entered the spotlight with his fund-raising campaign for the Shaukat Khanum Memorial Hospital (SKMH). Imran's growing populist support around the theme of political corruption and his born-again Islamist image created growing tensions with the Bhutto Government. It blacked out his appeal for donations for the SKMH from the state-run television network and blocked the contributions it received from *zakat* funds. By the time the opening ceremony of the 1996 Sixth Cricket World Cup began in Eden Gardens, Calcutta, on 11 February,

---

[35] For further details see Zahid Hussain, 'Who Killed Murtaza Bhutto?' *Newsline*, October 1996, pp. 23-30.

Imran, who had captained Pakistan's 1992 winning team, was *persona non grata*. He retaliated by securing international media coverage for the Princess of Wales's visit to his hospital and a fund-raising dinner a couple of weeks later.[36] Only on 25 April, after the unexplained bomb-blast which wrecked the outpatient wing of the cancer hospital, did Imran launch the Tehrik-e-Insaaf (Justice Movement). This was soon touted as an embryo 'third force' in Pakistani politics.

During the autumn of 1994 the confrontation intensified between Benazir Bhutto's government and the main PML(N) opposition party. Its 'train march' from Karachi to Peshawar was followed by a general strike on 20 September and a 'wheel jam' strike on 11 October. Despite the support from the Chambers of Commerce and Industry, who had their own grievances following the introduction of a new general sales tax, the 'Oust Bhutto' campaign rapidly ran out of steam. The conflict next shifted literally to the floor of the National Assembly. On 14 November, the occasion of the presidential address to the joint session of parliament, verbal insults and the unfurling of opposition banners gave way to physical assaults and intimidation. The rowdiness stemmed from the earlier arrest of Nawaz Sharif's elderly father, Mian Muhammad Sharif, on fraud charges. Nevertheless, from the end of 1994 onwards Nawaz Sharif, perhaps because of the growing number of legal cases he faced culminating in a treason charge, displayed a marked reluctance to make a fresh attempt to use street power to topple his rival.

Islamic militancy and sectarianism

The defeat of the religious parties in the 1993 elections was followed by an upsurge of militancy and sectarianism. This was particularly dangerous because of the continued twin backlash effects of the Afghan war – *jihad* mentality and Kalashnikov culture. Rival Sunni and Shia students fought each other with AK-47s in the Parachinar high school in the remote Kurram valley on 10 September 1996, sparking a week-long orgy of violence in the Upper Kurram Agency in which, at the most conservative estimate, 100 people were killed and scores more were wounded.[37] Earlier in November 1994, the Pakistan Government faced an armed Islamic insurrection in the Malakand region of the NWFP. This was led by the black-turbaned Tehrik-e-Nifaz-e-Shariat-e-Mohammadi (TNSM) followers of Maulana Sufi Muhammad. The TNSM had been founded in June 1989, but first came

---

36 *Newsline*, February 1996, pp. 83-5.

37 Amir Ziqa, 'Tribes and Tribulations', *Newsline*, October 1996, pp. 71-5.

to prominence on 11 May 1994 when its followers blocked the Malakand Pass as part of its campaign for the replacement of civil law by the *Shariat*. However, the legal vacuum created by the Supreme Court's declaration that the PATA regulation for the Malakand Division was null and void persisted.

Early in November, the TNSM stepped up its efforts for the enforcement of the *Shariat*. Roads were blocked for five days and TNSM activists took government officials hostage and occupied the Saidu Sharif airport. Amid evidence that the movement had been infiltrated by Afghan militants sponsored by the drug barons from the tribal belt, the Government took firm repressive action, calling on the services of the Frontier Corps at the same time as announcing the enforcement of the *Shariat*. Nevertheless, the deep scars caused by the agitation remained, and after a dispute over the refusal of an activist in Matta to pay 'un-Islamic' land revenue tax, the TNSM resumed its campaign on 18 June 1995. The Government's 'stick and carrot' approach, including the arrest of Maulana Sufi Muhammad, took the steam out of the agitation, although the poverty and underdevelopment of the region which had fuelled the unrest remained.

Fears that armed Islamic militancy might spread from the tribal areas, or even from the Afghan struggle of the ISI-backed student Taliban movement[38] to the plains of Punjab were intensified by such episodes as chanting by mullahs outside the Lahore High Court on 15 May 1994 during the hearing of the petition against the Blasphemy Law death sentence of Salamat and Rehmat Masih. They exhorted the Taliban to come forward to protect Islam in Pakistan, chanting '*Kabul ke baad Islamabad...Taliban, Taliban.*' (After Kabul, Islamabad...Taliban, Taliban).[39] The following October there was a heavily-armed rally by Allama Raza Naqvi Sipah-e-Muhammad Pakistan (SMP) at the Minar-e-Pakistan. The next month its workers attacked the offices of the Islamabad newspaper the *Pakistan Observer*, because of its alleged links with the hated rival Sunni SSP.[40]

In the increasingly anarchic city of Karachi the SMP and SSP fought pitched gun-battles. An assault on the Masjid-e-Akbar on 7 December

---

[38] For a recent restating of the dangers of backing the Taliban from both a strategic and domestic viewpoint see M.B. Naqvi, 'Creating a Monster', *Newsline*, Annual Issue 1996, pp. 115-16.

[39] For details on the Taliban and this incident see, Z. Hussain, 'Islamic Warriors', *Newsline*, February 1995, pp. 22ff.

[40] For details of this episode and the emergence in 1994 of the SMP with its heavily armed headquarters at Thokar Niaz Beg, a small town outside Lahore, see M. Zaidi, 'The Shias Strike Back', *Newsline*, February 1995, pp. 50ff.

1994 left eight dead including the city chief of the militant SSP.[41] Sectarian clashes also occurred in the Jhang district of Punjab. It was to this background that Major-General Zaheerul Islam Abbassi, Brigadier Mustansar Billah, Colonel Muhammad Azad Minhas and Colonel Innayatullah Khan plotted a coup attempt, which was to be accompanied by the declaration of Pakistan as a Sunni Islamic state. The conspirators along with some other junior officers had secured weapons from the tribal areas and planned to storm a commander's meeting on 30 September.[42] The conspiracy did not appear to have wide support within the Army and was significantly uncovered shortly before the retirement of the Chief of Army Staff General Abdul Waheed, who had established a reputation for non-intervention and professionalism. In keeping with this, he refused the Government's entreaties to extend his tenure on completing his term and handed over to General Jehangir Karamat in January.

Islamic militancy was paraded before an international audience, not only by the failed coup attempt but by the celebrated Salamat Masih and Rehmat Masih blasphemy trial[43] to which we have already referred. Its notoriety intensified when another of the accused, Manzoor Masih, was gunned down in Lahore on 5 April 1994 immediately after appearing at the trial. The vocal opposition of the mullahs prevented limited reforms of the Blasphemy Law despite its exploitation to settle grudges or to intimidate upwardly mobile members of minority communities.[44] For similar reasons the PPP's electoral promise of a review of the *Hudood* Ordinances had not been acted upon. The danger that the political battles being waged by Islamist groups in the Middle East might spill over into Pakistan was brought home by the suicide bomb attack on the Egyptian Embassy in Islamabad on 19 November, in which eighteen people were killed and sixteen injured.[45] Early investigations pinned the responsibility on the Al Jehad organisation which has been locked in a fierce struggle against the Mubarak regime. In the wake of the New York World Trade Centre bombing in 1992, Pakistan had already begun a crackdown on Islamist groups based in the country, many of whose members were veterans of the Afghan war.

41 *Newsline*, March 1995 p. 24.

42 *Herald*, Annual Issue, January 1996, p. 89.

43 See Aziz Siddiqui, 'The Law of the Mullah', *Newsline*, February 1995, p. 60 and ff.

44 See Aftab Alexander Mughal, 'Abused Law', *Newsline*, Annual Issue 1997, p. 120.

45 See Zahid Hussain, 'Wages of Terror', *Newsline*, December 1995, pp. 71-3.

Civil war in Karachi

Pakistan's post-1988 democracy faced its gravest crisis in the deteriorating law and order situation in Karachi. Any hopes of a reconciliation between the MQM(A) (Altaf Hussain Pachhou) and the PPP were dashed in April 1994 when MQM protesters at the Teen Hatti Bridge, dividing central and eastern Karachi, were fired on. As the present author personally witnessed, the violence in Karachi increased dramatically in the wake of the Army's hasty retreat early in December from a futile two-year operation in the city. In its first two weeks alone, there were over 100 deaths including the assassination outside his office of Muhammad Salahuddin, editor of the influential Urdu weekly *Takbeer* (Greatness). Also at this time the renowned social worker Abdul Sattar Edhi fled the country for London in mysterious circumstances.

The rumour factory worked overtime in the absence of clear responsibility for the violence. Much of the mayhem resulted from the clashes between the rival MQM factions of Altaf Hussain and Afaq Ahmed MQM(H) in Shah Faisal Colony, Korangi, Landhi and Pak Colony, among other localities. Sectarian violence also added to the death-toll. There were also claims of Indian involvement and of conflict arising from rivalries between Pakistani intelligence agencies.

There was little respite for the city during the opening months of 1995. In February a fresh wave of sectarian violence saw attacks on mosques and *imambaras*.[46] Twenty-five people were killed by unknown assailants in two incidents on 25 February alone. The next month, world attention was directed to the city following the killing in broad daylight on 8 March of two US consular officials when their van was ambushed by unidentified armed gunmen in one of Karachi's busiest roads, Shahrah-e-Faisal.[47] The ensuing security crackdown reduced the number of deaths as a result of acts of violence in April to just twenty-one. This was only a temporary respite: violence erupted again on 18 May with a day-long pitched battle between the security forces and the MQM(A) militants in North Nazimabad. In the week which followed there were repeated clashes in which more than seventy people were killed. The writ of the Government had collapsed in large areas of central, eastern and western Karachi.[48]

Some of the bloodiest fighting Karachi had ever witnessed between MQM factions and the security forces followed the claims on 22 June that a sixteen-year-old *mohajir* girl, Farzana Sultan, had been gang-raped

---

[46] The 25 February massacre at the Mehfil-e-Murtaza complex for example claimed sixteen lives.

[47] See Zahid Hussain, 'Murder in the Morning', *Newsline*, March 1995, pp.57ff.

[48] For details see *Newsline*, May 1995, pp. 22-30.

by PPP and Haqiqi activists.[49] Rocket-launchers were fired at the Pakistan Television Station and Liaqatabad police station, cars carrying government number-plates were attacked, and police and rangers' armoured cars were ambushed. The MQM(A) had the upper hand in what amounted to an insurgency until the end of June, after which concerted action by the security forces, involving extra-judicial means, made inroads into the militant strongholds of Orangi, Korangi and Gulbahar. The clearest evidence of the turning tide of battle was provided during the first week of August when the notorious militant Farooq Dada died in an encounter with the police near Karachi's Quaid-e-Azam international airport.

The May-June MQM campaign against government officials and the security forces, and the latter's sense of operating in 'foreign' territory, were dangerously reminiscent of events in East Bengal in 1970-1. The almost total alienation of the *mohajir* population from both the provincial Government of Chief Minister Abdullah Shah and the federal authorities was rooted in the excesses of law and order enforcement during Operation Clean-up. This was compounded by their lack of a political voice in the administration of the city following the Sindh Government's refusal to call elections for local bodies. An almost unbridgeable chasm existed between the political interests of rural and urban Sindh, and this lay at the heart of the failure to achieve dialogue between the PPP and the MQM(A). Yet this was essential both to restore peace to the city and to remove the wider threat its violence posed to the country's economic life and national unity. There was a flight of domestic capital to Punjab, while foreign investment dried up in the wake of the violence in Pakistan's leading commercial centre. During the first three months of 1995 alone, Rs.102 billion of market capitalisation was wiped off the Karachi stock exchange.[50]

The PPP leadership in Sindh continued to oppose dialogue with a 'terrorist' organisation. Karachi's problems were to be solved by time-honoured 'law and order' rather than political methods. Following the assassination of the American Consulate staff, the Army behind the scenes and the President more openly began to support the idea of a negotiated settlement,[51] and early in July the MQM(A) shifted its own hard-line attitude. The weekly two-day strike call was cancelled and talks tentatively began in the National Assembly building in Islamabad. This change of heart stemmed partly from the growing success

---

[49] See Muhammad Hanif, 'Dead End?', *Newsline*, pp. 24-34.

[50] It was also estimated that every one-day strike in the city cost the country a billion rupees in terms of revenue. See *Newsline*, March 1995, p. 95.

[51] See *Newsline*, July 1995, p. 26.

of government 'counter-terrorist' activities, personally directed by the Interior Minister Naseerullah Babar. It was also prompted by the way in which the PML(N) and other opposition parties had distanced themselves from the MQM following the launching of its May insurgency. Little progress was made however, as both sides raised their conflicting 21-Point and 18-Point 'charge sheets'.[52] The dialogue had not advanced beyond the abortive 10-point agreement of 19 October 1994 between the MQM(A) and the Sindh Government. It was clear by August that although the Government had achieved some success in breaking the networks of MQM(A) militants, the MQM's grassroots public support remained intact.

Karachi's violence thus continued unabated during the second half of 1995 – the body count between late August and early November alone stood at 500. In one especially gory incident, fifteen Saraiki-speaking labourers were murdered in cold blood. In December Nasir Hussain, the elder brother of Altaf Hussain, was kidnapped and murdered by unknown assailants. Two weeks later, Syed Ahsan Shah, the Sindh Chief Minister's brother, was killed in Karachi's Federal B area. These prominent deaths however marked the beginning of a return to relative normality rather than a fresh spiral of violence. The new atmosphere was most evident during the following spring, at the time of Ramadan and the Sixth Cricket World Cup fixtures which were held in the city shortly afterwards.

As had happened earlier in the Indian state of Punjab, counter-insurgency measures eliminated the 'terrorist' threat. Eleven police 'encounters' took place in January alone, resulting in the deaths of twenty-three MQM activists or sympathisers.[53] Such leading 'terrorists' as Naeem Sharri and Fahim Commando died in what appeared to be 'fake' encounters with the police, who along with the rangers seemed to have been given a free hand in dealing with the militants. In the absence of a meaningful political dialogue, however, the root of the disorder remained unchecked. Moreover, extra-judicial killings not only claimed their innocent victims, but further encouraged the brutalisation of Pakistani society.

Punjab

Punjab had proved the thorn in the flesh of the first Bhutto administration. In order to avoid a repetition, the PPP entered into a coalition provincial government with the PML(J) headed by Manzoor Ahmad Wattoo. By

---

[52] See A. Siddiqui, 'Sparring with the Enemy', *Newsline*, July 1995, pp. 29-30.

[53] *Herald*, February 1996, p. 74.

the summer of 1995, however, the Chief Minister was resented not only by the dominant PPP partners in the coalition, but by his own party members, as he attempted to turn the administrative services into his own personal preserve. He outmanoeuvred the PPP loyalist Faisal Saleh Hayat, who had been despatched as his 'minder' and principal adviser to secure almost a free hand in running the Punjab. In keeping with the pattern established by Nawaz Sharif, he ensured that development work was carried out exclusively in his own and his allies' constituencies. Open conflict surfaced in June following the death of the Governor Altaf Hussain who had collaborated closely with the PML(J) Chief Minister. Wattoo established 'back door' contacts with the PML(N), despite the fact that he had betrayed Nawaz Sharif during his 1993 tussle with Ghulam Ishaq Khan. The PPP for its part planned a no-confidence resolution against him with the support of such PML(J) rebels as Manzoor Ahmad Mohal.[54] Fearing the effect that a crisis in the Punjab would have on her power at the centre, Benazir Bhutto temporarily backed down, although it was clear to observers that Wattoo was living on borrowed time.

The political manoeuvring in Lahore which followed the Governor's dismissal of Wattoo under Article 234 for 'corruption, nepotism and violation of the PPP-PML(J) manifesto' could have either alienated the PPP's own supporters, or opened the way for a reunification of the Muslim League under Nawaz Sharif's leadership. In the event, Benazir Bhutto's personal intervention ensured the installation on 13 September of a PPP-PML(J) coalition under the much weaker figure of Sardar Arif Nakai, with the PPP now in the dominant position.[55] The matter did not however rest there: Wattoo lodged an appeal with the Lahore High Court, and Benazir Bhutto hurried to Lahore in the middle of July on a damage limitation visit. The Wattoo case remained unresolved, a constant threat to the coalition government in Lahore.

The fall from grace

The immediate background to Benazir Bhutto's dismissal was the mounting economic crisis, her clash with the judiciary, and deteriorating personal relations with Farooq Leghari. Economic storm-clouds had been gathering from the end of 1995 onwards. In addition to the longer-term problems of a narrow tax-base, low investment in human capital and political intervention in the commercial activities of publicly-owned

---

54 *Newsline*, July 1995, p. 25.

55 See M. Zaidi, 'Punjab's Political Opera', *Newsline*, September 1995, pp. 25-31.

banks and other financial institutions, the strife in Karachi had depressed both investment and production levels. Investment was further discouraged by the publication of the Berlin-based Transparency International's report, which ranked Pakistan as the second-most corrupt country in the world.[56] The financial crunch which really shook the Government came with the stalling of the privatisation programme and the increasing reluctance of the IMF to provide assistance. Hopes that the sale of state-owned assets would raise over Rs.40 billion foundered on the charges of corruption and lack of transparency which accompanied the sale of United Bank Ltd in April 1996.[57] Thereafter privatisation stalled, and the impending sale of 26 per cent of Pakistan Telecommunications was postponed indefinitely.[58] The inability of the Government to meet IMF requirements for tariff levels and the 4.5 per cent GDP budget deficit target, and its unilateral modification of these following the 'mild' June 1995 Budget, meant that it had to rely on a $600 million emergency standby loan rather than qualify for the 'cheap money' of an Enhanced Structural Adjustment Facility. Even this was withheld when IMF board members found evidence of fund shifting from state corporations to the State Bank of Pakistan in a bid to make bank lending to the Government appear to fall within IMF targets.[59]

The deteriorating situation was seen most dramatically in the fall of foreign exchange reserves. In addition to resorting to short-term loans at high interest rates, the Bhutto Government responded by raising taxes and devaluing the rupee by 7 per cent in an October mini-Budget in a bid to boost exports.[60] These measures were inevitably unpopular and did not address the underlying economic problems. The 13 June 1996 Budget was especially harsh in its efforts to bring the swollen deficit under control. This was caused by the still spiralling defence expenditure which was up 14 per cent on the previous year and reached Rs.131.4 billion. There was also the crushing burden of debt servicing. Political protests focused on both the extent of the new taxes (Rs.40.8 billion) and the fact that in the absence of effective agricultural taxation, the burden would be inequitably shared. As far as the man in the street was concerned, the higher General Sales Tax was seen as further adding

[56] *Far Eastern Economic Review* 159, no. 26 (27 June 1996,), p. 66.

[57] The group cleared to bid for the 26 per cent stake in UBL had claimed to be a Saudi-based company, but was found to be a front for a local group when it sought to raise the first installment of Rs. 300 million from a Hyderabad branch of the Muslim Commercial Bank.

[58] *Far Eastern Economic Review*, p. 67.

[59] Zahid Hussain, 'Juggling to Survive', *Newsline*, April 1996 p. 81.

[60] For details see Zahid Hussain, 'The Economic Squeeze', *Newsline*, November 1995, pp. 22-7.

to the cost of living. The task of appeasing both the IMF and domestic opinion appeared impossible. Benazir's meeting with the deputy managing director of the IMF, Stanley Fischer, on 3 October during a visit to New York to address the United Nations General Assembly failed to soften the IMF stance significantly. The Cabinet, faced by dwindling foreign exchange reserves, agreed a week later to implement the IMF's conditions designed to cut the budget deficit in order to receive the third tranche of the standby loan ($80 million) which had been refused. The imposition of fresh taxes appeared suicidal, however, in the light of the earlier public discontent.

Anti-budget demonstrations had been held in Islamabad and Rawalpindi on 24 June, in which three JI protesters were shot dead by the police. The Jamaat's leader Qazi Hussain Ahmed stood apart from the sixteen-party opposition alliance which was formed in July, but the JI did join the MQM and seven other parties in a strike called in Sindh on 21 July. This formed part of a wave of mounting protests in which the broad opposition alliance, led once again by the veteran of such groupings, Nawabzada Nasrullah Khan, was handicapped by its lack of ideological coherence and its appearance of responding to, rather than leading events.

The volatile political situation was intensified by a large bomb explosion at Lahore airport. This came at the end of a seven-month period in which more than eighty people had died in mysterious bombings in Pakistan's most populous province.[61] Lahore was to be rocked during the 1997 election campaign by an explosion at the district and sessions court which claimed nineteen lives. This apparently sectarian incident cost the life of the SSP chief Maulana Zia-ur-Rehman. It was soon followed by an attack on the Iranian Culture Centre,[62] after which the former Ambassador to the United States, Syeda Abida Hussain, claimed that Saudi Arabia and Iran were fighting their 'proxy war' by whipping up sectarian violence in Pakistan.[63] The danger of a recrudescence of violence in Karachi was brought home by the death of twelve SSP activists when unidentified gunmen opened fire on an Independence Day rally at Jamshed Road.

This gloomy situation coincided with a damaging stand-off between the Government and the judiciary. On 20 March 1996 the Supreme Court upheld the challenge mounted by the Rawalpindi lawyer Habib Wahabul Khairi to the PPP's legal appointments, in particular the appointment to the Lahore High Court of three female judges who lacked

61 *Newsline*, August 1996, p. 26.

62 *Dawn* (Internet Edition), 20 January 1997.

63 *Ibid.*, 2 March 1997.

the required ten years' High Court experience and who, in violation of the Constitution, had been recommended by the Government rather than the Lahore Chief Justice. Further controversy arose from the Government's appointment of Justices Ilyas, Munir and Hazar Khan Khoso as additional judges of the Supreme Court. The Supreme Court had agreed to hear Khairi's petition challenging the appointments and transfers of judges by the Bhutto Government on 5 November – a year to the day before Benazir's eventual dismissal. The ensuing attempts to pressurise the Supreme Court Chief Justice Syed Ali Shah through the intimidation of his son-in-law Pervaiz Shah caused immense damage to the Bhutto administration's image.[64]

The 20 March judgement[65] led to the dismissal of twenty High Court judges while also setting aside the constitutional amendment imposed by General Zia which allowed the transfer of High Court judges to the Federal Shariat Court without their consent. The Government refused to implement the Supreme Court orders, and lawyers in both Karachi and Lahore boycotted the PPP *ad hoc* judges in a move which further politicised the issue. The stand-off damaged the previously harmonious relations between the Prime Minister and the President, Farooq Leghari, and the question was raised for the first time publicly whether he would use his constitutional powers to move against the Government.[66] On 21 September the President filed a reference in the Supreme Court designed to expedite the 20 March judgement concerning the power to appoint judges to the superior courts. Less than a week later he met Nawaz Sharif for the first time since he had assumed the Presidency, and their five hours of discussions concluded with a statement in which Leghari significantly mentioned Article 52b under the Eighth Amendment of the Constitution which allowed the President to dismiss the Government. The same day Benazir addressed Murtaza's mourners and linked Leghari's moves with her brother's killing. The following day slogans appeared on buildings in Lahore accusing the President of Murtaza's murder.[67] This was a fateful development and precipitated the demise of the government.

Benazir Bhutto responded to the mounting political crisis by addressing large rallies in the Orangi district of Karachi and in a number of Punjabi towns. She also sought to shore up her position further by expanding the Federal Cabinet. The inclusion of her husband only

---

[64] See Zahid Hussain, 'The Government vs The Judiciary', *Newsline*, January 1996, pp. 16-27.

[65] For details see *Newsline*, March 1996, pp. 49ff.

[66] See Zahid Hussain, 'The President's Dilemma', *Newsline*, August 1996, pp. 22-9.

[67] Zahid Hussain, 'The President Also Rises', *Newsline*, October 1996, p. 49.

generated further controversy, as did the appointment of Haji Nawaz Khokhar as Minister of Science and Technology. The latter politician possessed a reputation for unscrupulous behaviour and had been arrested in 1995 on charges of loan default.

Punjab again proved the nemesis of the Bhutto regime. The Lahore Court precipitated a crisis by restoring Wattoo on 3 November to the post of Chief Minister and declaring Arif Nakai's government illegal. Asif Ali Zardari went to Lahore, allegedly to indulge in horse-trading on a grand scale as the PPP and its PML(J) ally mounted a no-confidence vote against Wattoo. In order to forestall this, the President finally decided to strike, secure in the knowledge that the Army supported his action. It appears both that the action was agreed upon hastily and that Benazir Bhutto was taken totally by surprise when she was notified of her dismissal.[68] Significantly this took place on the eve of the US presidential election when Washington's full attention was directed to domestic matters.

The caretakers

The caretaker administration headed by the octogenarian former PPP stalwart Meraj Khalid appeared a strange mixture of both its 1993 Mazari and Moeen Qureshi predecessors. Like the former it suffered a lack of credibility and neutrality[69] with the inclusion of such persons as Leghari's brother-in-law Dr Zubair Khan as Commerce Minister and Mumtaz Bhutto as Chief Minister of Sindh. The latter during a tour of northern Sindh baited the PPP, deriding a former provincial minister Nisar Khuhro as one of the 'third sex' and calling for Murtaza's murder to be avenged.[70] Simultaneously the caretakers sought to introduce major economic and financial reforms as Moeen Qureshi had done. These were entrusted to Shahid Javed Burki, a vice-president of the World Bank who became Meraj Khalid's economic adviser.

Burki engaged in a series of measures designed to stabilise the foreign exchanges and bring the fiscal deficit to the 4 per cent of GDP demanded by the IMF. Reforms included broadening the tax-base to include agricultural incomes which it was hoped would realise $2 billion, changes in the management of the state-owned banks, and the establishment of a Resolution Trust Corporation to deal with bad debts (amounting

---

[68] Zahid Hussain, 'Benazir Bhutto: Fall From Grace', *Newsline*, November 1996, pp. 24-31.

[69] The Pakistan Human Rights Commission report on the 1997 polls specifically criticised the caretakers for their blatant disregard of neutrality during the three preceeding months. *Dawn* (Internet Edition), 5 February 1997.

[70] *Newsline*, November 1996, p. 75.

to over Rs.100 billion) accumulated by state-run banks and financial institutions. The drive to cut public expenditure was symbolised by Meraj Khalid's closure of VIP lounges at airports and his example of air travel by economy class. Such measures seemed likely to lead to improvements only in the medium term, but despite Shahid Javeed Burki's public confidence in turning the economy around in a short time and of securing IMF funds without difficulty, this appeared increasingly unlikely.[71] To the general public, Burki's dispensation was associated only with price rises. For informed critics, it represented an expensive staving off of the economic reckoning by undertaking a number of short-term foreign loans which amounted to nearly $1 billion at high interest rates. Moreover as in 1993,[72] the continuing political uncertainty undoubtedly hit investment hard.

Under the terms of the Constitution, elections were scheduled for 3 February following the dissolution of the National Assembly, but there were serious doubts whether they would be held. These arose from statements by such cabinet ministers as Irshad Ahmed Haqqani, the Information Minister, and Sahibzada Yakub Khan, the Foreign Minister, who mentioned the possibility of postponement,[73] and from the uncertainty pending the outcome of Benazir Bhutto's appeal to the Supreme Court against her dismissal. The atmosphere was however very different from that of 1993 when Nawaz Sharif had been restored by the Court. The Bhutto Government's dismissal had been greeted with something akin to popular relief rather than resentment, most notably in commercial circles and in Karachi.[74] Even in the PPP heartland in the interior of Sindh, there were processions following Benazir's dismissal in which effigies of her husband and of the PPP Chief Minister Abdullah Shah were burnt. Large crowds flocked to glimpse Ghinwa Bhutto when she visited Thatta, Badin and Hala to express condolences to the families of Murtaza's slain bodyguards. She was greeted by such slogans as '*Ai Ai Ghinwa, gai gai Benazir*'(Ghinwa came, Benazir went).[75] Nevertheless, the caretakers were unable to bring any charges against

---

[71] See Zahid Hussain, 'Tall Claims', *Newsline*, Annual Issue 1997, pp. 93-5.

[72] In an interview to *Newsline* in December 1996 Burki maintained that the total economic outlook was much worse than in 1993 because of the siphoning of money from the system by loan defaults, the accelerating fall of the reserves and the loss of foreign confidence because of 'shoddy' economic managment and lack of transparency regarding privatisation. See Annual Issue 1996, pp. 96-100.

[73] President Leghari, who clearly held far more power in decision-making than Meraj Khalid, unambiguously supported the holding of elections in February.

[74] See Amir Zia, 'City of Joy', *Newsline*, November 1996, pp. 45-6.

[75] Hasan Mujtaba, 'Altered Scenario', *Newsline*, Annual Issue 1997, p. 76.

Benazir Bhutto which would have disqualified her from standing for election.

While the caretakers' inability to introduce an even-handed accountability process evoked considerable cynicism, two major institutional reforms were introduced during Meraj Khalid's tenure. The first, the introduction of adult franchise in Pakistan's Federally Administered Tribal Areas, was long overdue. Its implementation in the face of the bureaucracy's misgivings owed much to the efforts of the caretaker Interior Minister Omar Khan Afridi. The peaceful conduct of the elections fully justified the decision.[76] Tribal custom resulted in women being unable to exercise their right to vote in many places, but those who did represented a small but significant step forward.

The caretakers' second institutional reform, the formation of a Council of Defence and National Security (CDNS) was far more contentious.[77] The manner, constitutionality and timing of its introduction all raised criticism.[78] Qazi Hussain Ahmad, the JI *amir*, went further and claimed that the establishment of the CDNS strengthened the 'Washington Plan' of imposing the hegemony of the World Bank and the IMF and cutting the Islamic movements down to size.[79]

The idea that the Army should formally share decision-making with elected representatives dated back to Zia's post-Martial Law proposals for a National Security Council. It had been reiterated by the former Chief of Army Staff Aslam Beg on the eve of the 1993 polls. Despite its depiction as an advisory body which could be disbanded by an incoming elected government, the CDNS inevitably appeared as a formalisation of the power which the President and Army had wielded in the troika since the 1988 restoration of democracy. The notification order referred to fixing of priorities in the coordination of defence policy with external and domestic policies and of advising the Government on economic and fiscal policies affecting defence and national security, all of which certainly indicated a more than advisory nature.[80] Arguments that the CDNS's existence would prevent a military coup and ensure

---

76 See Rahimullah Yusufzai, 'A People Empowered', *Newsline*, February 1997, pp. 60-3.

77 The CDNS membership was to comprise the President, Prime Minister, Foreign Minister, Defence Minister, Interior Minister, Minister/Adviser for Finance, Chairman of the Joint Chiefs of Staff Committee, Chief of Army Staff, Chief of the Naval Staff and Chief of the Air Staff. Significantly, it was to be headed and convened by the President rather than the Prime Minister.

78 Although the CDNS proposal was supported by the caretaker cabinet, it was clear that the idea originated with the President, not Prime Minister Meraj Khalid.

79 *Dawn* (Internet Edition), 15 January 1997.

80 See Khalid Jawed Khan, 'Constitutionality of the CDNS', *Dawn* (Internet Edition), 27 January 1997.

continuity in economic and foreign policy appeared unconvincing, although Nawaz Sharif significantly did not commit himself to its dissolution. The official PML(N) line propounded by the Information Secretary Mushahid Husain was that the decision concerning retaining or disbanding the CDNS would be left to Parliament.[81] By the time of its second meeting on 28 January, it already appeared to have assumed a permanent character.[82]

Seen in a longer historical perspective, the CDNS appears to be a continuation of the viceregal tradition which has disastrously emphasised governance over participation; no provincial politicians were included in its membership. At the least, the CDNS could be regarded as Farooq Leghari's insurance policy for the election outcome, at worse as evidence of creeping centralisation and dilution of democracy. Earlier attempts at guided democracy had failed, and Pakistan's history indicates the desirability of less not more interference by the unelected institutions of the state.

The election campaign

The electioneering, or what passed for it, was the dullest in Pakistan's history.[83] Uncertainty as to whether the polls would go ahead, the Election Commission's restriction on posters,[84] party flags and loudspeakers, the influenza epidemic in Punjab, and the polls coinciding with Ramadan all contributed to the general lethargy. The JI's boycott had a more marginal impact.[85] The Supreme Court's verdict,[86] announced by Chief Justice Syed Sajjad Ali Shah to a packed court, upholding all the charges contained in the Presidential Proclamation of 5 November dismissing

---

[81] *Dawn* (Internet Edition),15 January 1997.

[82] In the wake of the PML(N) victory, the party's General Secretary Senator Sartaj Aziz declared that the CDNS could be a good advisory body to avoid the use of 58(2)(B) to dismiss governments. 'We would certainly like to watch the functioning of the CDNS', he told a press conference on 4 February, 'before finalising any opinion about it.' *Dawn* (Internet Edition), 5 February 1997.

[83] The party advertisements on PTV represented a novel development. The PML(N) spent some 40 million rupees during a 15 day advertising campaign. The PPP spent 30 million rupees. *Dawn* (Internet Edition), 2 February 1997.

[84] A number of enterprising candidates in Rawalpindi and Islamabad got round the poster and wall chalking prohibition by painting their cars with party flags and colours. See, *Dawn* (Internet Edition), 20 January 1997.

[85] Qazi Hussain Ahmad justified the JI's boycott in terms of the low turnout which he declared 'amounted to a rejection of the election process.' He also reiterated the demands that a census should be held, new voters lists prepared and constituencies should be demarcated afresh. See *Dawn* (Internet Edition), 4 February 1997.

[86] For the complete text of the judgement see *Dawn* (Karachi), 30 January 1997.

Benazir Bhutto's government,[87] finally removed any doubts from voters' minds. Its timing,[88] just four days before the votes were to be cast, undoubtedly damaged the PPP's prospects. The defection of its political heavyweights to the PML(N) and PPP(SB) and the decision of some to stand as independents[89] hinted at the PPP's impending débâcle, as did its weak position in the key Punjab province. But most media attention was devoted to the newcomers Ghinwa Bhutto and Imran Khan, supported on occasion by his photogenic wife Jemima.[90]

Ghinwa Bhutto rode the crest of a sympathy wave in the interior of Sindh. Her political progress also revealed the paradoxes and constraints surrounding Pakistani democracy. Despite her middle-class background and attachment to her late husband's radicalism, the bulk of the PPP(SB) candidates were large landlords,[91] many of whom had opportunistically jumped off the sinking PPP ship. Rather than representing a new beginning, Ghinwa was seen by Benazir's opponents as a useful spoiling factor. In the end the PPP(SB) had to rest content with one National Assembly seat and two Provincial Assembly successes in Sindh. Begum Bhutto defeated her daughter-in-law in the Larkana NA-164 constituency.

The course of the campaign also revealed that Imran Khan was not the hoped-for 'third force' in Pakistan politics, although few commentators expected him to score a duck in his first political innings.[92]

---

87 This included the charges of extra-judicial killings in Karachi, although the President's counsel Khalid Anwar could not present any evidence on this to the Court Bench. Nasir Malick, 'Anwar fails to provide evidence on extra-judicial killings', *Dawn* (Internet Edition), 28 January 1997.

88 The judgement had been delayed because the Supreme Court raised objections to Benazir Bhutto's initial petitions challenging the dissolution of the National Assembly and the dismissal of her government. It then gave the President, caretaker Prime Minister and Attorney General ten days to reply before hearing counsel. See Nasir Malick, 'Events Leading to SC Judgement', *Dawn* (Internet Edition), 30 January 1997.

89 Former PPP figures standing as independents included Malik Asad Sikander, and Ghous Bux Mehar from the Dadu and Shikarpur districts of Sindh. Virtually all the PPP legislators from the Jacobabad district had shifted to PPP(SB) and PML(N). Defectors in Punjab included the former PPP Defence Minister, Colonel Ghulam Sarwar Cheema, who contested for the PML(N) in Gujranwala.

90 She had made her public bow at the Pakistan Tehreek-i-Insaf's Womens' Convention in Islamabad on 23 January where she addressed a delighted audience in Urdu. She subsequently addressed a number of female gatherings in the Lahore NA-95 constituency where Imran was opposing Nawaz Sharif.

91 They included Allah Baksh Magsi and his son, Mir Manjoor Talpur, Pir Allah Shah Jilani, and Haji Abdullah Halepoto. Nafisa Hoodbhoy, 'PPP-SB Makes Inroads Into Sindh', *Dawn* (Internet Edition), 21 January 1997.

92 His Pakistan Tehreek-i-Insaf had put up around 150 candidates for National Assembly seats and 300 for Provincial Assembly constituencies. *Dawn* (Internet Edition), 7

The Sita White paternity scandal and the 'Jewish money' smear campaigns against him[93] laid bare the negative character of Pakistani electioneering. His floundering efforts also revealed the importance of patronage in political mobilisation and the effects of limiting the voting age to twenty-one. The majority of those who attended his rallies were too young to vote. Finally Imran's failure exemplified the difficulties surrounding simple Islamic appeals to an increasingly sophisticated and consumer-oriented urban population. His claim that Pakistan should follow Vietnam's example and hang those convicted of corruption beyond a certain sum of money led him to be labelled an extremist.[94]

In many rural constituencies in Sindh and in parts of the Punjab, patron-client and *biraderi* ties continued to hold the key to successful electioneering. The importance of personality rather than party was starkly demonstrated in the interior of the Sukkur and Ghokti districts of Sindh where the powerful Mehar clan was awarded no less than five PPP election tickets.[95] In a faint historical parallel with its electoral triumph half a century earlier, the Muslim League's eclipse of its rivals was to depend both on its manipulation of traditional networks of political mobilisation and on a groundswell of popular opinion. Indeed this explains the defection of political elites from the PPP, just as the Unionist Party had been deserted earlier. At a public meeting in Baghbanpura Lahore on the eve of polling, for example, the Arain leader Mehr Muhammad Aslam, a founder member of the PPP, joined the PML(N) with a large number of his *biraderi*. Similarly, leading Ghakkar PPP members orchestrated a mass departure to Nawaz Sharif's party.[96] The PPP's hold on the south-western region of Punjab was loosened by the estrangement from the Legharis. No less than five Legharis were elected as independent candidates from the Dera Ghazi Khan and Rajanpur districts, including the President's son Awais, who obtained two Provincial Assembly seats.[97]

February 1997.

[93] The PML(N) paid back with interest his attacks on Nawaz Sharif including the claim that he had allotted plots worth Rs. 5 billion against bogus ID cards. See *Dawn* (Internet Edition), 2 January 1997.

[94] Imran was unrepentant, declaring, 'We have reached a stage really where we have to choose between human rights and the freedom available to looters. The two cannot co-exist.' *Dawn* (The Internet Edition), 18 January 1997.

[95] Hasan Mujtaba, 'The Battle for Sindh', *Newsline*, January 1997 p. 57.

[96] *Dawn* (Internet Edition), 1 February 1997.

[97] *Ibid.*, 4 February 1997.

Fair and free polls?

During the campaign, Benazir Bhutto maintained that she would not accept the results if they were rigged. Although this stance was modified, she reiterated the claim on the eve of the elections that she suspected vote-rigging in sixty-five National Assembly seats.[98] Later the Punjab PPP President Mushtaq Ahmad Awan accused Leghari of 'computerised rigging' which had deprived the party of scores of seats.[99] Imran Khan also maintained that there had been rigging through increases in the number of votes in certain constituencies.[100] That such claims of executive influence in the electoral process were not mere paranoia was brought home by the former Chief of Army Staff Aslam Beg's admission to the Supreme Court on the eve of polling that the political cell of the ISI had received Rs.140 million from the Habib Bank during the 1990 elections.[101] The PML(N)'s decisive victory ensured that there was much less furore over the outcome than in 1990. As in earlier post-1988 elections, the polls were monitored by observers from the SAARC,[102] the European Union and the Human Rights Commission of Pakistan. The British High Commissioner personally visited a number of polling stations in the Hyderabad division.

This study has reiterated the importance of rigging claims in Pakistani political discourse. It has also pointed out that rigging of various kinds has been an ever-present political feature. In the narrow sense of the term, the widespread rigging which Benazir Bhutto claimed does not appear to have taken place. Disquieting anomalies nevertheless remain over the figure of a 35.92 per cent turnout, which conflicts with the physical evidence of deserted polling booths in many parts of the country on 3 February.[103] Qazi Hussain Ahmad declared as early as the middle of January that if the turnout exceeded 30 per

98 *Dawn* (Internet Edition), 2 February 1997.

99 *The Nation* (Internet Edition), 16 February 1997.

100 *Dawn* (Internet Edition), 23 February 1997.

101 *Ibid.*, 2 February 1997.

102 The 41-member SAARC group drawn from four countries visited over 400 polling stations in sixty-four constituencies including some in the FATA areas. Its report released on 6 February maintained that the elections were 'conducted substantially in accordance with the country's electoral laws and procedures'. But it continued: 'We feel that the micro-management of the polling marked a deterioration over the 1993 polls. There were problems and complaints with regard to the electoral rolls –a matter related to the absence of a proper census in Pakistan since 1981. The facilities in the polling stations including those relating to secrecy of voting were not uniformly available.' *Dawn* (Internet Edition), 7 February 1997.

103 At polling station no. 134 in NA-169 only 268 votes had been cast by mid-afternoon. For further details see *Dawn* (Internet Edition), 4 February 1997.

cent it would be the result of rigging.[104] Moreover, the official final figure did not square with President Leghari's statement on Pakistan Television as the results were coming in that the turnout was around 26 per cent. Furthermore, evidence of malpractice exists in some constituencies, for example the defeat in Multan of the former National Assembly Speaker Yousuf Raza Gilani.[105] According to the reports of the international observers this was sufficiently localised not to have altered the national outcome.

Procedural defects nevertheless called the absolute fairness of the polls into question. Moreover, the atmosphere of the caretaker regime was far from impartial. The announcement of the Supreme Court verdict so near polling-day further discouraged support for the PPP. The problems pointed out by international observers regarding earlier polls remained unresolved: the 1981 Census had still not been updated and constituencies redrawn accordingly; voting lists were inaccurate; widespread disenfrachisement resulted from the requirement of a national identity card; minorities continued to be marginalised in the absence of joint electorates; and voting by women was still discouraged in socially conservative rural areas. All these factors worked against the PPP. Its defeat, however, was primarily due to its widespread unpopularity.

The results

The PML(N)'s crushing victory inevitably grabbed the headlines. As Table 11.2 reveals, its triumph eclipsed that of 1990 and was on a par with the PPP's triumph in the 1970 West Pakistan elections.

The 135 seats which the PML(N) captured in the National Assembly made this the first occasion since 1985 that a party possessed an absolute majority. It was not just the number of seats which were captured but the margin of victory within them that was so impressive. Punjab once again proved to be its key area of support, but for a Punjab-based party it also made striking inroads into Sindh. The PPP, which had been decimated in Punjab where it won a paltry three out of 240 Provincial Assembly seats, was now no longer secure even in its traditional heartland. The party suffered a series of National and Provincial Assembly setbacks in the Nawabshah, Khairpur and Jacobabad districts. In Jacobabad, Mir Hazar Khan Bijarani was returned for the PPP(SB). In the Nawabshah district, the home of the Zardaris (even though the controversial Asif

---

[104] *Dawn* (Internet Edition), 16 January 1997.

[105] Some 35,000 votes were mysteriously cancelled in his constituency. See, I.A. Rehman, 'Not Quite Fair', *Newsline*, February 1997 p. 39.

Table 11.2.
PARTY POSITIONS IN THE NATIONAL AND PROVINCIAL
ASSEMBLY SEATS, FEBRUARY 1997 POLLS

| | Nat. Assembly | Provincial Assemblies | | | |
		Punjab	Sindh	NWFP	Balochistan
PML(N)	135	211	15	33	6
PPP	19	3	36	4	1
MQM(A)	12	0	28	0	0
ANP	9	0	0	31	0
BNP	3	0	0	0	10
JUI(F)	2	0	0	1	7
JWP	2	0	0	0	8
PPP(SB)	1	0	2	0	0
NPP	1	0	3	0	0
PML(F)	0	0	7	0	0
PML(J)	0	2	0	2	1
PKMAP	0	0	0	0	2
BNM	0	0	0	0	2
PDP	0	1	0	0	0
SNF	0	0	1	0	0
SSP	0	1	0	0	0
Independent	20	20	8	10	6

Source: Calculated from Zahid Hussain, 'Clean Sweep', *Newsline*, February 1997 p. 36 and 'Latest Party Positions' *Dawn* (Internet Edition), 5 February 1997.

Ali Zardari did not contest the polls)[106] the PPP vote slumped dramatically to the advantage of the PML(N). In addition to the rise of the PML(N), the elections confirmed two other long-term trends, the first being the electoral malaise of the Islamic parties. With the JI and JUP boycotting the polls, the spotlight had fallen on Fazlur Rahman's JUI. This captured just two National Assembly seats and eight Provincial Assembly seats (seven of which were in Balochistan).

The second trend is the continued strength of ethnic/regional identities for political mobilisation. Despite the shattering experience of state repression and the continued exile of Altaf Hussain, the MQM(A) retained its hold on urban Sindh, albeit with reduced majorities and two defeats at the hands of the PML(N) in Karachi. In all it captured twelve National Assembly and twenty-eight Sindh Provincial Assembly seats.

[106] Faryal Talpur his sister stood in his stead from Nawabshah city, but was defeated by the PML(N) candidate and former PPP stalwart, Shaukat Ali Shah.

Although the MQM(H) was able to intimidate its opponents in its Landi stronghold, it could not overcome the public perception of it as a creature of the Army and intelligence agencies. Other ethnic parties which strengthened their position included the ANP in the Frontier where it won thirty-one out of eighty-three Provincial Assembly Seats and the Jamhoori Watan and Balochistan Nationalist Parties which accounted for eighteen Balochistan Provincial Assembly seats. Political arithmetic ensures that such ethnic/regional parties have a marginal presence in the National Assembly. But the triumph of the PML(N) should not obscure the existence of strongly held ethno-nationalist identities. The task remains to strengthen the Pakistan polity by recognising its pluralism more fully through devolution.

Future prospects

In the post-election euphoria the Karachi Stock Exchange 100-share index soared to the 1700-point level. Nawaz Sharif signalled the intended austerity of the country's new rulers by driving in his own Pajero to the Prime Minister's House on his first day in office. Peace even seemed to have broken out in the National Assembly with the PML(N) leader promising to 'adopt a path of mutual trust and understanding with the opposition'.[107] Benazir Bhutto wished him well and hoped he would complete his term in office, despite the 'engineering' of the election results. She also said she would consider accepting the chair of the National Assembly's Foreign Affairs Committee if it was offered by the Government.[108] Hopes for improved relations with India were raised when, in an interview at his Lahore Model Town residence just two days after the 'silent revolution' of his election triumph, Nawaz Sharif declared: 'We have to learn how to be good neighbours – now is the time for serious dialogue.' [109] Shortly afterwards a foreign affairs spokesman declared that Pakistan was ready to settle the demilitarisation of the Siachen glacier with Deve Gowda's government.[110] Cynics, almost with a sense of relief, glimpsed a return to a more normal pattern of Pakistani politics with the appointment of Nawaz Sharif's brother Shahbaz as Chief Minister of Punjab.

The task which faced Nawaz Sharif was daunting. He had to evolve a working relationship with a President who had earlier been one of his major opponents. Much would depend here on how he responded

[107] *Dawn* (Internet Edition), 18 February 1997.

[108] *Ibid.*

[109] *Dawn* (Internet Edition), 5 February 1997.

[110] *Ibid.*, 2 March 1997.

to the issue of Farooq Leghari's re-election as President in 1998. Economic issues were however even more pressing. The need to repay $1.2 billion in loans by June 1997 occurred against the background of an increasing trade imbalance and rising prices. These circumstances not only boxed the Prime Minister in, but made it highly unlikely that Pakistan would meet the IMF target of current account deficit of 4.4 per cent of GDP for 1996/7. In his first televised address to the nation after assuming office, Nawaz Sharif, reading from his notes in Urdu, spoke emotionally about the economic crisis:

> 'Our rulers have plundered us in ways that even the enemy would not practice in occupied lands...they mortgaged the national interest to such an extent that we are not free to make our own budget. [...] Our donors order us around. [...] We are told to increase the price of flour which amounts to snatching the bread from people's mouths. [...] What sort of freedom is this? It is time for us to stand on the ruins of the last fifty years and pledge that we shall take back our freedom.'[111]

He talked even more expansively of establishing a participant democracy with primary education for all, the provision of health care for the poor, the enactment of progressive labour laws, and protection for the minorities and women. Similar promises had been made to the long-suffering populace before, and had not been honoured.

Would the new Prime Minister dare to use the mandate accorded by the 'silent revolution' of the 1997 polls to usher in fundamental institutional and structural reforms affecting the relationship of land and labour, state and society, male and female, Pakistan and India, thereby opening up the possibility of a peace dividend? Was Pakistan, on the eve of its golden jubilee, to enter, in Nawaz Sharif's words, a 'brighter tomorrow'? Or was it to sleepwalk towards the fate of a 'failed state'? Most pressingly of all, could economic collapse be averted at a time when indebtedness amounted to $500 per Pakistani inhabitant?

Some answers were provided during the first year of the Nawaz Sharif Government. The Prime Minister embarked on a series of populist measures designed to tackle the economic crisis. A new austerity era was meant to be signalled by the ban on serving food at weddings. The most striking populist measure was the '*qarz utaro, mulk sanaro*' (retire debt, develop the country) scheme in which overseas Pakistanis were asked to boost the flagging foreign exchange situation by depositing a minimum of $1,000 as an interest-free loan in Pakistani banks for

---

111 Eqbal Ahmed, 'A New Era or Flash in the Pan?', *Dawn* (Internet Edition), 2 March 1997.

two to five years. The 'brown' dollar was now being chased, having failed to attract investment from the 'white' dollar. This populist appeal immediately struck a chord and was supported by the former Pakistan cricket captain[112] Javed Miandad, along with other celebrities.[113] By the time Nawaz Sharif had gone through the formality of facing a vote of confidence on 19 February, some $150 million had already been repatriated.[114]

However, such gesture politics could not address Pakistan's deep-seated economic and political problems. In an economic reform package introduced by the Finance Minister Sartaj Aziz on 28 March, the Government changed economic direction, abandoning the austerity measures demanded by the IMF Standby Arrangement in favour of 'supply-side economics' designed to boost agricultural and textile production through tax-cuts and higher support prices. The 'growing out of problems' policy was prompted in part by domestic political considerations, but was mainly in response to the suspension of the IMF agreement a week earlier. Pakistan's international credit-rating nevertheless still depended on the IMF's endorsement. In July, Pakistan received the message it wanted from the IMF and was allowed to enter into a medium-term Enhanced Structural Adjustment Facility (ESAF). This in the short run reduced the balance of payments vulnerability, although questions still remained regarding how the breathing-space would be used to introduce the key economic reforms needed to widen the taxation-base, encourage greater direct investment and boost exports and agricultural production.

The economic euphoria induced by the ESAF agreement was mirrored by the political relief which greeted Nawaz Sharif's introduction of the Thirteenth Amendment on 1 April. This measure stripped the President of the power under Article 52(b) of the Eighth Amendment to dismiss the Prime Minister and dissolve the National Assembly. Benazir Bhutto unreservedly praised her rival for removing the Sword of Damocles which had hung over every elected government since 1988.

The large and unanticipated Muslim League majority had put the President on a collision course with a Prime Minister determined to flex his muscles. Tensions had first arisen over the appointment of the Sindh Governor as the PML(N) had held out the hope that a MQM(A) nominee be appointed, but President Leghari had insisted on an establishment figure – Lieutenant-General Moeenuddin Haider. Further tension was caused when Nawaz Sharif was forced to award a Senate

---

[112] As all cricket-lovers will know, Javed played in 124 tests and scored nearly 9,000 runs including 23 centuries.

[113] *The Nation* (Internet Edition), 16 February 1997.

[114] *Dawn* (Internet Edition), 20 February 1997.

ticket to the President's brother Maqsood Leghari, and by President Leghari's uneasiness with the Prime Minister's new supply-side economics. Nevertheless, commentators were taken aback by the speed with which Nawaz Sharif removed the legacy of Zia's check on the democratic process.

During the weeks which followed, talk was no longer of presidential power but of an elective dictatorship as Nawaz Sharif tightened his personal grip over the accountability process and passed the Fourteenth Amendment curbing the ability of legislators to defect from their parties. Moreover, the CDNS did not hold a formal meeting throughout this period. On the eve of Pakistan's golden jubilee, had power finally shifted from the unelected institutions of the state?

The months which followed were marked by the protracted and dramatic confrontation between Nawaz Sharif and the judiciary, culminating in the removal of the Chief Justice of the Supreme Court, Justice Sajjad Ali Shah, and the resignation of President Leghari on 2 December 1997. Nawaz Sharif presented this as a victory for parliamentary sovereignty. His position appeared to be further strengthened when Rafiq Tarar, an associate of his father the increasingly influential Mian Mohammed Sharif, was elected to the Presidency on New Year's Eve. With a pliant legislature, a docile President and a PPP opposition embroiled in the sensational though still unproven corruption charges surrounding Benazir Bhutto and her spouse, some commentators feared a 'democratic dictatorship' rather than viceregalism. In reality the PML (N) dominance was not as secure as it first appeared. However, before turning to this issue, we must briefly review the background to the constitutional crisis which dominated the last quarter of 1997.

The conflict was rooted in the encouragement to judicial activism given by the March 1996 verdict in the Judges Case. When Chief Justice Sajjad Ali Shah took notice on his own initiative of cases involving the government's handling of a wheat-shipping contract from the United States, and opened cases which had been pending concerning the alleged illegal distribution of residential plots by the Prime Minister, conflict became sharper. It further intensified following the Supreme Court's disapproval of the parallel justice system of summary trial courts introduced in August 1997 by the controversial Anti-Terrorist Law. This measure, which gave wider powers to the police and other security forces including the right to 'shoot to kill' and indemnity for acts done in 'good faith', met with international condemnation. On 3 August, just ten days before the Act was passed, Sajjad Ali Shah had publicly assured the Prime Minister that the judiciary would deal quickly with outstanding cases. The special courts for the Suppression of Terrorist Activities were not placed under the control of the superior judiciary.

Moreover, the federal government could determine where they would have their sittings, which might be a mosque or the 'place of occurrence' of a terrorist outrage. Such provisions contravened the presumption of a defendant's innocence until proven guilty, and prejudiced the possibility of a fair trial. This departure from established legal principles violated the constitutional guarantee of equality before the law.

The Anti-Terrorist Law had been urged by Shahbaz Sharif following the rising tide of sectarian violence in the Punjab which claimed 130 lives in the first half of 1997. However, the horrific January 1998 Mominpur graveyard massacre in Lahore, together with the failure to bring sectarian terrorist cases to court, made its ineffectiveness all too apparent. Shortly after its introduction, the Supreme Court Chief Justice named five judges who would be added to the bench to deal with a backlog of cases. But the Government delayed the notification of their appointment, thereby precipitating the first stage of the crisis.

This round was won by the uncompromising Chief Justice, who had earlier fought the second Bhutto Government on the issue of the political appointment of High Court judges. Following a challenge from the Supreme Court Bar Association, Nawaz Sharif had to retract an ordinance reducing the strength of the Supreme Court from seventeen to twelve. On 30 October the Supreme Court invoked Clause 190 of the Constitution to order President Leghari to intervene and notify the appointment of the five judges. Tension mounted in Islamabad as the President refused to accept Nawaz Sharif's advice to dismiss the Chief Justice, despite his censure by an emergency session of the National Assembly. On the evening of 31 October the Prime Minister apparently capitulated when he accepted the elevation of the judges as recommended by the Chief Justice.

However, he soon exacted his revenge, though at the cost of dividing the supposedly independent judiciary on clear party-political lines. The Balochistan circuit bench of the Supreme Court suspended Justice Shah and called for a full bench petition hearing to challenge his appointment shortly after Shahbaz Sharif had met Justice Irshad in Quetta. The Peshawar bench followed suit, paving the way for the existence of what amounted to two parallel Supreme Courts. A fight to the finish was signalled by the Chief Justice's decision to continue with a contempt of court trial against the Prime Minister. This occasioned the extraordinary scenes when PML(N) supporters, led by Senators and MLAs' stormed the Supreme Court building, forcing the trial to be abandoned.

President Leghari's condemnation brought him into direct conflict with the Prime Minister. Although the Thirteenth Amendment had clipped his wings, there were still fears that he might dissolve the National Assembly, and to forestall him the Government considered impeachment charges. In the final stages of the crisis the rival Supreme Court benches, led by Justice Shah and Justice Saeeduzaman Siddiqi, struck down and almost immediately reinstated the Thirteenth Amendment of the Constitution. The Crisis ended with the dramatic departure of both the Chief Justice and the President from the scene. This left Nawaz Sharif apparently in the strongest position of any elected Prime Minister since the days of Zulfikar Ali Bhutto.

It is important to realise that the Army had played a crucial role throughout the three months of the constitutional crisis. Indeed Nawaz Sharif had backed down on 31 October following a warning note from the military. The attitude of the Army COAS, General Jahangir Karamat, appeared equally decisive in the outcome of the second round: when military stepped back, this ensured that, in contrast to 1993, Nawaz Sharif would emerge triumphant from his conflict with the Presidency. The Chairman of the Senate, Wasim Sajjad, temporarily took Leghari's place before the indirect elections which saw the triumph of the surprise PML(N) nominee, Rafiq Tarar.

The Army, far from being excluded from national life by the now unchallenged political leadership of Nawaz Sharif, became closely involved in what might be considered routine civilian administrative tasks. The official explanation for this was to encourage a 'people-friendly' army, but in reality it was a response to the serious institutional decay which, throughout Pakistan's history, had undermined democratic stability. The corruption and politicisation of the administrative services by successive governments had accelerated this process. Nawaz Sharif's clash with the judiciary had of course further undermined an important state institution.

The Army was deployed for the first time during census enumeration when the much-delayed head-count was held in March 1998. The delays had been partly the result of anxieties in the Punjab establishment regarding the changing population balance between the provinces. The census was also expected to reveal a rapid population shift in favour of the urban areas, which would have important political repercussions in the redrawing of constituencies. Equally contentious was the balance it was likely to reveal between Sindhi and Balochi 'sons of the soil' and incomers. Resistance to the census was greatest among the Pakhtun population of Balochistan, who had long claimed that the Balochis overcounted their inhabitants. The Pakhtoonkhwa Milli Awami Party boycotted the census and organised increasingly violent protests; in one episode census returns were snatched from the premises of the Quetta *tehsil* office. In these circumstances the decision to deploy the Army was understandable, but it was nonetheless a dangerous development.

Even more so was the increasing tendency to call in the Army to carry out routine administrative tasks, which now seemed beyond the ability of the demoralised civilian agencies. The most striking instance was the use in the spring of 1998 of 1,400 Army teams to root out 'ghost schools' among the 56,000 government-funded primary schools in Punjab. The survey uncovered 4,000 such schools at an estimated annual cost to the exchequer of Rs. 1.4 billion. Shahbaz Sharif's decision to send in the military was reminiscent of his elder brother's populist touch. The public had long been concerned at a situation in which many teachers appeared only monthly to draw their salary, or in which local notables appeared on the payroll of 'ghost schools'. Nevertheless, the quick fix of military inspection did nothing to address the root of the problem, which required careful institution-building to address the collapse of the School Inspectorate System. Less well publicised but equally indicative of Pakistan's institutional crisis was the resort to Army contractors rather than their 'corrupt' civilian counterparts in a number of road-building projects in Punjab. Army personnel were also to be deployed in the province to investigate 'ghost' health centres, deliver educational services, and even tackle the Lahore Metropolitan Corporation's stray dog problem!

As well as these innovations, the PML(N) regime turned the clock back to old-style viceregalism in the Punjab Local Government (Amendment) Ordinance. This introduced a system of nominated village panchayats; rural Union Council members were also to be nominated. Thus beneath the district council level the elective principle was done away with.

If viceregalism was still thriving in Nawaz Sharif's Pakistan, so too were claims of the state's Punjabisation. These had been revived partly by the elevation of the Punjabi Rafiq Tarar to the Presidency instead of a minority province candidate, but it was noted too that the President, the Prime Minister, the Chairman of the Senate and the COAS were all from the Punjab. The dismissal of Chief Justice Shah was seen by some Sindhis as a further affront to their province. Sajjad Ali Khan came from an old-established Amirkhani Syed family which had settled in the eighteenth century in what is today the Lyari area of Karachi. The former chief justice was still remembered by older residents for his childhood pranks as a schoolboy at the Sindh Madrassa in the pre-Partition era.

The allocation of 1 billion dollars to Nawaz Sharif's beloved Islamabad-to-Peshawar motorway project when development funds were being frozen elsewhere in the country generated further criticism in cash-starved Balochistan and Sindh. Further disquiet was engendered by the decision to freeze Punjab's share of federal funds and level of political representation at current levels, regardless of the outcome of the census. The break-up of the marriage of convenience between the ANP and the PML(N) in the NWFP injected further bitterness into claims of Punjabi domination. The ANP left the coalition in February amid claims that Nawaz Sharif had reneged on his earlier support for the renaming of the North West Frontier Province as 'Pakhtoonkhwa' The protaganists turned to history in their increasingly bitter exchanges. Nawaz Sharif revealed the skeletons of opposition to the Pakistan movement in Wali Khan's cupboard, to which the octogenarian ANP leader retorted that the Punjabi Prime Minister was attempting to dominate the minority provinces in a way akin to the One Unit scheme of the 1950s.

By the anniversary of Nawaz Sharif's return to power, it appeared that his handling of Pakistan's economic crisis might seriously undermine his second term in office, just as it had the first. Supply-side economics and grandiose infrastructional developments appeared to be exacerbating the country's internal debt crisis, yet failing to lift the economy out of recession. The only bright spot, the containment of the foreign exchange deficit, was in part the result of falling imports induced by recession. It also stemmed from the simultaneous rise in overseas remittances, and appeared to justify the chase for the 'brown dollar'. The long-standing issue of the financial institutions' bad debt remained unsolved with only 4.127 billion rupees in unpaid loans recovered by the Government's February 1998 deadline. Moreover, budgetary cutbacks and downsizing of the banking sector at the IMF's behest threatened to preciptate the same unrest which had undermined Benazir Bhutto's government. Farmers in Balochistan blocked highways and roads, bringing the province to a standstill, in protest at the state-owned WAPDA's imposition of a water-metering system to meet IMF demands to eliminate subsidies. A greater test for the Government was the ability to retain its traditional support among the trader community in the Punjab following the introduction of a general sales tax. The only consolation in all this was the absence of opposition forces to channel the discontent arising from increasing inflation and unemployment.

The country could ill afford any of the increase in military expenditure which resulted from the escalating regional tension which followed the March 1998 emergence of a coalition government in New Delhi led by the BJP. Kashmir soon played its traditional role as a barometer of subcontinental relations. Claims of a return to 'normalcy' under the state Government of Faroq Abdullah were seriously questioned by the fierce battle between militants and Indian forces at Aagam. In April, Pakistan test-fired a long-range missile capable of hitting any target in India – it was named Ghauri after the Turkish Muslim invader of India in 1192. None of this however prepared the world for India's five tests as nuclear weapons beneath the Rajasthan desert in mid-May.

When the outrage which accompanied the initial three tests failed to prevent the final two in the series from taking place, President Clinton imposed sanctions under the 1994 non-proliferation law, which could cost India as much as $20 billion in aid. Japan followed suit, but other members of the G8 group, meeting in Birmingham, England, at the time, counselled caution. The US deputy secretary of state, Strobe Talbott, was sent to Islamabad to encourage restraint by Pakistan. Nawaz Sharif, returning visit to Kazakistan, rejected the US overtune, at the same time as Abdul Qadeer Khan reiterated that he was only awaiting orders to carry out a successful test.

Fifty years of nation-building based on animosity to the neighbouring 'other' state, which in turn had been preceeded by the politicisation of religious community and its essentialisation around the hostility of the religious 'other', culminated on 29 May 1998 with Pakistan's 'settling the account' and conducting its own five nuclear explosions at a test-site in Balochistan. Henceforth, Pakistan and India were to face each other across the Wagah border armed with the Hindu and Muslim bombs. The impact of sanctions on a Pakistan economy teetering on the brink of collapse led President Tarar to declare a state of emergency shortly after news of the detonations had received international condemnation. Nawaz Sharif, in an echo of Zulfiqar Ali Bhutto's famous phrase that Pakistanis would if necessary 'eat grass' to match India's nuclear capability, declared: 'If the nation will only take one meal a day, my children will only take one meal a day.' Glaring social inequalities, a deepening of the incidence of poverty, and massive inequalities in access to power all make such sentiments fatuous. As Tariq Ali wrote in *The Guardian* on 29 May, 'Those who make the decision never eat grass.'

If there is a silver lining to the nuclear cloud hanging over the sub-continent, it consists first of the hope that there will be renewed diplomatic pressures to resolve the Kashmir dispute, and, secondly, the burgeoning peace movements. Such groups as the Citizens' Peace Committee of Rawalpindi and Islamabad, the Joint Action Committee for People's Rights (Lahore) and the Karachi-based Action Committee Against the Arms Race called in July for the establishment of a National Campaign for Nuclear Disarmament in Pakistan. The Action Committee Against the Arms Race also launched a peace petition and sponsored a proposal to be presented to the SAARC Heads of State and Government meeting in Colombo on 25-27 July. Nevertheless, the voices for peace and regional cooperation remain weak amid the din of nationalist rhetoric and sabre-rattling in both India and Pakistan.

The immediate crises of ethnic and sectarian violence, indebtedness and even the regional nuclear tensions appear less daunting than the conditions likely to face Pakistan in the future. Diplomacy and security relations will have to be played out in the context of China's emergence as a superpower and India's position as a regional power with global aspirations. Technology and trade rather than military might are likely to be the keys to power. Pakistan must thus ensure national security without repeating the Soviet Union's historic fate of internal collapse resulting from the inability of the economy to bear the weight of the military superstructure. The late-twentieth-century trend for military expenditure in South Asia to increase while it is falling elsewhere must be reversed. The Indian nuclear tests torpedoed the hopes of many for a sane use of resources in a subcontinent which contains around 400 million illiterate adults, more than one-third of the world's poor (around 500 million people survive with an income equivalent to less than one US dollar a day) and where at least 293 million (the 1993 figure) are without access to safe drinking water.

The freeing of the economies of Pakistan and India from their military burden appears even more pressing in the light of their annual population growth rates of, respectively, 3.6 and 2.1 per cent. By the mid-twenty-first century, if the current growth-rates continue, India will have overtaken China as the world's most populous country and Pakistan, with 350 million, will have become the world's third-most populous country. Pakistan's task of feeding, clothing and educating a population more than two-and-a-half times the present level in a sustainable environment will be immense. Salinity, deforestation and soil erosion are already taking their toll. The dramatic increase in the use of pesticides and herbicides in the wake of the Green Revolution has also damaged the ecosystem, causing toxicity and lessening biodiversity. International environmental conferences have pointed out the impact of deforestation along the banks of the Indus on rainfall and soil erosion. The construction of the Indus dams has altered both the volume of the river and its course. The Indus dolphin and Indus salmon are among species that are now virtually extinct. Pakistan thus faces the twin threats of demographic and ecological disaster.

The country has survived seemingly overwhelming odds before because of the resilience and vitality – and the pride – of its people. This was demonstrated at Partition. Its prospects depend on the probity of its rulers and their willingness both to accommodate difference and embark on radical structural reforms of the economy and political system. They require not only courage and foresight, but a favourable relationship with India. Such a prospect seems bleak as the subcontinent appears to stand on the brink of a new and dangerous arms race. Yet it is only through the transformation of the security state bequeathed by the Raj into a participatory democracy that Pakistan will be equipped to meet its massive future challenges.

12

CONCLUSION

This study has sought to convey that Pakistan's post-independence political development has been considerably more complex than the traditional summing-up in terms of the 'three A's' – Allah, the Army and America, or of the official two-nation theory of history. Ambiguities and paradoxes abound, many of which derive from the era of British rule and the freedom struggle. Pakistan remains a highly plural society, not only culturally, but in the varieties of Islam it houses. The state's failure to embrace this pluralism has lain at the heart of its perennial problems of identity. Pakistan fifty years on is also still a hierarchical society. The failure to empower the mass of its population has lain at the heart of successive regimes' legitimacy problems.

Pakistan at fifty is in some ways very different than at the time of its creation. Karachi, for example, illustrates both the dynamism and the disorder flowing from rapid population growth and massive migration. Faisalabad, the 'Manchester of Pakistan', epitomises the strides in industrialisation which have been made from the low base inherited from the Raj. The crowded flights to London and New York and the mushrooming satellite dishes alike attest to increasing links to the global economy and communications networks.

Yet despite such changes, the political continuities of the post-independence era remain striking. The observation *'plus ça change, plus c'est la même chose'* seems particularly apposite. Despite incessantly changing political regimes, constitutions and institutions, the inherited democratic deficit of semi-feudalism, strategic insecurity and the viceregal tradition of the British Raj has remained influential. Ayub's experiment with guided democracy failed to bring about modernisation because it was unable to solve the problem of legitimacy which had beset its predecessors during the first decade of independence. Bhutto's new departure of populism foundered because it was unable to transcend the twin colonial inheritances of viceregalism and clientelist politics. Zia's Islamisation process exacerbated the divisions within Pakistani society based on religion, gender and ethnicity instead of healing them. As Lawrence Ziring has noted, 'Zia's Islamic state and the political system with which it is associated intensified and multiplied the divisions

368

that have plagued the nation since its birth.'[1] The restoration of democracy in 1988, despite the high hopes which attended it, ushered in a cycle of corruption, clientelism and political confrontation which created a crisis of governability. Democratic rulers, no less than the reviled military, have governed in an arbitrary fashion. Since 1988, no elected government has completed its term of office.

The political system and its practitioners in the 1990s appeared as ineffectual and bankrupt as their counterparts in the first troubled decade of independence. In both eras, politicians raised charges of corruption against their opponents while at the same time using patronage to secure power. The only difference is that with the passage of time both the resources available for corruption and the media's ability to uncover it have dramatically increased. Now, as during the 1950s, the disorderly struggle between opposition and government encourages military intervention in the political process. This very authoritarianism has in the past perpetuated the weakly institutionalised personalist politics which have become Pakistan's hallmark. Moreover, the cumulative effect of authoritarian rule has been to reinforce an inherited political culture which disavows cooperation and accommodation in favour of confrontation and intimidation. Thus it is hardly surprising that successive regimes have foundered in the attempt to forge a national consensus.

The two following assessments of Pakistani politics and society were made by a British observer towards the end of 1949. They could however have been uttered at any time during the state's half-century of existence:

> It may well be asked whether the present political manoeuvres (in Sindh) are of any real importance. The answer is that, of themselves they are probably not.[...] Indirectly, however, they are of real importance... they seem to increase the disgust felt by the important upper middle class section of the country, whose services are badly needed by Pakistan in... the administration, within the Muslim League, within politics as a whole.[...] Though Sind is doubtless an extreme case, the situation there is symptomatic of provincial public life throughout Pakistan, particularly in the revelation of the utter lack of idealism and public spirit and the complete ascendancy of personal motives.[2]

The 'Commonwealth Cricket Team' played two matches during their week's visit to Karachi. It is unfortunate that local politics,

---

[1] L. Ziring, 'Public Policy Dilemmas and Pakistan's Nationality Problem: The Legacy of Zia ul-Haq', *Asian Survey* 28, no. 8 (August 1988), p. 798.

[2] British Deputy High Commissioner's Report Sindh, Karachi, Balochistan, 18 November-24 November 1949, L/P&J/5/331 IOR.

which seem to permeate every aspect of life in Sind, should have affected the selection of the Sind team, three of the best players refusing to play owing to dissatisfaction with the methods of selection. The umpiring also left a great deal to be desired and the score cards were notable for a remarkable number of lbw decisions against the Commonwealth team. This lead to some unfortunate incidents, as a result of one of which Pepper, an Australian member of the team, is returning home to England.[3]

Mike Gatting's[4] infamous spat during the 1987 Faisalabad test match with the Pakistani umpire Shakoor Rana was thus not without historical precedent.[5] More important, there was never a golden age in Pakistani politics when idealism rather than cynicism and opportunism reigned. Horse-trading, the use of executive power to intimidate the opposition and the politicisation and corruption of the bureaucracy have all been rightly condemned in post-1988 Pakistan. They were all present at the birth of the nation as can be seen for example in any reading of Sindhi politics. What is new is only the extent of corruption made possible by increased resources and its infection of military as well as civilian life. Throughout its half-century of independent existence, Pakistan has functioned like an extension of the colonial viceregal state, while lacking its moral authority, legal order and tax-raising efficiency.

Another constant has been Pakistan's precarious strategic situation facing a hostile India and Afghanistan and, for many years, a potentially hostile Soviet Union. In military terms the Indian strategic threat has increased in the half-century since independence. Since November 1947, when Jinnah requested a $2 billion loan from the United States, successive Pakistani rulers have called the New World into existence to redress the balance of the Old. In Pakistani minds the Americans have frequently let down their loyal allies with the result that the People's Republic of China and the Gulf States have also been brought into the strategic balance. Indeed the Chinese have proved to be Pakistan's most constant allies. The American arms embargo at the time of the 1965 war rankled especially. Such episodes arose almost inevitably from the different

---

[3] British Deputy High Commissioner's Report Sind, Karachi, Balochistan, 2 December-8 December 1949, L/P&J/5/331 IOR.

[4] Gatting was the England captain at the time of this Second Test match of the Winter tour. His violent altercation with Rana captured international headlines.

[5] For the view that cricket propagated imperial values and reinforced the British self-image of superiority so that claims of Pakistani umpires and players being cheats is a continuation of the colonial 'demonising' of the other, see Asad Ali, 'Great Balls of Fire', *Newsline*, 8, no.2 (August 1996), pp. 18 and 19.

security perceptions of the United States and its 'most allied ally'. Even when Soviet troops were violating Pakistan's border during the Afghan struggle, Islamabad still perceived New Delhi rather than Moscow as the main threat and was eager to receive arms to counter this rather than for Cold War purposes.

In addition to a reliance on foreign allies to offset Indian dominance, Pakistan from its inception has attached great importance to the mobilisation of limited domestic resources for defence. This, along with the failure to introduce effective land reform, has perpetuated the social inequalities inherited from the colonial era. The 'over-development' of the military institution has encouraged authoritarianism in an environment of political opportunism and weak institutionalisation. The fact that the Pakistan Army has remained a predominantly Punjabi force has intensified the feeling of the smaller provinces that they are colonised by a Punjabi province which both benefits from this policy and has a stake in its continuation. Reduction of military expenditure in order to free funds for development is, as we have seen, high on a wish-list for Pakistan's future. Past experience, however, has created a not entirely unjustified fear of Indian hegemonistic impulses. Moreover, the constant sore of the Kashmir issue, the longest-running dispute before the United Nations, prevents the improvement in bilateral relations which is necessary for arms reductions and the establishment of a subcontinental security system. The twin pressures of economic globalisation and South Asian regionalism may eventually pave the way for a peaceful and co-operative subcontinental security environment, but in the immediate future no government in Islamabad could survive if it sought *détente* with India in order to make the necessary drastic arms reductions that would enable it seriously to address the mass poverty of its people. This would be depicted as a craven surrender of vital national interests.

Just as the imbalance of power between Pakistan and India has formed a constant context for the former's security and military policies, so its domestic politics have been continuously influenced by asymmetry between Punjab and the other provinces. Again, although fears of Punjabi hegemony are exaggerated, past experience has given the minority provinces sufficient cause for concern. Ethnic political consciousness among the *mohajirs*, Sindhis and, earlier, the Bengalis was rooted in part in a reaction to the domination of the Punjabi 'other'. Ironically the response to this 'Punjabi-bashing' was to strengthen Punjabi identity which had previously been subsumed under the wider Pakistani national identity.

Punjab is not monolithic, but only when the region's political boundaries are redrawn to acknowledge this reality will the fears of a Punjabisation of Pakistan cease. By creating three new provinces comprising two divisions with their headquarters respectively at Multan, Rawalpindi and Lahore, the imbalances in power which have undermined the country's stability will be addressed.[6] Moreover such a constitutional step would also accelerate the pace of development in the more backward parts of Punjab. The problem, as with arms control and *détente* with India, is how to get to this point in an atmosphere of mistrust and suspicion which would result in any radical changes being depicted as an attenuation of national security and state structures.

The reports of Pakistan's death have been greatly exaggerated. Tariq Ali's work, *Can Pakistan Survive? The Death of A State* now lies gathering dust. Pakistan's problems of identity and authority on the eve of the Twenty First Century are enormous, but not insoluble. This study has revealed for example that ethnic tensions are not based on the irreconcilable 'Dark Gods' of primordialism, but are circumstantialist. Sindhi, Baloch and *mohajir* nationalists have all 'cut ethnic identities to suit their political cloth'. The formation of a Punjabi and *mohajir* political identity in Sindh has clearly been influenced by economic and political competition with neighbouring groupings. The instrumentalist basis of identity is especially evident in the construction of a *mohajir* political identity by a leadership born in Pakistan. Although it never experienced migration it created 'foundational' myths of partition-related sacrifice which drew strength from a contemporary sense of disadvantage.

Similarly the state's weak legitimisation is not bound up in some irreconcilable conflict between Islam, democracy and the modern nation state, rather it has resulted from a lack of political participation. Rajni Kothari's recent critique of Indian democracy is especially apposite for Pakistan. 'Arenas of participation have been cornered by a few' Kothari maintains, producing for many a sheer struggle for survival in an increasingly iniquitous world'.[7] To consolidate Pakistan's procedural/formal democracy, the introduction of proportional representation, and restoration of a joint electorate with reservation of seats for minorities should be contemplated along with a restoration of reserved seats for women. The casting of a ballot in an election is however only part of the process of political empowerment. In order to achieve a substantive

---

[6] The three new provinces would have roughly the same size population as Sindh, the Frontier and Balochistan respectively. The proposal for the creation of new provinces is not in fact as radical as it seems as it was put forward by the Ansari Commission during the Zia era. On the anniversary of the dismissal of Benazir Bhutto's first dismissal, Rashid Ahmad a retired additional secretary to the government of Pakistan argued strongly for such a proposal along with a fixed three year life form provincial and national assemblies and local bodies See *Dawn Magazine*, 9 August 1991.

[7] R. Kothari, 'Pluralist Politics in India: Cultural Roots, Recent Erosions', p.45 Unpublished paper cited in N.G. Jayal, 'The State and Democracy in India', paper presented at India 50 conference, University of Sussex, 24-27 September 1997.

democracy there must be a search for social justice. This flows into such wider fields as legal reform, greater accountability and supervision of the police, perhaps by means of an Ombudsman, and a sustained literacy drive supported by an enforceable ban on child labour until the age of 14. Successive regimes have promised to achieve universal literacy, but fifty years on it remains as distant a goal as ever. Yet without increased literacy the social conditions do not exist for democracy to be consolidated.

Wider institutional political reform would include experiments with decentralisation in local government decision making to the *panchayat* and *mohalla* level, in the redrawing of provincial boundaries and even confederation in order to arrive at a workable political system. Such experimentation would not be entirely out of keeping in a country whose post-independence history has been marked by 'the casting aside of older political forms for newer political experiments.'[8] It would also mean a return to the original intentions of the foundational but now forgotten Lahore Resolution.

In dealing with political and economic trends both at a national and provincial level, this work has inevitably missed something of the essence of Pakistan – its millions of people living in thousands of towns and villages who remain its greatest asset. Their resilience in the face of the sufferings brought by migration, war and civil conflict has underpinned the nation's existence. In the day to day struggle for economic survival, they remain unconcerned about the infighting between politicians who continuously mouth slogans about the people's welfare while they live off the fat of the land. Yet it was from the ordinary people that the Pakistan movement drew its dynamism. The campaigns to unseat Pakistan's first military ruler and to secure freedom for the Bengalis were similarly rooted in the masses. If such popular outpourings could be channelled and institutionalised they would open the possibility of more participatory politics. These in turn would reduce clientalism and go some way towards solving Pakistan's persisting problems of regime legitimisation. In a virtuous cycle the way might then be open for the radical decentralisation to which we have referred above which is so urgently required to address the nation's long-established identity problems.

This conclusion commenced by arguing that Pakistan's politics could not be summed up in terms of the three 'A's'. We end on the note that further polarisation and instability can only be avoided by an internalisation of the five 'C's' of consensus, consent, commitment, conviction and compassion. In other words, Pakistan's best hope for the

---

[8] Ziring, 'Public Policy Dilemmas', p. 797.

future lies not in taking out the begging bowl to international governments and organisations, nor in sham populist or Islamic sloganeering, nor in successive bouts of authoritarianism designed to keep the lid on popular unrest. The way forward can only lie in the genuine political participation of previously marginalised groups such as women, the minorities and the rural and urban poor. This would not only redeem the 'failed promise' of 1947, but also provide hope that Pakistan can effectively tackle the immense economic, social and environmental challenges of the next century.

MUSHARRAF'S PAKISTAN: COUP, CRISIS AND CONFLICT

The October 1999 coup challenged Pakistan's democratic future. The aftermath of the World Trade Centre and Pentagon bombings on 9/11 called the state's survival into question. General Musharraf gravely warned that any wrong decision could spell disaster for its existence, and that the country was 'passing through its most critical phase since 1971'.[1] The Indian response to the 13 December 2001 attack on the Parliament building in New Delhi that resulted in nine fatalities brought the nuclear neighbours perilously close to war.

The pervading air of regional crisis and uncertainty contrasted sharply with the Musharraf regime's assured pronouncements on its wide-ranging domestic reform agenda. This had begun to acquire international credibility, before the post 9/11 response ended the diplomatic isolation arising from the coup and the Kargil war. While accountability possessed a familiar ring, the watchwords of decentralisation, devolution and empowerment had not so readily fallen from the lips of previous military rulers. Nevertheless, Musharraf's Pakistan increasingly resembled Ayub's failed modernisation and political reconstruction. The October 2002 national elections betokened not a brave new world of grassroots democracy, but the guided democracy of the Ayub and late and post-Zia periods. While journalistic attention focused on the dramatic consequences of 9/11, to seasoned observers Pakistan appeared to be stuck in a familiar historical groove. Good governance and political legitimacy remained elusive goals.

The coup of 12 October 1999

A PTV newsflash at 4.00 p.m. on 12 October 1999 announced the dismissal of the Chief of Army Staff, General Pervez Musharraf, who was then in-flight to Pakistan from Colombo. Shortly afterwards Nawaz Sharif taped a national address at the television station before returning

---

1 *Dawn*, Internet edn, 20 September 2001.

to his official residence in Islamabad. Lieut.-General Ziauddin, who had been appointed to replace Musharraf, had already been arrested. Unaware, Nawaz Sharif summoned a number of senior generals, but the discussions were interrupted by the arrival of the Commander, X Corps, Rawalpindi, Lieut.-General Mehmood Ahmad, with troops loyal to Musharraf. He abruptly ended Nawaz Sharif's second spell as Pakistan's Prime Minister.

Nawaz Sharif claimed that Musharraf had carefully planned the coup, and that his action had been prompted by criticism of the army's role in the mid-1999 Kargil episode and by the attempt to exert civilian control over the military.[2] In a national broadcast Musharraf echoed earlier justifications of coups, claiming that the army had intervened because of political mismanagement which had weakened the economy, encouraged provincial disharmony and undermined state institutions. He also dealt with the peculiar circumstances surrounding the need for a 'counter-coup' following his dismissal and the attempted hijack of his PK 805 Airbus as it returned from Sri Lanka.[3] The deposed Prime Minister was to be tried on these charges before an Anti-Terrorism Court.

Pervez Musharraf repeated the promise Zia made in 1977, when he declared that the armed forces 'have no intention to stay in charge any longer than is absolutely necessary.'[4] But unlike either Zia or Ayub, he exchanged the language of the service manual for development studies, when he spoke of the importance of 'good governance' and of the need for governments to 'serve' rather than 'rule' the people. 'Quite clearly what Pakistan has experienced in recent years', Musharraf opined, 'has been merely a label of democracy, not the essence of it. Our people were never emancipated from the yoke of despotism. I shall not allow the people to be taken back to the era of sham democracy, but to a true one.'[5]

These ringing phrases were accompanied by a seven-point programme, aimed at restoring national credibility and harmony.[6] At its heart was a drive for accountability. Investor confidence was to be regained by improvements in law and order and the documentation of the economy. Finally, Musharraf promised the empowerment of grassroots political

2 I. H. Malik, 'Pakistan in 2000: Starting Anew or Stalemate', *Asian Survey* XLI, 1 (January/February 2001), pp. 106–7

3 The Supreme Court was later to uphold the verdict of the Karachi court that Nawaz Sharif was guilty of conspiracy regarding the plane incident, although there were procedural problems surrounding the case which had been accompanied by the murder of Iqbal Raad, one of the deposed Prime Minister's attorneys.

4 *Dawn*, Internet edn, 18 October 1999.

5 *Ibid.*

6 The Points were as follows: 1, restoring national confidence and morale; 2, reducing inter-provincial disharmony and restoring national cohesion; 3, reviving the economy and restoring investors' confidence; 4, ensuring law and order and speedy justice; 5, strengthening and depoliticising state institutions; 6, devolving more power to the grassroots; and 7, imposing across-the-board accountability.

bodies through a process of decentralisation. The patchy record on the delivery of these promises is considered later. First we must turn to an analysis of the coup.

The coup appears to have been spontaneous, unlike either Ayub's or Zia's. There is no evidence that Musharraf planned a seizure of power on the lines of Zia's Operation Fairplay. The confused events at the PTV offices in Islamabad on the day it took place support this interpretation.[7] What could be termed a reactive 'counter-coup' thus took place on 12 October, although Nawaz Sharif maintained that he was entitled to dismiss the army chief. Unsubstantiated rumours have persisted that the DG ISI, Lieut.-General Ziauddin, forced the Prime Minister's hand. Whether he was pushed or not, Nawaz Sharif's personalisation of power had precipitated his downfall.

Nevertheless, questions remain regarding the military version of events. The army's intervention was not caused simply by Nawaz Sharif's political high-handedness. The military could have acted as early as October 1997 during the Prime Minister's confrontation with the Chief Justice, Sajjad Ali Shah. President Farooq Leghari sided with the Chief Justice, but stepped down on 2 December, when it was clear that the army remained neutral.

Nawaz Sharif alienated the army because of his interference in its affairs. Such civilian encroachment had also precipitated the 'constitutional coups' of 1990, 1993 and 1996, and the Prime Minister's removal of the Eighth Amendment had closed off this preferred military option. There are parallels in the ways that Nawaz Sharif and Zulfiqar Ali Bhutto in that both leaders had personalised power and so could only be removed by the generals. Moreover, they had both promoted their eventual nemesis to the position of army chief in preference to more senior officers; Musharraf had been appointed in October 1998 over the head of General Ali Quli Khan Khattak.[8]

During the following year tension had increased between the army chief and the Prime Minister. Musharraf objected to the military being blamed for the failed Kargil adventure, and he was further upset by the knowledge that information was being leaked from his monthly meetings with the nine powerful Corps Commanders.[9] The fear that Nawaz

---

7 Security forces apprehended the small force a surprised Lieut.-General Mehmood Ahmad despatched there, with the result that the broadcast was made of Musharraf's dismissal and replacement as COAS by the DG ISI, Lieut.-General Ziauddin. After this Mehmood Ahmed took more troops to the studios and also arrested Nawaz Sharif.

8 Nawaz Sharif had forced the COAS, General Jehangir Karamat, to retire early following a disagreement with him over the establishment of a National Security Council. It has been argued that General Khattak was overlooked as his replacement because Nawaz Sharif was not comfortable with a Pushtun general holding the most senior position.

9 The importance of the Corps Commanders' Committees was demonstrated after the seizure of power in that every one of Musharraf's cabinet members had to be unanimously approved by them.

Sharif was attempting to divide and rule the army, just as he had the judiciary in 1997, increased with his appointment of Lieut.-General Ziauddin as the DG of ISI, which placed him first in the line of succession. Ziauddin was seen as a Sharif man. He was an equally unpopular choice with the high command, because it seemed possible that for the first time someone outside the fighting branches of the army could become Chief of Army Staff.[10] The discipline of the Pakistan army chain of command, reinforced by these group loyalty feelings, ensured that Ziauddin was cold-shouldered on 12 October.

The 1958 and 1977 coups had been greeted calmly. Unsurprisingly, in the less fevered atmosphere of 1999, some people came on to the streets to welcome the army—thus providing a fitting epitaph for an era in which parliament was at worst a bear-pit, at best the fountainhead of patronage politics. Their action also reflected the long-term respect accorded to the army, especially in the Punjab. It was seen not only as the nation's guardian but as an employer, educator and provider of welfare services. Ironically Nawaz Sharif furthered the army's involvement in such civilian responsibilities as the national census, the inquiry into 'ghost schools' in Punjab, and the management of the Water Power and Development Authority. Ordinary consumers applauded its attempts to check 'electricity theft' by the large landowners.[11]

The May 2000 Supreme Court ruling justified the military intervention. Ayub's coup had been legitimised by reference to Hans Kelson's doctrine of revolutionary legality. Musharraf's by contrast received legal cover, as had Zia's, by reference to the doctrine of necessity, whereby it was maintained that the armed forces intervened to save the state from chaos. In one important respect the May 2000 ruling went beyond the 1977 verdict. It set a time-limit of three years from the coup for the new regime to hold national elections. International pressure kept Musharraf to this time-table.

Musharraf's leadership and relationship with the army hierarchy

Pervez Musharraf immediately portrayed himself as a moderate figure, more in the mould of Ayub than Zia, and he pointedly took the title of Chief Executive rather than Chief Martial Law Administrator. On 20 June 2001 he followed Ayub's and Zia's path by assuming the Presidency, a

10 The COAS has traditionally been drawn from the fighting branches of the army, i.e. cavalry, armour and artillery. Ziauddin came from the engineering branch. Bonds of army service including branch, combat experience and year of officer graduation are more important for networks of loyalty than ethnicity or religious affiliation.

11 The army's management of WAPDA was due to end on 31 March 2001, but was extended until 31 December 2002. *Dawn*, Internet edn, 17 January 2001.

move prompted in part by the forthcoming Agra summit[12] with the Indian Prime Minister.

Musharraf's moderate persona was necessitated by the country's post-coup diplomatic isolation. Furthermore, the International Monetary Fund had to be reassured if the breathing space of a further rescheduling of loans was to be won.[13] Musharraf was not play-acting. He lacked Zia's unctuous personal piety and was an instinctive consensus-builder. Nevertheless, his career reflected the significant changes in the Pakistan army since the 1980s. Indeed, in his training of Afghan *mujahideen* at the time of the Soviet occupation and his involvement in the planning of the Kargil operation, Musharraf was at the heart of the army's post-1979 strategic alliance with Afghan *mujahideen* and *jihad* groups, a policy designed to counterbalance India's regional supremacy. After the watershed of 9/11, he had to reverse a strategy to which he had been committed, not as an Islamist but as a 'soldier's soldier'.

Musharraf's abandonment of the Taliban prompted fears of a counter-coup, which could have been led by junior Islamist officers or by those close to the Afghan regime and *jihad* groups. Anxieties intensified on the eve of the US bombing campaign in Afghanistan. Musharraf superseded Lieut.-General Mehmood Ahmad, DG ISI, and General Muzaffar Hussain Usmani, deputy chief of army staff with the promotion of their junior colleagues Lieut.-General Aziz Khan and Lieut.-General Mohammad Yousaf.[14] Both Usmani and Mehmood had played crucial roles in the October 1999 coup, but were nonetheless seen as hardliners. Journalistic analysis ignored the fact that Musharraf had been building a core of loyalists since his appointment by Nawaz Sharif as Chief of Army Staff. He was following Zia's policy of the promotion of community members when he appointed a fellow Mohajir, Lieut.-General (retd) Moinuddin Haider to the key post of Interior Minister. Speculation regarding Mohajir-Punjabi splits, or for that matter Sunni-Shi'a[15] splits in

12 The summit marked a resumption of the Lahore process which had been disrupted by the Kargil episode. The summit failed over the central issue of Kashmir, although under US pressure the Indian and Pakistan governments agreed to the continuation of dialogue. In the aftermath of 9/11, tensions once again emerged in Indo-Pakistan relations, as New Delhi fretted that the Americans had too readily accepted the Pakistan regime as an ally in the war against terrorism.

13 This was achieved not just through Musharraf's moderate image and attempts at structural reform with respect to taxation, but by the appointment of Shaukat Aziz, formerly of Citibank, as Finance Minister.

14 *Dawn*, Internet edn, 8 October 2001. Mehmood was Musharraf's friend from their days in the Special Services Group. They had been close colleagues at the time of the Kargil conflict and, as we have seen, Mehmood had played a decisive role in the October 1999 coup.

15 Indeed the senior Shi'a generals, Saeed Amjad and Syed Tanvir Hussain Naqvi, were appointed to the important chairmanships of the National Accountability Bureau and the National Reconstruction Bureau.

the army hierarchy, ignored the importance of consensus and institutional loyalty. It also underestimated Musharraf's ability in the short term to safeguard national interests. This depended both on his diplomatic skills and his usefulness to the Americans. Zia had been a trusted leader of the front-line states in the struggle against communism because of his religious zeal. Musharraf's pragmatism and moderation were as valuable in the very different war in Afghanistan against terrorism.

Musharraf's reforms and achievements

Pakistani coup leaders have always justified their intervention in terms of national crisis. For Ayub Pakistan's salvation lay in a guided democracy dedicated to economic and social modernisation; Zia saw Pakistan's stability in Islamisation; and Musharraf has pinned his hopes on 'across-the-board accountability', the revival of the economy and 'devolution of power to the people'. The establishment of a grassroots democracy, cleansed of the political elite's corruption, echoed Ayub's Basic Democracy scheme. It followed the tradition of political experimentation within Pakistan.

The Musharraf regime linked accountability with both democratic consolidation and national economic renewal; more public-spirited newcomers would replace the old guard of corrupt politicians. The accountability drive would also revive the economy[16] by extending the precariously narrow tax-base[17] and by encouraging investment. Limited progress was made in the recovery of bad debts. Symbolic of the regime's intent was Nawaz Sharif's conviction, less than three months after he began his life sentence for hijacking, on corruption and tax evasion charges.[18]

The new National Accountability Bureau, which had been established by ordinance, exercised sweeping powers of investigation and arrest, but human rights organisations increasingly questioned its activities,[19] criticising its power to keep the accused in detention for up to ninety days without the need to appear before a court. Equally controversial was the denial of bail and the requirement that detainees prove their innocence. Disquieting reports of ill-treatment of high-profile detainees emanated from the forbidding Attock Fort. The Bureau's political motives were also questioned, since those convicted by it were prohibited from holding public office for twenty-one years. Opposition

16 The new regime inherited a situation in which the outstanding foreign debt stood at $42 billion and the domestic debt at $70 billion. Annual servicing of these debts took up to 60 per cent of the GDP.

17 In a country of 130 million inhabitants, just 1.2 million people paid tax.

18 On 22 July 2000 he received a further fourteen-years sentence and a Rs 20 million fine.

19 See, e.g., Human Rights Watch Report on Pakistan 2001
www.hrw.org/k1/wr2/asia/pakistan.html

leaders were further hamstrung by an amendment to the Political Parties Act in August 2000, which barred anyone with a court conviction from holding party office. The implications were serious for Benazir Bhutto in her Dubai exile, since she had been convicted of corruption during Nawaz Sharif's Premiership. Was the accountability process intended to eradicate corruption, or to disqualify the regime's opponents for the foreseeable future? By the beginning of February 2001, 242 politicians were under investigation for corruption and the misuse of their official positions.[20]

Cynicism replaced idealism when Musharraf allowed Nawaz Sharif, early on Sunday 10 December 2000, to go into exile in Saudi Arabia: he departed with twenty-two containers packed with furniture and carpets, accompanied by his family entourage, some of whom still had corruption charges hanging over them. In return for his release he promised to abstain from politics. Critics thereafter branded accountability as self-serving, rather than regarding it as central to institutional reform.[21]

By September 2000 the high-handed methods of the National Accountability Bureau were denting investor and business confidence. The midnight knock on the door for suspected tax-evaders was dispensed with. Its new chairman Lieut.-General Khalid Maqbool, who had been transferred from his position as a corps commander in Lahore in a series of military job transfers, presided over this change.

Decentralisation of power

Devolution of power was presented as central to the establishment of a 'true democracy', and on 14 August 2000 the Chief Executive highlighted its main features. The announcement had been preceded by widespread discussion of the National Reconstruction Bureau's proposals. The reforms involved local government bodies from district to village level. The plan for devolution of power contained two major elements designed to strengthen grassroots democracy. First, increased popular participation was encouraged through the reservation of seats for previously marginalised groups, and second, the district administrative service was made accountable to the voters. The twelve departments of the district administration were monitored both by special Union Council committees and by the creation of Citizens' Community Boards which reached down to the village level. The most important of the monitoring committees were the Public Safety and Justice Committees, which issued monthly reports on the police and the judiciary.

One-third of the seats in the district (*zila*), *tehsil*, union and village councils were reserved for women. In addition, 5 per cent each were re-

20 *Dawn*, Internet edn, 12 February 2001.
21 See www.Informationtimes.com 16 December 2000.

served for workers/peasants and minorities. The district-level administration and the police were placed directly under the control of local
representatives in the shape of the *Zila Nazim* (District Administrator)
and *Naib Nazim* (Deputy Administrator), who would be indirectly
elected as joint candidates by the union council members throughout
the district. The Union Councils possessed 21 members (18 of whom
would be elected). Their heads were automatically members of the *Zila*
council. Elections to the village council were to be by secret ballot with
the candidate who received the highest number of votes becoming
chairperson. The village councils were made responsible for promoting civic education, community learning and gender issues as well as
assessing finances required for projects and mobilising popular contributions.[22] In sum, the ambitious scheme was designed to recognise the
people's rights to development, participation and information. On paper
it represented a huge step forward towards governments which would
'serve' the people rather than 'rule' them.

The scheme linked grassroots democracy with the development process. This was pressing since the economic crises of the 1990s had dramatically increased poverty. At the beginning of the decade one in five
families was estimated to be living below the poverty line; by its close
this had risen to one in three.[23] Yet the scheme was not accompanied by
land reform. Critics seized on this to claim that the reforms were merely
an attempt to cash in on international donors' new-found belief that
good governance was vital for poverty alleviation.[24] By adopting this
agenda the Musharraf regime could achieve respectability abroad and
ensure funds to prop up the economy.

Whatever its motivations, the scheme ignored the highly skewed rural
power relations. The new regime ruled out land reform, although it
toyed with the idea of introducing productivity quotas in Balochistan
and Sind. If these were not met, owners would be forced to sell land privately. Without land reform the devolution of power would deliver the
administration into the hands of the local landed élites. This would both
limit participation[25] and pre-empt funds intended for the wider population—an outcome that became more likely due to the insistence that the
elections to local bodies should be 'partyless'; in the 1985 'partyless'
elections held by Zia, landowners relying on their local influence and
the manipulation of *biraderi* (kinship) networks had captured 117 out of
the 200 seats in the National Assembly.

22 National Reconstruction Bureau, *Local Government (Final Plan 2000)* (Islamabad,
2000).

23 Social Policy and Development Centre Karachi, *Social Development in Pakistan
Annual Review 2000: Towards Poverty Reduction* (Karachi, 2000) p. 2.

24 *Ibid.*, p. 124.

25 Participation was limited by the refusal of minorities to contest the elections in protest
at the continuation of separate electorates.

The four phases of elections to local bodies from December 2000 failed to usher in a new style of grassroots democracy. Voter turnout, and the pattern of electioneering, fell short of the government's hopes. Musharraf had frequently exhorted the voters to disregard the parties and the old-style politics they represented. The electoral rules were designed to assist this. The Election Ordinances contained a comprehensive 19-point list designed to exclude any candidate who had been convicted by a court for corrupt practices, who had been judged an intentional tax defaulter, or who possessed undeclared assets. The 25-Point code of ethics laid down by the Pakistan Election Commission banned candidates from holding public meetings, leading processions, waving flags or even displaying banners. Both sets of guidelines were circumvented. A number of party nominees who were under the shadow of corruption charges secured election.

On 31 December 2000 the first phase of elections for 956 Union Councils took place in eighteen of the country's districts.[26] Official figures revealed that only 3.9 million out of 8.9 million registered voters had cast their ballot. Contestants were also thin on the ground. In the Makran division of Balochistan, for example, there were only 1,519 candidates for the 1,407 seats. Hopes of empowering marginalised groups were dashed, as many seats reserved for women and minorities were left vacant,[27] or candidates were returned without a contest. Indeed, there were just eighty-eight contests in non-Muslim seats throughout the eighteen districts. In the Dera Ismail Khan district of the NWFP alone, 138 minority seats were uncontested. In the 3,822 reserved general seats for women 1,318 candidates were elected unopposed.[28] Many of these in 'backward' areas of NWFP and Sind had been put forward by tribal and *biraderi* leaders to increase their bargaining power at district level.

The ban on electioneering, which had been justified as a means of reducing costs and so allowing lower-class candidates to compete for office, was ineffectual. In Muzaffargarh, for example, candidates had arranged dozens of motor-cycles to transport voters to the polls. Others had hired rickshaws or cars. In Sargodha candidates painted their symbols on the rear windows of cars hired to transport voters. Earlier they had circumvented the ban on public meetings by calling these *iftar* parties.

The continued importance of *biraderi* ties hindered middle-class politicians. It was reported in Sargodha and Muzaffargarh that candidates contacted *biraderi* elders and bought their votes in bulk, procuring a

---

26 Elections were held in 8 districts of Punjab, 4 in NWFP, 3 in Balochistan and 3 in Sind.

27 In the Bannu district of NWFP, for example, 36/40 Union Councils had no female candidates. In the three districts of Balochistan where elections were held, only 4 candidates stood in the 51 seats reserved for minorities.

28 *Dawn*, Internet edn, 5 January 2001.

Epilogue

promise that these would be delivered by securing an oath of loyalty on the Quran. In the tribal areas of Dera Ismail Khan, Dera Ghazi Khan and Tank, the familiar names of Miankhel, Makhdoom, Leghari and Bhattani secured election.

The elections to local bodies similarly failed to banish political parties, because the patronage of 'discredited' political leaders remained vital. For example, the majority of council members elected in Sargodha City were loyal to the PML(N) leader Abdul Hameed who was in the National Accountability Board's custody on corruption charges. The so-called 'partyless' elections in the Punjab in fact saw a resurgence of the PPP[29] following its drubbing in 1997. The pattern of the 1993 assembly elections was repeated with the PPP winning in the countryside and the PML(N) in the towns.

On Wednesday 21 March 2001, the second phase of the elections to local bodies was held in twenty districts.[30] The Election Commission's figures recorded a higher national turn-out (52.45 per cent) than that of the previous December.[31] This was achieved by declaring a public holiday in these districts and allowing voters to cast their ballot without producing a national identity card.[32] Women were prevented from voting in the Mardan and Swabi districts of NWFP, following the decisions of tribal *jirgas*. Candidates backed by the government's political opponents won many seats. For example, in the Khairpur district of Sind the Awam Dost Panel, supported by the PPP, captured a majority of the 76 union council seats.[33]

The PPP repeated its success in Sind in the third phase of voting on 31 May 2001, capturing 32/64 seats in Mirpurkhas. A further 33 seats were won by PPP-backed candidates in the Latifabad and Qasimabad districts.[34] Women were again prevented from both casting their ballot and filing nomination papers in areas of the NWFP, especially the Hangu district. The Human Rights Commission of Pakistan condemned this violation of their fundamental rights.

The final polls were held on 2 July 2001 in 29 districts, including the major cities of Lahore, Karachi and Peshawar. The violence of the earlier rounds had increased. Harassment of women, low turn-out and party-backed candidates were again commonplace. The ballot was

---

29 The PPP made considerable inroads in the rural areas of Dera Ghazi Khan and Sargodha.

30 The districts were as follows in Punjab: Bahawalpur, Bahawalnagar, Rahimyar Khan, Gujranwala, Hafizabad, Gujrat, Mandi Bahauddin, Sialkot and Narowal; in Sindh: Sukkur, Ghotki, Khairpur, Naushahro Feroze, and Nawabshah; in NWFP: Kohat, Karak, Mardan and Swabi; in Balochistan: Nasirabad and Kachhi.

31 *Dawn*, Internet edn, 24 March 2001.

32 *Dawn*, Internet edn, 21 March 2001.

33 *Dawn*, Internet edn, 23 March 2001.

34 *Arab News*, Internet edn, 11 July 2001.

especially low in Karachi[35] as a result of the boycott by the two factions of MQM; on polling day markets, shopping centres and bazaars were deserted.[36] By contrast, electioneering was lively in Lahore, which had been a bastion of support for the deposed Prime Minister Nawaz Sharif. The high turnout of over 50 per cent was marred by claims of ballot-rigging in favour of pro-government groups such as the PML(QA) which included former Nawaz loyalists and the Qaumi Tajir Ittehad.[37] There was widespread violation of election rules, as candidates transported supporters to the polls and served them food. The elections in the seven districts of the NWFP were marred by violence, and in Peshawar one person was killed and forty others were injured. A further 30 people were injured in clashes at different polling stations in Rawalpindi. The activities of Maulana Sufi Mohammad's Tehrik Nifaz-e-Shariat-e-Mohammadi (TNSM) disenfranchised women; Maulana Sufi Mohammad maintained that 'permission to women to contest elections or cast their votes would lead to their independence, which Islam does not allow.'[38] All but seven of the twenty-seven female polling stations in the union councils of the Malakand Agency remained unused, and this was repeated in the Lower Dir district where none of the 137,199 women voters was allowed to vote.[39] In the less restrictive atmosphere of Peshawar in contrast, women participated both as electors and candidates. They took part in door-to-door canvassing, and even allowed their photographs to appear on publicity posters.

The second phase of elections in March 2001 produced over 50,000 candidates for the 20,005 seats in the nine districts of Punjab alone. The third phase for 1,575 union councils in eighteen districts of the country saw 16,345 polling stations in use, manned by 186,885 staff.[40] This was elective democracy on a vast scale. Yet the polls failed to transform politics. Traditional party allegiances and the power of *biraderi* networks prevented the emergence of a new type of politician. Social conservatism thwarted the intended empowerment of women.

Civil society

Musharraf stressed his liberal credentials by his promise to uphold press freedom. The monitoring of administrative services by citizens' groups

---

35 The official figure was 35 per cent. Unofficial figures placed this more realistically at 25 per cent. In MQM(A) areas such as Nazimabad, and Liquatabad it was less than 10 per cent, as it was in the MQM(H) Lines Area of Karachi.

36 *Dawn*, Internet edn, 3 July 2001.

37 *The News International*, Internet edn, 3 July 2001.

38 *Ibid.*

39 *Ibid.*

40 *Dawn*, Internet edn, 31 May 2001

was also an integral part of his proclaimed good governance agenda. Earlier military regimes had not spoken of participation, or of the need for Pakistanis to be 'masters of their own destiny'.

The success stories of civil society have been the growth of the press and non-governmental organisations (NGOs). According to the National Reconstruction Bureau, Pakistan possesses 424 daily newspapers, 718 weeklies, 107 fortnightlies and 553 monthly periodicals. NGOs, as in other developing countries, have recently provided the social services abandoned by an inefficient public sector undermined by declining revenues. They have been especially active in education, family planning and poverty alleviation, and a leading figure from the NGO sector, Omar Asghar Khan,[41] was appointed as a civilian cabinet minister.

Nevertheless, civil society remains weak in Pakistan. Its principal institutions have faced difficulties not only during the lengthy spells of military rule but at the hands of civilians. Nawaz Sharif's harassment in 1998–9 of the Jang Press Group and of Najam Sethi and the *Friday Times* is well known. His government also responded to Islamists' criticism of Western-financed NGOs bringing 'moral corruption'. In May 1999, on the grounds of misuse of funds, the Punjab government run by his brother Shahbaz dissolved 1,941 out of 5,967 NGOs working in the province. Thereafter NGOs had to seek clearance from the Intelligence Bureau before meeting the legal requirement of registering with the government. NGOs continued to be denounced in the more conservative areas of Pakistan. Male candidates associated with NGOs fared badly in December 2000 the NWFP Local Bodies elections because voters believed that they were supporting un-Islamic causes at the behest of their Western donors. The MMA success in the October 2002 polls raised NGO fears in the Frontier.

The civil society record of the Musharraf regime has been patchy,[42] and repression of national political parties contradicted the professed aim of empowering citizens. The unwillingness to curb the power of feudal élites and Islamist groups hampered improvement in the rights of women, minorities and the rural poor. Local and international human rights groups maintained that those rights declined in the year from October 1999.

Growing criticism of the regime's failure to deliver its promises created tensions with the press. When the respected *Dawn* newspaper claimed that the government was planning new curbs on press freedom, its Karachi offices were subjected to a thorough search on 27 September

41 The son of a prominent figure, Air Marshal (retd) Asghar Khan, he had run the Sungi NGO since 1987.

42 The most notable developments were the adoption of Pakistan's first juvenile justice law in April 2000, which included a ban on the death penalty for crimes committed under the age of eighteen and the establishment in September 2000 of a Commission on the Status of Women.

2000 by an army monitoring team.[43] Conversely the government stood aside when, the following January, supporters of Jamiat-i-Tulba (the youth movement of Jamaat-i-Islami) attacked the press council in Peshawar, their anger stemming from the arrest of five journalists from the *Frontier Post* under section 295-C of the blasphemy law.[44]

Sedition laws and the Maintenance of Public Order ordinance, along with the actions of the National Accountability Bureau, restricted political liberties. Repression was directed at first against the PML-N, but increasingly it was used against ethnic and labour parties. The biggest crackdown of all occurred in the face of the demand for immediate national elections from the 18-party opposition Alliance for the Restoration of Democracy.

Freedom of association was curtailed from 15 March 2000 when an order was introduced banning public rallies, demonstrations and strikes. A large number of PML-N leaders were arrested to prevent a procession from Lahore to Peshawar which was to have been headed by Nawaz Sharif's wife, Kulsoom Nawaz. A month earlier, activists from the Jeay Sindh Qaumi Mahaz and the MQM had been arrested after the parties protested against the downsizing of the labour force at the Pakistan Steel Mills. The parties again joined hands a year later around the issue of water distribution in Sind. Two people were killed and forty others injured in clashes between Jeay Sindh Qaumi Mahaz activists and police in June 2001;[45] such water disputes are likely to become increasingly prevalent as Pakistan faces worsening ecological problems. The army had come down heavily in Lahore on 23 March 2001 following an attempt by the Alliance for the Restoration of Democracy (ARD) to hold a rally at the famous Mochi Gate on Pakistan's national day. The area was cordoned off and around 2,000 political activists were arrested. As the ARD mass contact movement developed, there were further preventive arrests, as on 5–7 June 2001. The ban on political activities was to be lifted only shortly before the October 2002 polls, and even then rallies and processions were forbidden.

The government's failure to halt domestic and sectarian violence, along with growing attacks on the minorities, further weakened civil society. Musharraf had promised to replace a 'punitive Islam' with a 'liberal and progressive Islam'; he had also spoken out against honour killings, which had claimed 1,000 female victims in 1999 alone. However, little progress was made with these issues.[46] After an initial lull in

43 The ostensible reason for the inspection was to check electricity metering equipment in case of fraud.

44 *Dawn*, Internet edn, 31 January 2001.

45 The clashes occurred at Kotdiji, Ranipur, Nausharo Feroze, Dadu and Shikarpur. *Dawn*, Internet edn, 11 June 2001.

46 A legal aid unit was set up at Larkana to ensure that honour killings were treated as murder, but the rising trend of violence against women continued.

sectarian violence a spiral of killings threatened to get out of hand, as it had done in the closing months of Nawaz Sharif's rule. During the Moharram religious festival in April 2000, an attack on a Shi'a prayer meeting in Rawalpindi caused nineteen deaths. The following month the prominent Sunni leader Maulana Yousuf Ludhianvi was gunned down in an ambush in Karachi. In May 2001 the leader of the Sunni Tehrik, Saleem Qadri, was also assassinated in Karachi, provoking a series of strikes and disturbances.

Sectarian violence was encouraged by a Sunni *jihadi* culture fuelled by the proliferation of weapons, the spread of mosque schools and the backwash effects of the Afghan civil war and the Iranian revolution. As early as 1980 Allama Ahsan Elahi Zaheer, chief of the Ahl-i-Hadith, had declared Shia Islam a heresy and accused Shias of being Zionist agents in his book *Shias and Shi'ism*.[47] Sectarian *madrasas* spouted hatred. The registered *madrasas* in the Punjab rose from 1,320 in 1988 to 2,521 in 1997.[48] Many of these were linked with JUI. The collapse of the state educational sector and the lack of access, for all but the rich, to the growing English-language private sector left the *madrasas* as the only schooling option for the lower middle class. They provided not only the status of a religious education, but free food and clothing. Lurid Western fears of an imminent 'Talibanisation' of Pakistan were misplaced, yet the military government avoided challenging the more extreme groups and made only limited progress towards introducing a less restricted curriculum in the *madrasas* designed to increase their students' employability and 'civic' outlook.[49] Musharraf also backed down in May 2000 over a reform of the blasphemy law which would have limited its malicious use.[50] Reform had been prompted by such highly publicised cases as those involving Mohammad Nawaz, an Ahmadi leader, in the Okara district and two Christian brothers in Sialkot who had been accused of blasphemy by an ice cream vendor.

Musharraf's retreat over the blasphemy law followed strikes organised by the religious parties and traders who were protesting at the government's attempts to document the economy as part of the IMF-inspired

---

[47] M. A. Zahab, 'The Regional Dimension of Sectarian Conflicts' in C. Jaffrelot (ed.), *Pakistan: Nationalism without a Nation?* (New Delhi, 2002), p. 126.

[48] G. Dorronsoro, 'Pakistan and the Taliban: State Policy, Religious Networks and Political Connections' in Jaffrelot, *op. cit.*, p. 167.

[49] It was not until 2002 that President Musharraf introduced an ordinance making the imparting of sectarian hatred and militancy in *madrasas* a crime punishable by two years' rigorous imprisonment. It also drew up a 3-year project to provide government funds and technical assistance for the widening of the curriculum to include 'modern' general subjects. Foreign aid would be subject to the approval of federal and provincial *madrasa* boards, and if it came from a government source it would also have to be cleared by the Interior Ministry. *Dawn*, Internet edn, 21 June 2002.

[50] The limited reform would have taken the power away from local police officials to respond to blasphemy charges.

drive to expand the tax-base. The climbdown earned Musharraf the jibe that he was really CMLA rather than CE, but that the former stood for 'Cancel My Last Announcement'.

Liberals constantly called for curbs on *jihad* groups and for the state to distance itself from the Taliban. They linked Afghani developments with sectarian violence in Pakistan, and their nightmare scenario was of the return home by the 28,000 Pakistani combat-trained fighters based there. The army could ignore liberal opinion, but had to pay more attention to the Americans. In November 1998 the United States indicted Osama bin Laden and his Al-Qaeda network[51] for the bombings three months earlier of its embassies in Nairobi and Dar es Salaam. This turned the spotlight on Afghanistan, where Osama bin Laden had returned from Sudan in May 1996.

Washington requested the new Pakistan government to disown the Taliban regime, which faced US and UN sanctions for the continued hospitality extended to Osama bin Laden. The Pakistan government protested against the sanctions introduced on 19 January 2001, mandated by UN Security Council resolution 1333. Nonetheless, the State Bank of Pakistan complied by freezing the Taliban's assets, while the NWFP government sealed all the Taliban government's offices.[52] Despite this public stance, the Afghan opposition claimed that a number of new commando and artillery units had been despatched from Pakistan to aid Taliban attacks in the north-east of the country.[53] Pakistan remained one of just three governments which recognised the Taliban regime.

Security policy clung to the belief nurtured since Zia's time that a friendly government in Kabul provided Pakistan with strategic depth against its Indian rival. The army's number two, Lieut.-General Aziz Khan exercised a powerful influence over thinking regarding the alliances with Taliban and *jihad* groups fighting in Kashmir. The reverence in which he was held by militant groups increasingly embarrassed Musharraf and possibly Aziz himself. In the military reshuffle of 1 September 2000, Aziz was shifted to the role of Corps Commander Lahore, which removed him from day-to-day policy-making. This decision, made shortly before Musharraf attended a UN summit in New York, was designed to signal not only that he was in control, but that conservative forces would not hamper his liberal agenda.

During the following year the government took hesitant steps to curb *jihad* groups and to distance itself from the Kabul regime. The Taliban leadership struggle between moderates and hardliners, following the

51 For details on the evolution, ideology and structures of Al-Qaeda see R. Gunaratna, *Inside Al Qaeda: Global Network of Terror* (London, 2002)

52 See *Dawn*, Internet edn, 26 and 27 January 2001.

53 *Dawn*, Internet edn, 22 January 2001.

death of Mullah Mohammad Rabbani, caused friction with Islamabad. A goodwill visit by a Pakistani football team to Kandahar ended in the humiliation of its members by public head-shaving after the visitors had violated the Taliban dress code by wearing shorts. Pakistan appealed in February 2001 to the Taliban Information and Culture Minister, Mullah Qadratullah Jamal, over the fate of the Bamiyan Buddha statues. But the 2000-year-old sculptures were blasted from their cliff face, and within a month their remains were being sold to dealers in Peshawar. The decision to destroy them resulted from Osama bin Laden's growing influence over the Taliban government.[54]

The increasing number of refugees fleeing war-torn and drought-ravaged Afghanistan also created friction with Pakistan. Barbed wire was laid along the Torkham-Afghan border and the number of militia increased. Yet within a five-month period from September 2000 an estimated 170,000 Afghan refugees had entered Pakistan. The Interior Minister Moinuddin Haider talked of refugees' repatriation. Simultaneously he urged the Taliban to expel Pakistanis wanted for alleged terrorist attacks. During a visit early in 2001 to Afghanistan he also raised the issue of Osama bin Laden's continued presence in the country.

Within Pakistan measures were taken to control the networks of *madrasas* and militants which in Haider's words threatened the country by 'fanning sectarian violence and poisoning people's minds'.[55] On 19 August 2001 the government introduced a law which banned *madrasas* from receiving overseas funds without its approval. They were at the same time required to introduce modern education into their curricula. The following day the Sind government banned Islamic groups from publicly raising funds for *jihad* purposes, and ordered them to remove from public display the name of the *jihad* organisations they supported. On 22 August police raids took place in Karachi on the offices of a number of *jihad* groups including Jaish-e-Mohammad, Harakat-ul-Mujahadeen and Lashkar-e-Toiba. Over 250 people were arrested and 700 collection boxes were confiscated.[56]

This action marked a new departure, although its effects were limited. Most private funds for *jihad* groups were raised in mosques and not in public offices. Many *madrasas* were unregistered and therefore outside the government's purview. Finally, a ban in the North West Frontier Province of the type introduced in Sind would have signalled a more serious intent. Nevertheless, the Pakistan government was inching towards a curb on Islamic militancy in advance of the dramatic events of 9/11. These turned the spotlight on Osama bin Laden and his Taliban 'hosts'.

---

54 R. Gunaratna, *Inside Al Qaeda: Global Network of Terror* (London, 2002), p. 49.

55 Judith Miller, 'Pakistan Outlines Plans to Curb Militant Networks', *New York Times* (New York) 10 June 2000.

56 *Dawn*, Internet edn, 23 August 2001.

Terrorism against American interests was directed not from the Middle East, but the training camps at Sarobi village (Khost province), Ghazni training centre (Shashgao mountains), Jewara camp (Khost province), Mohammad training camp (Nangarhar province), Rishkur training camp (south of Kabul) and the Karaga camp (west of Kabul).[57]

The Aftermath of 9/11

The international outrage at the multiple suicide attacks of 9/11 forced the Musharraf regime to reassess its policy towards the Taliban and such Pakistan-based *jihad* groups as Lashkar-e-Toiba and Harakat-ul-Mujahideen[58] much more rapidly than it had ever imagined. The option of gradual disengagement no longer existed. The contradictions inherent in Pakistan's strategic policy and diplomatic obligations were starkly revealed. Ironically the architects of the Taliban government were now to provide the Americans with the intelligence information required to dismantle the Al-Qaeda-influenced regime. No civilian government would have dared such a dramatic strategic U-turn. No one could have conceived such a scenario before 9/11.

The decision to co-operate fully with the US war on terrorism was made following a seven-hour meeting of the Corps Commanders and other members of the military hierarchy on 14 September. A week later, with his face clearly betraying tension, Musharraf justified the decision in a national broadcast. He had cause for anxiety since this had not only aroused angry street protests but created tensions within the military and security establishment. The doomsday image was conjured up of the Pakistan state imploding as dramatically as the twin towers of the World Trade Centre.

The decision to accede to US wishes was made on pragmatic grounds. Non-compliance would open up for Pakistan not only the prospect of diplomatic isolation but the possibility of unpredictable military outcomes such as attempts to neutralise its nuclear assets. There was the certainty of economic ruin. The ailing economy, with debts of $38 billion and foreign exchange reserves of just $1.5 billion, would no longer be able to obtain the International Monetary Fund cash it needed to stay afloat. Joining the international coalition could bring economic benefits. The United States moved swiftly to end the sanctions it placed on

57 *Hindustan Times*, Internet edn, 20 September 2001.

58 Harakat-ul-Mujahideen (HUM) was listed by the US in 1999 as a terrorist organisation. It has received considerable support from the ISI over the years for its struggle in Kashmir. Musharraf claimed that HUM no longer had bases in Pakistan, although its headquarters was in Muzaffarabad in Azad Kashmir. The leading figure in HUM, Fazlur Rehman Khalid, has ties with Osama bin Laden. According to some reports, Musharraf's support for the US operation against bin Laden had been made conditional on the promise that HUM would not be a target.

Epilogue

Pakistan and India after their nuclear explosions of May 1998. When the US Secretary of State Colin Powell visited Islamabad on 15 October, the Americans promised an aid package of $650 million to assist in meeting Pakistan's increased military expenditure and to compensate for the loss of exports following the war in the region.[59] Canada and Europe also announced financial aid. On 16 October the European Commission announced textile trade concessions worth $1 billion.[60]

The India factor was equally compelling. Rivalry with India, centred on Kashmir, has driven Pakistan's security, military and diplomatic strategies ever since Partition. Involvement with radical Muslim groups in Afghanistan and support for Kashmir *jihad* groups stemmed from the goal of countering Indian regional predominance. New Delhi's speedy offer to the United States of the use of ports and airfields raised the prospect of Indian fighters flying over Pakistan airspace. In the longer term a successful military campaign in which Pakistan was sidelined would not only result in unprecedently close Indo-US military ties, but marginalise its regional influence. Islamabad especially feared a pro-Indian government in Kabul dominated by the West's new allies, the Northern Alliance. Only a year before, Pakistan Special Services Group personnel had directed Taliban military operations against that motley coalition of former warlords—Shiites sponsored by Iran, Tajiks, Turkmens and Uzbeks. The risk remained that even with Islamabad's involvement, a Northern Alliance government would come to power in Afghanistan, while the United States would walk away as in 1989 leaving Pakistan in turmoil. For decision-makers this had to be taken in the hope of minimising the shift in India's favour. In the event Washington stayed on after the end of the military campaign, but it was a Tajik-dominated post-Taliban government that held the reins of power in Kabul.

Musharraf's nimble diplomatic footwork displeased New Delhi. India's Parliamentary Affairs Minister, Pramod Mahajan, warned the American ambassador that if his country was serious in its war on terrorism it should consider the fact that it was co-operating with a country which had sponsored terrorism in the region.[61] Musharraf in his televised address of 19 September warned of Indian designs to ally itself with the United States to get Pakistan declared a terrorist state so that it could destroy its rival's nuclear and strategic installations and damage the Kashmir cause.[62] The mention of Kashmir touched a raw nerve. It raised the fear that the Americans would support Musharraf over Kashmir as a reward for his loyalty regarding Afghanistan. This was summed

---

[59] *Dawn*, Internet edn, 16 October 2001.

[60] *Dawn*, Internet edn, 17 October 2001.

[61] *Dawn*, Internet edn, 20 September 2001.

[62] *Ibid.*

up in the *Times of India* headline 'Musharraf Drops Taliban to Get Kashmir'.[63]

The Indian Prime Minister Atal Behari Vajpayee was stung by criticism not only from the Congress opposition but within his own coalition concerning the abandonment of non-alignment, and stalled the post-Agra summit dialogue process with Pakistan. While the aftermath of 9/11 had changed much in US thinking, policy-makers within the subcontinent were still preoccupied with Indo-Pakistan rivalries. When the British Prime Minister Tony Blair arrived in New Delhi on 5 October following a four-hour stopover in Pakistan to rally the pro-US coalition forces, he received a frosty reception. He was accused of 'double standards' in seeing Pakistan as an ally in the international struggle against terrorism while it was the instigator of terrorism in Kashmir.

Tensions mounted within Kashmir following the suicide car bomb attack of 1 October which killed over thirty people at the State Assembly in Srinagar. Responsibility was initially claimed by Jaish-e-Mohammad, a *jihad* group which is an offshoot of Harakat-ul-Mujahideen. Indian and Pakistan forces exchanged fire in the Akhnoor and Mendhar sectors of the line of control,[64] and there were even Indian calls for an invasion of Pakistan. Such stridency reflected growing anti-Muslim sentiment in India,[65] and arose too from bitterness at the realisation that the United States had become the military and diplomatic arbiter within South Asia; possible US mediation in the Kashmir dispute was as unwelcome in New Delhi as a revival of the Middle East Peace Process was in Tel Aviv. Years of failure to put the regional house in order had created the conditions for the sole superpower's intervention. For many Indians non-alignment had ended with the ignominy of the Foreign Minister Jaswant Singh's rush to provide bases for America—which had still not prevented it according Pakistan the status of a 'front-line' state.

Musharraf sought to halt Indian sabre-rattling. On 8 October he called Prime Minister Vajpayee asking him to resume the Agra peace process. The call was placed amid mounting street protests orchestrated by the Defence Council of Pakistan and Afghanistan, a coalition of religious parties dominated by Jamaat-i-Islami and the two factions of Jamiat-ul-Ulema-e-Islam (Fazlur Rahman and Samiul Haq groups). At one stage Jamaat-i-Islami had close ties with Zia, but these were never

63 *Times of India*, Internet edn, 20 September 2001.

64 Lashkar-e-Toiba threatened to launch suicide attacks against India in retaliation. *Dawn*, Internet edn, 16 October 2001.

65 Its saddest manifestation was the vandalism at the Taj Mahal on 14 October by a group of Bharatiya Janata Yuva Morcha members who were attending a Sangh Parivar meeting in Agra. Its most predictable manifestation was the fiery speech by the BJP minister Uma Bharti at this gathering. 'The US has announced it would take on countries that harbour terrorists,' she declared. 'In my opinion, the religion that promotes terrorism definitely gets destroyed.' *Dawn*, Internet edn, 15 October 2001.

reproduced·during the rule of his military successor. JI opposed Musharraf's government not only because of its 'moderation' but because of
its perceived attack, through the General Sales Tax and documentation
of the economy, on the economic interests of the Jamaat's core support
group of traders. Jamiat-ul-Ulema-e-Islam rallied to the Afghanistan
cause because many of the Taliban leaders had studied in its *madrasas*.
Traditionally it wielded the greatest influence in Pushtun areas of Pakistan, and it possessed close ties both with a number of militant Sunni organisations such as the Lashkar-e-Jhangvi, which had been banned by
the government on 14 August 2001, and with the Harkat-ul-Ansar,[66]
Jaish-e-Mohammad[67] and Lashkar-e-Toiba,[68] *jihad* organisations.

The fear of a military split was heightened by the sidelining of Lieut.-
General Mehmood Ahmad, who had developed close ties with the
Taliban while heading the ISI's Afghan Bureau.[69] Conversely it could be
seen as more firmly establishing Musharraf's control. With the earlier
transfer of Lieut.-General Aziz Khan, it removed from the inner circle
of policy-makers those who advocated continued patronage of extremist
groups.

The main religious parties of the Defence Council of Afghanistan
and Pakistan wielded most influence in the areas where there were con-
centrations of Pushtuns and Afghans.[70] These included the NWFP, its
adjoining tribal agencies and such cities as Quetta and Karachi. It was
for this reason that the call on 20 September for a national strike to ex-

---

66 This group was founded in 1993. HUA is based in Muzaffarabad in Azad Kashmir. It
allegedly possesses close ties both with JUI(F) and the ISI. A number of its members were
killed in the US cruise missile attack on Osama bin Laden's training camps in 1998.

67 Jaish-e-Mohammad was founded in March 2000 by Maulana Masood Azhar, who had
been freed from an Indian jail in December 1999 following the hijack to Afghanistan of an
Air India plane flying from Kathmandu. On 14 October 2001 the US government froze
Jaish-e-Mohammad's assests. The day before, a former leader of the organisation,
Abdullah Shah Mazhar, had been arrested in Karachi for leading violent anti-government
protests. It is claimed that Jaish-e-Mohammad, like HUA, has close links with JUI(F).

68 The headquarters of Lashkar-e-Toiba's parent organisation, Markaz Dawa Al Irshad,
cover a 200-acre site at Muridke, a small town 30 miles from Lahore. The Markaz, which
is Wahabi in religious orientation, was founded in 1987 to assist the Afghan struggle and
purge Pakistani Islam of 'Hindu' influences. It is claimed that the Markaz received funding in the past from Osama bin Laden.

69 It was rumoured that Mehmood had been ditched by Musharraf under Western pressure
following evidence from the FBI that he had personal links with Ahmad Omar Sheikh, one
of the hijackers of the December 1999 Air India flight from Kathmandu. This individual
had later provided over $ 100,000 to one of the suspected terrorists in the World Trade
Center Twin Towers attacks. The British-born and LSE-educated Omar Sheikh was arrested in February 2002 and later convicted for his role in the kidnap and murder of Daniel
Pearl, the *Wall Street Journal* reporter.

70 Pakistan possesses a Pushtun population of around 20 million and over 2 million
Afghan refugees.

press solidarity with the Afghans was only partly supported. Even in the city of Karachi, which was worst hit, the greatest impact was felt in such Pushtun- and Afghan-dominated localities as Sohrab Goth, Lasbella Chowk, Sultanabad, Quaidabad and Old Sabzi Mandi.[71]

Air strikes on Afghanistan following the launching of Operation Enduring Freedom increased the frenzy of anti-American demonstrators. The protests caused by the US Secretary of State Colin Powell's visit on 15 October 2001 were manageable, since they still only involved the small minority of the population who possessed an ethnic and ideological affinity with the Taliban.[72] In addition to promising military and economic support, Powell agreed with the need for a 'broad-based' government in Kabul including 'moderate' elements of the Taliban along with the Northern Alliance. He further gratified Musharraf by repeating at the Agra summit his refrain that Kashmir was 'central' to relationships between Pakistan and India.[73] A relieved Pakistan President promised off the record that the October 2002 elections would not be derailed. Unsurprisingly there was no red carpet, nor was Jaswant Singh present, to greet Colin Powell on his arrival in Delhi.

American hopes for an easing of Indo-Pakistan tensions so that efforts could be concentrated on the war against terrorism were shattered by the attack on the Indian Parliament building in New Delhi on 13 December. The Indian government accused Islamabad of supporting its Lashkar-e-Toiba and Jaish-e-Mohammad perpetrators. Troops were deployed on the international border and the line of control and the Prithvi short-range nuclear-capable missiles were deployed in East Punjab. Early in January 2002 diplomatic pressure on Pakistan intensified with telephone calls from President Bush and Colin Powell and a brief visit to the subcontinent by Tony Blair. The British Prime Minister signed a joint declaration with his Indian counterpart condemning all those who supported or financed terrorism. Musharraf's private decision to curb ISI backing for non-indigenous militant groups fighting in Kashmir was the key to defusing the crisis.

This was followed by a national television address on 12 January during which the Pakistan President announced a ban not only on Lashkar-e-Toiba and Jaish-e-Mohammad, but also on three sectarian organisations (Sipah-e-Sabha Pakistan, Tehrik-e-Jaferia Pakistan and Tanzim Nifaz-e-Shariat-e-Mohammadi) while the Sunni Tehrik was placed on a watch list.[74] Further measures included the registering of religious

---

71 *Dawn*, Internet edn, 22 September 2001

72 Lahore, Islamabad and Rawalpindi were largely undisturbed by strikes and protests. There were more strikes in the districts of Punjab and Sind than earlier. Karachi was gravely disrupted, but there were no fatalities. See reports in *Dawn*, Internet edn, 16 October 2001.

73 *Dawn*, Internet edn, 17 October 2002.

74 R. Gunaratna, *Inside Al Qaeda: Global Network of Terror* (London, 2002), p. 217.

schools and foreign students and teachers, and a limitation on the use of loudspeakers in mosques. While declaring continued diplomatic and political support for Kashmiris, Musharraf maintained that Pakistan would not be used for carrying out terrorist or subversive activities inside or outside the country. He also announced the establishment of 'speedy trial courts' to try those involved in terrorism and sectarian killing. Pakistani politicians gave the speech a mixed reception, but President Bush termed it 'candid, courageous and statesman-like'[75], while Tony Blair applauded its 'forceful defence of a tolerant and moderate Islam'.[76]

The crisis in Indo-Pakistan relations resurfaced when the melting of the winter snows was accompanied by an increase in infilitration across the line of control. New Delhi consequently dismissed the 12 January speech as mere rhetoric. The countries were brought again to the brink of war by the massacre of servicemen and their families at the Kaluchak army camp near Jammu on 14 May. The Lok Sabha unanimously adopted a resolution that criticised Pakistan for supporting cross-border militancy. The Indian navy was reinforced in the Arabian Sea. The Prime Minister Atal Behari Vajpayee, in a speech to soldiers at Kupwara on 22 May, called on them to be prepared for sacrifices because it was 'now time for a decisive fight'. In order to deter limited attacks on terrorist training camps in Azad Kashmir, Pakistan military spokesmen warned of a wider war. It is in this deterrence context that Pakistan's testing of short-range and medium-range nuclear-capable missiles over the weekend of 25–26 May must be understood. The following Monday President Musharraf, in a national address which had been trailed as likely to herald a breakthrough, upheld Pakistan's position in a resolute tone. Jaswant Singh, India's External Affairs Minister, termed the speech 'disappointing' and 'dangerous' and maintained that Pakistan was the epicentre of terrorism.[77] Intensive shelling along the line of control accompanied the diplomatic war of words.

The British Foreign Secretary Jack Straw, the US Deputy Secretary of State Richard Armitage and the Defense Secretary Donald Rumsfeld all shuttled to the subcontinent. The Pakistan authorities came under immense pressure to halt cross-border terrorism in which they had denied any involvement as recently as the Kargil conflict. The Hindu right was baying for war. The VHP president Ashok Singhal, for example, declared that it was 'unavoidable'.[78] There was talk in the media of fighting and winning a nuclear war, and this formed the context for the British and US governments on 31 May not only to advise their nationals against

75 *Dawn*, Internet edn, 14 January 2002.

76 *Dawn*, Internet edn, 15 January 2002.

77 *Hindustan Times* (New Delhi) 28 May 2002.

78 *Hindustan Times* (New Delhi) 31 May 2002.

travel to the subcontinent, but to offer the chance to return home to dependents and less essential government staff.[79] Within days the advice was upgraded to a warning that all British and US citizens should depart. The warning not only reflected the seriousness of the situation, but encouraged commercial pressures on the governments, especially from the powerful Indian software industry, to back away from war. In a repetition of the New Year crisis, Musharraf again secured military consensus for the cessation of cross-border infiltration by militants. Despite the easing of tensions, Indian officials made it clear that the military build-up would continue. Fears of an intensification of a subcontinental missile race were raised when, just a week before the Pakistan elections, Pakistan and India respectively 'routinely' test-fired medium-range ballistic and surface-to-air missiles.[80]

Throughout the standoff Musharraf had distinguished between support for 'genuine' Kashmiri freedom fighters and commitment to the war against terrorism. Pakistan itself was the victim of a growing number of terrorist outrages perpetrated by *jihad* groups which had close ties with, or had been infilitrated by, Al-Qaeda. The Christian minority suffered the brunt of these outrages because such attacks were seen as an easy way of hitting out at Western interests. There were attacks on the Protestant International Church in Islamabad (17 March 2002), the Christian Missionary School at Murree (5 August), the chapel of the Christian Hospital at Taxila (9 August) and the Karachi offices of the Christian welfare organisation, Peace and Justice (25 September). A new trend in violence was marked by a suicide car bombing on 8 May outside the Sheraton Hotel in Karachi. This claimed the lives of a busload of French naval construction workers. Another huge car bomb blast followed in June which killed eight outside the US Consulate in Karachi.[81] These attacks were designed to undermine the Musharraf government in the eyes of the West. It cooperated with the Americans not only in hunting down Al-Qaeda terrorists in Afghanistan; also, setting a precedent in Pakistan's history, the army operated in the Waziristan tribal area in support of the US Mountain Lion operation. By the anniversary of 9/11 a number of breakthroughs had been made in the apprehension of Al-Qaeda terrorists, including the capture of the Yemeni-born Ramzi bin al-Shibb following a dramatic Karachi gun-battle. From his base in Germany Ramzi had coordinated the financial transactions which made the US hijackings possible.

Musharraf's usefulness to the West reduced criticism of his increasingly tarnished good governance credentials. They had begun to lose their lustre following the 30 April 2002 Presidential Referendum. At the

---

79 Foreign and Commonwealth Office press release 31 May 2002.

80 *Dawn*, Internet edn, 5 October 2002.

81 For further details see *Dawn*, Internet edn, 14 June 2002.

outset of the campaign to secure support for a further five years in office in advance of the October 2002 general election,[82] Musharraf had declared: 'I want to bring real democracy to the country, because it is the only way out. I am not trying to deceive nor am I indulging in hypocrisy. Democracy is the only way and I want it.'[83] Although the speech began with a reference to Pakistan having reached an 'historical juncture', the phrase 'real democracy' echoed his initial condemnation of Pakistan's 'sham democracy' at the time of the October 1999 coup. He also harked back to the 7-Point Agenda, justifying the referendum in terms of the need to ensure continuity for its programme of restructuring and reforms. Just ten months earlier he had justified the assumption of the Presidency in the same way.[84] His contention 'I am neither Zia nor Ayub. I am Musharraf' was consonant with the efforts of the preceding twenty-seven months to distance his government from earlier military-led regimes.[85]

Sceptics saw the referendum as little more than an attempt to cover authoritarianism with the fig-leaf of a popular mandate. The referendum was challenged by five constitutional petitions to a special bench of the Supreme Court in the courts,[86] boycotted by the opposition mainstream parties and condemned as a return to the Zia era. The independent journalist Najam Sethi regarded the referendum campaign as not so much a legitimation exercise as an attempt to undermine the government's major opponents. This would ensure an outcome to its liking in the parliamentary elections.[87] Musharraf had in fact declared on 5 April: 'There are also a number of people who are fence-sitters waiting to go to this side or that side of the fence. There is confusion in their minds and I want to remove this uncertainty and confusion. Nawaz Sharif and Benazir Bhutto have no role in Pakistan's politics.'[88]

---

[82] This had been required to be held within three years of the 12 October 1999 coup by the Supreme Court verdict of May 2000.

[83] English rendering of the President's Address to the Nation, 5 April 2002. http://www.pak.gov.pk/public/Address-5April.htm p. 7.

[84] 'I have always been saying', he declared in June 2001, 'that I will ensure and guarantee the continuation and sustainability of all the reforms, all the restructuring that I and my administration have been doing.' http://www.InformationTimes.com 22/06/01.

[85] Military intervention in October 1999 had not been accompanied by a declaration of martial law; nor, as for example in 1958, was the Constitution abrogated. Musharraf himself had declared 'This is not Martial Law, only another path towards democracy.'

[86] The petitions were filed by Qazi Hussain Ahmad, Amir of Jamaat-i-Islami, Alliance for the Restoration of Democracy; Supreme Court Bar Association; Lahore High Court, Rawalpindi Bench Bar Association and Shahid Orakzai. The Supreme Court on 27 April ruled that the holding of the referendum was a valid exercise, but refused to pass judgement on its consequences, which were 'to be determined at a proper forum at an appropriate time'. *Dawn*, Internet edn, 28 April 2002.

[87] N. Sethi, 'The General and the Question that haunts all Dictators', *The Guardian* (London), 1 May 2002.

[88] President's address to the Nation, *op. cit.*, p. 10.

The Election Commission announced on 1 May a 70 per cent turnout in the referendum. Ninety-eight per cent of those who voted had stamped the 'yes' column, thereby providing an overwhelming democratic mandate for General Pervez Musharraf to serve as President for five years.[89] However, this was a pyrrhic victory. Voting irregularities, assisted by the absence of formal identification requirements and of electoral rolls,[90] had the result, in the words of the *New York Times*, that 'the balloting has actually diminished' General Musharraf's stature.'[91]

The voting irregularities invoked memories of General Zia-ul-Haq's 1984 referendum. There were reports of physical abuse and intimidation of public sector employees, who had earlier been bussed in large numbers to attend the pro-Musharraf rallies. Multiple voting was assisted by the positioning of the 90,000 polling stations in clusters. The use of Nazim's influence to canvass votes was a reminder of the role of the Basic Democrats in the Ayub presidential campaigns of the 1960s. The Human Rights Commission of Pakistan's independent assessment of the voting reported instances of 'voters marshalled by local councillors' enjoying 'the freedom to vote as many times as they wished', while 'polling staff, municipal councillors and the electoral commission's so-called neutral observers stamped ballot papers themselves.'[92]

Previous civilian politicians, as much as military leaders, have used the state machinery to mobilise voters. The misuse of public money and the promotion of blatant political opportunism had however been singled out as hallmarks of the 'sham democracy' to which Musharraf had vowed Pakistan would never return. Most damagingly the keystone of his local government reforms, the Nazims, had been inducted into this old-style politics. Mian Raza Rabbani, acting general secretary of the Pakistan People's Party, summed up Musharraf's loss of the moral high ground when he declared that 'the campaign for the referendum has once again burst the bubble of good governance of the regime.'[93] In a televised speech a month later, Musharraf publicly admitted that he had been informed of cases of vote rigging for which he expressed regret. The decision in June to sideline Major-General Ehtesham Zamir, head of the political wing of the Inter Services Intelligence, who had played a leading role in organising the referendum, indicated recognition that the victory that had been achieved was a hollow one.[94]

89 *Dawn*, Internet edn, 2 May 2002.

90 Many voters openly queued up to repeatedly vote. At one polling station a woman claimed to have cast her vote no less than sixty times. *Dawn*, Internet edn, 1 May 2002.

91 *Dawn*, Internet edn, 2 May 2002.

92 *Dawn*, Internet edn, 1 May 2002.

93 *Dawn*, Internet edn, 22 April 2002.

94 *Guardian Unlimited* 28 June 2000.
wysiwyg://1440/http://www.guardian.co.uk/pakistan/Story/0,2763,745475,00.html.

The referendum dispelled the favourable impression created by the reintroduction of joint electorates for the forthcoming parliamentary elections. Another innovation for them had been the reduction of the voting age to eighteen, thereby increasing the electorate by 5.2 million to around 72 million. The 22 June 2002 Ordinance requiring all candidates to be graduates was designed to encourage fresh faces among parliamentary aspirants as well as voters. In the event, despite some individual casualties such as members of the Abbasi royal family in the former princely state of Bahawalpur, this requirement did not undermine the sway of the feudal élite. The pro-government PML(Q) awarded many election tickets in such areas as the southern Punjab to the traditional political families.[95] The opposition PPP parliamentarians and PML(N) followed suit. Junior family members and better-educated wives and sisters were coopted by the traditional power-brokers. They not only ran the women's campaigns, but even ensured that they did not feature on election posters.[96] The roll-call of Daultanas, Legharis, Qureshis and Noons was the same as that of any election from the 1937 provincial polls onwards. While the graduation qualification did not curb the influence of the political families, it reinforced the élitist appearance of the political system, as an estimated 97 per cent of the country's population were disqualified from contesting the polls.

The graduation condition was one of a number of controversial measures introduced in the run-up to the 2002 elections. Opponents of the government claimed that its aim was to ensure a supine parliament by means of pre-poll rigging. The Political Parties Amendment Order of 28 June, which set eligibility requirements for parties to contest the polls, turned the clock back to the Zia period. The PPP only got round the 'disqualification' of its chairperson Benazir Bhutto[97] by forming a separate parliamentarians' group headed by the Sindhi landlord Makhdoom Amin Fahim to contest the polls. Another Presidential Ordinance issued on 6 July disqualified a person from holding office for a third time who had served twice as Prime Minister or Chief Minister, even if these periods of office had not been completed. This measure underlined President Musharraf's determination not to brook cohabitation after the polls with either Nawaz Sharif or Benazir Bhutto. It was especially damaging to the electoral prospects of the PML(N), which had been hit by a number of defections to the 'king's party' of the PML(Q) ever since the April Referendum. The eventual exclusion of the leading figures of the two main parties from the campaign itself contributed to its lacklustre character. According to one pre-election survey that covered fifty constitu-

95 For details see *Dawn*, Internet edn, 23 September 2002.

96 *Herald* (Karachi), October 2002, pp. 68 ff.

97 Benazir Bhutto's non-appearance in court on corruption charges had been made a convictable offence, thereby disqualifying her from holding party office.

encies, 50.2 per cent of prospective voters believed that Benazir Bhutto and Nawaz Sharif should have been allowed to contest the polls.[98] The issuing of the Legal Framework Order (LFO) on 21 August was the most controversial of the pre-election measures. It established a National Security Council that was to be chaired by the President rather than a future elected Prime Minister. It also restored the power—contained in Article 58–2(b) that Nawaz Sharif had removed—of the President to dismiss the Prime Minister. Musharraf saw these measures as a way of preventing further coups. 'If you want to keep the army out', he declared, 'you bring them in.'[99] This foreshadowed a guided rather than a restored democracy. It presupposed that the army was the saviour rather than the cause of Pakistan's political travail. The Pakistan Bar Council denounced the LFO as 'illegitimate' and designed to 'ensure a smooth and orderly transition' of the 'present regime dominated by generals'.[100]

The government's opponents maintained that in addition to these supra-constitutional amendments designed to ensure an outcome favourable to the Musharraf regime's interests, more traditional elements of pre-poll rigging were being deployed. These included transfers and appointments of officers from constituencies where it was sought to influence the electoral process;[101] intimidation to force candidates to join those parties favoured by the establishment;[102] and the use of the administration to favour pro-government candidates. A number of local police officials and nazims were reported to be assisting the Musharraf loyalist PML(Q) faction.[103]

The October 2002 elections

The October elections differed hugely from those of 1997 in terms of the rules, the numbers of constituencies and the character of the electioneering. The latter resembled the 1985 'partyless' elections and the local government polls of 31 December 2000–2 July 2001 more than

98 *Dawn*, Internet edn, 4 October 2002.

99 *Dawn*, Internet edn, 22 August 2002.

100 *Dawn*, Internet edn, 25 August 2002.

101 Such transfers occurred in spite of an Order issued by the Chief Election Commissioner in mid-July. During the next month 43 officers were transferred in the Larkana district alone. *Herald* (Karachi) October 2002, p. 27.

102 *Ibid.*

103 Among the many instances of alleged pre-poll rigging, the PML(N) candidate for Faisalabad accused the tehsil Municipal Administration and local police of running the election campaign of his PML(QA) rival, Mushtaq Ali Cheema (*Dawn*, Internet edn, 20 September 2002). It was claimed that Nazims in the Vehari district had spent millions of rupees for the benefit of PML(QA) candidates (*Dawn*, Internet edn, 14 September 2002). District and Tehsil Nazimeen in Faisalabad violated the Election Commission ban by canvassing for PML(QA) candidates and led processions of PML(QA) activists to Iqbal Park on 5 October (*Dawn*, Internet edn, 6 October 2002).

any of the post-1988 contests. In addition to the graduate qualification, the elections were fought for the first time since 1985 on a joint electorate basis. At the same time as bringing the minorities back into the mainstream, ten seats were reserved for them in the National Assembly, to be filled by nominees of political parties on the basis of their strength in the Assembly. Sixty reserved women's seats were also reintroduced, to be claimed by parties on the basis of proportional representation. The Election Commission announced after the 10 October polls that it had removed the 5 per cent general seat qualification for a share in the reserved seats. Overall the National Assembly was increased (in line with the 1998 census) from 217 seats in 1997 to 342. The provincial assemblies were to continue to form the electoral college for the Senate, which had its seats increased from 87 to 100.

Musharraf made clear that the elections would be conducted in a restricted atmosphere similar to that of the local polls. Only at the beginning of September was the ban on political activities lifted. The Election Commission introduced a code of conduct that allowed processions and rallies under specified conditions, but the government overruled this, ensuring that the elections were drained of much of their colour. The galvanising effects of Benazir Bhutto and Nawaz Sharif returning to the fray were never felt. The former went to the United States instead of Pakistan following the rejection of her nomination papers, and Nawaz Sharif in an unprecedented act of political solidarity withdrew his own nomination papers in protest at the 'blatant violation' of the Pakistan people's right to elect their leaders. While activists were demotivated by the absence of the party leaders, the apathy of ordinary voters[104] was bred of cynicism that nothing would subsequently change. The field was left open for political entrepreneurs and for the manipulation of traditional *biraderi*[105] rivalries and feudal influence.[106] It thus seemed that any genuine hopes for a new kind of politics entertained by the Musharraf regime had been shelved in the desire for a supine parliament.

Two new political groupings had come into existence since the distant days of Nawaz Sharif's 1997 landslide victory. The first was the Muttahida Majlis-i-Amal (MMA), a broader religious grouping than PIF (Pakistan Islamic Front). Headed by Maulana Shah Ahmad Noorani, this was the first Islamic alliance to bridge the Sunni-Shia divide as well as the traditional-Islamist one. The bringing together of JUI, JUP, Ahl-i-Hadith and Pakistani Islami Tehrik (representing the banned Tehrik-i-Jafria) was a major achievement; its driving force was the Jamaat-i-Islami. Sectarian differences were buried, at least temporarily, by the

---

104 *Dawn*, Internet edn, 6 October 2002.

105 *Dawn*, Internet edn, 3, 6 & 8 October 2002.

106 See for example the report on the Dera Ghazi Khan district by Tariq Saeed Birmani, *Dawn*, Internet edn, 27 September 2002.

MMA's anti-American stance: it decried the presence of US bases in Pakistan for the war on terrorism and the bombing of innocent Pushtuns in Afghanistan. The MMA's unequivocal resistance to US policy in Afghanistan undoubtedly increased its support at the expense of the nationalist parties in the Frontier and Balochistan which had adopted an ambiguous response.[107]

The Grand National Alliance was the second political grouping that had emerged since the 1997 polls. This arrangement brought together the so-called 'king's party' of the PML(Q) and the National Alliance of pro-government parties headed by the former President Farooq Leghari's Millat Party.[108] The PML(Q) was the driving force of the GNA. It had grown out of the Pakistan Muslim League (Like Minded) group which had been founded by factional rivals of Nawaz Sharif shortly after his dismissal in October 1999. In advance of the 2000 local bodies elections, the name was altered to the PML (Quaid-e-Azam). Its leading figures were the former Punjab governor Mian Mohammad Azhar (president PML(Q)) and the Chaudhurys of Gujrat, Pervaz Elahi (president of the Punjab PML(Q)) and Shujaat Hussain. In keeping with the tradition of Punjabi political opportunism, many supporters of Nawaz Sharif hitched themselves to the rising PML(Q) fortunes. In such districts as Sahiwal and Chakwal, the entire PML(N) leadership defected. The overwhelming majority of PML(Q) election aspirants in October 2002 were former members of the once powerful PML(N).

The Nawaz League's straitened circumstances contributed to its newfound harmony with the PPPP. There was talk during the run-up to the elections of large-scale seat adjustments to strengthen democratic forces and of presenting a restoration of democracy one-point common programme. Local rivalries conspired to prevent meaningful seat adjustments. This failure led the veteran president of the Alliance for the Restoration of Democracy, Nawabzada Nasrullah Khan, who had brought them on to the same platform, to scale down his campaign dramatically. The PML(N) thus entered the elections on the moral high ground following its 'illegal' 1999 dismissal, but precious little else.

The polls

The 272 general seats of the National Assembly and the 577 general seats of the four provincial assemblies were contested on 10 October by over 2,000 and 5,000 candidates respectively. Despite claims of extensive pre-poll rigging, no major party had decided on a boycott. The Musharraf regime could draw comfort from these facts, even before the

107 *Dawn*, Internet edn, 14 October 2002.

108 In addition to the Millat party, a key component of the National Alliance was the Sind Democratic Alliance formed in September 2001 by the ex-bureaucrat Imtiaz Sheikh.

results threw up the widely anticipated outcome of a hung parliament. No elections had been conducted under a fiercer international spotlight.[109] In addition to 1,300 field observers from the Human Rights Commission of Pakistan, there were 200 foreign election monitors from the South Asian Association for Regional Cooperation,[110] the European Union and the Commonwealth Observer Group led by the former deputy Prime Minister of Malaysia, Tan Sri Dato' Musa bin Hitam.[111] The EU team represented one of its largest-ever deployments of election monitors.[112] While the SAARC and COG teams arrived only shortly before the polls and concentrated their reports on the voting process, the EU monitors had been in Pakistan in the months leading up to election day and had carried out extensive interviews with party representatives. Significantly the preliminary report of the EU Election Observation Mission described the elections as seriously flawed and condemned the failure of the Election Commission to curb the misuse of state resources in favour of such parties as the PML(Q).[113] This criticism was almost as harsh as that of the locally-based Human Rights Commission of Pakistan.[114] The Commonwealth Observers on the other hand declared that the polls were 'for the most part transparent' although there were doubts over whether there was a 'truly level playing-field'.[115] More important, the State Department also gave the elections a clean bill of health, noting that voting day 'proceeded in a relatively free and orderly fashion', despite claims by the opposition to the contrary.[116]

The four most striking features of the results were, first, the rise to prominence of the MMA in a performance that far outstripped that of religious parties in previous polls; second, the demise of the PML(N) which was reduced to just 16 National Assembly Seats and 37 Punjab assembly seats; third, the even balance between the three main political groupings of the PPPP, the PML(Q) and the MMA in the National Assembly, assuring a hung parliament in which the MMA would emerge as influential powerbrokers; and fourth the continuation of distinctive regional political expressions. The MQM despite its efforts was unable

---

109 On the eve of the polls the US-based Human Rights Watch organisation had maintained that the entire election process was 'deeply flawed' and would prevent a meaningful transfer of power into civilian hands. *Dawn*, Internet edn, 10 October 2002.

110 These were coordinated by the Colombo-based International Centre for Ethnic Studies. The 38 monitors arrived in Karachi on 5 October.

111 Its report was to be submitted to the Commonwealth Ministerial Action Group which was to review Pakistan's status within the Commonwealth.

112 *Dawn*, Internet edn, 1 October 2002.

113 *Dawn*, Internet edn, 13 October 2002.

114 *Ibid.*

115 *Dawn*, Internet edn, 12 October 2002.

116 www.heraldelections.com./results.

to break out of its traditional heartlands. Similarly the MMA 'wave', for all its drama, was confined to the JUI's traditional Pushtun areas of influence, although its power was sufficient to sweep away the opposition of the ANP and the Pakhtunkhwa Milli Awami Party. Within the Provincial Assemblies, the PML(Q) seemed likely to form a majority Punjab government, while the MMA appeared in the position to form a government in NWFP. In Sind and Balochistan respectively, PPPP- and MMA-led coalitions emerged as likely outcomes.

Ep. 1. NATIONAL ASSEMBLY RESULTS, 2002: SEATS

	PPPP	PMLQ	PMLN	MMA	NA	MQM	ANP	Ind.	Other
Punjab	34	66	15	3	7	–	–	15	–
Sind	27	4	–	7	5	13	–	1	–
NWFP	–	4	–	29	–	–	–	–	–
Balochistan	–	2	1	6	1	–	–	1	–
FATA	–	–	–	7	–	–	–	5	–
Total	62	76	16	53	13	13	0	22	1

Source http://www.heraldelections.com/results/.

Ep. 2. PROVINCIAL ELECTION RESULTS, 2002: SEATS

	PPPP	PMLQ	PMLN	MMA	NA	MQM	ANP	INDP	Other
Punjab	60	127	37	6	12	–	–	39	–
Sind	50	10	–	13	12	28	–	5	1
NWFP	8	8	5	48	–	–	8	12	1
Balochistan	2	8	–	14	3	–	–	7	1
Total	120	153	42	81	27	28	8	63	3

Source http://www.heraldelections.com/results/.

The Western media focused primarily on the consequences of the MMA's rise to power for continued military operations against al-Qaeda groups in the border areas. Najam Sethi writing in the *Friday Times* echoed these concerns arising from MMA control of the police and civil administration. He roundly blamed the success of the 'extremists' on Musharraf's 'hostility' to the mainstream PPPP and PML(N) parties. 'The armed and unarmed *jihadis* inside and outside the establishment should be pleased by the election results,' he declared. 'Having 'lost' Afghanistan they have now acquired a large base area in their own land.'[117] Sethi pointed out that the MMA would use its powerful position in the Senate (arising from the equal representation of all provinces

---

117 Najam Sethi, 'Thank You General Musharraf', *Friday Times* (Lahore), 11–17 October 2002, vol. XIV, no. 33.

there) to introduce a stream of Islamisation measures. He also cynically opined that Musharraf, rather than being embarrassed in his support for the war on terrorism by the MMA rise, might draw comfort from it, as this would increase his leverage with the Americans. 'In time to come', Sethi concluded, 'the "election" may acquire the same ominous significance in the history of Pakistan as the 1970 elections under another 'sincere' military dictatorship.'[118]

The party leaders hurried to Islamabad to discuss ministry formation. Despite their ideological differences, the PPPP president Makhdoom Amin Fahim refused to rule out agreement with MMA. He held separate meetings with the JI leader Qazi Hussain Ahmed and the PML(N) chairman Raja Zafarul Haq and called for a consensus government of the three major groups in the National Assembly.[119]

It was not until 23 November, forty days after the elections, that the PML(Q) candidate Mir Zafarullah Khan became Prime Minister. The first Baloch to hold the office, he was clearly regarded as Musharraf's nominee. However his government's small majority in the National Assembly reduced his usefulness to the President. This was to be a major factor in the twelve-month constitutional deadlock in 2003. The MMA joined the secular opposition parties in the demand that the LFO must be given parliamentary assent and that President Musharraf should agree a date to vacate the office of Chief of Army Staff. The government response was that the LFO had become part of the Constitution because the Supreme Court ruling of May 2000 that upheld the 12 October 1999 coup authorised General Musharraf to make constitutional amendments needed for his reforms. The disputes were ultimately not about constitutional niceties, but about the extent of the army's influence and the terms on which it would be institutionalised in the political process. A key government aim in the protracted negotiations was to overcome its weak majority by driving a wedge between the secular and religious opposition groupings of the ARD and the MMA.

The former was weakened not only by the absence of Benazir Bhutto and Nawaz Sharif but by the death in September 2003 of its chief, the veteran opposition politician Nawabzada Nasrullah Khan. The MMA sought a more Islamic foreign policy and opposed the sending of Pakistani troops to Iraq. However, it cooperated with the ARD on the issue of resistance to the LFO. The terms on which the political stalemate would be ended became the focus for intense bargaining in the periodic rounds of negotiations between the government and opposition.

When the National Assembly was convened on 15 April 2003, the combined protests of the ARD and MMA disrupted its proceedings. The Speaker, Chaudhry Amir Hussain, adjourned the session amidst the

118 *Ibid.*

119 *Dawn*, Internet edn, 15 October 2002.

uproar of 'no LFO no' and 'go Musharraf go' slogans. This pattern was to be repeated in the Senate. The four and a half hours of slogan-chanting and desk thumping was the longest protest in Pakistan's parliamentary history.[120] The first attempt to end the deadlock involved the creation of an eleven-member joint government-opposition constitution committee. This was chaired by the president of the Pakistan Muslim League (Q), Chaudhry Shujaat Hussain. The joint committee held ten sessions over a two-week period, but failed to reach consensus on a constitutional package to be presented to Parliament for approval.

The government was hopeful by the beginning of June that a deal could be reached with the MMA which had reviewed its stand on the issue of Musharraf simultaneously occupying the posts of President and COAS, while putting forward ten demands concerning Islamisation,[121] provincial autonomy and the rights of minorities. Chaudhury Shujaat Hussain promised that the demands would be implemented, but the confrontation between the Centre and Akram Khan Durrani's MMA government in NWFP dashed these hopes. Their dispute revolved around the powers of the district *nazims*[122] (administrators). Following the adoption of a Shariat bill, Durrani's government was accused of seeking the Talibanisation of the province. MMA activists had torn down advertising signs that they regarded as obscene. Musharraf eventually intervened personally; he rejected the *nazims'* resignation while simultaneously directing the NWFP government to restore their powers concerning postings and distribution of funds as delegated by the 2001 Local Government Ordinance. On 8 June, in a speech organised by the Lahore Bar Association, he pointedly remarked that the 'people of Pakistan do not want a theocratic state and are strongly opposed to Talibanisation of society.'[123]

The combined opposition protests over the LFO resulted in a stormy budget debate on 7 June 2003. The opposition subsequently introduced a no-confidence motion against the National Assembly Speaker, Chaudhry Amir Hussain, on 20 June after he had had ruled that the LFO was part of the Constitution. The deadlock continued after a further round of talks between the government and its opponents failed to make

---

120 *Dawn* (Karachi, Pakistan), 19 April 2003.

121 The demands included the moulding of the economy, education and the media on an Islamic pattern, the introduction of Islamic subjects as part of the curricula, and the removal of obscenity and vulgarity from the electronic media. It would be left to parliament to decide whether Friday should become the day of rest.

122 All the twenty-four district *nazims* had stepped down and submitted their resignation to President Musharraf rather than to the NWFP Chief Minister. They had been elected on a non-party basis in the local government polls and did not share the MMA's ideological outlook. They claimed that the MMA had brought false corruption charges against them because they did not fit in with its priorities.

123 *Dawn*, 9 June 2003.

progress. The MMA still baulked at this juncture at splitting with the ARD. Only late in December 2003 was the deadlock broken when the MMA voted with the government ensuring the necessary two-thirds parliamentary majority for the 17th Constitutional Amendment to pass into law. The MMA had managed to extract seven concessions,[124] and claimed that parliamentary supremacy had been asserted by incorporating the LFO into the Constitution in this way.

In reality, however, the 17th Constitutional Amendment did little more than soften some of the undemocratic features of the LFO. The PPP secretary-general, Raja Pervez Ashraf, described it as 'the strangulation of democracy'.[125] The ARD promised to continue the struggle for parliamentary supremacy. Significantly the 17th Amendment retained the key presidential powers that had been set out in the original LFO: the power to dismiss the Prime Minister and to dissolve the National Assembly. The PPP legal spokesman Aitaz Ahsan appositely pointed out that the reference of the dissolution of the National Assembly to the Supreme Court would be of no relief, as had been shown by Pakistan's past history.[126] The permanent institutionalisation of the army in the political process through the establishment of the National Security Council also presaged a future 'guided democracy' albeit with the acquiesence of the politicians as the NSC's establishment now required an Act of Parliament. The 17th Constitutional Amendment Act indemnified all the actions and laws made by Musharraf since the October 1999 coup, thus repeating the 'cover' given to General Zia by the National Assembly in 1985 before his revival of the Constitution.

Musharraf further legitimised his position by safely negotiating a vote of confidence. However, the vote was less than a ringing endorsement following the abstention of the MMA and a boycott by the ARD and its smaller allies. The President was nevertheless pleased to secure a 56 per cent majority in the electoral college[127], in the wake of security lapses that had seen two attempts on his life within the space of eleven days in

---

124 These were as follows: (1) the government agreed to withdraw the three-year extension of the retirement age offered to superior court judges; (2) it would keep the local governments under the Sixth Schedule for six years; (3) it would set up the National Security Council under an act of parliament; (4) a decision to dismiss the Prime Minister and dissolve the National Assembly under article 58(2)b would be referred to the Supreme Court within fifteen days and the Supreme Court would decide within thirty days and its decision would be final; (5) the President would seek a vote of confidence from Parliament and the four provincial assemblies; (6) the President would consult the Prime Minister on the appointment of armed forces chiefs, but not be bound by the advice of the PM; and (7) the President would give up his uniform by December 2004.

125 *Dawn*, 29 December 2004

126 *Ibid.*

127 Musharraf received 658 votes of the 1,170-strong electoral college comprising the 342-seat National Assembly, the 100-seat Senate and the 728 members of the four provincial assemblies. *Dawn*, 2 January 2004.

December.[128] Moreover, the vote gave him a more legitimate position in which to work for a rapprochement with India on the sidelines of the 12th SAARC conference hosted by Islamabad on 4 January 2004.

Still, the President encountered a number of problems during the first half of 2004. On the international front the government had to face embarrassment following the revelations that Dr A.Q. Khan had sold nuclear technology to North Korea, Libya and Iran.[129] Although the former national hero was treated leniently by the authorities, there were continued concerns voiced by the opposition that Pakistan would relinquish its nuclear programme at America's behest. The MMA[130] further complained about the military operations in South Waziristan in pursuit of the US-led war on terror. In one episode thirteen civilians, including six children, died when helicopter gunships fired on their vehicles. The conviction of the acting president of the PML(N), Javed Hashmi, for sedition[131] and the immediate deportation[132] of Shahbaz Sharif, president of the PML(N), to Saudi Arabia on his return from exile on 11 May stirred further opposition. The Supreme Court had declared on 7 April that Shahbaz Sharif was free to return to Pakistan to face the cases pending against him. However, the major focus of unrest was the passing on 19 April of the National Security Council Act. This brought into being a thirteen-member National Security Council headed by the President and including the chairman of the Joint Chiefs of Staff Committee and the chiefs of the army, navy and air force. It thereby legalised the military's role in the governance of Pakistan. The government accused the MMA of going back on a pledge not to oppose the measure, but its members walked out at the start of the final debate. MMA spokesmen claimed that the President's legal team had added functions concerning 'crisis management'[133] that had not been present during its earlier discussions.

The Jamali government's lack of vigour, seen in the failure to finalise the award of the share of the provinces in federal revenues and in the fre-

---

128 Both attempts occurred within a couple of hundred yards of each other in the high security area of the Rawalpindi cantonment. Following the second attempt on 25 December involving suicide car bombers, a number of militants associated with the banned *Jaish-i-Mohammad* organisation were arrested.

129 The United States accepted the Pakistan government's claim that following its investigations it was clear that proliferation had been done by individuals for payment and that there was no official complicity.

130 *Dawn*, 18 March 2004. An amnesty, known as the Shakai Agreement was eventually granted on 24 April to local tribesmen who had been sheltering foreign fighters. A tribal lashkar was raised to force foreign militants who were hiding in the South Waziristan agency to register with the administration by 16 May.

131 See *Dawn*, 13 April 2004. He was found guilty of inciting mutiny in the army and was sentenced to twenty-three years in prison.

132 *Dawn*, 12 May 2004.

133 *Dawn*, 16 March 2004.

quent absence of ministers from the National Assembly, led to rumours
of a change of leadership. These coincided with the unification of the
five factions of the Muslim League—excluding of course PML(N)—
under the presidency of Chaudhry Shujaat Hussain. Real power lay with
the President rather than the Prime Minister. Musharraf remained, however deeply unpopular with large sections of Pakistan's population, and
the United States continued to work to shore up his position. There was
discreet pressure to end Pakistan's suspension from the Commonwealth.
Despite some disquiet because of the nuclear non-proliferation issue,
the Bush administration designated Pakistan a major non-Nato ally. It
thus joined Bahrain, Egypt and Jordan in acquiring this status, which
guaranteed priority for the delivery of defence equipment and assistance through defence export loan guarantees.

Rapprochement with India

The brinkmanship between India and Pakistan in 2002 was followed by
a thaw in relations that owed much to US influence. The Indian Prime
Minister Atal Behari Vajpayee also seemed eager to secure his place in
history by restarting the dialogue with Pakistan that had stalled at the
2001 Agra summit. A reduction in the infiltration of militants across the
border and the sense that India's economic potential and that of the
whole South Asia region[134] could only be fulfilled when political rivalries with Pakistan had been resolved, were other factors in the Indian
outlook. Terrorist outrages always threatened the rapprochement,[135] as
did domestic political pressures. Nevertheless, full diplomatic ties were
re-established. During June and July 2003 there were a number of private goodwill visits by parliamentarians and businessmen from both
Pakistan and India. An Indian delegation in August included the former
chief minister of Bihar, Laloo Prasad Yadav. On 11 July 2003 the Lahore-
Delhi bus service that had earlier been symbolic of Indo-Pakistan détente was restarted after an eighteen-month suspension. Agreement was
reached to start a bus service between Muzaffarabad and Srinagar on
1 August 2004.

Musharraf did not leave all the initiative to India. Pakistan responded
to Indian confidence-building measures regarding the restoration of
transport links and the resumption of cricketing rivalries with the declaration of a ceasefire along the line of control that came into force on

---

[134] Vajpayee declared at the SAARC summit that 'mutual suspicions and petty rivalries
have continued to haunt us. As a result the peace dividend has bypassed our region. History can remind us, guide us, teach us; it should not shackle us. We have to look forward
with a collective approach now.' *Dawn*, 5 January 2004.

[135] The most serious incident was the 25 August Bombay bomb blasts that killed fifty-
two people. The Deputy Indian Prime Minister Lal Krishna Advani dismissed Pakistan's
condemnation as 'a mere formality'. *Dawn*, 27 August 2003.

26 November 2003. Musharraf also referred to the readiness to meet India 'halfway on Kashmir'. He signalled a potentially important shift in policy just over three weeks later when declaring, 'We are for United Nations Security Council Resolutions. However now we have left that aside.'[136] Musharraf's critics doubted whether the architect of the Kargil war could be sincere. However, his response displayed a similar pragmatism to that at the time of the post 9/11 call by the United States to support the war on terror. Pakistan and India are both in an undeclared competition for US favour and Musharraf could not afford to appear inflexible. Moreover it is had been acknowledged for some time in Islamabad that a military solution to the Kashmir dispute was closed and that support for militant activity possessed both international and domestic drawbacks. A face-saving solution based on acceptance of the line of control as the international boundary, sweetened by a treaty with India and increased economic and people-to-people contact, might be regarded as the best deal on offer.

Musharraf and Vajpayee met during the 12th SAARC summit held in Islamabad in January 2004. The joint statement issued at its conclusion justified cautious optimism, rather than extravagant claims. A framework was established for a composite dialogue on all bilateral issues, including Jammu and Kashmir. Nevertheless, momentum had been established for another round in the long history of Indo-Pakistan dialogue over the vexed issue of Kashmir.

The thaw in Indo-Pakistan relations continued during the first half of 2004. This saw the restoration of air links between the countries and the resumption of cricketing ties. India embarked on a forty day tour of Pakistan on 10 March after a gap of fourteen years. A special visa camp was set up in Amritsar to facilitate the issuing of visas to a large number of Indian supporters who followed their team's successes in the One Day and Test series.[137] On 13 March Sonia Gandhi's son Rahul and daughter Pryanka Vadra attended the opening limited overs international match that was held in Karachi. Dina Wadia, after watching the final One Day match in Lahore accompanied by her son Nusli and grandsons Jehangir and Ness, visited the mausoleum of her father Quaid-i-Azam Mohammad Ali Jinnah on 26 March. 'May his dream for Pakistan come true,' she noted in the visitors' book.[138]

The long-drawn-out Indian election campaign did not sour the atmosphere. The expectation in Pakistan as elsewhere was of a BJP victory. Important talks on nuclear confidence-building measures and meetings at the foreign minister level on Kashmir had been timed to take place after the polls. Sonia Gandhi in the wake of her Congress Party's sur-

136 Reuters Foundation News Alert, 18 Dec. 2003.

137 India triumphed 3–2 in the One-Day Internationals and 2–1 in the three match Test Series.

138 *Dawn*, 27 March 2004.

prise return to power declared that the dialogue initiated by Vajpayee would be continued. She stunned her supporters, however, by declining the post of Prime Minister. This paved the way for the seventy-one-year old Sikh economist Dr Manmohan Singh to assume office. Another chapter of the peace process in the subcontinent was about to begin.

Pakistan since October 2002

The closing months of 2004 witnessed attempts by Musharraf to burnish his human rights record, while there was growing political opposition to his decision to continue to hold the dual office of President and Chief of Army Staff. However, the continued inability of the ARD and MMA to act in concert took some of the sting out of protests regarding the 'uniform' issue. The rapid turnover of Prime Ministers provided further evidence of the weakness of the parliamentary system. The prospects of an attempt by the Musharraf regime to restore relations at least with the PPP seemed to rise with the release of Asif Zardari, but there were again mixed signals following his brief re-arrest. Despite successes against al-Qaeda groups both in Pakistan's cities and in the tribal areas, the country continued to fall victim to terrorist outrages, which served the purpose of enhancing the perception that the country was 'off-limits' to westernisers. Even more worrying were the growing disturbances in Balochistan. In what seemed uncomfortably like a replay of the mid-1970s, nationalist sentiment was alienated by the regime's perceived disregard for the province's economic and political grievances. Increased sabotage activity against gas and rail installations by the self-styled Balochistan Liberation Army raised fears of a full-scale military crackdown.

On 15 May Musharraf called for a law to ban honour killing and emphasised that the Hudood Ordinance and the Blasphemy Ordinance should be 'studied afresh' to ensure that they were not misused. He also announced the creation of an independent National Commission for Human Rights.[139] Official statistics placed before the Senate on 9 July revealed that 4,000 men and women had been murdered in 'honour killings' during the previous six years. Double the number of women than of men had died.

The pro-Musharraf forces were further strengthened when the three-party National Alliance of former President Farooq Leghari merged with the unified Muslim League. A further blow was dealt to the opposition when the Speaker, Chaudhry Amir Hussain, used his discretionary powers to name the MMA secretary-general Maulana Fazlur Rehman as leader of the opposition—and hence eligible for a seat on the National Security Council—rather than the Alliance for the Restoration of Democracy candidate Makhdoom Amin Fahim.

[139] *Dawn*, Internet edn, 16 May 2004.

The continued threat of terrorism to Pakistan's stability was graphically brought home by the suicide bombing at the Imambargah Ali Raza in Karachi on 31 May. Outrage at this incident resulted in clashes between protesters and police.[140] The city was brought to a standstill on 1 June when funerals were held for most of the twenty-four victims of the blast. Equally serious was a bomb blast directed against the convoy of the corps commander Karachi in the first week of June. When the first meeting of the National Security Council was held on 24 June, it vowed to 'rid the country' of the terrorism and religious militancy that had claimed sixty lives since May.

However, the remote South Waziristan tribal region remained the frontline in the war on terror. The Pakistan army continued its operations to flush out 'foreign militants', and on 11 June the fighting escalated with bombing raids on suspected terrorist bases in the Shakai valley. The fighting continued sporadically in the Wana region over the following weeks. There were further air strikes on 20 July in the Santoi and Mantoi mountainous regions and on 9 September in the Kaikhel area of South Waziristan. The security services had more success in a series of raids that captured terrorists linked with the recent outrages and the December 2003 assassination attempts on Musharraf. The information yielded following the arrest of the 'terrorist computer expert' Mohammad Naeem Noor Khan prompted arrests in Britain and the foiling of an alleged plot to attack Heathrow Airport.[141] Further arrests on 21 August were claimed by the Pakistan authorities to have foiled an attack on official buildings and embassies in Rawalpindi and Islamabad. In a belated move the government shortly afterwards constituted a 45-member council of *ulema, masheikh* and intellectuals to campaign against terrorism in the country.

In an unexpected development Prime Minister Zafarullah Jamali resigned from office on 26 June. He was replaced as interim Prime Minister by the president of the PML, Chaudhry Shujaat Hussain. The interregnum gave time for the technocrat Shaukat Aziz to stand for election to the National Assembly and thereby be eligible to hold office. Jamali's resignation was linked to his rivalry with Chaudhry Shujaat Hussain, although it was recognised that crucially he had lost the support of the President. Musharraf publicly denied that he had forced Jamali to quit and said that it was the internal decision of the PML that he should go.[142] Chaudhry Shujaat Hussain was sworn in as Pakistan's nineteenth Prime Minister on 30 June after he had secured election by 190–76 as leader of the House in a vote boycotted by the MMA.

Shaukat Aziz stood for election to the National Assembly from the Tharparkar constituency in Sind and the Attock constituency in the Punjab. The latter election was marred by violence; there was a failed suicide

140 *Dawn*, Internet edn, 1 June 2004.

141 *Dawn*, Internet edn, 11 August 2004.

142 *Dawn*, Internet edn, 1 July 2004.

bomb attempt on his life on 30 July and three PPP activists were murdered. The opposition ML(N) and PPP parties had revealed their divisions in squabbles over securing a common candidate. It was only after the intervention of their leaders in exile that these disagreements were overcome.[143] The intervention of Asif Ali Zardari was necessary to secure the withdrawal of the MMA from the contests. Despite the clear run for the ARD candidates, Shaukat Aziz was elected by huge majorities in both constituencies in the 18 August polls. Immediately following the elections he took his seat in the National Assembly and within five days Chaudhry Shujaat Hussain had paved the way for him to become Prime Minister by stepping down after a fifty-seven-day transitional term. The opposition once again revealed its weakness by failing up till the last moment to agree a joint candidate to oppose the former finance minister in the prime ministerial contest in the National Assembly. Again the intervention of Benazir Bhutto and Nawaz Sharif was needed to prevent a split. The jailed PML(N) leader Makhdoom Javed Hashmi was finally agreed upon, but when he was not called from his Adiala prison cell to take part in the election process, the opposition boycotted the vote on 27 August, which secured Shaukat Aziz's election with 191 votes in the 342-member chamber. The following day he was sworn in as the second Prime Minister within two months. He promised to seek 'guidance' from President Musharraf in order to provide 'good governance' to the people.[144]

Opposition members declared that the farcical events revealed the weakness of democracy in Pakistan. They were further outraged when, on 6 September, the PML president Chaudhry Shujaat Hussain supported his party's Punjab General Council request that President Musharraf should continue to hold the post of Chief of Army Staff for another five years. He maintained that the 17th Amendment to the constitution did not make it mandatory for Musharraf to 'shed his uniform' as the MMA was demanding. The President received legal entitlement to continue in his post of Chief of Army Staff after The Dual Office Bill was rushed through the National Assembly on 14 October in the face of noisy protests from both the ARD and the MMA opposition groups. Spokesmen for the latter maintained that the President had broken his promise because he had agreed to remove his uniform in return for its support in the passage of the 17th Constitutional Amendment.[145]

The MMA protests early in 2005 consisted of strikes, 'million marches' and wheel-jams. The dual office issue remained at the forefront. However, the protests drew strength from the worsening economic situation for the ordinary consumer. Oil price rises contributed to the growing cost of living. By March 2005 inflation was running at 10 per cent.[146]

---

143 According to press reports, the disagreements had only been settled following Nawaz Sharif's telephone call to Benazir Bhutto. *Dawn*, Internet edn, 27 August 2004.

144 *Dawn*, Internet edn, 28 August 2004.

145 *Dawn*, Internet edn, 15 October 2004.

146 *Dawn* Internet edn, 12 April 2005.

While Musharraf remained resolute on the uniform issue, the federal cabinet met the MMA demand that a column recording religious affiliation should be restored in the new machine-readable passports; this was undoubtedly a blow for the President's policy of 'enlightened moderation'. The MMA less successfully tilted at the windmill of the 'un-Islamic' act of female participation in sports. On 3 April hundreds of activists disrupted a mini-marathon in which women competed in Gujranwala,[147] but the Punjab Assembly unanimously resolved the following day that this was an 'act of terrorism' and vowed to curb incidents that 'usurped the basic and constitutional rights of women.'

The MMA's activism was in part spurred on by the Supreme Court's release on bail of Benazir Bhutto's husband Asif Ali Zardari on 22 November 2004; he had been held in detention for eight years on corruption charges.[148] The PPP hotly denied rumours of a 'deal' between it and the establishment to secure Zardari's release, but he was quickly in the political saddle. When he attempted to go to the Punjab to address a political meeting a month later, he was briefly rearrested. A large number of PPP activists were detained as they attempted to greet him at Islamabad airport.[149] There were similar scenes when Zardari flew back to Lahore from Dubai on 16 April. Indeed it was claimed that more than 15,000 PPP activists had been arrested. There was some press speculation over whether government repression rested on the threat Zardari's presence posed to the Punjab Muslim League establishment more than to the President.

The ferment within Pakistan was undoubtedly embarrassing for Musharraf since it coincided with a fresh round of diplomacy with India. Chaudhry Shujaat Hussain's visit to New Delhi early in April 2005 injected new impetus into the ongoing round of confidence-building measures. The five-day visit, which included an eleven-member parliamentary delegation, furthered party-to-party contact and had its public highlight in an address to the congregation at the Jamia Masjid. However, the crossing of the Line of Control at Chakothi by passengers on the 7 April inaugural Srinagar-to-Muzaffarabad bus service was an even more potent symbol of the revived peace process.[150] At the close of President Musharraf's three-day visit to India which coincided with the One-Day Indo-Pakistan cricket series later in the month, a joint statement issued by him and Prime Minister Manmohan Singh declared that the peace

147 *Dawn* Internet edn 4 April 2005.

148 He was released on 22 November over the BMW case. He had previously been granted bail over eleven other cases and acquitted in three cases. *Dawn*, Internet edn, 23 November 2004.

149 *Dawn*, Internet edn, 22 December 2004.

150 The service was inaugurated on a fortnightly process and had been surrounded by security fears of terrorist attacks. The Indian Prime Minister, Manmohan Singh when he sent off the bus in Srinagar maintained that, 'The caravan of peace has started.' Special permits rather than passports or visas had been agreed as the required travel documentation thereby denying the Line of Control the status of an international border.

process was 'irreversible'. The two leaders also agreed to continue 'purposeful' discussions on the Kashmir issue in a 'forward-looking manner for a final settlement'.[151]

The positive steps in Pakistan's relationship with India contrasted with the mounting domestic problems. Like the MMA protests, ferment in Balochistan stemmed from the regime's legitimation problems arising from its narrow political base. The sabotage of gas installations and railway tracks raised the spectre of an 'army crackdown'. Nationalists remain resolutely opposed to the Gwadar port development,[152] claiming that the resulting population influx will convert Balochis into a 'minority' in their own homeland. The other bone of contention surrounds the establishment of cantonments in Sui, Kohiu and Gwadar, which are portrayed by nationalists as acting as an army of occupation in the province. The federal government wishes to 'modernise' Balochistan and to utilise its natural resources for Pakistan. Nationalists portray these steps as 'internal colonialism.'[153]

The government attempted to damp down the nationalist hostility by sending a twenty-eight-member parliamentary subcommittee to Balochistan to achieve dialogue and consensus. The centre-province disagreements in Balochistan are of the same kind as those relating to opposition in other provinces to dam construction (most notably the Kalabagh dam), which are made more difficult because of the law and order situation arising from the 'war on terror'. At a deeper level they can be linked to decades-old resentment at the 'Punjabisation' of Pakistan, which increases with each round of military intervention. Despite attempts at mediation by Chaudhry Shujaat Hussain, and the promise even of constitutional amendments to meet nationalist grievances,[154] the growing disturbances in Balochistan early in 2005[155] awakened painful memories of earlier struggles by ethnic nationalists against the Pakistan state. Were Pakistan politics once more moving in ever-decreasing circles?

May 2005

[151] Earlier Musharraf had declared to Indian editors that the Kashmir issue could erupt again, if it was left unresolved. For the text of the 18 April joint statement see *Dawn*, Internet edn, 19 April 2005.

[152] The first phase of this $250 million project which is being undertaken with the cooperation of the People's Republic of China was to be inaugurated early in January 2005.

[153] The secretary-general of the nationalist Jamhoori Watan Party, Agha Shahid Bugn, launched the so-called 'Bugti Dossier' on Balochistan's rights on 2 November. *Dawn*, Internet edn, 2 November 2004.

[154] *Dawn*, Internet edn, 1 February 2005.

[155] The catalyst for the deepening crisis was the alleged assault by army personnel on a lady doctor in Sui. The Frontier Corps had to take direct control of the Sui gas plant after national supplies were suspended following armed incursions. The disruptions were claimed by government spokesmen to have cost between Rs 150-200 million per day. There were also growing sabotage attacks on railway lines. By the end of January, night train services were suspended across the province. On 6 February, Quetta was for a time cut off from the rest of the country when the main railway line was blown up. See *Dawn*, Internet edn, 12, 15, 20, 26 January and 2. 8 February 2005

EPILOGUE

A TROUBLED TRANSITION

The Black Coat Revolt

Until the emergence of what has been termed the Black Coat revolt, General Musharraf appeared untroubled in his desire to secure Presidential re-election in advance of the parliamentary elections scheduled for the end of 2007. There appeared to be little prospect of a legal challenge and he had sufficient supporters in the existing assemblies which formed the electoral college to secure his vote. The opposition outside the assemblies could be contained; firstly because government dialogue with the mainstream opposition parties might divide them; secondly because previous ties between the military and the religious parties lessened the prospect of all-out conflict between them, despite their hostility to the Musharraf pro-western foreign policy[1]; thirdly prospects of access to power after parliamentary elections would distract opposition to the Presidential re-election. Pervez Musharraf's goal of securing Presidential re-election from the existing assemblies while still holding the office of Chief of Army Staff (COAS) thus appeared eminently achievable.

All this was turned on its head following the lawyers' mass protests at the 'suspension' of the independent-minded Chief Justice Iftikhar Muhammad Chaudhry on 9 March 2007.[2] Musharraf's decision was

1 It will be recalled that the MMA had supported the government in December 2003 in securing a two thirds parliamentary majority for incorporating the controversial Legal Framework Order as the 17th Constitutional Amendment. The LFO established a National Security Council and restored the power contained in Article 58–2(b) that Nawaz Sharif had removed of the President to dismiss the Prime minister.

2 The Chief Justice, who had assumed office in June 2005, had taken up the cases of those who had 'disappeared' during the military actions against Islamic militants. He had also annoyed the establishment by leading the Supreme Court bench which in August 2006 had overturned the privatisation of the Pakistan Steel Mills on the grounds that it was sold 'in indecent haste.' The opposition had subsequently tabled a no-confidence motion against Shaukat Aziz's government. President Musharraf made the Chief Justice 'non-functional' and sent a reference against him to the Supreme Judicial Council under Article 209 of the Constitution. Aitaz Ahsan led the panel of advocates which represented Justice Iftikhar.

based on the charge of the Chief Justice's misuse of authority. Former Chief Justice Sajjad Ali Shah who had clashed with Nawaz Sharif termed the action, 'as another step toward the ruination of the Constitution.'[3] A week later over 50 people were injured and 500 detained as police and protestors clashed near the Supreme Court in Islamabad.[4] The lawyers' agitation over the issue of the independence of the judiciary widened into an anti-Musharraf movement. Political protests were held across Pakistan on 26 March in which calls were made not only for the Chief Justice's reinstatement, but for Musharraf to step down.[5] The triumphant procession of Iftikhar Muhammad Chaudhry in a motorcade of over 2,000 vehicles from Islamabad to Lahore on 5 May revealed the depth of popular support for the Chief Justice. It was shortly after this show of opposition strength that the talk first surfaced of a declaration of an emergency. Significantly a number of TV channels including Aaj and Geo had their broadcasts of the motorcade blacked out.

Musharraf's attempt to muster political support in pro-government rallies was overshadowed by the pitched gun battles in Karachi on 12 May which shocked the nation. The Chief Justice's attempt to address a lawyers' convention on the premises of the Sindh High Court was the occasion for street gunbattles in which the pro-Musharraf regime Muttahida Qaumi Movement attacked activists coming to the city while the security personnel looked on. The main thoroughfare Sharae Faisal was turned into a battlefield. Clashes killed at least 34 people and injured 140 others. There were also attacks on a local private TV channel Aaj to prevent it from recording the events. The extent of the violence shocked opinion in the country and also revived memories of the lawlessness in Karachi during the troubled 1990s. There was adverse comment that Musharraf was playing the ethnic Mohajir card to sustain himself in power and that a pro-Government rally he was addressing in Islamabad continued despite news of the turmoil in Karachi.

Despite the Karachi killings, the campaign for the independence of the judiciary continued and the Chief Justice was received by further massed crowds during a fourteen-hour journey from Islamabad to Abbotabad at the beginning of June.[6] The dust had hardly settled from the motorcade when President Musharraf imposed fresh curbs on the electronic media, which were immediately greeted by street protests from journalists and human rights activists.[7] One of the proudest boasts of the Musharraf era had been the freedom of the press and media. This appeared now to be undone as the country lurched further into crisis. The turmoil continued

---

3 *Dawn*, Internet edn, 10 March 2007.

4 *Dawn*, Internet edn, 17 March 2007.

5 *Dawn*, Internet edn, 27 March 2007.

6 *Dawn*, Internet edn, 3 June 2007.

7 *Dawn*, Internet edn, 5 June 2007.

on 20 July when the Supreme Court reinstated the Chief Justice. Both Benazir Bhutto in the March 1996 Judges Case and Nawaz Sharif in his conflict with Chief Justice Sajjad Ali Shah had been embroiled in past clashes with the judiciary which had undermined their authority. The judges had always been supine, however, in the face of a military-backed regime. Indeed, as we have seen in this study, the Supreme Court had provided legal cover for Pakistan's coups under the 'doctrine of necessity.' The Supreme Court judgement which struck down the Presidential reference against the Chief Justice was thus not only unprecedented, but dealt a major blow to Musharraf's legitimacy.

The decision quickened Musharraf's talks with the PPP over a power-sharing agreement, indicating his weakening position.[8] It is clear that Washington pressed for this dialogue to shore up the position of its main ally in the war on terror and to strengthen the forces of Islamic moderation within Pakistan. Secret talks with Benazir Bhutto in Abu Dhabi at the end of July stalled on the issues of the removal of the President's uniform, the timing of the exiled leaders' return to Pakistan and Musharraf's desire to seek re-election from the current assemblies in advance of the projected general elections. Benazir Bhutto termed the ongoing dialogue with Musharraf as both 'erratic' and 'harrowing.'[9] It threatened the opening up of divisions in the mainstream political opposition. These became institutionalised by the PML-N's formation of the All Parties Democratic Movement which stood as a rival to the PPP dominated Alliance for the Restoration of Democarcy. The APDM made it clear in early August that it would take 'direct action' to obstruct Musharraf's re-election. These threats undoubtedly prompted almost 24 hours of speculation on 8 August about the imposition of an emergency. This action was apparently averted by the intervention of the US Secretary of State, Condoleeza Rice.

President Musharraf's Re-election

General Musharraf's re-election as President on 6 October was as controversial as the referendum in 2002 which gave him his first five year term in office. The 1,170 member electoral college was depleted by the resignation of the APDM opposition from around 200 seats in the National Assembly and the provincial assemblies. The MMA ruling alliance in the Frontier, because of divisions between its JUI-F and JI components, failed however to meet its intention to dissolve the provincial assembly before the Presidential vote. The PPP went ahead with its decision to abstain. Outside of the assemblies, the poll was greeted by strikes througout Balochistan and in Peshawar and Karachi. Lawyers led a number of protest demonstrations.

---

8 For Benazir Bhutto's account of these see, Benazir Bhutto, *Reconciliation: Islam, Democracy and the West* (London: Simon and Schuster, 2008), p. 223 & ff.

9 *Ibid.*, p. 229.

	Votes Polled	*Musharraf*	*Wajihuddin*	*Rejected*
NA & Senate	257	252	2	3
Punjab Assembly	257	253	3	1
Sindh Assembly	104	102	2	0
Balochistan Assembly	33	33	0	0
NWFP Assembly	34	31	1	2

Source: *Dawn* Internet edn, 7 October 2007

In the event just a handful of votes were cast for Musharraf's symbolic opponent, the former Supreme Court Judge, Wajihuddin Ahmed. But the fact that Musharraf received only 384 votes was hardly a ringing endorsement of his candidacy. More worrying for General Musharraf, however, was the fact that the Election Commission was unable to officially notify the results as a 11 member bench of the Supreme Court had to rule on petitions challenging his candidature for the Presidency.

The Emergency

Musharraf's goal throughout 2007 was to secure re-election as President in advance of parliamentary polls. Secure in another five year term of office, he could then address western pressures for parliamentary elections. It was the threat of legal rather than a political challenge to re-election which posed the greatest danger to Musharraf's plans. From the time of his ill-judged attempt to remove the Chief Justice, he painted himself into an ever tighter corner. Eventually, on 'Black Saturday', he was forced to introduce an Emergency through the Provisional Constitutional Order (PCO) of 3 November, although he realised this would anger his western supporters.[10] Musharraf maintained that judicial activism was 'destabilising' Pakistan. Police set up barbed barricades in Islamabad and blocked off access to public buildings. Lawyers' offices were raided in Quetta, Karachi and Lahore and the leading opposition lawyer Aitzaz Ahsan was arrested. The targeting of the lawyers followed the unprecedented attempt by seven judges of the Supreme Court to overturn the legal basis for the Emergency by rejecting the Provisional constitution order which accompanied it. The removal of the Chief Justice and sixty judges who refused to swear an oath of allegiance under the PCO prompted further protests by the opposition parties and the lawyers. The press was also muzzled along with independent TV companies which showed internationally embarrassing pictures of black-coated lawyers being tear-gassed and beaten by police outside the courts in Lahore and Islamabad. The lawyers were to be followed into detention by key politi-

---

[10] The Commonwealth suspended Pakistan from membership after Musharraf failed to either lift the emergency rule or resign as COAS within the ten day deadline set on 12 November.

cal figures as nationwide protests greeted the Emergency. When the PPP joined the opposition campaign, Benazir Bhutto was briefly detained. Imran Khan went on hunger strike following his detention in the Dera Ghazi Khan jail.

In order to placate western opinion, Musharraf had to continue with the election timetable as well as make the Emergency a short-lived affair. While this limited damage in the West, in Pakistan the Emergency gave renewed vigour to the lawyers' movement. It also raised the humiliating prospect that all the major parties would boycott the polls thereby undermining the President's credibility still further. His stepping down as Chief of Army Staff on 28 November in favour of the newly-appointed Vice-COAS, General Ashfaq Parvez Kanyani, who was widely regarded as a Musharraf loyalist, met the long-term opposition demands. Nevertheless, it was a case of too little too late as indeed was the ending of the Emergency just over two weeks later. When a poll boycott was avoided, it resulted from the urge to power of the main parties, not a conciliatory attitude to the now civilian President. Musharraf was not forgiven for the mass arrests, muzzling of the press and independent television stations and for the trampling of the judiciary's independence. The prominent role played by judges in the election process should not be overlooked, not only in terms of arbitration and oversight,[11] but in the fact that the key roles of Returning Officers and District Returning Officers were filled by session court judges, so the weakened judiciary raised public concerns about the fairness of the electoral process. Nawaz Sharif made the restoration of the sixty judges who refused to operate under the Emergency's Provisional Constitutional Order a major plank of his party's election campaign. The timing and manner of achieving this goal created differences between him and the PPP leadership in the early period of the post-independence coalition government and eventually culminated in its collapse.

Musharraf remained committed to the holding of national parliamentary elections, even if these were to take place in the circumstances of Emergency rule. In the event, the emergency was lifted just one day before campaigning began. The polls' fairness was further questioned both by the fact that the Election Commission was not independent and that the Interim Government headed by the Senate Chairman, Mohammadmian Soomro, which was sworn in on 16 November to oversee the polls, was partisan. Soomro had won the Senate election on a PML-Q ticket from Sindh. The visit to Islamabad of the US Deputy Secretary of State John Negroponte encouraged Musharraf to begin to release political opponents such as Imran Khan. Negroponte's visit coincided with a toning down of Benazir Bhutto's increasingly harsh criticism of Musharraf. He received a further bonus when a ten member bench of the reconsti-

---

11 On 5 January 2008, Musharraf appointed two High Court judges to the vacant Election Commission positions whose neutrality was considered as dubious.

tuted Supreme Court on 22 November dismissed the last petition challenging his right to seek re-election thus enabling the Election Commission to officially notify the results. The promulgation of a Presidential Ordinance officially described as the Constitution Amendment Order 2007 gave 'constitutional cover' to all the actions taken by him since the institution of the emergency. These legal steps enabled Musharraf to end the emergency on 15 December in advance of the polls as well as keep his promise to step down as Chief of Army Staff. His trusted supporter Ashfaq Pervaz Kiani had been promoted to Vice Chief of Army Staff in November. The symbol of the lawyers' revolt, Aitzaz Ahsan, President of the Supreme Court Bar Association remained in detention.[12]

The Lal Masjid Affair

The Red Mosque in the heart of Islamabad became the centre of a dramatic six month stand-off between the authorities and the radical students attached to its Jamia Hafsa and Fareedia *madrassahs*. Lal Masjid and Jamia Hafsa were extended into large complexes[13] on land illegally occupied by two cleric brothers Maulana Abdul Aziz and Maulana Abdul Rashid Ghazi.[14] They threatened violence when the Capital Development Authority attempted to recover the land. It was reported that the Jamia Hafsa with its 4,000 students possessed a stockpile of weapons and its female students had been trained and indoctrinated to carry out suicide attacks.[15] The episode which ended in a military storming of the compound was variously portrayed as symptomatic of Pakistan's 'creeping Talibanisation', or of the dangerous combination between the military and the *mullahs* which dated back to the Zia era.

Conspiracy theorists saw the Lal Masjid affair as a set up job, designed both to distract attention from the lawyers' movement and to secure western sympathy for the Musharraf regime as it battled to hold the line against militancy. The crisis originated in the students' attempts to enforce *sharia* law, under the encouragement of the mosque leadership of Maulana Abdul Rashid Ghazi and Maulana Abdul Aziz. The students' activities escalated from the occupation of a children's library, to the moral 'policing' of the nearby markets. The attempts to prevent the sale

[12] This was extended for a further 30 days on 2 February 2008.

[13] Jamia Hafsa covers an area of 6,500 square yards. This is thirteen times larger than the original area legally allotted by General Zia-ul Haq.

[14] They were the sons of the mosque's founder Maulana Abdullah, a fiery pro-*jihad* preacher who was assassinated within the mosque in 2001. Maulana Abdullah had gained close association with a number of Afghan *jihadist* figures during the Zia era and later developed close association with the Taliban. He was noted for his anti-Shia stance and had links with the militant Sipah-e-Sabha movement.

[15] See, Azfar-ul-Ashfaque, 'Students trained for suicide attacks: MQM report on Lal Masjid' *Dawn*, Internet edn, 23 April 2007.

of audio and video cassettes caused conflict with local traders. Liberal protestors carried placards and slogans against the Jamia Hafsa and Lal Masjid students containing such calls as 'No to religious extremism, Yes to life and music.' A number of the *ulama* in Islamabad considered that the female students' occupation of the children's library was not in line with the *shariah* and condemned Maulana Abdul Aziz's demands as a 'manifestation of extremism.' The educational board of Deobandi Madrassahs, Wifaqul Madariss Al-Arabia disaffiliated the twelve *madrassahs* run by the Lal masjis administration.

Lal Masjid had previously linked itself with the Pakistan Taliban cause. A conference of *ulama* issued a *fatwa* from Lal Masjid in 2003 which opposed Pakistan military operations in Waziristan and called for a boycott of the *namaz-i-janaza* of soldiers killed in the fight with Taliban militants.[16]

Female students from Jamia Hafsa occupied an adjacent Children's Library in protest at the Capital Development Authority's demolition of the Ameer Hamza Mosque situated on the Murree Road in Islamabad on 24 January 2007. Maulana Abdul Aziz encouraged them to widen their demands from a call for the reconstruction of the Ameer Hamza Mosque along with an apology from President Musharraf for its demolition, to an insistence on the immediate imposition of an Islamic order. In a note to the President they declared that, 'We are followers of Shariah which does not teach us to give and take. Rather it says that we firmly stick to the path of Islam and either be a martyr or a Ghazi. Therefore our demands are definitely unbending and we are not willing to withdraw any of our demands.'[17] This intransigence encouraged the Government to strike a reconciliatory pose in which the representatives of *Wifaq-ul-Madaris* (the national gathering of the Islamic seminaries in Pakistan) were encouraged to negotiate with Maulana Abdul Rashid Gazi and the Student Action Committee of Jamia Hafsa. A Government crackdown on 9 February was called off because of the fear of widespread violence. Following the kidnapping on 18 May of four policemen who were accused of 'spying' outside the mosque, meetings involving the police, the Interior Ministry and the army were held at the GHQ in Rawalpindi to find a 'permanent solution' to the Lal Masjid issue.

The six month stand-off was finally ended by a military assault codenamed Operation Silence which resulted in the death of fifty-five militants including the cleric Maulana Abdul Rashid Ghazi. The mosque seizure was followed by a wave of suicide bombings across Pakistan. These mainly affected the tribal areas and the NWFP and were directed at the security services. There was another failed assassination attempt on Pervez Musharraf on 6 July. The mounting tide of terrorist activity in the

16 Zaffar Abbas, 'The Creeping Coup' *Dawn* Internet edn, 31 March 2007. This would deny Pakistan army personnel a Muslim burial.

17 *Monthly Aab-e-Hayat* (Lahore) February 2007.

north west was accompanied by an ongoing mini-insurgency in Balochistan. The self-styled Balochistan Liberation Army blew up railway lines and gas pipelines in the increasingly troubled province.

The whole Lal Masjid episode highlighted the ambiguous relationship between the military and radical groups. The mosque originally owed its influence to Zia ul Haq's patronage. Despite its connections with sectarian extremist groups such as Sipah-e-Sabha and allegations that Maulana Abdul Rasheed Gazi had links with Al-Qaeda, no arrests were made to curb its influence. Despite growing lawlessness by the students of Jamia Hafsa it was only under the pressure of the Chinese government when its nationals were kidnapped that the government acted. The Lal Masjid affair thus came to be seen, as evidence that Musharraf was appeasing Islamic radicals rather than an example of the dangers of extremism.

The Troubled Tribal Areas

This sentiment had already began to take root because of growing Western dissatisfaction arising from the Miramshah peace deal signed in North Waziristan in September 2006. The withdrawal of Pakistan military forces in return for the tribal leaders' agreement to expel foreign militants was held to be responsible for the re-establishment of Taliban and Al-Qaeda safe havens. This issue caused increasing tension between Islamabad, the Karzai government and NATO commanders[18] and was a key factor in the downturn in US-Pakistan relations early in 2007[19] which saw mounting accusations that Pakistan was lukewarm in the war on terror. They were based on the continued activities of 'banned' organisations under a different name and the capture of high profile Al-Qaeda and Taliban figures only when the full international spotlight was turned on Pakistan. President Musharraf was increasingly angered by such criticisms. Indeed in a speech to the 2007 Land Forces Symposium in Islamabad attended by senior military officials from twenty-two countries, he warned that Pakistan would quit the international coalition against terrorism, if accusations of foot dragging continued. 'If we are bluffing each other, if I am bluffing and if Inter-Services Intelligence is bluffing, then we must be out of the coalition,' he asserted, continuing that, 'We have

[18] Tensions between the Pakistan and Afghanistan Governments were eased a little with the agreement on 30 April 2007 to set up a Joint Working Group to monitor progress in promoting peace and security in the region. This declaration followed talks between Pervez Musharraf and Hamid Karzai hosted by the Turkish Government in Ankara. Pakistan and Afghanistan agreed to deny sanctuary, financing and training to terrorists. Fighting between Afghan and Pakistani border guards on the 13th and 14th of May however once more strained relations between the two countries. See *Dawn*, Internet edn, 16 May 2007.

[19] Public criticism was muted by the spring and at the end of April 2007 a State Department Report praised the Pakistan Government's counter-terrorism efforts which were recorded as 'helpful' in the US-led fight against the Taliban in Afghanistan. See *Dawn* (the Internet edition) 30 April 2007.

suffered the maximum and we have contributed the maximum. Therefore, we will not accept that Pakistan is not doing enough in the war against terror.'[20] In July 2007, the US National Intelligence Estimate report went so far as to advocate unilateral US action in the troubled Tribal Areas. This threat of 'hot pursuit' resurfaced in 2008 as the security situation further worsened and western troops suffered increasing casualties in southern Afghanistan.

The Musharraf regime reacted angrily to such strictures. It pointed out that 80,000 troops had been deployed in the Tribal Areas and that around 700 of these had been killed in clashes with militants. Casualties among Pakistan troops increased in the wake of the Lal Masjid affair as convoys were targeted by militants in Waziristan. The consequences for army morale were difficult to ascertain following suicide attacks in high security areas in Rawalpindi and the Taliban's holding hostage of hundreds of troops in South Waziristan.

The tribal areas' socio-economic backwardness, poverty and conservatism are important factors in the support for the Taliban amongst its Pakhtun population. This is also linked with the legacies for the region arising from the 1979 Soviet invasion of Afghanistan. It was an important supply base and staging area during the first *jihad* against the Soviets. According to the International Crisis Group Asia report the North and South Waziristan Tribal Agencies were Osama bin Laden's operations base during the Afghan *jihad*. *Mujahideen*, supported by the West, assumed leadership roles in some of the Pakistani tribal areas. This influence continued after the end of the conflict and explains support for Taliban elements in the region whether of foreign origin or local who are engaged in what is termed the second *jihad* against the US and its allies in Afghanistan and Pakistan. Some foreign *jihadists* stayed on after 1979. They have been accepted in the region not only because of the *Pukhtanwali* code of sanctuary, but because of marriage ties with local populations. There was a further influx of Afghan Talibs and foreign *jihadists*, including Arabs, Uzbeks and Chechens into the Tribal Areas in the wake of post 9/11 US led offensives against Taliban and Al-Qaeda in Tora Bora in December 2001 and Shahikot valley in March 2002.

The writ of the government remains weak in the tribal areas. Without, peace and security, prospects are limited for socio-economic development. Yet the overcoming of the region's backwardness represents the best way forward for reducing the appeal of both homegrown and foreign religious extremism. It is thus crucial that there is sufficient stability in the region for the implementation of the projected $2 billion FATA Sustainable Development Programme. The Pakistan Government has agreed to provide $1 billion through the Public Sector Development Programme. It is incumbent on international donors to match this amount so that improve-

20 Ihtasham ul Haque, 'President warns of quitting war against terror', *Dawn*, Internet edn, 13 April 2007.

ments can be made in the key areas of roads, education and health.[21] It will be recalled that the Pakistan government proposed large scale investment when the Soviet Union left Afghanistan. It is not inconceivable that the expenditure of $3–4 billion in development programmes would have pre-empted the much larger expenditure of blood and treasure in the region since 9/11. A further important measure to bring FATA into the Pakistan mainstream would be to allow party candidates to campaign and operate in office. The present requirement for non-party polls in the name of maintaining tribal norms, not only breaches rights to freedom of association, but marginalises the region.[22]

Democratic opponents of the regime increasingly argued that extremism could only be effectively tackled by popularly elected representatives. 194 people were killed in suicide bombings during the first three weeks of July 2007 alone. The policy of dialogue which began with the April 2004 Shakai Agreement was taken up by the ANP in its election manifesto as the way to resolve conflict. Its adoption after the 2008 elections appeared to cede further influence to the militants and became increasingly controversial both in the West because of the security consequences within Afghanistan and amongst those Pakistani groups who feared creeping 'Talibanisation.' By September 2008, it had given way to more resolute military responses in the Khyber, Kurram and Bajaur political agencies as well as in Provincially Administered Swat, following the breakdown of an agreement with the pro-Taliban *TNSM*. Suicide bombings in Pakistan's major cities which had declined during the elections and in their immediate aftermath were resumed by the *Tehrik-i-Taliban Pakistan*. The government responded by banning the organisation.

The Return of Benazir Bhutto and Nawaz Sharif

Pakistan's political scene was transformed by the return from exile of its two leading figures within the space of a month in October-November 2007. The 2002 elections had been fought in the absence of Pakistan's two former Prime Ministers. President Musharraf at the beginning of 2007 could not have contemplated their return in advance of polls. Indeed when Nawaz Sharif had attempted to return on 10 September 2007, he had been unceremoniously bundled out of the country. Their return from exile was a sign of Musharraf's loosening grip on power, although few at the time had any inkling of the tumultuous events that were set to unfold. Behind the ending of their exile was respectively the hand of Washington and Riyadh. Musharraf's reluctant acquiescence revealed the extent to which the lawyers' revolt had diminished his power. Bhutto's return had been part of a long term western strategy to shore up the forces of mod-

---

[21] The US has committed $750 million for FATA development in the next five years.

[22] There was no EU Election observation in FATA at the time of the February 2008 polls.

eration against Islamic extremism. The National Reconciliation Ordinance, which lifted the legal threats against the Bhuttos, had been approved on the eve of Musharraf's Presidential re-election. In the preceding months, Benazir had steadfastly denied that 'back channel' contacts with Pakistan's ruler were taking place to pave the way for her return.[23]

Benazir Bhutto's homecoming to Karachi was marred by the suicide bombing of her slow moving motorcade in the Karsaz neighbourhood as she was taken in procession to the Quaid's mausoleum where she was scheduled to address a rally. 179 of her followers died and nearly 600 were injured in the two explosions.[24] Huge crowds had greeted her earlier arrival at Karachi airport on a plane from Dubai. Benazir Bhutto recalled that:

> It was truly a caravan of democracy, a way for an astounding three million Pakistani citizens—including huge numbers of women and children—to come Out and express their support for the PPP... Music pulsated from boom boxes, blasting the traditional anthems of thirty years of Peoples Party campaigns interspersed with the latest Pakistani pop music. Supporters danced around the vehicles, throwing rose petals and cheering my return and the return of democracy. People were hanging on from the trees and from telephone and telegraph poles, attempting to catch a glimpse of me and the other PPP leaders who stood on the flatbed truck.[25]

Other participants maintained that the welcome was more tumultuous than that which had greeted her arrival in Lahore in 1986. Benazir alleged that her long term opponents in the army and intelligence services were complicit in the failed Karachi suicide attempt.[26] Her relations with Musharraf further nosedived when he declared the Emergency on 3 November. Nevertheless throughout the following weeks, the PPP stance was less intransigent than that of the PML-N. This was seen most clearly in the PPP commitment to contest the polls. Nawaz Sharif wavered, but ultimately decided that it was too dangerous to leave the field open by boycotting. His decision to contest, left other members of the All Parties' Democratic Movement (APDM), which he had founded in London in July 2007, high and dry.[27] Both Jamaat-i-Islami and Imran Khan's, Tehreek-i-Insaaf had publicly committed to a boycott. They maintained

23 *Dawn*, Internet edn, 29 April 2007.

24 For Benazir Bhutto's own gripping account of the atrocity see, Benazir Bhutto, *Reconciliation*, pp, 11–13; 219–22.

25 *Ibid.*, p. 7.

26 The claims about security lapses were made in the press and found their way into her posthumous publication *Reconciliation*, see pp. 7–12; 218–21.

27 After a marathon seven hour meeting at Nawaz Sharif's Model Town residence in Lahore on 9 December, the APDM had failed to achieve a consensus on the election boycott issue.

that fighting the polls with Musharraf still as President lent him legitimacy. This was also the position adopted by the lawyers' movement.

The Assassination of Benazir Bhutto

Benazir Bhutto's shocking assassination near Liaquat Bagh, Rawalpindi on 27 December, less than six weeks after the failed Karachi cavalcade, stunned Pakistan and world opinion.[28] It ended long held western hopes of a stabilisation of moderate forces through a political arrangement between herself and President Musharraf. According to eyewitness accounts, the PPP leader was felled by an assassin's bullet as she was driving out of a park following an election rally. Her motorcade was also hit by a suicide bomber which claimed twenty-one other lives. Benazir Bhutto died nearby the spot where her father had been hung and also where Pakistan's first Prime Minister Liaquat Ali Khan had also been shot.

The violence during the three day period of mourning following her killing was especially severe in Sindh, with Karachi descending into anarchy, and raised fears of a resurgence of tension between this province and Punjab which Sindhis associate with the army. '*Pakistan na khapay*' (Don't want Pakistan) slogans were raised at her graveside. The fears were exaggerated however that the country would split along ethnic lines.[29] Nevertheless, approximately sixty lives were lost in the violence which broke out across Pakistan in the days immediately after her death. The economy and Pakistan's international image received a further setback.[30] Further political tensions were generated by the conflicting accounts of the circumstances of Ms Bhutto's death emanating from Government and her PPP sources. The PPP called for a UN investigation to uncover Government complicity in the murder. Scotland Yard detectives were sent to investigate the crime scene. Their evidence suggested the involvement of Al Qaeda militants along with the Waziristan Taliban tribal leader Baitullah Mehsud.

Benazir Bhutto was buried amidst tumultuous scenes at the *mazar* of her father in the ancestral Bhutto village of Garhi Khuda Baksh. Just eight weeks earlier she had returned to this spot to pray for the first time since the long years of exile. After she had showered rose petals on her

---

[28] See Zahid Husain, *Frontline Pakistan: The Path to the Catastrophe and Killing of Benazir Bhutto* (London, 2008).

[29] For a discussion of this see, Katherine Adeney, *Bad News Makes Headlines: Security Challenges Posed by Pakistan*, ippr Commission on National Security, Background Briefing Note 1 (January 2008), p. 5.

[30] Not only was domestic and international travel disrupted and industries and shops closed, but investor confidence was so badly affected that the Karachi Stock Exchange had to suspend trading for three days. When it reopened, it recorded the biggest one day fall in its history. *Dawn*, Internet edn, 1 January 2008.

father's grave, she had remarked to reporters that 'I now feel better about my security.'[31] Her subsequent death revealed the ways in which the country had changed since her exile. The last five years have witnessed a rising tide of suicide bombings and terrorist attacks. They have not been confined to the troubled border regions but have occurred in the heart of all of the country's cities. Benazir Bhutto was just one of the 2,000 victims of such attacks in 2007.[32]

Benazir Bhutto's political will vested leadership of the PPP in the Bhutto family dynasty with her husband Asif Ali Zardari acting as co-chairman until Bilawal Bhutto Zardari, a student at Oxford, was old enough to take up the party reins. Zardari had journeyed to Pakistan to accompany his wife's body to its final resting place at Garhi Khuda Baksh. The PPP decided to go ahead and fight the elections evoking a similar response from Nawaz Sharif's Muslim League. The violence following Benazir Bhutto's death led the head of the Election Commission Qazi Mohammad Farooq to postpone the election date for six weeks until 18 February. Opposition leaders claimed that this was because the ruling PML-Q feared a massive sympathy vote for the PPP in early polls. The election campaign continued to be fractious with widespread claims of Government attempts to ensure 'pre-poll' rigging. There was even talk of a further postponement and the formation of an interim government of national consensus. Nawaz Sharif made it clear however that this could only be achieved if President Musharraf stepped down from power and the Election Commission was reconstituted. These political developments continued against a backdrop of bombings, including a blast at the Shia Niaza Qaim Baig Imambargah at Peshawar, clashes between the army and militants in both Swat and Waziristan and deteriorating economic conditions.

The February 2008 Polls and their Aftermath

Benazir Bhutto's assassination, which had occurred just twelve days before the scheduled polling day, injected further uncertainty into Pakistan's tumultuous political scene. Western powers were nonetheless insistent that the polls be held. They supported the view that only fair and free elections could restore political legitimacy and thereby reverse the tide of increasing chaos. The polls were monitored by both foreign and domestic groups of observers; the latter were organised through the Free and Fair Elections Network. The EU Election Observation Mission[33] was almost

---

31 *Dawn*, Internet edn, 28 October 2007.

32 Massoud Ansari, '*Resurrecting Democracy?*' Dawn-Herald Elections 2008 http://www. dawn.com/weekly/herald/herald19.htm accessed 19/022008

33 This arrived on 9 December. On polling day it had 48 long term observers covering 65

bombarded by claims that there was an attempt at pre-poll rigging on a massive scale.[34] This took many alleged forms including, the bringing of false cases against PPP activists in the wake of the end of December disturbances, the use of government funds to pay for advertisements of PML-Q candidates, the use of threats against opposition candidates and activists, the buying of votes and the partisan support for the PML-Q by many *nazims*.[35] There was little public belief in the independence of either the Election Commission or of the caretaker governments in the provinces and at the centre. These had taken office when the term of the assemblies had expired. The caretaker Prime Minister, Mohammadmian Soomro had in fact been elected as Chairman of the Senate by the support of the PML-Q and was widely regarded as a close ally of Musharraf.[36]

The volatile security environment was cited as justification for restrictions on large scale processions and meetings. Electioneering was thus low key. Public broadcasting favoured the PML-Q, although cable and satellite stations, despite blocks and regular warning notices, provided coverage of opposition parties and leaders. Nevertheless in the words of the EU Election Observation Report, 'the combination of the existing regulatory framework, the curbs on the media and the arrest of more than 200 journalists in the aftermath of the declaration of emergency rule created an environment of tension and apprehension during the entire electoral period.'[37] The polls took place in an increasingly unfavourable economic background. This resulted in part from world trends of rising oil and food prices as well as domestic difficulties. The latter included: the withdrawal of overseas investments, in the wake of Ms Bhutto's death, inflationary pressures and power supply problems which led to factory shutdowns. State Bank of Pakistan figures revealed a worrying slowdown in the textile industry, which accounts for 65 per cent of Pakistan's exports. There was also a crisis in the availability of consumer necessities such as flour in part because of hoarding, as well as the impact on millers of the load-shedding problems .[38] Power was cut off to consumers across Pakistan for 8 hours on 2 January 2008. Shorter interruptions to supply continued for

per cent of constituencies. For its report and recommendations see, EU Election Observation Mission, Pakistan, *Final Report* (Islamabad, 2008).

34 Fot the litany of complaints made to the EU delegation when it visited Sahiwal on 29 January see, *Daw,n* Internet edn, 2 February 2008.

35 For details of all these allegations see the following issues of *Dawn*, Internet edn, 14 December 2007; 15 December 2007; 18 December 2007; 24 December 2007; 25 December 2007; 13 January 2008; 24 January 2008; 25 January 2008; 28 January 2008; 30 January; 31 January 2008, also see, *Daily Times*,Internet edn, 10 January 2008.

36 Nawaz Sharif alleged in a press conference held on 16 January in Lahore that the caretaker government was an extension of the PML-Q. *Dawn*, Internet edn, 17 January 2008.

37 EU Election Observation Mission, *Final Report*, p. 35.

38 Reduction in wheat grinding because of the suspension of power supplies aggravated the already serious flour crisis in the Punjab. *Dawn*, Internet edn, 5 January 2008.

the next two weeks. It was a sign of the PML-Q's desperation that the blame for consumer shortages was placed on the party's former Prime Minister Shaukat Aziz who had left for London on 6 January and was consequently playing no part in the campaign. Another harbinger of the party's subsequent defeat was the defection of members to the PML-N.[39] The PML-Q platform had been based on the economic achievements of the past five years, so these circumstances damaged its prospects.

Both the PML-N and the PPP made capital out of the shortages, rising costs of energy, education and rents. They provided various schemes to improve the conditions of the ordinary Pakistani. The PPP reprised Zulfiqar Ali Bhutto's slogans of the 1970s with the provision of food, clothing and housing (*roti, kapra aur makan*) for the poor. The PPP's key to poverty alleviation was the provision of a public works programme which would guarantee employment for at least a year to one member of the poorest 25 per cent of families in Pakistan.[40] The PML-N ambitiously aimed to establish a national education corps of unemployed graduates in an adult literacy drive. It also sought to provide free state run education up to the higher secondary level. Importantly for Pakistan's post-poll situation, both the party manifesto and Nawaz Sharif in fiery public speeches spoke of reinstating the deposed judges, disbanding the National Security Council and restoring the powers of the Prime Minister.[41] The PPP adopted a much more cautious approach to the issue of dismantling the changes brought by Musharraf. Indeed the PPP co-chairman Asif Ali Zardari left open the possibility of working with him.

Musharraf by this stage, however, had become so universally unpopular that the PML-Q had attempted to distance itself from him by removing his portrait from election materials. The 'King's Party' was now disowning its inspirer. The PPP in contrast drew succour from its deceased leader. Benazir's last election address at Rawalpindi was played to the crowds who were encouraged to take revenge by victory at the polls. The cry was frequently heard, 'Vote Bhutto *jo kariz aa*' (Voting for the Bhuttos is a debt we owe). Benazir's final speech was widely circulated on compact discs and cassettes. Some election addresses were barely veiled in their claims that the government was complicit in the assassination.[42] The ruling PML-Q suffered from a backlash in many Sindhi constituencies and found it impossible to undertake any electioneering. Angry rioters attempted to burn down the house of the former Sindh Chief Minister,

---

39 In December, for example, a number of leading party figures in Gujranwala defected to the PML-N after Nawaz Sharif's electioneering visit to the district. *Dawn*, Internet edn, 17 December 2007.

40 *Dawn*, Internet edn, 25 December 2007.

41 *Dawn*, Internet edn, 27 December 2007.

42 At a *chhelum* gathering at Mirpur Sakro in Sindh a PPP leader Ms. Sassui Palijo openly alleged the PML-Q Chaudries of Gujrat had 'conspired' to eliminate Benazir Bhutto. *Dawn*, Internet edn, 8 February 2008.

Liaquat Ali Jatoi, who was forced to flee in a car bearing the PPP colours as camouflage.[43] Even in rural Sargodha and Khushab in the Punjab, PML-Q election material and offices were burned.[44]

The polls delivered a resounding victory for the two mainstream opposition parties. The PPP emerged as the largest national party with 113 seats, the PML-N bagged 84 in the 342 member lower house. The PML-Q lost ground to Nawaz Sharif's party in its Punjab heartland. The PML-N's performance in the provincial assembly elections was even more impressive than for the national assembly with it capturing 102 Punjab seats to the PPP's 78 and PML-Q's 66 respectively. The PPP won the most seats in the provincial polls in Sindh and in the other provinces came second.

The PML-Q had lost so heavily in the Punjab that leading figures such as its President Chaudhry Shujaat Husain and Sheikh Rashid Ahmad, the former Federal Minister for Railways and Government spokesman, had been defeated in their 'ancestral seats' in Gujrat and Rawalpindi.[45] In the wake of this rout Imran Khan called for the President's immediate resignation because the election had been in effect a referendum against his personal rule.[46] The Musharraf factor alone did not however work against the PML-Q. It suffered as we have seen because of the declining economy.

Even in Balochistan where the PML-Q did sufficiently well to momentarily hold out the prospect of forming a government[47] this owed more to the boycott by the leading Pakhtun and Baloch nationalist parties than to its popularity or record in office. The party was also aided by the factional rivalries within the JUI (F) in the province. While support for the PML-Q held up in Balochistan, the MMA suffered major setbacks both there and in the NWFP. The pattern of pre-2002 elections was restored in which the religious-based parties were reduced to the margins. The MMA was left with just 6 of the 45 National Assembly Seats it had won in 2002. Both the ANP and the PPP triumphed at its expense. Indicative of the collapse of JUI (F) support was the defeat of its leader Maulana Fazlur Rehman at the hands of the PPP. The JUI (F) had been handicapped by the divisions between it and JI over the issue of boycott. The JI organisation

43 Massoud Ansari, 'Provincial Overviews—Sindh: PPP Broom Sweeps Clean', *Election 2008 Herald*

http:www.dawn.com/weekly/herald/herald22.htm accessed 22 February 2008.

44 *Dawn*, Internet edn, 5 January 2008.

45 Makhdoom Javed Hashmi who had led the PML-N during Nawaz Sharif's exile and served a long sentence in prison defeated Sheikh Rashid who had secured support for the creation of schools in Rawalpindi and for the controversial expressway between it and Islamabad over the Leh nullah.

46 *Dawn*, Internet edn, 20 February 2008.

47 In the event the PML-Q joined all other parliamentary groups in giving its backing for the PPP leader, Nawab Mohammad Aslam Raisani to take office as Chief Minister in an attempt at econciliation within the province.

had undoubtedly been important in mobilising urban voters on the MMA platform in the 2002 polls in the Frontier. JUI (F) also suffered from an anti-incumbency vote' arising from its failure to deliver on poverty alleviation. Critics argued that all it had achieved in five years in office in the NWFP was a kind of gesture politics, epitomised at the social level by the vandalising of hoardings which used women to advertise products and in parliament by the passage of the 2003 Sharia Act and the 2006 Hasba (accountability) Act. The latter Act, which created offices of *Mohtassib* (Ombudsmen), was criticised for its attempt to police public morals. It was also seen as a job creation scheme for MMA activists. Even before the passage of the Bill, the MMA had been accused of nepotism and patronage politics. Serious corruption charges were raised against MMA leaders in fact as early as the 2003 Senate elections. By the time of the parliamentary polls charges of personal profit from office were even more widespread. Indeed, the derisive term 'Land Cruiser Mullahs' had been coined.[48]

The Awami National Party (ANP), in contrast had put its 2002 divisions behind it. The party's claims that the Musharraf regime was responsible for the violence in FATA and Waziristan played well with the Pakhtun voters. The ANP also highlighted the spill over of violence into the NWFP. It held out the prospect for dialogue with militants as a way to restoring peace in the tribal and frontier regions. The polls restored the pre-2002 pattern in which the religious parties were a marginal force. While this was reassuring for Pakistani liberals, the outcome at a stroke undermined Musharraf's claims to the West that he alone stood as a bulwark against Islamic militancy.

The pattern of past elections was repeated in that weeks of horse-trading followed the polls before a Prime Minister and Cabinet could be announced. Initially it seemed as if Makhdoom Amin Fahim who had led the PPP in Parliament during Benazir Bhutto's exile would take up the reins of office. There were also signs that the PML-N would be happier to tend its former Punjab powerbase than to take responsibility in a national government. Following the Murree declaration, the PML-N entry into the federal cabinet was assured, with representation also going to the ANP, JUI-F and to an independent FATA MNA, Hameedullah Jan Afridi.[49] President Musharraf oversaw the swearing in not of Amin, but of Yusuf Reza Gilani as Prime Minister on 24 March in a ceremony which was boycotted by leading political figures such as Zardari, Nawaz Sharif, the JUI chief Maulana Fazlur Rehman and the ANP Chief Asfandyar Wali Khan. The tense and solemn occasion not only boded ill for future relations between the Parliament and Presidency, but hinted at future problems between the two major election winners in that a cabinet had still not been formed because of PPP and PML-N wrangling over portfolios.

---

[48] *Dawn*, Internet edn, 24 December 2007.
[49] He became Environment Minister.

When the cabinet was sworn in a week later, the PML-N members wore black armbands in protest at Musharraf's continuation in office. These circumstances led the political commentator Ishtiaq Ahmed to subtitle a piece on the new federal cabinet 'More of the same or something new?'[50] Asif Ali Zardari had discouraged Fahim's candidature as Prime Minister on the grounds of his contacts with the Musharraf regime. These had occurred at the same time as Benazir Bhutto was engaged in a discreet dialogue with the President. The real reason was that Fahim had his own powerbase in Sindh and would further consolidate this at the possible expense of the Bhuttos if he served as Prime Minister. Yusuf Reza Gilani appeared a better choice, not only because of his demonstrated loyalism to the PPP during a lengthy spell of imprisonment from 2001, but because as a Punjabi he could not threaten the Bhutto heartland. Nor was he likely to build up untrammelled influence in Punjab because of potential PML-N rivals in his home province. To further guard against the emergence of an uncontrollable Prime Minister, Zardari ensured that the Gilani family's traditional rivals in Multan politics, the Qureshis were represented in the Cabinet.[51] Makhdoom Shah Mehmood Qureshi, despite his inexperience in this area was given the important Foreign Affairs Ministry. In a further astute move, Zardari ensured that his friend, the Lahore industrialist and former jail companion, Chaudhry Mukhtar Ahmed was awarded the Defence Ministry. Ahmed too enthusiastically revealed his role as an intermediary with Musharraf[52] as he had to almost immediately deny a statement he had made on taking office that the President was a great asset to Pakistan. Conflicting attitudes between the PPP and PML-N to the President and the restoration of the pre-emergency judiciary existed from the outset of the coalition, despite its surface calm.

Just as Zardari sought to exert influence from behind the scenes, so Nawaz Sharif had sought to maximise his influence in the new cabinet. He ensured that two political heavyweights from his 1990 governments held key positions. Ishaq Dar reprised his role as Finance Minister.[53] Chaudhry Nisar Ali Khan, who had been Sharif's Special Assistant as well as Minister for Petroleum and Natural Resources during 1997–9, was awarded the post of Senior Minister, Communications with additional responsibility for Food, Agriculture and Livestock. The PML-N's

50 Ishtiaq Ahmed, 'The Pakistan federal cabinet: More of the same or something new?', *ISAS Insights* No. 27 (11 April 2008).

51 For the long term historical rivalries of the Gilani and Qureshi Pir families of Multan see, C. Baxter, 'The People's Party versus the Punjab Feudalists', in H. Korsen (ed.), *Contemporary Problems of Pakistan* (Leiden, 1974); 'Union or Partition: Some Aspects of Politics in the Punjab 1936–45' in L. Ziring et al. (eds.), *Pakistan the Long View* (Durham 1977); I. Talbot, *Punjab and the Raj! 849–1947* (New Delhi, 1988).

52 It was widely acknowledged that he had good relations with the President and the Army leadership.

53 His appointment aroused critical comment because he was a relative of Nawaz Sharif.

comeback in Punjab was further strengthened when Shahbaz Sharif secured victory in a by-election and promptly took up the post of Chief Minister. Legal barriers prevented Nawaz himself entering parliament by a similar route. The PPP sought to trump Shahbaz's re-emergence through the appointment of the forceful press baron Salman Taheer as Governor. Future battle lines were being drawn, even before the issue of Musharraf's position was resolved.

The prospects facing the new cabinet appeared uncertain on a number of fronts. It had taken office at a time of economic downturn, increasing security problems in the tribal areas, and mounting law and order problems.[54] There was the question of the extent to which its components could put the national requirement for unity, before party interests. National reconciliation had been talked of during the election campaign, but the long-standing tensions between a Punjab dominated centre and the provinces needed to be addressed in order to strengthen a fractious federation. Finally, the ways in which parliament could reassert its authority over the executive required careful handling, lest they precipitate a crisis similar to those which had previously invited military intervention.

Gilani held out hope that some of these issues could be addressed in his 100 day programme which combined austerity measures, a promise of a Truth and Reconciliation Commission, increased employment opportunities for the poor and reform of *Madrassah* Curriculum. New thinking on the security issue in the Tribal Areas was also proposed which would replace a purely military approach with dialogue backed up with development of the region. There were also signs that a new Eighteenth Constitutional Amendment would at some point clip the wings of the President with the aim of reducing the office to a ceremonial position.[55]

In the event the PPP-PML national coalition lasted a mere forty-two days. Talks in Dubai and in London could not secure the implementation of the agreement to restore the judges who had been out of office since 3 November within the timeframe of an agreement made at Bhurban on 9 March. The PPP's insistence on dealing with this issue in a 18th Amendment Constitutional package, rather than by means of a Resolution in the National Assembly strained its historic alliance with the PML-N. Nawaz Sharif gained the moral high ground as he resigned on the issue of the failure to implement the March pledge. Although the crisis was reported

---

54 Hopes that the opening session of the National assembly would usher in a process of national reconciliation were set back by incidents in Lahore and Karachi in which senior figures of the Musharraf regime Dr Arbab Rahim and Sr Sher Afgan Niazi were beaten by members of the lawyers' movement. This led to a clash between rival lawyers' groups in Karachi in which five people were killed in an arson attack. (see *Dawn* internet edn. 10 April 2008). Both MQM and PML-Q threatened an indefinite boycott of the Sindh Assembly. President Musharraf during his state visit to China warned of anarchy, while his opponents blamed the unrest on the dying embers of his regime in an all too familiar bout of mutual recrimination.

55 *Dawn* internet ed. 6 April 2008.

in terms of a breakdown over mechanisms rather than principles, the judges' issue revealed deep divisions. The PPP under Zardari was prepared to bide its time regarding the restoration of the judges and the move against the President. Nawaz Sharif was intemperate and remained implacably hostile to Musharraf. The restoration of the judges was for him a prelude to an assault on the Presidential power.

The Gilani government's political and economic problems intersected with the resignation of the experienced Finance Minister Ishaq Dar following the PML-N decision to quit the Federal Cabinet on 12 May. Inflation was running at a monthly increase of over 20 per cent; the rupee was depreciating alarmingly, despite the State Bank's 'stabilisation measures' and at the same time as energy bills for consumers were climbing, power shortages led to widespread load-shedding in such cities as Lahore and Karachi. The government appeared immobilised in the face of these problems.

The economic gloom was accompanied by growing security threats in the north-western regions. These resulted in the gradual abandonment of the ANP strategy of dialogue with militants. The PML-N complained before its withdrawal from the coalition that it had not been consulted, when military actions were launched in the Khyber Agency. Conflict continued in Bajaur and Swat. The new military drive was insufficient however to deter an impatient US from launching strikes in the tribal areas. A new threshold was reached when US Special Operations Forces killed Pakistani civilians in a raid on a village near Angoor Adda in South Waziristan on 3 September.[56] Pakistan-US relations reached their lowest ebb since 9/11 in its wake and the decision temporarily to halt fuel supplies to NATO forces in Afghanistan via the Torkham highway.[57]

Worryingly the mounting problems on the western frontier occurred against the backdrop of a downturn in relations with India. The establishment of a democratic government in Islamabad had not kick-started the stalled India-Pakistan composite dialogue. Internal developments within Indian-administered Kashmir which culminated in the introduction of federal rule in July and resumed firing along the line of control were depressing omens. New Delhi's claim that the bombing of its embassy in Kabul on 7 July bore an ISI imprint cast a pall over the fifth round of 'composite dialogue' between the Indian and Pakistan foreign secretaries a fortnight later. The advances in relations of the past five years, notwithstanding, a significant breakthrough seemed as far off as ever.

Musharraf's Resignation and Its Aftermath

Despite repeated claims that he would not run away from a fight, Musharraf tendered his resignation as President on 18 August. He announced

[56] *Dawn* internet ed. 4 September 2008.
[57] *Dawn* internet ed. 6 September 2008.

his decision during the course of a television address and, in keeping with earlier dramatic pronouncements during his nine year reign in office, claimed that he was putting the country and the nation before his own interests. It was clear however that he had taken the step to avoid the personal humiliation of impeachment, as the awareness dawned that the military establishment and Washington would not pull irons out of the fire for him. During the previous weeks he had become an increasingly isolated figure, with an ever narrowing group of advisors. Moreover, a steady haemorrhage of support from Independent and PML-Q MLAs was daily reducing his chances of defeating impeachment. Both publicly and in private, western politicians had counselled the former Commando against a last ditch stand which would further destabilise Pakistan's fragile polity.

Instantaneous judgements of Musharraf's legacy in the Pakistani and world press were at best mixed. Praise for his early institutional reforms and the freeing of the press were counterbalanced by vociferous criticism of his attempts to stifle civil society in the last year of his regime; the local government reform and accountability processes were regarded as partisan in intent and unlikely to survive; the record in the war on terror and with respect to Islamic moderation was seen as rhetorical and ambiguous in its character; even the macro-economic successes of the post-2001 period were regarded by many commentators at the time of his resignation as unsustainable for they had not been accompanied by structural reform, leaving Pakistan extremely vulnerable to inflationary pressures. Finally, while Musharraf could be praised for making efforts to restore dialogue with India, the likelihood of the process of confidence building measures culminating in a permanent rapprochement seemed far from certain by mid-2008.

Stepping back and viewing the Musharraf era within the longer historical context, it is clear that like Ayub and Zia before him, he was never able to secure legitimacy, despite the attachment of part of the political classes to his governments for opportunistic reasons. He found like, Ayub, that once he had shed military uniform, the army was no longer a reliable prop for his continuation in power. Its institutional interests as ever came first and foremost in responses to the impending impeachment of its former Chief. This does not mean however, that the army would readily countenance Musharraf's humiliation or trial. His hopes of enjoying his golf and brandy in retirement, rather than being hounded through the courts were in fact boosted by the eclipse of his nemesis Nawaz Sharif in the immediate aftermath of the 18th August resignation.

The removal of the common quarry was quickly followed by a final falling out of the PPP and PML-N. The fly in the ointment was again the judges's issue, although this masked the increasing differences between the erstwhile coalition partners. The entry of the PML-N into the opposition was marked by clear signs of a return to some of the more unsavoury aspects of the 1990s politics. Corruption charges against Nawaz Sharif

Epilogue

almost immediately resurfaced, as the National Accountability Bureau reopened the references of the Hudaibia Paper Mills, Ittefaq Foundry and Raiwind assets cases. There was fevered speculation that the PPP would replace the PML-N government in the Punjab in an unholy alliance with the PML-Q. This would further strengthen the PPP's grip on power within Pakistan.

The decision of the PML-Q to quit the government benches had been made precisely because of this evolving intention. Indeed the final straw for Nawaz Sharif had been Zardari's reneging on a signed agreement that a non-partisan pro-democracy figure would be elected to replace Musharraf if the Presidential office's wide-ranging powers remained intact. On the eve of the presidential polls, Zardari promised to ensure the supremacy of parliament, but by now he faced a considerable 'trust deficit'. For Sharif, it was essential immediately to remove the powers of the President to dissolve the National Assembly as the PPP was committed to this course in its joint Charter of Democracy with the PML-N. Moreover these powers could be used to establish a kind of 'elective dictatorship.' Previously Zardari had spoken of being a titular President. He continued to claim this was his goal, but such protestations appeared unconvincing to his critics.

The Presidential Election

The PML-Q decided to put up the longstanding Musharraf loyalist, Senator Mushahid Hussain as its candidate. The PML-N turned to the former Supreme Court Justice Saeed uz Zaman Siddiqui. Both men campaigned vigorously, despite the fact that Zardari was the overwhelming favourite to secure the support of the electors from the provincial assemblies and the national parliament. Many of the old charges of corruption, for which Zardari had spent years in prison, but had never been convicted were once again highlighted by his opponents. In this, Pakistan's second Presidential election within a five month period, the voting formula was as follows:

Voting Formula

		Total
National Assembly	1 person = 1 vote	342
Senate	1 person= 1 vote	100
Punjab Assembly	5.70 persons = 1 vote	65
Sindh Assembly	2.58 persons = 1 vote	65
NWFP Assembly	1.90 persons = 1 vote	65
Balochistan Assembly	1 person= 1 vote	65
		702

The National Assembly and Senate electors cast their votes in a joint sitting of parliament on 6 September, the provincial assemblies voted simultaneously, with their verdict being calculated in the voting formula set out in the above table. The outcome was hardly in doubt, but it revealed, interestingly, the dominance of the PPP following its alliance with MQM in Zardari's native Sindh, the continuing post-February 2008 decline of PML-Q which called its existence into doubt and finally that the PML-N remained a force to be reckoned with in the Punjab Assembly.

	Zardari	*Siddiqui*	*Hussain*
Parliament	281	111	34
Sindh Assembly	64	0	0
Punjab Assembly	22	35	6
NWFP Assembly	56	5	1
Balochistan Assembly	59	2	2

Source: dawn/news/special/zardari+wins+presidential/.

Addressing a victory rally at Prime Minister's House Islamabad, flanked by his daughters, Bakhtawar and Asifa, Zardari vowed to follow the policies of Zulfiqar Ali Bhutto and Benazir for democracy 'for which they had sacrificed their lives.'[58] In the same speech he had also reiterated that Parliament was sovereign and the President was subservient to it. Doubts remained however concerning the amount of power he would be willing to surrender. In addition there were anxieties regarding his political vision and statesmanship to overcome the grave security and economic problems which beset the nation. No President in Pakistan's history had entered office facing such challenges and with such open domestic and international disquiet about their ability to steer the ship of state into safer waters. Despite the high hopes generated by the February 2008 polls, Pakistan could once more face going back to the future. A fourth military intervention would be likely to imperil the federation's very existence.

58 *Dawn* internet ed. 7 September 2008.

APPENDICES

A

PAKISTAN HEADS OF STATE

Muhammad Ali Jinnah	Governor-General	Aug. 1947–Sept. 1948
Khwaja Nazimuddin	Governor-General	Sept. 1948–Oct. 1951
Ghulam Muhammad	Governor-General	Oct. 1951–Aug. 1955
Iskander Mirza	Gov.-General/President	Aug. 1955-Oct. 1958
Muhammad Ayub Khan	CMLA/President	Oct. 1958–Mar. 1969
Muhammad Yahya Khan	President	Mar. 1969–Dec. 1971
Zulfiqar Ali Bhutto	CMLA/President	Dec. 1971–Aug. 1973
Fazal Elahi Chaudhry	President	Aug. 1973–Sept. 1978
Muhammad Zia-ul-Haq	CMLA/President	July 1977–Aug. 1988
Ghulam Ishaq Khan	President	Aug. 1988–July. 1993
Wasim Sajjad	Acting President	July 1993–Nov. 1993
Farooq Leghari	President	Nov. 1993–Jan. 1998
Rafiq Tarar	President	Jan. 1998–June 2001
Pervez Musharraf	President	June 2001–August 2008
Asif Ali Zardari	President	September 2008–

PAKISTAN PRIME MINISTERS

Liaquat Ali Khan	Aug. 1947–Oct. 1951
Khwaja Nazimuddin	Oct. 1951–Apr. 1953
Muhammad Ali Bogra	Apr. 1953–Aug. 1955
Chaudhri Muhammad Ali	Aug. 1955–Sept. 1956
Huseyn Shaheed Suhrawardy	Sept. 1956–Oct. 1957
Ibrahim Ismail Chundrigar	Oct. 1957–Dec. 1957
Firoz Khan Noon	Dec. 1957–Oct. 1958
Nurul Amin	Dec. 1971–Dec. 1971
Zulfiqar Ali Bhutto	Aug. 1973–July 1977
Muhammad Khan Junejo	Mar. 1985–May 1988
Benazir Bhutto	Dec. 1988–Aug. 1990
Ghulam Mustapha Jatoi	Aug. 1990–Nov. 1990
Nawaz Sharif	Nov. 1990–Apr. 1993

Balakh Sher Mazari	Apr. 1993–May 1993
Nawaz Sharif	May 1993–July 1993
Moeenuddin Ahmad Qureshi	July 1993–Oct. 1993
Benazir Bhutto	Oct. 1993–Nov. 1996
Meraj Khalid	Nov. 1996–Feb. 1997
Nawaz Sharif	Feb. 1997–Oct. 1999
Zafarullah Khan Jamali	Nov. 2002–June 2004
Chaudhry Shujaat Hussain	June 2004–August 2004
Shaukat Aziz	August 2004–Nov. 2007
Mohammad Mian Soomro	Nov. 2007–March 2008
Syed Yusuf Raza Gilani	March 2008–

B

BIOGRAPHICAL NOTES

ACHAKZAI, KHAN ABDUS SAMAD KHAN (1907-1973) Pushtun active in Baloch politics known as the 'Baloch Gandhi' and 'Khan-i-Azarn'. He was repeatedly imprisoned both during the Raj and after independence for 'secessionist activities'. He opposed the One Unit Scheme. He was a member of the NAP, before forming a breakaway Pashtoonkhawa National Awami Party. He was a member of the Balochistan Provincial Assembly at the time of his assassination in December 1973. His son Mahmood Khan Achakzai was to become Chairman of the PKMAP.

AHSAN, AITZAZ (b.1945). Prominent lawyer, human rights activist, and author, Aitzaz Ahsan was born in Murree. He was educated at Aitchison College and Government College Lahore before studying law at the University of Cambridge. He was called to the Bar at Gray's Inn in 1967. He entered politics in 1975 and rose to the rank of a Minister in the Punjab Government. He subsequently resigned and was expelled from the PPP when he protested at the police firing on a lawyers' rally in Lahore during the PNA agitation. He rejoined the PPP during the Zia martial law era and played an important role in the Movement for the Restoration of Democracy. He was elected to the National Assembly during Benazir Bhutto's first ministry and took the post of Minister of the Interior. He was re-elected in 1990 but lost his seat in 1993. The following year he entered the Senate. During Nawaz Sharif's second government, he was leader of the opposition. He became increasingly prominent during the struggle for the independence of the judiciary which followed the suspension of the Chief Justice Chaudhry Iftikhar Mohammad Chaudhry in March 2007. He was the leading defence advocate when the Chief Justice appeared before the Supreme Judicial Council. Aitzaz Ahsan became a symbol along with the Chief Justice in the struggle against the authoritarianism of the Musharraf regime. Following the introduction of the Emergency, Aitzaz Ahsan was detained without charge. He continued to speak out in support of the Judges who had been dismissed because they refused to take an oath under the Provision Constitution Order. Ahsan supported the boycott of the parliamentary polls in order to deny legitimacy to the Musharraf regime. Following the elections, he continued to press the new parliamentarians to work for full judicial autonomy and the restoration of the Constitution to its pre-emergency status. In addition to these political roles, he became increasingly prominent in the legal profession. He currently holds the position of President Supreme Court Bar. Aitzaz Ahsan is also well known as a human rights activist and as an author. He published the book, *The Indus Saga and the Making of Pakistan* with Oxford University Press in 1996.

ALI, CHAUDHRI MUHAMMAD (1905-1980) Civil servant and later Pakistan Prime Minister born in Jullundur. He served in the Indian Audit and Accounts Service before independence. On the creation of Pakistan, he filled the most important bureaucratic post as Secretary-General to the Government. It was largely due to him that the Pakistan Civil Service emerged as a major pillar of the state. Unlike Ghulam Muhammad, his close friend and associate, he harboured no personal political ambitions.

In 1951 he became Minister of Finance and then in October 1955 succeeded Bogra as Prime Minister. He presided over the introduction of the One Unit Scheme and the 1956 Constitution, but was never at home in the political world of shifting allegiances. Especially after the creation of the Republican Party. His position became untenable when the PML withdrew its support from his coalition government. Mirza. Who did not want Suhrawardy to replace him as Prime Minister, tried unsuccessfully to prevent Chaudhri Muhammad Ali's resignation, but this was proffered on 8 September 1956.

During the early years of the Ayub regime, Chaudhri Muhammad Ali acted as an adviser to the National Bank of Pakistan and as Chairman of the PICIC. In 1962 he moved into the opposition ranks, leading the Nizarn-i-Islarn Party, Increasing frailty prevented him from playing a role in the post-Ayub political scene. His memoir *The Emergence of Pakistan* (New York, 1967) has become a classic account of a participant's view of the birth of the country and its immediate aftermath.

ALI, JAM SADIQ (1935-1992) Sindhi landowner and politician who was the controversial Chief Minister of Sindh from August 1990 until his death in March 1992. Jam Sadiq Ali came from an influential feudal Shia family. He entered politics in 1962 when elected to the West Pakistan Provincial Assembly. He was elected to the National Assembly in 1965 and to the Sindh Provincial Assembly in December 1970. He joined the PPP in 1972 and was appointed Minister for Local Government. He was re-elected in 1977 and remained in office at the time of Zia's coup. He fled arrest and began a twelve-year exile in London, resisting the Zia regime's efforts to implicate Zulfiqar Ali Bhutto. He returned to Karachi in April 1989 following Benazir Bhutto's assumption of power and acted as an adviser to her government. Following her dismissal by President Ghularn Ishaq Khan on 6 August 1990, Jam Sadiq Ali sided with her opponents and was appointed Caretaker Chief Minister of Sindh. One of his first actions was to order the arrest of Asif Ali Zardari. Jam Sadiq Ali used the machinery of the state to ensure that the PPP's hold on its Sindhi heartland was weakened in the 1990 polls. After the elections, he retained the post of Chief Minister.

His eighteen-month rule remains highly controversial. Supporters point to the relative tranquillity in the province after the highly charged *mohajir-Sindhi* clashes which had earlier brought it to the brink of civil war. However, it is undeniable that the Jam regime was marked by human rights abuses, with state terrorism being deployed against the Government's PPP opponents. Jam Sadiq Ali died of cirrhosis of the liver on 4 March 1992 and was laid to rest with state honours at his ancestral graveyard at Jam Goth (Sanghar) the following day.

AMIN, NURUL (1897-1974) Bengali Muslim League politician. He served as a member of the Bengal Assembly before independence and was its speaker in 1946. He joined Khawja Nazimuddin's cabinet after independence and replaced him as Chief Minister in 1948 on his becoming Governor-General. He suffered a humiliating defeat at the hands of the United Front in the 1954 provincial elections. Amin nevertheless remained President of the East Pakistan Muslim League at the time of Ayub's coup.

From 1962 Nurul Amin was a leading figure in the Council Muslim League which opposed Ayub's Convention League. He joined the National Democratic Front in October that year and was elected as one of its National Assembly candidates in 1965. Nurul Amin was heavily involved in the fruitless negotiations between the opposition parties and Ayub in March 1969. In the December 1970 elections he resisted the Awami League tide to secure election as a PDP candidate for Mymensingh. True to his long-standing Muslim League loyalty he opposed the Awarni League's movement for Bangladesh and migrated to Pakistan following the secession of the eastern wing. He held the post of VicePresident of Pakistan from December 1971 until its abolition two years later.

AMINUL, HASANAT (1922-1960) The fourth *pir* of Manki Sharif (Nowshera district), he succeeded his father Abdul Rauf in 1934. He openly supported the Muslim League after the 1945 Simla Conference and organised other *pirs* and *sajjada nash ins* in the Anjuman-us-Asfia which was founded in October 1945. He declared that Muslims should undertake a *'jihad'* for Pakistan and played a prominent role both in the civil disobedience against the Congress Government and in the referendum campaign. He was disillusioned when Shariat law was not introduced following the creation of Pakistan and came into conflict with

Abdul Qaiyum Khan. *Pir* Manki founded the Jinnah Awami League, but retired from politics in 1955. He was killed five years later in a car accident.

BEG, MIRZA ASLAM (b.1931) Pakistani Commander-in-Chief and leading figure in the Zia and post-Zia era. Beg was born and educated in Azamgarh, commissioned into the Pakistan Army in 1952 and served first in a Balochi infantry regiment before joining the Special Service Group in 1961. He saw active service during both the 1965 and 1971 Indo-Pakistan wars. After a spell at the National Defence College, he was promoted major-general in 1978.

Beg rose to prominence during the Zia era, becoming successively Chief of the General Staff (1980-5), Corps Commander (1985) with responsibility for a major part of the Pakistan-Afghanistan border, and Vice-Chief of Army Staff (1987). He was extremely influential in the smooth transition to parliamentary democracy following General Zia's death in 1988. From then until his retirement on 15 August 1991 he held the pivotal post of Chief of Army Staff. He formed part of a troika of powerholders which included the President and the Prime Minister. Ghularn Ishaq Khan would not have dismissed the Bhutto Government without Beg's support. He was later to disagree with Nawaz Sharif over Pakistan's policy during the Gulf War. This undermined the Prime Minister's position *vis-à-vis* his former Army backers as well as triggering intense conflict between the ISI and civilian Intelligence Bureau security agencies. On his retirement Beg cultivated the image of 'defender of democracy', but subsequent revelations by former colleagues have revealed his behind-the-scenes endeavours to secure the downfall of the first Benazir Bhutto administration. He raised the idea in 1993 of reconstituting the National Security Council as a Defence Committee of the cabinet. The CDNS later gave a similar constitutional role for the Army.

BHASHANI, MAULANA ABDUL HAMID KHAN (1885-1976) Left-wing peasant leader in East Pakistan, dubbed the 'red Maulana'. Bhashani led the Muslim League in Assam before independence, upon which he moved to his home province of East Bengal. He became the leader of the East Bengal Awami League which formed part of the United Front in the 1954 provincial elections. He resigned his post as Provincial President during Suhrawardy's Premiership because of his pro-Western foreign policy. Following a meeting in Dhaka in July 1957, he joined hands with Mian Iftikharuddin to form the NAP. This was revived following Ayub's lifting of martial law. He was interned in his home village of Kagmari following Yahya's assumption of power, but was freed to contest the December 1970 elections. He adopted a more radical stance than Mujibur Rahman and demanded on 10 December, shortly after the results were announced, that East Pakistan should be an independent and sovereign state.

BHUTTO, BENAZIR (1953-2007). Prime Minister 1988-90; 1993-6; PPP Chair 1993. The eldest of Zulfiqar Ali Bhutto's four children, Benazir was educated at Harward and Oxford Universities. She campaigned for her imprisoned father in 1977-9 along with her mother Nusrat, who assumed the Chair of the PPP. From 1977-84 she suffered long periods in detention, during which her health deteriorated. Benazir provides a detailed account of this traumatic period in her acclaimed autobiography *Daughter of the East* (1988).

After two years of British exile, Benazir had a tumultuous homecoming in April 19886. In July 1987 she married Asif Zardari, a member of a landowning family from Sindh. General Zia's death in August 1988 paved the way for election which the PPP won, although it did not obtain an absolute majority. On 1 December, Benazir Bhutto became the first female leader of a Muslim country.

Much of the ministry's energy was dissipated by her conflict with Nawaz Sharif. Chief Minister of the Punjab, and the leader of the national opposition IJI alliance. Following the collapse of the PPP-MQM alliance in October 1989, there was mounting ethnic violence between Sindhis and *mohajirs*. The May 1990 Pucca Qila incident in Hyderabad intensified the violence throughout Sindh. President Ghulam Ishaq Khan cited the deteriorating law and order situation when he dismissed the Bhutto Government on 6 August 1990. Benazir was charged with corruption and misuse of power, while her husband Zardari was arrested on a kidnap charge.

Nawaz Sharif held office after the October 1990 elections, and there was continuous conflict between him and Benazir during the next two years. In January 1993 a more conciliatory atmosphere emerged, which saw Benazir elected as Chair of the National Assembly's Standing Committee on Foreign Affairs. Zardari was released on bail shortly afterwards.

Benazir Bhutto returned to power following the October 1993 polls. Conflict continued with Nawaz Sharif's opposition Muslim League. Her relations with Nusrat were strained over her becoming sole PPP Chair and by her brother Murtaza's claim to his father's political legacy when he returned from exile in November 1993. The greatest threats to her government emanated from the unchecked violence in Karachi in 1994-5, her clash with the judiciary and the deteriorating economic situation in 1996. Her relations with President Farooq Leghari declined dramatically during the summer of 1996, especially in the wake of Mir Murtaza's death. Leghari on 5 November invoked the Eighth Amendment to dismiss her government. Benazir again campaigned vigorously in the February 1997 elections, as well as fighting the dismissal of her government in the Supreme Court. Her widowed sister-in-law Ghinwa Bhutto led a faction of the PPP loyal to the deceased Mir Murtaza, which opposed the PPP power-based in Sindh. Benazir's estranged uncle Mumtaz Ali Bhutto acted at this time as caretaker Chief Minister in the province. Benazir attributed the PPP's crushing defeat in the 1997 elections to rigging.

Benazir Bhutto spent eight years in political exile, in London and Dubai during which time a number of corruption and accountability cases were brought against her. She steadfastly maintained that these were designed to keep her away from Pakistani politics. Some commentators wrote off her prospects of ever holding power again. From 2006 onwards, however, in response to the changing situation within Pakistan, both London and Washington encouraged her to establish dialogue with President Musharraf in order both to strengthen the forces of moderation and provide legitimacy for the West's Presidential ally who was increasingly isolated. Benazir Bhutto's growing importance was reflected in the republication of her autobiography *Daughter of the East* and her increasing presence in the western media and in the corridors of power in Washington. She returned to Pakistan, following Musharraf's re-election as President on 6 October 2007 and the introduction of the National Reconciliation Ordinance which removed the threat of the legal cases against her. The homecoming to Karachi on 18 October was marred by a massive suicide bomb blast. Her relations with Musharraf were soured by accusations regarding the establishment's complicity in the attack and the introduction of the Emergency on 3 November. Nevertheless, Bhutto steered her party away from the boycott of the parliamentary elections which were scheduled for 8 January 2008. This forced Nawaz Sharif also to contest to the detriment of the All Parties Democratic Movement. Benazir Bhutto was assassinated in a bomb and shooting attack following an election rally at Liaquat Bagh, Rawalpindi on 27 December. The event shocked world opinion and threw Pakistan politics into turmoil. Both friends and opponents praised her courage and tenacity in returning to Pakistan. With her death a major player vanished from the political scene. Her immediate legacy was the defeat of the pro-establishment PML-Q in the February 2008 polls. Question marks surround whether her longer term legacy will be the consolidation of democracy within Pakistan.

BHUTTO, MIR MURTAZA (1954-1996) The eldest son of Zulfiqar Ali Bhutto. Like Benazir he was educated at Oxford and Harvard. He campaigned along with his younger brother Shahnawaz for his father's release following the Zia coup of 1977. When the Supreme Court upheld a death sentence he accompanied Jam Sadiq Ali and other PPP leaders to the Middle East to mobilise support for a clemency appeal.

After Bhutto's hanging, the Bhutto brothers founded the 'Al-Zulfikar' (The Sword) terrorist organisation, while Benazir and her mother worked for a democratic resistance to the Zia regime within Pakistan. Al-Zulfikar received financial support from a number of Middle Eastern countries and established training camps in Afghanistan. It achieved international notoriety following the hijacking of a PIA DC-10 in March 1981. Its activities provided the Zia regime with an excuse for repression of the opposition within Pakistan. The Afghan Government forced the closure of the camps. Shahnawaz settled in France, where he died in mysterious circumstances in July 1985. Mir Murtaza based himself in Damascus. Despite rumours of his return during the first ministry of his sister, he remained in increasingly frustrated exile. His hostility became directed towards Asif Ali Zardari, whom he denounced as a looter of the 'national wealth.'

Murtaza failed nominations in a number of Sindhi constituencies in the 1993 elections, although he remained in exile. Evidence of the growing family rift was provided by his mother Nusrat's campaigning on his behalf against official PPP candidates. He was eventually elected to the Sindh Assembly for the Larkana seat.

He returned to face a series of charges, but was surprisingly acquitted. Taking up residence at the family's Clifton home. He surrounded himself with activists, a number of whom had criminal records. He became an outspoken critic of his estranged sister's government and contemptuously derided her husband as the 'Black Prince of Islamabad'. Benazir was nevertheless grief-stricken at his death in a mysterious police encounter on the night of 20 September 1996. Her questioning four days later, and the role of the security agencies and even the President in the episode, were important contributory factors in her ouster.

BHUTTO, ZULFIQAR ALI (1928–1979) Foreign Minister 1963-6; President and then Prime Minister 1971-7. The son of a Sindhi feudal landowner, he was educated at Bombay Cathedral High School and the Universities of Oxford and California (at Berkeley). After Ayub Khan's 1958 coup, Bhutto became Minister of Commerce and Industries. He made his name as an expert on foreign affairs and held this cabinet office in 1963-6. His outlook was fervently anti-Indian. Bhutto clashed with Ayub over the Tashkent Treaty which followed the 1965 Indo-Pakistan war. In November 1967 he founded the PPP which propounded an ideology of Islamic Socialism. The PPP co-ordinated the campaign which led to Ayub Khan's replacement by the Army Chief Yahya Khan.

The PPP triumphed in the West Pakistan constituencies in Pakistan's first national elections in 1970. Sheikh Mujibur Rahman's Awami League similarly succeeded in East Pakistan. The inability to share power or to meet East Pakistani demands for autonomy resulted in the tragedy of the Bangladesh war. Pakistan's defeat by India ended Yahya's power. Bhutto replaced him in December 1971. Initially as Civilian Martial Law Administrator. He became Prime Minister following the introduction of the 1973 Constitution.

Bhutto's populism encompassed nationalisation, land reform and administrative reform designed to curb the power of the dominant elites. In foreign affairs, he shifted Pakistan into the Islamic and Third World orbit from its more traditional pro-Western stance. His greatest triumphs were the holding of the 1974 Islamic Summit in Lahore and the return of the 93,000 Pakistani prisoners of war following the June 1972 Simla Summit with Indira Gandhi.

By the March 1977 elections however, Bhutto's popularity appeared to be fading as his regime became more authoritarian and deserted its radical roots to form alliances with the Punjab's rural elite. The opposition PNA claimed that the PPP's sweeping victory resulted from widespread rigging. Its civil disobedience campaign was linked with the demand for an Islamic social order. Despite Bhutto's concessions, he was forced to introduce martial law in a number of cities. On 5 July Zia-ul-Haq launched the coup codenamed Operation Fairplay.

Zia cancelled the elections he had promised for October. The Lahore High Court found Bhutto guilty of the charge of conspiracy to murder a political opponent on 18 March 1978 and sentenced him to death, despite the weakness of the prosecution case. The Supreme Court upheld the sentence by a majority of one. Despite an international clamour for clemency, Bhutto was hastily executed on 4 April 1979 at Rawalpindi Central Jail.

Bhutto remains a controversial figure in Pakistani politics. While admirers point to his concern for the downtrodden, his dynamism and his foreign policy achievements, detractors emphasise his arbitrariness and vanity and claim that he was directly responsible for the dismemberment of Pakistan.

BOGRA, MUHAMMAD ALI (1901-1963) Bengali diplomat and Pakistan Prime Minister. He served as a parliamentary secretary and minister before independence, and then in the diplomatic service as Ambassador to Burma (1948), High Commissioner to Canada (1949) and Ambassador to the United States (1952-5). While serving in Washington, he acquired a pro-American reputation, a factor which was instrumental in his elevation to the post of Prime Minister following Khwaja Nazimuddin's dismissal. Bogra carried on as Prime Minister after Ghulam Muhammad's dismissal of the Constituent Assembly, although power lay with Ayub as Defence Minister and Mirza as Minister of the Interior. Bogra was replaced as Prime Minister in October 1955 largely because he opposed Mirza's replacement of Ghulam Muhammad as Governor-General. After another spell as Ambassador in Washington, Bogra served from 1962 until his death in 1963 as Minister of Foreign Affairs under Ayub.

CHISHTI, FAIZ ALI (b.1927) Lieutenant-General and important adviser to Zia-ul-Haq when he was in power. He was born in Jullundur on 13 June 1927 into a well-to-do Arain family, trained at the Officers' Training School, Bangalore, and commissioned in the Royal Indian Artillery in 1947. He saw active service on the Chhamb-Jaurian front during the 1965 war with India. The following year he was posted to the Command

and Staff College Quetta. He later served as Deputy Director of Military Training and Director of Research and Development in General Headquarters. He advised against the military crackdown in East Pakistan which culminated in the emergence of Bangladesh. During the Bhutto era he was Military Secretary at GHQ. He was Corps Commander of the Rawalpindi Division at the time of Zia's coup and executed the military takeover codenamed Operation Fairplay. In 1978 he was appointed Chief of Staff to Zia and served as a member of the Election Cell. He was persuaded with some reluctance to become a federal minister in April 1979, holding the portfolios of Labour, Manpower and Overseas Pakistanis; Petroleum and Natural Resources; Azad Kashmir and Northern Areas. Two months later he led a Labour delegation to the People's Republic of China.

General Chishti retired from service in March 1980, following the rule he had laid down himself of a four-year active tenure for officers of this rank. His relations with the military establishment thereafter became strained. His memoir *Betrayals of Another Kind: Islam, Democracy and the Army in Pakistan* (London, 1989) provides some informed insights into the early years of the Zia regime.

CHUNDRIGAR, ISMAIL IBRAHIM (1897-1960) A lawyer from Ahmadabad who was a close supporter of Jinnah in the Pakistan movement and briefly became Pakistan Prime Minister in 1957. He served in 1937-46 as a mcrnbei of the Bombay Legislative Assembly. In the latter year, he entered the Interim Government as Commerce Minister. After the emergence of Pakistan, he held the post of Ambassador to Afghanistan. In 1950-3 he served as Governor of the Frontier and of Punjab. He became Prime Minister on 18 October 1957, not because of his political standing in the Muslim League but because of his close friendship with President Iskander Mirza. Chundrigar's coalition ministry survived just two months in office and served only to further discredit the failing political process.

FAIZ AHMAD FAIZ (1911-1984) Revered Urdu writer and intellectual, born in Sialkot on 5 March 1911. His poetry ranged from traditional 'love' poetry to 'progressive' works such as 'Speak', His work remains popular in bOI India and Pakistan and has received international recognition. After service in the Indian Army Educational Corps. he took up full-time writing and following Partition became editor of the *Pakistan Times* where he displayed his pro-Soviet sympathies. In 1951 he was arrested for his involvement in the Rawalpindi Conspiracy Case and was not released from prison until 1955. In 1961 he was awarded the Lenin Peace Prize by the Soviet Union. During the Bhutto era he acted as Cultural Adviser. He left Pakistan following Zia's 1977 coup and spent some years in exile in the Soviet Union and Lebanon. He returned to Lahore in 1982.

FAHIM, MAKHDOOM AMIN (b.1939). Makhdoom Amin Fahim comes from the famous Sufi Pir family of Hala in Sindh. He was educated in his home town and at the University of Sindh. His father Makhdoom Talib-ul-Maula was one of the founders of the PPP. During the Zia era, the family were active in the Movement for Restoration of Democracy. Makhdoom Amin Fahim became a Federal Minister in the 1988–1990 and 1993–6 Benazir Bhutto governments. He acted as vice-chairman of the PPP and lead the party in the Assembly during her 8 years of exile from 1999. Following her death, he was widely expected to be the PPP Prime Ministerial candidate, but it became increasingly clear that Asif Ali Zardari was reluctant to give him this role as it would set up a rival powerbase in Sindh to the Bhuttos. By the time that the National assembly was convened on 17 March 2008, the tensions between the two men were barely concealed. Fahim was passed over as choice for Prime Minister, but insisted on his loyalty to the PPP. The possibility remained however of future factional conflict between him and the Zardari loyalists.

GILANI, SYED YUSUF REZA (b.1952). Syed Yusuf Reza Gilani became Pakistan's twenty fifth Prime Minister on 25 March 2008 following his nomination by the PPP. He was widely regarded as a party loyalist who would work closely with Asif Ali Zardari. He comes from a well known Pir family of Multan which had been active in electoral politics since the 1920s. His great grandfather, Makhdoom Raja Bakhsh Gilani served as a member of the Central Legislative Assembly from 1921–36.

Syed Yusuf Reza Gilani was educated at St. Mary's School and La Salle High School Multan and at the Punjab University where he received BA and MA degrees in Journalism. He commenced his political career in 1978 serving as Chairman of the Multan District Council. He was elected to the National Assembly in the 1985 non-party elections and was appointed the Minister for Housing and Works (April 1985–January 1986) and for Railways (January-December 1986) in the Mohammad Khan Junejo Government. In the 1988 elections he was returned on the PPP ticket. In the first Benazir Bhutto Government he served successively as Minister for Tourism and Minister for Housing and Works. He was also successful in the 1990 and 1993 polls and in the second Benazir Bhutto Government was elected as Speaker of the National Assembly. He held this position from 17 October 1993–16 February 1997. Defeat in the 1997 polls led to a downturn in fortune, although he was made senior vice-chairman of the PPP the following year. The National Accountability Bureau charged him with the misuse of authority as Speaker with respect to job allocations in the National Assembly Secretariat. He spent six years in jail from 2001–7. Many people saw his conviction as politically motivated. In the February 2008 polls he defeated the PML-Q leader Sikander Hayat Bosan. He was nominated as the PPP Prime Ministerial candidate ahead of Makhdoom Amin Fahim and easily defeated the opposition candidate Chaudhury Pervaiz Elahi by 264–42 votes. The hard bargaining between the PPP and PML-N meant that a Cabinet had still not been formed when he was sworn in as Prime Minister. For some commentators, he was merely a stop gap before Asif Ali Zardari assumed the post. Nevertheless, Gilani announced an ambitious 100 day programme which combined austerity measures with those designed to combat militancy and to improve the position of low income groups. The declining economic situation and the growing security problems in FATA, and Swat, together with the ongoing insurgency in Balochistan took much of the gloss off his government. Moreover, it was increasingly clear that the issues surrounding the President's future, the Judges' restoration and the resultant relations between the PPP and PML-N were being determined by the PPP Co-Chairman Asif Ali Zardari, not the PPP Prime Minister. The personal risks facing Gilani were brought home when shots were fired at his motorcade which was going to Islamabad airport to pick him up on 3 September.

HAQ, MAULVI ABUL KASEM FAZLUL (1873-1962) Lawyer and leading political figure known as the 'Tiger of Bengal', born in the Barisal district and educated in Calcutta. Haq was active in legislative and Muslim League politics from 1913 and served as AIML President from 1916-21. He represented the interests of a vernacular tenant and *mofussil* professional elite which creasingly clashed with those of the Urdu-speaking Muslim business and the downing elite. Haq institutionalised the interests of this new social format in the Krishak Praja Party (KPP) which he founded in April 1936. He came to office as Prime Minister in a coalition government with the Muslim League until December 1941. Following his public split with Jinnah, he formed a ministry initially allied with the Hindu Mahasabha which held office until May 1943. In the 1946 provincial elections, the Muslim League swept the Kris Praja Party aside.

After independence Haq resumed his legal career as Advocate-General of East Bengal. In 1954 he returned to active politics as head of the newly-formed Krishak Sramik Party (KSP), which triumphed along with its Awami League ally in the provincial elections. Haq became the Chief Minister of the United Front government. He lasted less than two months in office in the wake of the Adamjee Jute Mills riots and his 'indiscreet' remarks during a speech in Calcutta. After the lifting of Governor's Rule in June 1955 the KSP returned to form a coalition government. Haq was shortly afterwards made Governor of East Pakistan and attempted to bolster it against its erstwhile ally, hut now major rival, the Awarni Lengue. His efforts to replace Ataur Rahman's Awami League ministry in March 1958 with the KSP was opposed at the centre by both Firoz Khan Noon and Suhrawardy and culminated in his dismissal. Haq retired to relative obscurity and was senile at the time of his death in Dhaka Medical College on 27 April 1962. There ensued an unseemly squabble between Ayub's government and the opposition politicians over who should organise a condolence meeting. Some 2,000 people attended the government-sponsored meeting on 4 May, in stark contrast to the 50,000 who flocked to the Dhaka stadium for the unofficial one.

HAQ, ZIA-UL- (1922-1988) Chief of Army Staff 1976-88; Chief Martini Law Administrator 1977-8; President of Pakistan 1978-88. Zia came from a lowermiddle-class family in Jullundur and was educated at St Stephen's College in Delhi before joining the British Indian Army in 1944. He was commissioned into the cavalry and saw service in Burma, Malaya and Java. After his promotion to brigadier in 1 969, Zia was seconded to Jordan where he helped King Hussein's forces in their operations against the PLO. On his return home, he commanded the first Armoured Division for three years. He was still relatively unknown however when he became head of the Pakistan Army in the spring of 1976. He launched the coup code-named 'Operation Fairplay' against Bhutto on 5 July 1977. It ushered in Pakistan's longest period of military rule, and even when it was withdrawn on 30 December 1985. Zia retained his post as Chief of Army Staff and continued to wield power through the office of President. Indeed on 29 May 1988 he dismissed his hand-picked Prime Minister Mohammad Khan Junejo.

Zia's political survival rested on his skill in wrongfooting Opponents, and on the favourable external environment following the December 1979 Soviet occupation of Afghanistan. This transformed him overnight from an international pariah 10 America's front-line ally in the tight against communism. The Reagan administration provided $3.2 billion of military and economic assistance, despite concerns over human rights abuses and the nuclear programme.

The martial law era was punctuated by unfulfilled promises of national elections and by discussion of the relevance of democracy for an Islamic state. Zia maintained that a Western-style democracy was unsuitable for Pakistan. He eventually agreed to hold 'partyless' ejections in February 1985, following a referendum on his Islamic policies which was linked with his re-election as President. The eleven-party MRD alliance, which had mounted a major campaign in Sindh in 1983 against the Zia regime, boycotted both the polls.

Zia introduced special Shariat courts, with Islamic rules of evidence and punishments for certain crimes. Further measures included the provision of Islamic banking facilities and the government collection of *zakat* (alms) and *ushr* (agricultural tax). Islamisation, which was stoutly opposed by women's groups and human right's activists, stirred up sectarian tensions between Sunnis and Shias.

Karachi experienced mounting ethnic violence from 1986 onwards. Clashes between *mohajirs* and Pushtuns later extended to the Sindhi community. The growing lawlessness was encouraged by the ready availability of weapons and drugs as a result of the Afghan war. Zia justified his dismissal of Junejo in terms of the deteriorating security situation. Partyless elections were scheduled for November 1988, but Zia was killed on 17 August in the unexplained crash of his Col 30 aircraft.

Zia's supporters view him as a pious Muslim who halted his country's moral decay and contributed to the collapse of the Soviet empire. Detractors condemn him as an intolerant and vindictive ruler who cynically manipulated Islam to remain in power.

HUSSAIN, ALTAF (b.1953) Founding member of the APMSO and charismatic leader of the MQM from 1984 onwards, Altaf Hussain was born into a lowermiddle-class *mohajir* family in Karachi on 17 September 1953. He became politically active during his postgraduate studies in the Pharmacy Department at Karachi University, and was a founding member of the APMSO which wrested control of the campus from the 11T. The violence between student groups turned the hostels into armed camps and Altaf underwent several spells of imprisonment. Nevertheless some critics maintain that the security agencies of the Zia regime patronised APMSO in order to weaken its democratic opposition.

After a spell in the United States in which he worked as a taxi-driver in Chicago, Altaf returned to Karachi and launched the MQM, which drew its support from former cadres of the APMSO. The party rose to prominence against a background of ethnic tension between *mohajirs* and Pushtuns arising from rapid social change and the easy availability of drugs and guns because of the Afghan conflict.

Altaf manipulated a sense of disadvantage arising from preferential quotas to construct an aggrieved *mohajir* identity. He also cultivated his own personality cult. The MQM also thrived because of the collapse of state authority in the wake of ethnic riots. Its power was demonstrated in both the 1988 and 1990 national and provincial elections. After the collapse of the Karachi Accord with the PPP, Altaf threw all his influence behind the campaign to unseat Benazir Bhutto.

The heyday of the MQM was reached in the earlier period of Jam Sadiq Ali's ministry, when Altaf Hussain regularly received national and provincial leaders at his modest residence, 90 Azizabad. Splits within his party, based partly on ideological differences but also engineered by the security services, led him to retreat to London for medical treatment. From his North London residence he communicated by satellite, fax, telephone and e-mail with his supporters. The army crackdown which began on 27 May 1992 drove many of the MQM leaders loyal to Altaf underground, although their MQM(H) rivals lacked genuine support.

The continued influence of the MQM's distant *Quaid* was revealed in the 1993 provincial elections in which the MQM(A) took twenty-seven seats. The withdrawal of the army in November 1994 sparked fierce gunbattles between the rival MQM factions which paralysed Karachi. Throughout 1995 the MQM waged a virtual civil war against the PPP-controlled police and rangers.

To his loyalists he is venerated as the *Quaid* of their organisation. Opponents point to his fascist tendencies and his links with both domestic and Indian security agencies. Traitor or symbol of lower-middle-class *mohajir* aspirations, Altaf Hussain continues to be a potentially important power-broker in Pakistani politics.

IFTIKHARUDDIN, MIAN MUHAMMAD (1907-1962) Born to the leading Arain Mian family of Baghbanpura, Lahore, he was educated at Oxford and entered politics as a figure on the left wing of the Congress; even before this time, he had been involved in the Progressive Writers' Movement. He served as President of the Punjab branch of the Congress before joining the Muslim League in 1945. He played a leading role in the 1947 direct action movement against the Unionist Government. He founded Progressive Papers which, after independence, published the *Pakistan Times* and *Imroz*. Progressive Papers was taken over by Ayub Khan in 1959. Immediately after independence, he served as Minister of Refugees and Rehabilitation in the Punjab Government, but increasingly clashed both with the Prime Minister, the Nawab of Mamdot, and the Federal Minister for Refugees, Raja Ghazanfar Ali. He saw refugee rehabilitation as an opportunity to introduce land reform in the Punjab, but when this idea was rejected, he resigned from the Mamdot cabinet. In 1951 he was expelled from the PML and formed the Azad Pakistan Party. Five years later he played a leading role in the consolidation of anti-government parties in West Pakistan in the PNP. He worked with Maulana Bashani to forge an organisation which possessed a political presence in both wings–endeavours that bore fruit in 1957, when the Bhashani wing of the Awami league joined with the PNP to form the NAP.

Iftikharuddin's historic contribution to Pakistani politics can be explored through his *Selected Speeches and Statements* edited by Abdullah Malik (Lahore, 1971)

ISHAQ KHAN, GHULAM (1915-2006) Pashtun civil servant and President of Pakistan. After Punjab University, he entered the North West Frontier Province civil service and held various posts before independence. Following the creation of Pakistan he became Home Secretary. In 1956 he moved to the centre as Secretary for Development & Irrigation in the West Pakistan Government. In 1961 he became Chairman of W APDA, and in 1966 moved to the post of Financial Secretary, later becoming Cabinet Secretary (1970-1). He was Secretary of General Defence at the time of Zia's coup, and was given the status of a Federal Minister in Zia's cabinet in 1977-8. From 1978-85 he played a leading role in the development of the regime's economic policy.

Following his election to the Senate in the 1985 'partials' elections, Ghulam Ishaq Khan adopted a more visible political role as its Chairman. Zia's unexpected demise elevated him to the role of acting President in which he oversaw the democratic transition. From the 1988 polls onwards, he formed a leading part of the troika of President, Prime Minister and Chief of Army Staff. He dismissed the first Bhutto government on charges of corruption and inability to maintain law and order in Sindh. His relations with the new Prime Minister Nawaz Sharif were at first cordial, but later deteriorated over a range of issues. His dismissal of Sharif in 1993 precipitated a constitutional crisis when the Supreme Court upheld the Prime Minister's appeal. The stand-off was finally resolved through an army-brokered deal which saw the simultaneous resignation on 17 July of Ishaq and the Prime Minister.

JINNAH, FATIMA (1894-1967) Younger sister of Muhammad Ali Jinnah. After an early marriage and divorce, she devoted her life to acting as her brother's companion. She was regarded with immense respect and courted by both the Convention and Council Muslim League after Ayub's lifting of martial law. She attracted immense crowds when standing against him as a Presidential candidate in 1965. Ayub's control of the machinery of government in a restricted electorate ensured his victory, but her campaign severely undermined his moral authority.

JINNAH, MUHAMMAD ALI (1876-1948) Leader of the All-India Muslim League; founding father of Pakistan; President, Pakistan Constituent Assembly 1947-8; and Governor-General Pakistan 1947-8. The eldest son of a hide merchant, Jinnah was educated at the Sindh Madrassa; he qualified as a barrister at Lincoln's Inn, London. The future founder of Pakistan was first known as the ambassador of Hindu-Muslim unity. Indeed Jinnah only resigned from Congress in 1920 when he became disillusioned with the violence and communal passions unleashed by Gandhi's Congress-Khilafat civil disobedience campaigns. The division widened in 1928 when the Nehru Report rejected Jinnah' s 'Fourteen Points' constitutional proposals.

In 1921-35 Jinnah's political career was in the doldrums. He returned to India in October 1935 after a five-year exile in Britain to reorganise the Muslim League. It nevertheless lost heavily in the 1937 provincial elections. The Congress ministries' insensitivity to Muslim demands rescued it from oblivion, although Jinnah's leadership was equally crucial to its dramatic transformation. From 1940 onwards he propounded the two-nation theory as justification for Pakistan, and increasingly embodied the aspirations of the Indian Muslim community which acclaimed him as the *Quaid-i-Azam*, the great leader. Within the fractious politics of the Muslim League, he exerted an unquestioned moral authority which underpinned his formal power as President. Simultaneously he deployed his forensic skills in the complex constitutional negotiations with the British and the Congress.

Jinnah's successful claim to be the sole spokesman of Muslim India at the July 1945 Simla Conference greatly strengthened the Pakistan demand. During 1946-7, however, he suffered a series of reversals as the Muslim League lost its wartime bargaining power. He had to abandon his strictly constitutional approach to politics, but the resulting communal riots threatened civil war. Agreement for partition was finally reached on 3 June 1947, but the Pakistan which emerged did not consist of the full six Muslim provinces of Jinnah's dreams, but was a moth-eaten country shorn of West Bengal and East Punjab. Mass migrations and massacres accompanied Punjab's partition. The refugee crisis increased Pakistan's formidable security and administrative problems.

Jinnah, as both Governor-General and the Constituent Assembly President, assumed much of the burden for laying the state's foundations. He was by now seventy and appeared frailer and more emaciated than ever. It remains doubtful whether, had he lived beyond September 1948, Pakistan could have avoided its growing crisis of governability.

Jinnah is still revered as Pakistan's founding father. Islamists improbably and secularists more soundly have attempted to claim his mantle. Recent revisionist scholarship has speculated that Partition was the unintended consequence of his trumpeting the Pakistan demand as a bargaining counter for power in a united India.

JUNEJO, MUHAMMAD KHAN (1932-1993) Sindhi landlord and politician who became Prime Minister of Pakistan following Zia's lifting of martial law in December 1985. He had been active in politics since the 1960s and held minor office. He was hand-picked by Zia partly because he had the support of Pir Pagaro and was of his Sindhi background.

Despite his mild-mannered altitude, Junejo sought to carve out an independent sphere of activity. He attempted to organise the PML which he headed into a popularly-based party. He also launched a major programme of development and national renewal. His attempts to display independence increasingly irked Zia who was not temperamentally disposed to share power. Relations between the two men nose-dived when Junejo pressed forward with an investigation into the Ojhra camp explosion which threatened to embarrass the ISI.

When the President unexpectedly removed Junejo from office in May 1988, he cited the ethnic violence in Karachi and the Prime Minister's inability to bring forward a Shariat bill. In reality, Junejo's independent line on the Afghan settlement had been the major factor in Zia's hostility. The Prime Minister secured Pakistan's signature of the Geneva accords, but at the cost of his office. He was a latecomer to the Islamic Democratic Alliance which fought the 1988 elections and coexisted even more uneasily with Nawaz Sharif. Eventually, following his death, the PML was to split into Junejo and Nawaz Sharif factions.

KHALID, MALIK MERAJ (1916-2003) Caretaker Prime Minister following the dismissal of Benazir Bhutto on 5 November 1996, Meraj Khalid was largely unknown outside Pakistan, although he had been active in politics since the Ayub era when he joined the Convention Muslim League. He was one of Zulfiqar Ali Bhutto's earliest PPP supporters. After his election to the National Assembly in 1970 he became federal Minister for Agriculture. He briefly held office as Chief Minister of the Punjab amid the infighting between Ghulam Mustafa Khar and his opponents. He retained his National Assembly seat in 1977, although the opposition PNA claimed there had been rigging on a massive scale. Meraj Khalid was speaker of the National Assembly at the time of Zia's coup. Following Zia's death, he was elected for the PPP in the 1988 polls and resumed his role as Speaker, defeating the IJI candidate for the post, Sheikh Rashed Ahmad, by 134 to 72 votes. He increasingly clashed with Benazir Bhutto over his conciliatory attitude to the opposition. He lost his seat in the 1990 polls and did not receive a PPP ticket in 1993. When he accepted the post of Rector of the Islamic University in Islamabad, it seemed that his political career had ended. His period as caretaker Prime Minister was marked by the introduction of adult franchise in the FATA areas and by the formation of the CDNS.

KHALIQUZZAMAN, CHAUDHURI (1889-1973) A UP politician who quit the Congress to join the Muslim League after the failure to establish a coalition ministry in 1937, Khaliquzzaman was President of the PML from April 1949 until August 1950 when Liaquat Ali Khan assumed this office. In March 1953 he replaced Firoz Khan Noon as Governor of East Bengal. In the wake of the disturbances which followed the election of the United Front government he was dismissed by the Governor-General Ghulam Muhammad, but resumed his career as a leading organiser of the Convention Muslim League in 1962. His memoir *Pathway to Pakistan* (Karachi 1961) has enjoyed a wide readership.

KHAN, ABDUL GHAFFAR (1890-1988) Push tun nationalist and disciple of Gandhian non-violence who came from the village of Utmanzai in the Peshawar district of the NWFP. He was educated at the Municipal Board High School in Peshawar and the Edwardes Memorial Mission School, but quit before completing his studies in order to obtain an army commission. He reportedly abandoned this career because he had witnessed a British subaltern insulting an Indian officer. He then restlessly spent a brief spell in a school at Campbell pur and attended Aligarh College.

Despite his own chequered education, Abdul Ghaffar Khan worked from 1910 onwards to popularise schooling among the unlettered Pakhtun tribesmen of the Frontier. He clashed with the British in April 1919, when he organised a public meeting at Utmanzai to protest against the Rowlatt Act. He was arrested for the first time, but was released shortly afterwards. He thus embarked on a life of prolonged spells of imprisonment by both the British and Pakistani authorities. He resumed his educational

activities in 1921, opening an Azad High School at Utmanzai and forming the *Anjuman lslah-ul-Afghania* (Society for the Reform of the
Afghans) to carry on his work. By this date he had also been elected
President of the Provincial Khilafat Committee. His 'anti-British' activities culminated in arrest on 17 December 1921. On his release his followers honoured him with the title *Fakhr-i-Afghan* (Pride of the Afghans)
along with that of 'the Frontier Gandhi'.

In May 1928 Abdul Ghaffar Khan launched the monthly Pashto journal, the *Pakhtun*, which thereafter served as his mouthpiece. Through its
columns he expounded his philosophy of Pushtun nationalism, moral and
social reform, non-violence and Islam. The following year he embodied
these ideals in a new grassroots party called the Afghan Jirga. Three
months later in November 1929, he launched a parallel organisation, the
Khudai khidmatgars (servants of God) which was established on quasi-
military lines. This movement soon overshadowed the Afghan Jirga. Its
members wore uniforms dyed with red brick dust since their ordinary
white clothing showed the dirt too easily. The British thereafter dubbed
them the 'Red Shirts.'

The organisation's involvement in the civil disobedience struggles of
1930-2 strengthened the Congress's national claim to be a secular cross-
communal organisation. For his part, Abdul Ghaffar Khan allied with
Indian nationalists in the freedom struggle and quest for Hindu-Muslim
unity, but his first priority remained specifically Pushtun interests.

During the period from April 1930 onwards both Abdul Ghaffar Khan
and his brother Dr Khan Sahib served jail sentences. They were finally
released in August 1934, but externed from the Frontier and neighbouring
Punjab. Undaunted they travelled as far afield as Patna, Allahabad and
Calcutta to address meetings. They also stayed as guests at Gandhi's
Wardha ashram, where Abdul Ghaffar Khan was rearrested on 7 December 1934 after exactly 100 days' freedom. He served a two-year sentence
in Bombay and UP jails before being released in August 1936. Another
year passed before he could return to the Frontier. His homecoming
resulted from the formation of a Congress led Coalition Ministry headed
by his brother Dr Khan Sahib following the 1937 provincial elections.
Ghaffar Khan used his unaccustomed freedom to reorganise the *Khudai
Khidmatgars*.

Dr Khan Sahib's ministry resigned following the outbreak of the Second World War, although the civil disobedience movement in the Frontier
was very muted in comparison with other regions. Disturbances were
limited to the Mardan district. When he attempted to make his way there
in defiance of a government ban, Abdul Ghaffar Khan was arrested once
more on 27 October 1942, and spent the remainder of the war years in
prisons at Haripur, Abbotabad and Risalpur.

Ghaffar Khan attended the 1946 Simla Conference as a Congress delegate, Although the Congress retained power in the Frontier after the
1946 provincial elections, the Muslim League's advance in Punjab

strengthened its Pakistan demand. The Congress High Command reluctantly accepted the idea of partition as the price of independence. In Abdul Ghaffar Khan's eyes, however, this was an act of betrayal which threw the *Khudai Khidmatgars* 'to the wolves'. He exhorted his followers to boycott the June 1947 referendum on the Frontier's future, as it did not include an option for Pushtunistan along with those for India and Pakistan. The referendum result was a crushing blow for the Khan brothers. Over 99 per cent of the total number of votes were cast for Pakistan, although the turn-out at 51 per cent was admittedly low.

Within a week of Pakistan's creation, the Frontier Congress Ministry of Dr Khan Sahib had been dismissed. Abdul Ghaffar Khan took the oath of allegiance to Pakistan as a member of the Constituent Assembly. The *Khudai Khidmatgars* had earlier severed their connections with the Indian Congress and replaced the tricolour with the red flag as their party symbol. But the authorities were inevitably suspicious of his continued championing of Pakhtunistan at a time of tension with neighbouring India and Afghanistan. In May 1948, he attempted to spread the *Khudai Khidmatgars* movement throughout Pakistan. Within a month he was arrested with his son Wali near Bahadur Khel in Kohat on the charge of planning and fomenting open sedition against the state. The *Khudai Khidmatgars* were banned shortly afterwards.

Abdul Ghaffar Khan was first released in January 1954, but was again externed from the Frontier. The following year he headed the campaign against the merging of the provinces of West Pakistan into one unit. This caused conflict with the authorities. It also led to a breach with his elder brother Dr Khan Sahib, who in October 1955 become the Chief Minister of the newly-integrated West Pakistan. After a brief spell in prison, Abdul Ghaffar Khan joined Baloch and Sindhi nationalists and leftward leaning Punjabi and Bengali politicians to form the NAP in 1957. It called for the dissolution of the One Unit Scheme and demanded federal reorganisation which would give greater regional autonomy. Abdul Ghaffar Khan was arrested in October 1958 along with other opposition leaders. He was released the following April on account of his 'age and indifferent health'. But he was disqualified from being a member of any elected body and placed under restrictive orders. He defied these to tour the Frontier and was subsequently rearrested in Dera Ismail Khan on 12 April 1961. His health deteriorated alarmingly as he languished in the familiar surroundings of Haripur prison. Shortly after his release in January 1964, he journeyed to England for medical treatment.

Abdul Ghaffar Khan embarked on a lengthy self-imposed exile in Afghanistan in December 1964. He briefly visited India in November 1969 to receive the Nehru Peace Award. The formation of a NPP government in the Frontier in 1972 enabled him to return to Pakistan. A caravan of 6,000 lorries escorted him from the Afghan border. Within two months, however, the Bhutto regime had dismissed the Frontier Government and arrested Wali Khan and the other top NAP leaders for anti-state activities.

Abdul Ghaffar Khan was later arrested to prevent him returning to Afghanistan.

After the fall of Bhutto, General Zia-ul-Haq reversed the policy of repression.

After some hesitation, Abdul Ghaffar Khan was permitted to return to Afghanistan and he shuttled between it and Pakistan for the next two years. He again ran foul of the Pakistan authorities because he urged the refugees from the Soviet invasion to return home and denied that the Afghan conflict was a *jihad*. In December 1985 he attended the Congress centenary celebrations in India, but was now increasingly frail. On 15 May 1987 he was admitted to hospital in Bombay, but was discharged a month later and travelled to Delhi, where he suffered a stroke on 4 July 1987. From then until his death, he never fully recovered consciousness. After a bout of pneumonia, he died in Peshawar on the morning of 20 January 1988. The Governments of India, Pakistan and Afghanistan each declared a period of official mourning. An intensely religious man who lived an austere life, he nevertheless acted as the secular conscience of the Indian subcontinent.

KHAN, ABDUL QAIYUM KHAN (1901-1981) Frontier Congressman, later Muslim League leader who was born in Chitral of Kashrniri origin. After his education at Aligarh and at the London School of Economics he returned to Peshawar to practice law. He was elected unopposed as a member of the Central Legislative Assembly in 1934 and was a Deputy Leader of the Congress Assembly Party. He was for many years an admirer of the Khan brothers, although he later became their inveterate opponent. In 1945 he resigned from the Congress to join the Muslim League. The following year he was elected for the Peshawar City (Dual Constituency). As leader of the Frontier Muslim League, he orchestrated the civil disobedience movement against Dr Khan Sahib's ministry. He became Chief Minister after its dismissal by Jinnah and from 1947-53 was the strong man of Frontier politics. He joined the Bogra ministry at the centre in 1953, but was much Jess powerful in national than regional politics, although he became President of the PML in 1957. After Ayub's coup, he fell victim to the Elective Bodies Disqualification Order. With the lifting of martial law and the ban he joined the Council Muslim League. Factional rivalry with Mian Mumtaz Daultana led him to found the Qaiyurn Muslim League. He was elected to the National Assembly in 1970 and became Home Minister in the PPP Government in 1972. His defeat in the 1977 elections ended his political career.

KHAN, A.Q. (Dr) (b.1936): 'A.Q.' is considered to be the father of Pakistan's nuclear weapons programme. He was born in Bhopal and migrated to Pakistan at the age of sixteen. After graduating from Karachi University, he studied metallurgical engineering at a number of prestigious European universities. He worked for four years at the Physical Dynamics Research Laboratory in Holland before returning to Pakistan in 1975 where he offered his services to Zulfiqar Ali Bhutto's nuclear programme and allegedly supplied West German, Dutch and British UREN-CO blueprints and suppliers' lists. Until this time, Pakistan efforts had been directed towards the reprocessing route for nuclear weapons acquisition. Dr Khan provided an alternative that would be less vulnerable to international pressure through the enrichment of uranium at centrifuge plants at Sihala and Kahuta. During the 1980s components for the enrichment process were clandestinely acquired from high-technology Western firms. For professional and patriotic reasons Dr Khan was instrumental in Pakistan's *de facto* acquisition of a nuclear weapons capability.

KHAN, IMRAN (b.1952) Cricket captain and celebrity who entered Pakistan politics in 1996. Member of a famous cricket-playing family settled in Lahore, Imran was educated at the prestigious Aitchison College there and in Keble College, Oxford. He entered professional cricket as an all-rounder and was Pakistan's first genuine fast bowler. His dashing looks and style of play ensured him huge popularity both in England and Pakistan in an age when cricket was becoming an entertainment industry. Pakistan enjoyed its greatest-ever international success during his period as captain from 1982 onwards. The crowning point was the 1992 World Cup victory.

In the early 1990s, Imran Khan attempted to reinvent himself as a 'born-again' Muslim and critic of the 'brown sahib' culture which had nurtured him. As at the time of the 1997 election campaign, however, it was not always easy to live down his playboy past. His marriage to Jemima, heiress to the Goldsmith fortune, also raised accusations of Jewish funding for his activities.

Imran entered the political gaze as both a social worker raising funds for the Shaukat Khanum Memorial Cancer Hospital and as a critic of Pakistan's rampant corruption and mismanagement of finances. He appeared to be patronised by forces on the 'right' of Pakistan politics who were looking for a 'third option'. His relations with Pakistan's other great Western media celebrity, Benazir Bhutto, became increasingly cool. Indeed by the time of the February 1996 opening ceremony of the Sixth World Cup, jointly hosted by India and Pakistan, Imran was *persona non grata*.

After months of speculation, Imran finally founded his Tehrek-e-Insaff (Truth Movement) party on 25 August 1996. Immediately before this the outpatient wing of SKMH had been wrecked by an unexplained bomb blast. The February 1997 elections came too early for the fledgling party to establish itself. Imran also found himself beset with the Sita White scandal and the claim that Jewish money was funding his campaign. His party's failure to capture a single National Assembly and Provincial

Assembly seat was nevertheless unexpected. Imran maintained that here had been electoral rigging and determined to carry on his political carrier.

In 2007 Imran Khan increasingly opposed both the pro-western foreign policy of the Musharraf regime and its authoritarianism. He was a strong proponent of the lawyers' movement. He also was steadfast in the demand that Musharraf should step down and that to contest elections while he remained President would accord him legitimacy. Imran Khan's party Tehrek-e-Insaf was a founding member of the All-Parties Democratic Movement. He was briefly detained during the crackdown which accompanied the November 2007 Emergency. Along with Jamaat-i-Islami, his party boycotted the 2008 parliamentary elections, even although the main component of the APDM, the PML-N decided to contest them. After the polls, Imran Khan continued to cast himself as the political conscience of Pakistan warning that the issue of the restoration of the judges who had refused to take oath under the Provisional Constitutional Order should not be abandoned in a compromise with the President.

KHAN, NAWABZADA LIAQAT ALI (1895-1951) UP landowner, lawyer, Muslim League leader and first Prime Minister of Pakistan. During the Muslim League movement he served as General Secretary of the party and was acknowledged as Jinnah's right-hand man. He was Finance Member of the Interim Government in 1946. After partition, he took the post of both Prime Minister and Minister of Defence. However, Jinnah in the role of Governor-General remained the leading figure. Liaquat adopted a more dominant position following Jinnah's death. He encouraged the processes of centralisation, and publicly equated opposition to the Muslim League with hostility to Pakistan. The introduction of PRODA in 1949 contributed to the discrediting of politicians in the public mind. While Liaquat was Prime Minister, the Objectives Resolution was passed to provide an Islamic basis for future constitutions. He appeared to be on the verge of both reactivating the Muslim League and moving Pakistani foreign policy into a more Islamic ambit at the time of his assassination in October 1951. Liaquat is still revered as the *Quaid-i-Millat*. The MQM during the 1980s encouraged his veneration as a specifically *mohajir* figure.

The Nawabzada married Irene Pant in 1933, who after her conversion to Islam was known as Begum Raana'a Liaquat Ali Khan. She was the founder President of APW A, and held a number of public appointments including those of Ambassador to Holland and Italy. She served briefly under Zulfiqar Ali Bhutto as Governor of Sindh.

KHAN, MUHAMMAD AYUB (1907-1974) Chief Martial Law Administrator 1958; President 1958-69. Ayub came from a middle-income Pushtun family from the Hazara district of the North West Frontier. He was educated at Aligarh College and at Sandhurst, where he was commissioned in 1928. He served in Burma during the Second World War and in the Punjab Boundary Force at the time of partition. After his promotion to major-general he commanded the forces in East Pakistan, and in 1951 became the first Pakistani Commanderin-Chief. From October 1954 to August 1955 he was also Minister of Defence.

In the coup of 8 October 1958 he became Chief Martial Law Administrator, and shortly afterwards deposed Iskander Mirza and became President. Ayub sought to modernise Pakistan by introducing land reform and social reforms such as the celebrated Muslim Family Laws Ordinance of 15 July 1961, and by stressing economic development. In foreign affairs he maintained a pro-Western stance. Political parties were banned until July, 1962, and then Ayub favoured the system of guided democracy known as Basic Democracy. The 1962 Constitution created a powerful President who was to be elected by the 80,000 Basic Democrats.

From 1965 Ayub's fortunes declined as his growth-oriented strategy of channelling resources to an entrepreneurial elite generated increasing social and regional tensions. The 1965 Indo-Pakistan war following the failure of Operation Gibraltar's infiltration of armed volunteers into Kashmir was another major setback. Ayub was never comfortable with his new political role from December 1963 onwards as head of the Convention Muslim League. He had lost the campaign, although he won the tightly-controlled 1965 presidential election contest with Fatima Jinnah. Ayub had also created an Achilles Heel when he stood down as Commander-in-Chief of the army. The popular disturbances from November 1968 onwards Jost hi m the support of his former army colleagues. By March 1969 he had no choice but to step down in favour of General Yahya Khan.

Ayub is remembered as a hard-headed administrator whose modernising impulses foundered because his regime never acquired political legitimacy. He wrote a well-received autobiography *Friends Not Masters* (1969).

KHAN, WALI (1917-2006) The son of Abdul Ghaffar Khan and like him a leading Pushtun nationalist, he was President of the NAP, the main regional party in Balochistan and the Frontier, in the 1970s. He was arrested and faced a treason charge in 1975 in the wake of the bomb explosion which killed the PPP Frontier leader Hayat Muhammad Khan Sherpao. Wali Khan later founded the ANP and was ejected to the National Assembly in 1988.

KHAN, AGHA MUHAMMAD YAHYA (1917-1980) Pakistan Army Commander-in-Chief and President. He was born in Chakwal in the Jhelum district, the son of a police superintendent, commissioned in 1938 after his education at Punjab University and the Indian Military Academy, Dehra Dun. He fought in the British Eighth Army during the Second

World War. He rose through the Pakistan Army ranks after independence to become Chief of the General Staff in 1957. In 1966 he was promoted Commander-in-Chief. When Ayub resigned on 25 March 1969, Yahya replaced him as President. His period in office, which lasted until December 1971, was marked by a number of dramatic developments which changed the face of the nation. Yahya dissolved the One Unit Scheme and, after the introduction of the Legal Framework Order, oversaw Pakistan's first national elections under direct adult suffrage. He anticipated an inconclusive outcome in which he would play the role of broker. In the event, the parties Supported by the regime performed poorly and the PPP emerged as the dominant power in West Pakistan and the Awami League as pre-eminent in the eastern Wing. After negotiations appeared deadlocked, Yahya ill-advisedly authorised a military crackdown in East Pakistan on 25 March 1971, which set in train the events which culminated in the secession of East Pakistan and the Pakistan Army's humiliation at the hands of India. Its unconditional surrender on 16 December 1971 led to calls in West Pakistan that Yahya be tried as a traitor. He resigned from office and was sentenced to five years' house arrest.

KHAN SAHIB, Dr (1882-1958) Pushtun nationalist and West Pakistan Chief Minister, he was the elder brother of Abdul Ghaffar Khan with whom he worked closely in politics before independence. He was educated in England in medicine and joined the Hospital Corps during the First World War, serving in France. On his return to India he joined the Indian Medical Service before starting a practice in Peshawar. He was imprisoned during the 1930 Civil Disobedience movement and only released in 1934. Elected for the Hashtnagar South Constituency in 1937, he became Prime Minister after the short-lived United Muslim Nationalists ministry, and held office until November 1939, during which time a number of reforms were introduced designed to curb the power of the big Khans.

   Dr Khan Sahib returned to office at the end of the war and defeated the Muslim League in the 1946 elections. He remained as Prime Minister of a Congress-run province until after independence. He was imprisoned after his dismissal in August 1947, but re-entered politics in 1954 as Minister of Communications. He became Chief Minister of West Pakistan in 1955 and was a stalwart supporter of the One Unit Scheme, despite the break this involved with his brother and his Pushtun nationalist past. He was stabbed to death in Lahore on 9 May 1958 shortly after his fall from power.

KHATTAK, AJMAL (b. 1924) Pushtun political leader and writer, and a strong proponent of provincial autonomy. He rose to prominence as Secretary-General of Khan Abdul Wali Khan's NAP. After Zulfiqar Ali Bhutto declared it illegal he began a self-imposed exile in Afghanistan and was supportive of the Kabul regime. He returned to Pakistan during Benazir Bhutto's first administration.

KHUHRO, MUHAMMAD AYUB (1901-1980) Landowner from the Larkana district of Sindh. As a member of the Bombay Legislative Council in the mid 1920s, he played an active role in the campaign for Sindh's separation. From 1937 onwards he was active in the Sindh Muslim League, becoming its President in 1943: he had been appointed a Minister in 1940. He was deeply immersed in the intrigues of Sindh politics in the 1940s and was a leading opponent of the Syed faction. He was Prime Minister in 1947-8 and played the Sindhi card in dealings with the centre, particularly over the rehabilitation of refugees. The term 'Khuhroism' was coined for the factional patronage-based politics over which he presided. On three separate occasions during 1947-54, he was dismissed from office, but returned following the lifting of PRODA disqualification. He served as Federal Minister of Defence in the Cabinet of Firoz Khan Noon in 1958. After the imposition of martial law, he was banned under EBDO. He returned to politics and unsuccessfully contested the 1970 National Assembly election. His daughter Hamida held senior rank in G. M. Syed's Sindh National Alliance in the early 1990s.

LEGHARI, FAROOQ (b.1940) Landowner from the Balochi Leghari tribe of Dera Ghazi Khan. Educated at Oxford, he entered the political limelight as a PPP loyalist. He led the PPP parliamentary party in Punjab and served as Federal Minister for Water and Power in Benazir Bhutto's 1988-90 ministry. After her dismissal he acted as deputy opposition leader before briefly serving as a Minister in October 1993 following the dismissal of Nawaz Sharif. He became President in November, defeating the PML(N) candidate, former President Waseern Sajjad, by a majority of 106 votes. Leghari seemed at first to play second fiddle to Benazir Bhutto. His dismissal of Sabir Shah's government in the Frontier and Manzoor Ahmed Wattoos Government in Punjab indicated that he was a party loyalist head of state. Leghari's image was further undermined he claims that he was involved in the Mehran Bank scandal.

During the summer of 1996 his relationship with Prime Minister Benazir Bhutto sharply declined to the background of institutional collapse and a worsening economic situation. The situation worsened following her veiled attack on Leghari after Mir Murtaza Bhutto's death. The Prime Minister was nevertheless shocked when Leghari moved to dismiss her government on 5 November 1996. The President acted within his constitutional powers and promised that elections would he held within the statutory ninety-day period. Leghari appointed Meraj Khalid who had quit the PPP after many years in 1990 as caretaker Prime Minister. Despite some anxieties, the General Elections were duly held in February 1997.

MAMDOT, NAWAB IFTIKHAR HUSSAIN KHAN (1906-1969) Son of Nawab Shah Nawaz Khan, one of Punjab's leading Pashtuns and the largest Muslim landowner in pre-Partition East Punjab. Iftikhar succeeded him as President of the Punjab Muslim League in 1943 and was soon more active in its affairs. The Nawab of Mamdot was active in the anti-Khizr campaign in 1947. After Partition, he achieved his ambition of becoming Prime Minister. He increasingly clashed not only with Mian Iftikharuddin, but also Mian Mumtaz Daultana and Sardar Shaukat Hayat over the rehabilitation of refugees. Liaquat eventually dismissed the feuding ministry in January 1949 and handed Punjab over to Governor's rule, in advance of fresh elections. Shortly after his defeat at the hands of Daultana, Marndot formed a new party called the Jinnah Muslim League. In 1951 he joined forces with H.S. Suhrawardy in another party entitled the Jinnah Awami League. Cooperation with Suhrawardy lasted until 1953, when he rejoined the Muslim League. The same year he became Governor of Sindh. Marndor's continuing rivalry with Daultana led him to join the Republican Party in 1956. He served as a Minister in the new One Unit province of West Pakistan, but was banned from politics by Ayub under the PROD A Act.

MAUDUDI, MAULANA SYED ABUL ALA (1903-1979) Journalist and theologian who founded the JI in August 1941. Maududi came from a Sufi family and was educated and brought up in Hyderabad. He did not receive the traditional training of an *alim* but rather began a journalistic career. From 1924-7 he edited *Al-Jcuniat*, the publication of the Jarniat ul-Ulerna-i-Hind. He developed a vision of an Islamic state which would act as God's vice-regent on earth (Khalifa), Law was to be based on the Shariat and non-Muslims were reduced to the status of second-class citizens. Maududi formed the elitist Jamaat to act as a model for the future Islamic state and to work towards it. His conception was opposed to the Muslim League's Pakistan demand, but he moved his headquarters to Pakistan after its creation.

The 11 has not been successful in electoral terms, but it has played a role in undermining the secular understanding of the state espoused by Jinnah. The Jarnaat under Maududi's leadership played a key role in the Objectives Resolution and in the campaign against the Ahmadi heterodox community. It opposed the modernist MFLO and was in the forefront of opposition during the Ayub era. Maududi compromised with his ideals to support a woman, Fatima Jinnah, in her 1965 presidential campaign against Ayub.

Maududi was also in the vanguard of the Islamic opposition to Zulfikar Ali Bhutto and played a major role in his removal in 1977. The Jarnaat initially provided close support to the Zia regime, but by the time of Maududi's death disillusionment had crept in because of the slow pace of the Islamisation programme.

MIRZA, ISKANDER (1899-1969) Governor-General and President of Pakistan, born in Bombay of a Shia family from West Bengal. During the Raj he served in the Indian Political Service, while retaining his military commission (he was the first Indian to be commissioned from Sandhurst), He became Pakistan Defence Secretary in 1947 and Governor of East Pakistan in 1954. He was Interior Minister in Bogra's cabinet of talents which followed Ghulam Muhammad's dismissal of the Constituent Assembly. The following year he succeeded the ailing Ghulam Muhammad as Governor-General. Power had already slipped by this time from the politicians to the bureaucrats and their military allies. In order to provide a figleaf for this dispensation, Mirza encouraged the formation of the Republican Party. After the promulgation of the 1956 Constitution, he took the post of Pakistan President.

After a succession of weak Prime Ministers had come and gone, Mirza dissolved the National Assembly on 7 October 1958 and proclaimed martial law. This action has been seen as a pre-emptive strike to prevent elections which would have brought a threat to the establishment's foreign policy interests. As early as May 1958. Mirza had confided to the US Ambassador that only a 'dictatorship would work in Pakistan'. Mirza briefly shared power with Ayub Khan following the coup, but within three weeks he had been eased out of office and unceremoniously bundled out of the country to a London exile in his favour, he was neither a religious bigot nor a politician on the make. He was buried in Tehran.

MUHAMMAD, GHULAM (1895-1956) Civil servant and Governor-General of Pakistan who was a member of a Khakazai Pushtun family from Jullundur. He established his bureaucratic reputation under British rule as a financial expert both in the Indian Audit and Accounts Service and in administrative positions in Bhopal and Hyderabad. He was appointed Finance Minister following the creation of Pakistan. After Liaquat's death he became Pakistan's third Governor-General.

Although ailing, Ghulam Muhammad was a ruthless and ambitious figure who had little time for democratic politics. He hastened the demise of democracy in Pakistan by his dismissal of both Khwaja Nazimuddin as Prime Minister and of the Constituent Assembly. The courts supported his later action in the celebrated Tamizuddin Khan case. Ghulam Muhammad also proceeded with the support of Ayub and the military. Parliamentary politics were little more than a facade when he stepped down in 1955 as Governor-General, ostensibly for health reasons. He died shortly after Iskander Mirza succeeded him.

MUSHARRAF, PERVEZ (b.1943) Pakistan Chief of Army Staff and Chief Executive following the coup of 12 October 2000, President of Pakistan from 20 June 2001. Musharraf was born in Delhi into an educated Syed family, his father Syed Musharaff-ud-Din being a career diplomat. The family moved to Pakistan at the time of Partition. Pervez

Musharraf was brought up in Turkey from 1949-56 before completing his education in Pakistan at St Patrick's High School, Karachi, and Forman Christian College, Lahore. He joined the Pakistan Military Academy in 1961 and was commissioned into an élite Artillery regiment in 1964. He saw active service in the 1965 Indo-Pakistan war and was awarded the Nishan-e-Imtiaz for gallantry. He later volunteered and served for seven years in the Special Services Group, Pakistan's élite commandos. He was a company commander in a Commando battalion during the 1971 war with India. During the Zia era, he rose to command the Special Services group and was involved in the training of Afghan *mujahadin*. Staff and intstructional assignments he undertook during the these years included the role of the Director-General Military Operations at general headquarters. In 1991 he was prompted to major-general, and in 1995 he commanded the prestigious Strike Corps with the rank of lieutenant-general. In October 1998 Nawaz Sharif promoted Musharraf general and Chief of Army Staff over the heads of two more senior colleagues.

Musharraf seemed to confirm his anti-India reputation when he was not seen with the Pakistan Prime Minister during his celebrated bus diplomacy with his Indian Counterparts Atal Bihari Vajpayee in February 1999, and was widely acknowledged to be the architect of the military occupation of the Kargil hills in Indian Kashmir in June1999 which threatened a full-scale war. Nawaz Sharif's backing away from the conflict and attempts to blame the army for it ushered in a period of deteriorating personal relations with his Chief of Army Staff. The attempt to remove Musharraf while he was returning from a public engagement in Sri Lanka prompted the coup of 12 October.

Musharraf, in addition to castigating Sharif's 'sham democracy', promised economic revival and a restructuring of Pakistan's failing political institutions. He refrained from declaring martial law and took the title of Chief Executive. The national and provincial assemblies were suspended rather than abolished. The Supreme Court legitimised the coup, but ordered the holding of national elections by October 2002. Nawaz Sharif was sent into exile in Saudi Arabia after a lengthy trial in plane hijacking case. Musharraf's honeymoon period was ended by mounting international pressure for a definite road-map to the restoration of democracy, and rising hostility from business as he sought to increase the narrow tax-base. 'Non-party' local elections, rather than seeing the creation of a new class of political loyalists, led to the elections of many PPP and pro-Sharif Muslim Leaguers. In advance of a summit in India with Vajpayee, Musharraf surprised many by installing himself as President on 20 June 2001. The summit generated favourable publicity for this regime, but stalled on his insistence that Kashmir remained the central issue in Indo-Pakistan relations. The terrorist attacks on New York and Washington on 11 September faced Musharraf with the dilemma of abandoning long-term security and military links with Osama bin Laden's Taliban hosts, or risking international isolation and increased US-Indian ties in the subcontinent. He acted pragmatically in offering support to the US war on terrorism, despite the knowledge that the religious parties led by Jamaat-i-Islami and Jamiat-ul-Ulema and sections of the military and security establishment were bitterly opposed to this decision.

President Musharraf's position weakened throughout 2007. This was the result more of his own political miscalculations than the strength of his opponents. The suspension of the Chief Justice on 3 March unleashed the 'black coat rebellion' against his regime. The rise of judicial activism following the Supreme Court's reinstatement of Chief Justice Chaudhury threatened Musharraf's re-election as President for a further five year term. His ongoing dialogue with the PPP had ensured that the party did not embarrassingly boycott the indirect elections on 6 October. Musharraf's victory was not however notified by the Election Commission because of legal challenges to Musharraf's eligibility as a Presidential candidate. This formed the backdrop to the introduction of the Provisional Constitutional Order which introduced an Emergency on 3 November 2007. This was greeted with international disapproval. Pakistan was suspended from the Commonwealth when Musharraf failed to resign as COAS and to lift emergency rule within its ten day deadline. The Emergency complicated the powersharing arrangements between Musharraf and Bhutto favoured by the western powers. Eventually, Musharraf ended the Emergency on 15 December. He has also gone ahead with his promise to step down as COAS once a now supine Supreme Court had dismissed the petitions against his Presidential re-election. Musharraf handed over to General Ashfaq Parvez Kayani on 28 November. The following day he was sworn in as a civilian President for another five year term.

The return both of Benazir Bhutto and the Sharif brothers undermined the prospects of his loyalist PML-Q. This was further affected by Musharraf's extreme unpopularity both with Pakistani liberals and with the religious parties following Operation Silence against the Lal Masjid in Islamabad and the army's campaigns against Islamic militants in Swat and Waziristan. Musharraf was blamed by the politicians for the increasing terrorist outrages and lawlessness. Musharraf nevertheless continued to win support, especially from Washington. Even so there were tensions when US calls were made for military intervention against militants who were using the troubled tribal areas as bases for infiltration into Afghanistan. In order to allay western fears concerning the security of Pakistan's nuclear assets, Musharraf on 13 December 2007 established a National Command Authority under his Chairmanship. Benazir Bhutto's assassination just a fortnight later increased perceptions of Pakistan as being a nation in turmoil and raised once more talk of it being a 'failed state.'

The elections went ahead on 18 February 2008 amidst allegations of widespread pre-poll rigging. Musharraf constantly denied these as well as raising questions about the West's obsession with democracy when

Pakistan was facing severe security threats. The polls delivered a blow to Musharraf's supporters and generated immense euphoria. There were immediate calls for Musharraf to stand down. Nevertheless, by the time that the National Assembly convened, the situation appeared less bleak for the President. He continued to receive western diplomatic support. The squabbles of the politicians and the inability to come up with clear power-sharing arrangements and a Prime ministerial candidate also relieved some of the pressure on the President. Musharraf was however living on borrowed time as soon as it became clear that both his western allies and former military colleagues were ultimately unprepared to back him against the political forces seeking his resignation. The prospects of a protracted crisis arising from the President's impeachment were seen in the West as further distracting the government from the security challenges in the areas bordering Afghanistan. Musharraf first appeared to want to fight the looming impeachment proceedings, but finally agreed to resign on 18 August announcing this decision during the course of a national television address. The mixed legacy of nearly 9 years in office was reflected by the jubilant celebrations of political opponents and civil society groups, while the response of the business classes and of many ordinary citizens was more muted.

NAZIMUDDIN, KHWAJA (1894-1964) Member of the Nawab of Dhaka family and a leading Muslim League politician who in the pre-Partition era was a leading opponent of Fazlul Haq and a Jinnah loyalist. He opposed the progressive wing of the Bengal Muslim League associated with Abul Hashim and Suhrawardy. He held office as Prime Minister from 1943-5. After independence he returned to prominence following his marginalisation at the time of the 1946 elections. He gave up the post of Chief Minister of East Pakistan to succeed Jinnah as Governor General. Nazimuddin brought a much less interventionist role to this office. After Liaquat was assassinated, he became Prime Minister. He also held the post of President of the Pakistan Muslim League. The organisation atrophied under his leadership with important consequences for the country's future stability.

Nazimuddin alienated populist opinion in East Pakistan by his cavalier attitude to the burning Bengali-versus-Urdu language issue. His close ties with the *'ulama* also led him to vacillate at the time of the anti-Ahmadi disturbances in Lahore. This provided an opportunity for Ghulam Muhammad to dismiss him in April 1953. Nazimuddin displayed his lack of guile when he vainly attempted to telephone the Queen to order the dismissal of Ghulam Muhammad as Governor-General.

Nazimuddin was a leading opponent of the Ayub regime. After the lifting of martial law he played a key role both in the Council Muslim League and in the COP campaign. He died in October 1964 shortly before the Presidential elections.

NISHTAR, ABDUR RAB (1899-1958) Lawyer from Peshawar, educated at Aligarh. He was a leader of the Frontier Congress until his resignation in 1931. He was elected as an Independent for Peshawar in the 1937 Provincial Elections, but soon became Jinnah's loyal representative in the Frontier. He lost his seat in the 1946 elections partly because of his association with the unpopular Aurangzeb Khan ministry and partly because of the machinations of Abdul Qaiyum Khan. He was Jinnah's nominee at the May 1946 Simla Tripartite Conference to discuss the Cabinet Mission Plan. Nishtar was Member for Communications in the Interim Government and along with Liaquat, Patel and Nehru was a member of the Partition Committee. After the creation of Pakistan he served as Minister for Communications and Transport until 1949, when he became Governor of the Punjab in succession to Sir Francis Mudie. Two years later he became Minister for Industries. He was President of the PML from 1956 unti I his death on 14 February 1958.

NOON, FIROZ KHAN (1893-1970) Landlord and politician from the Sargodha district of the Punjab. He entered the Punjab Legislative Council in 1921 and held ministerial positions in 1927-31 and 1931-6. He then served as Indian High Commissioner in London for five years before being appointed to the Viceroy's Executive Council in J 941; the following year he became the first Indian to hold the defence portfolio. In 1945 after the Simla Conference he returned to Punjabi politics and campaigned against the Unionist Ministry of his kinsmen, Malik Khizr Hayat Tiwana. He played a part in the direct action campaign of March 1947. After independence he served as Governor of East Bengal in 1950-3. He then replaced Daultana as the Chief Minister of the Punjab in the wake of the anti-Ahmadi disturbances. However, the formation of a new Constituent Assembly provided Dauliana with an opportunity for revenge, and in advance of fresh elections he was dismissed by the Governor Nawab Mushtaq Ahmad Khan Gurmani (1905-81). With Suhrawardy's elevation to the post of Pakistan Prime Minister in September 1956, Firoz was rewarded with the post of Foreign Minister.

When Chundrigar resigned on II December 1957 after less than two months in office, Firoz Khan Noon formed a Republican Party coalition Government. His ministry was the last before Ayub's coup brought Pakistan's first parliamentary era to an end. The Ministry was weak from the outset as it relied on the support of Suhrawardy's Awami League which sat on the opposition benches. The political situation in East Bengal was increasingly disturbed, which provided the excuse for Ayub's coup which removed Noon from office. He did not hold further public office but his English-born wife Viqarunnissa was active during the Zia era as Minister of State for Tourism. Firoz Khan Noon's memoirs were published in *From Memory* (Lahore, 1966).

474   *Bibliographical Notes*

QURESHI, MOEENUDDIN AHMAD (b.1930) Banker and caretaker Prime Minister in 1993 after the dismissal of Nawaz Sharif, Qureshi established his economic expertise after obtaining a Ph.D. in economics at Indiana University. In 1977-80 he was Executive Vice-President of the International Finance Corporation. He then became Senior Vice-President of the World Bank (1980-7). During this same period he was Chairman of the International Development Association. It was this background that led to charges that he was an 'imported Prime Minister'. During his tenure as caretaker from July 1993 onwards he introduced a number of reforms designed to remove some of Pakistan's structural economic weaknesses. He also ensured that the Pakistan Banking Council published a list of loan defaulters. Many of his economic reforms were politically unpopular and did not survive the return of an elected PPP government. Nevertheless, his tenure in office pointed to the international financial pressures which now influenced Pakistani politics. There is some evidence that the Army hierarchy unsuccessfully encouraged him to take up the office of President.

RAHMAN, SHEIKH MUJIBUR (1920-1975) Bengali nationalist leader and founder of Bangladesh, he was born in Gopalganj in Faridpur district and involved in politics from his Calcutta College days as a member of the All-India Muslim Students Federation. Along with many other Bengali activists he became disillusioned with the Muslim League after independence over the language issue. On II March 1948 he was arrested while leading a language demonstration. Mujib was a successful Awami League candidate in its 1954 electoral rout of the Muslim League; he became increasingly important in the party organisation and was seen as Suhrawardy's successor. He was frequently imprisoned during the Ayub era and was convicted in Dhaka in September 1960 on a charge of criminal misconduct which carried a two-year prison term. He returned to political activity following his release and the lifting of martial law. In February 1966 he announced his Six Points for regional autonomy and was arrested the following month. After release, he was re-arrested in April 1967 and sentenced for making a 'prejudicial speech'.

Mujib was arrested on 18 January 1968 and implicated in the famous Agartala Conspiracy Case for collaboration with India to secure the secession of East Pakistan. Demands for Mujib's release formed a part of the anti-Ayub agitation in the eastern wing in 1968-9. He was released in 1969 and led the Awami League to a crushing victory in East Pakistan in the 1970 elections. Immediately afterwards Mujib demanded that the new Pakistan constitution be based on his Six Points for regional autonomy.

The negotiations over power-sharing between Zulfiqar Ali Bhutto and himself stalled and Bhutto threatened to boycott the National Assembly. When Yahya postponed the scheduled session at the beginning of March, Mujib led a nonviolent, non-cooperation movement. The subsequent constitutional talks with Yahya and Bhutto became deadlocked and led to the 25 March 1971 army crackdown with its accompanying massacre.

Mujib remained a prisoner in West Pakistan during the civil war which, following the Indian intervention of 3 December 1971, culminated in the emergence of Bangladesh. He was flown home to Dhaka via London after his release to become first Prime Minister and then President of the new country. He was assassinated on 15 August 1975.

SHARIF, NAWAZ (b.1949) Often cited as Pakistan's first industrialist leader, he rose to prominence in Punjab politics during the Zia era, building up a powerful political base as Finance Minister (1981-5) and Chief Minister from 1985 onwards. In 1988 he led the national opposition to the PPP, and came to power after the 1990 polls. His government introduced a number of populist measures such as the Yellow Taxi scheme. The Punjab Co-operative Banks scandal undermined his position. The religious allies in the IJI alliance were also increasingly restive at the slow pace of Islamisalion. Most dangerously he clashed with the Army commander Beg over the Gulf War and was increasingly at odds with Ghulam Ishaq Khan.

The President dismissed him, but Sharif won an appeal in the Supreme Court. He also used his Punjab power-base against the centre. The Army stepped in and both he and the President resigned on 17 July. His Muslim League party was by this time split into a faction of Mohammad Khan Junejo's followers and his own. The 1993 polls dealt a blow to his political fortunes, and he and his brother became embroiled in legal cases. The election of Farooq Leghari as President at first seemed to indicate a truce in the government-opposition conflict, but by 1994 he was involved in the same kind of extra-parliamentary efforts to unseat the PPP Government as he had condemned when they were used against him in 1990-3.

The 1994 'train march' from Karachi to Peshawar was followed by a general strike on 20 September and a 'wheel jam' strike on 11 October. These moves failed to oust Benazir Bhutto, and Nawaz Sharif showed little stomach for further street politics. In the wake of the popular opposition to the June 1996 budget, Sharif placed himself at the head of a sixteen-member opposition alliance hastily cobbled together. The dismissal of the second Bhutto ministry in November 1996 once more placed the Punjabi leader in a strong position to return to power. His Muslim League party swept to an even greater success in the 1997 elections than it had done some seven years earlier. However, he faced daunting economic problems, together with the need for major structural political reform.

Despite his continued exile in Saudi Arabia, Nawaz Sharif became politically more active in 2006. In May 2006 following negotiations with Benazir Bhutto, he signed the Charter for Democracy. This was designed to both unite the opposition against Musharraf and to map out the means by which to restore the authority of parliament against the executive. Ten-

sions later developed however between him and Benazir Bhutto because
of the contacts she established with the Pakistan government. The division in the opposition ranks was laid bare when Nawaz Sharif established
a rival to the PPP dominated Alliance for the Restoration of Democracy
with the creation of the All Parties Democratic Movement. Nawaz Sharif
attempted to return to Pakistan in July but he was unceremoniously bundled back on a plane to Saudi Arabia. President Musharraf's weakening
position and the return of Benazir Bhutto led the Saudis to force Islamabad to accept the return of Nawaz Sharif and his younger brother Shahbaz. Their arrival on 25 November 2007 enthused the ailing PML-N.
Neither brother stood for election, but they campaigned vigorously following hesitations as to whether the PML-N should contest the polls.
There were signs of reconciliation with Benazir Bhutto and following her
death the PML-N directed its fire against the pre-establishment PML-Q,
although there were never formal electoral arrangements with the PPP.
Nawaz Sharif adopted a much more strident tone against President Musharraf than did Asif Ali Zardari, especially with regard to the restoration of
the judges. After the polls, there were a series of talks between the PPP
and PML-N as to how they should share power. Nawaz Sharif wanted to
support the national government, but not to have seats in it. At the same
time, he wanted to build up a powerful PML-N government in Punjab.
The Murree agreement paved the way for power sharing between the PPP
and PML-N, although some commentators wondered how long the two
parties' traditional rivalries would remain submerged in the coalition
cabinet led by Yusuf Reza Gilani. Few expected, however, the coalition to
last a mere 42 days before it foundered on the judges question.

Nawaz Sharif achieved one major goal with the resignation of his bitter
enemy Pervez Musharraf. Hopes that this would reinvigorate the alliance
with the PPP were however almost immediately dashed. The precipitating
issue was again the vexed issue of the restoration of Chief Justice Iftikhar
Chaudhry; the final factor in leading him to openly join the opposition
ranks, however arose from the concerted effort to install Zardari as President with the office's constitutional powers (held under the 17th Amendment to the Constitution) untrammelled. Sharif saw these actions together
as clear evidence that Zardari was going back on his promises and that
his intention was to consolidate his grip on power. The government
claimed that it was merely coincidental that the National Accountability
Bureau's reopening of the three corruption references relating to Hudaibia
Paper Mills, Ittefaq Foundry and Raiwind Assets followed soon after
Nawaz Sharif's movement into opposition and declaration that he was
determined to secure election to the National Assembly.

SOOMRO, MOHAMMADMIAN (b.1950). Mohammadmian Soomro
was born on 19 August 1950 into the leading Sindhi Soomro family. His
father Ahmed Mian Soomro was Deputy Speaker in the West Pakistan
Assembly. Mohammadmian was initially educated at Forman Christian

College Lahore, before studying at Masters level in the USA and at the Punjab University, Lahore. He embarked on a career in banking and commerce serving as a director of numerous companies and as a member of the governing council of the Institute of Bankers (1997–2000). Mohammadmian Soomro entered public life following the Musharraf coup. He became Governor of Sindh in 2000. After holding this position for two years, he became Chairman of the Senate. He was widely seen as a confidant of Musharraf. He was elected the Chairman of the Senate through the support of the PML-Q. For this reason his partiality was questioned when he became caretaker Prime Minister on 16 November 2007. He oversaw the elections which delivered a victory for the main opposition parties. Soomro stepped down as Prime Minister when the new National Assembly was convened.

SUHARWARDY, HUSAIN SHAHEED (1893-1963) Leading Bengali politician and Pakistani Prime Minister. Born in Midnapore, West Bengal, the son of a Calcutta High Court judge, he was educated at St Xavier's College, Calcutta, and at Oxford. He entered politics through the Calcutta Corporation and was Deputy Mayor under C.R. Das's patronage in 1923. He also established an important power-base in the Bengal National Chamber of Labour. From 1936 onwards he was active in Muslim League politics. He served as a Minister between 1937-41 and 1943-5. Suharwardy was increasingly at odds with the Dhaka Muslim League old guard, and elbowed Khwaja Nazimuddin aside at the time of the 1946 elections, thereby assuring himself of the post of Prime Minister. His actions at the time of the 16 August 1946 Great Calcutta Killing remain highly controversial. Immediately preceding Partition he worked with Abul Hashim, Surat Bose and Kiran Shankar Roy for the idea of a sovereign United Bengal state. He remained in West Bengal after the creation of Pakistan and worked with Gandhi to maintain communal harmony.

In February 1950 he founded the Pakistan Awami League. To fight the 1954 East Bengal Legislative Assembly elections he joined with Fazlul Haq's KSP in the United Front in order to put forward the demand for provincial autonomy. The United Front dealt a devastating blow to the Muslim League. Haq became Chief Minister, while Suhrawardy entered the central cabinet. The Governor-General dismissed the United Front government after less than two months in office. Suhrawardy led the fight against the insertion of a number of 'Islamic' provisions in the debates on the constitution. With the formation of the Republican Party he attempted to forge a national coalition which would keep the Muslim League out of office. Mirza at first put obstacles in its way, but after the resignation of Muhammad Ali, he allowed an Awami League Republican combination to hold power. Suhrawardy's Muslim League opponents were prepared to compromise their principles over the One Unit scheme in order to undermine his coalition ministry. Mirza used the growing rift between the

Republicans and Suhrawardy to present him with the ultimatum to resign or face dismissal.

Suhrawardy was an implacable opponent of the Ayub regime. His arrest in Karachi in January 1962 under the Security of Pakistan Act sparked off widespread student disturbances in East Pakistan. Following his release, he led in October 1962 the broad-based National Democratic Front directed against the Ayub regime, but following a heart attack in January 1963 he had to restrict his activities. He settled in Beirut a couple of months later and was about to depart for medical treatment in Switzerland when he died.

SYED. G.M. (SYED GHULAM MURTAZA SHAH) (1904-95) Controversial Sindhi nationalist born into a pir landowning family in the Dadu district. He was active in the Sindh Legislative Council in the 1920s and supported the movement for separation from the Bombay Presidency. After the formation of a Sindh Provincial Assembly he organised a Syed factional grouping within it. It was only in 1938 that he joined the Muslim League. He was arrested during its Manzilgarh agitation. Even during the Pakistan movement, he rep¬resented a regionalist perspective based largely on hostility to Punjabi 'outsiders', although in 1943 he became President of the Sindh Muslim League and a Member of the AIML Working Committee.

Syed was heavily involved in the Sindh Muslim League's factional infighting between its Mir and Syed groups, which was institutionalised in terms of a clash between the ministerial and organisational wings of the party. This conflict led to his temporary expulsion from the League in January 1946.

After the creation of Pakistan, Syed quickly gravitated towards the Muslim League's opponents. After being imprisoned for opposing the decision to place Karachi under federal administrative control, he formed the Azad Pakistan Party on his release. His opposition to Sindh's incorporation in the One Unit scheme landed him in prison again, this time for almost a decade. On his release in 1966, he formed the Bazrn-e-Soofia-e-Sindh (Organisation of the Mystics of Sindh). His later publication on religion, *Jeenain Ditho Moon* (As I saw it) was condemned by many of the orthodox 'ulama. Syed also wrote extensively on Sindhi literature and history.

He contested the 1970 elections on the platform of the Sindh United Front, but was defeated in his own Dadu district by a PPP rival. Growing disillusionment with Pakistani politics led him in 1972 to launch the Jiye Sindh (Life to Sindh) movement and to raise the demand for Sindhu Desh (Land of the Sindhis).

During the Zia era, Syed's dislike for the PPP led him to stand aloof from the 1983 MRD agitation in Sindh. As part of the martial law administration's tactics of divide and rule, he had greater freedom than ever to express his views and even spoke publicly in India, The return of the PPP to power in 1988, however, cast the aged Sindhi leader in his more traditional opposition role. Syed was arrested following an episode at Sukkur airport in October 1989 in which some of his Sindh National Alliance supporters burnt the Pakistan flag. The wheel turned once more with the dismissal of Benazir Bhutto and the installation of Jam Sadiq Ali. G.M. Syed was courted by the authorities because of his hostility to the PPP, but detained again in 1992 following a controversial speech at his birthday celebrations in Karachi's Nishtar Park. It was only while comatose for several weeks before his death on 25 April that he was granted bail.

TARAR, RAFIQ (b.1929) Tarar, born at Pirkot on 2 November 1929, was a little-known figure before becoming President of Pakistan on 31 December 1997. His nomination for the post by the ruling PML(N) had come as a surprise even to Cabinet members. Indeed, it was rumoured that he owed his elevation to support from 'Abbaji' Mian Mohammad Sharif, patriarch of the Sharif family.

Tarar, who came from a modest background, was educated at college in Gujranwala before entering Law College in Lahore where he obtained his LL.B. in 1951. He established a practice in Gujranwala before rising to the post of Chairman of Punjab Labour Court in 1970. He entered the High Court four years later, and became Chief Justice of the Lahore High Court in 1989. He reached the pinnacle of his legal career two years later when he joined the Supreme Court, escaping the limelight since he dealt mainly with criminal cases rather than the politically contentious constitutional cases that have featured so prominently in Pakistan's history. Nor was he a prominent member of the Senate, which he entered on the PML(N) ticket in March 1917 following his retirement from the judiciary.

Some commentators have depicted Tarar as a conservative who is hostile in his attitude to the minorities, and whose elevation exemplifies Pakistan's 'creeping fundamentalism'.

ZARDARI, ASIF ALI (b.1954) Highly controversial spouse of Benazir Bhutto, whom he married in December 1987. He is the son of a Sindhi landowner and businessman Hakim Ali Zardari. According to Benazir Bhutto, Zardari has been the victim of a massive disinformation campaign designed to discredit her politically. Zardari has been variously described as a wife-beater, 'Mr Ten per cent' and 'the billion dollar man'. Opponents claim that his corruption brought down both the Bhutto governments and that his political influence contributed to the estrangement between Benazir and her mother Nusrat.

Before his marriage Zardari was known more as a playboy than as a politician, although he had unsuccessfully contested the 1985 party less elections. He played an important role in distributing PPP tickets at the time of the 1988 elections and was subsequently alleged to have accumulated a fortune through the sale of permits and licences. He spent the best part of two and a half years in prison on a series of charges of which he was eventually cleared, and was elected for the Karachi Lyari National Assembly constituency in 1990 while in prison. After the PPP returned to power in 1993, he was again accused of receiving huge commissions and kickbacks. The criticism generated by his appointment as Minister of Investment in August 1996 has been cited by some analysts as an important factor in the dismissal of the Bhutto government.

For the following see the political organisations mentioned in Appendix C: Nawabzada Nasrullah Khan, Democratic Action Committee and Pakistan Democratic Party; Asghar Khan, Tehrik-i-Istiqlal; Ghulam Mustafa Jatoi, Na¬tional People's Party; Mufti Mahmud and Fazlur Rahman, JUI; Allama In¬ayatullah Khan Mashriqi, Khaksar Tehrik.

Zardari's eight year imprisonment ended in 2004 following behind the scenes negotiations between the PPP and the Musharraf regime. He adopted a low profile in which he lived largely separately from Benazir. He spent some time in the USA receiving treatment for diabetes and his back problems. Benazir Bhutto's assassination thrust her husband into the limelight. He became co-chairman of the PPP and in effect ran the party as his son Bilawal who was also co-chair continued his studies at Oxford University. Zardari did not contest a seat in the elections, but made a number of campaign speeches. Following the polls he was involved in discussions with Nawaz Sharif. The Murree declaration paved the way for the creation of a coalition government. When Zardari later backed out of his commitment to restore the judges deposed following Musharraf's Emergency, relations eventually broke down between him and Nawaz Sharif.

It became clear after the polls that Zardari did not want the former PPP Vice-President Makhdoom Amin Fahim as prime minister as it would strengthen the power of a rival political grouping within Sindh. In the event Syed Yusuf Reza Gilani was chosen in a move not only designed to nullify rival groupings to the Bhuttos within the PPP, but to balance Sindhi and Punjabi regional interests and to balance PPP and PML-N interests within Punjab. The reconciliation between Zardari and Altaf Hussain early in April 2008, although it did not meet with full PML-N approval was another step to boost the Bhutto influence in Sindh. Within the PPP, Zardari quickly established his power, even being prepared to sideline some of Benazir's former friends and loyalists in order to achieve this.

The post-election period clearly revealed that power lay with Zardari rather than the Prime Minister. It was Zardari, for example who led the rounds of talks between the PPP and PML-N over the judges issue. Zardari's relations with Nawaz Sharif became increasingly strained, although cordiality was maintained in public. It became clear that all the while, Zardari sought to strengthen his grip on power. This became even more evident once Musharraf resigned as President as he swiftly became the front runner for the polls scheduled for 6 September. Zardari was duly elected President with two thirds of the votes cast in the electoral college, comfortably defeating the PML-N candidate, Justice (Retd) Saeeduzzaman Siddiqui.

C

PAKISTAN POLITICAL PARTIES AND ORGANISATIONS

ALL PARTIES DEMOCRATIC MOVEMENT (APDM) This coalition of over 30 parties opposed to the Musharraf regime was founded by Nawaz Sharif in July 2007. The main components were the PML-N, MMA, PTI and ANP. The PPP was a notable absentee. Benazir Bhutto stated that another opposition alliance alongside the Alliance for The Restoration of Democracy was unnecessary. Moreover, she refused to sit alongside the MMA members within the new coalition. It was regarded at the time however that the major factor in her party's aloofness was its dialogue with the Musharraf regime. The APDM attempted to orchestrate opposition to Musharraf's Presidential re-election in October 2007. The call for legislators to resign from the National Assembly and four Provincial Assemblies which formed the electoral college created tensions between the JUI-F and JUI. The APDM subsequently protested about the imposition of the Emergency. On 24 November it announced that it would boycott the parliamentary polls. Nawaz Sharif's reversal of this decision and the PNL-N's contesting the polls virtually signalled the death knell of the short lived APDM coalition. JI and PTI along with the PKMAP did however persist with the boycott strategy.

AL-ZULFIQAR Al-Zulfiqar was a terrorist organisation founded in Kabul in February 1981 by Murtaza Bhutto, which grew out of the Pakistan Liberation Army which had been established by Murtaza and his brother Shahnawaz. It sought the overthrow of the Zia regime and drew on support from Libya and Afghanistan. It claimed responsibility for a number of acts of sabotage and for the assassination of such Zia supporters as Chaudhri Zahur Elahi.

ALL-PAKISTAN MOHAJIR STUDENTS ORGANISATION (APM-SO) This organisation, the precursor of the MQM, was founded in Karachi on 11 June 1978 by Altaf Hussain, Aziz Ahmed Tariq, Saleem Haider, Imran Farooq and ten others. The background to *its* formation was *mohajir* anger over domicile fraud in the operation of admissions quotas to colleges and universities. The APMSO soon eclipsed the Jarniat-i-Tuleba, the student wing of Jl, and gained a reputation for militancy. Indeed both Altaf Hussain and Aziz Ahmed Tariq were expelled from Karachi University because of their activities in 1980 following an earlier spell in prison. The fierce battle between the APMSO and the PSF resulted in the militarisation of the Karachi University campus in 1989. Many former APMSO students joined the MQM in March 1984. Thereafter the APMSO acted as a quasi-independent student wing of the party.

ALL-PAKISTAN WOMEN'S ASSOCIATION (APWA) This is the oldest established organisation in Pakistan dedicated to promoting women's social, economic and political rights. It has established a number of schools, colleges and industrial homes. Perhaps the greatest achievement was its role in paving the way for the 1961 Family Laws Ordinance through the Family Laws Commission.

Founded in Karachi on 22 February 1949, it was seen for most of its existence as an establishment movement made up of do-gooder *begums* under the leadership of Begum Raana Liaquat Ali Khan, widow of Pakistan's first Prime Minister. During the Zia regime the movement was radicalised and took an active stance over the Law of Evidence, the Law of *Qisas* and *Diyas* and a number of the recommendations which emanated from the Ansari Commission, which had been established in 1982 to report to the President on those elements of Pakistani society which were repugnant to Islam. APWA nevertheless still remained a much more conservative organisation than the Women's Action Forum which led the fight against the discriminatory measures of the Zia regime.

AWAMI LEAGUE The Pakistan Awami League was founded by Suhrawardy in 1950, and increasingly became centred in Bengal, gaining support following the 1952 Bengali-language disturbances. It fought the 1954 East Pakistan provincial elections in the United Front alliance with the KSP. Following the dismissal of the United Front government, Haq split the Awami League. It took up the 6-Point Programme calling for the establishment of full provincial autonomy in East Pakistan on the basis of the Lahore Resolution. The centre would only be left with responsibility for defence and foreign affairs. An Awami League government led by Ataur Rahman was established in Dhaka in August 1956, and tension grew between it and the national coalition Awami League-Republican Party of Suhrawardy.

The party was in opposition during the Ayub era. Following Suhrawardy's death, Mujibur Rehman became the leading figure. The party secured a staggering victory in East Pakistan capturing 160 out of 162 National Assembly seats at the time of the 1970 polls. The inability to secure an agreement between it and the West Pakistan based PPP led to growing tension and militancy. The army operation of March 1971 paved the way for the establishment of Bangladesh under the Awami League's leadership.

AWAMI NATIONAL PARTY (ANP) This leftist party was founded in 1986 following the merger of the National Democratic Party, the Awami

Tehrik of Sindhi nationalist Rasul Bux Palejo and the Pakistan National Party of the Baloch nationalist Mir Ghaus Bux Bizenjo. Wali Khan, son of the 'Frontier Gandhi' Abdul Ghaffar Khan, became its first President. However, the party split shortly after its creation and its influence remained limited to the Frontier, although even here dissidents broke away to form the Pakhtun Liberation Front. The ANP aligned itself with former leading opponents the Muslim League and Jamaat-i-Islami in the IDA in 1990. Ajmal Khan Khattak held office in Nawaz Sharif's federal cabinet. The ANP continued its anti-PPP alliance with Nawaz Sharif in the 1993 elections and although it had more strength than the PML(N), it threw its weight behind the Muslim League Chief Minister Sabir Shah in the Provincial Assembly. It went into opposition when this government was toppled by Aftab Sherpao of the PPP. In the 1997 elections it again allied itself with the PML(N) and captured 31 out of 83 Frontier Assembly seats along with nine National Assembly constituencies.

It finally split with the PML(N) over Nawaz Sharifs 'betrayal' regarding the remaining of NWFP as Pukhtoonkhwa.

AWAMI TEHRIK This Maoist-based party was active in Sindh under the leadership of Rasool Baksh Paleejo, who was arrested by the martial law authorities in 1979. The Awami Tehrik joined the MRD on 26 January 1984, and was a founder-member of the Awami National Party in July 1986.

BALOCHISTAN NATIONAL PARTY This was formed in 1996 by the ex-Chief Minister, Attaullah Khan Mengal, who had earlier worked with Akbar Bugti's Balochistan National Alliance after the 1988 polls. The Balochistan National Party cut into the Makran support-base of Mengal's former factional rival and head of the Balochistan National Movement (BNM), Dr Abdul Hayee Baloch in the 1997 polls. It emerged with ten seats to the BNM's two and was in a position to form a coalition government with Akbar Bugti's Iamhoori Watan Party.

CONVENTION MUSLIM LEAGUE This party was founded in May 1963 by Chaudhri Khaliquzzaman, the former UP Muslim League leader and East Pakistan Governor as a pro-Government grouping in the National Assembly. General Ayub Khan became its President in December 1963. Many of those elected to the National Assembly in 1965 claimed allegiance to the party. But it was almost entirely without popular roots and dependent on government patronage for its functioning. Significantly, it polled less than 5 per cent of the votes in the 1970 elections. The party continued its existence as a minor political force following Ayub Khan's retreat from power, but was dissolved on 5 July 1977 following Zia's promulgation of martial law. The Khwaja Kairuddin faction of the Muslim League was heir to the Convention League. It joined the MRD in 1981 and later became known as the PML(Chatta group).

COUNCIL MUSLIM LEAGUE The Council Muslim League comprised old-style Muslim Leaguers opposed to the Convention Muslim League. and was led by the former Governor-General and Prime Minister Khwaja Nazimuddin. After his death in 1964, the leadership was held by another Bengali, Nurul Amin. In 1968 the Council League joined the Democratic Action Committee movement against the Ayub regime. The heir to it was the PML(P), later the PML(J), which. unlike the Chatta faction, co-operated with the martial law regime. For a time it was known as the Pakistan Muslim League under the leadership of Muhammad Khan Junejo. After the former Prime Minister's death in 1993, a formal split emerged between this and the Nawaz Sharif faction of the Muslim League. Pir Pagaro also went his own way and founded the Muslim League (Functional) grouping.

DEMOCRATIC ACTION COMMITTEE (DAC) This broad-based coalition against the Ayub regime was convened in 1968 by Nawabzada Nasrullah Khan. Major components of the coalition included the Awami League, the Council Muslim League and the NDP. The DAC called for a federal system of government to replace the 1962 Constitution. It participated in the March 1969 Round Table discussions which culminated in Ayub's hand-over of power to Yahya Khan, whereupon it disbanded. Like later broad anti-government coalitions, it lacked ideological coherence and any positive programme of action.

HIZBE JIHAD Small Shia grouping founded by Murtaza Pooya in the wake of Pakistan's growing sectarianism. It originally formed part of the IJI.

ISLAMI JAMHOORI ITTEHAD (IJI) (Islamic Democratic Alliance) This nineparty alliance was organised in September 1988 by the military-controlled ISI in order to co-ordinate electoral opposition to Benazir Bhutto's PPP. The alliance included such unlikely partners as the ANP, the PML and the JI, as well as a number of smaller parties such as the TI. Its main success came in the Punjab where it drew on Nawaz Sharif's influence. The PPP secured a national majority in the October elections with ninety-three seats to the IJI's fifty-five, but was out of office in the key Punjab province. The IJI increasingly posed as a protector of Punjabi interests against the centre, and was also stridently anti-Indian in its political approach. It joined with other opposition parties to form a Combined Opposition Party under Ghulam Mustafa Jatoi's leadership in June 1989.

The IJI came to power after its triumph in the October 1990 elections, when it captured 105 National Assembly seats to the PPP-led PDNs forty-five. The PDA claimed that the elections were rigged, although this did not receive international support. However, there were growing tensions in the governing IJI coalition however between the ANP and JI and between the PML and JI over the issue of a Shariat Bill and the introduction of a non-interest-based economy. The JI eventually quit the IJI over the issue of its Afghanistan policy. The IJI henceforth was the Nawaz Sharif faction of the Muslim League writ large, and was dissolved before the 1993 elections. The PML(N) contested these alone, facing a challenge not only from the PPP but from the JI-Ied PIF. The latter grouping captured just three seats.

JAMAAT-I-ISLAMI (JI) (Islamic Movement) This Islamist movement was founded by Maulana Abul Ala Maududi in 1941 in opposition to the Muslim League-led Pakistan movement. It opposed both the secularist orientation of the League leadership and the modernist reconciliation of the nation-state concept with Islam. Following the creation of Pakistan the JI moved its headquarters from East Punjab and sought to work for an Islamisation of the state.

The JI, like the modernists, accepts the concept of independent judgement in areas of Islamic interpretation, thereby marking itself out from 'traditionalist' *'ulama*, but adopts a 'fundamentalist' approach to the removal of what Maududi called 'deviant' behaviour and to political organisation. Hence the party's support for an 'Islamic democracy' whose features are reproduced in microcosm in its hierarchical and elitist organisation. The strict membership requirements have limited the JI's development, but its organisational strength and discipline have been displayed in the numerous street agitations it has joined against un-Islamic governments. The JI led the 1953 anti-Ahmadi agitation and opposed both Ayub (especially because of the MFLO) and Zulfiqar Ali Bhutto in 1977. It was active in the IJI opposition to Benazir Bhutto under the leadership of Amir Qazi Hussain Ahmad, although it eventually split with Nawaz Sharif.

The JI was closest to the seat of power during the early period of the Zia regime when its Amir was Mian Tufail Muhammad. It eventually parted company with Zia because of its criticism of the 'cosmetic' nature of the statesponsored Islamisation programme and because of the restrictions on its powerful student organisation Jamiat-e-Tuleba-e-Pakistan in 1984. The JI closely supported Gulbuddin Hekmatyar's 'fundamentalist' Hezb-i-Islami during the Afghan conflict and following the Soviet withdrawal. The JI has similarly supported Kashmiri militants and earlier backed such opponents of the A wami League in 1970-1 as Al-Sharns and Al-Badr.

Despite the JI's opposition to Western-style democracy, with the exception of the February 1997 polls, it has contested national and provincial elections including the 1985 party less elections, but has met with little success because of its inability to expand beyond a narrow lower-middle-class urban support base. It has even been prepared to compromise its principles as in the support it gave to Fatima Jinnah during the 1965 presidential election campaign. Electoral failure should not obscure JI's ability to influence politics through both street agitation and in setting a national Islamic agenda to which all parties have to respond.

JAMIAT-UL-ULEMA-I-ISLAM (JUI) This organisation reflects the reformist and scripturalist Islam of the Deoband movement, which grew up in nineteenthcentury British India with an emphasis on education, opposition to Sufi and Shia practice, and individual moral responsibility. In 1919 the Jamiat-ul-Ulemai-Hind was formed to represent Deobandi views. It was pro-Congress in orientation and this stance was maintained during the Pakistan movement. A minority of Deobandi scholars led by Shabbir Ahmad Usmani formed the JUI in November 1945 as a rival organisation to support the Pakistan demand.

Since independence the JUI has developed strong roots in Balochistan and the Frontier and as a result has polled more consistently than the other *'ulama* parties. It formed coalition governments with the NAP in both provinces, although these were dismissed by Zulfiqar Ali Bhutto. This experience led the JUI to take its place in the anti-PPP Pakistan National Alliance in 1977. However, the JUI under Maulana Fazlur Rahman's leadership distanced itself from the Zia regime, and took its place in the eleven-party MRD launched in February 1981. Five years later, Maulana Fazlur Rahman was appointed its convenor. Despite the collapse of the MRD before the 1988 elections, the JUI remained in opposition to the IJI and captured eight seats in the National Assembly. The JUI remains opposed to the Islamist approach of the JI, but its greatest rivalry is with the Barelvi and Shia Islamic groupings.

JAMIAT-UL-ULEMA-I-PAKISTAN (JUP) The organisation was founded in 1949 out of the rivalry between the Deobandi and Barelvi schools of *'ulama*. The Barelvis wanted a party to rival the JUI. Unlike the JI and the majority of the Deobandi *'ulama*, the Barelvis actively supported the Pakistan movement. The greatest difference between them and the other *'ulama* parties remains their upholding of traditional Sufi practices including intercession at shrines. This is anathema to the Deobandis and lies behind the history of violent clashes between the two movements: these intensified during the Zia era which encouraged sectarianism. The JUP under its leader Maulana Noorani actively criticised the Zia regime.

The JUP has been less electorally successful than the JUI and the JI because it lacks the former's regional power base and the latter's discipline and ideological unity. Sindh was for many years its main source of support. The MQM however undermined its Karachi base, while the PPP and the nationalists out manoeuvred it elsewhere in the province. Noorani's public support for Saddam Hussain during the Gulf War temporarily raised the JUP's profile to the discomfort of Nawaz Sharif.

JAMHOORI WATAN PARTY This Baloch nationalist party was formed by the tribal leader Akbar Bugti after the dismissal of Benazir Bhutto's first administration in August 1990. In the November polls it captured 13 out of 43 Baloch Provincial Assembly seats, but was unable to capture the Chief Ministership. It fought the 1997 elections on a platform of provincial autonomy and called for the redemarcation of provinces within Pakistan. It captured eight Assembly seats and two National Assembly constituencies.

KHAKSAR TEHRIK Allama Inayatullah Mashriqi (1888-1963) formed this lower-middle-class volunteer movement in April 1931. Khaki-clad Khaksars drilled with sharpened *belchas* (spades) and engaged in social welfare projects. The movement spread from its Punjab base to Sindh, Balochistan and the Frontier late in the period of British rule. The Khaksars opposed both the 'loyalisrn' of the Unionists and the 'communalism' of the Muslim League. During the war years they were placed under a banning order and Mashriqi was arrested. The police fired on a Khaksar rally in Lahore on I March 1940, killing a number of volunteers. The Khaksars' influence declined because of their opposition to the Pakistan movement. Oneoftheir volunteers, Rafiq Sabir, attempted to assassinate Jinnah on 26 July 1943. The Khaksar Tehrik has operated as a small radical urban movement since independence. In 1977 it formed a component part of the PNA.

KRISHAK PRAJA PARTY (KPP) Radical Bengali tenant party founded by Fazlul Haq in April 1936. It fared especially well in the East Bengal constituencies in the 1937 elections, and formed a coalition government with the Muslim League from 1937-December 1941. After Haq's split with the Muslim league it formed a leading component of the Progressive Coalition Assembly Party which survived in office until March 1943. By the time of the 1946 provincial elections it had lost a large number of its members to the Muslim League. After independence KPP supporters formed the nucleus of Fazlul Haq's Krishak Sramik Party which played an important role in the United Front's crushing victory over the Muslim League in the Spring 1954 East Pakistan provincial elections.

MOHAJIR QAUMI MAHAZ (MQM) This party, founded in March 1984 by Altaf Hussain and other cadres of the APMSO, appealed especially to the lowermiddle-class *mohajirs'* sense of alienation arising from the state's preferential politics regarding employment and admission to educational institutions. It also grew out of the tensions arising from rapid socio-economic change in such cities as Karachi and Hyderabad. The MQM also reflected the ethnicisation arising from the depoliticisation of the Zia era.

The MQM's rapid rise to power in Karachi was primarily at the expense of the JI, It was aided by the spread of ethnic riots between *mohajirs* and Pushtuns from the mid-1980s onwards. Altaf Hussain's personality cult and the construction of a fifth *mohajir* 'nationality' accompanied the MQM's rise to prominence in local bodies' elections. The movement acquired a reputation for violence and intimidation of opponents along with a commitment to such social works as free bazaars, establishment of field hospitals and urban 'beautification' campaigns.

The MQM possessed considerable leverage following its capture of thirteen National Assembly seats in the 1988 elections. Informed part of the PPP coalition both nationally and in Sindh following the Karachi Accord. Relations with Benazir Bhutto's government became frosty over its failure to implement the Accord, *mohajir* claims of police *zulm* (wrongdoing), and the contentious issue of the repatriation of Biharis from camps in Bangladesh. The MQM decision to support Nawaz Sharif's September 1989 no-confidence motion against the PPP Government took the latter by surprise. Thereafter the law and order situation declined dramatically in both urban and rural Sindh, culminating in the notorious Pucca Qila incident in Hyderabad on 27 May 1990 in which police opened fire in a *mohajir* locality. The ensuing violence sealed the fate of Benazir Bhutto's first administration.

The MQM reaffirmed its dominance in the 1990 elections. For the next nineteen months it ruled in Sindh during the chief ministership of the renegade PPP leader Jam Sadiq Ali. The violence arising from a split between supporters of Altaf Hussain and Aamir Khan on one side and Afaq Ahmed's 'Haqiqi faction'–MQM(H)–on the other formed part of the background to Operation Clean-Up in May 1992. Army raids revealed torture chambers and arms caches in areas of Karachi previously controlled by the MQM(A). Army sponsorship of the rival MQM(H) did not bring long-term electoral dividends. Despite Altaf Hussain's continued exile in London, the MQM(A) swept all rivals aside in the 1993 provincial elections which followed the dismissal of Nawaz Sharif, although it boycotted the national polls.

After a short-lived reconciliation, the MQM(A) resumed street fighting with the PPP following the controversial decision to form a new Malir district of Karachi in March 1994. The withdrawal of the army in December 1994 led to violent gun battles between the rival factions of the MQM which coincided with rising sectarian clashes and *mohajir-Sindhi* violence. During May-June 1995 a virtual civil war was fought out in Karachi between the MQM(A) and the police and rangers. Talks between the PPP and MQM(A) failed to bring about peace, but ruthless counter-insurgency operations brought a relative calm to Pakistan's metropolis by the spring of 1996. Charges of extra-judicial killings were later used by President Farooq Leghari against the Bhutto administration. MQM supporters rejoiced at the dismissal of the Government on 5 November, although they were less happy with the appointment of the Sindhi nationalist Mumtaz Ali Bhutto as caretaker Chief Minister. The MQM(A) won 28 Sindh Assembly seats and 12 National Assembly seats in the February 1997 elections, once again eclipsing the MQM(H) although there was some evidence of the PML beginning to erode its support-base. Instructions continued to be relayed to the local leaders by the self-exiled Altaf Hussain.

MOVEMENT FOR THE RESTORATION OF DEMOCRACY (MRD) This was launched in February 1981 to pressurise Zia to hold 'free and fair elections under the 1973 Constitution'. Like the PNA earlier, the alliance contained a very disparate group of parties–eleven in all–which did not share any common ideological ground. Indeed four of its members allied with the PPP – the JUI, @Text:NDP, PDP and TI–had earlier been in the PNA directed against Zulkikar Ali Bhutto in 1977.

The first phase of the MRD campaign was quashed by the repression which followed the hijacking of a PIA flight allegedly by the Al-Zulfikar organisation in March 1981. In the summer of 1983, however, the MRD launched an agitation which was widely supported in Sindh, and considerable force was required to bring it under control. The Punjab remained quiescent, thereby ensuring the stability of the Zia regime. The MRD parties boycotted the December 1984 referendum and February 1985 elections, but cracks began to appear in the alliance resulting from tensions between the PPP and the smaller parties. In 1986 the TI left the alliance, which by November 1987 was in considerable disarray. It was finally dissolved shortly before the 1988 elections; with hindsight this appeared to be a mistake on Benazir Bhutto's part.

MUSLIM LEAGUE There have been numerous heirs in Pakistani politics to the All-India Muslim League which was founded in Dhaka in 1906 and successfully led the demand for a Muslim homeland in the 1940s. A number of writers have pointed to the League's weak institutionalisation and faction-ridden provincial branches even in its 1940s heyday. The future functioning of Pakistani democracy was also hampered by the League's latecomer status in the 'Pakistan' areas, the lack of governmental experience of many of its leaders, and the political culture of confrontation which had grown up following its clashes both with the Indian National Congress and such regional political opponents as the Unionist Party, *Khudai Khidmatgars* and KPP. Another handicap was its *mohajir* leadership's lack of a political base in the Pakistan provinces.

After independence, the Muslim League's inability to function as successfully as its Congress counterpart in ensuring stability was a major factor in the different political trajectories of the South Asian neighbours. The Muslim League was badly hit not only by Jinnah's death but by the unfolding Urdu-Bengali clash in the eastern wing. Its routing by regionalist forces in the 1954 provincial elections in Bengal was a major turning-point in Pakistan's history. The formation of the Republican Party two years later was a further blow and paved the way for the emergence of a national non-Muslim League leadership.

The Muslim League was dissolved along with other parties in the Ayub martial law era, but in 1962 the Convention and Council Muslim Leagues came into existence. This set the trend for a proliferation of largely personality-based Muslim Leagues all of which have attempted to claim the historic mantle of the founders of Pakistan. After Zia's lifting of martial law in 1985, Muhammad Khan Junejo formed a Pakistan Muslim League (PML). After his death and during the constitutional crisis of 1993, it split into PML(N) and PML(J) factions. The latter, headed by Hamid Nasir Chattha, sided with the PPP in both the 1993 and 1997 polls. Its relationship with the Punjab branch of the PPP was uneasy during Benazir Bhutto's second administration.

The PML(N)'s founding convention was held the day after Nawaz Sharif's dismissal by President Ghulam Ishaq Khan. This enabled its propagandists to claim that in contrast with other post-independence Muslim Leagues it was founded on anti-establishment lines. While this point should not be overplayed and should be understood in the context of Nawaz Sharif's entry into politics as Zia's protégé, it is nevertheless incontestable that by the time of the 1997 elections the PML(N) had gathered considerable popular support. It had distanced itself both from the Zia legacy and from its earlier ties with Islamist groups. Punjab remained its heartland, but it had also established a considerable presence in Sindh and the Frontier. It eclipsed not only the PPP in the 1997 polls but also other claimants to the 'magic' of the Muslim League title including the PML(J) and the PML(F) of Pir Pagaro. Another claimant to the Muslim League mantle was the PML(Q), a faction headed by Malik Qasim which supported the MRD.

NATIONAL PEOPLE'S PARTY (NPP) This party was founded in August 1986 by Ghulam Mustafa Jatoi, a former Sindh PPP President who had left the party after disagreement with Benazir Bhutto, and in August 1990 following her dismissal he was appointed acting Prime Minister. The IJI fought the elections separately from the COP label of Jatoi. The NPP joined the ruling coalition, but in March 1992 it was expelled by Nawaz Sharif because of Jatoi's alleged cooperation with the PPP against his government. By the October 1993 elections, however, Jatoi had quarrelled with Benazir and was out in the cold. Although he secured election for his Naushero Feroze Sindhi constituency, this was the NPP's only success.

NIZAM-I-MUSTAPHA Small religious party founded by Maulana Abdul Sattar Khan Niazi who is (also a leading figure in the JUP), which is working for the establishment of the system of the Prophet in Pakistan. It was active in both the PNA and IJI.

PAKISTAN DEMOCRATIC PARTY (PDP) The long-time opposition figure Nawabzada Nasrullah Khan founded the PDP in June 1969, merging together four parties–the Justice Party, the National democratic Front, Nizam-i-Islarn and the West Pakistan Awami League. The PDP has never expanded beyond its personalist base, but it has played a part in wider opposition campaigns such as those of the PNA and MRD. During Nawaz Sharifs first ministry, Nasrullah Khan formed an opposition 'third force' called the All Parties Conference. His component was the National Democratic Alliance which replaced the PDP. It contested the 1993 elections, securing one National Assembly seat and two Punjab Provincial Assembly seats.

PAKISTAN NATIONAL ALLIANCE (PNA) This coalition was formed in January 1977 to oppose the PPP in the national elections. It included the JI, JUP, JUI, Muslim League, TI, PDP, NDP, Khaksar Tehriq and Muslim Conference. Despite the large crowds which it attracted, the PNA did poorly in the 1977 elections winning only 36 seats to the PPP's 155. This led to allegations of ballot-rigging by the bureaucracy. The PNA organised a street agitation in order to force Bhutto to hold fresh polls. The military had to restore order in Lahore and a number of other cities. Following negotiations between Zulfiqar Ali Bhutto and the PNA, General Zia initiated 'Operation Fairplay' on 5 July 1977.

When the PNA split over the issue of political cooperation with the martial law regime, some of its component members went into opposition, while the JI developed close links with the regime in its early days.

PAKISTAN PEOPLE'S PARTY (PPP) This 'left-of-centre national party was founded on 30 November 1967. Its populist approach was reflected in the slogan 'Islam is our faith; democracy is our polity; socialism is our economic creed; all power to the people.' This image, which attracted professionals, students and intellectuals who were disillusioned with the Ayub regime, was further burnished during the period November 1968-March 1969, when the PPP under the charismatic leadership of Zulfiqar Ali Bhutto co-ordinated the popular disturbances against his former mentor, Ayub.

The PPP swept to power in West Pakistan in the December 1970 elections campaigning under the slogan *'Roti, Kapra aur Makan'* ('Food, Clothes and Shelter'). The Awarni League achieved even greater success in East Pakistan where the PPP did not contest a single seat. The failure to secure an acceptable power-sharing arrangement between the PPP and Awami League formed the background to the military crackdown in the eastern wing on 25 March 1971 which plunged Pakistan into civil war.

The PPP came to power the following December in the wake of the separation of East Pakistan. Bhutto served initially as a Civilian Martial Law Administrator.

Bhutto's regime drifted towards authoritarianism and personalism with increasingly heavy-handed treatment of dissent and atrophy of the PPP organisation. The socio-economic reforms went far enough to alienate vested interests without transforming the basis of political and economic power. The Army, which had been in disarray following the Bangladesh debacle, re-entered public life via its utilisation in Balochistan. In the 1977 elections, Bhutto turned to many of the traditional landholding families for support. The PPP won a massive victory against the PNA, but the latter's supporters took to the streets amidst claims of fraud and rigging. The PPP-PNA confrontation paved the way for the imposition of martial law by General Zia-ul-Haq.

The repression of the Zia era, including the banning of the party, failed to break the spirit of PPP activists. Following Bhutto's execution in April 1979, Begum Nusrat Bhutto assumed the chairmanship of the party, Benazir Bhutto later becoming co-Chair. The PPP was the dominant force in the MRD. The PPP's Sindh heartland was the centre of the 1983 agitation against the Zia regime. Along with the other MRD parties it boycotted the 1985 party less elections. Benazir Bhutto returned to Pakistan from exile in London in April 1986 to a tumultuous reception. Zia was not however to be swept from power and splits developed within the PPP between Benazir and the 'old guard'. The new generation of leaders were seen by some as marking a shift to the right on economic issues and relations with the United States.

The PPP came to power in December 1988 following the elections and military transfer of power after Zia's death in August. It did not however hold power in the key Punjab province which remained under the control of Nawaz Sharifs Muslim League. The first Bhutto administration was a great disappointment to many PPP supporters, with little legislative achievement or party institutionalisation. The PPP accord with the MQM broke down amidst mutual recrimination and spiralling violence, while there was constant confrontation between the Government and the IJI opposition.

The PPP was dismissed from power in August 1990 by President Ghulam Ishaq Khan. Ghulam Mustafa Jatoi, a former PPP leader who had formed the rival NPP, headed a caretaker government. In the 1990 elections the PPP-led coalition, the PDA, fared badly especially in the Punjab. Benazir Bhutto claimed that the polls had been rigged but this was not supported by international observers. PPP activists in Sindh suffered considerable persecution during the nineteen-month ministry of another former PPP leader, Jam Sadiq Ali. Both Benazir Bhutto and her husband Asif Ali Zardari were embroiled in legal cases. This did not prevent the PPP co-chairman leading a popular agitation against Nawaz Sharif in

November 1992 which fed on the popular anger caused by the cooperative banks fraud. It was the rift between Sharif and the President Ghulam
Ishaq Khan, however, which opened the way for the PPP to return to
power in late 1993. Unlike five years earlier, the PPP was able to wield
power in a coalition government in the Punjab as well as at the centre.
The second Benazir Bhutto government repeated many of the disap-
pointments of its predecessor. The PPP organisation continued to atrophy
and the politics of patronage totally overwhelmed those of principle. Confrontation with the Muslim League opposition and a declining economy
as a result of the ongoing crisis in Karachi prevented any meaningful
reform. The PPP's feudal assembly members also blocked any attempts to
widen the very narrow tax-base. The clash between the judiciary and the
Government paved the way for the former PPP loyalist, President Farooq
Leghari, to dismiss Benazir Bhutto and dissolve the assemblies on 5
November 1996.

The PPP faced the opposition of Mir Murtaza Bhutto's supporters in
Sindh in the February 1997 elections. Murtaza's mysterious death in a
police encounter was blamed by some on his estranged sister. His widow
(who had been his second wife) Ghinwa Bhutto, headed the PPP(SB) faction. It secured the support of a number of leading Sindhi landowners.

Benazir Bhutto did not persuade the Supreme Court to overturn President Leghari's dismissal of her government, although the hearing failed
to turn up evidence of the 'extra-judicial' killings in Karachi which had
formed part of Leghari's 'charge sheet' against her. The PPP suffered a
crushing defeat in the 1997 polls amidst familiar claims of rigging.

PAKISTAN PEOPLE'S PARTY (SHAHEED BHUTTO) PPP(SB) This
faction of the PPP was founded by Mir Murtaza Bhutto early in 1996.
Following his return to Pakistan after sixteen years in exile, he had been
elected to the Sindh Provincial Assembly in 1993. The faction argued
for a return to the original radical ideals of Zulfikar Ali Bhutto's PPP
and was critical both of Benazir's leadership and of Asif Ali Zardari's influence within the PPP. After her husband's death in a police encounter,
Ghinwa Bhutto took over as Chair of the party. The PPP(SB) ran 35 National Assembly candidates and 55 Sindh Provincial Assembly candidates in the 1997 polls. Despite the sympathy for Ghinwa in the interior
of Sind, she was defeated by Begum Bhutto in the Larkana constituency.
The PPP(SB) emerged with just one National Assembly seat and two
seats in the Sindh assembly.

PAKISTAN TEHRIK-E-INSAAF (PTI) This party was founded by Imran Khan in 1996 with the message of removing corruption from Pakistani politics and society. It grew out of the former international cricket
star's attacks on 'brown sahib' culture and his work for the Shaukat Khanum Memorial Cancer hospital. The mid-term polls took the party by

surprise, as *was* seen by the fact that in the absence of a grassroots structure it had to invite applications for election tickets through the post. In the end the PTI fielded 150 Nationl Assembly candidates and 300 candidates for the provincial assemblies. Many of these were youthful and inexperienced newcomers, although some opportunists joined the bandwagon hoping that Imran's media celebrity would carry them to victory. In the event the party failed to capture any National or Provincial Assembly seats. The lack of organisation and a local power-base was decisive. It also had to contend with the entrenched support for the PML(N) in many of the constituencies it was contesting. The party's prospects had not been helped by the 'Jewish money' and Sita White smears which surrounded its leader. In the immediate aftermath of the polls, Imran Khan gave every indication that he would carry on the fight to establish a political presence.

PUSHTUNKHWA MILLI AWAMI PARTY (PKMAP) This party was founded in the late 1960s by Khan Abdus Sarnad Khan Achakzai after his split with the NAP. Following his death in a bomb blast, his son Mahmood Khan Achakzai took over its leadership. He went into exile in Afghanistan in October 1983, but returned after the election of Benazir Bhutto. The party seeks support from Pushtuns resident in Balochistan and its primary demand is for the incorporation of the Pushtun areas of the province into a greater NWFP called Pushtunistan. In the 1997 elections the PKMAP captured just two Provincial Assembly seats.

SAWAAD-I-AZAM This militant Sunni organisation was formed in the increasingly sectarian atmosphere of the late I 970s. Under its leader Maulana Azam Asvandgar it sought to establish Pakistan as a Sunni Islamic state.

SIPAH-I-SAHABA-I-PAKISTAN Militant Sunni organisation which has been involved in violent clashes with Shia activists. A number of its leaders have been assassinated from the death of Muhammad Ghiasuddin in May 1992 onwards. The organisation's strength lies in its Jhang heartland.

TEHRIK-I-ISTIQLAL This party was founded in 1969 by the retired Air Marshal Asghar Khan who was a leading opponent of Ayub Khan. Its centrist position limited its appeal to a small urban middle-class following. Asghar Khan was defeated by Khurshid Hasan Mir of the PPP in the 1970 elections along with all the other TI candidates.

Asghar Khan remained in the opposition ranks during the Zulfikar Ali Bhutto era and returned to prominence at the time of the PNA agitation in 1977, although his party had again emerged seatless in the preceding elections. The Tehrik distanced itself from the Zia regime from the outset and joined the MRD in 1981. Asghar Khan found working within this

PPP-dominated alliance difficult and left the MRD in 1986. The following year his meeting with the Kabul Communist regime resulted in a number of Frontier and Balochistan leaders quitting the Tehrik. It was thus not surprising when the Tehrik-e-Istiqlal again failed to return a candidate in both the Provincial and National Assemblies in the 1988 elections.

The circumstances surrounding the dismissal of Benazir Bhutto's first administration led Asghar Khan to ally his party with the PPP in the PDA in the October 1990 elections. With the return of the PPP to power, the TI once more moved into opposition. It joined with the JI in boycotting the February 1997 polls.

TEHRIK-E-NIFAZ-E-FIQH-E-JAFRIA (TNFJ) The movement for the implementation of the Shia code was founded in 1979 in response to Zia's states-ponsored Islamisation which favoured *Sunnifiqh*. The movement was registered as a political party in 1987. Three years later it joined the PDA in opposition to the HI. By the time of the 1993 elections however it had split from the PPP, for which Shias nonetheless continued to vote. Its influence was further diminished by its factional divisions. TNFJ has been involved in violent clashes with SSP both in Karachi and in a number of Punjabi cities.

WOMEN'S ACTION FORUM (WAF) This organisation was founded in 1982 in the wake of the impact on women of Zia's Islamisation process. It was confined to upper-class and educated middle-class women. It was active in public protests in Lahore and was far more radical in its stance than APWA. By the mid-1990s it had atrophied as it failed to appeal to a younger generation. Many of its original members did, however, playa role in the foundation of NGOs such as the ASR Resource Centre in Lahore and the Aurat Foundation. War Against Rape was also founded in 1989 by a subcommittee of WAF. Its objectives included providing legal, medical and psychological support to rape victims.

SELECT BIBLIOGRAPHY

PRIVATE PAPERS

Caroe Papers, India Office Library, London, Mss. Eur F203.
Cunningham Papers, India Office Library, London Mss. Eur 0670.
Linlithgow Papers, India Office Library, London, Mss. Eur F125.
Mian Fazl-i-Husain Papers, India Office Library, London, Mss. Eur F325.
Mountbatten papers, University of Southampton.
Mudie Papers, India Office Library, London, Mss. Eur F164.
Quaid-e-Azarn Papers, National Archives of Pakistan, Islamabad.
Tiwana and Unionist Party Papers, University of Southampton.

GOVERNMENT RECORDS

India Office Library
Records of the Political and Secret Department 1928-47.
Records of the Public and Judicial Department 1929-47.
Records of the Military Department 1940-2.

National Archives of India
Records of the Home Political Department 1927-45.

National Archives at College Park
State Department Central Files 1960-3, 1964-6.

National Security Archives, George Washington University
LBJ Presidential Files Country Files (Pakistan).
India-Pakistan (4 boxes).

Freedom Movement Archives
All India Muslim League Records.
Committee of Action 1944-7.
Working Committee 1932-7.
Provincial Muslim League Records.

NEWSPAPERS AND JOURNALS

Dawn (Karachi)
The Nation (Lahore)
Herald (Karachi)
Newsline (Karachi)
Nawa-i-Waqt (Lahore)

498   *Select Bibliography*

INTERVIEWS

Alan Campbell-Johnson (1993)
Altaf Gauhar (1996)
Rafi Raza (1997)
Maleeha Lodhi (1996)
Robert Oakley (1996)
Selig Harrison (1996)
Altaf Hussain (1997)

Ahangar, Parveena, Founder of the Association of Parents of Disappeared Persons (APDP), Srinagar, July 2006.
Ahmad, Sheikh Nazir, General Secretary of the National Conference, April 2008.
Ali, Suraiya, Vice Chairperson of Behboodi Khwateen, an Organization for the Upliftment of Downtrodden Women and Children, Srinagar, March 2008.
Dhar, Amar Nath, Professor of English, and Scholar of Lalla-Ded's Religious Philosophy, April 2008.
Duda, P.N., Retired Senior Advocate of the Supreme Court of India, April 2008.
Firdous, Shamim, Former Member of the Legislative Council, Assembly of Indian Administered Jammu and Kashmir, and Current President of the Women's Wing of the National Conference, Srinagar, July 2006.
Malik, Yaseen, Chairman of the Breakaway Faction of the Jammu and Kashmir Liberation Front, April 2008.
Mattoo, Neerja, Emeritus Professor of English at Maulana Azad Government College for Women, Srinagar, April 2008.
Misri, Krishna, Former Principal of Government College for Women, Nawakadal, Srinagar, and Maulana Azad Government College for Women, Srinagar, April 2008.
Naeem, Hameeda, Professor of English at the University of Kashmir and Human Rights Activist, Srinagar, July 2006.
Pathani, Begum, Gujjar Matriarch, Srinagar, July 2006.
Political Activists of the National Conference and the People's Democratic Party, Srinagar, July 2006 and 2007.
Rehmani, Mohammad Farooq, Convener of the Pakistan Chapter of the All Parties Hurriyat Conference (APHC) and Chairman of the Jammu and Kashmir People's League, April 2008.
Shah, G. M. Former Chief Minister of Indian Administered Jammu and Kashmir, and President of Awami National Conference, April 2008.
Singh, Karan, Former Crown Prince of the Princely State of Jammu and Kashmir and Sadr-i-Riyasat (Governor) of Indian Administered Jammu and Kashmir, New Delhi, July 2007.
Wahid, A., Retired Chair of the Department of Internal Medicine, Sher-i-Kashmir Institute of Medical Sciences, Srinagar, March 2008.
Zameer, Sajjida, Member of the 1947 Women's Militia Organized by the National Conference, and Former Director of the Education Department, Indian administered Jammu and Kashmir, April 2008.

International Documents

Amnesty International. *"If They are Dead Tell Us": Disappearances in Jammu and Kashmir*. London: Amnesty International, Feb. 1999.
———. "India." November 2005. http://web.amnesty.org/report2004/ind-summary-eng (accessed December 15, 2005).
———. "India Must Prevent Torture." *Article*, 1995. Kashmiri-Canadian Council, November 2005. http://www.kashmiri-cc.ca/quarterly/kq2–4/AMNESTY2.htm (accessed January 10, 2007).
Asia Watch, Reports, June 1993.
Census of India, 1981. Series 1: India. Part II-B (i). New Delhi: Office of the Registrar General, 1983.
Human Rights in Kashmir, Report of a Mission, International Commission of Jurists, Geneva, November 1994.
Human Rights Commission of Pakistan, January 1994 *Newsletter*.
Indiagram, The Embassy of India, Washington D.C., No. 333, November 18, 1953.
Security Council Official Records, Third Year, Nos. 1–15, 65.
Speeches and Interviews of Sher-e-Kashmir Sheikh Mohammad Abdullah. Srinagar: Jammu and Kashmir Plebiscite Front, 1968. 2 vols.
United Nations Security Council. *Security Council Official Records*. United Nations Publishing. Third Year. Nos. 1–15.

Speeches on the Status of Jammu and Kashmir within the Indian Union, 1951–1954

Opening Address by Honorable Sheikh Mohammad Abdullah, Jammu and Kashmir Constituent Assembly, Srinagar, 1951.
Nehru, Jawaharlal. Speech on the Floor of the Indian Parliament. 11 Aug. 1951. Vol. 2 of *Jawaharlal Nehru's Speeches: 1949–1953* (Delhi: Government of India, 1963).
Nehru, Jawaharlal. Speech. 17 Sept. 1953.
———. Speech. House of the People, 29 Dec. 1953

Books

Abdullah, Farooq. *My Dismissal*. Delhi: Vikas, 1985.
Abdullah, Sheikh Mohammad. *Flames of the Chinar: An Autobiography*. Translated by Khushwant Singh. New York: Viking, 1993.
Aitchinson, C. V., ed. *A Collection of Treaties, Engagements and Sanads, Vol. XII Part I*. Calcutta: Government of India Central Publication Branch, 1931.
Akbar, M.J. *India, The Siege Within: Challenges to a Nation's Unity*. New York: Penguin, 1985.
Ali, Tariq. "The Story of Kashmir." In *The Clash of Fundamentalisms: Crusades, Jihads and Modernity*, 217–52.. London: Verso, 2003.
Bamzai, Prem Nath Kaul. *Culture and Political History of Kashmir*. Delhi: M.D. Publications, 1994. 3 vols.
Bazaz, Prem Nath. *Daughters of the Vitasta*. New Delhi: Pamposh Publications, 1959. Reprint, Srinagar: Gulshan Books, 2005. Page references are to the 2005 edition.

———. *Inside Kashmir*. Mirpur, Azad Kashmir: Verinag Publishers,1941. Reprint, Srinagar: Gulshan Publishers, 2002. Page references are to the 2002 edition.

———. *Kashmir in Crucible*. New Delhi: Pamposh Publications, 1967. Reprint, Srinagar: Gulshan Books, 2005. Page references are to the 2005 edition.

———. *Truth about Kashmir*. Delhi: Kashmir Democratic Union, 1950.

Behera, Navnita Chadha. *Demystifying Kashmir*. Washington, D. C.: Brookings Institution Press, 2006

Bhattacharjea, Ajit. *Kashmir: The Wounded Valley*. New Delhi: U.B.S. Publishers, 1994.

Bose, Sumantra. "Hindu Nationalism and the Crisis of the Indian State: A Theoretical Perspective." In *Nationalism, Democracy and Development: State and Politics in India*. Edited by Sugata Bose and Ayesha Jalal, 104–164. Delhi: Oxford University Press, 1997.

Bose, Sumantra. *Kashmir: Roots of Conflict, Paths to Peace*. Cambridge: Harvard University Press, 2003.

Bose, Tapan, et al. "India's Kashmir War." In *Secular Crown on Fire: The Kashmir Problem*. Edited by Ashghar Ali Engineer, 224–253. Delhi: Ajanta, 1991.

Brecher, Michael. *The Struggle for Kashmir*. Toronto: Ryerson Press, 1953.

Butalia, Urvashi, ed., *Speaking Peace: Women's Voices From Kashmir*. Delhi: Kali for Women, 2002.

Butler, Judith. *Bodies that Matter: On the Discursive Limits of "Sex."* New York: Routledge, 1993.

Chadha, Vivek. *Low Intensity Conflicts in India: an Analysis*. New Delhi: Sage Publications, 2005.

Chengappa, Raj. "End the Wink and Nudge Approach." In *Weapons of Peace: The Secret Story of India's Quest to be a Nuclear Power*, 352–366. New Delhi: Harper Collins Publishing India, 2000.

Clifford, James and George E. Marcus ed. *Writing Vulture: The Politics of Ethnography*. Berkley: University of California Press, 1986.

"'Cloth' saith Custom. Doth that sanctify?" In *The Word of Lalla the Prophetess*. Translated by R.C. Temple. London: Cambridge University Press, 1924. Reprint with introduction by Shafi Shauq. Srinagar: Gulshan Books, 172–173. Page references are to the 2005 edition.

Cohen, Stephen P. *The Idea of Pakistan*. Washington: Brookings Institution Press, 2004.

Copeland, Ian. "The Abdullah Factor: Kashmiri Muslims and the 1947 Crisis." In *Political Inheritance of Pakistan*. Edited by D. A. Low, 218–254. London: Macmillan, 1991.

Das Gupta, Jyoti Bhusan. *Jammu and Kashmir*. The Hague: Martinus Nijhoff, 1968.

Gandhi, Leela. *Postcolonial Theory: A Critical Introduction*. New York: Columbia, 1998.

Ganguly, Sumit. *The Crisis in Kashmir: Portents of War, Hopes of Peace*. New York: Woodrow Wilson Center Press, 1997.

Ganju, M. *Textile Industry in Kashmir*. New Delhi: Premier Publishing Company, 1945.

Gottlieb, Gidon. *Nation against State: A New Approach to Ethnic Conflicts and the Decline of Sovereignity.* New York: Council on Foreign Relations, 1993.

Grierson, G.A. *Standard Manual of the Kashmiri Language.* Calcutta: Asiatic Society, 1911. 2 vols.

Gupta, S. *Kashmir: A Study in India-Pakistan Relations.* Bombay: Asia Publishing House, 1966.

Hagerty, Devin T. *South Asia in World Politics.* Lanham, MD: Rowman and Littlefield, 2005.

Hassnain, F. M. *Freedom Struggle in Kashmir.* New Delhi: Rima Publishing House, 1988.

Hoodbhoy, Pervez Amirali and Abdul Hameed Nayyar. "Rewriting the History of Pakistan." In *Islam, Politics, and the State: The Pakistan Experience,* edited by Asghar Khan, 164–177. London: Zed Books, 1985.

Jain, R.K. ed. *Soviet-South Asian Relations: 1947–1978.* Vol. 1. Atlantic Highlands, N.J.: Humanities Press, 1979. 2 vols.

Jayawardena, Kumari. *Feminism and Nationalism in the Third World.* London: Zed Books, 1986.

Jha, Prem Shanker. *Kashmir, 1947: Rival Versions of History.* Bombay: Oxford University Press, 1996.

Kampani, Gaurav. "Kashmir and India-Pakistan Nuclear Issues." In *South Asia in World Politics.* Edited by Devin T. Hagerty, 161–186. New York: Rowman and Littlefield Publishers, 2005.

Karim, W. "The Nativised Self and the Native." In *Gendered Fields: Women, Men and Ethnography.* Edited by D.P.C. Bell and E.J. Karim, 248–251. London: Routledge, 1993.

Kaul, R. N. *Kashmir's Mystic: Poetess Lalla Ded, Alias Lalla Arifa.* New Delhi: S. Chand and Co., 1999.

Kaura, Uma. *Muslims and Indian Nationalism: The Emergence of the Demand for India's Partition 1928–40.* Columbia: South Asia Books, 1977.

Kaw, M. K., ed. *Kashmir and its People: Studies in the Evolution of Kashmiri Society.* New Delhi: A.P.H., 2004.

Khan, Amanullah. *Free Kashmir.* Karachi: Central Printing Press, 1970.

Khan, Mohammad Ishaq. *History of Srinagar, 1846–1947: A Study in Socio-Cultural Change.* Ann Arbor, MI: University of Michigan Press, 1978.

———. *Kashmir's Transition to Islam: The Role of Muslim Rishis.* New Deli: Manohar, 1994.

Khan, M. Zafarullah. *The Kashmir Dispute.* Karachi: Institute of International Affairs, 1958.

Kishwar, Madhu. *Religion at the Service of Nationalism and Other Essays.* Delhi: Oxford University Press, 1998.

Kodikara, Sheldon U. "South Asian Security Dilemmas in the Post-Cold War World." In *South Asia after the Cold War: International Perspectives.* Edited by Kanti P. Bajpai and Stephen P., 47–65. Cohen. Boulder, CO: Westview Press, 1993.

502   *Select Bibliography*

Korbel, Josef. *Danger in Kashmir*. Princeton: Princeton University Press, 1954. Reprint, New York: Oxford University Press, 2002. Page references are to the 2002 edition.

Krishen, Rajbans. *Kashmir and the Conspiracy Against Peace*. Bombay: People's Publishing House, 1951.

Kumari, Abhilasha, and Sabina Kidwai. *Crossing the Sacred Line: Women's Search for Political Power*. New Delhi: Orient Longman Publishing, 1998.

"Lal Ded's Vakhs." *Kashmiri Saints and Sages: Ancient and Modern Ascetics in Kashmir.* Kashmir Overseas Association Inc. http://www.koausa.org/Saints/LalDed/Vakhs1.html, (accessed March 2005).

Lamb, Alastair. *Kashmir: A Disputed Legacy, 1846–1990.* Hertingfordbury: Roxford Books, 1991.

Lawrence, Walter R. *The Valley of Kashmir*. London: H. Frowde, 1895. Reprint, Srinagar: Gulshan Books, 2005. Page references are to the 2005 edition.

Madhok, Balraj.*Kashmir: Center of New Alignments*. New Delhi: Deepak, 1963.

Mahjoor, Ghulam Ahmad. "Vwolo Haa Baagvaano," [Come, Gardener!]. Translated and edited by Trilokinath Raina. *An Anthology of Modern Kashmiri Verse (1930–1960)*.Poona: Sangam Press, 1972.

Malik, Iffat. *Kashmir: Ethnic Conflict International Dispute*. Karachi: Oxford University Press, 2002.

Margolio, Eric S. *War at the Top of the World: The Struggle for Afghanistan, Kashmir, and Tibet*. Toronto: Key Porter Books, 1999.

McClintock, Ann. *Dangerous Liasons: Gender, Nation and Postcolonial Perspective*. Minneapolis: University of Minnesota Press, 1997.

Mehta, Jagat S. "Resolving Kashmir in the International Context of the 1990s." In *Perspectives on Kashmir: The Roots of Conflict in South Asia*. Edited by. Raju G. C. Thomas, 388–409. Boulder: Westview Press, 1992.

Minh-ha, Trin T. *Woman, Native, Other*. Bloomington: Indiana University Press, 1989.

Mir, Imraan. *A New Kashmir: Religion, Education and the Roots of Social Disintegration*. Napa Valley: Valley House Books, 2003.

Mohanty, Chandra. *Third World Women and the Politics of Feminism*. Bloomington, IN: Indian University Press, 1991.

Murphy, Paul E. *Triadic Mysticism: The Mystical Theology of the Saivism of Kashmir*. New ed. Columbia: South Asia Books, 1999.

Nandy, Ashis, et al. *Exiled at Home: Comprising, at the Edge of Psychology, the Intimate Enemy, Creating a Nationality*. New York: Oxford University Press, 1998.

———. *The Intimate Enemy: Loss and Recovery of Self Under Colonialism*. Oxford: Oxford University Press, 1983.

Natsional'nyi Vopros I Angliiskii Imperialism v Indii. Ogiz, 1948.

Newberg, Paula R. *Double Betrayal: Repression and Insurgency in Kashmir*. Washington DC: Carnegie Endowment for International Peace, 1995.

Noorani, A.G. *The Kashmir Question*. Bombay: Manaktalas, 1964.

Parimoo, B. N. *The Ascent of Self: A Reinterpretation of the Mystical Poetry of Lalla-Ded*. Delhi: Motilal Banarsidaas, 1978.

Perkovich, George. *India's Nuclear Bomb: The Impact on Global Proliferation.* Berkeley: University of California Press, 1999.

Puri, Balraj. *Jammu and Kashmir: Triumph and Tragedy of Indian Federalism.* Delhi: Sterling, 1981.

———. *Kashmir: Towards Insurgency.* New Delhi: Orient Longman, 1995.

Qasim, Syed Mir. *My Life and Times.* New Delhi: Allied Publishers, 1992.

Rahman, Mushtaqur. *Divided Kashmir: Old Problems, New Opportunities for India, Pakistan, and the Kashmiri People.* Boulder: Lynne Rienner, 1996.

Rai, Mridu. *Hindu Rulers, Muslim Subjects: Islam, Rights, and the History of Kashmir.* Princeton: Princeton University Press, 2004.

Ray, Sangeet. *En-Gendering India: Woman and Nation in Colonial and Postcolonial Narratives.* Durham: Duke University Press, 2000.

Ray, Sunil Chandra. *Early History and Culture of Kashmir.* New Delhi: Munshiram Manoharlal, 1970.

Razdan, P. N. *Gems of Kashmiri Literature and Kashmiriyat, the Trio of Saint Poets.* New Delhi: Samkaleen, 1999.

Rogers, A., trans. *The Tuzuk-i-Jahangir or Memoirs of Jahangir.* Ed. H. Beveridge.Vol. 2. London: Royal Asiatic Society, 1914. 2 vols.

Rushdie, Salman. "The Assassination of Indira Gandhi." In *Imaginary Homelands: Essays and Criticism 1981–91*, 41–6. London: Granta Books, 1991.

———. *Shalimar the Clown.* New York: Random House, 2005.

Said, Edward. *Culture and Imperialism.* New York: Knopf: Distributed by Random House, 1991.

Saxena, Hari Lal. *The Tragedy of Kashmir.* New Delhi: Nationalist Publishers, 1975.

Schofield, Victoria. *Kashmir in Conflict: India, Pakistan and the Unending War.* 2nd rev. ed. London: I. B. Tauris, 2002.

Singh, Karan. *Karan Singh: Autobiography.* New Delhi: Oxford University Press, 1994.

Sibtain, Tahira. "The Genesis of the Kashmir Dispute." In *Kashmir: Now or Never.* Edited by, Abdul Hafeez Touquir. Islamabad: National Book Foundation, 1992.

Singh, Tavleen. *Kashmir, A Tragedy of Errors.* New Delhi: Viking, 1995.

Smith, Vincent H. *The Oxford History of India.* Oxford: Clarendon Press, 1928.

Soz, Saifuddin. *Why Autonomy to Kashmir?* New Delhi: India Centre of Asian Studies, 1995.

Spivak, Gayatri Chakravorty. *Critique of Postcolonial Reason: Toward a History of the Vanishing Present.* Cambridge: Harvard University Press, 1999.

Stromquist, Nelly P. "The Theoretical and Practical Bases for Empowerment." In *Women, Education and Empowerment: Pathways towards Autonomy.* Edited by Carolyn Medel-Anonuevo, 12–22. Hamburg: UNESCO Institute for Education, 1995.

Sufi, Ghulam Muhyi'd Din. *Islamic Culture in Kashmir.* New Delhi: Capital Publishing House, 1979.

—. *Kashir, Being a History of Kashmir From the Earliest Times to Our Own.* 2nd ed. New Delhi: Light & Life Publishers, 1974. 2 vols.

504 Select Bibliography

Talbot, Ian. *Pakistan: A Modern History*. London: C. Hurst, 1999.

Taseer, Bilquis C. *The Kashmir of Sheikh Mohammad Abdullah*. Lahore: Feroze Sons, 1986.

Tellis, Ashley. *Stability in South Asia: Prospect of Indo-Pak Nuclear Conflict*. Dehradun: Natrag Publishers, 2001.

———. "Toward a Force-in-Being: Understanding India's Nuclear Doctrine and Future Force Posture." In *India's Emerging Nuclear Posture: Between Recessed Deterrent and Ready Arsenal*, 251–475. Santa Monica: Rand, 2001.

Temple, Richard Carnac. *The Word of Lalla the Prophetess*. London: Cambridge University Press, 1924. Reprinted with introduction by Shafi Shauq. Srinagar: Gulshan Books, 172–173. Page references are to the 2005 edition.

Verghese, B. G. "Kashmir: The Fourth Option," *Defence Today* 1:1 (1993). Quoted in Robert Wirsing. *India, Pakistan, and the Kashmir Dispute*. 229. New York: St. Martin's Press, 1994.

Verma, P. S. *Jammu and Kashmir at the Crossroads*. New Delhi: Viking, 1994.

Widmalm, Sten. *Kashmir in Comparitive Perspective: Democracy and Violent Separatism in Kashmir*. New York: Routledge, 2002.

Wirsing, Robert. *India, Pakistan, and the Kashmir Dispute*. New York: St. Martin's Press, 1994.

Younghusband, Sir Francis. *Kashmir*. New Delhi: Sagar, 1970.

Ziring, Lawrence. *Pakistan in the 20thCentury: A Political History*. New York: Oxford University Press, 2000.

Zutshi, Chitralekha. *Languages of Belonging: Islam, Regional Identity, and the Making of Kashmir*. New York: Oxford University Press, 2004.

Articles

"Another Pugwash on Kashmir." *Daily Etalaat*, April 3, 2008, http://etalaat.net/english/?p=10 (accessed April 8, 2008).

Akhtar, Shaheen. "Elections in Indian-held Kashmir, 1951–1999." *Regional Studies* 18.3 (2000): 12–29.

Armitage, Richard. Interview. PBS transcript. Aug 30, 2002. http://www.outlook-india.com, (accessed July 4, 2006).

"Army Commanding Officer, Bodyguards Killed in Blast," *Kashmir Times*, August 20, 2002. http://www.kashmirtimes.com/archive/0208/020820/index.htm, (July 2004).

Barve, Sushobha. "Bridging Divides." *Dawn*, February 5, 2008. http://www.dawn.com/2008/02/05/op.htm, (accessed March 12, 2008).

Battye, Michael. "Angry India Accuses U.S. Tilt to Pakistan." *Reuters*, October 30, 1993.

Bisnath, S., and D. Elson. "Women's Empowerment Revisited." UNIFEM. November 2002. http://www.undp.org/unifem/progressww/empower.html (accessed August 10, 2006).

Bhagat, Pamela. "Women in Kashmir: Citizens at Last." *Boloji Media*. November 2005. http://www.boloji.com/wfs/wfs110.htm (accessed November 2005).

Bhatnagar, Rashmi Dube, Renu Dube, and Reena Dube. "Meera's Medieval Lyric Poetry in Postcolonial India: The Rhetorics of Women's Writing in Dialect as a Secular Practice of Subaltern Coauthorship and Dissent." *Boundary 2* 31.3 (2004): 1–46.

Chaudhuri, Pramit Pal. "Why a War against Terrorism Has Pakistan Terrified." *Hindustan Times* [Delhi], September 16, 2001. www.hindustantimes.com; http://www.ofbjp.org.news/0901/10html (accessed August 2006).

Das, Tarakhnath. "The Kashmir Issue and the United Nations." *Political Science Quarterly 65.2* (1950).

Delhi Express January 1, 1952.

"Delhi Positions Missiles on Border." *Dawn*, December 27, 2001. http://www.dawn.com/2001/12/27/top4.htm (accessed December 2007).

Delhi Radio. Indian Information Service, Delhi. 31 Mar. 1952.

Desmond, Edward W. "The Insurgency in Kashmir 1989–1991." *Contemporary South Asia* 4.1 (1995): 5–16.

"Eleven Policemen Indicted for Custodial Murder of Two Civilians." *Greater Kashmir*, March 20, 2008, http://www.greaterkashmir.net/full_story.asp?Date 21_4_2008&ItemID=22&cat=1, (accessed March 20, 2008).

"Family Seeks Whereabouts of Youth." *Greater Kashmir*, March 25, 2008. http://www.greaterkashmir.com/full_story.asp?Date=26_3_2008&ItemID=54&cat=14 (accessed March 20, 2008).

"Five Lecturers Among 30 Injured: Protests Continue in Sopur. " *Greater Kashmir*, September 13, 2007. http://www.greaterkashmir.com/full_story.asp?Date=14_9_2007&ItemID=52&cat=1 (accessed December 2007).

"Foreign Minister Speaks on Kashmir Issue, NPT, Relations with India, USA." *BBC Summary of World Broadcasts*, January 10, 1995. http://web.lexis-nexis.com (accessed August 2006).

Friese, Kai. "Hijacking India's History." *New York Times*, sec. A: 17, December 30, 2002.

"GOI Responsible for Exodus of Kashmiri Pandits." *Greater Kashmir*, November 12, 2007. http://www.greaterkashmir.com/full_story.asp?Date=13_11_20 07&ItemID=23&cat=1 (accessed November 12, 2007).

"Grave Concern." *Greater Kashmir*, March 31, 2008. http://www.greaterkashmir.com/fullstory.asp?Date=10_4_2008&ItemID=15&cat=10 (accessed November 12, 2007).

Guha, Ramachandra. "Opening a Window in Kashmir." *World Policy Journal, Reconsiderations* 21.3 (2004): 1–17.

Hayward, C. R. "De-facing Power." *Polity* 31 (1998): 22–34.

The Hindu, [Madras, India], March 26, 1952.

The Hindustan Times [Delhi], October 26, 1953.

India Today March 31, 1987, 26; April 15, 1987, 40–3; November 15, 1983, 43; April 30, 1990, 10; March 31, 1993, 27.

Iqbal, Anwar. "Outgoing Prime Minister Says Kashmir at Root of Nuclear Arms Race." United Press International, October 18, 1993 http://web.lexis-nexis.com.

Johnson, Robert. "Russians at the Gates of India? Planning the Defense of India, 1885–1900." *The Journal of Military History* 67.7 (2003): 697–743.

Kabeer, N. "Resources, Agency, Achievements: Reflections on the Measurement of Women's Empowerment." *Development and Change* 30 (1999): 435–64.

Kampani, Guarav. "India's Compellence Strategy." *CNN Research Story of the Week*, June 10, 2002. http://cns.miis.edu/pubs/week/020610.htm (accessed November 2007).

Kashmir Human Rights. "Impact of Conflict on Children and Women in Kashmir," http://kashmirahrchk.net/mainfilephp/articles.45 (accessed November 2005).

Kashmiri Women's Initiative for Peace and Disarmament. "Probe Gimmick." *Voices Unheard: A Magazine*. http://www.geocities.com/kwipd2002 (accessed November 2005).

Kelly, John H. "Prepared statement by John H. Kelly, assistant secretary for Near Eastern and South Asian Affairs before Subcommittee on Asian and Pacific Affairs, House Foreign Affairs Committee." U.S. Department of State, November 2, 1990. http://web.lexis-nexis.com (accessed April 2, 2008).

Kohli, Atul. "Can Democracies Accommodate Ethnic Nationalism? Rise and Decline of Self-Determination Movements in India." *Journal of Asian Studies* 56 (1997): 325–44.

Lok Sabha. "Obituary References." 2000. http://parliamentofindia.nic.in/lsdeb/ls13/ses4/24072.htm,(accessed August 2005).

The London Times, September 6, 1950.

Mattoo, Neerja. "Lalla-Ded as the Voice of the Marginalized," Paper presented at the Series on Mystic Masters. India International Center, New Delhi, India, March 2007.

"Militancy in Kashmir Valley Completes Fourteen Years." *Kashmir Times* August 1, 2002, http://www.kashmirtimes.com/archive/0208/020801/index.htm (accessed March 2004).

Misri, Krishna. "Kashmiri Women Down the Ages: A Gender Perspective." *Himalayan and Central Asian Studies* 6.3–4 (2002): 3–27.

Pickering, Sharon. "Undermining the Sanitized Accounts: Violence and Emotionality in the Field in Northern Ireland." *The British Journal of Criminology* 41 (2001): 485–501.

Prasad, Shally. "Medicolegal Response to Violence Against Women in India." *Violence Against Women* 5 (1999):478–507.

Puri, Balraj. "Analysis of the J & K Permanent Resident Bill." *PUCL Bulletin*. April 2004. PUCL. http://www.pucl.org/Topics/Law/2004/jk-pr-bill.htm (accessed November 2005).

Ramachandran, Sudha, "Suicide, just another way to fight in Kashmir." *Asia Times Online*. July 24, 2002, http://www.atimes.com/atimes/South_Asia/DG24Df02.html, (accessed March 2008).

Reuters. "Pakistan Court Expected to Rule on Gang-Rape Case." *Khaleej Times*, August 27, 2002. http://www.khaleejtimes.co.ae/ktarchive/270802/subcont.htm (accessed August 24, 2007).

Rushbrook-Williams, L. F. "Inside Kashmir." *International Affairs* 33.1 (1957): 26–35.

Schofield, Victoria. "Pakistan's Northern Areas Dilemma." BBC News, August 15, 2001. *BBC News Online.* http://news.bbc.co.uk/1/hi/world/south_asia/1491179.stm (accessed March 15, 2008).

"Sentimental Return for Pandits." *Tribune News Service* 2000, http://www.tribuneindia.com/2000/20000610/j&k.htm#3, (accessed January 2008).

Sherif, Bahira. "The Ambiguity of Boundaries in the Fieldwork Experience: Establishing Rapport and Negotiating Insider/Outsider Status." *Qualitative Inquiry* 7.4 (2001): 436–47.

"Soldiers Go Berserk in Pulwama." *Greater Kashmir*, September 13, 2007. http://www.greaterkashmir.com/NewsItem.asp?Date=14_9_2007&Show=1 (accessed January 2008).

"Statement Unrealistic." *Greater Kashmir*, March 22, 2008, http://www.greaterkashmir.net/NewsItem.asp?Date=3_3_2008&Show=10, (accessed March, 2008).

The Statesman. [Calcutta], September 15, 1950: 16.

Talbott, Strobe. Interview. *Hindu* [Chennai, India] 14 Jan. 2000, http://www.hinduonnet.com.

"Text of PM, Musharraf Statement." *Hindu* [Chennai, India], January 6, 2004, http://www.hindu.com/2004/01/07/stories/2004010706041100.htm, (accessed July 2007).

The Times [London], April 26, 1952.

"U.S.—South Asia: Relations under Bush." *Oxford Analytica* 2001 http://www.brook.edu, (accessed March 2008).

Whitehead, Andrew. "Kashmir's Conflicting Identities." *History Workshop Journal* 58 (2004): 335–40.

Wirsing, Robert. "Kashmir in the Terrorist Shadow." *Asian Affairs* 33.1 (2002): 91–7.

ADDENDUM

PUBLICATIONS SINCE FIRST EDITION

Adeney, Katharine, *Federalism and Ethnic Conflict Resolution in India and Pakistan* (New York, 2007).

Afzal, M. Rafique, *Pakistan History lind Politics, 1947-1971* (Karachi, 2001).

Ahmed, Ishtiaq, 'The Pakistan Federal Cabinet: More of the Same or Something, New?' *ISAS Insights* 27 (11 April 2008).

Akhund, Iqbal, *Trial and Error: The Advent and Eclipse of Benazir Bhutto* (Karachi,2000).

Arnin, Shahid M., *Pakistan's Foreign Policy A Reappraisal* (Karachi, 2000).

Arif, K. M., *Khaki Shadows: The Pakistan Army, 1947-1997* (Karachi, 2000).

Baxter, Craig, *Pakistan on the Brink: Politics, Economics and Society* (Lanham, MD,2004).

Bhutto, Benazir, *Daughter of the East: An Autobiography* revised edition (London, 2007).

Reconciliation: Islam, Democracy and the West (London, 2008).

Cohen, Stephen Philip, *The Idea of Pakistan* (Oxford, 2004).

Correra, Gordon, *Shopping for Bombs: Nuclear Proliferation, Global Insecurity and the Rise and Fall of the A.Q. Khan Network* (London, 2006).

Daechsel, Markus, *The Politics of Self-Expression: The Urdu Middle Class Milieu In Mid-Twentieth Century India and Pakistan* (London, 2006).

EU Election Observation Mission Pakistan, *Final Report* (Islamabad, 2008).

Faruqui, Ahmad, *Rethinking the National security of Pakistan* (Aldershot, 2003).

Ganguly, Sumit, *Conflict Unending: India-Pakistan Tensions since 1947* (New York, 200 I).

Grare, Frederic, *Rethinking Western Strategies Towards Pakistan: An Action Agenda for the United States and Europe* (Washington DC, 2007).

Haqqani, Husain, *Pakistan: between Mosque and Military* (Lahore, 2005).

Hassan, Abbas, *Pakistan's Drift into Extremism: Allah, the Army and America's War On Terror* (Armonk N.Y. 2005).

Hussain, Zahid, *Frontline Pakistan: The Struggle with Militant Islam* (London, 2007), *Frontline Pakistan: The path to the catastrophe and killing of Benazir Bhutto* (London, 2008).

International Crisis Group, *After Bhutto's Murder: A Way Forward for Pakistan* (Islamabad/Brussels, 2008).

Jaffrelot, Christophe (ed.), *A History of Pakistan and its Origins* (London, 2002).

———, *Pakistan: Nationalism without a Nation?* (New Delhi, 2002).

Jamie, Kathleen, *Among Muslims: Meetings at the Frontiers of Pakistan* (London, 2002).

Jones, Owen Bennett, *Pakistan: Edge of the Storm* (Lahore, 2002).

Jones, Philip E., *The Pakistan People's Party Rise to Power* (Karachi, 2003).

Kazimi, Muhammad Reza, *Liaquat Ali Khan: His Life and Work* (Karachi, 2003).

Kennedy, Charles H., Kathleen McNeill, Carl Ernst, David Gilmartin (eds), *Pakistan at the Millennium* (Karachi, 2003).

Khan, Adeel, *Politics of Identity: Ethnic Nationalism and the State n Pakistan* (London, 2005).

Khan, M. Asghar, *We've Learnt Nothing from History: Pakistan-Politics and Military Power* (Karachi, 2005).

Khan, Yasmin, *The Great Partition: The Making of India and Pakistan* (Yale, 2007).

Khan, Gul Hassan, *Memoirs of Lt. General Gul Hassan Khan*, Karachi: Oxford University Press, 1993.

Malik, Iftikhar Haider, *Culture and Customs of Pakistan* (Westport, Conn. 2005).

Mazari, Sherbaz Khan, *A Journey to Disillusionment* (Karachi, 2000).

Mazari, Shireen M., *The Kargil Conflict. 1999: Separating Fact from Fiction* (Islamabad, 2003).

Select Bibliography 509

Mumtaz, Soofia, Jean-Luc Racine, Imran Anwar Ali (eds), *Pakistan: The Contours of State and Society* (Karachi, 2002).

Musharraf, Pervez, *In the Line of Fire: A Memoir* (London, 2006).

Nadeem, Azhar Hassan, *Pakistan: The Political Economy of Lawlessness* (Karachi, 2002).

Nasr, Sayyed Yali Reza, *Maududi and the Making of Islamic Revivalism*, New York: Oxford University Press, 1996.

Niazi, Amir Abdullah Khan, *The Betrayal of East Pakistan*, Karachi: Oxford University Press, 1998.

Pande, Sivita, *Politics of Ethnic and Religious Minorities in Pakistan* (New Delhi, 2005).

Pandey, Gyanendra & Samad, Yunas, *Fault Lines of Nationhood* (Delhi, 2007).

Paul, T.V. *The India-Pakistan Conflict: An Enduring Rivalry* (Cambridge, 2005).

Patel, Dorab, *Testament of a Liberal* (Karachi, 2000).

Pirzada, Sayyid, A. S., *The Politics of Jamiat-i-ulema-i-Islam Pakistan. 1971-1977* (Karachi, 2000).

Rahman, Tariq, *Language and Politics in Pakistan* (Karachi, 1996).

Sayeed, K. B., *Western Dominance and Political Islam: Challenge and Response*, Albany: State University of New York Press, 1995.

Siddiqa, Ayesha, *Military Inc. Inside Pakistan's Military Economy* (London/ Anne Arbor 2007).

Swami, Praveen, *India, Pakistan and the Secret Jihad: The Covert War in Kashmir 1947–2001* (Milton Park, Abingdon, 2007).

Syed, Anwar Hussain, *The Discourse and Politics of Zulfiqar Ali Bhutto*, Basingstoke: Macmillan, 1992.

Talbot, Ian, *Divided Cities: Partition and its Aftermath in Lahore and Amritsar 1947–1957* (Karachi, 2006) (ed) *The Deadly Embrace: Religion, Politics and Violence in India and Pakistan, 1947–2002* (Karachi, 2007).

————, 'Pakistan in 2002: Democracy, Terrorism, Brinkmanship', *Asian Survey* 43, I (January/February 2003), pp. 198-208.

————, 'Pakistan in 2003: Political Deadlock and Continuing Uncertainties', *Asian Survey* 44, 1 (January/February 2004), pp. 36-43.

Weiss, Anita, M. Gilani and S. Zulfiqar (eds), *Power and Civil Society in Pakistan* (Karachi, 2001).

Wirsing, Robert, 'Pakistan's Transformation: Why it Will Not (and need not) Happen', *Asia-Pacific Centre for Security Studies* 4, 2 (2005), pp. 1–6.

Zaheer, Hasan, *The Times and Trial of the Rawalpindi Conspiracy, 1951: The First Coup Attempt in Pakistan*, Karachi: Oxford University Press, 1998.

Ziring, Lawrence, *Pakistan: At the Crosscurrent oj History* (Oxford, 2003).

PRINTED SECONDARY WORKS

Abbasi, Nasreen, *Urbanisation in Pakistan, 1951-1981* (Islamabad, 1987).

Ahmad, Aijaz, 'The Rebellion of 1983: A Balance Sheet', *South Asia Bulletin*, 4, no I (spring 1984), pp. 27-44.

Ahmad, Farid, *The Sun Behind the Clouds* (Dhaka, n.d).

Ahmad, Iftikhar, *Pakistan General Elections 1970* (Lahore, 1976).

Ahmad, Manzooruddin (ed.), *Contemporary Pakistan: Politics Economy and Society* (Karachi, 1982).

Ahmad, Syed Nur, *From Martial Law to Martial Law: Politics in the Punjab 1919-1958* (Boulder, CO, 1985).

Ahsan, Aitzaz, *The Indus Saga and the Making of Pakistan* (Karachi, 1996).

Akhtar, Rafiq, *Pakistan Year Book, 1987-88* (Karachi, 1987).

Akhtar, Rashid, *Elections '77 and Aftermath: A Political Appraisal* (Islamabad, 1981).

Alavi, Hamza, 'Nationhood and Communal Violence in Pakistan', *Journal of Contemporary Asia*, 21, 2 (1991), pp. 152-78.

Ali, Imran, *The Punjab under Imperialism, 1885-1947* (Princeton, 1988).

Ali, Tariq, *Can Pakistan Survive? The Death of a State* (Harmondsworth, 1983).

Amin, Tahir, 'Pakistan in 1993: Some Dramatic Changes', *Asian Survey 34*, 2 (February 1994), pp. 191-9.

————, 'Pakistan in 1994: The Politics of Confrontation', *Asian Survey* 35, 2 (February 1995), pp. 140-6.

Ansari, Sarah, *Sufi Saints and State Power: The pirs of Sind, 1843-1947* (Cambridge, 1992).

Arif, Gen. KM., *Working With Zia: Pakistan's Power Politics 1977-1988* (Karachi, 1995).

Ayoob, Muhammad, 'Dateline Pakistan: A Passage to Anarchy?', *Foreign Policy* 59 (summer 1985), pp. 154-73.

Ballard, Roger, 'The Context and Consequences of Migration: Jullundur and Mirpur compared', *New Community* II, 1/2 (autumn/winter 1983), pp. 117-36.

Barlas, Asma, *Democracy, Nationalism and Communalism: The Colonial Legacy in South Asia* (Boulder, CO, 1995).

Bashir, 1. K., *NWFP Elections 1970* (Lahore, 1973).

Baxter, Craig (ed.), *Zia's Pakistan: Politics and Society in a Front-Line State* (Boulder, CO, 1985).

————, 'A New Pakistan under a Revised Bhuttoism', *Middle East Insight* 6, 4 (winter 1989), pp. 23-8.

———— et al., *Government and Politics in South Asia*, 3rd edn (Boulder,CO, 1993).

————, 'Pakistan Votes-1970', *Asian Survey* 11, 3 (March 1971), pp. 197-218.

Bray, John, 'Nawaz Sharifs New Order in Pakistan', *Round Table* 318 (1991), pp. 179-90.

Bhutto, Benazir, *Daughter of the East: An Autobiography* (London, 1988).

Bhutto, Zulfiqar, *The Great Tragedy* (Karachi, 1971).

Brines. Russell, *The Indo-Pakistani Conflict* (New York, 1968).

Brohi, A.K., *Statement in Supreme Court of Pakistan* (Islamabad, 1977).

Burki, S. Javed, *Pakistan Under Bhutto, 1971-1977* (London 1980).

————, 'Development of Towns: The Pakistan experience', *Asian Survey* 15, 8 (August 1979), pp. 751-62.

————, 'Pakistan under Zia 1977-88', *Asian Survey* 28, 10 (October 1988), pp. 1082-100.

————, 'Social and Economic Determinants of Political Violence: Case Study of Punjab', *Middle East Journal* 25, 4 (1971), pp. 465-80.

———— and Craig Baxter, *Pakistan under the Military: Eleven years of Zia ul-Haq* (Boulder, CO, 1991).

———— and Craig Baxter, 'Socio-Economic Indicators of the People's Party Vote in the Punjab: A Study at the Tehsil level', *Journal of Asian Studies* 34, 4 (August 1975), pp. 913-30.

Carroll, Lucy, 'Nizam-i-Islam: Processes and Conflicts in Pakistan's Programme of Islamisation, with special reference to the position of women', *The Journal of Commonwealth and Comparative Politics* 20, I (March 1982), pp. 57-95.

Chaudhri, M.A., *Government and Politics in Pakistan* (Dhaka, 1968).

Cheema, P. I., 'The Afghanistan Crisis and Pakistan's Security Dilemma', *Asian Survey* 23, 3 (March 1983), pp. 227-43.

Chishti, Lt.-Gen. F.A., *Betrayals Of Another Kind: Islam, Democracy and the Army in Pakistan* (London, 1989).

Cohen, S.P., *The Pakistan Army* (Berkeley, CA, 1984).

Cordovez, Diego, and 5.S. Harrison, *Out of Afghanistan. The Inside Story of Soviet Withdrawal* (Oxford, 1995).

Dewey, Clive, 'The rural roots of Pakistani Militarism' in D.A. Low (ed.), *The Political Inheritance of Pakistan* (Basingstoke, 1991), pp. 255-84.

Embree, Ainslee T.(ed.), *Pakistan's Western Borderlands* (Durham, NC, 1977).

Feldman, Herbert, *The End and the Beginning: Pakistan, 1969-1971* (Karachi, 1976).

Ganguly, Surnit, 'Explaining the Kashmir Insurgency: Political Mobilization and Institutional Decay', *International Security* 21, 2 (autumn 1996), pp. 76-108.

Gauhar, Altaf, 'Pakistan: Ayub Khan's Abdication', *Third World Quarterly* 7, 1 (January 1985), pp. 102-3 I.

————, *Ayub Khan: Pakistan's First Military Ruler* (Lahore, 1994).

Gilani, S. Z., 'Bhutto's Leadership: a Psycho-Social View', *Contemporary South Asia* 3, 3(1994), pp. 217-37.

Gilmartin, D., *Empire and Islam: Punjab and the Making of Pakistan* (Berkeley, CA, 1988).

Girardet, E. R., *Afghanistan: The Soviet War* (London. 1985).

Gordon, S., 'South Asia After the Cold War: Winners and Losers', *Asian Survey*, 35, 10 (October 1995), pp. 879-95.

Gustafson, W. E., 'Economic Reforms Under Bhutto', *Journal of Asian and African Studies* 8, nos. 3-4 (July-October 1973), pp. 241-58.

————, 'Pakistan 1978: At the Brink Again?', *Asian Survey* 19,2 (February 1979), pp. 157-64.

Haq, Farhat, 'Rise of MQM in Pakistan. Politics of Ethnic Mobilization', *Asian Survey* 35, II (November 1995), pp. 990-1004.

Hardin, Russell, *One for All: The Logic of Group Conflict* (Princeton, 1995).

Hardy, P., *The Muslims of British India* (Cambridge, 1972).

Harrison, S.S., 'Baluch Nationalism and Superpower Rivalry', *International Security* 5, 3 (1980/1), pp. 163.

————, 'Nightmare in Baluchistan', *Foreign Policy* 32, (fall 1978), pp. 136-60.

Hasan, K. Shamsul (ed.), *Sindh's Fight for Pakistan* (Karachi, 1992).

Hasan, Mushirul, *India's Partition: Process, Strategy and Mobilization* (New Delhi, 1993).

Hassan, Riaz, 'Islamisation: An Analysis of Religious, Political and Social Change in Pakistan', *Middle Eastern Studies* 21, 3 (July 1985), pp. 263-84.

Hollen, Eliza Van, 'Pakistan in 1986: Trials of Transition', *Asian Survey* 27, 2 (February 1987), pp. 143-55.

Horowitz, D., *Ethnic Groups in Conflict* (Berkeley, CA, 1985).

Human Rights Commission of Pakistan, *State of Human Rights in Pakistan 1993* (Lahore, 1993).

Iqbal, Javed, *Ideology of Pakistan*, 2nd edn (Lahore 1971).

Islam, Safiqul, 'Failure in State Building: The Case of Pakistan', *Asian Profile* 12, 6 (December 1984), pp. 579-90.

Ispahani, M. Z., *Roads and Rivals: The Political Uses of Access in the Border-lands of Asia* (Ithaca, NY, 1989).

Jahan, Rounaq, *Pakistan: Failure in National Integration* (New York, 1972).

Jalal, Ayesha, *Democracy and Authoritarianism in South Asia: A Comparative and Historical Perspective* (Cambridge, 1995).

————, 'Inheriting the Raj: Jinnah and the Governor-Generalship' (Issue) *Modern Asian Studies*, 19, I (1985), pp. 29-53.

————, *The Sole Spokesman: Jinnah, the Muslim League and the Demand for Pakistan* (Cambridge, 1985).

————, *The State of Martial Rule: The Origins of Pakistan's Political Econo-my of Defence* (Cambridge, 1990).

————, 'Conjuring Pakistan: History As Official Imagining', *International Journal of Middle East Studies* 27 (1995), pp. 73-89.

James, Sir Morrice, *Pakistan Chronicle* (London, 1993).

James, William E., and Subroto Roy (eds), *Foundations of Pakistan's Political Economy: Towards an Agenda for the 1990s* (New Delhi, 1992).

Jansson, Erland, *India, Pakistan or Pakhtunistan? The Nationalist Movements in the North-West Frontier Province, 1937-47* (Uppsala, 1981).

Kak, B. L., *The Fall of Gilgit: The Untold Story of Indo-Pak Affairs from Jinnah to Bhutto* (New Delhi, 1977).

Kapur, Ashok, *Pakistan in Crisis* (London, 1991).

————, *Pakistan's Nuclear Development* (London, 1987).

Kazi, Aftab A., 'Ethnic Nationalities, Education and Problems of National Inte-gration in Pakistan', *Asian Profile* 16, 2 (1988), pp. 147-61.

Kennedy, C.H., *Bureaucracy in Pakistan* (Karachi, 1987).

———— (ed.), *Pakistan in 1992* (Boulder, CO, 1992).

———— and R.B Rais (eds), *Pakistan in 1995* (Boulder, CO, 1995).

————, 'Islamisation in Pakistan: Implementation of the Hudood Ordinanc-es', *Asian Survey* 28, 3 (March 1988), pp. 307-16.

————, 'The politics of ethnicity in Sindh', *Asian Survey* 31, 10 (October 1991), pp. 938-55.

Khan, M. Asghar, *Generals in Politics: Pakistan, 1958-1992* (New Delhi, 1983).

Khan, M. Ayub, *Friends Not Masters: A Political Autobiography* (London, 1967).

————, *Speeches and Statements* (Karachi, 1961).

Korson, 1. Henry and M. Maskiell, 'Islamization and Social Policy in Pakistan: The Constitutional Crisis and the Status of Women'. *Asian Survey* 25, no. 6 (June 1985), pp. 589-612.

Kurin, Richard, 'Islamization in Pakistan: A View from the Countryside', *Asian Survey* 25, 8 (August 1985), pp. 852-62.

Laporte, Robert, 'Pakistan in 1995: The Continuing Crises', *Asian Survey 36*, 2 (February 1996), pp. 179-89.

Lodhi, Maleeha, *The External Dimension* (Lahore, 1994).

Low. D. A. (ed.), *The Political Inheritance of Pakistan* (Basingstoke, 1991).

Malik, I. H., *State and Civil Society in Pakistan: Politics of Authority, Ideology and Ethnicity* (Basingstoke, 1997).

————, 'Ethno-Nationalisrn in Pakistan: A Commentary on Muhajir Qaumi Mahaz (MQM) in Sindh', *South Asia* 18, 2 (1995), pp. 49-72.

————, 'Identity Formation and Muslim Party Politics in the Punjab 18971936: A Retrospective Analysis', *Modern Asian Studies* 29, 2 (1995) pp. 293-323.

————, 'The State and Civil Society in Pakistan: From Crisis to Crisis', *Asian Survey* 36, 7 (July 1996), pp. 673-90.

Maniruzzaman, T., *Group Interests and Political Changes: Studies of Pakistan and Bangladesh* (Delhi, 1982).

Mascarenhas, A., *The Rape of Bangladesh* (Delhi, 1971).

McGrath, Allen, *The Destruction of Pakistan '05 Democracy* (Karachi, 1996).

Monshipouri, M. and A. Samuel, 'Development and Democracy in Pakistan: Tenuous or Plausible Nexus?, *Asian Survey* 35, 11 (November 1995), pp. 973-89.

Mumtaz, Khawar, and Farida Shaheed (eds), *Women of Pakistan: One Step Forward Two Steps Back* (London, 1987).

Murshid, T. M., *The Sacred and the Secular: Bengal Muslim Discourses, 1871-1977* (Calcutta, 1995).

Musa, Muhammad, *My Version: India-Pakistan War*, 1965 (Lahore, 1983). Nasr, S.V.R., 'Democracy and Crisis of Governability in Pakistan', *Asian Survey* 32, 6 (June 1992), pp. 521-37.

Niazi, Zamir, *Press in Chains* (Karachi, 1986).

Nornan, Omar, *The Political Economy of Pakistan, 1947-85* (New York, 1988).

Noon, Feroz Khan, *From Memory* (Lahore, 1966).

Pataudi, Sher Ali, *The Story of Soldiering and Politics* in *India and Pakistan* (Lahore, 1983).

People's Democratic Alliance, *How an Election was Stolen* (Islamabad, 1991).

Piscatori, J.(ed.), *Islamic Fundamentalism and the Gulf Crisis* (Chicago, 1991).

Qureshi, *S.A.*, 'An Analysis of Contemporary Pakistan Politics: Bhutto Versus the Military', *Asian Survey* 19, 9 (September 1979), pp. 910-21.

Rahman, Tariq, 'The BalochilBrahvi Language Movements in Pakistan', *Journal of South Asian and Middle Eastern Studies* 19,3 (spring 1996), pp. 71-88.

————, 'Language and Politics in a Pakistan Province: The Sindhi Language Movement', *Asian Survey* 35, 11 (November 1995), pp. 1005-16.

Rais, Rasul B., 'Pakistan in 1988: From Command to Conciliation Politics', *Asian Survey* 29, 2 (February 1989), pp. 199-207.

Rakisits, C.G.P., 'Centre-Province Relations in Pakistan Under President Zia: the Government's and the Opposition's Approaches', *Pacific Affairs* 61, 1 (spring 1988), pp. 78-97.

Randhawa, M.S., *Out of the Ashes–an Account of the Rehabilitation of Refugees from West Pakistan in Rural Areas of East Punjab* (Chandigarh, 1954).

Rashid, Harun-or, *The Foreshadowing of Bangladesh: Bengal Muslim League and Muslim League Politics, 1936-1947* (Dhaka, 1987).

Richter. W.L., 'Islamic Resurgence in Pakistan", *Asian Survey* 19,6, pp. 547-57.

————, 'Pakistan in 1984: Digging In', *Asian Survey* 25, 2 (February 1985), pp. 145-54.

————, 'The 1990 General Elections in Pakistan' in e.H. Kennedy (ed.), *Pakistan in 1992* (Boulder, CO, 1992), pp. 19-43.

Rittenberg, S.A., *Ethnicity, Nationalism and Pakhtuns: The Independence Movement in India's North-West Frontier Province, 1901-1947* (Durham, NC, 1988).

Rizvi, H. A., *The Military and Politics in Pakistan 1947-86* (Delhi, 1988).

————, 'The Legacy of Military Rule in Pakistan', *Survival* 31, 3 (May-June 1989), pp. 255-68.

————, 'The Civilianization of Military Rule in Pakistan', *Asian Survey* 26, 10 (October 1986), pp. 1067-81.

————, 'The Paradox of Military Rule in Pakistan', *Asian Survey 24*, 5 (May 1984), pp. 534-55.

Robinson, F., 'Origins' in Wlliam E. James and S. Roy (eds), *Foundations of Pakistan '05 Political Economy: Towards an Agendafor the 199005* (New Delhi, 1992), pp. 33-58.

————, *Separatism among India Muslims: The Politics of the United Provinces' Muslims, 1860-1923*, (Cambridge, 1974).

Rose, Leo. E., 'The Politics of Azad Kashmir' in R.G.C. Thomas (ed.), *Perspectives on Kashmir: The Roots of Conflict in South Asia* (Boulder, CO, (992), pp. 235-53.

Samad, Yunas, 'The Military and Democracy in Pakistan', *Contemporary South Asia* 3, 3 (1994), pp. 189-203.

Sayeed, K.B., *Pakistan: The Formative Phase, 1857-1948* (London, 1968).

————, *Politics* in *Pakistan: The Nature and Direction of Change* (New York, 1980).

————, 'Pakistan in 1983: Internal Stresses More Serious Than External Problems', *Asian Survey* 24, 2 (February 1984), pp. 219-28.

————, 'The Three Worlds of Democracy in Pakistan', *Contemporary South Asia* I, I (1992), pp. 53-66.

Schofield, V., *Kashmir* in *the Crossfire* (London, 1996).

Shafqat, Saeed, 'Pakistan Under Benazir Bhutto', *Asian Survey* 36, 7 (July 1996), pp. 655-672.

Shah, Syed Waqar Ali, *Muslim League in NWFP* (Karachi, 1992).

Siddiqi, A.H., *Baluchistan (Pakistan): Its Society, Resources and Development* (Lanham, MD, 1991).

Syed, Anwar H., 'Pakistan in 1976: Business as Usual', *Asian Survey* 17, 2 (1977), pp. 181-90.

————, *Pakistan: Islam, Politics and National Solidarity* (New York, 1982).

————, 'The Pakistan People's Party and the Punjab: National Assembly Elections 1988 and 1990', *Asian Survey* 31, 7 (July 1991), pp. 581-97.

Talbot, Ian, 'Back to the Future? The Punjab Unionist Model of Consociational Democracy for Contemporary India and Pakistan', *International Journal of Punjab Studies* 3, 1 (January-June 1996), pp. 65-75.

————, *Freedom's Cry: The Popular Dimension in the Pakistan Struggle and Partition Experience in North-West India* (Karachi, 1996).

————, *Provincial Politics and the Pakistan Movement: The Growth of the Muslim League in North-West and North-East India, 1937-1947* (Karachi 1988).

Titus, P. (ed.), *Marginality and Modernity: Ethnicity and Change in Post-Colonial Balochistan* (Karachi, 1996).

Waseem, M., 'Pakistan's Lingering Crisis of Democracy', *Asian Survey 32*, 7 (1992), pp. 617-34.

————, *The 1993 Elections in Pakistan* (Lahore, 1994).

————, *Politics and the State in Pakistan* (Lahore, 1989).

Weinbaum, M.B., 'The Politics of Afghan Resettlement and Rehabilitation', *Asian Survey* 29, 3 (March 1989), pp. 287-307.

————, 'The March 1977 Elections in Pakistan: Where Everyone Lost', *Asian Sunrvey* 17, 7 (July 1977), pp. 599-618.

Weiss, A.M., *Culture, Class and Development in Pakistan: The Emergence of an Industrial Bourgeoisie in Punjab* (Boulder, 1991).

————, (ed.) *Islamic Reassertion in Pakistan: The Application of Islamic Laws in a Modern State* (New York, 1986).

————, 'Women's Position in Pakistan: Socio-Cultural Effects ofIslamisation', *Asian Survey* 25, 8 (August 1985), pp. 863-80.

Whaites, A., 'The State and Civil Society in Pakistan', *Contemporary South Asia* 4, 3 (1995), pp. 229-54.

Wilcox, W., *Pakistan: The Consolidation of a Nation* (New York, 1963).

Wilder, A., 'Changing Patterns of Punjab Politics in Pakistan: National Assembly Election Results 1988 and 1993', *Asian Survey* 35, 4 (April 1995), pp. 377-93.

Wirsing. R.G., 'The Arms Race in South Asia: Implications for the United States', *Asian Survey* 25, 3 (March 1985), pp. 265-91.

————, *Pakistan's Security Under Zia, 1977-1988: The Policy Imperatives of a Peripheral Asian State* (Basingstoke, 1991).

————, *The Baluchis and Pathans* (London, 1987).

Wriggins, W.H., 'Pakistan's Search for a Foreign Policy After the Invasion of Afghanistan', *Pacific Affairs* 57, 2 (summer 1984), pp. 284-303.

Zaheer, Hasan, *The Separation of East Pakistan: The Rise and Realization of Bengali Muslim Nationalism* (Karachi, 1994).

Ziring, L., *Pakistan in the Twentieth Century: A Political History* (Karachi, 1997).

————, *Pakistan: The Enigma of Political Development* (Boulder, 1980).

————, 'Pakistan: A Political Perspective', *Asian Survey* 15,7 (JUly 1975), pp. 629-44.

————, 'Pakistan in 1989: The Politics of Stalemate', *Asian Survey 30*, 2 (February 1990), pp. 126-35.

————, 'Public policy Dilemmas and Pakistan's Nationality Problem: The Legacy of Zia ul-Haq', *Asian Survey* 28, 7 (july 1988), pp. 795-812.

UNPUBLISHED DISSERTATIONS

Akhtar, S., 'Pakistan since Independence: The Political role of the Ulerna', D PhiL, University of York, 1989.

Deal, J.S., 'Love and Mysticism in the Punjabi Qissas of the Seventeenth and Eighteenth Centuries', M.Phil., School of Oriental and African Studies, University of London, 1996.

Hussain, F.A., 'The Problem of Federalism and Regional Autonomy in Pakistan', M.PhiL, London School of Economics, 1989.

Lodhi, M., 'The Pakistan People's Party', Ph.D., London School of Economics, 1979.

Mitha, Y.A., 'Linguistic Nationalism in Pakistan: With Special Reference to the Role and History of Urdu in the Punjab', M.Phil., University of Sussex, 1985.

Rahman, M., 'The Emergence of Bangladesh as a Sovereign State', Ph.D., Institute of Commonwealth Studies, University of London, 1975.

Shah, S.W.A., 'Muslim Politics in the North-West Frontier Province 1937-1947', D.Phil., University of Oxford, 1997

Warren, A., 'Waziristan, The Faqir of Ipi and the Indian Army–The North-West Frontier Revolt of 1936', Ph.D., Monash University, 1996.

INDEX

Afghanistan 222, 55, 99, 267, 317; war against terrorism 380, 389, 395, 397; Afghan refugees 269-7

Afghan war 14, 33, 45, 249, 252, 26570, 288; see also Geneva Accords Agartala conspiracy 188-9

Ahmad, Lt.-Gen. Mehmood 376, 377, 394

Ahmad, Qazi Hussain 36, 351, 355; see also Jarnaat-i-Islarni

Ahmadiss 35, 141, 282-3, 288, 392; see also Blasphemy Ordinance

Aitaz, Ahsan 18, 301

Alavi, Hamza 7, 54, 66-7, 89

Ali, Chaudhri Muhammad 64, 132, 144

Ali, Jam Sadiq 1981, 219, 305, 322-3

Aligarh Movement 28, 66, 91, 150; see also Islam, Modernism

All Pakistan Mohajir Student Organisation (APMSO) 68, 221, 304, 306

All Pakistan Women's Association (APWA), see Appendices and women

Al-Qaeda 389, 391, 397, 412

Aminul, Hasanat Pir, 86; see also Appendices

Amnesty International 250

Ansari Commission 260

Awami League 126, 144-5, 182, 188, 190, 195, 198-9, 200-3, 207

Awami National Party (ANP) 267, 270

Awami Tehrik, see Appendices

Ayub Khan: 11, 37, 141-2, 146-8, 160, 188; background 148-52; loss of power 179-84; compared with Musharraf 376, 378, 380, 398;see also Basic Democracies, Kashmir, land reform, Muslim Family Laws Ordinance, US-Pakistan relations

Azad Kashmir 18, 22, 42-3, 116-17, 155-6, 192, 308, 315, 330; Azhar, Mian Muhammad 403

Aziz, Shaukat 413, 414

Babar, Naseerullah 344

Balochistan, Baloch 5, 10, 14, 29, 38, 43-4, 45, 51, 55-7, 59, 62, 135, 200, 216, 224, 226, 243, 269, 313, 355, 403, 412, 416

Balochistan National Party, 400-1

Bangladesh 1, 6, 39, 186-7, 206, 208, 236-7

Barelvis 28, 160, 251, 403; see also JUP

Basic Democracies 148, 153-6, 161, 164

Beg, Mirza Aslam 285, 316, 351, 355

Bengal 58, 60, 63, 87-91, 93; see also East Bengal, East Pakistan

Bengali language 90, 133, 141, 188

Bhashani, Maulana Abdul Hamid Khan 136, 195, 374

Bhutto, Benazir 4, 16, 47, 258,
    262–3, 287, 293, 305, 311,
    321, 381, 400, 401, 402, 406,
    414; (1988–90 administration)
    15, 308–10; (1993–6 adminis-
    tration) 38, 335–49; *see also*
    Appendices
Bhutto, Ghinwa 338, 335, 353
Bhutto, Mir Murtaza 259, 297,
    334, *337–8, 348; see also*
    Appendices
Bhutto, Mumtaz Ali 302
Bhutto, Nasrat 257–8, 322, 337
Bhutto, Zulfiqar Ali 1, 4, 37, 146,
    157, 172, 177–9, 213, 234–5,
    256–8, 303, 377, 398; and
    break-up of Pakistan 203–5,
    216; characteristics 215–17,
    244; *see also* Appendices,
    Constitution 1973, land reform,
    nationalisation, Pakistan
    People's Party, Simla Agreement
    (1972)
Biharis 209, 306
Biraderis 10, 24, 30, 70, 73, 156,
    192, 261, 265, 294, 313, 354,
    382, 383–4, 385, 402
Bizenjo, Mir Ghaus Bakhsh 245,
    286
Blair, Tony 393, 395, 396
Blasphemy Ordinance 35, 341,
    412; *see also* Ahmadis
Bogra, Muhammad Ali 120,
    142–3; administration, 53–65;
    see also Appendices, British
    rule, viceregalism
British rule in India 53–64, 66–7
Burki, Shahid Javed 39, 165, 197,
    233, 246, 329, 349–50
Bush, George W. 395, 396

China 173–5, 178, 212, 22–1,
    235, 317
Chishti, Faiz Ali 249, 258
Chundrigar, Ismail Ibrahim 126,
    1–15

Constituent Assembly 26, 126,
    134–5, 138, 142–3, 152
Constiruuon: (1962) 11, 157–8:
    (1973) 223, 228–9; *see also*
    Eighth Amendment
Council for Defence and National
    Sccurity 3, 327, 351–2, 161

Dacoits 323–4
Daultana, Mian Mumtaz 133, 192
Democratic Action Committee
    182; *see also* Appendices
Deobandis 29, 150, 160, 251; *see
    also* JUI
Dhaka 133, 141, 144–5, 151,
    205–6, 207–9, 211
Dual Office Hill 414

East Bengal 24–5, 31, 90–1, 133,
    186
East Pakistan 16, 33, 50, 98, 100,
    105, 137–8, 145, 162, 170,
    180–3, 118, 199, 203, 206, 211
EBDO (Electoral Bodies Disquali-
    fication Order) 154, 163
Eighth Amendment 262, 293, 310,
    325, 334, 348, 360
elections: 2–3, 15–16, 30, 88;
    (1954) 131, 142; (national,
    1962) 10; (1970) 1994–201;
    (1977) 232, 239–41; (1984) 10,
    30; (1988) 294–7; (1990)
    310–14; (1993) 19, 16, 294,
    331–3; (1996) 325–8; presiden-
    tial (1965) 30, 169–1; and
    rigging 238–41, 313–14, 355–6;
    East Pakistan (1954) 131, 142
Elahi, Pervez 403

Fahim, Makhdoom Amin 412
Faiz, Ahmed 138; *see also*
    Appendices
Family Laws Ordinance 28,
    167–9, 183
Federal Security Force, 222–3
Frontier Crimes, Regulation 11, 59

Gandhi, Indira 210, 218, 223, 233, 235–6, 268
Gandhi, Rajiv 287, 301
Gandhi, Sonia 410, 411
Gahhar, Altaf 178–9
Geneva Accords 266
Ghulam Muhammad 64, 126, 128, 129–30, 140–3, 152; *see also* Appendices
Green Revolution 153, 184
Gulf War (First) 315–17, 319

Haider, Lt.-Gen. Moinuddin 379
Hameed, Abdul 384
Haroon, Abdullah 76–7
Haq, Fazlul 64, 87, 160; *see also* Appendices
Haq, Zia-ul: 1, 4–5, 32, 34–5, 48, 222–3, 243, 245, 289, 303, 376, 398, 408; compared with Musharraf 376, 377, 378–80, 400, and Islamisation, 251, 256, 259, 270–83, 286, and referendum (1984) 399; *see also* Afghan war and Appendices
Hashim, Abul 87–9, 122
Hashmi, Makhdoom Javed 414
Hayat, Shaukat 255, 296
Hayat, Veena 321–2
Hikmatyar, Gulbuddin 317
Hindus 5, 24, 33, 69, 71, 75, 77, 97, 101–2, 104–5, 109, 111, 120–1, 124
Hizbe Islami, *see* Appendices
Hudood Ordinance 48, 274–6, 288, 341, 412
Huntington. Samuel H. 8, 9, 51, 148, 153
Hussain, Atlaf 110, 221, 304, 306–77, 312, 324, 342, 357; see also APMSO Mohajirs, MQM, Appendices
Hussain, Chaudhry Amir 406–7, 412
Hussain, Chaudhry Shujaat 403, 410, 413, 414, 416

Hyderabad 216, 303; Pucca Qila episode 307

Iftikharuddm, Mian Muhammad 121, 3, 154
IJI (Islami Jamhoori Ittehad) 294–5, 249–301, 303, 306, 309, 312, 314
India, Pakistan's relations with 222, 98–9, 124, 138, 329, 336, 375, 392–7, 410–12; 1965 war, 177, 189; 1971 war, 210–11; Indu waters dispute 112–13, 121; *see also* Kashmir, Simla agreement
International Monetary Fund 379, 391
Iqbal, Allama, Mohammad, 66
ISI (Inter-Services Intelligence) 269, 295, 309
Islam: 1, 27–30; modernism 27, 157; sectarian violence, 289–90, 323, 335, 339–41, 387–8; *see also* Aligarh Movement, Barelvis, Blasphemy Ordinance, Deobandis. Mizam-i-Mustafa. Pirs, 'Ulama, Zia-ul Haq and Islamisation; individual Islamic parties
Islamabad 164, 301, 321, 326, 133, 347
Ishaq Khan, Ghulam 278, 285, 287, 292, 303, 306–7, 310, 320–1, 325, 327–9; *see also* Appendices

Jalal, Ayesha 11, 54, 127, 129, 130–1, 137–8, 204
Jamaat-i-Islami (JI) 28, 36, 158, 160, 181, 196, 267, 280, 304, 313, 330–1, 347, 351–2; *see also* Qazi Hussain Ahmad, Maulana Maudoodi, Appendices
Jamali Zafarullah 413

Jamiat-ul-Ulema-i-Islurn (JUI) 29, 35–6, 196, 226, 310, 312, 318, 331
Jamiat-ul-Ulema-i-Pakistan (JUP), 29, 35–6, 196, 316
Jatoi, Ghulam Mustafa 94, 263, 299, 310–12
Jehangir, Asma 36
Jhang 34, 200, 294, 341
jihad groups 389, 390, 391, 392, 394, 405
Jinnah, Fatima 156, 160–1, 382
Jinnah, Muhammad Ali 5, 28, 35, 68–9, 79, 85, 90, 101, 127, 134–55, 139, 411; s *ee also* Appendices
Junejo, Muhammad Khan 37, 245, 248, 261–3, 266–7; *see also* Geneva Accords

Kalabagh dam 416
Kalat 56, 152, 225; *see also* Balochistan
Karachi 16, 17, 22, 40, 43–4, 45–6, 49, 51, 53, 99, 104, 138, 164, 224, 232, 298, 304, 322, 334, 340, 342–4, 346; *see also* Mohajirs
Karachi Declaration (1998) 102, 305
Kargil war (1999) 375, 376, 377, 379, 396
Kashmir 95, 100, 106, 112–16, 124, 172, 174, 176, 188, 236, 336, 389, 392–3, 396, 411, 415–16; *see also* Azad Kashmir, Indo-Pakistan relations, 1964 war
Khaksars, 62, 157
Khalid, Malik Meraj 300, 349, 51
Khaliquzzaman, Chaudhry 159, *see also* Appendices
Khan, Dr A.Q. 409
Khan, Abdul Ghaffar 14, 63, 82–3, 86, 134, 154; *see also* Appendices

Khan, Abdul Qaiyum, 87, 132, 154, 196; *see also* Appendices
Khan, Asghar 258; *see also* Appendices
Khan, Lt-Geu, Aziz 379, 389, 394
Khan, Imran 2, 49, 338–9, 353–4; *see also* Appendices
Khan, Liaqat Ali 15, 26, 93, 110, 118, 131–2, 136–9
Khan, Mir Zafarullah 406
Khan, Muhammad Naeem Noor 41
Khan, Nasrullah 182, 403, 406; *see also* Appendices
Khan, Sahib 128, 134, 143
Khan, Syed Ahmed 27; *see also* Aligarh Movement, Islam, Modernism
Khan, Wall 1, 86, 199, 216, 270; *see also* Appendices
Khan, Yahya 16, 148, 183, 185, 200–13, 223; compared with Ayuh Khan 191–3; see also elections 1970
Khan, Ghulam Mustafa 219, 299, 300, 333
Khattack, Gen. A.Q.K. 377
Khudai Khidmatgar 82–3, 85, 99
Khuhro, Muhammad Ayub 77–9, l08, 128, 140, 154; *see also* Appendices
Krishak Praja Party 64, 87; *see also* Maulvi Abul Kaeem Fazlul Haq

Lahore 13, 15, 34, 44, 49, 53, 66, 86, 97, 101, 107, 110, 151, 177, 179–80, 204, 212, 237, 294, 300, 327, 332, 347, 349
Lahore Resolution (1940) 2, 5, 66, 89, 124, 188
land reform 165–6, 218, 230–2
Larkana 76, 179, 182, 202, 253
Legal Framework Order (1970) 193–4

Leghari, Farooq 17, 299, 326,
333–4, 337–8, 345, 348, 377,
403, 412; *see also* Appendices
Lodhi, Maleeha 9, 47, 336
Lyari 44, 49, 311

madrasas 388, 390
Majlis-r-Shoora 259–60, 281
Malakand 595, 339
Malik, Iftikhar 47, 67
Maqbool, It.-Gen. K. 381
Mamdot, Iftikhar Hussain Khan,
133; *see also* Appendices
Maududi, Maulana, Syed Abdul
A'la. 158; *see also* Jamaat-i-
Islami, Appendices
middle classes 46–7
Mirza, Iskander 64, 128, 141–4,
146–7, 164; *see also* Appendices
MMA 402 ff.
Mohajirs 13, 93, 106–7, 109–10,
114, 121, 220, 265–6, 307; *see
also* Altaf Hussain, Karachi,
MQM
Movement for the Restoration of
Democracy 248, 251, 252–3,
256, 259–61, 291, 297
MQM 6, 16, 41, 45, 50, 265–6,
303–4, 306, 3322, 343; *see also*
Altaf Hussain, Karachi,
Mohajirs
MQM (Haqiqi) 324–5, 332,
342–4
Musharraf, Gen. Pervez: October
1999 coup, 375–8; reforms and
character of regime 380ff.
passim; see also Ayub Khan, Zia
ul-Haq
Muslim League: (pre-1947)
68–73, 7481, 81–7, 100;
Convention Muslim League
159, 161; Council Muslim
League 159; Pakistan Muslim
League 10, 131; unified 112; *see
also* M.A. Jinnah, Nawaz
Sharif, Pakistan movement

National Accountability Bureau
380–1; National Committee for
Human Rights, created 412
National Security Council 412,
413; nationalisation 233–4
Nazirnuddin, Khwaja 87–9, 131,
136, 140—2, 159; *see also*
Appendices
Nehru, Jawaharlal 114, 116, 142
Nishtar, Abdur Rab 92, 133; *see
also* Appendices
Nizarn-i-Mustapha 243, 255, 272
Noon, Firoz Khan 86, 145; *see
also* Appendices
North West Frontier Province 59,
61–2, 81–7, 96, 216, 383, 384,
390, 403; *see also* Abdul
Ghaffar Khan, Abdul Qaiyum
Khan, Awarni National Party,
Khan Sahib, Pushtuns,
Pushtunistan
Nothern Areas 117–18

Ojhri camp 266, 284
One Unit 126, 134, 143, 149,
163, 185
Operation Brass Tacks 268
Operation Clean-up 324–6
Operation Gibraltar 177
Operation Searchlight 208
Osama bin Laden 389, 390, 391n.

Pakistan: Army, 3 fn, 4, 9,
99–100, 118–19, 222–5, 325,
329, 341, 351–2, 366, 380ff.
passim; bureaucracy 100,
16–12, 227–8, 247; economy
23, 38–9, 97, 171–2, 230, 247,
277–8, 315, 330–1, 346–8,
349–50, 359–60; historiography
4–55, 12, 255–6; languages
25–7; nuclear proliferation
238–9, 250, 285, 312, 337;
Pakistan movement 5–6, 12,
30–1, 66–94; political culture
2–4, 7, 10, 13, 25–6, 30–1, 34,

64, 93; population growth
23–4, 39–40; *see also* Balochistan, East Bengal, Islam,
Muslim League, relations with
India and United States, North
West Frointier Province, Punjab,
Sindh
Pakistan National Alliance 240–3
Pakistan People's Party 9, 16,
180–2, 197–8, 200, 206,
218–20, 2673–4, 2922, 22944,
2296–7, 305, 353, 3567; *see
also* Benazir Bhutto, Nusrat
Bhutto, Z.A. Bhutto, elections,
land reform, nationalisation
Pakistan Tehrik-i-Insaf, *see* Imran
Khan Partition (1947) 95–124
pirs 13, 29–30, 36, 37, 70–1, 76,
80, 166, 251; *see also* elections,
Islam press freedom 385–7
Powell, Colin 392, 395
PRODA (Public Office Disqualification Act) 54, 92, 139–77,
142, 290
Punjab: 42, 60–2, 344–5; and
army 3, 15, 62, 344–6; 'Pun-
jabisatiori' of Pakistan 4,
14–15, 31–2, 127, 163, 249,
279; regions 16, 366–7; *see also*
elections, Nawaz Sharif,
Pakistan Army, Pakistan
People's Party
Pushtun 1, 7, 113, 14, 19, 32, 41,
43, 57, 81–2, 115, 149, 252,
403; *see also* Abdul Ghaffar
Khan, Khan Sahib, North West
Frontier Province, Pakistan:
languages
Pushtunistani/Pakhtunistan 7, 99;
see also Afghanistan
Pushtunkhwa Milli Awami Party
14

Quetta 55–6, 63, 225
Quaid-e-Azam *see* Muhammad Ali
Jinnah

Qureshi, Main 329–31, 249; *see
also* Appendices

Rahman, Sheikh Mujibur 88, 163,
182, 185, 189–90, 205–7; *see
also* Agartala conspiracy,
Awami League, Bangladesh,
East Bengal, East Pakistan
Rarnzi bin al-Shibb 397
Rawalpindi 139, 156, 174, 179,
181, 243, 305, 327
Rawalpindi conspiracy 138, 151
Red Shirts, *see* Khudai Khidmat-
gar Rehman, Maulana Fazlur
412
Republican Party 131, 143, 145,
161; Research and Analysis
Wing (RAW) 22, 336
Robinson, Francis 66
Rumsfeld, Donald 396

Samad, Yunus 92, 130–1
Saraiki Qaumi Mahaz 16, 302; *see
also* Pakistan: languages
Schofield, Victoria 11
sectarian violence 387–8
Sethi, Najam 386, 405–6
Sharif, Mian Nawaz 2, 3, 16, 110,
288, 292, 300–2, 309, 314,
333, 339, 352, 381, 398, 400,
401, 402, 406, 414; dismissed
(1993) 325–6, 327–9; and
Islamisation 317–18; dismissed
(1999) 375–6, 381; *see also*
Gulf war, Pakistan Muslim
League, Punjab, Appendices
Sharif, Shahbaz 2, 409
Shias 28, 168, 278; *see also* Islam:
sectarian violence, TNJF, *zakat*
Sikhs 18, 102–4, 111, I 15, 121–2
Simla Accord (1972) 235–6
Sindh 19, 40, 41, 62, 74–81, 96,
10710, 163, 221, 253, 319,
323–5, 350; nationalism 27,
80–1, 164, 252–3; *see also*
Mumtaz Ali Bhutto, Movement

for the Restoration of Democracy, Pirs, G.M. Syed
Sindhi Language Bill (1972) 220–2; *see also* Pakistan: languages
Sindhi, Sheikh Abdul Majid 77
Singh, Manmohan 412, 415
Sipah-i-Sahbah-i-Pakistan 34, 271, 340, 347
South Waziristan 413
Suhrawardy, Husain Shaheed, 88–9, 92, 102, 132, 144; *see also* Appendices
Syed, G.M. 13, 37, 74–55, 79, 80, 154, *192; see also* Appendices

Taliban 379, 389, 390, 392
Tehrik-i-Nafraz-i-Shariat-i-Muhammadi 59, 339–40
Tehrik-i-Nifazi-Fiqh-i-Jafria (TNJF) 34, 271
terrorism threat 413
Tiwana, Khizr 12, 69, 71, 74
Tiwana, Rahila 323

'Ulama, Anti-Ahmadi movement, *see* Ahmadis, Blasphemy Ordinance, Islam, Islamic parties and leaders, sectarian violence
Union Councils 381, 382, 383
Unionist Party 5, 12, 2267–73; *see also* Khizr Tiwana
United States of America and Pakistan 22, 119, 130, 146, 172–4, 178, 211, 149, 288, 310, 312, 316, 320, 335–6, 365; post 9/11 391 ff.; *see also* Afghan war, Pakistan: nuclear proliferation

Urdu 26, 141, 164, 278; *see also* Mohajirs, United Provinces
Ushr 278
Usmani, Gen. M.H. 379
Uttar Pradesh/United Provinces (UP) 66, 92, 105, 108; *see also* Mohajirs, Urdu

Vajpayee, A.B. 393, 396, 410, 411, 412
viceregalism 54, 132, 183, 327; *see also* British rule

Waseem, Muhammad 65, 110–11, 154, 244, 331
Wattoo, Mian Manzoor 328, 345, 349
Water and Power Development Authority (WAPDA) 248, 299
women: 47–8, 51; and voting rights, 384–5; and honour killings 387; *see also* Family Laws Ordinance, Hudood Ordinance
Women's Action Forum (WAF) 36, 276, 281; *see also* Appendices

Yadav, Laloo Prasad 410
Yousaf, Lt.-Gen. M. 379

zakat, 251, 271–2, 278
Zardari, Asif Ali 293, 297, 311, 3211, 326, 334, 349, 357, 412, 414, 415; *see also* Appendices
Zikris 35, 252
Ziring, Lawrence 9